This edition
has been limited to
2,000 numbered copies
of which this is
No. *1475*

The Somerset Home Guard
A Pictorial Roll-call

The Somerset Home Guard
A Pictorial Roll-call

Jeffrey Wilson

Millstream Books

To the men and women of the Somerset Home Guard

"They also serve who only stand and wait." (Milton)

First published in 2004 by Millstream Books, 18 The Tyning, Bath BA2 6AL

Set in Times New Roman
Printed in Great Britain by The Amadeus Press, Cleckheaton

© Jeffrey Wilson 2004

ISBN 0 948975 71 7

British Library Cataloguing-in-Publication Data:
a catalogue record for this book is available from the British Library

All rights reserved. No part of this publication may be reproduced, stored in a retrieval system, or transmitted in any form or by any means, electronic, mechanical, photocopying, recording or otherwise, without the prior permission of Millstream Books.

Preface

by
Jimmy Perry, O.B.E.,
creator of the BBC Television Series *Dad's Army*.

On 20th September 2003, I celebrated my 80th birthday – well, not exactly *celebrated*; I kept it as quiet as possible, except for a few people who are very close to me. When you get to my age, no matter how hard you try, your memory is not always as sharp as it was. You can remember what happened 60 years ago but you can't remember what you had for dinner last night. So when Jeffrey Wilson asked me to write a foreword to this splendid book, the memories came flooding back.

It seems only yesterday that, as a boy of 17, I was queuing up to sign on for the Home Guard. I'd wanted to join at 16 when it was first formed ("We want large numbers of men from 17 to 65," said Anthony Eden in his radio appeal). No one bothered too much about your age and they would have taken me like a shot, but my mother bothered; I was too young and that was that. She had a brother who had been dreadfully wounded in the First World War and it broke her heart to think of me in uniform but, just like all young boys, I couldn't wait to get my hands on a rifle.

When the Home Guard was first formed there was a shortage of weapons but by the time I finally joined, President Roosevelt had sent over two cargo ships of P14 and P17 rifles that had been used by the US Forces in WW1. Amongst this huge consignment of weapons there was a quantity of Thompson sub-machine guns (Tommy guns as used by Gangsters). When the day came when I was, at last, issued with my American P17 rifle I was overjoyed – it was *mine*, to care for and to keep. We were lectured very severely on how to treat it: "Never point it at anyone. Always see that the safety catch is on. Always cock it and fire in the air as a double check that it's not loaded." There was only one snag; as young boys we were never given any ammunition to take home – that was for the older ones.

14789618 Gunner Jimmy Perry, photographed in 1944

In the event of the church bells ringing (to signal that the Invasion had started) we were to get on our bikes and pedal like fury to Headquarters and draw our 50 rounds. It's interesting to contemplate that there were more than three million firearms with ammunition kept in homes throughout the British Isles, yet no one, as far as I know, used them to hold up banks, mug people in the street or rob factories and big firms of their wages. True, a few wives shot unfaithful husbands with them but apart from that the guns were in safe hands. Within a year of its formation the Home Guard became a well-armed, well-trained auxiliary force. One of their duties was to guard strategic points such as railway goods yards and factories that were turning out vital war supplies. This set the Regular Army free to serve overseas.

A couple of years ago I was being interviewed by a woman presenter on radio: "What you're really telling us, Jimmy," she said, "is that *Dad's Army* is a send-up of the Home Guard." "No," I replied, managing to suppress my anger. "You clearly have no idea of what the Home Guard was about. They were a well-disciplined force of men who would have fought to the last to defend this Country, not a bunch of idiots." There was an awkward pause and I sat there and remained silent for the rest of the programme. I never intended to poke fun at the Home Guard but to pay a tribute to their steadfastness and courage. I was proud to have served in their ranks. I wanted the viewers to laugh *with* them, not *at* them. I like to think that I reminded the British People of the time when this dear country of ours stood alone against the most evil regime the world has ever seen. Yes, we stood alone and were not found wanting.

Jimmy Perry
London 2003

Introduction

In the early 1980s I was shown a postcard-sized photograph of members of a local Home Guard Unit by one of those included in the photograph. After a lapse of some 40 years he was still able to identify all of those present. Finding this of interest and not having seen any other similar photographs of local Home Guard Units, I took a copy and made a note of the names. Several years later, as a result of a chance encounter with another ex-Home Guard, a formal photograph of Nether Stowey Platoon was discovered. Sadly, the owner was not able to identify all his comrades. This posed the question, could anyone else identify the remainder? As an exercise, I sent a copy to *The Bridgwater Mercury* with an appeal to readers. The result was staggering. Within a couple of weeks all but one of the faces had been identified. (A name was provided for this last one some five years later.) Together with the names came a mass of other information and anecdotes about the Home Guard.

Such a response posed a multitude of questions. How many formal and informal photographs had survived fire, flood and house clearance during the last 40 years? How many faces could be identified by the dwindling numbers of ex-Home Guards?

To collate information that might be lost forever I produced a simple questionnaire which was sent sent to ex-Home Guards who contacted me. This requested information on Platoon names, numbers, officers and N.C.O.s commanding, weapons, rifle ranges and, finally, any short amusing incidents.

Being in full-time employment was a help rather than a hindrance because during the next few years opportunities arose to meet many of the wartime generation and much information was volunteered or suggestions made as to who might be able to help. As time progressed, more and more photographs and details came to light. Questionnaires were sent out and invariably returned with much new information including original documents. Much arrived unsolicited with comments such as: "Best of luck with your research; please return the photos when you have finished with them".

With retirement looming I decided to include all the information in one book. At this stage I had studied only part of the old County of Somerset. To ensure the whole of the traditional County of Somerset was covered, I contacted every Parish Council and Church Council with an appeal for information and photographs of the Home Guard. The response was most gratifying with some 50% of councils publishing the appeal. Many Somerset-based newspapers also heard of this work and copied the appeals.

A visit to the Somerset Archive & Record Office in Taunton and an examination of the Bushell Collection provided an insight into the structure of the Home Guard in Somerset. This enabled me, with a little detective work, to put titles to the majority of photographs. Some proved impossible to place with certainty so an educated guess had to be made. Unlike the first photograph received, most of the 'troops' were unidentified. Only in about four photographs out of nearly 500 were those featured contemporaneously named. From an early stage it was my intention to record the names of those featured for posterity, for what contribution is made to our history by a photograph without a caption? In another generation or so who would be alive to identify those featured?

The amount of success varied considerably. Bert Whatley, in his 90s and the last surviving member of Newton St. Loe Platoon, provided names for all of those in his Platoon photograph hanging in his living room. Other photographs came from families where only one relative was identified. Here the press once again came to the rescue by publishing the photographs with an appeal to readers. This invariably provided several more names. Not once was there no response. Faces identified on one photograph often appeared on another. Many hours were spent with a powerful lens comparing photographs. Where facial features were obscured by shadows, other features sometimes made identification possible. Despite the men being in uniform, their uniforms were by no means 'uniform'. The cut of the collars, folds in epaulettes, creases in battledress blouses, badges of rank, service stripes, chevrons, angle of caps, field service all helped. Close study of the better-quality photographs also showed medal ribbons of long-forgotten campaigns.

Let the reader not forget that many of those who volunteered in May-June 1940, now standing proudly to attention, had already been through the horrors of the First World War. They had experienced the slaughter of the Somme, the ill-fated Gallipoli Campaign, the mud of Flanders and numerous other battles. These were the men, now a little thinner on top and fatter in the middle, peering through spectacles at the cameraman, who had gone 'over the top' and across no man's land leaving their dead and dying comrades behind, and who were often driven back and exhorted to 'hold the line and dig in' only to find they were digging into temporary graves of their chums who had joined up with them in the summer of 1914. Others had survived epic naval battles fought on the high seas. Here, sometimes, survival relied on being rescued from an open boat or floating débris having had their ship sink beneath them. Many Home Guards still bore the scars, both mental and physical, of that conflict only 22 years before.

Many of the photographs also show fresh-faced young men who had joined the Home Guard whilst waiting for their call-up. For some families this proved to be the last image of the son or brother who never returned to the bosom of his family.

Whilst every attempt has been made to ascertain the correct names and ranks of those featured, after nearly 60 years errors will have occurred. Initially 'other ranks' in the Local Defence Volunteers of Home Guard were given the rank of 'volunteer', whilst later in the war, the rank of 'private' was used. In order not to offend, the titles 'volunteer' and 'private' have been omitted unless copied from original documents. Other ranks are as provided or confirmed from the photographs. Confusion occurs in some cases where veterans of the First World War continued to use their First World War rank whilst serving in the Home Guard.

Similarly, names have often been provided orally, with no written evidence, and the passage of so many years will inevitably have resulted in some of them being misspelt, e.g. Morris for Maurice, Derrick for Derek, Hedley for Headley, let alone a variety of surnames.

If any ranks or names have been incorrectly recorded the author unreservedly apologises for the unintentional error to those whose efforts and sacrifices all those years ago made it possible to write this book.

Acknowledgmemnts

It would not have been possible to produce this book without the unselfish and willing help of many hundreds of people from around the world but especially those of Somerset. Many responded to appeals kindly published in newspapers, magazines and parish newsletters. The majority of the photographs have been lent unreservedly by these kind people. They are credited with their photographs. Many others assisted with the loan of original documents, personal reminiscences or provided useful leads. Many of those are included in the list below. If I have omitted anyone this is purely accidental and apologies are offered.

Tom Atlay, Dennis Attrill, Tony Bailey, Bill Baker, I. Banwell, Mrs. M. Barandij, *The Bath Chronicle*, Dennis Bawden, Mrs. Nora Beer, Mrs. Gwen Bellinger, Iris Bendall, Ken Betty, Len Beviere, Stan Bevin, Jim Bicheno, F.A. Biffen, P. Bodman, Alec Bowditch, Alec Bown, Arthur Bown, Mrs. F. Bowyer, Stan Braddick, John Brain, *The Bridgwater Mercury*, David Bromwich, Lt. Col. (ret'd) Donald S. Brown, Mrs. D. Burge, Ken Burston, V.H. Butchers, Mrs. Audrey Carver, Frank Challoner, John Chamberlin, Mrs. Julia Chandler, *The Chard and Ilminster News*, *The Cheddar Valley Gazette*, *The Chew Valley Gazette*, Stanley Chedzoy, S.F. Chidgery, George Chislett, Reg Clack, Roy Clapp, The Archive Department of C. and J. Clark, John L. Clarke, The Trustees of The Coldharbour Mill, Len Coles, Commonwealth War Graves Commission, Phil Cook, Mrs. Cooper, Mr. Couzins, Jack Crane, Leslie Cranfield, Bob Crees, Mrs. S. Crocker, Mrs. Ann Crockford, Fred Cross, Gerry Cryer, Mrs. Culliford, Mrs. Ann Dale, Mrs. B. Darch, Mr. W.A.C. Davies, Mrs. Mary Davys, Mrs. J. Denis-Meira, Mrs. M.L. Digby, Mrs. O'Donnell, Clifford F. Dowden, Mrs. B. Dru, Francis Edward Duck, Harry Duke, Mr. E.F. Dunn, Edwin Dunning, P.A. Elliott, Ron Farley, Mr. Harold G.W. Ferdinando, David Ford, A.J. Fox, Steven Fox, Ted Frost, Mr. H.J. Fursland, John Gallop, Mrs. G. Garland, Peter Garrett, Mrs. M. Gibbs, George Gifford, Mr. C.J. 'Jack' Gilson, Mr. R.G. Gilson, Reg Glandfield, Jack Gooding, Mr. K.S. Grabham, Mrs. Shirley Grant, Mrs. Diana Gready, Mr. A.J. Greswell, Mrs. Gudge, Mr. T.G. Hallett, Dave Hares, Margaret Harvey, Mac Hawkins, Alan Hembrow, Mrs. Jackie Henley, John Hill, Ken Holley, G. Hooper, Hazel Hudson, Mrs. M.J. Hughes, Mrs. Ann Humphries, David Hunt, Richard Hunt, W. Husland, Tony Hutt, Mrs. Sheila Ingram, Mrs. Edie Jenkins, C.W. Jones, Peter Jones, M. Jons, Maureen Joyce, Mr. Keirle, Mr. P.E. Kerton, D.L. King, Eric Kingston, J. Knox, Nelson Lane, Ken Langworthy, Mrs. D. Larcombe, David Leat, John Lee, Penny Lewis, M.B.E., Mrs. Jane Lloyd, Graham Lock, Norton Look, John Loosemore, Sheila McKenn, Mr. R.A. Major, Judy Marsh, H.J. Martin, Reg Marker, Charles Maunder, *Mendip Magazine*, Len Miles, Sam Miller, Millfield School Archive Department, Iris Mitchard, Mrs. Jan Morland, E. Ann Newman, Mrs. Ailsa Newton, Ken Nicholls, Mrs. J. Nipper, Andy Norman, Leslie Norman, John Page, John Maurice Parrett, A. Parsons, Mrs. C. Parsons, Dennis Parsons, Mrs. Myrtle Parsons, David Patten, Miss W.M. Pearce, Miss J. Pelly, Norman A. Perriman, Christopher Perry, J. Perryman, Bill Pertwee, Ann Pibworth, *The Portsmouth News*, Gerald Quartly, R.A.F. Museum, Hendon, Bill Read, Deirdre Rickard, Elizabeth Ricketts, Mr. N.E. Ricketts, O.B.E., Mrs. Edna Rideout, Alex Rogers, Mr. K. Rogers, Terry Rowles, Royal British Legion (Banwell Branch), R. Russell, Mrs. Sage, John Salter, Alison Shinn, Mrs. E. Simmonds, Mrs. E. Sims, Brian Slocombe, Keith Smart, Mrs. Enid Smith, Gerald Smith, Margaret Smith, *The Somerset County Gazette*, Mr. Spratling, The Reverend Terry Staples, Ron Stevens, David Strawbridge, Mr. R. Stroud, Fred Sweet, Sam Sullivan, R.H. Symons, Mrs. Greta Thrush, Ken Trego, Mrs. M. Trott, Ruth Uffindell, Steve Venus, Alan Viney, Mr. K. Ward, William Ward, Stanley Webb, Mr. A.J. Webber, Don Webber, *The Wellington Weekly News*, Radley Wheeler, Tom White, Brenda Whitby, Jan Wilcox, Clive Williams, Miss Willis, Brian Wills, Tim Wray, Peter Wright and R.W. Wyatt.

A special mention must be made of Colonel (retired) David Hunt, O.B.E. who, whilst pursuing his own line of research into the Taunton Stop Line, unearthed much previously unseen information on the Home Guard which he willingly passed on.

I should like to record my thanks to the following people without whose help 12 years of work would have never seen the light of day. The late Donald Smith of Douglas Allen Associates copied the first 100 or so photographs before he sadly passed away prematurely. Richard Sainsbury of Delmar Studio, Taunton, kindly agreed to continue Donald's work and his photographic expertise brought many photographs 'back to life'. For typing, correcting and checking the first draft, my thanks go to Jacqui Sainsbury whose patience over some 15 months has enabled my handwritten notes to be proof-read by the following: Mike Pauley, Richard Derry, Christine and Alan Hammond. I also appreciate the help, encouragement and trust placed in me by my publisher, Tim Graham of Millstream Books. A special mention must be made of my son Edward who produced the drawing which accompanies the dedication. Finally, my thanks go to my wife Pauline, who not only carried out proof-reading but has helped so much over the years, including 'surrendering' the dining room table for weeks on end.

Finally, all our thanks go to Jimmy Perry, O.B.E., for kindly writing the foreword. If it had not been for his television series, *Dad's Army*, sowing the seed of interest in the Home Guard, this book would have never been started.

Arrangement of the Book

By 1944, for command purposes, the County of Somerset had been divided into two Home Guard sectors, North and South, and the book follows this division. The two sector commanders, who had their own headquarters staff, were responsible for the General Service Battalions in their sector, and, again, the Battalions within each sector are recorded in order. Command below this level roughly followed Regular Army practice with battalions being divided into companies, companies into platoons and platoons into sections. Unlike the Regular Army, the Home Guard was a local force based in its own area and it proved impossible to form units of regulation size.

Unless stated, commanders listed are as at 1944. Officers whose names appear in brackets following are the predecessors to the 1944 commanders.

Photographs are inserted in the book on the above basis except for the majority of Railway, Motor Transport and Post Office Units which have been included in the chapter covering the General Service Battalion in their respective area.

Prologue

> I am speaking to you from the Cabinet Room at 10 Downing Street. This morning the British Ambassador in Berlin handed the German Government an official note stating that unless we heard from them by eleven o'clock, that they were prepared at once to withdraw their troops from Poland, a state of war would exist between us. I have to tell you now that no such undertaking has been received, and consequently this country is at war with Germany.

These were the opening words of Prime Minister Neville Chamberlain's wireless broadcast to the nation at 11.15 a.m. on Sunday 3rd September 1939. On the same day the British Expeditionary Force embarked for France where the majority of the force was stationed along the Franco-Belgian border. Here they waited. In May 1940, after a successful campaign in Denmark and Norway, the German war machine turned its attention to the Western Front. Bypassing the Maginot Line, the full might of the German army and airforce was unleashed on the British and French forces who, after some initial success, were forced into a tactical withdrawal towards the coast at Dunkirk.

At home, as the worsening news unfolded, it was obvious that Hitler was not going to stop at the Channel Coast. Great concern was being expressed about the perilous state of the nation's defences. Various sections of the community, especially veterans of an earlier conflict, were demanding an opportunity to be able to defend their homeland. With the situation now desperate, those tuning in their wireless sets on Tuesday 14th May 1940 heard an appeal being made by Anthony Eden, the Secretary of State for War.

> ... We want large numbers of such men in Great Britain, who are British subjects, between the ages of 17 and 65, to come forward now and offer their services in order to make assurance doubly sure. The name of the new Force which is now to be raised will be 'The Local Defence Volunteers'. This name describes its duties in three words. It must be understood that this is, so to speak, a spare-time job, so there will be no need for any volunteer to abandon his present occupation ...

With the creation of an official force the population lost no time in organising patrols, the first of which took place the following day. Virtually unarmed and known as Parashots, these patrols operated at dawn and dusk, the times thought most likely for an airborne assault. The first item of equipment issued was a brassard with printed letters L.D.V. This was so the wearer, if captured, would be accorded the protection of the Geneva Convention. However, Hitler had other plans. He threatened to treat them as *francs-tireurs* and have them shot.

By the end of May the situation for the B.E.F. was desperate and Operation Dynamo was mounted to rescue the British and French troops whose perimeter defences around Dunkirk were shrinking daily. By 4th June some 330,000 allied soldiers had been snatched from under the nose of the enemy. However, the situation did not look good. Left behind were some 68,111 troops dead, wounded or captured. In addition, 2,472 guns, 63,879 vehicles, 20,540 motorcycles and half a million tons of stores and ammunition were lost. Some 243 vessels were sunk including several destroyers. Great Britain stood alone. The younger reader brought up on a diet of U.S.-made films should be reminded that the U.S.A., as in the First World War, did not join the fight until later in the war, although unofficial help was forthcoming in the autumn of 1940.

Meanwhile, the L.D.V. was growing up fast. Initially, it had been estimated that some 150,000 men would volunteer and on this basis it was proposed that the L.D.V. would be organised into Groups and Zones with Companies being formed in the police areas of the counties. With the numbers volunteering exceeding this estimate, some 250,000 responding within 24 hours of the appeal and numbers swelling to 300,000 by the end of May, a rapid reorganisation took place. Companies were upgraded to Battalions and Platoons were upgraded to Companies. At a lower level, Platoons and Sections were formed, their numbers and strength depending on population densities and distribution, especially in rural areas.

With ordnance factories working flat out to make up for the losses sustained at Dunkirk and in anticipation of a protracted war, Home Guard requirements were a low priority. Here the British reputation for ingenuity, inventiveness and enterprise came to the fore. Appeals for weapons were met with donations and loans of many privately-owned firearms, whilst museums were scoured for anything of use. Eley, the cartridge manufacturers, produced solid ball cartridges for 12- and 16-bore shotguns which were, in some areas, the only weapon available. The New York Police Department sent over a shipment of confiscated weapons.

Even when a vast amount of .300" rifles arrived from America in late 1940 there were still three-quarters of a million men with no personal weapon. To absorb the numbers of unarmed volunteers and improve the armoury of the Home Guard (as the L.D.V. was known from July), various engineering firms and private individuals developed weapons including the Blacker Bombard, Northover Projector, Smith gun, E.Y. (Edwin Yule) Grenade Projector, Flame Fougasse and probably the best known of all weapons, the Sten gun.

With training being given by WW1 veterans, Regular Officers and the Home Guard Travelling Wing, the Home Guard developed into a creditable force. All units down to sections became part of an integrated defence force with pre-planned schemes to harass the enemy should he attempt to invade.

As the war progressed, pressure came from various quarters to allow women to join the Home Guard as 'nominated women', a title soon changed to 'Women Home Guard Auxiliaries'. These auxiliaries were not permitted to carry weapons or wear uniforms, although a 'blind eye' was turned to the latter instruction. Duties included acting as secretaries, telephonists, signallers and cooks.

After June 1944, with the allies firmly established in Europe, the role of the Home Guard diminished. In September 1944 they were not surprised (although perhaps relieved) to hear an announcement that as from 6th September duties would no longer be compulsory.

With the Stand Down Parades, held on Sunday 3rd December 1944 throughout the county, many of the 22,000 men of the Somerset Home Guard assembled for the last time. On the following Sunday the Motor Transport Column held their Stand Down Parade in Wells. A force that at its height totalled 1,800,000 men was no more.

As we approach the 60th anniversary of this event little survives. The youngest volunteers and conscripts are now senior citizens. Their slit trenches, ambush points, shelters and store sheds built so rapidly all those years ago have mostly disappeared. Perhaps the most tangible 'monument' to these men are the pillboxes built in the dark days of late 1940 and early 1941, now devoid of their camouflage, quietly gathering the moss and lichen of the passing years. One wonders how many people, who see these pillboxes on their travels, spare a thought for the men of the Regular Army and their contemporaries in the Home Guard who were prepared to defend their homeland 'to the last round, to the last man'.

North Somerset Group/Sector

HEADQUARTERS	Drill Hall, Bridgwater (to 14.3.43)
	15, Johnstone Street, Bath (after 14.3.43)
DATE FORMED	21.10.40
COMMANDING OFFICER	Col. G.H. Rogers, O.B.E., D.L.
	(Col. A.B. Incledon-Webber, C.M.G., D.S.O.)
2ND IN COMMAND	Lt. Col. A.M. Stancombe

H.Q. STAFF:

INTELLIGENCE OFFICER	Lt. R.R. Henshaw
LIAISON OFFICER	Capt. A.I. Ingram
GAS OFFICER	Capt. A.J. Gould
SECTOR SIGNALS OFFICER	Capt. A.W. Allan
STAFF OFFICER	Major G.St.J. Strutt, C.B.E.
O/C SECTOR SIGNALS	2nd Lt. K.P. Gooder
SECTION SECRETARY	Mrs. Priestley

The North Somerset Group comprised 4th (Frome) Battalion, 5th (Bath City) Battalion, 6th (Bath Admiralty) Battalion, 7th (Long Ashton) Battalion, 8th (Weston-super-Mare) Battalion, 9th (Wells) Battalion & 13th (Axbridge) Battalion.

4th Somerset (Frome) Battalion

HEADQUARTERS (Admin.)	Drill Hall, Frome
HEADQUARTERS (Battle)	No. 2 Market Place, Frome
DATE FORMED	May 1940
COMMANDING OFFICER	Lt. Col. Huntley G. Spencer, T.D., D.L. (from 1.2.41)
2ND IN COMMAND	Major T.T. Foster, M.C.

HQ STAFF:

A & Q	Capt. J.P. Merrifield, General List
ADJUTANT	Capt. C.I.P. Holroyd, General List
AMMUNITION OFFICER	2nd Lt. J.B.T. Armstrong
GAS OFFICER	Lt. E.S. Robbins
INTELLIGENCE OFFICER	Lt. L. Ruegg
MEDICAL OFFICER	Major G. Walker, Capt. Gibb Thompson, Capt. P. Taeffe-Finn
MILITARY INFORMATION CENTRE	Capt. F.C.C. Ensor, O.B.E., Lt. S.F. Adams
SIGNALS OFFICER	2nd Lt. C.H. Dainton
TRANSPORT OFFICER	2nd Lt. A.G.P. Evans

(left) **Headquarters Staff of 4th Somerset (Frome) Battalion.**
Back Row: 2nd Lt. C.H. Dainton; 2nd Lt. J.B.T. Armstrong; Major G. Walker; Unknown
Front Row: R.S.M. Glover; Capt. C.I.P. Holroyd; Lt. Col. H.G. Spencer; Major T.T. Foster; Capt. J.P. Merrifield; Sgt. Major Stone
(Reg Glover collection)

(right) **Officers of 4th Somerset (Frome) Battalion.**
Back Row: 2nd Lt. C.H. Dainton; Unknown; Unknown; 2nd Lt. J.B.T. Armstrong; 2nd Lt. E.H. Badder; Lt. P.A. Valton; Unknown
Middle Row: Major G. Walker; Capt. J.P. Merrifield; Unknown; Lt. Bernard Wheeler; Unknown; Unknown; Capt. C.I.P. Holroyd
Front Row: Lt. Philip Brend; Lt. F.G. Sheppard; Major R.W.H. Vallis; Lt. Col. H.G. Spencer; Major T.T. Foster; Capt. N.F. Read; 2nd Lt. Haywood
(Reg Glover collection)

NORTON ST. PHILIP COMPANY

COMMANDING OFFICER	Major E.C.R. Baily
	(Major C.I.P. Holroyd)
2ND IN COMMAND	Capt. F.C.C. Ensor, O.B.E.

Despite numerous appeals, no further information has been forthcoming on this Company.

'A' (FROME) COMPANY

COMMANDING OFFICER	Major R.W.H. Vallis, M.B.E.
	Major W.E. Arnold (Evans Company)
2ND IN COMMAND	Capt. N.F. Read
	Capt. Ford (Evans Company)
	Lt. D. Kennedy (Evans Company)

By October 1940 the strength of the Frome Home Guard had risen to 500 all ranks, plus 300 rifles. At the time work was well in hand to turn Frome into an anti-tank island. Eight sites had been selected and surveyed for siting anti-tank guns and a further eight for anti-tank rifles. Additionally, various nodal points had been earmarked for the installation of road blocks consisting typically of removable railway lines which could be inserted into pre-installed sockets to prevent the passage of tanks. However, at the time calculations showed that to man the defences fully a further 200 troops would be required. An optimistic comment suggested that in the event of German troops arriving with armoured support before the guns were made available, Molotov Cocktails thrown from the gun sites by Home Guards would have to suffice!

(below) 'A' Frome Company in September 1941.
Back Row: Percy Knee; 'Chalkie' White; Mr. Lapham; Mr. Bracey; Unknown; Mr. White; Mr. Lawrence; Roy Burge; Ken Taylor; Roy Walwin; Mr. Sainsbury; Mr. Cross; J. Lambert; Mr. Martin; Unknown; K. Lambert; Mr. Whalley; Mr. Badder; Mr. Button; Mr. Walton; Mr. Woods; Mr. Wines; Mr. Barter; Unknown
Second Row: Mr. Caple; Mr. Hares; Unknown; Unknown; Unknown; Unknown; Mr. Johnson; Unknown; Stephen Cruttwell; Mr. Rossiter; Unknown; Mr. Painter; Unknown; Unknown; Unknown; Mr. Churchill or Wilkins; Mr. Carpenter; Unknown; Mr. Badder; Mr. White; Unknown; Unknown; Unknown; Unknown; Unknown; Mr. G. Stewart or Martin; Mr. Withy; Unknown; Unknown; Unknown; Unknown
Third Row: Mr. Lambert; Unknown; Mr. Sainsbury; Mr. C. Dyer; Unknown; Unknown; Unknown; Mr. S. Bennett; Mr. E. Coward; Tommy Cox; Mr. A. Silcocks; Mr. Armstrong; Unknown; Unknown; Unknown; Unknown; Mr. James; Mr. Martin; Unknown; Mr. Hawker; Mr. Colman; Unknown; Mr. Ellis; Unknown; Unknown; Unknown; Mr. Belcham; Mr. Reynolds; Mr. John Garman; Mr. Glover Jnr.; Unknown; Unknown; Unknown; Unknown; Mr. J. Robbins; Mr. Ragbourne; Mr. Axon; Unknown; Mr. Wren; Unknown
Fourth Row: Mr. K. Hucker; Unknown; Mr. George Lake; Unknown; Mr. Coleman; Mr. L. Allcott; Mr. Archie Haskell; Mr. G. Singer; Mr. Bruzas; Unknown; Mr. Totterdale; Mr. Davage; Mr. Chivers; Mr. Pritchard; Mr. Newport; Mr. Edwards; Unknown; Unknown; Mr. Butler; Unknown; Geoff White; Mr. Cornish; Unknown; Mr. York; Unknown; Mr. White; Mr. Ledbury; Mr. Milsom; Unknown; Mr. Knight; Mr. Winterbourne; Mr. Matthews; Mr. Parfitt; Mr. Trivett; Unknown; Unknown; Mr. Knight; Unknown; Mr. T. Sheet; Unknown; Unknown
Fifth Row: Unknown; L/Cpl. Davis; L/Cpl. Pain; Cpl. Reg Stent; Unknown; Sgt. Crowe or Spital; Sgt. Darlow Humphries; Sgt. Eric Lewis; Sgt. A.E. Franks; Sgt. King; Unknown; Frank Walter Parker; Capt. Merrifield; Mr. B.M. Stone; Mr. Ragbourne; R.S.M. Glover; Capt. P.A. Valton; Lt. S.F. Adams; Major R.W.H. Vallis; Major T.T. Foster; Capt. Nelson F. Read; Lt. Phillip Brend; 2nd Lt. Bernard Wheeler; Unknown; Sgt. Major Singer; Sgt. L. Haywood; Sgt. E. Midgley; Unknown; Sgt. Churchman; Unknown; Sgt. Major J.F. Burt; Bandmaster Cross; Cpl. Ellis; L/Cpl. Durnford; Cpl. Bennett; Cpl. Bull; Cpl. Knight; L/Cpl. W.H. Scammells; Cpl. Herbert Dark; Unknown
In the foreground: Master David Ragbourne.
(Mrs. D. Burge collection)

Frome in 1940, showing sites of proposed defensive positions designed to turn the town into a tank-proof island, reproduced from a 1902 Ordnance Survey Map.

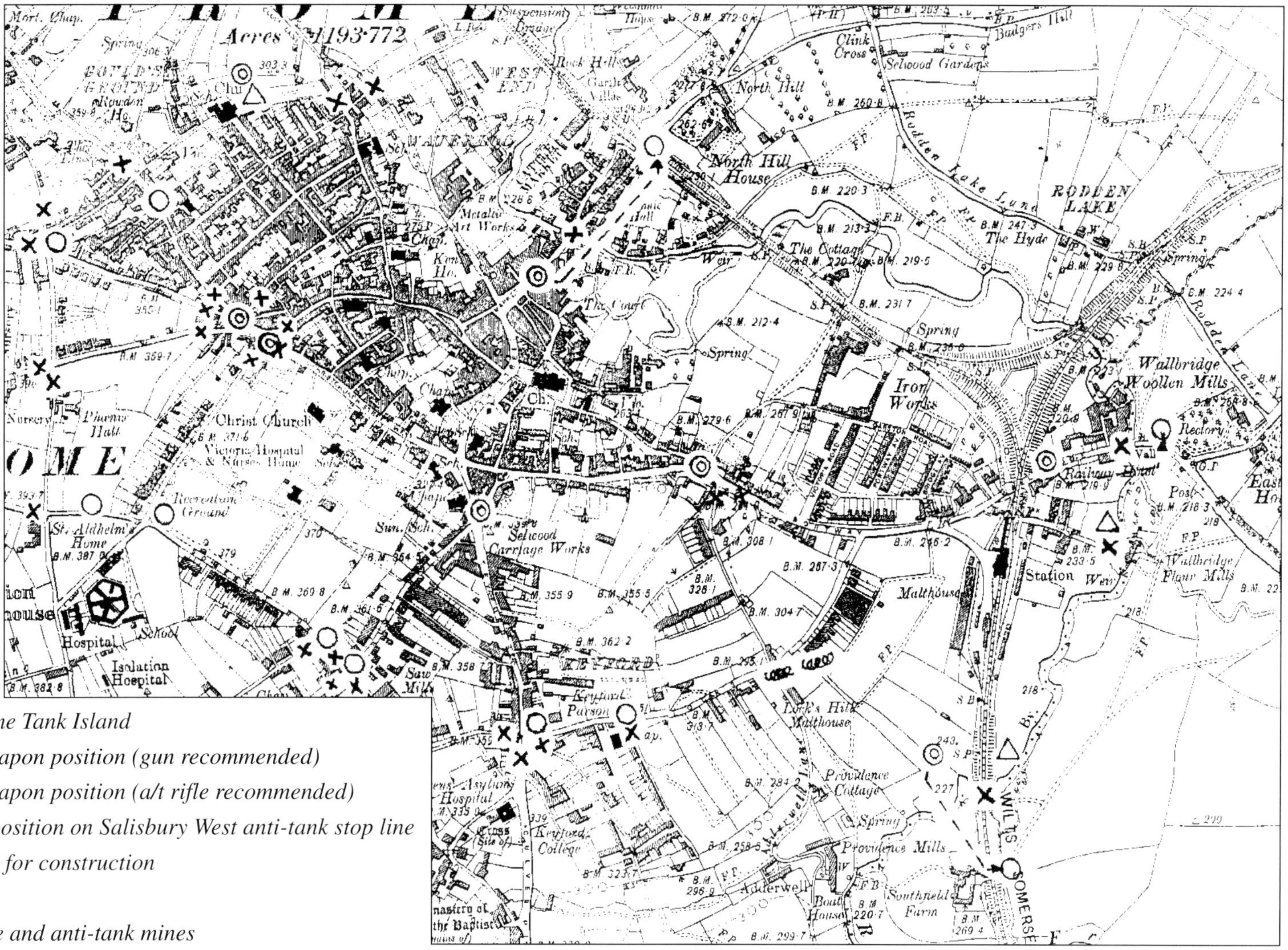

Key for Frome Tank Island
- ◉ Anti-tank weapon position (gun recommended)
- ○ Anti-tank weapon position (a/t rifle recommended)
- ---▶ Alternative position on Salisbury West anti-tank stop line
- △ Infantry post for construction
- ✕ Tank stop
- ෴ Dannert wire and anti-tank mines

EVANS AND COMPANY HOME GUARD

Evans and Co. was established in the 1920s, setting up business in Oyster Street, Portsmouth, where they initially carried out the business of motor engineers. As business increased they moved to Goldsmith Avenue, purchasing further premises in the road as business expanded. Early contracts included piston-grinding for Petters of Yeovil.

One day in 1941 the management of Evans and Co. received a telephone call from a Government Department informing them that they had been allocated factory space away from the bombing, at the printing works of Butler and Tanner in Frome. Within 24 hours the first low-loader arrived at the works to move the machinery to Frome.

Reg Clack, then the 32-year-old personnel manager, remembers being instructed to hire a convoy of coaches to move employees and their dependants to Frome, their new 'home', the staff numbering some 200 at the time. Jim Bicheno, a few years younger than Reg, unmarried and employed as a progress chaser, was one of those moved to Frome. Arriving in a strange town he joined other employees in the search for lodgings. Determined not to return to Portsmouth that night with others unsuccessful in finding accommodation he spent a couple of weeks sleeping on the floor of the boiler house at his 'new' factory before he found temporary lodgings with Mrs. Ludlow in Bath Road. He subsequently moved to Mr. and Mrs. Pickford's home in New Buildings Lane. Mr. Pickford was also employed in war work, working for Cockey's of Frome, a subsidiary of Stothert and Pitt of Bath.

Bill Evans, being one of the senior management, established himself in a smallholding at Trudoxhill, earning himself the nickname of 'Lord Trudoxhill'.

Evans and Co. worked full-time, producing complete undercarriages for Halifax Bombers and Horsa Gliders in addition to undercarriage legs for Hawker Typhoons and Tempests.

Other products included flap controls for the Bristol Aircraft Company, bomb release levers for the Folland Aircraft Company, machine parts for Armstrong Siddeley and quick-release mechanisms for barrage balloons. During the war many factories mounted 20 mm. Hispano-Suiza machine guns on their roofs and again Evans and Co. was involved, manufacturing the gun mounts. Precision products included hydrostatic fuses for the Navy.

Distinguished visitors to the factory included H.R.H. Queen Mary and Sir Stafford Cripps who, by November 1942, was Minister for Aircraft Production.

Whilst the initial strength of the Factory Home Guard in Portsmouth was approximately 12, the unit expanded to nearly 100 in Frome, enabling Evans to boast their own Home Guard Company. Air Raid Shelters were constructed in the factory grounds. The works was patrolled during the hours of darkness by the factory Home Guard. Because of its size, Evans Home Guard was able to assist the local Home Guard in other duties. The Company also boasted their own Spigot Mortar which would be taken on a special trailer pulled by a works van to Chapmanslade for practice shoots.

After the end of hostilities, Evans and Co. moved back to Portsmouth where they continued in business, manufacturing nose wheels for Meteor and Hunter jets and later the outriggers for Hawker Harriers.

The company closed in the 1980s, Goldsmith Avenue works being re-developed for housing, but not before the factory had its swan-song, as the setting for some indoor scenes in the film *Tommies*.

(below) ***Evans and Company Home Guard***.
Back Row: Jim Loan; Charlie Baker; Jock Ballantyne; Arthur Scarbrough; Sid Hughes; Len Clarke; Walter Disney; Bob 'Bubble' Woods; Leslie Wheeler; Unknown; Unknown; Unknown; Vic Stewart; Bob Feasey; Charlie Turner; Les Searle; John Howarth; Unknown; Unknown; Bill Hayter; Ron Redman; Fred Fuller; Norman Gleed; Ken Ashman; Unknown; Doug Harding; Ernie Simmonds; Unknown; Ken Spicer
Second Row: Tom Cobb; John Standing; Henry Woodward; Unknown; Alex Clough; Les Horler; Basil Hayward; Steve Arnold; Unknown; Bill Butcher; Bert Robinson; Unknown; Jim Bicheno; Unknown; Ron Murray; Frank Lillicrap; Ron Miller; Robert Frank Pibworth; Les Clarke; Sid Hinge; Andy Anderson; Sid Stewart; Alan Thorning; Len Butcher; Unknown; Unknown; Ted Colyer; Bert Goater; Steve Matthews; Arthur Waldron

(right) **Officers of Evans and Company**.
*Back Row: Lt. Don Kennedy; Unknown;
  Sgt. Major Hector Cook; Lt. James Harris Cannon
Front Row: Capt. Ernie Ford; Major W.E. Arnold;
  Lt. Jim Weldon
(Muriel Cole collection)*

Jim Cannon, who was born on 10th September 1915 in Glasgow, joined the Royal Navy at the age of 13. Suffering a serious injury to his hand when a hatch fell on it, Jim was invalided out of the Navy in February 1940 and subsequently joined Evans and Co. He died on 17th September 1998, aged 83.

*Third Row: George Smith; L/Cpl. Reg Clack; L/Cpl. Ben Oman;
  L/Cpl. Jack Horner; Unknown; L/Cpl. Stan Baldwin;
  Cpl. Jock Valentine; Sgt. Jack Calderwood; Sgt. Harry Read;
  Sgt. Terry Stevens; Sgt. Basil Trayfoot; Sgt. Major Hector Cook;
  Lt. Don Kennedy; Capt. Ernie Ford; Major W.E. Arnold; Lt. Jim Weldon;
  Lt. James Harris Cannon; Unknown; Sgt. Major Fred Waldron;
  Sgt. Bill Sannigar; Sgt. Pat Paterson; Cpl. Bill Ross; Cpl. Bill Mead;
  Cpl. Henry Proost; Unknown; L/Cpl. Arthur Lillicrap; L/Cpl. Bert East;
  L/Cpl. Jeff Arnold; Unknown; L/Cpl. Eddie Palmer
Front Row: Jim Robbins; Alf Bounton; Stan Penny; Tom Coates;
  Johnny Hugo; Tony Defazio; Stan Newton
(Muriel Cole collection)*

(right) **No.1 Platoon Frome Company**, September 1941.
Back Row: Mr. Sainsbury; Unknown; Mr. Martin; George Lake; Mr. Sainsbury Jnr.; Unknown; Unknown; Unknown; Unknown; Unknown
Second Row: Archie Haskell; Mr. Singer; Unknown; Unknown; Mr. James; Mr. Woods; Unknown; Unknown; Unknown; Mr. Allcott; Mr. Milsom; Unknown; Unknown
Third Row: Mr. Chivers; Mr. Newport; Unknown; Unknown; Mr. Rowe; Mr. Ledbury; Mr. Martin; Unknown; Unknown; Mr. Badder; Mr. Lambert; Mr. Badder
Fourth Row: Unknown; L/Cpl. Walton; Unknown; Unknown; Sgt. Cross; Sgt. (later Lt.) L. Haywood; Unknown; Sgt. Major Singer; Sgt. Eric Lewis; Cpl. Horler; Unknown; L/Cpl. Stephen Cruttwell; Unknown
Sitting: Unknown; Unknown; Sam Bennett; Mr. Armstrong (Reg Glover collection)

(below) Unknown Platoon.
Back Row: apart from No. 6, Mr. Edwards, none of the others have been identified although all their faces appear in the photograph on pp.11 & 12 as follows:
 2nd Row No. 28; 2nd Row No. 24; 4th Row No. 38; 4th Row No. 18; 4th Row No. 25; Mr. Edwards; 4th Row No. 2; 4th Row No. 4; 3rd Row No. 24; 3rd Row No. 25; 3rd Row No. 32
Middle Row: Mr. Wren; Mr. Caple; Unknown (3rd Row No. 33); Mr. Hares; Unknown (3rd Row No. 22); Mr. Ellis; Unknown (2nd Row No. 29); Mr. C. Dyer; Mr. J. Robbins; Mr. Withy
Front Row: Cpl. Johnson; Unknown (2nd Row No. 11); Cpl. Herbert Dark; Sgt Major. J.F. Burt; Capt. Valton; Major Vallis; Capt. Merrifield; Unknown (Front Row No. 30); Unknown (2nd Row No. 30); Cpl. Ellis; L/Cpl. Durnford
(Pauline Cox collection)

(above) **'A' Company Band**, photographed outside Frome Drill Hall.
Back Row: Roy Burge; Mr. Lapham; Mr. McDonald; Unknown; Mr. Button; Unknown; Mr. Walton; Mr. White
Middle Row: Unknown; Mr. Sainsbury; Unknown; Unknown; Unknown; Unknown; Unknown; Roy Walwin; Unknown; Mr. Cross; Mr. Lambert
Front Row: Cpl Corbin; Mr. Badder; Unknown; Bandmaster Cross; Major Vallis; R.S.M. Glover; Percy Knee; Unknown
(Reg Glover collection)

(left) **N.C.O.s of Frome Company**.
Back Row: Unknown; Drum Major R.J. Pickford; Sgt. D.W. Humphries; Unknown; Sgt. A.E. Franks; Sgt. Edwin 'Pop' York; Unknown; Unknown; Unknown; Unknown; A Sgt. V.W. Martin; Sgt. H.J. Bull; Sgt. R. Stent
Front Row (sitting): Unknown; Unknown; possibly Sgt. A.G. Churchman; Sgt. E. Lewis; R.S.M. Glover; Sgt. Major Burt; Sgt. Major Stone; Unknown; Sgt. L.A.C. Badder
(Reg Glover collection)

(right) Apart from Sgt. Major Burt, front row number 3, and Lt. Valton, number 4, no one else has been identified. It may well be they are featured on pages 11 & 12.
Note: The eagle-eyed reader may notice Sgt. Major Burt is wearing the badge of rank of a Warrant Officer Class II, typically a Company Sergeant Major. It is believed that this was the rank held by Sergeant Major Burt in a previous conflict.
(Reg Glover collection)

(left) Back Row: Fred Doel; Unknown; Unknown; Unknown; Unknown; Unknown; Unknown
Second Row: Unknown; Unknown; Unknown; Unknown; Unknown; Unknown; Mr. Ellis; Mr. Reynolds
Third Row: Unknown; Unknown; Mr. Whiting; Unknown; Mr. Haines; Unknown; Unknown; Unknown; Unknown
Front Row: Unknown; Unknown; Unknown; Unknown; Unknown (possibly landlord of *The Ring of Bells*); Cpl. Knight
(Reg Glover collection)

(left) Back Row: Unknown; George Lake; Unknown
Middle Row: Unknown; Unknown; Unknown; Peggy Ragbourne; Maureen Joyce; Cpl. H.T. Vranch; Cpl. Darlow Humphries; Unknown
Front Row: Unknown; Sgt. 'Pop' York; Sgt. Eric Lewis; Capt. Nelson Read; Major Vallis; Lt. Bernard Wheeler; Sgt. Major Burt; Sgt. Franks

Peggy Ragbourne and Maureen Joyce were both 'nominated women'. Maureen remembers back over 60 years when the photograph was taken as, unlike Peggy, she had not received her Home Guard badge in time to sew it on.
(Reg Glover collection)

(right) Back Row: George Trivett; Unknown; Unknown; Unknown; Unknown; Unknown
Second Row: Unknown; Unknown; Tom Cox; Unknown; Unknown; Unknown; Unknown
Third Row: Francis R.J. Treasure; Unknown; Unknown; Unknown; L/Cpl. W.H. Scammells; Unknown; Unknown
Front Row: Unknown; Sgt. H.J. Bull; Unknown; Lt. F.G. Sheppard; Sgt. R. Stent; Unknown
(Reg Glover collection)

(left) Back Row: Mr. Smith; Mr. Martin; Unknown; Unknown; Unknown; Unknown; Mr. Sainsbury; Unknown; Unknown
Second Row: Unknown; Unknown; Cpl. Bennett; Unknown; Unknown; Archie Haskell; Unknown; Unknown; Mr. Ballam
Third Row: Unknown; Unknown; Unknown; Unknown; Unknown; Unknown; L/Cpl. R.C. James; Mr. Rowe
Front Row: Sgt. V.W. Martin; Unknown; 2nd Lt. L. Haywood; 2nd Lt. E.H. Badder; Sgt. L.A.C. Badder; Sgt. Edwards; Unknown
(Reg Glover collection)

(right) Apart from Mr. Ayres (back row No. 3), George Rose (third row No. 1) and Mr. Bond and Drum Major Pickford (front row Nos. 4 and 6), no others have been identified.
(Reg Glover collection)

(left) **Drum and Bugle Band**, photographed at Victoria Park, Frome.
Back Row: Maurice Watts; Unknown; Unknown; Donald Wright; Unknown; Unknown; Charlie George; Unknown
Middle Row: Unknown; Unknown; Mr. Lambert; Unknown; Unknown; Unknown; Unknown; Mr. McDonald; Unknown; Unknown; Unknown; Unknown
Front Row: Unknown; Unknown; Major Vallis; Capt. Read; Drum Major Pickford; Cpl. Percy Knee; Unknown; Unknown
(Reg Glover collection)

(right) Lt. P.A. Valton with fellow Home Guards outside his home, 'Sandusky', Berkley Road, Frome, in 1944. (Gerald Quartley collection)
Back Row: Sgt. W. Vernon; Cpl. W.W. Quartley; 2nd Lt. E. Midgley; Capt. H. Frampton; Mr. A. Edwards; Sgt. H.E. Painter
Middle Row: Cpl. F. Green; Mr. W. Evemy; Sgt. Major J.F. Burt; Lt. P.A. Valton; Sgt. W.B. Johnson; Sgt. S.A. Banton; Cpl. E.R. Dunford; Mr. E.J. Ellis
Front Row: Lt. H.R. Harding; Capt. W.J. Horseman; Cpl. B. Marsh; Cpl. H. Butler
Lt. Harding and Capt. W.J. Horseman are wearing 'Cadet Force' shoulder flashes and the county badge of Somerset. William Quartley was a lorry driver for Frome Rural District Council whilst J.F. Burt was employed by the Urban District Council as a steam roller driver. E. Midgley worked for the G.W.R. as a clerk. Roads Reconstruction employed H.E. Painter whilst P.A. Valton was one of its directors. E.J. Ellis was the owner of 'Wessex Engineering'. H. Frampton was the local Bank Manager whilst Mr. Edwards was the chief clerk at Westminster Bank, later joining the Army Cadet Force. At the beginning of the War the Coopers' Company School moved to Frome from London bringing with it Mr. W.B. Johnson, a Biology teacher known to his pupils as 'Bio Bill'.

(left) Lt. Col. Huntley Spencer inspects men of **Frome Company, probably No. 1 Platoon**, drawn up for their last parade on 3rd December 1944 in Market Place, Frome. Note the reflections of the men on the rain-soaked road and members of the A.C.F. in the background.

Left to right: Major Vallis; R.S.M. Glover; Capt. Holroyd; Lt. Col. H. Spencer; Sgt. Major J.F. Burt; Lt. L. Haywood

Today little has changed; the buildings remain but the men, who for the previous four years were prepared to 'give their all', have all but faded away, replaced by a society they would not recognise.
(Reg Glover collection)

(below) In May 1940, within 12 hours of Anthony Eden's appeal for a Local Defence Force, there was a 100% response from Frome Tax Office. The list gives an indication of the experience of the volunteers. Of the three too young to have served in the First World War two still had experience in military matters.

NUNNEY COMPANY

COMMANDING OFFICER   Major E.J. Loring, M.C.   2ND IN COMMAND   Capt. S.W. Fry
(Capt. S.H. Berry)

*Members of **Nunney Home Guard** pose with their Company Commander in front of a defensive work from a much earlier era, Nunney Castle.*
Back Row: Sgt. Bill Hall; Arthur Hughes; Sgt. Joe Richards; Cpl. Reg. Herridge; Bill Howlett; Frank Bradley; Charlie Howlett; Alfie Hillier; Cecil 'Mick' Bartlett; Oliver Brooks; Albert Seviour
Front Row: L/Cpl. Silvester Seviour; Herbie Seviour; Sgt. Fred Fowler; Captain Bradshaw; Major E.J. Loring; Sgt. Blacker; Sgt. Monty Conibear; Bill Vince; Fred Hiller; Mr. Anderson

Note the two fabric patches on L/Cpl. Silvester Seviour's right sleeve comprising a square and below it a strip. The square was the proficiency badge introduced in 1941. In May 1943 revised conditions for awards were introduced taking into account new training methods and weapons. Those who qualified for the new award wore the red felt square and a 1" x 1/4" red felt strip below. In May 1944 regulations permitted the wearing of proficiency badges by sergeants.
(Bette Bullus collection)

Many members of Nunney Platoon were employed in Coleman's Quarry. These included Reg Herridge, Bill Howlett, Charlie Howlett, Cecil Bartlett, Oliver Brooks, Bill Vince and Fred Fowler who was employed as a driver. Arthur Hughes was a council employee, Alfie Hillier a farmworker. Frank Bradley's skills were always required, being the local blacksmith and plumber. Fred Hillier's inclusion suggests he had been a member of the Home Guard and had been called up subsequently.

Cecil 'Mick' Bartlett passed away in August 2003, the last surviving member of the group photographed above.

(right) The local observation point was at map ref. ST 728 457 where a small hut, on wheels, provided shelter. The same hut is now in retirement, having recently had its shingled roof felted. The hole in the centre of the door towards the bottom was not made by mice but is the result of a 'negligent discharge' by Bill Vince. Another result of forgetfulness was the finding, many years after the war, of four hand grenades in Sgt. Bill Hall's loft. (Author's collection)

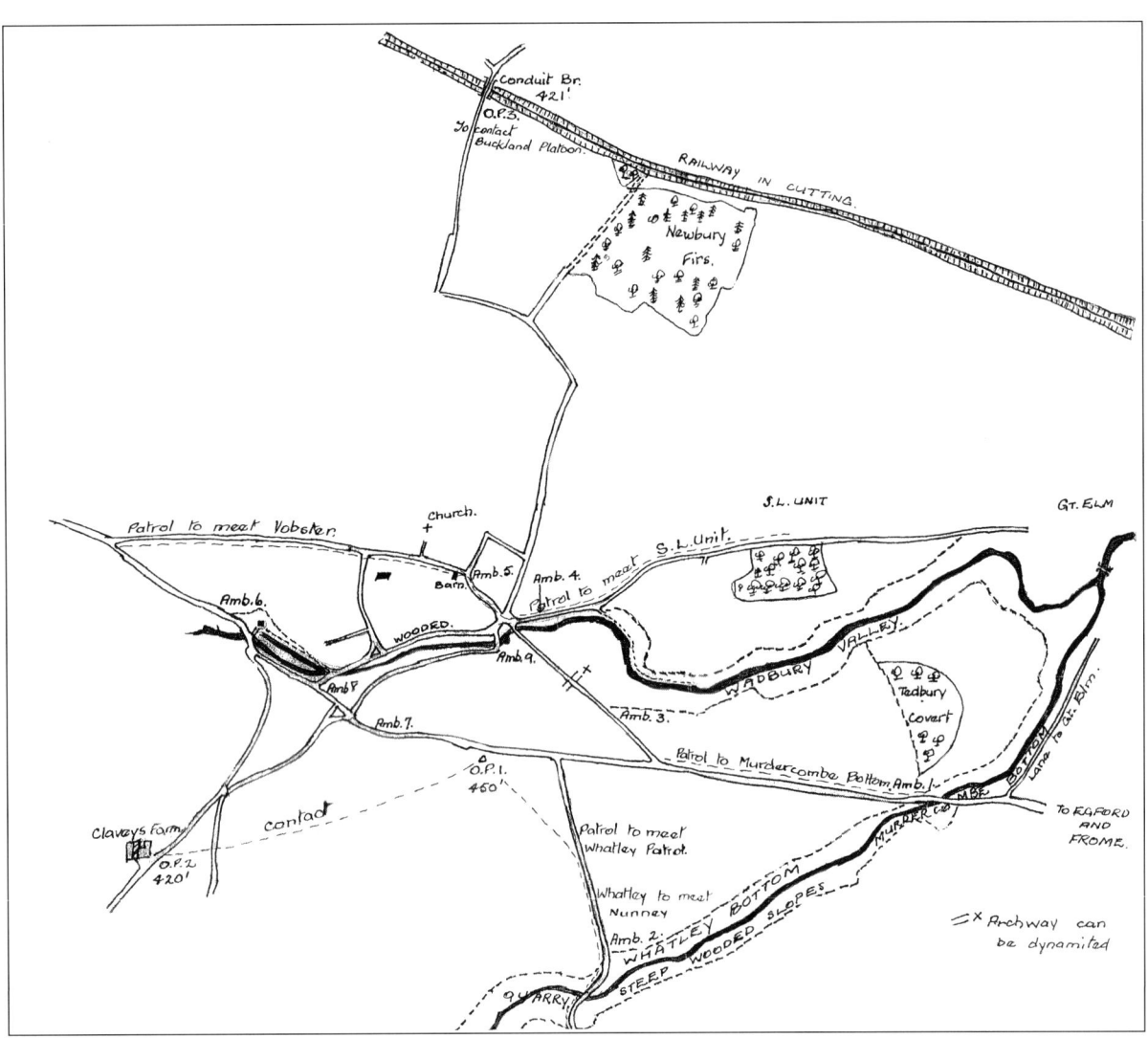

Two miles to the north of Nunney lies the village of Mells. The map (left) belonged to R.S.M. John Glover of Frome Company. Close examination shows the location of the observation points and the routes the nightly patrols were to take. Note the number of pre-selected ambush sites, No. 1 being appropriately at Murder Combe Bottom. Even a minor bridge had been earmarked to be dynamited. Reference has also been made to a Searchlight Unit which, no doubt with a little detective work, would enable the map to be dated.
(Reg Glover collection)

Trudoxhill, Marston and Tytherington Home Guard, photographed in 1944 by A.J. Ashby of Frome.
Back Row: Unknown; Mr. Cox; Ted Giles; Unknown; Fred Howlett; Ken Salmon; Herbie Taylor; George Marklew
Second Row: Unknown; Unknown; Unknown; Unknown; Unknown; Harold Andrews; Ron Bratten; Ern Weeks; Laurie Starr
Third Row: Cpl. Bill Elmer; Sgt. George Wareham; Sgt. Archie Starr; Capt. Richard Shore; Sgt. Jack Hillier; Unknown; Cpl. Reg Rayner
Front Row: Cpl. Ted Woods; Ted Starr; Unknown; Unknown; Unknown
Ted Starr is wearing an unidentifiable shoulder flash.
(Joyce Stride collection)

Trudoxhill Home Guard, again photographed by A.J. Ashby.
Back Row: Ted Starr; Ern Weeks; George Marklew
Middle Row: Ronald Bratten; Ted Giles; Harold Andrews; Fred Howlett; Laurie Starr
Front Row: Reg Rayner; George Wareham; Richard Shore; Archie Starr; Bill Elmer
(Joyce Stride collection)

BATCOMBE HOME GUARD

Batcombe, some 2½ miles to the north of Bruton, was the southernmost parish in Nunney Company's area. Although no photograph has been located, the author is indebted to Mr. D. Sage for his reminiscences.

Batcombe's famous platoon formed part of the Somerset 4th Battalion under the command of Col. H.G. Spencer of South Hill House, Cranmore, whose battle HQ was at No. 2 The Market Place, Frome. Local control came under Lieutenant David Britten, the dentist who lived at Church Farm House, and 'square bashing' was the job of Company Sergeant Major Fred Priddle, landlord of *The Three Horseshoes*. How Batcombe came to have a company sergeant major in charge of just one platoon is not known. It was, nevertheless, in keeping with Batcombe's idea of its status that they should have one. Their operational instructions were contained in a War Office directive of 28th June 1940 (part 6) which included:

> The Home Guard are to deal with all parachutists, fifth columnists and enemy motor-cyclists who may penetrate or appear in disguise at unexpected places.

Following the loss of weapons at Dunkirk, most of the rifles went to the Regular Army, and it was only after anxious messages from Churchill to Franklin Roosevelt, the U.S. President, that one million .300 Springfield rifles arrived from America for the Home Guard at the end of July 1940. Smart uniforms, caps and boots also arrived from our own factories.

Everyone who attended the Sunday services during the summer of 1940 will recall the 'clump, clump, clump' of those army boots marching up and down the road outside the church, interspersed with the seemingly exasperated commands of Sergeant Major Priddle. No, this was not the cream of the British Army, but it was Batcombe's very own Home Guard, and we were all very proud of them. About 20 in number they were a complete cross-section of our more senior residents: the tall, the stout, the short and the rather frail. There was Fred Massey, standing 6' 6" tall who, while working on the farm could throw a whole hile of corn sheaves by one pitchfork toss on to a well-loaded wagon; and not so tall William Gibbons, the postman. With a few, their uniforms fitted perfectly, and for one conscientious patriot, so the story goes, there was often only one man in step. In fact they were the image of 'Dad's Army' and all the village lads thought they were wonderful.

By the time we came out of church the local militia had often retired to the rifle shooting range in Gold Hill paddock. From just over the wall beyond the war memorial, the range faced across the valley to the butts constructed in the field beside Home Farm at map ref. ST 390 691. The remains of the butts could still be seen in 1995. They consisted of a deep trench where two brave markers took cover, and above them were timber frames on which two five-feet-square targets pivoted. Communication to the butts from the firing point was by loud blasts on a whistle. It was their earlier night-time patrols in pairs with shotguns that gave the Batcombe contingent their skills in shooting as well as providing a much needed supply of rabbit meat to the village larders; and this skill was often evident in competition with other platoons from neighbouring villages.

As in many villages the Home Guard Headquarters was at the pub, home of Sergeant Major Priddle, where meetings were held and spare ammunition kept. It would seem that Batcombe's first line of defence between the village and Germany was the boundary ridge of Saite Hill, for it was the site of the platoon's forward base – a large chicken house hidden amongst the briars near the top of Copplesbury Lane. Certainly it can be said that the Germans did not break through these defences during the last war, but it is still debated in 1995 as to which was the greater enemy – hostile troops or sheer boredom. During those long nights of sentry work, the activities that took place up there are still considered classified information, although it is known that cider and other comforts helped them through, and in the circumstances, not many stripes were lost due to spot checks by senior officers.

Members of Batcombe Home Guard included:

Lieutenant David Britten (school dentist)
Sergeant Major Fred Priddle (publican)
Arthur Coombs (Sergeant) (roadman)
George Veasey (farmworker)
Gilbert Veasey (Gilb) (farmworker)
Jeffrey Cox (Jeff) (roadman)
Charles Cox (Charlie) (farmer)
James Cox (Jim)
Gilbert Cox (Gilb)
George Wiltshire (engineer/bus driver)
Reginald Wiltshire (Reg) (farmer/contractor)
John Wiltshire (Jack)
Gilbert Wiltshire (Gilb)
Harold Clothier (farmer)
Frederick Massey (Fred) (farmworker)
William Gibbons (Billy) (taxi driver/postman)
Harold Shears (farmer)
Stanley Shears (Stan) (farmer)
Harold Brown (Harry)
Richard Walls (Dick)
Edward Longman (Eddie) (farmer)
William Noaks (Bill)
Ernest Charlton (Chick) (mason)
Bertram Thorn (Bert) (steamroller driver)
Charles Firth (retired)
Jack Gould (farmworker)
Richard Watts (Dick)
Jack Dyke
? Hawke
? Bourne (retired)
Thomas Padfield (Tom) (retired)
? Craig (poultry dealer)

MIDSOMER NORTON COMPANY

COMMANDING OFFICER   Major A.F.B. Thatcher
2ND IN COMMAND   Capt. Gordon Hillier

Despite numerous appeals, no further information has been forthcoming on this Company.

RADSTOCK COMPANY

COMMANDING OFFICER   Major C.F.P. Clerihew
2ND IN COMMAND   Capt. I.F.H. Beauchamp

(below) **Men of the Radstock Company**.
Back Row: Frank May; Fred Hillman; Unknown; Unknown; L. Perry; Chris Carpenter; Unknown; Len Woodhouse; Beresford Carpenter;
Second Row: all unknown except No. 4 captioned 'R.E.'
Third Row: all unknown except No. 3 captioned 'F.H.', No. 8 captioned 'E.C.' and No. 17 Bert Edwards
Front Row: No. 1 captioned 'S.M.'; No. 7 Major C. Hill; No. 8 captioned 'L.C.'; No. 10 captioned 'C.C.'
The reference to Major C. Hill was obtained from a postwar press cutting. It is possible that Major C.F.P. Clerihew has over the years become Major C. Hill.
(Radstock Museum collection)

*The **Radstock Railway Home Guard** were members of the 22nd Devonshire (5th Southern Railway) Battalion. They pose here in 1940, in their newly issued battledress, not before sewing on their campaign medal ribbons from a previous conflict.*
(Radstock Museum collection)

(below left) Terry Benwell was a dispatch rider in the 4th Somerset Battalion Home Guard, based at Tunley. Note the Sten gun magazine opening has been rotated through ninety degrees to keep the action protected from dirt and no doubt to feel more comfortable for Terry. Other members recalled by Terry were George Macey, George Mondrell, Charlie Hawkins, Jim Domesa, Mr. Gardiner (senior), Noel Chapman, Charlie Baker, Jim Spering. The Officer in Command was Captain Reg Brimble with Jim Barnes as Sergeant and Corporal Stanley Rowsell. (Terry Benwell collection)

Sadly no group photograph seems to exist nor information on the platoons covering this area south-west of Bath. In November 1942 Terry left the Home Guard and joined the Royal Electrical and Mechanical Engineers. Jim Spering also left the Home Guard having been found on duty one night the worse for wear.

(below right) Young George Macey at the 'on guard' with his P17 rifle and bayonet while George Mondrell looks on. (Terry Benwell collection)

SHEPTON MALLET COMPANY

COMMANDING OFFICER   Major C.B. Radway (Major F. Luff)
2ND IN COMMAND   Capt. W.H. Morgrove (Capt. R.K. Franks)

DITCHEAT PLATOON

Part of Shepton Mallet Company, Ditcheat Platoon was commanded by Lt. A.H. Scutts of Factory House, Ditcheat. Factory House was used for meetings in the summer months whilst activities were transferred in the winter to the skittle alley of *The Green Tree Inn*, since demolished.

In the early days, when there were insufficient weapons, rifles were handed back to Lt. Scutts in the mornings when the guards came off duty. It was on one such occasion when what could have been a fatal accident occurred. It was the practice when returning rifles to 'ease springs' which entailed the rapid opening and closing of the bolt until all live rounds had been cleared from the rifle. On completion the bolt would be closed and the trigger squeezed. In theory nothing should happen as the breech should be empty. On this occasion, Jack Lintern left a live round in the breech. The bullet went through the open door of Factory House and past Lt. Scutts. It ricocheted off the tiled floor, through a grandfather clock and embedded itself in the ceiling. One Home Guard present at the 2001 reunion clearly remembers the hem of his greatcoat lifting with the muzzle blast!

A poultry hut was obtained for Home Guard use which was made from old shipping crates for motor vehicles. It was erected on Ditcheat Hill at map ref. ST 618 368. Inside, the 'facilities' consisted of bunk beds and a paraffin stove. Two Home Guards would patrol for two hours at which point they would be relieved by the next pair. On one cold night discipline slipped and the hut was occupied by all eight of the sentries, fast asleep. On this occasion Lt. Scutts happened to carry out a spot check. He quietly recovered their rifles and took them home. The next morning eight very sheepish Home Guards reported to Lt. Scutts that they had lost their rifles. History does not record what was said! However, it was not long before East Pennard Home Guard heard of this incident and soon after they paid a night-time visit to their Home Guard colleagues, creeping up to their shelter and vigorously beating the sides with sticks!

No. 76 Sticky bomb practice was carried out in a disused quarry whilst for rifle practice a range was established to the north of the village between map references ST 628 369 and ST 627 375 where shooting took place across a small stream with the butts on the north side. For longer range shoots Yoxter camp was used, on some occasions the platoon members contriving to return home with more ammunition than they took. The platoon members appear to have led a charmed life. Having narrowly missed shooting Lt. Scutts, grenade practice resulted in yet another close call. On this particular day the Platoon were instructed to throw grenades over a high bush. Everything went well until it was Tom White's turn. His grenade caught the top of the foliage and fell down through the undergrowth. Col Harrison, who was watching, shouted, "Get down". Unfortunately Lt. Heywood from Pilton, who was less agile, due to a wound sustained in the First World War, was unable to move fast enough and was hit by shrapnel. Private Look, the platoon medic, rushed forward and dressed the wound, being very proud of his first-aid handling of the casualty. Several days later Lt. Scutts asked him why he had not dressed the other wound which he had missed. This turned out to be the exit hole for the shrapnel.

Ammunition and weapons were distributed around the village. A wooden pig hut in Jackass Field was used for some ammunition whilst the Lewis gun was kept at Cpl. White's house. Lt. Scutt's garage was used to store the Northover Projector. Plans were made to defend the access roads into Ditcheat. At suitable points sand bag 'walls' were built at the edge of the roads to give cover to Home Guard members who would lay in wait with Sticky Bombs. As the threat diminished, such 'defence works' were abandoned. During the build-up to D-Day, Ditcheat Home Guard shared in the guarding of Southwood Viaduct on the Somerset and Dorset Railway. At the end of the war, whilst the collection of small arms was well organised, it would appear that little thought was given to the disposal of munitions. Many years later Lt. Scutt's garage was found still to be stocked with grenades and small arms ammunition.

No. 1 Section Ditcheat Home Guard, pictured outside Ringwell House, Ditcheat, in June 1941. This is one of the few photographs contemporaneously captioned. Note the well-stocked bandoleers, no doubt as a result of a visit to Yoxter Camp!

Back Row: K.J. Parker, garage mechanic; W.J. McLeod, cheesemaker for S.W. Gullidge of Highbridge Farm; S.H. Ford, schoolteacher; H.A. Billing, farmworker; R.W. Taylor, farmworker; H.R. Longman, farmer; E.S. Dyke, farmer; S.J. Sullivan, general labourer involved in the construction of army camps; G.T. Golledge, farmer at Lower Wraxhill; H.N. Golledge, farmer, son of S.W. Golledge; T.N. Yeoman, farmworker.
Centre Row: A.C. Trim, baker at Ditcheat; L/Cpl. R.N. Look, farmer; Cpl. G.T. White, farmer; Lt. A.H. Scutts, oil and tyre dealer; Col. N. Harrison, retired Army officer; Sgt. E.R. Lewis, milk factory worker at Evercreech; Cpl. J.K. Longman, farmer; R. Longman, farmer; P.W. Moody, farmer.
Front Row: M.A. Wilcox, baker's 'boy', assisted Mr. Trim; I.H. Lye, 'tea boy' at Dimmer Munitions Dump; F.T. Golledge, farmer; H.G. Dukes, self-employed hedger and ditcher; E.F. Vaux, son of bakery owner, 'Vaux of Ditcheat'.

Apart from Col. N. Harrison, only Sgt. E.R. Lewis is known to have definitely had previous military experience – as a boy soldier in the Boer War. (Norris Yeoman collection)

Colonel R.N. Harrison, O.B.E., the son of Colonel N. Harrison, remembers his involvement in Ditcheat Home Guard as a young man:

During the War my parents lived at Ringwell House, Ditcheat. My father (Lt. Col. J.S.N. Harrison, D.S.O.), commanded our unit, though Mr. Scutts who lived in a house only 50 yards from the drive leading to Ringwell House was the Platoon Commander.

During school holidays, because I was an N.C.O. in Haileybury College Corps, I remember, as a 17-19 year old, drilling the stalwart Ditcheat Platoon in the roadway at the north end of Ditcheat. I believe reserve ammunition was kept in a chicken house in one of Mr. Barker's fields.

There was a hut on top of Ditcheat Hill, where, at night, constant patrols were mounted. I remember doing my stint during the holidays. We patrolled along the hill as far as the Fosse Way to the west. There was excitement when a shot was fired at something white during one night. However, the target turned out to be a cow. The shot missed!

We used to throw grenades in the re-entrant on the south side of Ditcheat Hill. Slit trenches were dug beside the roads leading to the village.

East Pennard Home Guard.
Back Row: Ted Kent; Archie Kent; Bert Whitehead; Cecil Warren; Len Hatcher; Jim Hoare; George Pearse; Bill Newport; Reg Raikes (worked at Lower Withial Farm for William Moody, lived in a cottage opposite Higher Withial Farm)
Second Row: Les Whitemore; Harry Allen; Bill Woolley; Mr. Newport; Austin Moody; John George; Arthur Billing; Roy Rogers; Walter Spirrell
Third Row: Will Bryant; Fred Whitemore; 'Squire' Walter Napier; Alan Raikes; Fred Norman
Front Row: Jim Woolley; John Gould; Eddie Gifford; Herbert Bryant; Harry Gifford; John Maidment
Others in the platoon included David England, Alan Nurse, Arthur Yeoman, Thomas Hutchins, Arthur Down, Maurice Allen and Dick Allen, the platoon's 2nd in Command.
Austin Moody, Cecil Warren, brothers Eddie and George Gifford, and John Gould were all farmers, whilst John George was a local garage proprietor.
(Mrs. Kathleen Nurse collection)

Pennard House, the home of 'Squire' Napier, was used for Sunday parades; grenades and ammunition were kept in a Nissen hut in an area near the greenhouses known as Carpenter's Yard (ST 598 375). Cpl. Fred Norman was, like his father before him, head gardener at Pennard House and was responsible for the ammunition stored there. Two wooden huts were erected to provide shelter at the observation posts, one at Boxbush Hill (ST 582 373), the other at Wraxall Hill. Below this point, in the south-east corner of the cross roads, at what was known as the 'Wraxall Arms', slit trenches were dug to provide cover for troops defending the cross roads.

Evercreech Home Guard at a Stand Down meal in The Bell Inn.
Back Row: Sam Carew; Unknown; Jim Rayes; Harry Bryant; Unknown; George Reakes; Walt Rabbits; Edgar Rabbits; Hedley Lester
Second Row: Unknown; Reg Read; Ted Belfield; Theo Matthews; Unknown; Unknown; Dick Durnford; Jim Doble; Kenneth Hill
Third Row: Unknown; Unknown; Unknown; Ted Gardiner; Unknown; George Oliver; Percy Hill; Jack Crago
Fourth Row: Fred Hicks; Sgt. Reg Moody; Mr. Melville; Col. Spencer; Lt. Jim Dudd; Unknown; Sgt. Reg Goverd; Viv Moxey
Fifth Row: Tom Rabbits; Doug Dunford; 'Butcher' Haines; George Parker; Claud Wiltshire; Norman Stone; Ern Riggs
Front Row: Fred Hartnell; Bill Upshall; Sam Cox; Charlie Joyce; Bill Feaver; Fred Taylor; Ken White
Included in this photograph are some N.C.O.s from Shepton Mallet Home Guard. It is believed that Fred Ackerman is also in the photograph.
(G.J.H. Doble collection)

NO. 5 (PILTON) PLATOON

The following five photographs have kindly been provided by the Pilton Local History Group. Unfortunately, none of the photographs were captioned at the time and the names provided are as a result of enquiries nearly 60 years later.

(top left) Back Row: Bill Appleby; Cpl. Frank Stockwell; Capt. Hayward; Capt. Franks; Cpl. Fred Morgan; Fred Padfield; Sgt. Bert Dew, M.M.
Front Row: Bill Carter; Sgt. Cyril Chapman; Royston Connock; Bert Rymes

(top right) Back Row: Unknown; Cpl. Frank Stockwell Jnr.; Jack Harris; Maurice Watch; Frank Miell; Doug Fleming
Front Row: Sgt. Cyril Chapman; Frank Stockwell Snr.; Unknown; Gerald Plumley; Mick Leonard; Sgt. Bert Dew; Captain Franks

(above) Back Row: Captain Hayward; Geoff Williams; Jack Harris; Bert Rymes; Fred Padfield; Ford Tilley; Joe Eavis; Gus Rodgers; Frank Stockwell Jnr.; Mick Leonard
Front Row: Unknown; Bill Appleby; Art Ball; Cpl. Fred Morgan; Royston Connock; Alec Green; Eddie Harris; Cyril Chapman

The above three photographs were taken in the grounds of Pilton Manor with the tower of St. John the Baptist Church just visible in the background. The quality of the photographs makes confirmation of some ranks difficult.

(left) Sgt. Bert Dew, M.M.; Jim Rogers; George Windsor; Alf Dew; Jack Harris; Eddie Harris; Alec Green; Bill Appleby; Cyril Chapman

(right) Pilton Home Guard gather for a final photograph, probably on 3rd December 1944.

The following extracts have been taken from a notebook entitled 'No. 5 (Pilton) Platoon Home Guard Fund':

At a meeting held in The Hut on 11th October 1943 Lt. Cooper suggested that a committee be formed to deal with the Home Guard Fund which amounted to £17-13-2½d. As a result the following committee was formed:

Chairman, Secy. & Treasurer	2nd Lt. A.B. Cooper (later replaced by Sgt. A. Dew, M.M.)	
Committee	No. 1 Section	Cpl. Morgan, Pte. Appleby
	No. 2 Section	Cpl. Stockwell, Pte. Stone
	No. 3 Section	Sgt. Chapman, Pte. Padfield

As Stand Down approached in 1944, the Committee decided to spend 10/- on a Home Guard party. On 6th October a meeting was held to decide what was required for the evening. The following accounts indicate the form the party took:

9 gallons of beer	£3-12-0d	1 doz. Minerals	4-0d
2 doz. Pale Ale	£1- 8-0d	4 Guinness	4-4d
1 doz. Home Brewed	14-0d	Caretaker	5-0d

Not all monies were spent on self-indulgence. On 15th November 1944 the Platoon held a Home Guard Social and were able, on 20th November, to hand £22-5-0d to a Miss Dashwood for the Prisoners of War Fund.

One interesting entry in the accounts mentions a payment of 14/- for damage to Pilton Working Mens' Club. It must have been some party!

The final entry in the accounts refers to another Home Guard Party held on 17th October 1945. Expenses for beer, cigarettes and cleaning the hut put a large dent in the fund, leaving a balance of £1-9-6d which was paid to the Welcome Home Fund. We can only hope that the £1-9-6d was well spent.

ASHWICK COMPANY

COMMANDING OFFICER   Major Hamilton Price
2ND IN COMMAND   Capt. A.C. James
                                  (Capt. W.W.T. Moore)

*This photograph of **Ashwick Company** is hand-captioned 'Downside, Stratton. Ashwick Company Parade 4th Som. HG 1943'.*

  At the head of the parade is Major Hamilton Price who lived at Ashwick Court. Behind him, left to right, are Capt. John 'Jumbo' Moore of Downside School, Lt. Bert Skirton (Oakhill Platoon), Lt. Cobb, Capt. A.C. James (Company 2nd in Command), 2nd Lt. Harry Durbin, Dr. P. Taeffe-Finn (Company M.O.), 2nd Lt. Wisdom (Stratton Platoon), Lt. Bennett Greenway (Holcombe Platoon), Lt. Jack Brittain (Leigh-on-Mendip), Lt. Lionel Brewer (Stoke St. Michael) and Lt. S.W. Fry. The third from the rear on the extreme left-hand column is Sgt. A.C. Britton. Halfway down the left-hand column is the figure of C.S.M. Wyndham Gilson who was a regular in the Somerset L.I. from about 1912-19. A quarry accident in the 1920s resulted in the loss of most of his right arm but this did not prevent him from continuing to drive his motorcar. He sunsequently became a member of Holcombe Platoon before he left to become responsible for training members of other platoons in Ashwick Company. These were based on Oakhill, Stoke St. Michael, Holcombe, Stratton-on-the-Fosse (No. 4 Platoon), Chilcompton and possibly Leigh-on-Mendip and Coleford. Some weapons and stores were kept at Holcombe Manor. Grenade practice was carried out at Vobster whilst Stratton Moor was used for rifle practice.

(above) **Stoke St. Michael Home Guard**.
Back Row: D. Wilkins; Fred Parfitt; G. Banfield; L. Wilkins; David Treasure; Percy Francis; D. Gilson; Edgar Massey; E. Griggs; 'Jumbo' Massey; R. Emery
Second Row: H. Taylor; R. Burnett; D. Isaacs; R. Tucker; D. Swain; P. Witcombe; W. Hiscox; C. Lovelock; S. Berryman; L. Colbourn; Ted Treasure
Third Row: Gordon Treasure; C. Cullen; F. Griffen; L. Vincent; 'Shotter' Lambert; E. Fuller; Len Treasure; Bill Lambert; Walter Lambert; Walt Francis; G. Taylor
Front Row: Alec Parfitt; Alf Parfitt; L. Browning; Edgar Massey; A. Perkins; Lt. Lionel Brewer (Platoon Commander); Ron Parfitt; Sgt. V. Butt; H. Tapscott; Cpl. G. Derrick; Frank Parfitt
It is likely that all the front row are N.C.O.s but the quality of the photograph prevents correct identification of most ranks.
(Bob Lambert collection)

(left) For identification purposes, the columns have been lettered A-O from left to right and the ranks numbered 1-27 from front to back.

A1 Herb Allen; A2 Bert Emery; A6 Sgt. A.C. Britton
B1 Les Padfield; B2 Bob Marks; B4 Frank Thorner; B5 Ivan Webb; B6 Frank Turner
C1 Sid Barnett; C2 Maurice Skirton; C4 Bill Williams; C5 Cecil Burr; C6 Tony Thorner; C7 Dick Gill
D1 Lance Purnell; D2 D. Miller; D4 Perce Hockey; D5 Reg Reeves; D6 Cyril Hockey
E1 Bob Rolls; E2 John Gilham; E4 Raymond Davey; E5 Vic Attwood
F1 Jack Gilson; F2 Ted Williams; F3 Bob Steeds; F4 Jack Flower; F5 Mr. Walters; F6 Bill Fricker
G1 Arthur Gilson; G2 Henry Tucker; G3 Jack Barnett; G5 Bill Flower; G6 Hewart Snook
H2 Harold Tucker; H3 Claude Godfrey; H4 Nelson Bown; H5 Powell Dudden; H6 Nelson Thorner
I1 Dennis Rossiter; I4 Herb Rossiter; I6 Edgar Smith
J1 Reg Challenger; J2 Gilb Gilson; J3 Mr. Bevan; J4 Bill Wilkins
K1 Henry Witcombe; K2 Mr. Syrup; K4 Edwin Hill; K5 Tom Purnell; K6 Les Charlton; K7 Bill Wells (injured in a cup discharger accident at Daly's Quarry)
L1 Reg Trippick; L2 Godfrey Alford; L3 Mr. Padfield; L5 Morris Hill; L6 Bill Diamond
M1 Mr. Bryant; M2 Bill Feltham; M5 Mike Reakes
N1 Albert Bromwell

Another photograph exists, obviously taken just after the one displayed here, which shows Bill Lovell standing in front of Albert Bromwell in Column N.
(Mrs. Gwen G. Nielson collection)

Platoon stretcher-bearers for Stoke St. Michael Home Guard were Walter Lambert, L. Colbourn and Len Kerton. First aid was practised by them at Dr. Taeffe-Finn's home every Sunday morning.

Desmond Wilkins joined the Home Guard in 1942 when he was 18 years old. The platoon built a rifle range at Moons Hill Quarry. Wainwright's Quarry was used for grenade practice. Exercises were varied; Glen View House at Nettlebridge was 'attacked' one Sunday morning whilst an all-night scheme involved marching to Midsomer Norton to attack the railway. The field behind the Old School at Stoke was used as an observation post, a wooden hut being provided for shelter. Desmond can recall a period when duties were discontinued on the hill. This may well have saved his life as afterwards the Germans dropped a stick of bombs, one sending a large stone clean through the hut. A memory he will never forget was in June 1944 when O.P. duties were being carried out at Cranmore Tower. One early morning the sky was filled with a seemingly endless stream of aeroplanes, so many that Desmond could not understand why they did not collide; it was D-Day, 6th June.

Live firing also took place at Edford, Holcombe, Hinton Charterhouse near Norton St. Philip and on the Beacon Range, north-east of Shepton Mallet. The exact location of the first three ranges has not been determined.

The late Gerry Burr of Yeovil, in a letter to the author, recalled his memories of the Gurney Slade Home Guard.

My first memories of 'Slade Home Guard' was seeing outside *The George Inn* a parade of our local middle-aged men proudly displaying their L.D.V. arm bands. We in the village of Gurney Slade invariably referred to our local Home Guard as Slade Home Guard although the unit consisted of Binegar men as well. All the parades were held in Gurney Slade, either midweek at the Village Hall or Sunday mornings outside *The George Inn*. Whatever the training programme, the parades always dismissed outside *The George*.

Their Commanding Officer was Major Hamilton Price, a resident of Ashwick. (Gurney Slade has no parish and shares parishes with Binegar and Ashwick.) Hamilton Price was a retired Army Major and in appearance a typical portrayal of military men of the day. Sporting a monocle and upturned white moustache he could be no other than an old soldier. Unfortunately time had taken its toll on his bearing and he had quite a humped back but nevertheless he carried himself quite well. He drove a small Austin Seven two-seat tourer identical to those used in early war years by the army, just to suit his image. Hamilton Price had once owned property in Malaya (tea, I believe) but the Japanese invasion had caused him problems. Captain Hillier, also from the neighbouring parish of Ashwick, was the other senior officer. It seemed that we had a shortage of senior officer material in our village. Later on, a sergeant was promoted to Lieutenant and he too was from Ashwick. He was Mr. Cobb, a representative for the Oakhill Brewery.

A nightly guard was mounted on the local Somerset and Dorset Railway Station, Binegar. The Guard occupied a small gangers' hut from which they did their patrols. Hamilton Price paid them a visit on one occasion to test out their 'Halt, who goes there' ability and went away quite satisfied. Many of the Home Guard were World War 1 veterans who hadn't forgotten their training. A couple of holes appeared in the hut roof over the years when the off-watch guard returned and emptied their magazines by the old 'ease springs' method. You only had to miscount and with one left up the spout away went a round skyward over Binegar Station. Raymond Davey, a local quarryman with an unfortunate stutter cleared his magazine one night and when looking for the discharged rounds on the floor could only find three. While Raymond was stuttering to his colleague about the lost two rounds there were two loud explosions as they flew from Raymond's rifle over his shoulder into the stove. When the story was related to me next day I was told that old Tom Ford was asleep on the bunk at the time and in the two seconds between round one and round two going off, Tom was up, boots on and outside. Slight exaggeration, perhaps, but apparently he did move well for an old 'un.

A quiet man, Tom, but a very sincere member of the Home Guard and proudly held the rank of Lance Corporal. During one night of manoeuvres against a neighbouring section, Tom, together with Private Hewart Snook, was confronted by a low wall. In the total darkness they decided to climb over, keeping as low as possible and advance upon the enemy position. Neither could see that the wall concealed a drop of 12 feet on the other side. The result was two casualties, Hewart with a broken leg and Tom with bruises and a broken rifle.

Minor casualties did crop up from time to time. Harry Foxwell from Emborough was the proud possessor of a motorbike, a Montgomery JAP, for which he was allocated petrol for use as a dispatch rider. Harry had a busy night on one occasion and altogether knocked down five members of his own side. I suppose this comes under the category of 'friendly fire'. That particular night our Home Guard had a 'battle' with the Farrington Gurney Section. The first attempt at this battle was unsuccessful as they turned out on the wrong night. Bill Flower, another quarryman and Lance Corporal, led his section against the opposing side that night. It is hard now to imagine how dark the countryside was during those years of blackout. Bill edged forward to see if he could discern any movement.

Meanwhile back in the platoon the men were getting a bit bored and one asked his comrades if they knew what time it was. Neither knew, only the N.C.O. had a watch. I think it was one of the Hockeys who edged forward slowly and quietly, as he was trained to do, and reached a point close to Bill without Bill hearing his approach. He tapped Bill on the shoulder: "What time is it?" The shock was too much for Bill who let out a cry of alarm and had to retreat with an acute laundry problem.

Transport was never a problem. Our local Haulage Contractor, E. Wareham and Sons, and Arthur Harvey, Licensee, both possessed tipper lorries that could be used as personnel carriers. Hamilton Price however, always used his little Austin. I remember very well one Wednesday evening outside the Village Hall watching the men parade. This was done in the main road but passing vehicles were rare then so no hold-ups ever occurred. Hamilton Price stepped back as the men were given the open order march and vanished. He had failed to see the overgrown ditch behind him and was lying in it, flat on his back.

You can imagine my friends and I at the age of about 14 finding this episode hilarious. I was at Downside College, Stratton-on-the-Fosse, when the 4th Somerset were disbanded. A huge parade was brought together in lorries and out the front once again, in all his glory, was Major Hamilton Price. We had heard his parade ground voice so many times as each year he led the parade to the local church on Armistice Sunday. This was his great day and he took an almighty breath and called, "PARADE", in a voice that echoed across the field. He then collapsed choking as unfortunately his teeth had become dislodged and it was the quick thinking of his Lieutenant who thumped him on his arched back that saved the day. This caused quite a bit of polite chuckling 'amongst the ranks'.

I remember watching the weapon training when new weapons became available to our temporary troops, namely the Blacker Bombard and the Cup Discharger. Cyril Hockey was trained to use the Blacker Bombard and one evening was demonstrating the technique to a bunch of interested privates. Unfortunately Cyril had a couple of misfires and being rather 'fiery' by nature started using a few adjectives that were not in the book. One more go then 'click', another misfire. Cyril got up from his prone position, kicked the gun and went on home. Fortunately you didn't get put on a charge in the Home Guard. Bill Wilkins, a private, was once reprimanded by Ivan Webb, his Sergeant, for not calling him Sergeant whilst on duty. This ended up in a fist fight.

There are many incidents that can be told with humour about any Home Guard but there were also occasions we remember that brought sadness to the village. One Sunday morning the troops were training in an old disused quarry (Dally's Quarry on Marchant's Hill). The object of the exercise was to learn how to use the 'Cup Discharger', an attachment to the end of a rifle designed to fire a Hand Grenade further than that normally thrown by hand. On this occasion the grenade exploded in the cup, killing Captain Hillier and causing serious arm injuries to Sergeant Bill Wells. In those days it was necessary to run the half mile or so to the pub and telephone Shepton Mallet Ambulance Station. It was the best part of an hour before they received any attention from the ambulance but in the meantime my future father-in-law, Charlie Mears, had done his best with bandages. Charlie was a qualified first-aider in the local coal mines and a stretcher-bearer with the Home Guard.

Leaving school at the age of 14 in 1942, I was employed as barman in *The George*. I would open the pub at 12 noon on Sundays but as that time coincided with the morning parade falling out I would go in a few minutes early and line up the drinks ready on the bar. I knew all the 'usual' drinks and soon sorted out the invasion of about 20 or 30 thirsty troops. We all tend to laugh at the 'Dad's Army' of that era. They certainly did provide some laughs. One annual duty was to erect an anti-tank barrier across the A37. The location of this was right on the pub forecourt and across to the garage opposite. Holes had been prepared in the crossing and rectangular concrete covers fitted into them. The rails that fitted into them were old railway lines and when inserted formed an inverted 'V', known as hairpins. There were several rows of these and they would certainly have presented quite a barrier to any tanks. Had the Germans invaded and reached that far inland I could have witnessed their frustration from my bedroom window! These concrete sections were removed towards the end of the war, except for one. If you look on the door-step of our old cottage (*right*), now part of *The George's Restaurant*, you can still see the rectangular cover of one of the holes.

Anti-tank trenches were also dug by excavators all along the railway and many pillboxes were constructed; the latter are still to be seen.

Well, they were never put to the test, our part-timers in khaki, but my bet is as far as the Mendip troop was concerned, that they would have had a go and done their best. Looking at it one way they were our best. In fact, they were all we had.

*Lt. Bert Skirton and some of the **Oakhill Platoon** parade in Oakhill Village. Behind him on his left is D/R Bill Cox on a Calthorpe whilst D/R Harold Tucker sits astride his Royal Enfield. Leading the column nearest the house is Thomas Perkins. Behind Sgt. Maurice Skirton, leading the centre column, is Henry Tucker. Note Sgt. Skirton's chevrons on his left sleeve only, the correct method of wearing chevrons in the Home Guard. At the head of the column nearest the camera is L. Padfield with the tall figure of A. Gilson behind.
(Dorothy Tucker collection)*

The **Oakhill Platoon**, photographed at 'The Beeches', at the time the offices of the Oakhill Brewery. The front rows are standing or sitting on beer crates marked 'The Bristol United Breweries Ltd'.
Back Row: Arthur 'Snowy' Barnett; Sid Barnett; Len Bevan; Reg Passey; Harold Tucker; Unknown; Arthur Gilson; A. Weeks; Harry Tucker; Mick Reeves; Bob Steeds; Reg Trippick
Second Row: Unknown; Lance Purnell; Gilb Gilson; L. Harding; R. Emery; Unknown; John Gilham; F. Reeves; Unknown; Jack Gilson; Unknown; Hubert Padfield; Henry Witcombe; Maurice Skirton
Third Row: W. Foxwell; Mr. Daniel; Mr. Mencam; P. Trippick; Bill Feltham; Godfrey Alford; D. Miller; Fred Searle; Unknown; Jack Barnett; Unknown
Front Row: Cpl. Les Padfield; Unknown; Sgt. B. Melhuish; Lt. Bert Skirton; Sgt. Davies; Unknown; Cpl. Hibbs
(Dorothy Tucker collection)

LEIGH-ON-MENDIP PLATOON

Although no photograph has been located, Leigh-on-Mendip Platoon comprised more than 30 men. Platoon Headquarters was the Church Reading Room which could be contacted by dialling Mells 17, the telephone number of the house next door. The Platoon Commander was Lt. Jack Brittain. A note in the Leigh-on-Mendip War Book records the death of Pte. H. Day in September 1942 whilst on an exercise. The war book, now lodged with the Somerset Archive & Record Service, lists the members as follows:

Pte. W.T. Abel, L/Cpl. W.F.T. Ashman, Pte. C. Berry, Pte. P. Berryman, Pte. L.W.T. Bodman, Cpl. K.R. Britten, Pte. H.E.M. Britten, Pte. A.G.J. Candy, L/Cpl. H.G. Chapman, Cpl. L.A. Clark, Pte. J.E. Cox, Pte. C.E. Day, Pte. H.F. Day, L/Cpl. L. Duck, Pte. A.J. Erswell, Pte. D.H. Evans, Sgt. W.H. Evans, Sgt. J. Griffin, Cpl. A.J. Hiscox, Sgt. E. Jelly, Pte. H.E. King, Platoon Sergeant E.E. King (2nd in Command), Cpl. W.J. March, Pte. L.A. Moon, Sgt. W.J. Paradise, Pte. L.T. Potts, Pte. W.E. Reakes, Pte. H.O. Saunders, Pte. E.T. Stock, Pte. E.V. Trim, L/Cpl. E.J. Trim, Pte. A. Tucker, Pte. O.S.A. Tucker, Pte. F.H. Vining, Cpl. P.G. Wheeler, Pte. J.E. Whitmarsh, Pte. L.J. Wickham, Pte. J. Witcombe, Pte. F.M. Withey.

Holcombe Platoon, *photographed in August 1943.*
Back Row: Mr. Young; Harold James; Bill Young; Ken Ashman; Bill Robbins; Gerald Perkins; Cyril Treasure; Eric Swift
Second Row: Percy Taylor; Henry Moore; Harold Padfield; Ron Lodge; Ted Salvidge; Unknown; Ernie Chivers; Harry Winters; Howard James; Robin Candy
Third Row: Maurice Dodimead; Mr. Staunton; Jack Head; John Moore; Stan Lane; Walter Moore; Charlie Paget; Fred Pearce; Bob Wheeler
Front Row: Sgt. Harry Raikes; Sgt. Charlie Britten; Sgt. Frank James; L/Cpl. Len Hoskins; Lt. Bennett Greenway; L/Cpl. Archie Harding; L/Cpl. Malonski; Cpl. Jesse Edwards; Cpl. 'Nobby' Clarke
(A.C. Britten collection)

5th Somerset (Bath City) Battalion

HEADQUARTERS	15, Queen Square, Bath
DATE FORMED	May 1940
COMMANDING OFFICER	Lt. Col. L.R.E.W. Taylor, D.S.O.
	(Col. G.H. Rogers, O.B.E., D.L.)
2ND IN COMMAND	Major A.O. Day, T.D.

H.Q. STAFF

A & Q	Capt. S. Leverton, General List.
	Capt. L.E. de Ridder, General List
ADJUTANT	Capt. E.F. Radcliff, General List
ADMIN. OFFICER	Lt. L.E. de Ridder
AMMUNITION OFFICER	Capt. R.T. Field
ARMOURER	2nd Lt. A.T. Selman
BATTERY OFFICER	Lt. L.E.C. Baker
CAMOUFLAGE OFFICER	2nd Lt. C.W. Ellis
CHEMICAL WARFARE OFFR.	Lt. N. Morton (Capt. A.J. Gould)
GUIDES OFFICER	Lt. W. Moger
INTELLIGENCE OFFICER	Lt. H.A. Mealand
	(Major G. St. J. Strutt, C.B.E.)
LIAISON OFFICER	Major J.B. Heron (Civil Defence)
	Capt. J. McKee (North Sector)
	Lt. M.S. Macdonnel (Police)
MEDICAL OFFICER	Major S. Marle,
	Major E.J. Boschi
	(Major J.B. Bennett)
	(Capt. D.A. Mitchell)
MESSING OFFICER	Lt. W. Lewis
RANGES & ANTI-AIRCRAFT LIAISON OFFICER	Capt. F.W. Willis
SIGNALS OFFICER	Lt. V.G. Roberts
	(Lt. Pooley)
WEAPON TRAINING OFFR.	Lt. D.A. Pike
	(Capt. H.M. Howell, M.B.E.)
WORKS OFFICER	Lt. A.H. Axford

HEADQUARTERS COMPANY

HEADQUARTERS	19a, Monmouth Place
COMMANDING OFFICER	Major W.H.M. Richards
2ND IN COMMAND	Capt. F.W. Ashpole

"THE SOUL OF ANZAC" INSPECTS BATH HOME GUARD.

*Field Marshal Lord Birdwood inspecting a guard of honour of the **Headquarters Company** at Bath Pavilion in February 1941. Colonel Guy Rogers, the Battalion Commanding Officer, is on the left of the picture. As General Sir William Birdwood, he had taken part in the Gallipoli Campaign of the First World War. On 15th May 1915, he had his hair parted by a Turkish bullet while he was looking through a periscope. The wound turned septic but he remained in command. He died in 1951 in his 87th year. (Bath Weekly Chronicle & Herald, 15th February 1941, via Mrs. Theobald)*

Bob White, a member of Headquarters Company, recalls the names of other members: Lt. Cyril Harris, 2nd Lt. John Williams, C.S.M. Richardson, Sgt. (later Lt.) George Hovey and Cpl. Cavill. 'Other ranks' included Bert Chick, Rex Jones, Cyril Sharpe, Ken Saunders and John & Ron Legg.

An isolated spot at Lansdown in the vicinity of map ref. ST 725 703 was used for Sten and Tommy gun practice whilst an adjacent quarry was used for live grenade practice.

NO. 1 (SOUTH EAST) COMPANY

HEADQUARTERS   Normal – 5, Warminster Road
                            Operational – The Hut, North Road

COMMANDING OFFICER   Major K. Stewart
                                    (Capt. A. Stuart Black)
2ND IN COMMAND   Capt. C. Gordon

(above) **No. 1 Company** *believed to have been photographed on 8th October 1944.*
Back Row: none identified
Second Row: No. 3 Gudge Tucker; No. 18 Tommy Punter
Third Row: No. 11 Harold Player; No. 13 Fred Arnold; No. 19 Dick Dowding
Fourth Row: No. 2 Frank Green; No. 9 Major Stewart; No. 12 Lt. Stokes; No. 16 Eric Stoffels
Front Row: No. 2 Richard Green; No. 4 Ray Cook *(Tony Green collection)*

(right) **'C' Platoon (Claverton and Claverton Down) No. 1 Company**
Back Row: Mr. Cook; Unknown; Cpl. Frank Green; Dick Dowding; Unknown; Gudge Tucker; Gerald Rich; Unknown
Middle Row: L/Cpl. Harold Player; Unknown; Unknown; 2nd Lt. Fred Stokes; Unknown; Unknown; Cpl. Tom Punter; Ray Brooks
Front Row: Herbert Mays; David Butcher; Ray Cook; Tony Candy
    Other members of the Platoon included Herbert Francis Croon, Dicky Dafforn, Bert Feasy, Reg Hancock, Mr. Lodge, Bill Maidment, Charlie Maslen, Mr. Mottram, Pete Myson, Reg Player and Bill White.
(Tony Green collection)

The original meeting place for 'C' Platoon was the school at Claverton but later it moved to Claverton Manor. Arms were kept in the front room of No. 1 Brassknocker Hill, the home of Corporal Croon. A road block was manned by the platoon at Claverton Down Road at a site now occupied by the entrance to Bath University. Guard duties were carried out at the top of Bathwick Hill.

Small-bore shooting took place in an old quarry at Lime Kiln Lane and at Monkton Combe School, where the butts were still standing in 2000, and at Vineyards Farm where full-bore shooting took place across a valley. Grenade practice took place at Hampton Rocks. Despite several appeals the site of the rifle range at Vineyards Farm has not been determined.

Ray Brooks recounted the following story after the war. Corporal Green served in the Army Veterinary Corps. in the First World War. One night he was detailed to meet a contingent from the Admiralty Home Guard at Claverton Down and take them to Claverton School. He selected a route that kept clear of the roads and proceeded through Claverton Woods. By the time the Admiralty arrived at the rendezvous it is maintained they were nervous wrecks, because every rustling branch and cracking stick underfoot convinced them they were being followed by Germans!

One evening's training, which took place at Spring Hill, Claverton Down, entailed pairs of Home Guards having to advance silently up to a sentry without being detected. Privates Brooks and Mottram slowly and quietly crawled towards the sentry, 'freezing' every time he turned. Suddenly the silence was punctuated by screaming and shouting and waving of arms from the two 'attackers' who were promptly captured. Unknown to them until it was too late, our intrepid pair had crawled through a bees' nest.

For many Home Guards who were not used to being in the countryside in the dark, noises and shadows played tricks on their imagination. One incident, not in Somerset, concerned two Home Guards who stalked a pair of 'German Paratroops' moving slowly along a ditch. After a considerable time they realised the 'enemy' were two hedgehogs snuffling their way along the top of the bank.

NO. 2 (NORTH EAST) COMPANY

HEADQUARTERS	Normal – Horse Showground, Lambridge
	Operational – Griffin's Garage, Swainswick
COMMANDING OFFR.	Major W.M. Huntley
	(Commander A. Pakenham)
	(Major A.O. Day, T.D.)
2ND IN COMMAND	Capt. E.J. Hart

'A' Platoon No. 2 Company, *photographed outside Oriel Hall in Swainswick.*
Back Row: Roy Cambourne (gardener); Selwyn Shepherd (music teacher); Mr. Godwin (farmer); Chris or Phil Blanchard; John Painter (quarryman); Alfred Bath (farmer); Leslie Bath (son of Alfred, farmer)
Middle Row: Reg Cambourne (gardener); Len Daniels (Admiralty employee); Ken Stephens; Cpl. George Sartain (building trade); Les Greenslade; Eddie Eastment (farmer); Mr. Headley (printer)
Front Row: Cpl. Merchant (building trade); Cpl. Jefferies (Bath Wholesale Fruiterers); Lt. Hewitt Hart; Lt. Page (Bath Cabinet Makers); Sgt. Oram; L/Cpl. Eddie Nicholls (building trade).
Missing from the photograph is Ted Gibbs. Note the interesting hair style sported by John Painter.
(Gladys Jeffries collection)

Roy Cambourne believes that 'A' Platoon was unique in that it had its own signal section. It comprised five members aged 16 at the time who trained in semaphore signalling with flags under the guidance of Fred Jeans, an old soldier who had served with the Royal Signals.

Rifle ranges used were at Box, Chilcombe Bottom and Newton St. Loe whilst grenade practice was carried out at Cheddar and Newton St. Loe. Transport to get to distant ranges was provided by lorries owned by Swainswick Garage.

Night-time exercises were sometimes fraught with danger. One night young Roy Cambourne clambered up over a wall, jumped off into the darkness and fell a considerable distance into a stream.

Men of 'A' Platoon No. 2 Company.
Back Row: John Turner Griffin; Eddie Nicholls; Unknown
Middle Row: Unknown; Dennis Daniels; Unknown; Unknown; Selwyn Shepherd; Reg Merchant
Front Row: Unknown; Cpl. Jefferies; Unknown; Lt. Page; Capt. Hewitt Hart; Unknown
John Turner Griffin later became a sergeant in 'A' Platoon and it was his garage at Swainswick that became the operational Headquarters of No. 2 Company.
(Mrs. Maude Griffin collection)

(right) Henry Charles Pickford, Somerset's first Home Guard fatality, with his daughter Marianne. Harry, as he was known to everyone, was a member of the 5th (Bath City) Battalion Home Guard. In the early hours of Saturday 17th August 1940, Harry was part of a detail guarding the as yet unfinished Charmy Down Airfield. There were no witnesses to the incident but it is believed that having placed his rifle and dog in his car, before going home, Harry returned to the vicinity of an unexploded bomb. Suddenly the tranquility of the early hours was shattered by a violent explosion. Harry was killed instantly together with a civilian. He left a young widow and Marianne, his four-year-old daughter. For weeks after, Marianne waited patiently every evening at the cottage window for her father to return home. Harry lies at rest with other members of his family in Langridge Churchyard. (Mrs. Marianne Brunt collection)

This scroll commemorates

Private H. C. Pickford
Somerset Home Guard

held in honour as one who served King and Country in the world war of 1939-1945 and gave his life to save mankind from tyranny. May his sacrifice help to bring the peace and freedom for which he died.

*(below) Taken on a winter's day in Tadwick Lane, Upper Swainswick, members of **Swainswick Home Guard** pose for the cameraman.*
Back Row: centre, Sgt. Malcolm Shackell
Front Row: left, Henry Davis
(Caroline Davey collection)

'B' Platoon No. 2 Company, photographed at the Horse Showground, Lambridge, Bath.
Back Row: H. Ricketts (Stothert & Pitt employee); Mr. Merritt Jnr.; Mr. Midgley (electrician); Unknown; Mr. Clancy (tool maker); Unknown; Mr. Williams (Stothert & Pitt employee)
Middle Row: Unknown; G. Cross (builder); George Banks (maintenance engineer at Fortt's Biscuit Factory); W. Elley (gardener); Unknown; Unknown; Unknown; Unknown
Front Row: Cpl. Hamilton (decorator); Cpl. McNamara (decorator); Sgt. Merritt (motor mechanic); Unknown; Lt. William Hart (ladies and gents hairdresser in Orange Grove, known as Hart and Godwin in 1937, renamed Hartwin by 1957); Capt. Hewitt Hart; Sgt. Room (Stothert & Pitt engineer); Sgt. Clem McNamara
(Gordon Banks collection)

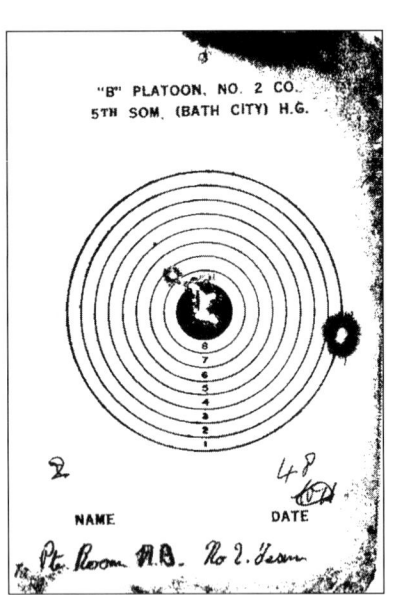

Apart from an indoor rifle range built at Chudleigh Villa (see below), an outdoor range was built nearby which was damaged by a direct hit during the air raids of 1942.

(right) Work being carried out at Chudleigh Villa in 1940, converting the building in the background to a .22" rifle range for the Home Guard. When the building was subsequently demolished in the 1990s a dozen or so targets were found. The score on one shot by Pte. Brown, a creditable 48 out of 50 (above).
On the roof: Unknown; Unknown; Mr. Coles; Fred Freeman; Charlie Rhymes; Mr. Wheatley; Sgt. Clem McNamara
Foreground: Fred Mines; William Hart; Unknown; Unknown; George Banks; Les Room; Bert Room; Unknown; Mr. Matthews; Gordon Banks
(Gordon Banks collection)

Members of the Home Guard at Fairfield Park, Bath collecting scrap metal. Their Headquarters was originally at Fairfield Stores, owned by Mr. Cook, a Captain in the First World War. Later Headquarters moved to Chudleigh Villa in Fairfield Road. The motorcycle with the Bath registration number is either a Triumph Tiger 80 or 90, a popular single-cylinder machine of the late 1930s.
Back Row: Mr. Coles; Charlie Rhymes; Les Room; Mr. Wheatley; Maurice Gordon Oatley; William Hart; Clem McNamara
Front Row: Mr. Matthews; Unknown; Unknown; George Banks; Unknown; Bert Room; Unknown
Kneeling: Fred Mines; Fred Freeman.
Maurice Gordon Oatley subsequently joined the Northamptonshire Yeomanry and was killed in Holland on 30th October 1944 aged 20. He lies in Plot 9, Row A, Joint Grave 10-11 Bergen-op-Zoom. (Gordon Banks collection)

*Photographed in front of the present Bath Rugby Clubhouse, members of **Fairfield Park Home Guard** march past, led, possibly, by Lt. Crozier Cole. Note the band which was painted red on the rifle fore ends, signifying rifles chambered for .300" rimless ammunition, typical Home Guard issue. (Gordon Banks collection)*

NO. 3 (NORTH WEST) COMPANY

HEADQUARTERS	Sion Lodge, Sion Hill
COMPANY COMMANDER	Major R.R. Glynne-Jones, O.B.E., T.D.
	(Major T.A. Davis)
2ND IN COMMAND	Capt. L. Hunt, M.C.
	Capt. T.J. Castle, O.B.E., M.C.

Sadly, no photograph of the Company or of any of its Platoons has been located.

NO. 4 (SOUTH WEST) COMPANY

HEADQUARTERS	Normal – 30, Gay Street
	Operational – Southdown Hall, Mount Rd.
COMPANY COMMANDER	Major T.J. Castle, O.B.E., M.C.
	(Major R.H. McKeag)
2ND IN COMMAND	Capt. J.W. Holloway

Note: Normal Headquarters in this case is at June 1943, the private residence of Major R.H. McKeag. Presumably Normal Headquarters would have moved to Major T.J. Castle's address when he took command after June 1943. This address is unknown.

(above) **Men of No. 4 Company**.
Back Row: No. 6 Mr. Morris; No. 26 A. Llewellyn
Second Row: none identified
Third Row: No. 5 George Lewis; No. 10 W.A. Curtis; No. 21 Cpl. L. Miles
Front Row: No. 6 Sgt. Ernie Chivers; No. 12 2nd Lt. Harold Holton;
 No. 17 2nd Lt. Hone; No. 18 Lt. A. Cox; No. 21 Lt. Clark; No. 22 Lt. Wheeler;
 No. 24 Mr. Wheeler (brother of No. 22); No. 27 Sgt. Philip Nowell;
 No. 28 Edwin Curtis Williams; No. 30 Sgt. Bert Brown, M.M., B.E.M.

Edwin Williams was a veteran of the First World War, having been wounded by shrapnel, as were so many of his contemporaries; he spent his working life at Ware's Nurseries. Sgt. P. Nowell worked at B.A.C. in Corsham; Sgt. Chivers, a resident of Southdown, was a local plumber. W.A. Curtis was employed by Stothert and Pitt whilst another Southdown resident, Mr. G. Lewis, worked for Mr. Bennett at Bath Market.
(Mrs. B. Temlett collection)

(right) **'A' Platoon No. 4 Company**, photographed at St. Philip's Primary School, Odd Down.
Back Row: Mr. Cox; Unknown; Mr. Morris; Unknown; Jim Hunt; Unknown;
 Unknown; Mr. Prewer; Gerald Plummer; Unknown
Middle Row: Unknown; Unknown; Unknown; Reg Hobbs; Jack Barratt;
 Sam Hallett; George Morris; Mr. Cartman; Unknown; Unknown;
 Bert Stride; Unknown; Unknown
Front Row: L/Cpl. George Stanton; Cpl. Bill Yewlands; Cpl. Len Miles;
 Lt. Clark; Lt. Doubleday; Sgt. Bert Brown, M.M., B.E.M.; Cpl. George Bond;
 Unknown; L/Cpl. Collins
(Mrs. Patricia Moore collection)

Len Miles, born in December 1905, was a baker by trade. When Bath suffered its first air raid Len attempted to join the Fire Service but was told he was too old and warned that as he was in a reserved occupation as a baker he could be sent anywhere in the county. Len then joined the Home Guard, drawing his kit and rifle from the Wessex Drill Hall, becoming a member of 'A' Platoon No. 4 Company. Having been sent on a Spigot Mortar course he joined 'A' section who were responsible for the Platoon's mortar. This bulky piece of equipment was kept at *The Burnt House* Inn run by a fellow Home Guard, Bert Stride. *The Burnt House* also provided a meeting place and .22" rifle range in the skittle alley. Later the Platoon moved to a new HQ built in a stone quarry on Bloomfield which consisted of a Nissen hut. Training was carried out in an open field at Kelston View. Improvisation was the order of the day and when it was decided that a moving target would be useful to train the Platoon members, a door was fitted with pulley wheels and suspended on a wire rope. Outdoor rifle ranges were used at Newton St. Loe and Englishcombe. Jim Hunt, the local coal merchant, loaned his lorry for Platoon transport. Platoon duties included guarding both ends of the railway tunnel and the Gas Works.

Sgt. Bert Brown was a native of Culmstock, Devon who served in the 8th Devonshire Battalion during the First World War at Ypres where he won the Military Medal.

Whilst living in Bath he was a member of No. 4 Company of the 5th Battalion, living at 8, Eastover Grove. He was employed by Mallory's, looking after all the local church clocks, including Bath Abbey. In the summer of 1940 he spent several nights away from Bath with fellow Home Guards manning the General Headquarters Stop Line Green, some 90 miles long, which finally boasted some 319 pill-boxes and 20 miles of anti-tank ditches stretching from Highbridge to within six miles of Gloucester via Freshford and Stroud.

During an air raid in April 1942 Mr. V. Sellar's drapery establishment and home on Bear Flat received a direct hit. Mr. Sellar's home was occupied by his wife, two daughters, a girl billetee and himself who were all sitting under the dining-room table when the bomb struck. The three girls managed to crawl out but Mr. Sellar was pinned down by fallen masonry.

Hearing footsteps they cried out for help but the footsteps faded away. Shortly after, the footsteps returned. Sgt. Brown apologised for not attending sooner but he explained he was carrying a wounded comrade to safety. At this stage the air raid was still in progress with bombs continuing to fall, together with random machine gunning. Sgt. Brown removed the masonry from Mr. Sellar and then released Mrs. Sellar. He then escorted the occupants of the wrecked house to a shelter, lending his greatcoat to one of the girls as she was only in her night clothes. For his actions Sgt. Brown was awarded the British Empire Medal.

(above) **Odd Down Platoon**.
Back Row: Len Rosenburg; Bill Stride; Dennis Meddick; Norman Gray; Theo Trim; Mr. Lovegrove; Unknown; Dai Thomas; Maurice Bailey; Unknown
Second Row: Unknown; Reg Day; Albert Cox; Joe Brennan; Unknown; Unknown; Harry Biggs; Roy Hardick; Mr. Prosser; George Player; Alan Pocock; Unknown
Third Row: Unknown; L/Cpl. Valdimir Austin Nelson Bampfylde; L/Cpl. Ernest 'Con' Flower; Roy Russell; Brian Carpenter; Unknown; Major Bert Mullins; Mr. Cartman; Ron Mullins; Unknown; Cpl. Shawcross
Front Row: Cpl. Bert Hulance or Bill Yewlands; Cpl. Dick Franklin; Sgt. Holbrook; Sgt. (later Lt.) Doubleday; Unknown; Capt. Holloway; Mr. Cutler?; Sgt. Bert Brown, M.M., B.E.M.; Mr. Bell?; Unknown
In June 1941 the following were known to be Members of 'A' Platoon: H.J. Biggs, E. Brown, H.S. Chick, A.H. Cox, H. Doubleday, E.W. Flower, V. Franklyn, L.M.P. Grath, J. Lovegrove and R.F. Russell.
(Len Cox collection)

(right) **Englishcombe Home Guard**.
Back Row: Fred Hallett; Ivor Harding; Bill Butler; George Barrett; Bob Lane; Tom Smith; Alfie Legg
Middle Row: Cpl. Geoff Rowe; Des Salter; Peter Lane; Peter Date; Bill Sawyer; Roy Meddick; Bill Bax
Front Row: Sid Dyer; Fred Rose; Len Harding; Lt. Walter Burden; L/Cpl. Fred Knott; Bobby Purnell; Fred Peach
Many members of Englishcombe Home Guard appear to have been employees of Manor Farm. Frederick Peach and Fred Hallett were the shepherds, Peter Lane was a general farmworker, Alfie Legg a rick thatcher. Ware's Nurseries employed Roy Meddick and Fred Knott. Fred Rose was a farmer's son of Rectory Farm whilst Peter Date's father farmed at Inglesbatch. George Barrett and Bill Butler were also farmworkers at Inglesbatch. All these men had passed away by 2001. Des Salter, a Platoon member still living in Englishcombe in 2003, was a foreman working for Stothert and Pitt of Bath.
(Mrs. Pat Stamp collection)

The undulating countryside around Englishcombe provided a site for a short rifle range with a natural amphitheatre forming the stop butt. This was situated in a field to the west of a minor road on a WNW/ESE axis with the butts at map ref. ST 714 620. As the minor road passed above the butts it was necessary to post lookouts on the road to warn traffic. Cartridge cases recovered during the war indicate that both .300" and .303" rounds were fired here.

Newton St. Loe Home Guard. *(Bert Whatley collection)*
Back Row: Norman Payne; Ted Davis; Ron Fletcher; Bob Hapgood; Bert Bailey; Bert Whatley; Jack Smith Jnr.; Jack White
Middle Row: Harry Ricketts; Ted Bailey; Tony Tuckwell; Lt. McDougall; Jack Gay; Arthur Tovey; Arthur Reginald Buoy; Ray White
Front Row: Norman Fletcher; Bill Wright; Cpl. Fred Hawkes; Lt. Carter; 2nd Lt. Hone; Sgt. Alec Chave; Cpl. George Hughes; Cpl. Jack Smith Snr.; Hubert William Shailes

The building in the background was the Girls' School at Newton St. Loe. By the time the photograph was taken this building had become The Men's Club and Platoon meeting place. By May 2000 all Platoon members, apart from Bert Whatley, had passed away. Hubert Shailes, remembered by Bert as an excellent shot, joined the 2nd Battalion Duke of Cornwall's Light Infantry. He was killed on 30th June 1944 aged just 19. He lies in Plot 4 Row C Grave No. 5 in the Assisi War Cemetery, Italy.

Arthur Buoy worked for the Bath Artcraft Company in Twerton. During the war this company manufactured parts for gliders; he joined the Royal Artillery in 1944 and died in 1951 aged just 43. Ted Bailey fought in World War One and was subsequently captured by the Germans and put to work in the German Salt Mines. George Hughes was a well-known chrysanthemum grower whilst Lt. Hone owned a laundry on the Lower Bristol Road. Harry Ricketts was the signalman at Twerton Signal Box throughout the War.

Newton St. Loe Home Guard in 1944.
Back Row: Bert Davis; Tony Cook; Ray White; William Jones; Bob Dale; Bill Parsons
Middle Row: L/Cpl. Arthur Reginald Buoy; L/Cpl. Bert Whatley; Cpl. Jack Smith; Cpl. Fred Hawkes; Cpl. George Hughes; Ron Fletcher
Front Row: Sgt. Dick Anderson; Capt. J.W. Holloway (Company 2nd in Command); Lt. McDougall; 2nd Lt. Hone; Sgt. Jack Harris; Ted Davis

Platoon duties before the air raids included guarding Bath Gas Works once a week. Platoon transport was provided by George Hughes, who loaned his fruit and vegetable lorry. Sgt. Alec Chave farmed at Claysend Farm, Newton St. Loe, which provided suitable land for rifle practice. It was here the Gloucester Regiment manned a searchlight and Lewis gun where accommodation existed in the form of a Nissen hut. Bert Whatley recalls a Spitfire crashing nearby. The R.A.F. recovered the ammunition and gave it to Bert for Home Guard use.

(Bert Whatley collection)

During the war many Americans were stationed in and around Bath and it was not long before they became involved in the social life of the area which included many dances held to support the war effort in one way or another. One such function was a fancy dress dance and Bert was press-ganged by his chums to join in the fun. However, he was at a loss for ideas regarding his costume. On the night of the dance, Bert and his friends arrived at the dance but one Land Army girl was refused admission for failure to attend in fancy dress. After a hurried consultation with the doorman they were all allowed in, including the stunningly attractive Land Army girl who soon caught the eye of a G.I. who, having spent some time with her, arranged to meet again the following Saturday at a local pub. A week later the G.I. turned up and was watched by Bert and his pals as he complained of being stood up by a 'broad'. Bert did not have the heart (or courage) to admit to the American that the Land Army girl was in fact himself!

In the 1980s the remaining two .303 rifles and approximately 1,000 rounds of ammunition belonging to the Platoon were found at Claysend Farm and handed in after lying forgotten in a loft for some 40 years.

*A very early photograph of members of **'C' Platoon No. 4 Company**, taken at Lambridge in 1940. Despite an appeal in* The Bath Chronicle *only two faces have been identified. On the extreme right is Ernest Budge of Fairfield Park whilst on the extreme left is Bill Venn, an employee of* The Bath Chronicle *who died c.1941 as a result of an accident. Like some members of the Admiralty Home Guard these men were issued with long Lee Enfield rifles, a weapon introduced in the 1890s. Other Platoon members included Mr. Ham, Mr. Symonds and Mr. Burnell. (John Venn collection)*

'C' Platoon No. 4 Company, photographed in the grounds of St. Michael's Church, Twerton in 1944. What a contrast to the above photograph. This is one of the few captioned Home Guard photographs.

Back Row: Ptes. C.Stevens; H. Stockdale; A. Rogers; L. Folland; L/Cpl. A. Maggs; Ptes. F. Dauncey; H. Maidment

Second Row: Ptes. H. Palmer; L. Stebbings; A. Dowding; F. Kettley; A. Goding; F. Bryan; W. Humphries; Cpl. E.E. Kettley; Ptes. A. Smith; E. Frost; W. Gay

Third Row: Ptes. F. Sellick; A. Llewellyn; W. Densley; C. Bond; L/Cpl. W. Edwards; Sgt. Willavoys; Sgt. R. Morris; L/Cpl. V. Harris; Ptes. J. Parratt; J. Hemmings; S. Perry

Fourth Row: Cpl. L. Wells; Cpl. S. Thurgar; Cpl. R. Rogers; Sgt. D. Pocock; C.S.M. E. Wotton; Lt. A. Cox; 2nd Lt. H. Holton; Sgt. E. Vezey; Cpl. E. Rogers; Cpl. P. Smith; L/Cpl. S. Crump; Cpl. A. Cook

Front Row: A. Campbell; P. Wheeler; R. Morrison; C. Cook; A. Maslen; C. Rawlings; W. Evans; W. Vines; A. Perkins; H. Brooks

The Platoon's local drill hall was probably that at Brougham Hayes, East Twerton, since demolished. Tony Llewellyn remembers that his father was required, together with other Platoon members, to man a searchlight on Pennyquick Bridge in Twerton after putting in a full day's work as a nurseryman at Ware's Nurseries where he worked for 54 years. Lt. Alfred Cox was the Platoon Commander having served in the Rifle Brigade before WW1. (Tony Llewellyn collection)

(right) 'A' Platoon No. 6 Company.

Back Row: Aubrey Rich (market gardener); Unknown; Earl Carpenter (Stothert and Pitt employee); David Taylor; Unknown; Fred Godwin (head gardener); Jeff Harding (market gardener); Charlie Cook (prison officer); Dennis Harding; Haddon Batt; Bert Forsey (local grocery delivery man); Bert Bartram (carpenter); Bert Harding

Second Row: Stan Harding; Stan Rawlings (market gardener); Ted Lovell (butler); Tommy Evry; Harry James; Charlie Davis (farmworker); Bill Hawker (foreman and part owner joinery firm); Sam Anderson (Bradford Paper Mill employee); Les Vernon; George Cottle; Laurie Harding; Mr. Giles (market gardener); Stan Rich; Vernon Rowlands (owner of local grocery shop)

Third Row: Mr. Wyatt (Stothert and Pitt employee); Arnie Moss (builder/decorator); Walter Hervin; Fred Bartram Jnr.; Bill Harding (lorry driver); Unknown; Mr. Skrine; Jack King (market gardener); Len Walker (Stothert and Pitt employee); Frank Lovell (Stothert and Pitt employee); Ron Hancock (boy!)

Front Row: Ern Hill; Roy Hallett (milk roundsman); Harry Dennis (coach painter); Fred Bartram Snr. (carpenter); Wilf Reynolds (painter/decorator); Herbert Watson (butler); Walter Moss (builder/funeral director); Ern Hancock (carpenter); Ron Rich (market gardener); Les Nicholls (electrician); Len Hawker (plumber)

(Audrey Duncan collection)

NO. 5 (SOUTH) COMPANY   COMPANY COMMANDER   Major C.C. Parmee
                                                                                      (Colonel Bendall)
HEADQUARTERS   Normal – Gilfach, Grosvenor, Bath   (Major H.M. Howell, M.B.E.)
               Operational – Sledmore, Bradford Road, Combe Down   2ND IN COMMAND   Capt. R.D. Hole

No. 5 Company. No.12 in the back row is Hubert Dancey, Latin master at City of Bath Boys' School. First row from the back, No. 16 is Fred White. (Bob White collection)

Arthur Temlett joined the Home Guard in 1942 aged 16 where he trained as a signaller at the Church Rooms, Combe Down. Guard duties included protecting the canal at Limpley Stoke and at the Dundas Viaduct. .22" rifle practice took place in the skittle alley of *The Viaduct Hotel*, Monkton Combe and at Prior Park. A full-bore range was used at Priston for rifle and sten gun practice whilst Spigot Mortar practice took place on Claverton Down, now the Sulis Sports Club.

NO. 6 (NORTH EAST) COMPANY

HEADQUARTERS   Normal – The Sycamores, Bathford   COMPANY COMMANDER   Major W.H. Sheppard
                    Operational – Lower Northend Farm   2ND IN COMMAND   Capt. W.R. Griffith, M.C.

'C' Platoon No. 6 Company, photographed at the rear of Sycamore House, Church Street, Bathford. Before the war this was the local Scout Headquarters, then it became the 'normal' Headquarters of No. 6 Company. In recent years it became associated with another 'company' formed to keep another form of 'foreign body' at bay, being the home of Dyson vacuum cleaners.

Back Row: Unknown; L/Cpl. Hunt (paper mill employee); Stan Cutter (Stothert & Pitt electrician); Les Morgan (Stothert and Pitt chargehand); Jim Hodder (Westinghouse Brakes employee); Jimmy Compton

Second Row: Charlie Bachell (Admiralty employee); Vic Cottle; Sgt. Jim Gray (paper mill employee); Mr. Gay; Louis Gage (Stothert and Pitt employee); Norman Ingram (farmer); Cpl. Walter Thyer; Bill Hoskill, R.N.; Unknown; Arthur Brown (hairdresser); Unknown

Third Row: Sgt. Ernie Tugwell; Unknown; Lt. or 2nd Lt. Harry Makin (Admiralty employee); Lt. D.R. Cooke (solicitor); Staff Sgt. Leonard William Gage (dairy owner); Sgt. George Matthews (paper mill employee); Unknown; Unknown

Front Row: (with hands clasped) Mr. Davis; Cpl. Sid Henry Waldon (master baker and paper mill employee); Unknown; 'Pop' Brown; Unknown; Roy Mitchell.
(Louis Gage collection)

The Platoon's Army Book 527 (Register of Hours of Attendance) has survived and from this it has been possible to provide a list of active members as of April 1942. The numbers following the name indicate the section to which the men belonged:

R.G. Allen (2); Sgt. W.G. Ash (1); C.E. Bachell (2); J. Beazer (4); A. Brown (1); S.W. Brown (5); A.H. Burden (2); F.L. Brockliss (3); Cpl. P.H. Cahill (1); H.C. Chapman (4); V.H. Cockle (4); W. Cockle (3); W. Coles (1); Cpl. P.R. Collett (4); E.G. Clewer (1); W.H. Churchill (5); R. Churchill (4); H.J. Farrant (5); L/Cpl. E. Follom (4); T.C. Fish (1); L.J.L. Gage (2); L.W. Gage (5); H.A. Godwin (3); P.J. Gouldstone (5); Sgt. J. Gray (2); L/Cpl. W. Gray (1); A.F.E. Griffiths (1); J.E. Hawker (1); V.F. Hunt (5); W.J. Hunt (1); W.H. Hoskill (3); J. Hancock (4); J.W. Harris (3); J.R. Hodder (2); V.G. Hartland (1); F.D. Hughes (3); J.N. Ingram (4); L/Cpl. W. Johnson (2); K.F. Kernery (1); W.H. Lewis (4); A.E. Lodder (1); W.M.H. Lyles (3); G.E. Lavington (2); K.J. Lavington (4); T.E. Lavington (4); Sgt. G.A. Matthews (3); F. Mole (2); Morgan (3); F.H. Mulcock (1); N. Mellor (1); C.F. Norris (2); Cpl. E.H. Pollard (5); K.H. Pollard (4); Cpl. H. Pegler (3); R. Reynolds (3); A.E. Slater (3); G. Staddon (2); H.F. Small (3); E.F. Stephenson (3); Cpl. W. Thyer (3); Sgt. A.E. Tugwell (4); A.S.P. Treble (2); Sgt. L.D. Vernon (1); J.H. Waldon (4); Cpl. S.H. Waldon (2); Sgt. F.E. Waller (2); W. Ward (3); G. Walters (4); M.G. Young (5)

(left) 'C' Platoon No. 6 Company marching along Ashley Road, Bathford, also known as Brewery Lane. Leading the column nearest the camera is Sgt. George Matthews whilst to the right of him is Sgt. Ernie Tugwell, his unusual gait being the result of a badly set leg after a rugby accident. Leading the centre column is Cpl. Sid Waldon. The building in the background was a brewery supplying the many pubs of Bathford, later used by a dairy company.
(Miss Karen A. Waldon collection)

```
                HOME  GUARD
                              12 John Street,
                                Bristol, 1.
                              10th Novr. 1941.
Dear Sergeant Gage,
        I should like to write and thank you for
all the interest you took and the work you did in
connection with yesterday's Armistice Parade. It was
a great success. The Captain was very pleased, and I
happened to meet him again this morning, strangely
enough, and he repeated his appreciation of the way
in which everything was organised, and I told him the
work had been done by you.
        I am asking the Sergeants to collect from
the men something towards the wreath and the bugler,
as I think they should bear part of the expense at any
rate of the Parade.
                        Yours faithfully,

Sergeant L. W. Gage,
Bathford Dairy,
BATHFORD,
Somt.
```

NO. 7 (CITY) COMPANY

HEADQUARTERS	Wessex Drill Hall, Upper Bristol Road
COMMANDING OFFICER	Major G.D. Scott, M.B.E.
	(Major M. Hopkins, M.C.)
	(Major J.B. Heron)
2ND IN COMMAND	Capt. T.J. Hodgkinson
	(Capt. J.C. Lambert, D.C.M.)

This photograph (from The Bath Weekly Chronicle and Herald *of 15th February 1941, via Mrs. Theobald) was captioned 'Capt. Adrian Hopkins and Major Heron leaving a parade, 9th February 1941. Capt. Hopkins is rejoining his old regiment, The Royal Artillery. Major Heron will be taking over command of Headquarters Company.' In the absence of other evidence, apart from the cap badge, it would appear that Capt. Hopkins is on the left.*

On one occasion during the war Capt. Hopkins was in the process of dismantling a weapon during a demonstration when the telephone rang. A voice at the other end said that an enemy bomb had blown out the windows of his home. "Tell them I'll be there when I have put this lot back," he replied.

Note the method Capt. Hopkins is using to carry his steel helmet. Throughout the war the Army Council issued a mass of instructions covering every facet of military life as in Army Council Instructions 1900 of 1941 below:

<u>Carrying of Steel Helmets</u>

1. As the only practicable means of carrying a steel helmet at present is by slinging it around the respirator haversack, which results in damage to the haversack and the steel helmet chin strap, it has been decided that steel helmets will not be carried except when necessary.

2. Steel helmets will be carried on the following occasions
    (a) when absent from quarters or places of duty for periods exceeding 24 hours.
    (b) on training or operations.

    Steel helmets may be carried at any time on the instructions of the unit commander who will issue orders to this effect if he considers that it is operationally necessary.

    This A.C.I. will not be interpreted as forbidding the wearing of the steel helmet by individuals when it appears to them to be a reasonable precaution in view of hostile activity.

3. Whenever the steel helmet is carried it will either
    (a) be worn on the head or;
    (b) be carried on the point of the shoulder.

    The method of carrying the steel helmet slung around the respirator will be discontinued forthwith.

4. The provisions of this A.C.I. will only apply to formations and units at home. Commanders abroad will issue orders, based on these instructions, to suit their peculiar circumstances.

Gordon Pearce Lanning attended King Edward VI Grammar School, joining the Officer Cadet Training Corps. In May 1940 those over the age of 17 were asked to join an 'interesting' unit which was being set up, although the Local Defense Volunteers was not specifically mentioned. It was several days later when the formation of the L.D.V. was publicly announced.

NO. 8 (WORKS) COMPANY

HEADQUARTERS 15, Queen Square, Bath

COMPANY COMMANDER Major N.H. Fortt
2ND IN COMMAND Capt. W.E. Tucker

*(above) **No. 8 (Works) Company** in front of Norfolk Crescent. The majority were employees of the Electricity, Gas Works or the Railway Companies.*

Back Row: Unknown; Ernest Weston (Gas Co.); Unknown; Lou Adams (railway fitter, brother of George Adams); Unknown; Unknown; Unknown; Harold Ward (Gas Co.); Jack Chivers (engineer, Aldridge and Ranken); Arthur James King (engine driver); Charles Woodward (jointer, Electricity Co.); Frederick Epps (passed fireman); Jack Barber (fireman)

Second Row: Ted Cross (builder); Unknown; Bart Westcombe (Gas Co.) or Arthur Bolomue; Edwin 'Ted' Tucker (engine driver); George Adams (foreman fitter); Ralph Hooper (engine driver); Unknown; Unknown; Albert William Stephen Fear (woodworker); Arthur Rowett (foreman, Bath Green Park Station); Harold Barber (engine driver); George Arlett (engine cleaner); Unknown (platelayer); Unknown; Douglas Holden (fireman); Unknown; Percy Hurd (clerk, Green Park Loco. Dept.); Ronald Shearn (engine cleaner); Unknown (passed fireman)

Third Row: Bill Ebdon (Gas Co.); Unknown; Unknown; Ted Hefferman (porter at Green Park Station); Unknown; Archie Gunning (passed fireman); Ralph Holden (engine cleaner); Unknown; Len West (passed fireman); Harold Reginald 'Reg' Scott Hake (carpenter, Gas Co.); Unknown; Stan Hilleard (Water Board); Unknown; Unknown; Unknown; Mr. King (engine cleaner); Ken 'Spider' Norris (engine cleaner); Unknown; Unknown (bar boy); Unknown; Unknown

Front Row: Douglas Brown (Gas Co.); Francis Edward Duck (Gas Co.); Fred Allard (Gas Co.); Bert Reed (engine driver); Sgt. Tommy Hughes (Gas Co. employee for more than 50 years); William Baggs (Gas Co.); Dick Tidball (engine driver); Mr. Seal (Electricity Co.); Unknown; Unknown; Capt. W.E. Tucker, Company 2nd in Command (Gas Co.); Major N.H. Fortt, Company Commander (owner of restaurant and cake shop in Milsom Street); Lt. Fred Jefferies (engine driver); Unknown; Unknown Lt. (fitter, Green Park Loco. Dept.); Unknown; Tom? (water softening plant attendant, Green Park Loco. Dept.); Unknown (carriage and wagon fitter, Green Park Station); Unknown; Unknown (fitter, Green Park Loco. Dept.); Unknown (carriage and wagon fitter, Green Park Station); Bert Harding (Gas Co.); Unknown. *(Keith Ward collection)*

(above) **L.M.S. and S.& D. Home Guard** at Bath Green Park Station, 1943.
Grades: D = Driver; F = Fireman; PF = Passed Fireman; PC = Passed Cleaner; Fr = Fitter; SF = Senior Fitter; FM = Fitter's Mate; GS = Goods Shunter; GG = Goods Guard; BB = Bar Boy; S = Signalman; SR = Steam Raiser

Back Row: Unknown; Dennis Clem (D); Edward Tucker (D); Ern Buffrey (PF); Ron Bean (PC); Walter Weston (PC); Roy Pearce (D); Albert Fishlock (GS); Henry Waldron (F); Fred Epps (F); George Coles (F); Edward Bullock (FM)

Second Row: Robert Clothier (SR); Charles Brown (D); Fred Meader (PF); Fred Brooks (D); Robert King (PC); William Lee (D); Herbert Hulance (PC); Bill Williams (S); Doug Holden (F); William Wiles (S); Ronald Shearn (PC); Dennis Emery (PC); George Adams (SF); Percy Hurd (Loco Department Clerk); Unknown

Third Row: Sgt. Thomas Hilton (Water Softener Plant Attendant); Cpl. Len West (F); Cpl. Stan Hayward (Carriage & Wagon Examiner); Sgt. Gordon King (PC); Archie Gunning (PF); Sgt. Lou Adams (Fr); Capt. Fred Jefferies (D); Arthur Tidball (D); Cpl. Albert Reed (D); Sgt. Albert Chapman (Fr); Unknown; Sgt. Robert Ford (F); L/Cpl. Ralph Hooper (D)

Fourth Row: George Stott (GG); Sidney Maslen (F); Unknown (Goods Office Clerk); L/Cpl. Harold Barber (D); L/Cpl. Norman Rosenburg (D); L/Cpl. Arthur King (D); Lt. Reg Iley (Fr); Lt. Ernie Cross (SR); Charlie Crocker (D); L/Cpl. Arthur Rowett (S); L/Cpl. Bob Cannings (S); Cpl. William Tosseano (D); Unknown; Charles Herbert (PC)

Front Row: William Mantle (PF); John Barber (PC); Norman White (S); Thomas Every (BW); Tom Gunning (PF); George Quinn (Control Office, Bath Green Park); Ken Hartley (PC); Ken Norris (PC)

Whilst many railway employees were members of the 22nd Devonshire (5th Southern Railway) Battalion, those featured are wearing the cap badge of the Somerset Light Infantry (compare this photograph with those of 7th Battalion Glastonbury Railway Home Guard on page 118). Several men above have also been identified in the photograph of No. 8 (Works) Company (left, above) although doubt must exist in some cases. However, there is no doubt about Fred Jefferies except that in the photograph above he is listed as a Captain whereas previously he is given the rank of Lieutenant. It may well have been that the title Captain was due to his service in the First World War. (John Stamp collection)

(left) **Stothert and Pitt Platoon**.
Back Row: No. 7 Norman Stanley Trott; No. 11 Bert Room; No. 14 Reg Fellows
Second Row: No. 4 Leonard George Bally; No. 10 R.G. Hodges
Third Row: No. 9 Ron Lewis; No. 13 Jack Symonds; No. 17 A. Golledge
Fourth Row: No. 6 Paul Barber; No. 7 Vic Holmes; No. 11 Jack Garret; No. 12 Arthur Ball; No. 14 Reg Whitcombe; No. 15 Jack Frankcom; No. 19 Peter Bilsdon
Front Row: No. 3 Gerry V. Cryer; No. 6 Jack Hills; No. 9 Capt. W. Lane; No. 10 possibly Col. Franklyn; No. 13 Jack White; No. 19 Randolph Webb

Col. Franklyn was a director of Torrance and Son of Bitton, a Stothert and Pitt company. Jack Hills in the front row was an observer in the Royal Flying Corps during the First World War. Boxing historians may have heard of Leonard Bally who was a well-known boxer from Bath. He was born in 1908 and died in 1996. Stanley Trott was born in 1911 and joined Stothert and Pitt in 1924, passing away in 1954. Capt. Lane lost his life on a firing range on 12th August 1944, less than four months before the Home Guard held their final parade.
(Mrs. Julia Chandler collection)

22ND DEVON (5TH SOUTHERN RAILWAY) BATTALION

BATTALION HEADQUARTERS	Central Station, Exeter, Devon
COMMANDING OFFICER	Lt. Col. A.H. Greening
2ND IN COMMAND	Major F.H. Baker

Two of the Companies from this Battalion had their Headquarters in Somerset:

'A' COMPANY (YEOVIL)

COMMANDING OFFICER	Major H.J. Hooper
2ND IN COMMAND	Capt. J.F.K. Bridle

'E' COMPANY (BATH AND TEMPLECOMBE)

COMMANDING OFFICER	Major H. Barry (at Bath)
	Major R. Paton (at Templecombe)
2ND IN COMMAND	Capt. W.W. Newman

(right) A Bathonian, Harold Walter Barry, like his father, was a railway employee all his life. He joined the Territorial Reserves in 1912 and was called up for service at the outbreak of the 1914-18 War. He served in the Royal Army Medical Corps when this photograph was taken and spent most of his time in Military Hospitals in Palestine. After the war he returned to work in the offices of the Somerset and Dorset Railway in Bath. Later he was transferred to Bristol.

During the Second World War Harold Walter Barry was seconded to work full-time in the Railway Home Guard and became Commanding Officer of 'E' Company of the 22nd Devonshire (5th Southern Railway Battalion), with the rank of Major. His work entailed the safety of rail transport of essential goods, foodstuffs and army equipment.
(Sonia Barry collection)

(left) Harold Walter Barry at Wells, proudly wearing his medals. They appear to be The First World War War Medal and Victory Medal, together with the Territorial Force War Medal, Territorial Efficiency Medal and the Defence Medal. Harold died in May 1976, aged 87. (Sonia Barry collection)

6th Somerset (Bath Admiralty) Battalion

HEADQUARTERS	Originally 6, Edward Street and at the The Holburne Museum, Bath. Later at The Empire Hotel, Bath
DATE FORMED	May 1940
COMMANDING OFFICER	Lt. Col. W.C. Brown (from 6.12.43) (Lt. Col. D.C. Morrison, Commander R.N.ret'd)
2ND IN COMMAND	Major G.J. Dear

H.Q. STAFF

A & Q	Capt. L.F. Lynham, General List
ADJUTANT	Capt. C.G. Moss, The Queen's Royal Regiment
ADMINISTRATION OFFICER	Major Howard
AMMUNITION OFFICER	Lt. K.L. Miller
CAMOUFLAGE OFFICER	(Lt. J.M. Rounthwaite)
CHEMICAL WARFARE OFFICER	Lt. E.L. Harrington
FIELD TRAINING OFFICER	Capt. P.T. Williams
FIELD WORKS OFFICER	Lt. S.A. Gothard (Capt. C.H. Cotten)
INTELLIGENCE OFFICER	Lt. N.B. Henderson
MEDICAL OFFICER	Major S. Marle (Major J.B. Bennett, Major D.A. Mitchell)
MESSING OFFICER	Lt. H.L. Longhurst (Lt. C.J.O. Whitaker)
MUSKETRY OFFICER	Lt. S.O. Grant
SIGNALS OFFICER	Lt. L.A.W. Davis (Lt. A.L. Farr, Lt. W.A. Richmond)
TRAINING OFFICER	Capt. G.T. Powlesland
TRANSPORT OFFICER	Capt. P.J. Ryan (Capt. H.W. Birchby, M.B.E.)
WEAPONS TRAINING OFFR.	(Capt. B.R. Elliston)

OFFICERS SECONDED

NORTH SECTOR SIGNALS	Capt. A.W. Allan
BATH GARRISON SIGNALS	Lt. K.P. Gooder
SCOUT UNIT	Capt. L.A. Aves, Capt. J.G. Spearman, Lt. F. Bradbury, Lt. A. Simpson

This photograph, taken on 'The Rec' at Bath, appeared in a Civil Service Magazine in 1990 and was captioned:

> *Major W.C. Brown, Lieut. Patterson, Colonel Morrison, Lord Louis Mountbatten, J. Russell, C. Hall, B. Williams, C. Fisher, W. Smith, H. Palmer, H. Overy, A. Weeks, S. Benzing. Major Brown was well known to the old Admiralty as Head of Common Services. He succeeded to Lt. Col. rank and was 'Colonel Brown, M.B.E.' until he retired in 1958 aged 62. His limp was due to a wound received in the First World War.*

In front, Colonel Morrison talks to Lord Louis Mountbatten. Behind Colonel Morrison are Major W.C. Brown and Lt. Patterson. In the front rank, from left to right, are J. Russell, C. Hall, B. Williams, C. Fisher, W. Smith, H. Palmer and H. Overy. Behind are A. Weeks and S. Benzing.

Note the mixture of rifles, Short Magazine Lee Enfield and its predecessor the Rifle Magazine Lee Enfield, whilst Charlie Hall and Jack Russell are both carrying Sten guns. Jack remembers that the Company also had either P14 or P17 rifles. Today the site of the inspection echoes to other commands more familiar to the post-war generation, being the home ground of Bath Rugby. (Jack Russell collection)

HEADQUARTERS COMPANY

COMMANDING OFFICER   Capt. P.J. Ryan
2ND IN COMMAND   Lt. E.L. Harrington

(right) Lt. Edmund Lynn Harrington, the Battalion Chemical Warfare Officer, salutes as members of the Battalion march through The Rec. Lt. Harrington was a veteran of the First World War, serving in France and Belgium as a dispatch rider. The men following could well be members of Headquarters Company. (Lynn Harrington collection)

Mrs. Joan Gilmour (née Griffin) was an Admiralty employee, moving to Bath on 10th August 1942. Joan was also employed in carrying out secretarial duties to senior battalion officers including Major G.J. Dear, Capt. Lynham and Capt. Moss. The offices were initially at 6, Edward Street. During air raids the basement was used as a shelter which Miss Griffin thought was highly dangerous as it was stacked with arms and ammunition. Joan remembers Col. Morrison as an extremely blustery man – it seemed to her the building shook when he arrived every morning and as soon as he had sat down he immediately began summonsing his secretarial support for dictation and running errands which included taking his dog Rio for walks.

'A' COMPANY

COMMANDING OFFICER   Major H.H. Owens
    (Major G.J. Dear, Major E.G. Neate)
2ND IN COMMAND   Capt. L.F. Moorse

'A' Company comprised Platoons Nos. 1 – 4 and was based at Foxhill.

'B' COMPANY

COMMANDING OFFICER   Major T.T.J. Leonard, M.M.
    (Major W.E. Cowan-Dickie)
2ND IN COMMAND   Capt. C.F. Watts

'B' Company comprised Platoons Nos. 5 – 8 and was based at Ensleigh.

'C' COMPANY

COMMANDING OFFR. Major H. Lamerton
                                 (Major W.C. Brown)
                                 (Major C.I. Hunt, M.M.)
                                 (Major A.C. Ridlington, M.C.)
2ND IN COMMAND   Capt. A.J. Fell
                                 (Capt. G.T. Powlesland)

Based in the centre of Bath, 'C' Company comprised Platoons Nos. 9-12 made up of electrical (D.E.E.) staff working in the Technical College and the Holburne Museum. An exception was No. 9 Platoon based on Dockyard Department staff working in The Pulteney Hotel. It was commanded by Jack Murphy, a photo printer in the Empire Hotel, with Jack Russell as platoon sergeant.

(right) **No. 9 Platoon 'C' Company**, *photographed on Bath Recreation Ground in 1944. Note The Carfax Hotel in the background.*
Back Row: Unknown; D. Burrows; R. Frith; L/Cpl. T. Griffiths
Middle Row: S. Benzing; J. Whalebone; E. Holford or Hulford; Sgt. E. Ovenden; R. Lamswood; A. Jury; Cpl. H. Palmer
Front Row: Cpl. N. Freeman; Unknown; R. Creighton; Sgt. J. Russell; Sgt. E. Clacton; W. Hackett; Unknown; E. Burch. *(Jack Russell collection)*

John Frederick Russell joined the Home Guard on the day of its inception. Writing in 1996 'Jack' Russell recalled that the Platoon was originally a large collection of all sorts of volunteers among staff working in the Pulteney Hotel and was merged into No. 7 Platoon 'B' Company. The first Platoon Commander was a Naval Architect called Craig, soon succeeded by a Naval Stores Officer called Bartlett. Mr. Bartlett was transferred to London, his place being taken by Mr. Patterson. On the renumbering of the Platoon to No. 9 of 'C' Company, the Commander became Jack Murphy. The Commanding Officer of 'B' Company was at the time Major Cowan-Dickie whilst Horace Lamerton (a senior draughtsman) commanded 'C' Company. Battalion Commanding Officers were Capt. Morrison, R.N. and Bill Brown, a senior civil servant. The Adjutant from the Regular Army was Captain Geoffrey Moss assisted by two Regular C.S.M.s named Gray and Field. Following the Blitz on Bath in April 1942 he helped to repair gas mains, dig out bodies and generally tidy up.

Having access to Naval Stores, the first weapons 'Jack' Russell remembered were Maxim machine guns, a weapon dating back to the First World War and before. Later on, Northover Projectors and the No. 74 Sticky bomb came on charge. Some .22 rifle ranges were established in Admiralty buildings whilst a range at Box was used for service rifle shooting. Grenade practice took place in a quarry at Sham Castle.

'Jack' Russell remembered vividly an exercise when the Home Guard was detailed to attack the aerodrome at Colerne. Unfortunately, nobody thought to tell the R.A.F. sentries and 'Jack' and his companions were nearly shot whilst penetrating the perimeter fence.

(left) **No. 7 Platoon 'B' Company (later No. 9 Platoon 'C' Company)**. *The Platoon was based in The Pulteney Hotel and this photograph was taken at the rear of the hotel. After the Home Guard was reorganised it became No. 9 Platoon 'C' Company. The Platoon Commander was Captain Bartlett who had just succeeded Capt. Craig. Later Captain Bartlett was replaced by Capt. Patterson.*
Back Row: Mr. Smith; Unknown; Mr. Brooker; Unknown; Unknown; Mr. May; Unknown; Mr. Bright; Unknown; Mr. Hackett; Unknown
Second Row: No. 5 Mr. Weeks; No. 8 Mr. Ovenden
Third Row: No. 1 Mr. Thomas; No. 3 Mr. Creighton; No. 12 Mr. Lamswood; No. 14 Mr. Overy
Fourth Row: Mr. Shapter; Unknown; Cpl. Hambly; Unknown; Sgt. Ford; Sgt. Craig; Capt. Bartlett; Sgt. Banks; Sgt. Patterson; Sgt. Light; Unknown; Mr. Sidell; Unknown
Front Row: Cpl. Hall; Mr. Palmer; Unknown; Mr. Benzing; Mr. Sweetman; Mr. Williams; Cpl. Woodley; Unknown; Unknown; Mr. Brown; Cpl. Fisher; Jack Russell.
(Jack Russell collection)

William Henry Pascoe, now living in Exmouth, was another member of the Admiralty Home Guard. He recalls his Home Guard Days:

Having qualified as an Electrical Draughtsman in Devonport Dockyard before World War Two (1938) I was not surprised at receiving an order in June 1940 to report to the Drawing Office of Branch V of the Department of the Admiralty in Bath. They had moved from London a short while previously to requisitioned property in that city.

The actual organisation of the 6th Somerset Battalion and the appointment of its Officers took a little time. The 6th Somersets were in the command of Lt. Col. D.C. Morrison, Commander R.N., later Lt. Col. W.C. Brown. Our Platoon was commanded by Captain Fell. One of our N.C.O.s was Corporal Bevan. 'Other ranks' included Privates Pascoe, Elliott, Evans, McCall, Kingdon, Tack, Waller and Russell. Though we were all known to each other, it was very interesting to see ourselves in a completely different environment. The uniform and rifles (.303 Lee Enfield) were issued and we slowly got accustomed to them. Rifle drill in a public street was a frequent activity.

We were taken to a rifle range at Box at map ref. ST 818 681 to the east of the city and there fired our first rounds at still and moving targets. The ability of each man was being tested and I found that I was one of the six best shots in the Company. This led to taking part in inter-Platoon, inter-Company and inter-Battalion shoots in which the six of us were very often to take part. The best individual marksman in our Company turned out to be Pte. Steve Elliott, an old friend from our days in the Instrument Room in Devonport Electrical Shop.

Normal routine was an assembly on Thursday evenings in Stall Street and then to whatever pattern of training was to follow. On Sunday mornings we were off on a route march (anything up to 14 miles) with a recce over our area of country which extended from Sham Castle hills in the east, along Combe Down, Odd Down to Twerton and Newton St. Loe, in the south-west. In poor weather we met in the basement of the Technical College. We were well trained there, only once did a bullet go up through the ceiling. It was there that Sergeant Johnny proposed that we form a Camouflage Unit. We were three at first but brought in another one or two as necessity demanded in the various demonstrations we gave. With sheets of canvas and some coarse netting we designed and painted rough stone walls, hedges and trees and bushes. They were used to cover us in exposed positions and we were soon to discover how very effective they could be.

Unfortunately I did not keep diaries of those days of over 50 years ago but by punishing my memory I can recall certain events of the period.

One evening's exercise took us across Sham Castle Golf Course to some quarries at the far end where we practised throwing hand grenades. We each had two or three throws at targets in the quarry. The evening passed and the Camouflage Unit slipped away to get their disguises on and get into position in the quarry. The Company were formed up to march through the quarry on their way back to Bath. But not one of our three disguises was spotted. Major Lamerton did an about turn and marched them back again – still unspotted – so one of us fired a shot. Shock ensued.

I was also a Scout and was asked to lead the Company back home. I could see Sham Castle silhouetted on the skyline half a mile away and set course for it. The company, trailing rifles in the darkening gloom, followed. I hit every bunker on that Golf Course and so did every man behind me – what language as they each fell into a sandy pit!

There were occasions when we were proud to prove the efficiency of our disguises – even against the men of the 5th Battalion in the town. But the occasion that really stands out in my memory was a particular Sunday exercise by the whole company up on Odd Down. It was arranged that the Major (who was in the know) would lead the whole company on the completion of their exercise across a certain field on the way back. They had to cross a stile into the field where we, the Camouflage Unit, had put our Sergeant with a Lewis gun. I was halfway along with my back to a large tree with another man on the opposite side, he and I with just our rifles and another Lewis gun at the far end. The company approached, crossed the stile and marched on. As they reached the middle the Sergeant opened fire – blanks of course – and we all followed suit.

What then followed was utter chaos. The Company just scattered, some did fall down (the correct action) but the others were off in all directions except for the stunned few who just stood still in shock! The Major shouted and yelled at them, "Stop! Stand Still! What are you doing? Where did the shots come from?" When he had got them together and each of us had fired one shot – they were challenged to say where the shooting had come from. They did not know, so we each fired another shot. Again they were still vague – we were not spotted. So I fired one more and then the puff of smoke was seen but I had to stand up before anyone could say I was real! It was the greatest lesson we could give and the Major was delighted. And the men had learned a lot!

Another big exercise was a call-out one weekend. I was busy on my allotment one Saturday afternoon when a motorbike arrived. The order was to report fully equipped, in uniform, overcoat, gas-cape and mask, haversack and rifle and report in Stall Street within the hour. Whilst daylight lasted we were marched out of the city and by the time it was dark we were established in a wood to the south-west about five to six miles away. We were to expect an attack at any time. Groundsheets were hung overhead to keep the rain off and to mask any lights. Groundsheets on the ground were for sleeping on. I was on first sentry duty from 10 p.m. till midnight, in an area I did not know but managed to find the limits of my beat by walking in each direction until reaching another poor lad who was also lost! When relieved I was taken back to the wood and lay down to sleep in my overcoat. The smell of frying bacon woke me about six o'clock. Afterwards we were assembled and formed up to resist an attack by the 5th Battalion who had also moved up during the night to a base for attack. It was not an affair with a determined target but it passed away most of the morning with a few blanks being fired at each other until our HQ Unit had packed up all the kit and we were ready to march back into Bath and home to our Sunday roast dinners.

'C' Company, photographed on The Rec with St. Mary's, Bathwick behind.
Back Row: Unknown; Unknown; William Hackett; Norman Parr; Unknown; Unknown; Unknown; K. Fradd or Frith; Unknown; Mr. Attolls; Unknown; W. Marsh; Eddie Ovenden; P. Poulson; G. Wemys; Unknown; G. Brockway; W. Cracknell or Wally Smith; T. Yates
Second Row: Unknown; Eric Holford or Hulford; Unknown; Unknown; Hughie Fielder; J. Barker; Unknown; Matt Gill; George Ch.....; Derek Jeffery; Unknown; Unknown; Frank Wickins; S. Akers; Unknown; Unknown; Unknown; Alf Jury; Unknown
Third Row: D. Francis; Unknown; Eric Burch; G. Stanworth; Dougie Blake; L/Cpl. Bernard Eugens Vieyra; R. Lamswood; H. Bennett; J. Johns; R. Digby; H. Jackson; M. Slater; Unknown; W. Beaven; Steve V. Elliot; Unknown; Unknown; Unknown; Jackie Blanchard; Aubrey Hawkes
Fourth Row: Sgt. I. Fraser; Unknown; W. Hassett; C. Merrett; Unknown; Bill Tutt; Lt. W. Sykes; Lt. McDermot; Capt. A. Jimmie Fell, Major Horace Lamerton; Mr. Sutherland; Jack Murphy; Bill Miller; Unknown; Ken Sidell; F. Rowe; R. Moore; Maurice Hales; Jackie Whalebone
Front Row: Unknown; Tommy Griffiths; W.H. Pascoe; Harold Palmer; Unknown; W. Williams; Frank Hedger; Mr. Francis; Unknown; S. Hawke; Unknown; Unknown. (Bernard Vieyra collection)

'D' COMPANY

COMMANDING OFFICER	Major G.W.F. Reeves
	(Major W.C. Brown)
	(Major P.A.N. Phillips)
	(Major A.C. Ridlington, M.C.)

No. 15 Platoon 'D' Company, photographed in front of the Cricket Pavilion, since rebuilt. The photograph was contemporaneously captioned.
Back Row: Pte. Slator; L.Cpl. Thomas; Pte. Lynch; Pte. Cannon
Second Row: Pte. Hender; Pte. Starks; Cpl. [Arthur Samuel Bailey] Lewis; Pte. Hughes; Pte. White; Pte. Kitchener
Third Row: Pte. Trevis; Cpl. Sugrue; Sgt. Vivian; Sgt. Futcher; Pte. Powell
Front Row: Pte. Smart; Sgt. Botting; Lt. Neal; Sgt. Hughes; Pte. Anderson
(Penny Lewis collection)

'D' Company comprised Platoons Nos. 13-16 and was based at the Admiralty offices in Warminster Road and The Spa Hotel.

Before the war, Arthur Lewis worked for the Admiralty in London as a draughtsman of ship design, travelling from his home in Portsmouth daily. At the outbreak of war in 1939 he was moved to Bath, as were so many other employees of the Admiralty. The Admiralty was very quick in forming its own Home Guard unit out of approximately half of its able-bodied staff, the other half becoming members of A.R.P. and fire-fighting contingents working together to ensure the safety of the Admiralty Buildings. Cpl. Lewis was a member of the Admiralty Home Guard from 2.7.1942 to 31.12.1944. Platoon duties included guarding Cleveland Bridge.

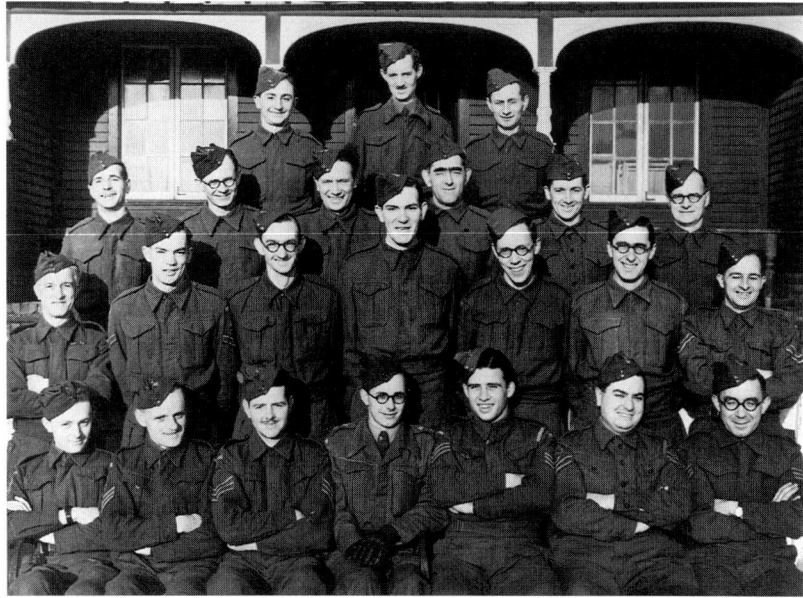

Although not confirmed, these men were part of 'D' Company in 1940, the clue being the background, the colonnade at The Spa Hotel. With rifles, bayonets fixed and ammunition pouches from an earlier conflict, they are ready for duty.
Left to right: Aubrey Smith; J. Spearman; Les Rawlings; Ted Sargent; Roy Iles and George Watkins. (Andrew Jeffrey Spearman collection)

Unlike the photograph on the previous page, this one is sadly uncaptioned but may well be another Platoon from 'D' Company. Note the shadows on the wall behind have moved very little between exposures. The only face identified is that of Alexander Bertram Chandler, front row, right-hand side. For many years he was involved in the East Bath District Scouts as badge secretary, retiring from the Scouts in 1977 after 25 years. (Penny Lewis collection)

Town Fighting Instructors, 1942-43.
Back Row: Sgt. Hands; Pte. Lester; Cpl. Hayes; Sgt. Mogg
Front Row: Cpl. Marshall; Lt. Miller; Sgt. Probst; Cpl. Cooper; Sgt. Russell; Cpl. Canavan; Lt. S.A. Gothard.
Jack Russell writes that this specialist group was commanded by Capt. P.T. Williams who took the photograph. "We had completed an army course at Birmingham and trained the rest of the Battalion via demonstrations, exercises, lectures etc. A 'party piece' included throwing a German soldier out of a high-level building; this impressed viewers of our normal demos in bombed out buildings and was a sensation when we did it from the top of the damaged Rugby stand during a Military Tattoo on Bath Rec. The dummy 'lived' with us between exercises: my wife wasn't too pleased about this but the children were delighted!

Williams and Gothard were chartered civil engineers and Mogg, Marshall and Canavan were civil engineer assistants. The others pictured were either constructive, mechanical or electrical engineering specialists, originally trained and educated in Royal Dockyards. The availability of such people is one reason why our Battalion had considerable advantages compared with the rest of the force.

This photograph was taken in the Kingsmead area of Bath, about 50 yards from The Theatre Royal, near the site of Bath College. The area was devastated during the Bath Blitz air raids in April 1942 which left acres of destroyed and partially destroyed buildings. We practised and taught street fighting in the shells of what had once been a row of terraced houses and it was here we posed for the above photograph." Note the commando toggle ropes. These could be joined to make a climbing rope or even a suspension bridge. *(Jack Russell collection)*

*Members of **Bath Admiralty Home Guard** pose for their photograph. Sadly none have been identified. (Mrs. Marion Martin collection)*

Members of an unknown Admiralty Platoon pause for refreshments during an exercise. With Balaclavas much in evidence, the group huddled against the stone wall and a leafless tree, one can understand the lack of smiles. Note the Lewis gun with its magazine removed and Lee Enfield rifles. (Mrs. Marion Martin collection)

Members of an unknown Admiralty unit pose at what is believed to have been near Sham Castle. On the skyline appear to be some form of agricultural machinery and car bodies, whilst to the right, a flag is just discernible. It is known that a rifle range was used at Vineyards Farm by the Admiralty Home Guard but at the time of writing its location is unknown. To add confusion the hillside is very similar to the rifle range at Englishcombe. (Mrs. Marion Martin collection)

*Members of **Bath Admiralty Home Guard** train near Lansdown on a beautiful summer's day. Only Arthur George Ashfield (No. 6) has been identified.*
(Mrs. Betty Ashfield collection)

Men from the same unit pose with their Lieutenant. Note, unlike the majority of Home Guards, these men are armed with the Rifle No. 1, no doubt obtained from Admiralty stocks. Again Arthur George Ashfield has been identified (centre row No. 6).
(Mrs. Betty Ashfield collection)

Admiralty Home Guard Auxiliary Units were formed from members of the Home Guard and others from outside having carried out basic Home Guard training. They were formed into small patrols operating independently of any military establishment. Should the country be overrun by Germans, these cells would harass the enemy behind their lines, carry out sabotage and murder. Life expectancy would not have been very long.

***The 203rd GHQ Reserve Home Guard**, photographed outside the Cricket Pavilion at Bath.*
Back Row: E. Dwane; A.P. James; N.J. James; W.W. Curry; J. Blair; S.R.G. Saunter; L.M. Pusey; H.D. Rees, B.E.M.; W.F.E. Emmerson
Second Row: H. Masters; C.J. Gates; L/Cpl. R.A. Partridge; S.L. Baldery; F.N. Jermy; H. Banham; R.A.D. Heward; A.P. Morgan; P.F. Carter; T.F. Pope; L/Cpl. R.N. Reeds
Third Row: R.M.B. Judson; L/Cpl. S.F. Phillips; E. White; Sgt. E.A. Steane; Sgt. N.W.S. Baker, B.E.M.; Sgt. N.E. Shephard; L/Cpl. E. Roscorla; N. Armstrong; J.O'B. Canavan
Front Row: Sgt. D.F. Stevenson; 2nd Lt. G.R.M. Hutchings; Lt. L.A. Aves; Capt. J.G. Spearman; 2nd Lt. I.McG. Phillips, B.E.M.; Sgt. R.W. Bennet
(Andrew Jeffrey Spearman collection)

A smaller group formed from those in the previous photograph.
Back Row: A.N. Armstrong; L/Cpl. S.F. Phillips; J. Blair;
  R.M.B. Judson
Middle Row: J.O'B. Canavan; Sgt. Norman E. Shephard;
  Capt. J.G. Spearman; Sgt. E.A. Steane; E. Dwane
Front Row: Lt. L.A. Aves; 2nd Lt. Ivor McG. Phillips;
  2nd Lt. G.R.M. Hutchings
(Andrew Jeffrey Spearman collection)

From time to time it was necessary for Capt. J.G. Spearman to travel to Taunton to collect stores for his auxiliary unit. On one occasion the return journey was broken at The Rose and Crown *in East Lyng for refreshments. Above, looking east towards Burrowbridge, are, from left to right, J.G. Spearman, L.A. Aves, Ivor Phillips and G.R.M. Hutchings. Right, looking west towards Taunton, G.R.M. Hutchings, J.G. Spearman and L.A. Aves pose besides their Morris 8.* The Rose and Crown *still survives but what of the motor cars?*
(Andrew Jeffrey Spearman collection)

'E' (ANTI AIRCRAFT) COMPANY

No further information has been forthcoming on this Company.

COMMANDING OFFICER Major L.G. Bolton, O.B.E., M.C.
2ND IN COMMAND Capt. A. Fisher, M.M.,
  Capt. E.R. Evans

7th Somerset (Long Ashton) Battalion

HEADQUARTERS (Admin)	Wraxall House, Wraxall
HEADQUARTERS (Battle)	Long Ashton Research Station
DATE FORMED	May 1940
COMMANDING OFFICER	Lt. Col. Sir H.J. Tweedie, K.C.B., D.L., Légion d'Honneur (Admiral, retired) (from 1.2.41)
2ND IN COMMAND	Major J.C. Jesser-Coope
	Major T. Wallace, M.C.
H.Q. STAFF	
A & Q OFFICER	Capt. E.L. Curtis, The Rifle Brigade
ADJUTANT	Capt. C.E. Hardwicke, General List
	Capt. A.N. Lister, The Buffs
ADMINISTRATIVE ASST.	(Lt. W.S. Whiting)
AMMUNITION OFFICER	Lt. H.N. Grundy
	(Lt. K.S. Saunders)
CAMOUFLAGE OFFICER	Lt. H.W. Miles
CHIEF STAFF OFFICER	Major C.T. Hudson Harrison, M.C.
INTELLIGENCE OFFICER	Capt. J.S. Bennett,
	Lt. J. Hunt,
	Lt. H.C. Boyes
MEDICAL OFFICER	(Major N.H. Kettlewell)
SIGNALS OFFICER	Capt. W. Latimer,
	Lt. H.C. Crowlie, D.C.M., M.M.,
	Lt. J.E. Gray
TRANSPORT OFFICER	Lt. E.R. Cockbaine
WEAPONS TRAINING OFFR.	Capt. J. Thistlewaite,
AND GAS OFFICERS	2nd Lt. F.R.C. Love,
	2nd Lt. R. Stewart

Whilst Lt. T.A. Bushell of the 2nd Taunton Battalion deposited in the County Record Office a list of Company Commanders and 2nd in Commands for all Companies in Somerset, Lt. Col. Sir H.J. Tweedie wrote an extremely detailed report, produced as a book, on the formation and organisation of the 7th (Long Ashton) Battalion. It is through his endeavours that such a comprehensive list of officers exists for all the Long Ashton Companies. His list includes all officers who served at one stage or another.

Headquarters Staff of 7th Somerset (Long Ashton) Battalion.
Back Row: No. 2 Lt. H.C. Boyes; No. 4 Lt. H.N. Grundy
Middle Row: No. 4 Capt. J.S. Bennett
Front Row: No. 5 Lt. Col. Sir Hugh Tweedie;
   No. 6 Major T. Wallace, M.C.
(Stephen Boyes collection)

Company Commanders of the 7th Battalion, photographed in 1944.
Back Row: all unknown
Middle Row: No. 4 Capt. H.A.H. Fraser; No. 7 Major F.B. Leman
Front Row: No. 3 Lt.Col. Sir Hugh Tweedie
(Mary Campbell collection)

NO. 1 (LONG ASHTON) COMPANY

COMMANDING OFFICER	Major G.W. Stacey (Major T. Wallace, M.C.) (Major W.E. Berry)	2ND IN COMMAND	Capt. N.C.H. Glide (Capt. W.E. Berry) (Capt. G.W. Stacey)

PLATOON COMMANDERS
Capt. R.H. Elton
Capt. S.H. Knight
Capt. D.N. Robertson, M.C. (Group of Platoons)
Lt. F.S.G. Barnett, M.C.
Lt. G.C. Brooks
Lt. H.E. Croxall
Lt. N.C.H. Glide
Lt. A. Hirst
Lt. G.H. Lewis
Lt. H.S. Rex
Lt. J.H. Savory
Lt. A.W. Southway
2nd Lt. J.H.M. Budgett
2nd Lt. R.E.B. Harris
2nd Lt. R.J. Knight
2nd Lt. J. MacGregor
2nd Lt. A.H. Mainstone
J.W.F. Footman, O.C., Clifton College O.T.C.

OTHER OFFICERS
Capt. W.J. Paramore, M.O.
Lt. J.D.G. Baker
Lt. H.C. Crowlie, D.C.M., M.M.
Lt. R.W. Marsh
Lt. G.T. Spinks
Lt. J.L.R. Wood
2nd Lt. D.G. Ashford
2nd Lt. H.S. Crabtree
2nd Lt. D.T. Dufty
2nd Lt. N. Elliott
2nd Lt. J.A. Farrell
2nd Lt. W.S. Goodbody
2nd Lt. W.A. Jones
2nd Lt. R.W.M. Melvin
2nd Lt. A.G. Morgan
2nd Lt. F. Pembury
2nd Lt. G.C. Popham
2nd Lt. E.M. Savory
2nd Lt. J.G.R. Scarff
2nd Lt. A.E. Thorne, M.M.
2nd Lt. E.H. Wilkinson

(Bristol Evening World, via Penelope Harris)

Accompanying the above press photograph of August 1940 was an article about early mounted Home Guard troops. It reads as follows:

"Horses and men are ready on the outskirts of Bristol to greet Hitler's paratroops if ever they land in the vicinity.

"A day or two ago I watched these mounted Home Guards at training", writes an 'Evening World' reporter, "and was convinced of their earnestness and their usefulness.

"Their official title is the Mounted Troop, Long Ashton Division Home Guard, and they consist mostly of Bristol Businessmen who are contributing their horsemanship and their leisure to national safety.

"In addition they are paying out of their pockets about £50 per week for maintaining the troop. Fodder is one of the most expensive items.

"Week-end Training

"Formed about the end of May, the men have overcome many difficulties to reach their present state of preparedness. Week-ends are devoted to training and general exercises, and men of the troop are on patrol each night.

"The troop headquarters are at Barrow Court, stately home of Lt. Col. and Mrs. William Gibbs, whose stables have been placed at the disposal of the troop. One or two other stables in the area are being used for the duration as sub-sections. The Troop Commander is Mr. J.S. Thompson and the 2nd in Command is Mr. C.H. (*sic*) Crowlie.

"The idea of forming a mounted troop originated at a riding school which many of its present members attended [believed to be at Flax Bourton].

"Primary Duty

"Now they have given up hunting and their riding-for-pleasure and turned their skill in the saddle to a more practical purpose.

"Their horses, many of them expensive hunters, were loaned to them for the duration by people in Gloucestershire and Somerset. They are stabled at Barrow Court and two or three other stables in the area and are groomed and fed by the men themselves.

"The troop's primary duty is patrolling and dispatch-riding over a wide area stretching from Clevedon to Keynsham and Dundry. Twelve men, patrolling in twos, are on duty each night, and each carries a revolver, haversack, gas mask, torch, notebook and map. Some of the members come from as far away as Weston-super-Mare. Private cars are used to get to and from Headquarters, and that accounts for most of the petrol ration.

"Week-ends are devoted to map-reading practice, cavalry drill and rifle and revolver practice."

During World War Two, Mervyn Pragnell (photographed on the previous page, eighth from the camera in the front row) was Managing Director of Oliver Pragnell and Co., paint manufacturers of Broadmead and a member of the above troop. His daughter writes:

Mervyn Pragnell held every field rank commissioned and non-commissioned in the British Army. In camp at Aldershot in 1897 he was one of the four soldiers who chaired Lord Kitchener round the camp on a vociferous welcome home following on a Sudan victory. He was one of the first hundred to volunteer for service in the South African War, serving in the Mounted Sharpshooters Corps. Previous to this he was in the 1st North Hants. Volunteer Engineers. In the Great War he fought with the 12th and 6th Battalions of the Gloucester Regiment, and the 16th London Queen's Westminster Rifles, attached to the Australian Mining Corps. He also served with the Royal Engineers. During the Great War he was recommended for the D.C.M. He was 'blown up' on the Somme, took part in all subsequent battles on the Western Front and also saw service in East Africa and India.

NO. 2 (KEYNSHAM) COMPANY

COMMANDING OFFICER Major W.S. Scammell, M.C.
2ND IN COMMAND Capt. F.W. Partington (Capt. H.A.H. Fraser)
OFFICERS COMMANDING Capt. G.E.A. Richards, M.C.
   GROUPS OF PLATOONS Capt. F.A. Venn

PLATOON COMMANDERS
Lt. H.J. Bewley
Lt. G.H. Blain
Lt. W.H. Conn
Lt. R.E. Cornick
Lt. R.H. Gillard
Lt. H.P. Gray
Lt. P. Grossett, D.F.C.
Lt. F. Harding, D.C.M.
Lt. H.E. Learoyd
Lt. W. Morris
Lt. H.F. Palmer
Lt. N.G. Sutton, M.C., Croix de Guerre
Lt. C.W. Trussler
Lt. F.A. Venn

OTHER OFFICERS
F.W. Tennant, B.E.M. (Major, retired)
Capt. N.D. Gerrish (M.O.)
Lt. W.M. Bond
Lt. L.J.C. Bunker
Lt. A. Campbell-Smith
Lt. G.F. Clark
Lt. J.I. Derriman
Lt. H.F. Dominey
Lt. G.C. Fray
Lt. C.K. Godwin
Lt. G.E. James
Lt. D. Kirkwood
Lt. A.J. Membry
Lt. A.G.C. Paget
Lt. A.W. Powell
Lt. A. Pym
Lt. H.G.S. Thomas
2nd Lt. J.P.T. Briggs
2nd Lt. M.E. Brodie
2nd Lt. W.J. Frost
2nd Lt. C.J. Horlick
2nd Lt. G. Palmer
2nd Lt. F.C. Smailes
2nd Lt. G.M. Weir

Stanton Drew Home Guard, photographed outside Mill Place, Stanton Drew, the home of Capt. (later Major) Fraser. He was 2nd in Command of No. 2 Company before being promoted to Officer in Command of No. 3 Company.
Back Row: Ernest Beacham (miner); Jack Bates (miner); Mr. Palmer (miner); Unknown; Jack Burge (miner); Fred Filer (farmworker)
Second Row: Wally Smart (village blacksmith); Fred Ashley (miner); Reg Brimble (miner); John Young (farmer); Mr. Hawkins (miner); Bert Hudson (miner); Mr. N. Coles (market gardener)
Third Row: Arthur Penney (local builder, lived at Box Bush); Ken Hawkins (miner/building worker); Farnham Stevens (farmer); Percy Howe (miner, from South Wales); Bill Power (miner until Bromley Colliery closed); Stan Brimble (miner until Bromley Colliery closed); Edwin Winstone (farmer); Bill Ashley (miner and farmworker)
Fourth Row: Edward Ashley (miner, WW1 veteran); L/Cpl. Jack Harvey (miner/pit blacksmith); Sgt. Norman Tovey (driver and rep. for Smith's Potato Crisps); Lt. H.F. Palmer; Capt. H. Alistair H. Fraser (employee of Wills Tobacco, Bristol); 2nd Lt. Gilbert Palmer (miner); Cpl. Cathcart (farmer); L/Cpl. H. Bourne (miner); L/Cpl. G. Bown (rep. for Pinjar Stuffings and Sausage Fillers)
Front Row: Harold Hewish (miner); Maurice Brown (miner/Scout Master/church chorister)
(Mrs. Lily Spear collection)

NO. 3 (TEMPLE CLOUD) COMPANY

COMMANDING OFFICER	Major H.A.H. Fraser
	(Major A.D. Eshelby)
2ND IN COMMAND	Capt. J.L.S. Melville, M.B.E.
	(Lt. F.D. Vaughan)

PLATOON COMMANDERS
Lt. Thomas Walter Blanning
Lt. P.A. Briscoe
Lt. E.J.M. Fenton
Lt. L.G. Pritchard
Lt. A.B. Scott, M.C.
Lt. H.C. Shearn, M.M.
Lt. F.J. Terrell
Lt. J. Thistlewaite
Lt. W.S. Whiting

OTHER OFFICERS
Capt. H.W. Kettlewell (Lt. Col. retired)
Capt. A.J.B. Miall (M.O.)
Lt. F.C. Collyer
Lt. J. Coxon
Lt. E.W. Curtis
Lt. D.J. Kathro
Lt. S.W.D. Knight
Lt. G.H. West
Lt. B.L. Woodland
2nd Lt. W.E. Dobson
2nd Lt. L. Flower
2nd Lt. J.H. Murison
2nd Lt. F.E. Reeves

No. 3 Company, with their Headquarters at Temple Cloud, covered the areas around Ston Easton, Farrington Gurney, Paulton, Hallatrow, Timsbury, Farnborough, Clutton and High Littleton.

(left) **Officers of No. 3 (Temple Cloud) Company**.
 Opinions differ as to what should be the correct title for this photograph. Close examination reveals that the majority are wearing officers' 'pips'. Thomas Walter Blanning, standing on the extreme right, appears to have some form of fabric strips sewn on the left sleeve of his battledress. At the time of Stand Down he was certainly a Lieutenant. Others identified in the front row are No. 3 Major H.A.H. Fraser, No. 4 Lt. Peter A. Briscoe and possibly No. 1 Lt. Lewis G. Pritchard.
 Thomas Blanning's stance is explained by the fact that he is suffering from a stiff leg occasioned by a 'botched' cartilage operation following a rugby accident – he used to play for Bath. He badly wanted to join the Royal Navy and was bitterly disappointed when he was turned down at his medical examination.
(Sally Blanning collection)

(right) **No. 1 (Temple Cloud) Platoon**, *photographed at the rear of* The Temple Inn, *Temple Cloud. (Bob Williams collection)*
Back Row: Les Smith; H. Thatcher; Jim Bailey; Lionel Abbott
Middle Row: Mr. Tancock; Wally Lovell; E. Elver; Ken Gallop; Wilf Perry; Cliff Chivers; Fred Oldham
Front Row: E. Williams; Sgt. John W. 'Bill' Knott; Lt. Eric J.M. Fenton; Lt. S.W.D. Knight; Cpl. Bertram Chivers; L/Cpl. Fred Lewis

The author is indebted to Bob Williams for providing the above names and following notes:
 Lt. Fenton lived at High Littleton where he was Headmaster of the primary school. Lt. Knight also lived at High Littleton. All others lived in Temple Cloud/Cameley. Sgt. Knott served in the Rifle Brigade in WW1. There were a number of earlier members who were called up for military service.
 Other platoons in the company had their photographs taken at the rear of *The Temple Inn*, including No. 3 (Farrington Gurney/Hallatrow Platoon). The Temple Cloud Platoon was based at the 3rd Company Headquarters which occupied a lean-to office attached to The Old Wool House, Peterside, Temple Cloud (still there in 2002). They also used a Nissen hut in the yard that was demolished after the war. From 1942 they also used the hall of the local primary school one evening a week.
 Major A.D. Eshelby, the first Company Commander, was an officer in WW1 and a prominent member of the British Legion. His 2nd in Command was Lt. F.D. Vaughan, believed to be the son of the local doctor. Major H.A.H. Fraser was the next Company Commander from about 1942. His deputy was Captain James L.S. Melville, who was the West of England representative of Leyland Motors, based at Brislington, Bristol. He rented a cottage (demolished in the 1960s) next to the Company Headquarters in Peterside, where he lived with his family for the duration of the war.

Officers and N.C.O.s of No. 3 Platoon (Hallatrow and Farrington Gurney) No. 3 Company, photographed at the rear of The Temple Inn, *Temple Cloud in 1944.*
Back Row: L/Cpl. Jarman (Hallatrow); L/Cpl. Kingman (Farrington Gurney); Unknown
Middle Row: Cpl. C. Hobbs (Farrington Gurney); Cpl. Ron Speed (Paulton); Cpl. Glyn Teek (Farrington Gurney); Cpl. Gillard (Hallatrow); Cpl. Clifford Weeks (Hallatrow)
Front Row: Sgt. Treasure (Farrington Gurney); Sgt. Sharman (Paulton); Lt. Peter A. Briscoe (Temple Cloud); Lt. Thomas Walter Blanning (Hallatrow); Sgt. Graham Stock (Hallatrow); Sgt. Ford (Farrington Gurney)
(Charlie Blanning collection by courtesy of Sally Blanning)

Gwen Stock remembers that her back bedroom was used as the Home Guard magazine. Shelves were put up and the ammunition stored there until her adopted daughter Tessa arrived. The magazine was then relocated to Sally Blanning's grandparents' home, 50 yards down the road. When the house was cleared in the 1970s, following the death of Sally's grandmother, a quantity of pistol ammunition was recovered from a cupboard under the stairs.

The first night that the Hallatrow and Farrington Gurney Platoon met at their Headquarters, the waiting room at Hallatrow Station, Tom Blanning, the officer in charge, was addressed by one of the 'other ranks'. "Right Mr. Tom, up you go and get the beer", (*The Station Hotel* being at the top of Station Road). "I can't go," said Tom, "I'm in charge." "You bloody well go," was the reply, "You are the youngest." He was and he did.

Tom Orchard was a member of the Platoon very much like Pte. Godfrey in *Dad's Army*. One night he was so incensed when he saw German planes returning from bombing Bristol he fired at them with his rifle, only succeeding in extinguishing the search lights to the annoyance of the other men.

Paulton Platoon.
Back Row: Cyril Vowles or Mr. Snelling; Oliver Atkins
Second Row: P. Chivers; Joe Chivers; Unknown; Alfie Hillman or L. Bourton; Roly Sage; M. Padfield; B. Carter; Jo or Walt Brown; Donovan Sherbourne; L. Hanney; N. Woodall; Mr. Banks; Lionel Wall; Fred Burge; Unknown; V. Rogers or Mr. Weeks
Third Row: Bert Carter; B. 'Topper' Woodall; Arthur Chivers; A. Baker; L. Chivers; Alfie Hillman; Archie Hayward; Mr. Redwood; Rex Wells; George Beal; Tony Whitehead or Ken Churchill; Ronnie 'Pinky' Chivers; Unknown; Mr. Cooper; Unknown
Front Row: Ray Wells; Charlie Bourton; Cpl. 'Sonner' Harrington; Sgt. Fred Brooks; Sgt. C. Parfitt; Lt. F.C. Collyer; Lt. H.C. Shearn, M.M.; Dennis Catherole; Sgt. Reg Bennett; Charlie Exten; Cpl. H. or A. West; L/Cpl. V. Sage
Kneeling behind the Machine Vickers .303" Mk. 1 is Wilfred Callow. One other volunteer known to have been a member of this platoon was Mr. Banks. Sgt. Fred Brooks, ex-Grenadier Guards, was a miner who worked at Old Mills Colliery, Paulton. (Joe Chivers collection)

Sunday drill for the platoon commenced at 10 a.m. with parades being held at Pow's Garage, Ham Lane, the Platoon Headquarters, afterwards adjourning to *The Red Lion* at 12 noon. Rush Hill on the Mendips was used for training in field craft. A rifle range was used at Temple Cloud.

It was planned that a photograph of the platoon was to be taken on Sunday 17th September 1944 and the men were gathered together for the photographer when disaster struck. A Horsa glider, on its way to Arnhem, broke up overhead and crashed nearby. Naturally all thoughts of taking a photograph were abandoned in the wake of such tragedy – the photograph being taken the following Sunday.

Timsbury Home Guard, photographed at Kingwell House, destroyed by fire in the 1950s.
Back Row: Jack Rhymes; Roy Purnell; Unknown; L. Boulton
Middle Row: Norman Meek; Mr. Gregory; Unknown; G. Smith; Henry Biggs; Fred Mitchard
Front Row: Cpl. Gerald Dyer; Sgt. W. Gunter; Lt. S.W. Donald Knight; Lt. Eric J.M. Fenton; Sgt. David Payne; Sgt. G. Boulton; Cpl. Barnes.

Lawrence Berry was a member of Timsbury Home Guard from late 1941 until he joined the Royal Navy in March 1943. Other members remembered by Lawrence were Cpl. Cecil Bridges, Herbert Payne, Frank Lodge, Edward 'Teddy' Shearn, George Sperring, Cyril Bird, Fred Berry, Ted Curtis, Bill Packham and possibly Rob Dyer.
(Jack Gunter collection)

> Brenda Dibble was the daughter of Ernest Moxham. In 2002 she wrote:
>
> My father was the village blacksmith and he owned two ancient motorcars, a 1920 SCAT and a 1928 Bean. Both vehicles were commandeered by 'Major' Walters, and placed in Leves Hill to serve as a road block in spite of my father's plea that they would be useless as a tank could go through the hedges and bypass the obstacle. The SCAT was one of only eight made in Italy and in 1948 an ex-Italian P.O.W., who either saw or heard of it, came over from Italy and tried to buy it.

The Unit's original meeting place was at No. 8, Lansdown Crescent, Timsbury, the home of Sgt. Gunter who joined the Home Guard on 10th June 1940. Subsequently a more suitable 'home' was found with the offer of the use of a farm building at Kingwell Farm. An observation point had been established on The Sleight, Timsbury at the entrance to the reservoir compound at map ref. ST 657 593. Here a Nissen hut was built, with its lower half below ground level. This, it is believed, served as a store and shelter for the pickets.

Other information received suggests a wooden hut was built for the same purpose on the left of the track to Sleight Farm at map ref. ST 664 591 whilst a dug-out was built just to the west at map ref. ST 660 592. The large field opposite the turning to Sleight Farm was considered suitable for landing gliders and was therefore 'planted' with stakes to deter such activity.

To the south-west of Timsbury is the disused Lower Conygre Pit. Land at the mine was used as an unofficial rifle range.

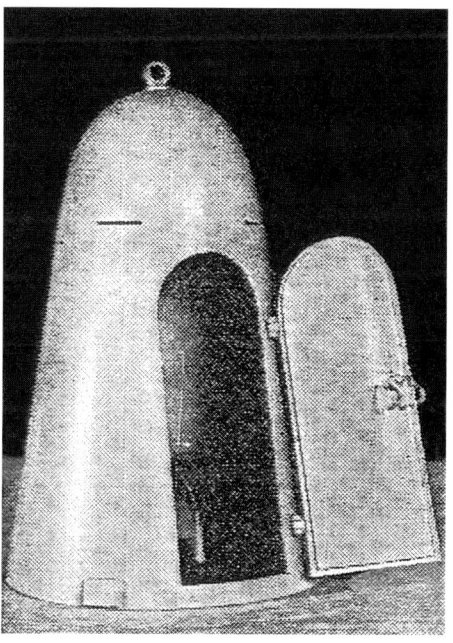

Although not strictly 'Home Guard', this Solent bell shelter (left) was spotted in Timsbury. Enquiries revealed that its first 'home' was at St. Anne's Paper Mill, Keynsham where it provided shelter for the firewatchers. How many of us would relish the thought of sitting in this during an air raid? At least it was furnished with two seats.

NO. 4 (PORTISHEAD) COMPANY

COMMANDING OFFICER	Major J.H. Gove	Lt. R.S. Gunson	Lt. W.C. Stuart-Low
	(Major G.S.J.F. Eberle, D.S.O., T.D.)	Lt. R.J. Hamilton	Lt. P.J. Stidard
	(Major Frank H. Williams)	Lt. F.L. Hodges	2nd Lt. H.L. Cheston, M.M.
2ND IN COMMAND	Major G.S.J.F. Eberle, D.S.O., T.D.	Lt. H.G. Lock	2nd Lt. B.J.A. Holder

PLATOON COMMANDERS		OTHER OFFICERS	
Capt. A.J. Organ	Lt. G. Mounter	Capt. J.E. McCornick (M.O.)	Lt. C.F.H. Walters
Lt. R. Dickenson	Lt. V.E.W. Nock	Lt. L.A. Didlick	2nd Lt. H.S. Crabtree
Lt. D.P. Farrant	Lt. H.C. Parsons	Lt. J.L. Packard	2nd Lt. W.S. Jones

*Field Marshal Lord Birdwood inspects men of **No. 4 Company** in Leigh Woods in May 1941.*
Left to right: Ernest Robbins of Portishead; Bill Andrew, M.M.; Geoffrey Tebbutt; Ronald Jarrett; Field Marshal Lord Birdwood; Major Frank H. Williams (Company Commander). To the right of the picture nearest the camera is Lt. Col. Sir Hugh Tweedie and on the extreme right of the photograph is Reg Knowland. Geoffrey Norman Tebbutt subsequently joined the R.A.F. On the night of April 24th 1944 Sgt. Tebbutt took off from R.A.F. Coningsbury in a Lancaster III OL-C serial No. ND469, with other aircraft from 83 Squadron for a raid on Munich. Sadly it was to be his last mission. Geoffrey lies at rest in the German War Cemetery at Durnbach, plot 7 row J collective grave 8-11; he was aged just 22.

John Richardson, who took part in the parade, and whose shadow appears on the left of the photograph, recalls that it was an extremely hot day with some members of the Home Guard fainting. He also remembers an incongruous part of the Field Marshal's uniform that day. He was carrying a civilian-pattern respirator in its cardboard box, the strap of which is visible in the photograph. (Mrs. J. Holley collection)

John Richardson was one of the first twelve to join the L.D.V., reporting to Portishead Police Station. Initially the Headquarters was at the Police Station, moving on to Forehill Quarry where a rifle range was established. The final 'resting place' of the Platoon was the golf club premises. One night a young officer cadet from Clifton College, on leave, proffered his services for that night. The platoon had at this stage been issued with Canadian Ross Rifles which were not fitted with a magazine cut-off. Insufficient training with this weapon resulted in the cadet closing the bolt on a live round, and squeezing the trigger, thus joining the growing number of Home Guards who had shot holes in sundry walls, floors and ceilings. This occurred in a circular tower of about twenty feet diameter. The oil lamp blew out with the blast. Bill Andrew, in charge of the detail, found his box of matches to relight the lamp. Having been shell-shocked in the First World War, the discharge in such an enclosed space brought back terrible memories. It was maintained by those present that the box of 'England's Glory' matches sounded like a biscuit tin of pebbles being shaken vigorously as poor Bill attempted to regain his composure and strike a light.

Portishead Home Guard.
Back Row: Albert Savory; Gordon Hayman; Unknown; Fred Peacock; Unknown; Unknown; Unknown; Norman Berg; Unknown
Middle Row: Tom Maggs; Unknown; Unknown; Fred Palmer; L/Cpl. Arthur 'Sonner' Rowles; Unknown; Unknown; Unknown; Les Wade; Unknown; Unknown; Unknown; Harry Skinner; Unknown; L/Cpl. Jim Brooks
Front Row: Victor 'Neppy' Holder; Edward 'Kingy' O'Connell; Cpl. Seward 'Sonny' Chapman; Arthur Selvey; Sgt. Albert Hawker; L/Cpl. Tom Coles
(Castle Cary and Ansford Living History Group collection)

Rifle shooting was not the preserve of male members of the Home Guard; ladies were also encouraged and were equal to the men, especially shooting .22" rifles.
Standing: Doreen Jenkins; Unknown; Kitty Almond; Iris Thayer; Esme Hampton; Sgt. George Rogers; Lt. H.C. Parsons; Sgt. Reg Shepherd
Prone: Lt. J.L. Packard; Iris Sellick
(Ken Crowhurst collection)

Portishead Home Guard Signals Platoon.
Back Row: Jimmy James; Clifford Edwards; Mr. Skinner (Captain WW1); Bert Luke; Ray Davies; Stuart Ekless; Ken Selvey
Second Row: Ivor Johnson; Charlie Norris; Mr. Dickinson; Ken Tucker; Iris Sellick; Kitty Almond; Cissie Wood; Iris Thayer; Esme Bown; Unknown; L/Cpl. Stan Aston
Third Row: Sgt. Reg Shepherd; Sgt. A.T. Selvey; Lt. H.C. Parsons; Capt. E.L. Curtis; Sgt. George Rogers; Sgt. Reg Parsons
Front Row: Fred Palmer; John Ives; Reg Spear; Ron Lane; John Butt
(Ken Crowhurst collection)

NO. 5 (CLEVEDON) COMPANY

COMMANDING OFFICER	Major G. de S.H. Middlemass	**OTHER OFFICERS**
2ND IN COMMAND	Capt. H.A. Lenaton, M.C.	Capt. R.G. Turner (Colonel Ret'd), C.M.G., D.S.O., M.O.

PLATOON COMMANDERS
Lt. G.R. Brodie
Lt. C.A. Buxton
Lt. J.L. Chaffe
Lt. A.W. Hand
Lt. R.J. Hoddell
Lt. R. Latham, M.C.
Lt. F.E. Reeves
Lt. W.J. Simmons, M.M.
Lt. L.H. Tiley

G. Christie
Lt. R.D. Cousins
Lt. E. Haines
Lt. F.D.B. Morton
Lt. T. Roynon

2nd Lt. P.R. Edwards
2nd Lt. J.McA. Hutton
2nd Lt. M. I'Anson
2nd Lt. G.C. Lucas
2nd Lt. D.J.N. Sawkins
2nd Lt. A.G. Smith

No. 1 (West End) Platoon.
Back Row: Unknown; Unknown; Unknown; Charlie Marsh
Second Row: Joe Laver; Unknown; Unknown; Harry Hancock; G. Horsey; E.A. Weaver; Unknown; Cyril Marks; Victor Pepler; Cecil Guest; Unknown; Unknown; Unknown
Third Row: Unknown; Unknown; Unknown; Unknown (manager of local butchers); M.E. Stephens or Stevens; S.D. Crisp; Edward George Vowles; Unknown; Reg Ford; Ted Weaver; Unknown; Unknown; Unknown; Unknown
Front Row: Alvin Newton; George Jarrett; Unknown; Sgt. Vic Summers; Lt. T. Roynon; Lt. C.A. Buxton; WO2 Arthur Williams; Sgt. E. Spencer; Unknown (possibly manager of Eastmans); Unknown; Unknown
Victor Pepler was the local coal merchant in Clevedon, George Jarrett was a farmer and journalist whilst Lt. C.A. Buxton was the Headmaster at St. John's School, Clevedon. Reg Ford was a local market gardener.
(Miss C.Y. Jarrett collection)

No. 1 (West End) Platoon.
Back Row: Unknown; Reg Ford; Reg Ewins; Mr. Fletcher; Unknown; R. Woollard; Unknown; F. Dallimore; Unknown; E. Cunliffe; E. Derrick; R. Mogg; Unknown
Second Row: Unknown; Mr. Hanson; Unknown; H. Farndon; Unknown; M. or F. Hack; Unknown; Charlie Marsh; F. Blackmore; Unknown; Victor Pepler
Third Row: Ted Weaver; Sgt. Vic Summers; Unknown; Lt. T. Roynon (2nd in Command); Lt. C.A. Buxton (Platoon Commander); S.D. Crisp; G. Christie; Rev. J. Pugh; Unknown; Cpl. H. Mortimer
Fourth Row: Mr. Plumley Snr.; E. Spencer; Unknown; Unknown; Arthur Williams; Mr. Bettles; Unknown; Unknown; T. Cridland or Bill Durbin
Front Row: Unknown; B. Goddard; Edward George Vowles; G. Cleverley; Reg Ellis; Unknown; George Jarrett; Unknown; Unknown; D. Hack; Reg Tredinnick.
(Mrs. Jean Binding collection)

Harry Mortimer had been a regular soldier since 1887, travelling to many parts of the world. He was one of the first to volunteer for the L.D.V. and was accepted although he was over the age limit, being born on 10th April 1866. He was put in charge of the stores and later became a sergeant at the parade for 'Salute the Soldier Week' in 1944, when he accompanied Col. E.G. Gidley Kitchen. Harry died in 1948 at the age of 82 and was given a semi-military funeral; his coffin was draped with the union flag and was borne by four former members of the Home Guard: T. Houghton, E. Spencer, B. Godwin and E. Vowles.

Sgt. Vic Summers was an extremely lucky man. Experimenting with a home-made bomb he lost his hand. After the war he could be seen cycling around Clevedon with a bucket and ladder cleaning windows, providing for his family.

West End Platoon was based at The Pill, the site before the war of two redundant artillery pieces. Here they had a hut, probably the one in the background. One training exercise involved setting up a breeches-buoy to transport personnel across the local river. It was quite surprising how certain unpopular N.C.O.s found out that for some inexplicable reason they were always subjected to an 'unfortunate' dunking in the river.

Part of No. 4 Platoon's orders was to clear civilians from the slopes of Wains Hill in the evenings before commencing their patrols from their hut on the hill. One evening Reg Tradinick and Reg Ewins could see a courting couple around the side of some bushes. Reg closed on the couple and in a very loud voice shouted, "Come on there, clear the hill." To the amazement of the two men, heads popped up everywhere, "just like mushrooms".

During the war the Walton Park Hotel at Clevedon was taken over by the Bristol Aeroplane Company for their drawing offices, having moved from Filton. In 1943 Stanley Ewins left school at 14 and joined as an apprentice draughtsman. Lt. Chaffe was the Platoon Commander at Walton whilst working for B.A.C. and it was not long before young Stanley was enrolled into the Platoon, Lt. Chaffe adding two years to Stanley's age. Stanley subsequently left the Home Guard and joined the Central Inspectorate Team, R.E.M.E. In a letter of 2001 he recalled some lighter moments:

My brother was in the L.D.V. When it started, they had only armbands. Over a period of time he was issued one further item when it became available. One day he came home with a helmet. He told us proudly that this helmet would stop shrapnel and even bullets, whereupon he put it on and told me to hit it with something as hard as I liked. I picked up my Mother's shoe and hit it with the heel. He was horrified when he saw the dent I had made in it.

One night about 12.30 a.m. my father woke me to say that the church bells were ringing – warning of invasion. I got dressed and started cycling to Walton-in-Gordano. On the way I stopped to knock at the door of another Home Guard colleague. After knocking for quite a while his father opened his bedroom window. I said, "Tell your son to get dressed, it's an invasion!" He replied: "He is still asleep and won't be coming this time." And, with that, he shut the window.

One Sunday when we were on parade, Lt. Chaffe announced, "We are going to have field training." We were marched to Sir Charles Miles' lower field where two tractors were working around the edge of the field cutting the wheat. We were given lumps of wood and told to line up around the edge of the field and work our way towards the centre looking for rabbits. At the end of the day we each had three or four rabbits and were all feeling the effects of the cider provided by the farmers.

(above) **No. 2 (Kenn Road) Platoon**, *photographed outside Clevedon Station, now the Triangle Development.*
Back Row: Doug Hand; Albert Webb; Unknown; Cecil Guest; possibly Mr. Powell; Unknown
Second Row: Unknown; Unknown; Unknown; Unknown; possibly Mr. Coles; Unknown; Unknown; Sam Dyer; Mr. Jones
Third Row: Tom Hussey; Fred Strickland; Unknown; Walter George Hollyman; Jack Morgan; Mr. Selwood; Unknown; Alan Thomas; Bill Clark; Stan Chapple
Front Row: Cpl. Bill Moss; Sgt. Albert Nichols; Unknown; 2nd Lt. J. Mc A. Hutton; Lt. E. Haines; Lt. A.W. Hand; 2nd Lt. A.G. Smith; Sgt. Fred G. Marshall; Sgt. Bill Grigg; Sgt. Fred Walker; Unknown
(Clevedon Civic Society and Living History Group collection)

(right) **No. 3 (East Clevedon) Platoon**, *photographed in October 1944 at Court Farm, East Clevedon. Note the order on the door 'H.G. Keep Out'. This was the unofficial Home Guard urinal! Ray Strickland, who provided the majority of the names, joined the L.D.V. in 1940 but was shortly after ordered to leave as someone told the Platoon Commander he was only 15.*
Back Row: Bill Waite; Unknown; Tom Chappel; Unknown; Harry Tucker; Ray Strickland; Gruff Whiting
Second Row: Jimmy Frake; Ben Cooper; Unknown; Albert Brimble; Frank Ashman; Bob Hasnip; Unknown
Third Row: Ernie Scribbins; Bill Taylor; Unknown; Harry Pym; John Wallis; Unknown; Sid Peck; Sam Harris; 'Gomer' Lloyd; Mr. Howard
Front Row: D/R Cpl. Geoffrey Broadhurst; Cpl. Newman Young; Cpl. Reg Bray; Sgt. Norman Fisher; Sgt. Archie Burlingham; Lt. Fred E. Reeves; Sgt. Fred Cantor; Cpl. Gordon Forbes; Cpl. Stanley Webb; Cpl. Sid Morrish; D/R Alfie 'Pop' Izzard.
By the time this photograph was taken Jimmy Frake had ceased to be a member of the Home Guard, having joined the Royal Tank Regiment in 1942, surviving the War. (Ray Strickland collection)

Sadly Ray Strickland died shortly after this photograph was lent and only a few occupations can be confirmed. Frank Ashman was the local milkman, Bob Hasnip a butcher. Ernie Scribbins worked at the local sawmills whilst Sam Harris was a blacksmith. Reg Bray was a local baker and Norman Fisher worked for Wake and Dean. Lt. Fred Reeves and Sgt. Fred Cantor were both market gardeners whilst Sgt. Archie Burlingham was a draughtsman at B.A.C.

All Saints Hall in Old Street provided a Platoon meeting place whilst an indoor small-bore range was used at *The Star*, the steel plate behind the targets only having been removed in the late 1990s. Outdoor shooting took place on the 600-yard range to the south of Clevedon. At the junction of Court Lane (now Manmow Lane) and Tickenham Road there existed a stone-built barn where Molotov Cocktails/Self-Igniting Phosphorous (S.I.P.) were stored for use in the event of attack. In the summer of 1940 Ray recalls the Platoon practising one evening with Molotov Cocktails against an apple tree. The effect was most spectacular. The tree burst into flames and burnt furiously, well past the commencement of the blackout!

*(left) Members of an unidentified **Clevedon Platoon, possibly No. 4 (Walton St. Mary)**.*
Back Row: C.M. Sykes; Albert Nichols; Wilfred Hammond
Second Row: none identified
Third Row: No. 2 Sgt. Herbert Wilkins; No. 6 has been identified as Harry Mortimer. However, looking at Harry Mortimer in the No. 1 Platoon photograph, where he was identified by his daughter, there are subtle differences, such as the medal ribbons
Front Row: 2nd Lt. J. Mc A. Hutton; Unknown; Unknown; Lt. E. Haines; Unknown; Unknown; Aubrey Crane; 2nd Lt. A.G. Smith; Arthur Williams
(Clevedon Civic Society and Living History Group collection)

*(right) **No. 5 (Tickenham) Platoon**.*
Back Row: William Summerell; Unknown; Maurice Brown; William 'Dinger' Bell
Second Row: Vernon Moses; Oliver Summerell; Unknown; Leslie Bye; Unknown; Unknown; Unknown, possibly Mr. Bax; Ivor Trigg; Charles Francis; Wallace Canter; Gordon 'Podge' Roberts
Third Row: Roy Rickards; John Morrish; Cpl. R. Woodward; Cpl. D. Morton; Sgt. Len Tiley; Lt. W.J. Simmons, M.M.; Sgt. Edwin Dyer; Cpl. Alan Lindsey; L/Cpl. George Fussell; Tom or William Durston; William or Tom Durston
Front Row: Charles Tavener; L/Cpl. D. Olive; L/Cpl. Frank Day; Ernest 'Nung' Summerell; William Selman; L/Cpl. J. 'Ted' Bowen; Reg Masters
(Clevedon Civic Society and Living History Group collection)

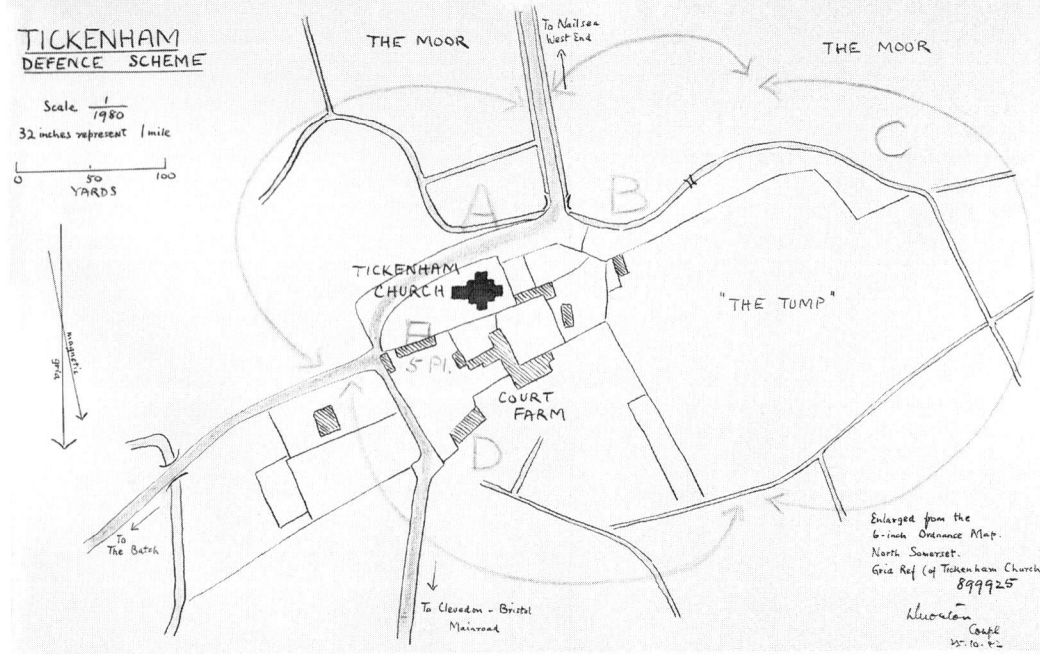

(left) Tickenham Defence Scheme.
Plans dated 25th October 1942, now lodged with the Somerset Archive & Record Service, cover the method of defending Tickenham. It was intended that the village was to be prepared for all-round defence, denying the enemy the use of all roads leading into it. Special attention was to be given to the road leading over the moor from West End, Nailsea, which was considered to be the most likely line of attack.

The Platoon comprised four sections with Platoon Headquarters in a building to the south-west of the church. The deployment of men is shown on the left.

With the possibility of being totally surrounded, outnumbered and outgunned, each man was to be issued with 60 rounds of rifle or 128 rounds of Sten gun ammunition. The Lewis gun team was to carry five full 97 round magazines. Ammunition for the Northover Projector and grenades are also listed, with ammunition reserves being held at Platoon Headquarters. There were no plans for withdrawal.

Walton-in-Gordano Home Guard, *photographed in a field beside Manor Drive, near to where the Home Guard had a hut.*
Back Row: Richard Young; Jack Virgo; Unknown; Unknown; Unknown; Jack Griffiths
Middle Row: Unknown; Bert Bessant; George Hurdle; Unknown; Lt. J.L. Chaffe; Sgt. Harry Banwell; Cpl. Edward Blake; Unknown; D/R Jack Gilling
Front Row: Unknown; Unknown; Unknown; Graham Coles, Fred Kempster
(Gordon Russell collection)

Another photograph of **Walton-in-Gordano Home Guard**.
Back Row: Unknown; Unknown; Unknown; Sgt. Harry Banwell; Lt. Chaffe; Unknown; Richard Young; Jack Griffiths or Jim Moorhouse
Middle Row: Unknown; Arthur Dunn; Cpl. Charles Young; Fred Kempster; Unknown; Unknown; Edward Blake
Front Row: Unknown; Unknown; Unknown; Jack Gilling; Unknown; Unknown; Unknown
Although Lt. Chaffe has been identified in the back row, his appearance differs from that in the previous photograph and he is not wearing a collar and tie as one would expect from a Platoon Commander.

Jack Virgo was a market gardener, living at Myrtle Cottage. Bert Bessant was a local farmworker whilst George Hurdle was a smallholder. Edward Blake, in addition to being employed by Jack Virgo, was the local milk delivery man. Jack Gilling was employed by the Bristol Aircraft Company as a draughtsman. Sgt. Harry Banwell was Sir Charles Miles's chauffeur, having served as his batman in India during World War 1 and recorded 21 years of Army service.
(Gordon Russell collection)

(left) Deployment of men for the Tickenham Defence Scheme. An asterix signifies men earmarked for providing an emergency reserve.

Platoon Headquarters.
Lt. W. Simmons, Sgt. L. Tiley, L/Cpl. G. Fussell, Ptes. I Trigg, W. Penny & K. Penny.

'A' Section.
Cpl. D. Morton*, L/Cpl. D. Olive, L/Cpl. B. Day*, Ptes. L. Withers, C. Moses*, L. Bye*, G. Jefferies & T. Durston*.

'B' Section.
Sgt. E. Dyer, Ptes. R. Masters*, E. Summerell*, W. Summerell*, J. Bewen, F. Smith, A. Bax & C. Tavener.

'C' Section.
Cpl. R. Woodward, Ptes. Francis, G. Roberts, W. Selman, M. Townsend & K. Staple.

'D' Section.
Cpl. A. Lindsey, Ptes. J.P. Brown, W. Durston, Bush, H. Bax, W. Bell, W. James, M. Brown & Richard Santer.

NO. 6 (YATTON) COMPANY

COMPANY COMMANDER	Major Frederic Baring Leman	OTHER OFFICERS	2nd Lt. C.C. Clarke
2ND IN COMMAND	Capt. W. Twiston Davis, M.C.	Lt. F. Chick, D.S.O.	2nd Lt. R.V.C. Cook
PLATOON COMMANDERS	Lt. P.G. Cardew	Lt. H.N. Grundy	2nd Lt. J.J. Harding, M.S.M.
Capt. L.F. Adams	Lt. J.A. Dommett, M.C.	Lt. C.C.W. Havell, M.C.	2nd Lt. W.R. Mumford
Capt. H. Drewett, M.C.	Lt. G. Lenaton	Lt. E.C. Tuckey, D.S.O.	2nd Lt. A.M. Parsons
Lt. T.R. Atlay	Lt. A. Shaw	2nd Lt. H.S. Boddey	2nd Lt. F.G. Smallman

(left) **Officers of No. 6 Company** in July 1942.
Back Row: Lt. H.N. Grundy; Lt. F. Chick; Lt. T.R. Atlay; Lt. C.C.W. Havell; Lt. E.C. Tuckey; Lt. P.G. Cardew
Front Row: Capt. H. Drewett; Lt. J.A. Dommett; Major J.C. Jesser-Coope, Battalion 2nd in Command; Major F.B. Leman; Capt. Twisden Davis
Major Leman lived at Bickley. Mrs. Leman, being of a slightly nervous disposition, did not approve of her husband holding meetings away from Bickley, especially in the winter. Consequently the Home Guard HQ was moved to Bickley where the cart shed was used for ammunition storage.
(Nailsea and District Local History Society)

(above) Ammunition storage Home Guard style – the Company ammunition store some 58 years later. How many similar buildings around the county stand quietly mouldering away belying their crucial role in the defence of the Realm? Perhaps it was here that the ammunition for the Blacker Bombard position at the end of Rhodyate Lane was stored. *(Author's collection)*

(left) **Signal Section of No.6 Company** in 1944.
Only Major F.B. Leman (front row no. 3) and Sir Hugh Tweedie (front row no. 4) have been identified.
(Mary Campbell collection)

(left) **Members of No. 6 Company** *marching through Yatton. (Mary Campbell collection)*

(below) **Members of Yatton Platoon** *pose for their photograph on the forecourt of* The Bridge Inn *in 1944, the building in the background being* The Old Forge.

Key to residence, where known: Y = Yatton; K.S. = Kingston Seymour.

Back Row: Clifford or Len Hale (plant attendant at local sewage works); Reg Pitts (furniture maker); Hilary Simms (K.S.); Ben Boulter or Dennis Hume; Frank Stuckey; Ken Simms (Y) (local transport company employee); Harry Trott; Frank Chappel (K.S.) (farm labourer); Stewart Galloway (furniture maker); Martin Marlowe (furniture maker); Frank Maynard (K.S.) (farmer at Kingston Seymour)

Second Row: Bill Smith (K.S.) or Bert French (Y); Cecil Neath (K.S.) (farm labourer); Walter Neath (K.S.) (highway maintenance employee); Cyril Parsons (K.S.) (farm labourer); Unknown; Peter Davis; Unknown; Alan Viney (aircraft industry); Mr. Newton; Tom Atlay (Yatton Garage employee); Ern Norton (K.S.); Bob Brice (Yatton Garage employee)

Third Row: Arthur Short (K.S.) (farm labourer at Kingston Seymour); Don Howell or Mr. Hippisley; Gordon Spratt (K.S.); Frank Trott (Co-op butcher in Yatton); Unknown; 'Trixey' Price (Y) (farmer); Len Manley (manager of Wyman's bookstall on Yatton Station); Tom Dale (Y) (furniture maker); Fred Deacy (furniture maker); Bert Fowler or Jim Symons; Jessie Strange (furniture maker); Albert Pearce (Y); Alf Moore

Front Row: L/Cpl. Stanley Watkins (Y) (builder); L/Cpl. Jack or Harry Marshall (employee of Wyke and Dean); L/Cpl. Harold Major (Y) (employee of Wyke and Dean); Cpl. Jack Crease (probation officer); Cpl. Arthur Challenger; Sgt. Tom Evans (Y); Lt. T.R. Atlay (Y) (proprietor of Yatton Garage); Sgt. Jenkins (Y) (garage trade in Bristol); Sgt. Charlie Parsons (K.S.) (farm labourer at Middle Lane Farm, Kingston Seymour); Cpl. Bert Savage (Y); Cpl. Malcolm Stone (Y) (schoolmaster); Cpl. Tom Waygood (K.S.) (farm labourer); L/Cpl. Philip Harris (K.S.) (farmer).

Wyke and Dean was a local firm which employed all those listed above as furniture makers. Note the four years' good conduct stripes on Sgt. Tom Evans's sleeve.
(Mrs. Gwennie Lyddon collection)

Alan Viney recalls joining the Home Guard as a messenger, together with Tom Atlay and Brian Warburton. He was issued with a uniform and webbing when he was about 17½. Keen on rifle shooting he recalls the Platoon being issued with American P17 rifles. The unit also possessed a Lewis machine gun, ex-Royal Flying Corps, and a Northover Projector, Cpl. Malcolm Stone being responsible for the Northover.

[The Northover Projector was produced for the Home Guard in a rush to provide some form of platoon weapon. It was issued in late 1940 or early 1941 and consisted of a hollow metal tube supported by a cast-iron tripod. Capable of firing self-igniting phosphorus grenades, No. 36 grenades or the No. 68 anti-tank grenade by means of a charge of gun powder, it had several drawbacks. Firstly, the cast-iron tripod tended to break if dropped. In wet weather the propelling charge sometimes failed to ignite. Some rounds when fired could fall dangerously short. On other occasions the S.I.P. grenade, which was made of glass containing phosphorus, would ignite in the barrel because the charge was too powerful. If the projector team managed to fire off a round, their position would be given away by a cloud of smoke which also obscured the target, making it impossible to aim a second round until the smoke cleared. Despite its drawbacks the issuing of the Northover Projector continued and by the summer of 1941 some 8,000 were in service nationally.]

1941 also saw the introduction of a new weapon, the Sten gun. Alan remembers the Platoon's first instruction on the weapon. "Never seen one before," was the Regular Sergeant instructor's comment on being handed the weapon, hardly surprising for it had been designed with the Home Guard in mind. Alan also remembers their Platoon being issued with cup-dischargers for their rifles. This enabled the grenade No. 36 to be fired up to 200 yards, considerably further than the 25-35 yards that the grenade could be thrown by hand. In addition to this, the cup-discharger also enabled the rifle to fire the anti-tank grenade No. 68. The rifle range was situated on the coast south of Clevedon between map ref. ST 396 701 and ST 390 702 where it was possible to fire up to 600 yards, the 'danger' area being the Bristol Channel. Later on the Platoon received a Browning Automatic Rifle (B.A.R.).

Tom Atlay's father, like many of the older Home Guard members, had experienced the tragedy of the Great War. Both his brothers were killed within days of each other on the Somme. Lt. Atlay was subsequently gassed and returned to England. On recovery he took up flying, taking his first flight in 1918, just before the cessation of hostilities. On the outbreak of the Second World War he was directed by the R.A.F. to report to Filton where he was to instruct potential R.A.F. air crew. It soon became apparent to Lt. Atlay that aviation had changed somewhat since 1918 and he thus concentrated his war effort on the Home Guard which he had joined at its formation.

One of the Platoon's duties was to share in the defence of Lulsgate Airport. One night whilst on duty Jack Crease slipped down a bank at Brockley Combe. Unfortunately, he was carrying a box of Swan Vestas and the inevitable happened. The resulting conflagration burnt a hole in his battledress trousers.

NO. 1 PLATOON NO. 6 COMPANY

Whilst no photograph has been located of these men, the roll has and this has been reproduced (*left*) in the hope that memories will be jogged and a photograph may be forthcoming.

Fortunately some of the War Diary for No. 1 (Yatton) Platoon has survived and the author is indebted to Mrs. M. Campbell for providing extracts which give an indication of the duties and responsibilities of the Home Guard whilst on and off duty.

HOME GUARD

No. 6 Company

Yatton Platoon (No. 1)

Record of Guard Duty and Patrols

Oct. 8th   (1940) – Report of a bright light showing from the top south-east window of the Railway Hotel at 12.55 a.m.

Oct. 9th   (1st Suffolks) missed last train to Cheddar 12.30, reported to Guard Room Yatton Railway Station and Village patrols 4-6th Oct. 1940 8.00 p.m. to 6.30 a.m.

Oct. 5/6th   Strong SW gale with frequent squalls. Red lamp on loan from Railway Co. About 20 cars were halted between 12.00 and 4.00 a.m. and several pedestrians – nothing to report Village Patrol ... owing to heavy rain not all the route specified was patrolled ...

Oct. 12/13th	Areas patrolled Railway Bridge – all cars stopped.
Oct. 17th	Found car ... YW 9224 with front doors unlocked. Found car ... HW 8664 with all doors unlocked.
Oct. 20th	All cars stopped as per orders.
Oct. 17th	Station – Cycle and car found unlocked.
Oct. 19/20th	11.00 p.m. Car No. 1848 GL, side lights left on.
Oct. 25/26th	Cpl. Nicholls with two men of the Clevedon Home Guard reported at Guard Room with message saying that plane was believed brought down in the neighbourhood of Kenn and Yatton Moors. Detailed two men of my section to go with Cpl. Nicholls and his men, to search in the direction of Kenn Pier who eventually came back with nothing to report.
Oct. 28/29th	Alert already on at 10.30 p.m. Raiders passed at 11.40 a.m. Night fine but uneventful.
Nov. 5/6th	Weather very inclement. Rain and half a gale. Raiders passed signal 2.30 a.m.
Nov. 12th	A quiet night, nothing to report.
Nov. 15/16th	(Patrol) 1. Proceeded by car to Kingston, walk to sea wall and patrol. In view of report given to Commander, direction N to NNW 1.45 a.m. Three red lights from sky falling to ground – believed to be rockets fired – in view of flashes from ground – or balloons descending in flames. (Patrol) 2. Generally quiet – plane heard returning at 3.30 a.m.
Nov. 17th	Report of plane seen burst high in the air over Clevedon.
Nov. 30th-Dec. 1st	Owing to the Field Exercise to be held on Sunday 1st December and the need for as many of the section to turn out as possible, it was arranged that a station platform sentry should do a 50 minute duty only, thus enabling the (detail) to get a fair amount of rest.
Dec. 1st	No air raids, clear night.
Dec. 2nd	Heavy air raid in progress, probably in Bristol. All Clear 12.00 Midnight.
Dec. 12th	12.00-1.30 a.m. – The patrol observed 3 cycles outside one council house and 4 cycles outside another, Claverham. The occupants concerned were awakened and warned that the practice must cease, the people concerned promised that our instructions would be carried out.
Dec. 15/16th	A quiet night with no incident to report, weather stormy. Air raid in progress on mounting guard, All Clear at 11.30 p.m.
Dec. 16/17th	Patrol noticed about 17 bicycles around the factory, that were left out and warned the owners that they must keep them in at night.
Dec. 21st	Air raid in progress on mounting guard, All Clear at 12.40 p.m.
Dec. 27th	Many men of the Green Howards stranded on the station. Failed to get a reply from their unit at Winscombe in spite of frequent attempts. It struck me that a similar thing could happen in the event of the Home Guard requiring assistance.
Jan. 3rd 1941	Constant enemy air activity all night and large fires seen in the direction of Bristol.
Jan. 4/5th	Enemy activity all night over widely separated area.
Jan. 14th	Air raid in progress at time of mounting guard. Heavy gunfire over Bristol and District.
Feb. 9/10th	Weather stormy. Air raid Purple at 10.30 p.m. White at 12.30 p.m. Nothing else to report.
Feb. 12th	Loud explosion heard at 3.28 a.m. in the direction of Weston and at 3.45 a.m. it was repeated.
Feb. 27th	Vivid white flashes in sky at various points of the compass between 3.00 and 4.00 a.m., but no reports heard.
Mar. 13/14th	Air raid in progress at time of assembly. All Clear at 2.48 p.m. Nothing else to report.

(gap until November 1941)

Nov. 1st/2nd	The whole section operated in one hour 20 minute duties and ( ) during an air raid. All Clear at 11.23 p.m. – weather very cold, heavy cloud wind NE veering to NW. No incident to report.
April	Note from Company Commander to say that the Guard Commander need not remain alert throughout his tour of duty. After positioning his sentries he should get what sleep he can, arranging that a sentry arouses him in time to post the next relief.

Section Leaders Please Note:

The following have been reported unofficially from G.W.R. Yatton:

1. Communication cords in carriages pulled and vacuum released.
2. Carriage seats incorrectly placed.
3. Lights switched on and coach batteries exhausted.

These practices must cease if duty is to be allowed to continue to have convenience and comfort of the coach in question.

(The book ends on 20th June 1944)

(left) **No. 3 Section No. 2 Platoon No. 6 Company**, *photographed on the Playing Fields at West Backwell.*
Back Row: Mr. Endicott; Mr. Farrant; Mr. Aulman; J. Ryder; J. Ready
Second Row: Unknown; Unknown; Mr. Ball; Unknown; H. Young; Mr. Hyde
Third Row: Mr. Waite; M.F. Pearce; E.H. Udall; Mr. Nutman; O.J. Jeanes; Mr. Luckwell; Mr. Marsden
Front Row: Cpl. Williams; 2nd Lt. A.M. Parsons; Lt. A. Shaw; Major F.B. Leman; 2nd Lt. C.C. Clarke; Sgt. R.A. Hayes; L/Cpl. Brookhouse-Richards; L/Cpl. Floyd.
A.M. Parsons was the founder of Blackfriar's Paints.
(John Brain collection)

(right) **No. 3 Platoon No. 6 Company**.
Back Row: Fred Long; Walt Webber; Unknown; Cliff Llewellyn; Robin Reed; Mr. Brown; Mr. Bryne; possibly Mr. Taylor; Charlie Maine; Mr. Boxall
Second Row: Mr. Newman; J. Stock; George Wood; G. Ridge; J. Durbin; Harry Cripps; Mr. Goodliffe; H. Ford; Edward Court; H. Shears; R. Cox
Third Row: Edgar Hobbs; Walt Young; Unknown; Unknown; Mr. Smallman; Unknown; George Pane; Harold Parker; Mr. Hunt; G. Pippit; Jack Caldwell; Cecil Hills; Jack Durant
Fourth Row: Mr. Hicks; Albert Trott; Mr. Pippit; Tim Luxton; Bill Weeks; Bill 'Fishy' Elverd; A. Kelland; Gilbert Carey; Len Stokes; Unknown; Unknown; Unknown; Unknown; Fred Aish; George Gallop; G. Llewellyn
Front Row: Cpl. Young; Unknown; Sgt. Robert Hobbs; Unknown; Capt. Tuckey; Major Leman; Lt. Col. Tweedie; Capt. H. Drewett.; Capt. Chick; possibly Mr. Brown; Sgt. Bill Stokes; Sgt. Hector Shepherd; Cpl. Chapman.

'Capt.' Tuckey is wearing Lieutenant's 'pips'. 'Capt.' Chick is also listed as a Lieutenant in the Battalion history.
(Mary Campbell collection)

No. 4 Platoon No.6 Company. *Only the five members of the back row have been identified:*
S. Barnes; Mr. Cox; Mr. Coombs; B. Stokes; J. Neate
(Mrs. E. Clark collection)

NO. 7 (CHEW MAGNA) COMPANY

COMMANDING OFFICER   Major F.J. Terrell
2ND IN COMMAND   Capt. A. Tyte (Capt. A.B. Scott, M.C.)

PLATOON COMMANDERS
Lt. H.W. Buckland   Lt. R.L. Stevenson
Lt. F.H. Moss   Lt. M.F. Symes
Lt. A.B. Scott, M.C.   Lt. J. Thistlewaite
Lt. S.F. Smith   Lt. A. Tyte

OTHER OFFICERS
Capt. A. Hebert   Lt. P.S. Wills
Capt. F.W.F. Hughes (M.O.)   2nd Lt. E.A. Chapman
Lt. T.H. Hancock   2nd Lt. P.R. Chivers
Lt. C. Maynard   2nd Lt. W.C. Forse
Lt. W.A. Rogers   2nd Lt. J.G. Hoare
Lt. M. Richard Ryder   2nd Lt. H.D. King
Lt. W.J.S. Simmons   2nd Lt. S.W.I. Mayo
Lt. W.S.S. Whiting   2nd Lt. R.C. Rainford
Lt. J.H.A. Wilkins   2nd Lt. C.C. Todd

(left) **Chew Magna Platoon**. *(Mrs. Sheila Walker collection)*
Key to residence, where known: B.S. = Bishop Sutton; C.M. = Chew Magna.
Back Row: Unknown; Jim Harris (B.S.); Mr. Osmond (C.M.); Unknown; Jeff Hasell (C.M.); Bill Hasell (C.M.); Patrick Walker (C.M.); Mr. Trendell (C.M.)
Middle Row: Lt. M. Richard Ryder (C.M.); Bill Sage (C.M.); Unknown; Sgt. Hubert Clark (C.M.); Sgt. Bert Bown (B.S.); Cpl. Arthur Perry (B.S.); L/Cpl. Tom Pierce (C.M.); L/Cpl. Roy Perry (Newtown); Unknown; Mr. Stephenson (Stowey, B.S.)
Front Row: Oliver Ware (B.S.); Unknown; Cpl. Jim Patch (C.M.); Jack Marsh (C.M.); George Perry (B.S.)
The main observation post for this Home Guard unit was on the top of Knowle Hill Tump which provided views over a wide area.

(right) **Chew Stoke Home Guard**. *(Mrs. Pat Huggins collection)*
Back Row: Nelson Read; L/Cpl. Bert Harris; Cpl. Bert Wedlake; L/Cpl. George Bond
Front Row: Sid Clark; Sgt. Francis George Cox; Roland Clarke; Cpl. George Lane; Gilbert Wedlake
Many members of the Home Guard had received serious injuries in the First World War. L/Cpl. George Bond, however, received his after the war, losing his left hand in a mangold cutter. This did not prevent him from joining his local Home Guard unit and posing with his comrades in the summer of '44. Note the medals being worn by Roland Clarke.

(below) **Chew Stoke Home Guard**. *(Mrs. Pat Huggins collection)*
Back Row: L/Cpl. Bert Haskins; Gilbert Wedlake; Francis Stallard; Harvey Cainey; L/Cpl. Michael Francis; James Churches; George Horler; Cpl. Nelson Read
Middle Row: Cpl. Alfred Perkins; possibly Mr. Wilson; Edward Cooke; Harry Chapman; Leonard Thornet; Roland Clarke; Cpl. George Lane
Front Row: Cpl. George Weaver; Vivian Weston; Sgt. Francis Cox; Sgt. William Brawn; possibly James Trimm; Kenneth Wedlake; Sidney Clark; Cpl. Herbert Wedlake

Edward Cooke joined Chew Stoke Home Guard in 1942. Drill took place at Rectory Hall where they were joined by men from Nempnett Thrubwell. The armoury and stores were located at the home of Lt. Thistlewaite. Other officers remembered were 2nd Lt. W.C. Forse, 2nd Lt. P.R. Chivers and Lt. H.W. Buckland. N.C.O.s included Cpl. Dagger, Sgt. Cox and Sgt Brawn. At one stage during the war a nightly guard duty was maintained at a local high spot known as The Tump, local coal lorries providing transport.

Sunday morning drill was remembered with affection. On favourable days the Platoon would proceed in a north-westerly direction in arrowhead formation with weapons at the trail. On arriving at *The Star Inn*, Breach Hill, at 12 noon, thirsts would be quenched before the return march along the lanes to be dismissed at the Rectory Hall. For grenade practice old lead workings on the Mendips were used.

*(above) A group of unidentified stretcher bearers from **No. 3 (Ubley) Platoon No. 7 Company**. (Mrs. Sheila Weatherall collection)*

(above) **Ubley, Nempnett Thrubwell and Chew Stoke Home Guard.**
Back Row: Unknown; Gilbert Wedlake; Edward Cooke; Vivian Weston; Unknown; Unknown; Unknown; Unknown; Harry Chapman; Sidney Clark; Leonard Thornet; Unknown; Michael Francis
Middle Row: Bert Haskins; Ivan Brock; Unknown; Mr. Wilson; Francis Stallard; James Churches; Kenneth Wedlake; Harvey Cainey; Unknown; Unknown; Roland Clark; George Bond; Raymond George Simmons
Front Row: Unknown; George Lane; Alfred Perkins; Unknown; Sgt. William Brawn; 2nd Lt. S.W.I. Mayo; Unknown; Sgt. Francis Cox; George Weaver; Nelson Read; Herbert Wedlake
George Simmons was a dispatch rider who owned a 1928 348cc. A.J.S. motorcycle which he used on official Home Guard business. (Mrs. Maisie Simmons collection)

(above) **Ubley and Nempnett Thrubwell Home Guard.**
Back Row: Ivan Brock; Len Weaver; George Symes; Arthur Jefferies; Reg Weaver; Alex Flower; Arthur Yates; Jack Satchel
Front Row: Raymond George Simmons; Lestor Norman; 2nd Lt. S.W.I. Mayo; Len Baker; George Bond.
(Mrs. Maisie Simmons collection)

(right) **Chew Stoke, Ubley and Nempnett Thrubwell Home Guard.** *2nd Lt. S.W.I. Mayo, in the centre of the picture, marches his men towards* Stoke Inn *on the West Harptree road past Norman Brain's Garage. The second figure behind is Lestor Norman whilst the moustachioed figure of George Bond can be seen further back. Bringing up the rear on the left is Sgt. Francis George Cox who fought with the North Somerset Yeomanry in the Great War. One can almost hear the crunch, crunch of boots marching along the tarmac road. (Mrs. Maisie Simmons collection)*

West Harptree and Compton Martin Home Guard. (Jon Budd collection)

Although no one has been identified in this photograph, those residents of West Harptree who served in the Home Guard are commemorated on a roll of honour erected at St. Mary's Church in 1997. Their names are listed below:

H. Baber	G. Farrow	R. Maggs
L. Baber	R. Haines	I. Mayo
C. Blacker	F. Harris	W. Seward
M. Blannin	G. Harris	V. Sheppard
H. Body	M. Harvey	M.F. Symes, Lt.
E. Boyd	I. Hodgson	P. Warford
F. Boyd	E.M. King	R. Weeks
J. Branch	G. King	W. Weeks
J. Burdge	J. Lyons	F. Wyatt
E. Clift	L. Lyons	S. Wyatt
F. Farrow		

Whilst M.F. Symes's rank has been included no others have been recorded including that of S.W.I. Mayo who is known to have been a 2nd Lt.

Lt. Wilfred Joseph Simmons joined the Home Guard at its formation, being too old to be 'called up'. With his brother-in-law Thomas Hancock and Arthur Tyte they formed No. 4 Platoon. Patrols covered East Harptree, through Coley, around the reservoir and through to Litton. Patrols also extended up to *The Castle of Comfort* on The Mendips.

Manoeuvres took place in The Park at Harptree Court. It was on one such occasion that Lt. Simmons was wounded. Acting as an umpire during the exercise Lt. Simmons came face to face with a home guard who promptly shot him in the chest with a blank round. As Lt. Simmons bent forward he was promptly shot again, the blast and débris from the discharge removing the lobe from his ear. Arriving home with his head bandaged Mrs. Simmons greeted him with the comment: "I thought you were umpiring, not out with the British Army". On enquiring what he said to his assailant Lt. Simmons simply replied: "I told him never to point a gun at anyone unless he intended to shoot them". Many Home Guards were not so fortunate, over 1,000 losing their lives through accidents. With the shortage of blank ammunition for P17 rifles, use was sometimes made of cracker blanks (*right*). Tied to the muzzle of a rifle, gun fire could be simulated by gently pulling the string. Use of cracker blanks would have saved Lt. Simmons's ear lobe.

The rifle range was situated on The Common, South Widcombe, East Harptree. The firing point was approximately at map ref. ST 582 565 and the butts at map ref. ST 585 564. Meetings took place at The Theatre, East Harptree. Others who attended would have included Sgts. Ted Jennings and Arthur Smith, as well as L/Cpl. Frank Cooke.

Members of East Harptree, Litton and Hinton Blewitt Home Guard.
Back Row: Frank Cooke; Norman Curl (or Currell); Unknown; Seward Payne; William Derrick; George Drake
Middle Row: Sgt. Edward Jennings; L/Cpl. Fred Tucker; Cpl. Maurice Weeks; Arthur Smith; Basil Guy; Seward Wareham; Harold Durbin; Eric Leach
Front Row: Lt. Wilfred J.S. Simmons; Lt. Arthur Tyte; Lt. Thomas H. Hancock
(Mrs. Pat Huggins collection)

(left) Lts. Wilfred Simmons, Arthur Tyte and Thomas Hancock
(Mrs. Mary Wyatt collection)

(below) Sgt. Arthur Smith, Lt. Wilfred Simmons and Cadet Donald Simmons
(Mrs. Mary Wyatt collection)

Jonah Weeks astride his Rudge Special. (Mrs. Brenda White collection)

Maurice Weeks (brother of Jonah) and William Derrick with their Savage Lewis .30 machine gun. In America, where it was manufactured during WW1, it was known as the Lewis .30M 1918. (Mrs. Brenda White collection)

NO. 8 (BISHOPSWORTH) COMPANY

COMPANY COMMANDER	Major R.H. Elton
2ND IN COMMAND	Capt. J. MacGregor

PLATOON COMMANDERS
Capt. A.H. Mainstone
Lt. R.E.B. Harris
Lt. G.M. Hopson
Lt. A.V. Mereweather
Lt. W.D. Mereweather
Lt. F. Pembury
Lt. G.C. Popham

OTHER OFFICERS
Capt. M.K. Dunlop (M.O.)
Lt. N. Elliott
Lt. E.S. Jenkins
Lt. E.C. Park
Lt. L. Smith
Lt. C. Winfield, M.M.

No. 8 Company comprised nine Platoons including HQ, Ambulance and Signals. Company Headquarters was at St. Peter's Hill, Bishopsworth and totalled 297 all ranks.

Officers of Bishopsworth Home Guard.
Back Row; No. 2 Sgt. Fred 'Butch' Davies. He was later promoted to Captain and was i/c Local Army Cadets long after the Home Guard was stood down.
Middle Row: No. 3 Lt. (the Rev.) Norman Elliott, the local Congregational minister and Home Guard padre. No. 6 Lt. George C. Popham
Front Row: No. 3 Major Roy H. Elton. He lived in Bishopsworth and was a primary school Headmaster in Bristol.
(Malago Society collection)

No. 8 Company was the first to build its own rifle range in one of Mr. Rudd's fields behind Margaret Road, Broadoak Hill, Dundry Slopes. On the left, senior officers inspect the targets and the scoring 'paddle'. The value of the shot would be signalled by use of the scoring paddle or flag as laid down in Small Arms Training Vol. 1, Pamphlet No. 1, Weapon Training, 1942. *Note the senior officer nearest the camera wearing puttees, and the 'tin hat' aiming mark on the target face off centre to enable rifles to be shot at a range shorter than the lowest sight setting. On the right, the firing point at Rudd's Field which was so constructed to prevent ricochets off the target areas. An officer nearest to camera is holding a No. 1 rifle correctly whilst the private behind manages to operate his P14/P17 rifle left-handed. (Malago Society collection)*

Captain A.H. Mainstone was subsequently promoted officer i/c Heavy Ack Ack Home Guard Bedminster Down where Sgts. Reakes and Hammond won promotions to officer rank. Sgt. Derrick became Battery Sergeant Major and was later awarded the B.E.M.

Below is a letter to Sgt. Reakes from Major Elton appreciating his efforts in Exercise Raider. Some exercises were quite extensive lasting complete weekends, day and night. On the Monday morning exhausted Home Guards would return to their civilian occupations some even subsequently falling asleep at work.

```
                            No. 8. Coy (7th Bn).,
                            SOMERSET HOME GUARD,
                            St. Peter's Hall,
                            BISHOPSWORTH.

                    4th Oct. 1943.    RHE/LP.

Dear Sergt. Reakes,

        I would like to say a special word in
appreciation of your own personal part in "EXERCISE RAIDER".
        I appreciate most sincerely the work you
did at so short a notice and knowing you were manning A. A.
the following evening.
        Your report was a pattern and I am sure
will be of very great assistance to the Bn. Commander in
assessing the value of the Exercise.
        Very well done indeed; a really good
show.
                            Yours sincerely,

                            R.L. Elton
                                Major

Sergt. Reakes,
"Northview",
Main Rd.,
BISHOPSWORTH.
```

Whilst it is uncertain if the following extract from Sir Hugh Tweedie's book on the history of the 7th Battalion refers to Exercise Raider, it gives an idea of how some weekends were spent:

An example of weekend training was an operation to attack a village guarding an Aerodrome in a neighbouring county. Saturday afternoon: ordinary Platoon Parade, dismiss 1700 hours; on parade again 2200 hours (it was a wet night and meant three and a half hours across country in pitch darkness); returned to HQ at 07.45 Sunday; 09.30 on Parade for a camouflage display. In the course of the night-attack six men had been gassed and were violently sick, one having to be left behind in hospital. The squad had been on the move from 14.30 on Saturday 'till noon on Sunday, with a short break. Many similar weekends were spent in training, always, wet or fine, under the strictest field conditions.

Our last exercise on the bigger scale was to take part with some 2,000 Regular troops in the attack on a town in mid Somerset, the local Home Guard defending. We got into the town and lay up undetected. We then had to find our way out again and report to the HQ of the Highland Light Infantry in a Sector previously indicated.

The night squad led the way through gardens and lanes, past C.D. and Police, and eventually we rolled, one at a time, across the main road and into a cemetery. We then got into some kale which was very wet, crossed several railway tracks, passed through the yard of a big factory, and after some trouble located the HQ in a farm. It was then about 03.00. At 05.30 hours the attack was to go in. We had to pass again through the defences and lay a smoke screen near some ponds which were indicated.

We had no difficulty in getting into the town again, and promptly at 05.30 we fired a green light: the pre-arranged signal. We lit our smoke-candles unobserved, and our job was finished.

These smoke-candles were No. 20 and contained gas, and we suffered from this and were glad to get out of it. At 06.30 we left the town full of smoke and gas, and the civil population must have taken a dim view of the proceedings.

'X' Platoon's work is done. That work was spontaneous and hard. This is only a very abbreviated account of the work of one platoon among perhaps 50,000, all imbued with the same spirit. There has been no fighting for the Home Guard, but a great mutual respect has arisen among its members, and no time spent in such a cause could be time wasted.

NO. 9 (LEIGH WOODS) COMPANY

COMPANY COMMANDER	Major D.N. Robertson, M.C.	OTHER OFFICERS	
2ND IN COMMAND	Capt. G.C. Brooks	Lt. J.F. Boucher	Lt. E.M. Savory
PLATOON COMMANDERS		Lt. J.H.M. Budgett	Lt. J.H. Savory
Lt. T.H. Alger	Lt. B. Strange	Lt. H.S. Crabtree	2nd Lt. W.A. Jones, O.B.E.
Lt. W.S. Goodbody	Lt. W.C. Stuart-Low	Lt. J.G.R. Scarff	2nd Lt. C.E. Sibley, M.M.

Despite numerous appeals no photographs have been forthcoming on No. 9 Company. The following letter from P.H.F. Clarke, a student at Clifton College and at the time in the College's L.D.V., to his father Richard Clarke in London, gives an indication of the activity experienced by members of No. 9 Company.

... I hear that there have been masses of rumours rushing around London about the bombing of Bristol; they are all exaggerated horribly which I think is the result of the air of mystery around it by a rather futile censorship; this reached the peak of its futility in Tuesday's *Evening Post* whose headlines were "THREE KILLED IN BOMBING IN SOUTH WEST TOWN", the rest of the paper was equally silly and looked absolutely crazy to those who knew all about it.

On the first night of bombing (Monday June 24) I was doing L.D.V. on Beggar's Bush and it was a grand sight. When we first got there the weather was so bombish that I said that there was a 50% chance that there would be a raid, everyone was very scoffish and said 10% at the most, hence when a couple of hours later the sirens began wailing, I crowed like anything.

At midnight we returned from patrol and I settled down to try to get some sleep before going on sentry duty at 2.30 a.m. At 12.15 I was nearly asleep when I heard a distant drone of bombers. I was more or less hoping that they were Germans (!) and I wondered if the sirens would start; ten seconds later to my surprise they did. We jumped into our trenches and from then on had a first-class view of the fun and games.

There were only two bombers; at first they circled round a few times at a colossal height (about 20,000 ft I guess); they then came down into the clouds which were very conveniently just above the balloons (8,000 ft) and had a look round by crossing from cloud to cloud. After identifying Temple Meads by the light of the moon (quite bright) they came just below the clouds and did some pretty accurate bombing for six or seven minutes dropping nearly 20 High Explosive bombs and quite a large number of incendiary bombs. These H.E. bombs caused three deaths in Brislington and did very little damage beyond putting Temple Meads out of action for a few hours. I heard that eight bombs fell actually on the lines or on the surrounding platforms etc. Most of the incendiary bombs were put out quite quickly, the only damage they did was to gut completely a soda water factory; this provided a grand sight from Beggar's Bush, the whole sky was lit up by a red glow. The planes then flew off towards Avonmouth and after a quick look round dropped about five H.E. bombs which apparently did no damage. The planes then returned to the clouds and went off over East Bristol, still remaining however within earshot. After circling around for about twenty minutes they separated and resumed the attack, one over Bristol and the other over Avonmouth; the latter did little if any damage, but the one over Bristol dropped a line of about six bombs one of which fell in Old Market and another fell on a corner shop just by the Eye Hospital killing two people, and neatly cutting off the corner to show all the rooms in section; hundreds of windows were broken. The bombs bursting made a grand sight. This plane then came over us making us jump back into our covered trenches hastily; the planes then joined together again and after circling round a few more times, climbed again and made off southward. During the whole raid, lasting exactly seventy minutes, not a single anti-aircraft gun was fired and not a single fighter went up ...

During Tuesday several fighters flew over here practising, as if they had only just come here from the east coast, and on Tuesday night they succeeded in shooting down one bomber down near Avonmouth; AA guns were also active then; there were two warnings, about five planes took part but no casualties were caused. They first appeared about 12.15 [a.m.] and stayed for three-quarters of an hour dropping about 15 bombs around Avonmouth, they then went and the all clear sounded. Six of these bombs fell in one field near Portbury, the craters were not very large yet a wooden five bar gate was smashed to bits and a bomb splinter hit a bar of an iron gate and cut it neatly in half. Half an hour after the all clear the wardens began ringing their hand-bells to signify that there was no gas about, and in the middle of this the siren went again and so they put down their bells and got out their whistles again. The planes circled round for about ten minutes but I don't think they dropped any bombs although the A.A.s were active; they went away again and so I went to bed. One hour later I was woken by five colossal bangs in succession which were bombs at Pill; five minutes later they went away again and the all clear was sounded.

For the last four nights there have been no warnings and no bombs dropped, but there have been plenty of German planes about and masses of A.A. fire particularly on Saturday night.

8th Somerset (Weston) Battalion

HEADQUARTERS (Admin)	Salisbury Terrace, Weston-super-Mare
HEADQUARTERS (Battle)	R.E. Drill Hall, Langford Road, Weston
DATE FORMED	May 1940
COMMANDING OFFICER	Lt. Col. A.W.A. Bruce
	(Lt. Col. A.H. Yatman, D.S.O., D.L.)
2ND IN COMMAND	Major G. Wood, Major A. Henniker

H.Q. STAFF

A & Q	Capt. L. Barker, The Queen's Royal Reg't
ADJUTANT	Capt. E.T. Trevelyan, Gloucester Reg't
ADMINISTRATION OFFICER	2nd Lt. H.A. Tibbetts
AMMUNITION OFFICER	Lt. H.C. Sewell-Grant
GAS OFFICER	Lt. W.C. Noakes
INTELLIGENCE OFFICER	Capt. F.W. Robins
LIAISON OFFICER	Capt. A.E. Philpott (Sector)
	Capt. R.A.C. Wright (Cinema)
	Capt. C.J. Walker (Military Info. Centre)
	Lt. E.L. Dauncey (Press)
MEDICAL OFFICER	Major A.W. Hooper, C.M.G., D.S.O.
MESSING OFFICER	Lt. M.E. Georgy
PADRE	Capt. S.R. Hosbons
PIGEONS OFFICER	Lt. P.J. Parrett
SIGNALS OFFICER	Lt. V.E. Dimoline
	(Capt. W.L. Eveleigh)
TRANSPORT OFFICER	Lt. Lawton H. George
WEAPONS OFFICER	Lt. A.O. Williams

(above) **Officers of the 8th Somerset (Weston) Battalion.**
Back Row: No. 4 2nd Lt. Reed; No. 5 2nd Lt. Trevor; No. 6 Lt. Gray
Front Row: No. 4 Capt. Atkinson; No. 5 Major P.C. Nicholls; No. 6 Major George Wood, J.P.; No 7 Lt. Col. A.W.A. Bruce; No. 8 Capt. E.T. Trevelyan; No. 11 Capt. A.E. Phillpott.
(reproduced by courtesy of Weston-super-Mare Gazette*)*

Members of Weston-super-Mare Home Guard *pose outside the swimming pool. With furled flags and wireless sets, the signal section must be represented in this photograph.*

No doubt the photograph of officers on the previous page includes the Battalion Pigeons Officer, Lt. P.J. Parrett. Lt. Parrett fought in the First World War in the Royal Artillery, subsequently spending two years in hospital having been both severely wounded and gassed. During the war pigeons were used by the armed services and the police. The message carriers were hollow cylinders of coloured bakelite fixed to a ring on the pigeons' legs. They were colour coded to identify the service on which they were employed as detailed below:

> Green – Special Pigeon Service
> Grey – Special Pigeon Service
> Red with coloured disc in cap –
>   Special Pigeon Service
> Red (plain) – Normal Army Pigeon Service
> Blue (plain) – R.A.F. Pigeon Service
> Blue with coloured disc in cap – R.A.F. Pigeon Service
> Blue with white patch on side – R.A.F. 'S.O.S.'
> Black – Civil Police
> Yellow – Commercial

The colours identified the address to which such messages should be forwarded. Interestingly, Special Pigeon Service messages were to be sent to the C.S.O. Army Pigeon Service, 'Wing House', Piccadilly.

Lt. Parrett trained pigeons for message carrying from foreign countries back to England. He would collect pigeons from various lofts in the south-west of England and, together with his own, would, after a period of training, release them from resorts such as Weymouth, Lyme Regis and Sidmouth. The War Office would then take suitable birds.

HEADQUARTERS COMPANY

COMMANDING OFFICER   Major George Wood
2ND IN COMMAND   Capt. F.W. Robins

Kenneth Trego was a member of HQ Company before joining the Royal Engineers Bomb Disposal Unit. His contemporaries included Ptes. Alan Bailey, Ralph Bailey, Peter Banwell, Norman Cook, Terry Dicker, Henry Gill, John Hiscocks and Ray Jones. Their commander was 2nd Lt. Bob Browning. All of them had been members of the Army Cadet Force and joined the same platoon before being called up for military service. Mr. Taylor, a retired police sergeant, was the company QMS, the stores being kept in a disused shop in Oxford Street.

On one occasion young Ken and his colleagues were called out to Puxton in the early hours of the morning to search for German airmen reported to be in the vicinity. It was as well they did not come face to face with the enemy. Their sergeant had forgotten to bring along any ammunition!

After leaving the Home Guard and joining the Regular Army, Ken's final posting was with the 6th Airborne Division in Palestine after the war, an experience he would rather forget.

'A' COMPANY

COMMANDING OFFICER   Major P.C. Nicholls
    (Major G. Wood)
2ND IN COMMAND   Capt. Percy Atkins

No. 3 Platoon marching past Lt. Col. Bruce and Mayor Alderman P. Culling outside Weston Town Hall after attending a Company Church Service in 1943.
Column nearest Lt. Col. Bruce: Unknown; Unknown; Mr. Rooke; L/Cpl. W. Amesbury; Unknown; Mr. Gallop; Unknown; Unknown; Unknown; Unknown
Centre column: Mr. Bateman; Mr. Osborne; Unknown; Unknown; Unknown; Unknown; Unknown; Unknown; Unknown; Cpl. Popham
Column nearest camera: Mr. Doule; Unknown; Unknown; Mr. Davis; Unknown; Unknown; Unknown; E. Amesbury; Mr. Coles; Unknown
(Weston-super-Mare Gazette *via Bill Amesbury*)

(above) **No. 3 Platoon 'A' Company** at Langford Road Drill Hall.
Back Row: Auxiliary; Auxiliary; Mr. Doule; Unknown; Unknown; Mr. Dudley; Unknown; Mr. Goodman; Unknown; Unknown; Unknown; Unknown; Mr. Davis; Auxiliary; Auxiliary
Second Row: Bill Amesbury; W. Osborne; E.C. Berkley; Unknown; Mr. Coles; Unknown; Unknown; Unknown; Unknown; Mr. Briggs; Lawrie Turner; Mr. George Lock; Unknown; Unknown; Mr. Rooke
Third Row: Unknown; Unknown; Cpl. Popham; Unknown; Sgt. Major Council; Unknown; Capt. P. Atkins; Major Nicholls; Lt. Philpott; 2nd Lt. Reed; Cpl. Heybern; Sgt. Goodman; L/Cpl. Clarke; Sgt. W.J. Huff; Sgt. M. Wilson
Front Row: P.O. Johns; Unknown; Unknown; Unknown; Unknown; L/Cpl. M. Price; Unknown; Mr. Gibbs; Ted Amesbury; S. Gallop; B. Miller, R.N.
Other members of 'A' Company included Herbert Alford and Arthur Fear, who had both served in the Royal Engineers in World War One; Mornington Merrick, an ex-Somerset Light Infantry WW1 veteran; and Bert Fear.
(Mary Armstrong collection)

In addition to standard Home Guard weaponry, Weston-super-Mare also boasted a Boys anti-tank rifle. Whilst a pre-war rifle range had existed to the south of Uphill between map refs. ST 314 576 and 315 583 this appears not to have been used fully by the Home Guard. Only the area around the butts below St. Nicholas's Church was used for small-bore shooting. Full-bore shooting took place on a new range established on the west side of Uphill Pill between map refs. ST 312 580 and 311 585. In a letter written in 2003, Bill Amesbury confirmed that the remains of the butts are still visible, the danger area behind being the mouth of the River Axe. The beach nearby was also used by the Weston Home Guard for occasional practice shoots with their Spigot Mortar. A small-bore range at R.A.F. Locking was also made available to them.

In a letter of January 2002 Bill Amesbury writes:

When I heard the appeal on the radio for volunteers to enrol for a new force to be called the Local Defence Volunteers, I went to the Police Station the next morning to enrol. A few days later I received a letter telling me to report to the Drill Hall in George Street. On arrival, there was another form to complete giving next of kin, etc. It was then explained what was expected of us and we were placed into groups and told to bring a broomstick or the like for Drill instruction. This was held in the Christ Church School playground, a 1914/18 veteran putting us through our paces.

My first duty was on the Birnbeck Pier. We had to patrol the Pier and also place a lookout at a suitable location to scan the Channel and the coastline north and south of Birnbeck Island. On duty I carried a truncheon which I had made from a piece of rubber hose lined with metal tube for a handle, the top of which was bound with insulation tape. One day an incident happened when we were on duty. We received a message from the coast guard that there was a floating object in the Channel heading in our direction, which we were to report if sighted. It was a very high tide that night and we did see something floating nearer to the Island. It came in on the tide and floated between the piles supporting the Pier. It looked like a mine and it passed under the Pier and out to sea past the lifeboat slipway. We reported back to the coast guard and later that day there was an explosion out to sea. This duty ceased when the Navy took over the Pier in 1941. We had a rest-room in one of the buildings near the entrance of the Pier. It was left to us to arrange our own duty roster depending on the number of men on duty.

I also did a spell of duty at the Cable Office (Atlantic Cable) in Richmond Street. In the winter of 1940/41 I was on duty at Drove Road Railway Bridge and the perimeter of the Gas Works. We used a gangers' hut by the railway line as a rest-room. This was very convenient because the engine drivers used to drop off coal for use in the fire inside the hut.

On all these duties we wore our respected L.D.V. armbands. Later we received an issue of denim uniforms and caps. We had to wait for our boots and we received them when our size was available. Late 1940 we received a number of American P17 .300 rifles. These had been in store for years and were coated in grease. One of our members owned a bakery and as one of his ovens was not used for baking he lit the oven and used it to de-grease the rifles. At this time we also received a number of Aircraft Lewis guns converted for ground use, by the fixing of a bipod to the body of the weapon. It was heavy but served the purpose until we received the Bren L.M.G.

As the military stores began to arrive we received our uniforms, steel helmets, greatcoats, respirators and webbing. Our military look was now complete and the Battalion was now divided into Companies, including an HQ Company. Weston Town was divided into two through the centre of Town, 'A' Company on the south from the Grand Pier to the River Axe along the foreshore and inland to the factory boundaries; 'B' Company to the north of the town. 'F' Company was responsible for defence of the factories, the remaining four companies covered the rest of the Battalion area. My platoon, 'A' No. 3 Platoon, had beach huts as their quarters, and patrolled the beach north to the Royal Hospital and south/south-east along the River Axe. A further platoon patrolled the beach from the Royal Hospital north to the swimming pool and another platoon from the swimming pool north to the Grand Pier. The platoon that used the beach huts near the Royal Hospital suffered no casualties when their huts were destroyed by bombs which fell on the sand dunes near the hospital, but there were casualties in the Home Guard when bombs damaged the swimming pool. The husband of one of my cousins had shrapnel wounds to the back.

We were lucky one night when one enemy aircraft attempted to shoot out a searchlight. We had dived for cover and the rounds fired from the aircraft ploughed across the ground a few yards ahead.

Prior to D-Day the platoon was transferred to a new billet at Lympsham Wharf, an old cow shed. We had to clean it out before we could use it. We had to patrol the main railway line from the railway bridge at Bleadon to Brean Down Station. This line was used to carry war materials and supplies to the South Coast in preparation for D-Day. It was a very busy line taking arms, equipment and supplies from Avonmouth. One night it was very windy and we had to jump for our lives. An American locomotive, which we had not heard owing to the wind, almost ran us down. My brother, who was also in the patrol, lost two of his teeth hitting his Sten gun as he fell.

(left) **Members of No. 3 Platoon** *parade in late 1941, shortly before testing their respirators by passing through a van into which gas had been introduced. Note that the respirators are being carried in the alert position.*

Back Row: Unknown; Unknown; Sgt. Reed; Unknown; Unknown; E.C. Berkley; Mr. Perkins; Unknown; Sgt. Goodman; Unknown; Unknown; Unknown; Mr. Dudley; Unknown; Unknown

Middle Row: Mr. Gallop; Sgt. Huff; Unknown; Bill Amesbury; E. Amesbury; Lt. Hess (later became Gas Officer for 13th Battalion); Capt. Atkinson; Lt. Philpott; Unknown; Cpl. Heybern; Unknown Sgt.; Sgt. Wilson; Unknown; Mr. Banwell

Front Row: Unknown; Unknown; L/Cpl. Gibbs; Unknown; Unknown; Unknown; Unknown; Unknown

(Bill Amesbury collection)

We attended classes at the Drill Hall for instruction on field craft, map reading, weapon training etc. On Sunday mornings we paraded at our training area at Uphill where we put what we had learnt indoors into practice, using the rifle ranges at Uphill and Clevedon. At Yoxter we were able to fire all the weapons including anti-tank rifles and grenades. The week-ends we spent at Yoxter were the best. We had members of the Regular Army to instruct us in every field of infantry tactics. Some Sundays we had inter-platoon exercises. This gave us the opportunity to know the advantages and disadvantages of our own location. One of the most successful exercises carried out against the Regular Army was at the Ack-Ack site on the Golf Links. Whilst the Platoon put in a frontal attack from the beach and a flank attack from the wooded area two men in a milk float, one disguised as a milkman the other as a paper man with a bag full of papers, drove straight up to the gates. When they were at the entrance an officer approached and the gates opened. They drove in and the paper man pointed his bag at the officer and informed him he had been shot. They then proceeded to throw dummy missiles at other troops. One other member crawled under the wire netting towards the radar station and took it single-handed. The army had to admit defeat and at the debriefing they conceded it was a glorious victory to the Home Guard.

The beach in front of the radar station and Ack-Ack site was patrolled from dusk to dawn by my platoon, two members doing two hours on and four hours off. The winter months were the worst, bitterly cold and on most nights driving rain. We had no heating in the huts with which to warm or dry ourselves, but we were able to make hot drinks. One night we were startled by the firing of the heavy coastal guns located on Brean Down and Steep Holm; we never did find out why. The beach had no anti-invasion defences i.e., wire, poles or mines. There were pillboxes in the sand dunes and the farm land from the beach following the River Axe inland across the county in the direction of Wells, Radstock and Bath, which represented the G.H.Q. Stop-line Green.

The Home Guard was not only trained to carry out their military commitments but also trained to assist the other emergency units in the event of heavy air attacks on the town, of which there were many. There were four of us who lived in the centre of the town and we teamed up and assisted the Fire and Rescue services if we were not on duty at our respective Home Guard posts. One incident which stands out in my mind, was on 28th/29th June 1942. During the previous week we had received our issue of Sten guns, and on the weekend Weston received one of its heaviest air raids. My section of the platoon was sent to stop members of the public approaching a bombed area where there were many casualties and unexploded bombs. We were located on each road approaching the area. I was on duty at the railway bridge near the most devastated site and not too far from the unexploded bomb. A member of the public approached me and said, "I see you have one of the new weapons, the Sten gun". He could tell me all about it because he had heard it on the news that morning. He told me they were being produced in large numbers and would eventually be dropped to the resistance organisations in Europe.

When the air raids started at Weston, the first bomb to fall in our Company area was on 14th August 1940, with an attempt to bomb the railway line in October; this failed and no damage or injuries were sustained on either occasion. In January 1941, Weston received the first of its heavy raids with high explosive bombs and incendiaries. A serious incident occurred in the road where I am now living, Rectors Way, a terrace of houses received a direct hit. My colleague and I went to this location to assist in search and recovery. Most of the casualties had been removed but we came across the body of a girl whose body had been burnt in half by a gas jet and we had to remove it in two halves. All of the family in the house were killed. In June a barrage balloon in our Company area broke loose and fouled the electric grid and the area was without electricity until it was repaired. In November mines were dropped in Weston Bay near the Atlantic Cable post and one U.X. parachute mine was washed up on the beach near the low tide mark. In June 1942 there was one of the heaviest raids on the town with H.E. bombs and incendiaries over most of the town and surrounding area. My colleague and I on this occasion assisted the Fire Service and then went to another location where bombs had fallen and people were trapped. When we arrived we could see that the corner of the building had collapsed with two people trapped on the top floor. We were told that the fire service was going to rescue them and we were asked to start a search of the ground floor. We cleared a way to the stairs and under the stairs discovered the bodies of a boy and an old lady, both dead. The little boy had a small wound on the side of his head; otherwise there were no injuries to either body, presumably killed by blast.

March 1944 marked the last of the heavy raids on Weston. This was concentrated on the factories at Oldmixon and Banwell but with little success. Most of the bombs fell on open land but some property was damaged, causing loss of life and casualties. All the aforementioned incidents were within the Company area. There were many other incidents outside of our Home Guard duties to which we responded but these often involved 36-48 hours without respite. The Battalion also had two anti-aircraft troops and a bomb disposal unit. During the air raids on the town two members of the Home Guard were killed and a number of others wounded. Two other members were killed and these were listed as range accidents. To assist in catering, when required, 16 members of the W.V.S. were enrolled into the Home Guard and their service was much appreciated when we were on exercises or assisting the other emergency services.

Following the Stand Down of the Home Guard my friend and I were approached by a professional associate of ours who was the C.O. of the Weston Army Cadet detachment. He stated that he could do with some extra adults to assist in their training. We visited the Drill Hall one training evening to see what was required, had a discussion with the C.O. and offered our help. After a few months we were interviewed by a Col. Harvey who recommended that we attend an officer's training course at Taunton T.A. Centre. This we did and after an exam and test we were informed that we had passed the requirements to be promoted as officers in the T.A. Auxiliary Force. We continued training the Cadets for a number of years.

When the Home Guard was re-formed in 1952 we both volunteered, retaining our rank as Lieutenants, and we were enrolled in the same Company. But this is another period of time when the Home Guard again became one of Britain's 'Forgotten Armies'. When the Home Guard was stood down once more in 1955, I finished with the service.

No. 4 (Uphill) Platoon 'A' Company, taken at Uphill Castle, now a hotel.

Back Row: Stan Pickett; Dr. William Crawford; John Thoday; Len Trowbridge; Les Varder; F.S. Brown; Mr. Holt; W. Wright; Rex Coward

Middle Row: F.W. Matthews; L/Cpl. G. Milton; Cpl. W. Robins; Sgt. T.F. Palk; Lt. Jay; Cpl. Davidson; L/Cpl. C. Gamblain; Fred Gamblain; Mr. Pearce

Front Row: J. Geary; David Minifie; Mr. Parsons; Mr. Walters; Mr. Macdonald; Mr. Lake.

C. and F. Gamblain were brothers, Charlie being a First World War Veteran. Corporal Davidson was killed in one of the air raids on Weston-super-Mare. Young Mr. Walters was called up and subsequently killed in action. The Platoon Commander, Lt. Jay, was well known in Weston-super-Mare as he owned Jay's Mineral Waters. Rex Coward ran the local Post Office whilst David Minifie was the local plumber and W. Wright swept chimneys. Sgt. Palk owned a butcher's shop in Uphill. Les Varder was one of three Home Guards selected from the Battalion to represent the unit at the Stand Down Parade in London held on 3rd December 1944. (Len Trowbridge collection)

No. 4 (Uphill) Platoon 'A' Company. This photograph was taken after the one above as C. Gamblain is now a full Corporal.

Back Row: Cpl. Brown; Les T. Varder; Mr. Parsons; Unknown; Unknown; Stan Staples; Mr. Lane; Unknown; Unknown; Mr. Palmer; Jim Upham

Second Row: Sgt. Vickery; Unknown; Unknown; Unknown

Third Row: Unknown; Mr. Cole; Sgt. T.F. Palk; Unknown; Unknown; Mr. Usher (wearing glasses); Unknown; Mr. Edwards; John Thoday

Front Row: Sgt. Cliff Greedy; Rex Coward (on leave); L/Cpl. Sidney Clark; Sgt. Len Driver; Unknown; Sgt. Jack Webber; Lt. Jay; 2nd Lt. Trevor; Unknown; Cpl. Gamblain; Unknown; Unknown; G. Milton

(Len Trowbridge collection)

Perched on the hill to the south of Weston-super-Mare is the isolated and windswept remains of a windmill. There is nothing today to remind the casual observer of the vital role this building took during the war. It was from here that the men of No.4 Platoon mounted their night-time vigils. The facilities provided were somewhat primitive. Heating was by means of a paraffin stove and lighting by candles. Bunks were provided for those not on watch. If it was necessary to communicate with the outside world a runner would be sent down the hill to the telephone in Sgt. Palk's butcher's shop, near *The Dolphin* Public House. Fortunately one of the two platoon diaries known to have existed has survived and the following entries for 1940 have been reproduced to give an insight into how the Home Guards spent their nights.

June 20th	Lights showing 10-10.20 at Rossiter and Newbury Porch. Back rooms and bedrooms 1st and 2nd house on left and 2nd on right Ellesmere Road.
June 28th	12.50 a.m. searchlights went on beginning in S.E., then all round from Burnham direction through Brent Knoll, Banwell, Bristol to South Wales. Several flashes seen low down and detonations heard from area from south of Barry to Cardiff.
June 30th	Planes passed over towards Welsh coast 12.45 p.m. The sirens sounded in the town when the planes had passed. Too late!
July 5th	2.30 Gamblain and Thoday reported seeing car proceeding towards Weston south of Uphill Station (main road). It apparent car was signalled to stop by someone with red light. From the vantage point the car did not appear to obey the signal.
August 1st	4.30 a.m. Two officers of the Somersets visited post. Challenged. 4.45 Colonel commanding area also visited post with A.D.C. Challenged and proved identity.
Sept 7th	[The night of the invasion scare] Macdonald, Crawford, Trowbridge, Sansom 8.30-11.00 p.m. all on guard. 11.00 p.m. to 2.00 a.m. J. Macdonald and W.H. Crawford on guard. Warnings sounded 10.47. Enemy aircraft overhead. Searchlights active Bristol district. 11.45 enemy plane went over the Welsh coast and dropped bombs. Mr. Palk visited us at 1.30 and told us General Alarm sounded – to stay on duty until 7.30 a.m. On duty 2.00 a.m. until 5.00 a.m. L.F. Trowbridge and W.H. Sansom. From 5.00 a.m. until 7.30 all on duty. [There is a corresponding note in the back of the log book: "7.30 a.m. 8.9.40 General Alarm, 20 rounds of small arms ammunition received from Sgt. Palk."] [It would appear that the post was manned throughout the daylight hours of Sunday 8th September and through to the morning of 9th September, some Home Guards logging 11 hours' continual duty.]
Sept 29th	R.A. patrol challenged 06.20. Officer no identification. Private O.K. (believed R.A.).
Oct 6th	19.15 on guard F.C. Holt, G.E. Willingham, S. Clark, T.F. Palk. 22.10-03.15 high cold wind, heavy storms, visibility poor. Nothing to report. 03.15-4.45 searchlight activity south of town and also S.S.E. Heavy clouds preventing distance judging. 04.45-06.45 nothing to report except Barry searchlight sweeping the channel 06.00 to 06.20.
Oct 7th	W. Foy, J. Geary, J. Thoday and J. Holt. 19.00 Foy, Geary and Thoday. 20.00-22.00 E.V. Fry on patrol <u>ALONE</u> The above ALONE has been duly noted and this act has been reported to HQ London T.F.P. [obviously a serious matter].
Oct 14th	6.15 Several H.E. bombs dropped in Bleadon village and hill. It is believed that two <u>nearer</u> bombs are still unexploded. Knocked off (*sic*) 7.00 a.m.
Oct 25th	Candles required.
Dec 3rd	N.B. The Union Jack is flying upside down.
Dec 7th	Nothing to report only that it was "damn cold". No candles thanks.
Dec 17th	Candles needed. Oil soon needed. Wick of stove getting short.
Dec 18th	No more candles in box.
Dec 23rd	Could do with some more blankets – please.
Dec 25th	Oil and candles needed.

Note: the lack of paraffin and candles seems to be an ongoing problem. The entry for January 16th 1941 mentions, in addition to 30 rounds being returned, the absence of candles. March 7th sees a request for more oil which obviously went unheeded for on March 30th the entry reads: "heaters went out at 3.30 a.m. (no oil)".

Thus during the winter of 1940/41 the men of the Home Guard took turns at the nightly vigil through storm and tempest, watching helplessly as the Luftwaffe bombed and strafed their fellow countrymen. After each nightly vigil they returned to their homes for a quick shave, breakfast and work.

From the log book covering 20th June to 31st December 1940 the following members of the Home Guard took post at the windmill at various times:

E. Baker, C.C. Beamish, E.C. Berkley, W. Blunt, F.S. Brown, Burrows, N.M. Clark, S. Clark, J.D. Courtenay-Smith. W.H. Crawford, D.R. Coward, H. Davidson, M.N. Davidson, J.C. Davies, J.H. Davies, Drakeford, W. Foy, A.J. Francis, G.A. Franklin, E.V. Fry, C.C. Gamblain, J. Geary, N. Gill, W. Harris, Hayes, F.C. Holt, J.D. Holt, R. Hope, T. Hussey, T. Hutton, R.W. James. E. Jenkins, W.B. Judd, G. Langford, M. MacNaughton-Wainwright, J. Macdonald, W.A. Matthews, W.E. Matthews, G. Milton, D.R. Minifie, W. Minifie, R. Owen, T.F. Palk, Parsons, S.H. Picket, E.C. Pople, E. Reakes, A. Reed, W. Robins, R.S. Robinson, W.H. Sansom, F.W. Simpson, E. Smart, J.C. Smith, J. Thoday, H.A. Thompson, R. Thorpe, L.F. Trowbridge, F.C. Turner, L.T. Varder, L.R. Vowles. J.C. Wall, Wallace, R.S.L. Walters, G.W. Webb, Weeks, E. Williams, F. Willingham, G.E. Willingham and W. Wright.

1941 and Lt. Jay leads **No. 4 Platoon** *along the sea front at Weston-super-Mare past the junction with Clarence Road South.*
Column Nearest Camera: Sgt. Palk; Les Varder; Unknown; Unknown; Rex Coward; Fred Gamblain; remainder Unknown
Centre Column: Sgt. Cliff Greedy; remainder Unknown
Column Furthest from Camera: Unknown (hidden by Lt. Jay); Mr. Holt; Unknown; Unknown; Unknown; Len Trowbridge (joined L.D.V. aged 17); remainder Unknown
Standing on the extreme right of the photograph behind an unknown captain is Major Percy C. Nicholls, Company Commander of 'A' Company. This photograph is obviously one of a series taken on the same by the Weston-super-Mare Gazette *day of the platoons forming 'A' Company. Only this photograph and the following one have been found.*
(Joe Thomas collection)

No. 5 Platoon *marches past the same spot. Behind can clearly be seen the figure of Sgt. Palk of No. 4 Platoon. In the right foreground, the officer may well be Captain P. Atkins.*
(Ken Durston collection)

Probably taken in May 1940 this photograph was endorsed on the back 'First Patrol'. With the situation in Europe going from bad to worse and the British Expeditionary Force carrying out a 'tactical withdrawal' to the Channel coast, patriotic members of the population were forming themselves into armed bands to resist German paratroops. This action forced the Government to apply some order and channel efforts of the population by forming the Local Defence Volunteers. Note the 'weapons' – one shotgun, two coshes, two road lamps for signalling traffic to stop and an unidentifiable weapon being carried by Sid Gallop. The absence of L.D.V. brassards would have precluded these men from the protection of the Geneva Convention. Captured by the Germans they would have (at best) been lined up against a wall and shot as franc tireurs.
(left to right) W. Osborn; W.J. Huff; S. Gallop; M. Price; S. Banwell
(Weston-super-Mare Gazette via Mary Armstrong)

No. 5 (Bleadon) Platoon in 1944.

Back Row: John Gardner (in civilian clothes); Bert Wiltshire; Clifford Durston; Ronald Harvey (aged 17); Unknown but worked for B.A.C.; Unknown; Unknown; Reginald Durston; Dick Scotchmer (on leave from Rifle Brigade); Unknown; Unknown (on leave from Tank Corps)

Second Row: Mr. Apps; Ivor Budden; Unknown; Unknown; Unknown; Unknown; Unknown; Unknown; Unknown; Unknown (partly hidden by previous unknown); George Harris (on leave from Welsh Guards); Arthur Ling (at 5 o'clock to George Harris); Unknown; Unknown; Unknown; Barry Davies (in civilian clothes); Walter Ling

Third Row: Unknown; Unknown; Unknown; Unknown; Unknown; Lt. Yaldwin; Unknown; Unknown; Sgt. Edgar Goodman; Unknown; Unknown

Front Row: Jack Gore (arm resting on knee); Frank Woolacott; Fred Kerton; Bob Say; Unknown; Cliff Millard; Metford Crandon; Unknown; Unknown; Unknown

Many of those not identified were employees of the London Assurance Company. Bob Say was responsible for maintaining the local roads. He was a well-known squeezebox player whose instrument was lodged at The Victoria Inn. His musical repertoire precluded him from ever having to buy himself a drink. (Mrs. J. Henly collection)

Kenneth John Durston was a member of the platoon, putting a year on to his age so he could join as a cadet. The photograph of Cadet Ken (right) was taken when he was just $15\frac{1}{2}$ years of age. Although not required to carry out night-time duties he was employed as a messenger during exercises, cycling from unit to unit. In December 1943 Ken joined the Army, being demobbed in 1947. Some six months after joining the Army Ken was given ten days leave. He struggled home with all his kit comprising rifle, kit bag, greatcoat, small pack, gas mask and steel helmet. It was not until Ken arrived home that he realised he had left his greatcoat on the train. Enquiries during the next few days proved negative – Ken's greatcoat was not to be seen again. Although it was mid-summer, at some stage Ken would undoubtedly be required to wear his coat but where was he to obtain a new one? The problem was partly solved by borrowing his father's greatcoat. As his father had two brothers in the Bleadon Platoon he would borrow one of theirs when required and if this was not possible he would merely miss the parade. Some months later Ken passed his army driving test and was allocated to the Quartermaster's stores, becoming the quartermaster's personal pick-up driver. Surrounded by greatcoats it was not long before Ken had a brand new coat and his father's coat was returned.
(Ken Durston collection)

Of his days in No. 5 (Bleadon) Platoon Ken Durston writes:

> Parades and training were held in Bleadon Quarry. In the summer-time, outdoor training took place on South Hill. The long barn-type building at the bottom of Quarry House was used as a rifle range and ammunition store.
>
> Night duties and patrols covered the area from the junction of Bleadon Hill with Roman Road to the top of Canada Coombe including the anti-aircraft site at the far end of Roman Road and the Barrage Balloon site at the Bleadon Hill end. A shelter for the off-duty sentries was in the form of an old railway carriage standing in Bert Wiltshire's market garden in Roman Road. However, the attraction of the W.A.A.F.'s barrage balloon site was greater and many happy hours were spent drinking tea in their guardhouse. In addition to myself there were four other members of the Durston family in the Home Guard. Reginald Durston, my father, who had served in the Hampshires and the Gloucesters between the wars; his brothers Clifford and George. George, because he owned a motor cycle and was a lorry driver, was seconded to the Motor Transport Battalion at Frome. Clifford Millard, a brother-in-law made up the quintet.
>
> Grenade practice with inert grenades took place at South Hill where a local lad was injured whilst collecting the grenades for re-use. Rushing up to collect recently thrown dummies he was hit in the face by the last grenade to be thrown and knocked unconscious. He still carries the scar on his forehead to this day.

*An early photograph of members of **Weston-super-Mare Home Guard**.*
Front Row: Bill Huff; 'Monty' Price
Sitting: Sgt. Atkinson; Lt. Sainsbury; Cpl. Philputt
Standing: Stan Banwell; Sid Gallop; Bill Osborne; Bert Millier
(Mary Armstrong collection)

'B' COMPANY

COMMANDING OFFICER   Major R.M. Smith
(Lt. Cdr. S.L. Bonning, Major J.C. Walker)

Despite the clarity of this photograph only one face has been identified. That is of Lt. A.M. Wilmot (third row from front, third from right). He was in business near Bristol Temple Meads Station, manufacturing agricultural machinery. (Miss Barbara Wilmot collection)

No. 3 Platoon 'B' Company, photographed at The Newtons. Sadly, although some faces have been recognised, their relative positions in each row are unknown.
Back Row: Jack Thyer; Bert Smith; Jack Wride; William Perks; Wilf Kingsbury; Jack Hack; David Morris; Len Griffiths; Peter Chaplin; Percy Prewitt; Len Venn
Second Row: Maurice King; Reg Hunt; Harry Knight; Harry Phippen; Ellis Chaplin
Third Row: Mr. Rogers; Tim Starr; Walt Williams; Mr. Trego; Jack Hutchins; Reg Palmer; Jack Vinning; Horace Ackland; Mr. Pope; Mr. Burrows
Front Row: Frank Phillips; Gordon Pope; George White; Jack Watkins; Fred Williams; Mr. Beacham
(Anthony Moger collection)

No. 6 Platoon 'B' Company was a factory platoon formed by employees of Varley Pumps. Their Drill Hall was in George Street where there was a .22" rifle range.

Ernest Mathewson had been an employee of Varley Pumps at its original factory in Park Royal, London. Late in 1940 his factory received unwelcome attention from the Luftwaffe. The photograph shows employees standing outside the bombed-out building. Involved in Government contracts, no time was wasted in dragging out the damaged machinery from the wrecked factory, installing it in other factory units nearby and having repaired it, resuming production of essential items including the hydraulic firing mechanisms for aircraft Browning machine guns.
(Ernest Mathewson collection)

In 1941 Varleys was moved to the relative safety of Weston-super-Mare, occupying Grove Park Garage, Lower Road, but not before the owner had been threatened with imprisonment for refusing to relinquish his premises.

Varley's staff were progressively transferred to Weston. Ernest and his father, also an employee, packed their worldly possessions into Ernest's motorcycle combination and drove down to the West Country, a journey made more difficult by having no idea where Weston-super-Mare was and the total lack of road signs.

Despite the passage of some 60 years, Ernest clearly remembered walking into the factory one day and on noticing a pretty local girl saying to a friend, "That's the girl for me". Today Ernest has been happily married to his "girl for me", Dulcie for 58 years, a result of a factory bombing so many years ago.

Members of No. 6 Platoon, photographed in Grove Park.
Back Row: No. 6 Mr. Knight; No. 8 Bill Smith; No. 9 Charles Grey
Middle Row: 3rd from right Reg Salt
Front Row: No. 1 Charles Grenough (the spelling is suspect as Charles was French; his pre-war occupation was a tea-taster); No. 2 Jack Budd
Sitting: No. 1 Ron Freeman

> Whilst unfamiliarity with weapons resulted in the accidental shooting of floors, walls, ceilings, weather vanes and town hall clocks, occasionally events took a tragic turn. Jack Crocker Raines, a member of 'B' Company was a 33-year-old member of the Weston-super-Mare Home Guard. In the early hours of 18th September 1940, he was preparing to go out on patrol from the windmill on Worlebury Hill, his picket post, with fellow Home Guard, 19-year-old Harold Singleton. As the tower light was extinguished prior to opening the door, Harold was caught unawares in the process of loading his rifle. As the light was rekindled at his request, his rifle was accidentally discharged, the bullet striking Jack Raines in the leg. Despite a prompt attempt at stemming the flow of blood and the rapid arrival of the ambulance, Jack died at 3.00 a.m. in a local hospital. The funeral at Worle Parish Church was attended by some 60 officers and men of the Weston-super-Mare Home Guard, together with some 200 Worle residents.

'C' COMPANY

COMMANDING OFFICER   Major D.W. Ware, T.D.
2ND IN COMMAND   Capt. S.C. Dawes

Despite numerous appeals, no further information has been forthcoming on 'C' Company.

'D' COMPANY

COMMANDING OFFICER   Major P.D. O'Connell
2ND IN COMMAND   Capt. J.W. Vinson

MAJOR P.D. O'CONNELL, 1899–1978

Patrick Dominic O'Connell served in the 2/5 Norfolk Regiment and the 1st Battalion The Hertfordshire Regiment from 1915 to 1919, seeing action in France. He was demobbed in March 1919.

In 1939 he became the joint founder of the 290 Weston-super-Mare Squadron O.T.C. He joined the L.D.V. in May 1940. On 1st June 1940 he was appointed Platoon Commander and was immediately appointed Transport Officer, raising the Transport Section locally, using his own initiative. This was in addition to his civilian occupation of Company Director of the United Bill Posting Co. which proved a useful contact when he designed his recruiting poster (*right*). He was appointed Lieutenant on 21.3.1941, Captain on 5.1.1942 and Major on 1.10.1943.

In June 1942 he founded the 1st Weston-super-Mare Army Cadet Force, becoming its first Commander enrolling 70 youths under the Lord Lieutenant's Commission. He later became Company Commander of 'D' Company with Capt. S.C. Dawes as his 2nd in Command.

Patrick O'Connell worked tirelessly for the people of Weston-super-Mare. Between 1941 and 1945 he was Chairman of the local Savings Committee whose powerful aid to the nation's finances sustained our victorious forces. He organised Weston's D-Day appeal in 1944 and was Parade Marshal and organiser of the Drumhead Service for the Army Blood Transfusion Service. He marshalled four large parades for 'Wings for Victory Week' raising funds for the town's Spitfire appeal. The Weston-super-Mare Spitfire Mk II was taken into R.A.F. Service in 1941 and survived the war, being 'demobbed' in about 1947. Its subsequent history is unknown. Further parades for 'Salute the Soldier Week' were also organised by him. An indicator board erected on his authority outside the Town Hall showed the final money raised for the War effort was £424,728.

Pat O'Connell served with the Home Guard until it was stood down in December 1944. At the cessation of hostilities he organised parades and church services that were held on 13th May 1945 and 19th August 1945 to celebrate V.E. and V.J. day. When the Home Guard was reformed in the early 50s, Major P.D. O'Connell was appointed Deputy Commander of the 12/13th Battalion Home Guard.

He died in 1978, aged 79, leaving his wife Nora, six children and fifteen grandchildren. The Requiem Mass celebrated by the Bishop of the Diocese, 18 priests and a huge congregation was some indication of the high esteem that Major P.D. O'Connell was held by his fellow countrymen.

(Anthony Keys collection)

Motor Transport Section Headquarters Platoon in *November 1941.*
Back Row: B. Snell; D. Weber; D. Snelgrove; S. Williams; S. Ball; F. Reynolds; W.J. Coles; H. Wheatley; L. Day; G. Snelgrove; Jack Johns (H.G. weapons instructor, proprietor of John's Bakery)
Middle Row: J. Drew (owner of a grocery shop); O. May; L. Blanning (dairyman); L/Cpl. J. Martin (manager of Shell Petrol Depot); Cpl. W. Stuckey; L/Cpl. H. Lovell; H. Dyer; M. Dare; E. Mitchell (shoe repairer); R. Coles
Front Row: Sgt. L. George; Sgt. G. Marshall; Platoon Sgt. F. Arlotte (quarryman at Butts Quarry); Lt. P.D. O'Connell (Platoon Commander); Capt. H.J. Ormerod (Adjutant); C.Q.M.S. F. Hook; L/Sgt. J. White; Sgt. F. Blackmore; Cpl. E. Stanier
Sitting: L/Cpl. A. Hynd; L/Cpl. H. Hess (accountant)
(Anthony Keys collection)

'E' COMPANY

COMMANDING OFFICER	Major H.J.W. Rush (Major H.S. Pennycott)
2ND IN COMMAND	Capt. R.H.S. Kemps

No further information has been discovered about this Company.

'F' COMPANY

COMMANDING OFFICER	Major H.J.W. Rush (Major E.C. Lovell)
2ND IN COMMAND	Capt. J. Mew

Norman Perriman was a member of 'F' Company, joining on 16.1.1942. He writes:

On January 16th 1942, stating I was 17 years of age although I was just 16, I joined the Weston Aircraft Factory Home Guard. This was officially known as 'F' Company, of the 8th (Weston) Battalion of the Somerset Home Guard.

Major E.C. Lovell was the Commanding Officer. He was also in charge of all factory security. The full-time Sergeant Major was C.S.M. Harris. Among my pals in 'F' Company were Bob Adams, Ted Mason, Bill Cornish, Ron Maxted and 'Ginger' Poole.

Dai Morgan was the youngest Sergeant in the Company, and the smartest in the Battalion. He later joined the Royal Marines and soon gained promotion, and came back to lead one of the large military parades through Weston.

The Home Guard Armoury at the time was a brick building on the side of the road that ran between the erecting hall and the quarantine building. There was also a bungalow just over the railway line, and outside the airfield perimeter at Hutton Moor, where most of the Home Guard clothing etc. was stored.

We were very well kitted out, more so than most of the other companies in the Battalion, and it was a proud day when I first dressed in my full uniform: boots, gaiters, battledress, overcoat (the best I had ever had), belt, pouches, gas-mask (army type), steel helmet with camouflage net, and forage cap with the 'Jellalabad' badge of the Somerset Light Infantry, which my father had worn whilst serving in the Somersets from 1914 to 1918. Most important we were issued with .303 Lee-Enfield rifles, which at that time were not too plentiful. I wore my uniform, as was the practice, to and from work and felt ready to face up to anything, with my double-breasted overcoat to keep me warm, and the .303 rifle for company.

Night guards had to be carried out on a regular basis, at various locations in the factory and around the airfield. As a rule it was two hours on sentry duty, then four hours off through the night. We tried to sleep most of the time whilst 'off guard' in the Nissen huts on the airfield, mostly at Hutton Moor, or in the canteen building. We also covered for the factory police whilst they left their police boxes to have a meal break during the night.

Field training would be done after work hours, which were quite long anyway, and we would often train across the fields as far as the top of the hill over Hutton. (I realise now why some of the older members of the company found the going rather tougher than we 'young-uns' did!) Jimmy Rush was our Training Officer and he gave us every encouragement and certainly led by example.

We would use Yoxter ranges at Priddy for live rifle shooting practice on a Sunday, and also learnt to make Molotov Cocktails which would have been used for attacking tanks or setting fire to any enemy vehicles. Thank goodness we never had to use them.

A minus point was the frost and at times snow on the airfield, especially on a wild and windy night, black as pitch, feet freezing, no glamour then. "Why, oh why had I joined?" I asked myself as I tried to go to sleep for an hour or so in a freezing Nissen hut!

The subsistence allowance for Home Guard duties for 'F' Company was 15 shillings per guard (75p) which was equal to what was in my pay packet for working a full 48-hour week. Now and again I would do two guards a week and get 30 shillings (£1.50) which with my wages would give me a grand total of £2.5s.(£2.25) which was very good money at that time for my age. (Was that the reason I so eagerly joined? I think not as it was good to be involved and I was a bit of a 'show-off' I suppose.)

The day soon came when the Home Guard said that the official subsistence would be reduced to three shillings a guard (15p) right through the country.

I can well remember some of us going up to C.S.M. Harris and saying, "Sergeant Major, we wish to resign". We were too wet behind the ears to know any better I guess, and his reply was so loud it made the whole factory shake, and was certainly unprintable. We had no doubt about the course we had to take, so whilst standing to attention and with a very loud "Yes, Sir", we carried on with our duties, but our pockets were a lot lighter and we would make sure that in future it would only be one guard per week, unless ordered otherwise.

One night whilst on guard at the police post, (at the double iron gates near to the Hutton Moor flight shed) the telephone rang. On going into the box I picked up the phone and a garbled message came through, and then the phone went dead. I went outside again and slung my rifle over my shoulder and tried to puzzle out the message. The truth then hit me like a bomb. I rushed and opened wide the first gate in record time, and as I got the second gate open I heard a lorry very close in the darkness. It seemed to be going very fast, but in reality it was going about ten miles an hour. It swept through the gates assuming of course that they had already been opened for it.

With my heart pounding I realised that the message had come from the police post at the entrance to the airport road for me to open the gates as a lorry was coming through with a Beaufighter in tow from the Banwell Shadow Factory. The road from the factory at Elborough had been specially widened so that the aircraft they made could be brought to the Weston Factory for spraying in the dope shop, and then tested in the flight sheds before being test flown from the airfield. The tail wheel of the Beaufighter was attached to the bed of the lorry, which pulled it backwards. So as not to be seen in the black-out, the lorry, as with all vehicles, was only showing a small slit of light from the headlamps.

When the P.C. arrived back from the canteen he casually asked if everything was in order, and as my heart was just about back to normal, I answered in the affirmative, vowing to myself to keep secret the night that I nearly wrote off a Beaufighter before it had even been in action. I prayed that the aircraft concerned would have a charmed life in its service. With a Private in the Home Guard like me – who needs the enemy?

```
8th (WESTON) BN., SOMERSET HOME GUARD.

        "F" COMPANY
            WESTON AIRCRAFT FACTORY,
                    WESTON-SUPER-MARE.
YOUR REF:
                        20th March, 1944.


Certificate of H.G.Service.

    This is to certify that N.A.Perriman
joined 'F' Coy, 8th Somerset (Weston) Bn.
Home Guard on 16.1.42 and joined H.M.Forces
7.1.43.



                        for Major,
                    O.C. 'F' Coy.,
            8TH SOMERSET (WESTON) BN. H.G.
```

Another night I was on guard on the main factory road between the canteen and the main office block with orders to stop and check everyone coming through. Anyone approaching received the warning "Halt! Who goes there?", and on receiving the correct answer of "Friend", I would then shout "Advance and be recognised". If there was more than one person the shout would be "Advance one, and be recognised", and on producing a pass, or paybook if they were in the armed forces, they would be let through for duty or to the canteen (one at a time).

On this particular night about 23.00 a group of soldiers and A.T.S. girls approached, and by the noise and laughter I guessed that they had been off-duty and had returned from Weston after a good night out, and had consumed plenty of beverage of the type that I was to get used to. At the same time I knew that my duty officer and the guard N.C.O. were due on their rounds to make sure that all was in order.

On the shout by me of "Halt! Who goes there?", the group of soldiers and A.T.S. girls stopped, with the exception of one figure who kept walking. I again shouted "Halt", and could then see the figure was that of an A.T.S. girl. My next shout should have been "Halt! Or I fire" (knowing that I did not have any rounds in my rifle anyway), but by then she was right up to me, and on giving me a kiss on the cheek said, "You wouldn't shoot me, would you?"

I knew that the duty officer and the guard N.C.O. were standing back listening, and I was glad that in the black-out they could not see my scarlet face. I stood there praying for a hole to appear in the ground so that I could fall into it. It was certainly not the time to be thinking about being 16, a virgin, and being kissed by a soldier girl. I then told her in no uncertain terms to push off to the canteen and not try it on again. Her mates came up one at a time in the proper manner and one of them shouted out to tell her how stupid she was. I then waited to know what the duty officer would say, but he passed on without saying a word (from then on he was my favourite officer!).

Worse was to come, though, when my relief turned up and I went to the canteen for a break. I was ribbed by the gunners from the ack-ack site and the A.T.S. girls. It was one more experience of growing up in a cruel world – at least it seemed cruel at that particular moment.

The winter of 1942 was very, very cold, with severe frosts on the airfield. Being off-duty in the Nissen huts meant that even overcoats stayed on, and with only a couple of army type blankets, and not much of a fire in the stove, it was certainly not a place for luxury, but then we did volunteer to play soldiers. (And all for three bob a night – Sergeant Major!)

On guard we were only issued with one clip of five rounds for each rifle, but I always carried an extra clip in my pocket – self-preservation being the priority – and if a budding armourer could not wangle a few extra rounds – who could?

```
DEFENCE (HOME GUARD)
REGULATIONS, 1940.
APPENDIX A.C.1. No.872 of 1942.
To......Pte.N.Perriman. 401/1972
You are hereby warned to report for Guard Duty at O.Mixon
on   14 SEP 1942          Time
                                20.30 hrs
You are required to sign the Duty Roster on reporting Duty and
it will be the duty of the N.C.O. i/c to see that this is carried
out.   Failure to perform this duty renders you liable to prosecution
under the above order.

              E.C.Lovell. Major. 'F' Coy.

Note.  If you are required to work overtime authorisation must be
obtained from your Superintendent.  This authorisation must be
handed in to the Security Office before 5 p.m. on the day you are
detailed for duty.

              Commencing Time
              Finishing Time
              Signature of Superintendent
```

The official notification for guard duty, with the usual 'failure to do so would result in prosecution' wording, was generally put with the time card at the 'clocking in and out' station, which in my case was in the erection hall. 401/1972 after my name related to the department number 401 – and 1972 my works number.

Norman left the Home Guard on 7.1.43, his 17th birthday, and joined the Fleet Air Arm as an Air Mechanic (Ordnance) when he sailed on *H.M.S. Indefatigable*. His subsequent service in the Far East was undertaken on the American-built Ruler Class Escort Carriers, *Rajah, Empress, Khedive, Emperor, Shah* and *Ameer*, which all survived the war.

(below) Two views of Weston Airfield in 1995. On the left, the Guard Room and on the right, a pillbox, probably a modified type 27. The absence of weathering on the lower surfaces indicates that additional protection would have been provided by soil being built up around the structure which has since been removed. (Norman Perriman collection)

John Hill, a member of No. 2 Platoon 'F' Company, left in November 1943 with a rank of Platoon Sergeant, joining the R.E.M.E. Names he remembered were Capt. Hammond, C.S.M. Harris, Platoon Sergeant David Morgan, L/Cpl. Derek Whyte, Lt. Thomas and Les Carpenter. 'F' Company's principal task was to guard the airfield and factory buildings, (and as John remembers, with affection, the girls of the barrage balloon unit). One night the Home Guard was turned out on the receipt of a report of parachutists on the airfield. Before investigating further, John and his comrades were ordered to remove their rifle bolts as a safety precaution! It was just as well that the parachutists turned out to be members of the R.A.F.

(right) **British Aircraft Corporation, Banwell Home Guard** *in December 1941.*
Back Row: No. 2 'Bill'
Second Row: No. 7 Fred or Jack Gamblin; No. 9 Mr. Bains
Third Row: No. 2 Jim Sheppard; No. 5 S. Jim Chidgey;
*   No. 10 Mr. Reeves*
Front Row: No. 1 'Gilbert'; No. 2 'Gussie'; No. 4 2nd Lt.
*   Pryser Jones; No. 5 Lt. C. Thomas; No. 6 Sgt. Jack Taylor;*
*   No. 8 Bill Bartlett*
(S.Jim Chidgey collection)

(above) **Members of Weston-super-Mare Platoon 'A' Company 13th Gloucester (Post Office) Battalion** *pose outside St. Margaret's Terrace.*
Back Row: No. 2 Frederick William Sheather; No. 3 Ron Jenkins; No. 4 Mr. Harding; No. 8 'Dickie' Bird
Second Row: No. 10 Colin Bass
Third Row: No. 6 possibly 2nd Lt. Dobbins
Front Row: No. 9 Paddy Earls
(Mrs. Anita Melluish collection)

'A' LIGHT A/A TROOP	**'B' LIGHT A/A TROOP**
COMMANDING OFFICER Capt. R.A. Vickery ('E' Company)	COMMANDING OFFICER Capt. A.G.L. Langfield ('F' Company)

BOMB DISPOSAL UNIT

COMMANDING OFFICER   Lt. J.K. Brown

No further information has been forthcoming on these three units.

*Members of the **Home Guard Comrades' Club** on their first outing on 5th September 1948.*
Back Row: No. 3 Maurice Watts; No. 6 Tommy Goodwin; No. 14 Sid Gallop
Front Row: No. 1 Billy Huff; No. 2 Mr. Milton; No. 8 Roy Popham.

The original of this photograph was found literally trampled into the mud in a garden shed in Weston-super-Mare. Fortunately the finder was aware of the author's project and it was saved just in time but what of other photographs? (Author's collection)

9th Somerset (Wells) Battalion

HEADQUARTERS	15, Union Street, Wells
DATE FORMED	October 1940
COMMANDING OFFICER	Lt. Col. James McDonnell (from 1.2.41)
2ND IN COMMAND	Major H.F. Scott Stokes, M.C.

H.Q. STAFF

A & Q	Capt. E. Keeling Stamp, General List
ADJUTANT	Capt. I.V. Yeatman, King's Liverpool Regiment
AMMUNITION OFFICER	Lt. P. Wellstood White
GAS OFFICER	Lt. G. Taunton
INTELLIGENCE OFFICER	Lt. G.H. Glass (Lt. J.S. Stotesbury, M.C.)
MEDICAL OFFICER	Major T.R.G. Melrose (Major R.M. Ainsworth) (Major A.C. Hinks, M.C.)
SIGNALS OFFICER	Lt. N.S. Warner
SECTOR LIAISON OFFICER	Lt. W. Barnard
TRANSPORT OFFICER	Lt. R.A.E. Loder

Lt. Col. J. McDonnell, 1893-1966. A veteran of The Great War in which he served with the Wiltshire Regiment, Lt. Col. James McDonnell became the manager of the Unigate Dairy at Wells. The following poem, penned by an unknown hand, records the early history of the Wells Home Guard in a form readily recognised by any ex-member. (Mrs. Margaret Lees collection)

McDONNELL'S OWN

When his country stood at bay
And the peril seemed at hand
Brave McDonnell rose to slay
Th'invader of this cherished land,
Gathering round him all alike
Drawn from office, pub and farm,
Armed with shotgun, fork or pike,
Ready for the dire alarm.

Chorus: McDonnell's Own, McDonnell's Own,
        Boys of the Old Brigade!
        Now shall the foe be overthrown,
        Now shall he low be laid!
        Rushing ahead with their Blackers,
        Spigotting all they see,
        Ripping away their knackers
        And chucking 'em back to the Spree!

Clad in suit or corduroy,
Shod with shoe or gardening boot,
From farmer's lad to old McCoy
Away they went in hot pursuit;
Whither no one knew nor cared,
Fresh from *Mermaid*, *Swan* or *Star* –
Rabbits, pigeons, none was spared
As Mendip felt the breath of war.

            McDonnell's Own, etc.

Now in denims, on they go
(Let all lazy slackers scoff!)
On to disembowel the foe
With a dose of Molotov.
And on lonely Mendip top,
Though the peril lurketh near,
Strive to drain another drop
From that dwindling case of beer.

            McDonnell's Own, etc.

Rifles now and bayonets
Flow in from America.
Grenades (with or without dets.)
Clutter up Max Crease's car.
War has come to Wells itself
And everyone must do or dare
When bombs adorn the mantel shelf
And ammo. fills the hollow-ware!

            McDonnell's Own, etc.

All in battledress arrayed,
Marching to the Market Square,
Ankle deep in bumph they wade,
Now the danger is not there.
And if any foolish Hun
Dares to drop in from the skies,
Let him fear the fire of gun
Less than death by A.C.I.s!

            McDonnell's Own, etc.

WELLS CITY COMPANY

HEADQUARTERS	Bishop's Barn, Wells	COMMANDING OFFICER	Major O.W. Berry, M.B.E.
(Battle)	4 Chamberlain Street	2ND IN COMMAND	Capt. A.G. Johnson
	(Defended Location)	WEAPONS TRAINING OFFICER	Capt. S.G. Harwood

The boundary of Wells City Company encompassed the civil parishes of Wells, North Wootton and parts of St. Cuthbert without. The Company comprised No. 1 to No. 6 Platoons. Their officers and duties in 1944 were as follows:

No. 1 Platoon

Platoon Commander	Lt. E.M. Crease
Platoon Officer	2nd Lt. V.H.E. Klinge
Static Headquarters	Milton Lane, Wells
Battle Headquarters	1, New Street, Wells (Defended Location)

No. 2 Platoon

Platoon Commander	Lt. F.H. Vinnell
Platoon Officer	2nd Lt. D. Pointing
Static Headquarters	St. Thomas Vicarage, Wells
Battle Headquarters	1, St. Thomas St., Wells (Defended Location)

No. 3 Platoon

Platoon Commander	Lt. P.A. Hole
Platoon Officer	2nd Lt. H.E. Southwell
Liaison Officer	Lt. W. Barnard
Static Headquarters	Bishop's Barn, Wells

Battle Headquarters	1, St. Thomas St., Wells (Defended Location)

No. 4 Platoon

Platoon Commander	Lt. W. Pearce
Platoon Officer	2nd Lt. G.C. Marsden
Headquarters	Burcott Road, Wells
Battle Headquarters	1, New Street, Wells

No. 5 Platoon

Platoon Commander	2nd Lt. B. Saxby
Headquarters	Chapel Farm, North Wootton
Battle Headquarters	Coombe House, North Wootton
	Little Fountain, Dulcote

No. 6 Platoon

Platoon Commander	2nd Lt. G.J. Culling
Headquarters	Greyholm Hut, Coxley
Battle Headquarters	Coxley Mill, Coxley

No. 1 Platoon Wells City Company, photographed on Wells Recreation Ground.
Back Row: Unknown; Mr. Parker; Fred Scott; Mr. Lukins; Mr. Collins; Unknown; Unknown; Kenneth Holley (aged 16)
Middle Row: Ern Holley; Frank White; Fred Merchant; Unknown; Unknown; Mr. Rogers; Unknown; Mr. Bengefield
Front Row: Sgt. Stokes; Sgt. Bill White; Lt. Max Crease (Platoon Commander); 2nd Lt. Bengefield; Sgt. Stan Fudge; Sgt. Norman Spearing
Frank White was home on leave from the Royal Marines but sadly was later killed in action. During the war Ern Holley worked for the builders Melhuish and Saunders, as did his son. Mr. Rogers was a local A.A. man whilst Lt. Max Crease was a Wells grocer.
(Mr. D.G. Holley collection)

No. 2 Platoon Wells City Company, photographed at Dulcote Quarry.
Back Row: Unknown; Mr. James; Harry Gerrish
Second Row: No. 1 Percy Alfred Gallop;
　No. 3 Fred Speed
Third Row: No. 5 Mr. Chamberlain; No. 6 Mr. Faulk;
　No. 9 Albert Uphill; No. 11 Arthur 'Tom' Horsey
Front Row: No. 1 Mr. Addicott; No. 5 Jack Micklewhite;
　No. 8 Mr. Hicks
(Mrs. Valerie Malcolm collection)

No. 2 Platoon Wells City Company at Dulcote Quarry. This is a 'second take' of the previous photograph except that those who had steel helmets on the day are now wearing them. *(Mrs. Jill Venn collection)*

No. 3 Platoon Wells City Company.
Back Row: W. Dupuy; S. Loxton; Unknown;
　H. Hollinshead; Unknown; F. Lush; Unknown
Middle Row: G. Ravenhill; D. Mosley; A. Radford;
　J. Miller; S. Caines; H. Swain; H. Loxton;
　F. Maybury
Front Row: Sgt. J. Clarke; Lt. W. Barnard (Liaison
　Officer); Lt. Percy A. Hole (Platoon Commander);
　2nd Lt. H. Southwell (Platoon Officer); Unknown
(Mrs. Winifred Ware collection)

No. 3 Platoon Wells City Company, *taken in the Burcott Lane area of Wells.*
Back Row: No. 2 Van Eyking; No. 8 Mr. Edwards; No. 11 George Baker; No. 12 Stanley J. Guise; No. 13 Jimmy Reakes
Middle Row: No. 5 Wilf Pitman; No. 6 'Pop' Norris; No. 7 Mr. Stott; No. 11 Sgt. Baker
Front Row: No. 7 Lt. Roly Gunning; No.8 Lt. Hargreaves
Almost the whole platoon assembled for this photograph to be taken on an early spring day in 1941. Mr. Guise joined No. 3 Platoon Headquarters as a 14-year-old boy. The Platoon Commander at one stage was Roly Gunning of Gunning's Garages, Priory Road. Later Mr. Guise was attached to the Platoon signal section. (S.J. Guise collection)

A rifle range near Burcott was used whilst live grenade practice was carried out in Dulcote Quarry. The Platoon's night-time patrol area included 'Forty Acres', an area around Platoon Headquarters. A large building in the field provided sleeping quarters for the Home Guards resting between patrols.

One night Stanley Guise and George Baker, Sgt. Baker's son, spotted a lonely figure on the moor. Having issued the correct challenge, which went unanswered, and shaking in their boots, the figure was promptly dispatched with ferocious thrusts from their bayonets but refused to 'die'. The scarecrow was too well-fixed to its post!

Church Parade, 1940. Capt. Sylvester George Harwood (front row, nearest the camera) leads his men out of Market Square, Wells. (Mrs. Betty Mattick collection)
Column nearest camera: Percy Hole; Jack Whiting; Sam Gaines; Bill Holcombe; Bert Cook
Centre column: Walt Pearce; Unknown; Unknown; Stan Cook
Column furthest from camera: Unknown; Sid Hoskins; Unknown; Unknown; Unknown; H. Loxton

In a recent letter Stanley Guise summed up his personal thoughts of his days in the Home Guard:

Really the backbone of the L.D.V. were the veterans of World War 1, men who had been 'over the top' and up to their necks in mud and carnage. Like *Dad's Army*, in many cases we were led by Bank Managers but without these old soldiers I don't think the Home Guard would have ended up the creditable force it was.

One had only to take notice at the time of their thoughts and attitudes – no thought of losing the war came into anyone's head.

We came within a whisker of losing. I joined the Royal Navy at 17 and was involved in the latter stages of the Battle of the Atlantic. Had it not been for the courage, tenacity and sacrifice of our merchant seamen of whom 31,000 lost their lives, we would never have made it. Those who survived being torpedoed in mid-Atlantic, adrift, often wounded in open boats, were hardly cheered on by the fact that their pay stopped from the moment they 'lost' their ship. Thousands were never rescued, left to watch their convoy steaming onwards.

*Taken outside The Bishop's Barn, probably **Officers and N.C.O.s of Wells City Company** pose for the cameraman.*
Back Row: No. 3 Lt. H. Gordon Glass;
No. 4 Lt. Max Crease
Middle Row: No. 3 Capt. George Harwood; No. 12 Lt. Percy A. Hole; No. 13 Lt. William Barnard
Front Row: No. 8 Lt. Col. J. McDonnell (Battalion Commander) (Mrs. Betty Mattick collection)

"But what is the Home Guard supposed to do?"

At a social meeting in February 1943, somebody asked the question above. This prompted a wag to write the following lines.

Members of the unpaid, unfed, unthanked, part-time, part-town, sockless, shirtless army known as the Home Guard, are supposed, in the first place, to be crack shots with a rifle, bayonet fighters and expert throwers of hand-grenades. They are supposed to know the weight and length of the rifle and all its parts. The weight, characteristics, contents, parts and destructive power of several kinds of grenades and bombs, and all are supposed to be tommy-gunners. There are many other weapons they are supposed to use too, but as only 1,700,000 men know about them, they are too secret to be mentioned here.

Apart from this, they are supposed to know the exact position of local post and telegraph offices, railway stations and petrol-filling stations, the distances and routes to neighbouring villages and towns, and the telephone systems and the position of available instruments.

They are supposed to know the names of their section, platoon and company commanders, to recognise by sight their Colonel, whom they have probably never seen, and know the name of their Zone Commander, they have often never heard of. They are supposed to know the address, location and nearest route to platoon, company, battalion and zone headquarters, which are sometimes changed overnight without their knowledge, and to be experts on field-craft, street-fighting, map-reading and defence in depth.

They must know how to deal with paratroops, how to camouflage their positions from air observation, how to use natural cover, how to move unseen and unheard, how to crawl on a middle-aged tummy through undergrowth and how to convert themselves from a clerk or businessman who wouldn't hurt a fly in the daytime, into an assassin with a dagger at night. They are supposed to know how to destroy tanks and erect road blocks, how to deal with all known gases, and how to provide for themselves an iron ration, without points.

Incidentally, they are supposed to earn their living and mount a 12-hour guard at least once a week, for which they are paid 54 whole pennies to spend on whatever luxuries they can find.

And now all Home Guards must attend first-aid lectures. This means they should have a working knowledge of pressure points, bandaging, splinting, artificial respiration and should be able to treat cases of poisoning, concussion, fainting fits and shock. They must be able to drive W.D. vehicles and private cars, motorcycles, and ride bicycles.

Not one of us will be surprised if we are expected to take a course in midwifery in our spare time – to prepare us to give a hand in an emergency!!!

CHEDDAR VALLEY COMPANY

HEADQUARTERS (1944)	Wookey Vicarage, Wookey		COMMANDING OFFICER	Capt. G.J.S. Lane, M.M.
HEADQUARTERS (Battle) (1944)	Southview, Hollybrook			(Capt. The Reverend H.L. Walker)
				(Capt. A.W. Powell)
			2ND IN COMMAND	Lt. E. Butterfield

In 1944 the composition and deployment of the Cheddar Valley Company as detailed in the Street Invasion Committee War Book was as follows:

	HQ	Battle HQ		HQ	Battle HQ
No. 1 Platoon			No.3 Platoon (continued)		
Pl. Com. Lt. A.E. Sealey	Memorial Hall, Draycott	Tom's Cottage, Hollybrook (Defended Location)	Pl. Officer 2nd Lt. H.C. Lunnon	No. 10a Sec. St. Cuthberts Mill Haybridge	Shepperd's Cottage Hollybrook (Defended Location)
No. 2 Platoon				No. 7 Sec. Sunday School, Wookey	
Pl. Com. 2nd Lt. A.G. Packer	Memorial Hall, Westbury	Mr. Frank's House, Hollybrook (Defended Location)			
Pl. Officer and Coy. I.O. 2nd Lt. F.W. Cressy			No. 4 Platoon		
			Pl. Com. Lt. T.G. Cunans	No. 7a Sec. Henton Hut Henton	Henton Hut Henton (Defended House)
No. 3 Platoon			Pl. Officer 2nd Lt. W.H.J. Harding		
Pl. Com. 2nd Lt. E.C.L. Rose	No. 10 Sec. Bowling Pavilion, Wookey Hole	Dennis's Farm Hollybrook (Defended Location)		No. 7b Sec. Day School, Godney	

(left) **Officers and N.C.O.s of No. 19 Platoon** in June 1941.
Back Row: No. 2 Gilbert Cook; No. 5 Sgt. Coleman
Front Row: No. 4 Capt. The Reverend H.L. Walker
  No. 19 Platoon's area included the village of Henton. The battle plan for the Platoon was to act as a Recce and Fighting Patrol in the Henton-Wookey area based on the Defended Locality at Westbury-sub-Mendip where 150 men were earmarked to deny enemy use of the Wells-Cheddar road.
(Maisie Simmons collection)

(right) **Members of Rodney Stoke and Draycott Home Guard, part of No. 1 Platoon**.
Back Row: No. 5 Mr. Taylor; No. 8 Mr. Dalley; No. 9 David Hale; No. 11 Jack Huish
Middle Row: No. 5 Lt. Arthur Sealey (Platoon Commander); No. 8 Mr. Trickey
Front Row: No. 2 Mr. Carey; No. 5 Mr. Moore; No. 6 Jack Masters
No. 1 Platoon's Headquarters was the Memorial Hall, Draycott whilst the Battle Headquarters was Tom's Cottage, Hollybrook.
(Betty Moore collection)

MENDIP COMPANY

		H.Q. STAFF	Capt. H.E. Reynolds
			2nd Lt. H. Keen
COMPANY HEADQUARTERS	Green Ore Farm		2nd Lt. B. Green
COMMANDING OFFICER	Capt. H.E. Reynolds		C.S.M. R.G. Gilson
2ND IN COMMAND	2nd Lt. B. Green		Private R.E. Reynolds
			Private W. Dallimore

Mendip Comany in 1944.
Back Row: Unknown; Ern Mullett; Maurice Winter; Henry Dyke; Ern Young; Aston Sparkes; Ronald Weston; Arthur Payne; Unknown; William James; Frank Hicks; Bob Dyke; Mr. Guy; Unknown; Unknown; William Weston; Unknown
Second Row: Unknown; Ollie Wareham; Unknown; Unknown; John Thayer; Unknown; Unknown; Cpl. Jack Duck; Unknown; Unknown; Unknown; Unknown; Unknown; Unknown; Unknown; Unknown; Unknown
Third Row: Cpl. Stan Russell; Unknown; Unknown; Bob Reynolds; Lt. Charlie Packer; Capt. H.E. Reynolds; Lt. E. Douglas-Dufresne; Unknown; Company Sgt. Major Raymond Gordon Gilson; Unknown; Sgt. E. John Hicks; Unknown
Front Row: All unknown
(Ron Gilson collection)

Ronald George Gilson, son of Company Sgt. Major Raymond Gordon Gilson, was 8½ years old when the war ended. In a letter of 2000 he wrote:

I lived during the war in a farm cottage near Green Ore on the Priddy Road. My father appeared to be employed full-time in the Home Guard, responsible for supplies. He had spent the First World War in India and Mesopotamia. Capt. Reynolds, Company Commander, lived at a house which I believe burnt down, probably after the war. It was on a site now occupied by Pinelea Farm, Green Ore. It was here that Nissen huts were built for the storage of A.W. Bombs. They took their name from Allbright and Wilson, the manufacturers of these weapons, otherwise known as No. 76 (Self-Igniting Phosphorus) Grenades.

At the end of the war these grenades were disposed of by dropping them down a disused lead mine. I remember the wonderful blast of flame that came back up the shaft.

I can remember the area was also used for the storage of vehicles prior to D-Day. The B3135 from Green Ore towards Red Quar Farm and Green Ore to Whitnell Corner was full of vehicles with sentry huts at Green Ore and Whitnell Corner. Midway between Whitnell Corner and Green Ore there was a vehicle maintenance depot which included a vehicle ramp long enough to accommodate several vehicles. Parts of this still remain.

In January 2003 an original type-written list of company members compiled by M/4221 C.S.M. R.G. Gilson was lent to the author. Their names follow in the relevant sections. Those listed without rank were at the time privates or volunteers.

Nedge Hill Section, Green Ore Platoon in 1944.
Back Row: Frank Hicks; Ollie Wareham; Unknown; Ronald Weston; William James; Mr. Guy; Mr. Guy
Front Row: William Weston; Sgt. E. John Hicks; Lt. E. Douglas-Dufresne; Unknown; John Thayer
(Nigel Hicks collection)

Green Ore Platoon comprised two sections, Nedge Hill and Pen Hill, under the command of Lt. E. Douglas-Dufresne.

Members of Nedge Hill Section included:

Sgt. J. Hicks	W. Crockett	O. Speed
Cpl. F. Battle	C. Guy	E. Stanton
Cpl. W. James	O. Guy	G. Stanton
C.F. Ball	F. Hicks	J. Thayer
K. Bishop	C. Norris	R. Uphill
C.A. Carter	L. Norris	O. Wareham
R. Chappell	E. Pirkins	B. Weaver
A. Church	H. Perry	W. Westaway
W. Clavey	R. Randall	A. Willis
	C. Rolls	W. Weston

Members of Pen Hill Section included:

Sgt. W.T. Mantle	L. Dors	G.C. Powell
Cpl. R.D. Towler	J.E. Hawkins	C.W. Roberts
L/Cpl. E.E. Beacham	W.H. Hawkins	W. Rogers
W.L. Beacham	M.W. Hillier	J.W. Rogers
I.L. Bown	W.C. Mantle	R.G. Rogers
M.H. Bown	A.L. Ollis	A.E. Sealy
A. Crockett	H.B. Parfitt	A. Weeks
G. Dallimore	G.H. Pearce	J.R. Weaver

Sergeant E.J. Hicks of the Nedge Hill Section kept much paperwork from his days in the Home Guard including a register of equipment issued to him which shows just how much each Home Guard was equipped with by 1942 (*right, above*).

Some members, even at the age of 17, would be issued with a Browning Automatic Rifle. With four in a B.A.R. team the notes on the next page indicate what was expected of them in battle.

Although initially it was hoped that the Home Guard would not become a casualty of paperwork this proved not to be the case and circulars, questionnaires, A.C.I.s and returns became part and parcel of Home Guard life. See page 112 for samples of Part II orders recording the movement of staff.

Nedge Hill Section, as did so many other units, organised social functions for needy causes. The accounts reproduced indicate the sort of monies isolated communities up on Mendip could generate. Of interest is the proceeds of the auction. A local man on leave from the services came home with two bananas and a lemon which were auctioned, raising over £10.00, a fortune in those days.

Another document found in Sgt. Hicks's collection referred to a shoot on Burcott Range in May 1944. Burcott Range was situated to the south of Ben Knowle Hill, Wookey. A map of the 1880s shows a flagstaff at map ref. ST 517 448 and targets at map ref. ST 517 446. Firing points are shown at 100-yard intervals back to 800 yards with supplementary firing points at 550, 650 and 750 yards. No doubt men of the Wells Battalion spent many Sunday mornings practising shooting, either Application or Rapid. One score sheet also records their scores under the heading of 'Gas'. This would refer to the requirement to shoot wearing their service respirators. Needless to say the scores were considerably lower, 7 shooters out of 22 failing to hit the target at all under this condition!

REGISTER OF EQUIPMENT.

Batt. No. 4292

Surname **HICKS**
Christian Name **E. JOHN**
Address **PRESTONS COTTAGE, CHEWTON MENDIP**

Date of Issue	Ammun.–Rev.	Ammun. .30 Amer.	Anklets	Anti-gas Capes	Anti-gas Ointment	Armbands	Badges Cap	Battle Dress Blouse	Battle Dress Trousers	Signature of Volunteer
19-6-42		60	1	1	1		1	1	1	E.J. Hicks

Date of Issue	Bayonets	Belts Waist	Blankets	Boots	Boots A.G. Rubber	Camouflage Nets	Caps F.S.	Cudgels	Cases, Eye-shields	Signature of Volunteer
19-6-42	1	1		1	1		1	1	2	E.J. Hicks
10.5.43					1			1	4	E.J. Hicks

I, **E. JOHN HICKS**, Volunteer of the Home Guard, having received into my care the articles of Clothing, Arms, etc. signed for on this Register, do hereby engage to take charge of, keep in good order, and produce the same when called upon to do so.

Date of Issue	Field Dressings	Frogs	Gloves, A.G.	Greatcoats	Ground Sheets	Haversacks H.G. Flashes	Mess Tins	Oil Bottles Pull-through	Respirator	Face Veils	Signature of Volunteer
19-6-42	1	1	1	1	1	1 4	1	1 1	1	1	E.J. Hicks

Date of Issue	Ret Numbers Revolvers HOODS A.G.	Rifles .30 Amer.	Scabbards	Slings Rifle	Steel Helmets	Water Bottle Cover	Cases Webb. Bott. Pouches Gas Detec. Sleeve	Signature of Volunteer
19-6-42	4 1076658 1	1	1	1	1	1	1	E.J. Hicks

1.

.300" BROWNING AUTOMATIC RIFLE

			lbs.	oz.
TEAM	4 Men.			
EQUIPMENT	1 B.Aut.Rifle with sling and carrier			
	14 Magazines loaded (280 rounds)			
	1280 Rounds .300 S.A.A.			
	1 Bottle Oil			
	1 Rod Cleaning			
NO.1	Will carry 1 Rifle, complete with sling & carrier		15	12
	4 Magazines, loaded (80 rounds)		6	8
NO.2	" " 1o Magazines, loaded (200 ")		16	4
	1 Bottle Oil			
	1 Rod Cleaning			
NO.3	" " 500 Rounds S.A.A.		30	0
NO.4	" " 500 " "		30	0

DUTIES

NO.1   Will fire the rifle in single shots or in short bursts according to the target, and is responsible for the setting of the sights and of the change lever, changing of magazines and rectifying of stoppages with the help of NO.2.

NO.2   Will place full magazines in the rifle when directed by NO.1, and will pass empty magazines back to NO.3.

NO.3   Will help to load magazines and pass them to NO.2, and will spot targets.

NO.4   Will load magazines.

GOING INTO ACTION

NO.1   Will take up his firing position, either standing, kneeling or lying.

NO.2   Will take a position to the left of NO.1 and near enough to fix the loaded magazines.

NO.3   Will when possible take a position at least 10 yards to left rear of NO.2, or some other position as location necessitates.

NO.4   Will when possible take a position at least 10 yards away from NO.3.

N.B.   In block houses NOS.1 & 2 will be in one compartment, and NOS. 3 & 4 will each be in the other compartments.

ACTION

NO.1   When a magazine is empty he will say "OUT", and as soon as NO.2 has grasped the magazine NO.1 will press the magazine release stud. When the new magazine has been fired he will recock the rifle and continue Action.

NO.2   Will provide himself with full magazines. When NO.1 says "OUT" he will grasp the empty magazine with his left hand and remove it, and place a full magazine in the gun with his right hand. He will then pass the empty magazine to NO.3.

NO.3   Will spot targets and keep NO.2 supplied with full magazines and convey empty magazines to NO.4. He will also help load magazines when necessary.

NO.4   Will load magazines, taking care to keep both magazines and rounds free of grit and dirt.

CASUALTIES   Replace upwards. Example:- If NO.1 is hit NO.2 takes his place. NO. 3 comes up to NO.2 and NO.4 comes up to NO.3 but continues to load magazines. If NO.2 is hit NO.3 takes his place etc.

```
                    H O M E   G U A R D
                      PART II ORDERS
                  (Officers and other Ranks)
Company: WELLS CITY        Battalion: 9th SOMERSET (WELLS). Serial
         CHEDDAR VALLEY                                    No.49
         MENDIP
         GLASTONBURY & STREET
             Station: WELLS      Date: 5.12.41
        Last Part II Orders issued No. 48 dated 28.11.41.
..................................................................
Item No.
         WARRANT & NON-COMMISSIONED RANK
   1.    The following is promoted to the rank of Corporal with effect
         from  31.10.41
            W 4532 L/Cpl. Spearing, N.A.   (Wells City Coy)
         EXTENSION
   2.    The following is permitted to continue over age limit for
         period of 6 months from 1.12.41. (Authority: Zone Cmdr. HGB/Ext.
         dated 2.12.41
            W 4208 Fry, C.W.               (Wells City Coy)
         TRANSFERS
   3.    The following has been transferred from the Mendip Coy to the
         8th Somerset Bn. (Wrington Coy)
            M 4668 Yarde, K.
   4.    The following has been transferred from the 12th Hants Bn.
         and posted to the Cheddar Valley Coy
            C 40013 Ridges, W.H.J.
         DISCHARGES
   5.    The following have been discharged - services no longer re-
         quired - joined H.M. Forces.
            3735  Warman, H.W.             (Glastonbury & Street Coy)
            W4664 Wollen, W.G.             (Wells City Coy)
   6.    The following have been discharged at own request on expiry
         of period of notice.
            W4040 Bayliss, J.W.            (Wells City Coy)
            W4570 Tate, J.H.                  "     "    "
         ENROLMENTS
   7.    The following have enrolled and been posted to the under-
         mentioned Coys.
            3990  Perry, B.L.              (Glastonbury & Street Coy)
            3991  Culliford, C.T.             "        "     "    "
            3992  Clarke, R.J.S.              "        "     "    "
            M40013 Weston, R.S.            (Mendip Coy)
         ENROLMENTS - ERRATA
   8.    B.R.O. Serial No.44 dated 31.10.41  Item 6 - delete "C 40013-
         Ridges, W.H.J."  Authy: HGB/TFRS/318 dated 27.11.41.
```

```
                    H O M E   G U A R D
                      PART II ORDERS
                  (Officers and other Ranks)
Company: WELLS CITY        Battalion: 9th SOMERSET (WELLS). Serial
         CHEDDAR VALLEY                                    No.50
         MENDIP
         GLASTONBURY & STREET
             Station: WELLS      Date: 12.12.41
        Last Part II Orders issued No. 49 dated  5.12.41
..................................................................
Item No.
         WARRANT AND NON-COMMISSIONED RANK
   1.    The following is promoted to the rank of Corporal with effect
         from  9.11.41
            M 4210 Furze, W.J.             (Mendip Coy)
   2.    The following are  appointed to the rank of Lance Corporal with
         effect from 9.11.41
            M 4193 Ford, H.                (Mendip Coy)
            M 4661 Withey, J.                 "     "
            M 4555 Storey, G.A.               "     "
         DISCHARGES
   3.    The following have been discharged - services no longer required-
         joined H.M.Forces.
            3016   Attwood, E.             (Glastonbury & Street Coy)
            M 4695 Durbin, G.O.            (Mendip Coy)
            W 4972 Davis, R.A.             (Wells City Coy)
            W 4506 Sambourne, W.H.            "     "    "
   4.    The following have been discharged at own request on expiry
         of period of notice
            W 4906 Barnard, W.             (Wells City Coy)
            W 4972 Davis, J.R.                "     "    "
            3492   Burt, W.R.N.            (Glastonbury & Street Coy)
            3319   Helliker, B.H.             "        "     "    "
   5.    The following has been discharged - services no longer required
            W 4082 Browne, R.R.            (Wells City Coy)
         ENROLMENTS
   6.    The following have enrolled and been posted to the Cheddar
         Valley Coy
            C 40015 Eames, E.J.
            C 40016 Allen, R.
```

```
                    NEDGE HILL SECTION
                       H.G. Dance.

           In favour of:

                    KING GEORGES FUND FOR SAILORS.

              CREDIT.                         DEBIT.

                  £ -s-d.                         £ -s-d-


           Sale Tickets   22-15-0    Band              4-15-0
           Auction sale   10- 0-3    Hire of Hall      1-10-0
                                     Refreshments      1-14-6
                                     Prizes:Savings Stamps  10-0
                                     Floor Polish         2-9
                                                      _____
                                                       £8-12-3
                                     Balance sent to:
                                     KING GEORGES FUND
                                         FOR SAILORS:  £24-3-0
                          _____                    _____
                          £32-15-3                    £32-15-3
```

(above, left and right) The Part II Home Guard orders issued to Sgt E.J. Hicks of Green Ore Platoon.

(right) The accounts for a Home Guard dance held by the Nedge Hill Section of Green Ore Platoon.

Priddy Platoon in 1944.
Back Row: Henry Dyke; Ern Mullett; Ern Young; Aston Sparkes; Arthur Payne; Bob Dyke; Maurice Winter
Front Row: Cpl. Stan Russell; Lt. Charlie R. Packer; Cpl. Jack W. Duck
In the background is, possibly, Sgt. E. John Hicks.
(Author's collection via Mrs. Thelma David)

Priddy Platoon:

Lt. Charlie R. Packer (Platoon Commander)
Sgt. F. Dunford
Cpl. J.W. Duck
Cpl. E.C. Harris
Cpl. S. Russell
G.R. Bird
Mr. Bishop
H. Dyke
R. Dyke
H. Hillard
S. Hulin
G. James
W. Kilmerster
S. King
G. Lane
E. Mullett
A.H. Payne
K. Payne
O. Payne
R. Payne
F. Pitman
W. Simmons
H. Sparkes
A. Sparks
A.R. Speed
E.J. Speed
A.T. Weeks
B. Weeks
D. Weeks
H.R. Weeks
L. Weeks
M.J. Winter
E. Young

Horrington Platoon:

2nd Lt. M. de Kremer
2nd Lt. H. Keen
Sgt. O. Howell
Cpl. E.J. Allen
L/Cpl. A.O. Allen
L/Cpl. E. Mitchell
J. Alderman
G.W. Baker
L. Baker
G.G. Brown
A.I. Chard
R.A. Chard
J. Gibbon-Pimlett
W.G. Harding
W. Hasell
L.J. Heal
W.H. Malcolm
F. Mitchell
H. Nineham
S. Oatley
B.R. Palmer
D. Tucker
H. Tucker
W. Williams

Chewton Hill Platoon

Unfortunately, no photograph has been located of the Chewton Hill Platoon. Additionally, the original records are damaged and the name of the Platoon Commander is not legible but it is known that a Lt. C. Stevens was Platoon Commander until 11.4.43. By 1944 the Platoon Commander was 2nd Lt. V. Anderson.

Sgt. W. Randall
Cpl. F. Battle
Cpl. V.H. Church
Cpl. H. Ford
Cpl. J. Keen
Cpl. J. Withey
L/Cpl. C. Green
G.C. Baker
S.C. Ball
J.C. Bartlett
J.A. Black
G.M. Church
A. Ford
C. Ford
H.L. Green
S. Heal
W.J. Heal
J.E. Hewish
S. Humphries
R. Prior
H.G. Pullin
W.H. Rogers
N.F. Speed
R.J. Stock
W.I. Thomas
F. Whitfield

GLASTONBURY COMPANY

COMMANDING OFFICER   Major G.H. Harland
2ND IN COMMAND   Capt. C.S. Grunsell

In May 1940 the towns of Glastonbury and Street formed part of No. 3 Company, coming under the command of Brigadier-General A.B. Incledon Webber, C.M.G., D.S.O. with Captain A.M. Stancombe, R.N. as second in command. The headquarters were in Bridgwater.

When Glastonbury and Street Companies were formed Lt. G.H. Harland became Company Commander of Glastonbury Company with the rank of Major whilst Sgt. C.S. Grunsell became Company 2nd in Command, with the rank of Captain. The Company's Headquarters was the Drill Hall which also served as the Headquarters for Nos. 1 and 2 Platoon. The Commander of No. 1 Platoon was Lt. F. Durston. Liaison Officer was Lt. L.R. Dunthorn whilst the Platoon Officer and Quartermaster was Lt. S.A. Haimes. No. 2 Platoon was commanded by Lt. H.W. Jefferies, his Platoon Officer being 2nd Lt. A.J. Pearce. Battle Headquarters was at the defended location at the top of Glastonbury High Street at ST 503 390.

The following lists of volunteers have been extracted from the original Street and Glastonbury Company records. Although undated, evidence suggests they were compiled between September 1940 and Spring 1941. Note that Platoon Commanders are without rank. Home Guard ranks were not introduced until Spring 1941. As time progressed various volunteers became N.C.O.s and this was annotated on the original typewritten roll in pencil. These have been included in brackets as have dates referring to volunteers' membership of the Home Guard.

Key: (T/F) = transferred
       (R) = resigned
       (C) = called up
       (D) = discharged
       (J) = joined H.M. Forces

Note: Many of the dates associated with their subsequent future are the same, probably indicating the date of notification in Part II orders.

Glastonbury Platoon

Platoon Commander: G.H. HARLAND

ALLEN Percival James (casualty 15.10.41)
ANDREWS Harold S.
ATTWOOD Edward (J. 12.12.41)
ATWELL Wilfred (D. 16.5.41)

BAKER R.H. (Sgt.)
BARNSTAPLE L.H.
BAULCH Plassy
BLYTHMAN Thos. Powell (C. 4.7.41)
BOWN Kenneth Philip
BRAKE Alexander Frederick (D. 1.8.41)
BRASS Alb. Ed. (Cpl.)
BREWER Ivor Headly Frank
BROWN A.L.
BROWN Charles
BROWNING Herb.
BUCKINGHAM Claud Irish
BURDEN Thomas
BURKIN R.K.
BURROW Charles George
BURT William Robt. Norton (D. 12.12.41)

CANNIFORD William John
CARTER Frank (Cpl.)
CARTER Harry (C. 8.8.41)
CHAMPION W.A. (Cpl.)
CHAPMAN Gilbert
CHAPMAN Reg. Henry (C. 12.9.41)
CHAUNCY Edward St. Martin Blanc
CHISLETT Henry (D. 2.5.41)

CHIVERS Edward (C. 4.7.41)
CHIVERS R.V. (Cpl.)
CHRISTOPHER Alf.
CHURCHES Joseph Edward
CLARK George
CLARK Harry
CLARKE Robert John Samuel
COLENUTT Dennis Ronald (L/Cpl.)
COOMBS Oliver C.
COX Bertie John
COX Ernest Ger. (Cpl.)
COX Stan. Bertie (D. 11.10.41)
COX Wm. Frank
COX Wm. James (allowed to continue over age limit for 6 months beginning 1.1.41)
CROCKER Duncan (D. 1.8.41)
CULLIFORD Herb. (D. 9.5.41)

DAVIS Cliff. Hy. (D. 2.5.41)
DAVIS Ernest Ewin
DAVIS Harold
DEAN Jack Loftus
DODGE Wm. Alfred (D. 25.4.41)
DONLEY Leo. C.
DOWDEN Wallace
DOWDNEY Francis Cecil
DOYLE Geo. Arthur
DOYLE Walter J.
DRAPER Richard Jack (Cpl.)
DUNTHORN Leslie R. (Cpl.)
DURSTON F. (Sgt.)
DYER Wm. Samuel

DYER Wilfred
DYER George (C. ?.8.41)
DYMOND John

ENGLAND Wm. Thos.

FEAR Cliff. Ed.
FIELD Derrick Bertram
FIELD L.R
FIELD Reg. Stan (C. 15.8.41)
FLEMINGTON Alan (Cpl.)
FOOKS Ger. Bertrand
FOURACRES Arthur (D. 25.4.41)
FRASER Stanley (D. 9.5.41)
FRIEND Arthur J.
FRIEND Walter G (J. 31.10.41)
FUSSELL Alb. Ed. (Sgt.)

GANE Edwin Charles
GIFFORD Albert Jas. (D. 15.8.41)
GILBERT T.V. (Cpl.)
GILL Alfred George
GINN A.W.
GINN Nathaniel
GODDARD Ernest John
GOULD Lewis James (J. 31.10.41)
GREEN Dennis
GREEN Harry (15.8.41)
GREEN Percy Ernest Thomas
GRUNSELL Charles Stuart (Sgt.)
GRUWYS Wm. Lionel (J. 31.10.41)

HAIMES S.A. (C.Q.M.S.)

HALLETT Fred. J.
HALLETT John
HATCH Arthur John Louis (North Somerset Electric Supply Co. Section)
HEAL Leslie John
HEAL Roy Bertram
HELLIKER Bertram Henry (D. 12.12.41)
HENNESSEY John
HIPPISLEY W.H.J. (L/Cpl.)
HITCHCOCK James Vincent
HOLBROW Bernard T.
HOLLOWAY Ernest Philip
HOLLOWAY John Henry (D. 18.7.41)
HOOD Fred. William (D. 11.4.41)
HOWE Fergus Henry (Sgt.)
HUXTER Roland Chas. D. (C. 4.7.41)

JAMES Martin
JEFFERIES H.W. (Cpl.) (North Somerset Electric Supply Co. Section)

KING Horace John
KNIGHT Francis Wm.

LACEY John William
LACEY Peter James
LANGDON Oliver Geo
LEE Leonard Percy
LEGGE James Victor
LINHAM Ralph Stanley

MADDAFORD William
MAPSTONE Horace Jas
MASTERS Robert
MATTOCK Arthur W.F.
MATTOCK Stanley Thos.
MELMOTH Horace Joseph
MILES Wm. Charles
MILLER John Henry
   (North Somerset Electric
   Supply Co. Section)
MOULE Lancelot
MULLINS George Arthur John
MULLINS Walter
MUNDY Edward Overton

NAPPER D.C.
NASH Leslie Richard
NURSE Leslie John

PALMER Stanley Fitz-James
PARSONS Albert Ed. (L/Cpl.)
PARSONS Eric Wm.
PAYNE Lewis Albin
PEARCE Allan John
PEARCE Eric Robt.
PEARCE Reginald (L/Cpl.)
PINNEGAR T.K.
POPHAM John Thos.
PORCH M.P. (Sgt.)
PRETTYMAN Alfonso

RENDELL Thos. John
RICE George
RICE Hartnell
RIDOUT Alf. James (D. 18.7.41)
ROBINS Dennis Cecil
ROOD Frederick Wm.
ROWSELL Albert Henry
RUSSELL Clifton Henry

SARTIN Gordon Dennis George
SARTIN Wm. George

SHARP Albert Hamilton
SHENTON Jeff
SHORT Leonard Robt.
SHORT Walter Robt. (Cpl.)
SMALL Jeffrey Nelson
SMITH George Henry
SMITH Kenneth Robert
SNELL Wyatt
SNOOK Herbert Richd. (D. 11.4.41)
SQUIRE Fredk. John
STOODLEY Robert Arthur (L/Cpl.)

TAYLOR Allan Henry (C. 29.8.41)
TAYLOR Frank (D. 9.5.41)
TAYLOR Leslie Samuel Chas.
THOMAS Fred. Wm.
THYER A.G.
TINCKNELL Reg. F. (J. 13.6.41)
TOWNHILL Peter Wilham
TUCKER Allan Wilfred
TUCKER Richard Hy.

TUCKER Wilf. Harry
TURNER Ernest (Cpl.)
TURNER Henry John

WASON Arthur C. Daniel
   (D. 31.10.41)
WEATHERILL Reg. Owen
   (D. 31.10.41)
WEBB William James
WELLMAN Alfred Geo. (Cpl.)
WEST William L.
WHITEHEAD F.S.
WHITEHEAD Robert (Cpl.)
WILLIAMS Cyril John B.
WILLS Henry
   (granted extension of six
   months from 16.9.41)
WILLS Kenneth James
WITNEY Frank (Cpl.)
WYNNE Leonard Percy
WOODS Hubert

No. 3 (West Pennard) Platoon.
Back Row: Jack Hembury; Cpl. Lionel Selway; Jack Miller;
   Sgt. Ted Garland; Alfie Petheram; Dick Merrifield
Front Row: Lt. Len Selway (Platoon Commander);
   Wallace Gifford; Claude Guildford; Joe Kent; Sid Ridout;
   Eddie Cooper; Bill Friend
(Mrs. Myra Collins collection)

Early records indicate that West Pennard Home Guard was a section rather than a platoon. After the formation of Glastonbury Company, West Pennard Section was re-designated No. 3 Platoon, Glastonbury Company.

In the early days the Platoon drilled at West Pennard Station before moving to *The Red Lion* which became Battle Headquarters and a Defended House. Defended Houses were properties that had been earmarked from a survey that would, by suitable modification, provide cover for troops whilst engaging the enemy. Modification would entail removing windows and replacing them with sand bags, punching loopholes through walls and mouseholing interior walls to allow movement within the building. Defended Locations could include several Defended Houses (see the Wells City Company details on page 104 for examples).

The Village Hall became static headquarters with 2nd Lt. A.J. Ritchie of Meare as Platoon Officer, his Platoon Commander being Lt. L.J. Selway. In common with other Home Guard units an Observation Post was established, West Pennard's being on Pennard Hill behind the church where a wooden hut was built as a shelter for the picket.

One night members of the Platoon were alerted by the flashing of a light at Edgarley Hall (then a private house). This was duly reported to the police who apprehended a foreign domestic the following day.

George Gifford remembers clearly one exercise when half the platoon concealed themselves in a wood whilst the remainder were detailed to clear it. At the end all but two had been accounted for – one, who had covered himself in bracken in a ditch, and George who hid in a tree. Lt. Selway stopped at the foot of George's tree and discussed at length with another member of the search party the possible whereabouts of the missing two. Unable to contain himself any longer, George gave his position away.

As with other local units Dulcote Quarry was used for grenade practice whilst land at Higher Farm, Wick was used as a 50-yard and 100-yard rifle range.

West Pennard Platoon

Section Commander: L.J. SELWAY (Sgt.)

BOWN Metford Arthur *

CARTER E.H.C.
CLARK Harry
COOPER Edgar Charles
COOPER Geo. Ed.
COOPER Walter Horace
COX Thomas *
CREED Roy Stanley Carey

DAY Ernest Reginald

FEAR Edward *
FRIEND William Dunster (Cpl.)

GANE Walter (D. 11.4.41)
GARLAND Edward Walter (Cpl.)
GARTHWAITE William Brian
GIFFORD George
GIFFORD Wallace
GREEN Robert
GUILDFORD Claude Clifford Louis
    (J. 26.9.41)

HEAL Horace Geo.
HEMBURY John Arthur Wm.
HIGDON Alb. Ed. (D. 11.4.41)
HILL Fred. Walt. (Cpl.)

KENT H.H.
KENT Joseph H.

MERRIFIELD Henry Richard
MILLER George (Cpl.)
MILLER Jack *

PATTISON Stuart Arthur
PETHERAM Alfred Ed. H. * (Cpl.)
PHELPS Albert Henry (D. 11.4.41)
PHELPS Herbert Frank

SELWAY L. (Jnr.)
SHADWELL Alfred Farr (L/Cpl.)
SWEET Percy

VEALE John Edwin *
VICKERY Albert Bruce
VICKERY Reginald Mark
VOWLES Frank Harry

WALL Wm. *
WALTERS Godfrey James
    (D. 29.11.41)
WHITEHEAD Louis Fredk. Stanley

* These members carried out duties at West Pennard Railway Station.

*(left) George Gifford and (right) Eddie Cooper from **West Pennard Platoon**. Both photographs show windows covered in sticky tape to reduce the damage caused by flying glass after a bomb explosion. Even West Pennard was not safe from enemy bombs, a particularly large one falling in the fields behind Higher Sticklinch Farm.*
(Myra Collins collection)

Meare Section had similar battle duties to the West Pennard Section. It was tasked with carrying out reconnaissance and forming fighting patrols. On reorganisation of Street and Glastonbury Home Guard into two Companies, Meare Section became No. 4 (Meare) Platoon, Glastonbury Company.

Sgt. T.J.H. Powell became Platoon Commander with the rank of Lieutenant. His Platoon Officer was 2nd Lt. C.E. Driver. Static Headquarters was at the Central Hall in Meare, whilst Battle Headquarters was at *The Ring of Bells* Hotel which became a defended house.

Meare Section

Section Commander: T.J.H. POWELL (Sgt.)

ALLEN R.J. (C. 25.7.41)

BAKER Arthur Noel
BAKER Dennis R.
BAKER Geo. Thos.
BAKER John W.
BAKER John Wm. (Cpl.)
BAKER Leonard Frank (D. no date)
BAKER Leslie Arthur
BELL M.C.W.
BURRIDGE Jesse
BURTON Ronald

COX Richard (L/Cpl.)
CRANE James (D. 8.4.41)
CRANE Wm. Henry (D. 3.10.41)
CROSSEY Wm. Harold (C. 1.8.41)
CURLE Ed. Geo. (D. 14.11.41)

DIFFORD Abram
DIFFORD Herb. John
DOWNER Robert West

FEAR Dennis Reg. John
FEAR Harold Aubrey James (C. 25.7.41)
FOSTER Fredk. C.R.
FRANKS Reg. Stewart (D. no date)

HAYES Ivor John
HUGHES F.R.

JACKSON James (L/Cpl.)

LONSDALE Edwin

MARTIN A.G. (Cpl.)
MARTIN Wm

MARTIN Ivor
MILTON H.C.F. (D. 6.6.41)
MOXLEY Edward Horace

PARSONS Geoffrey (D. 8.4.41)

REDMAN Wilfred George
REED Arthur George
RITCHIE Alex. John
ROGERS Wm. Joseph Edward
ROOD Vernon (D. 6.6.41)
RUSSELL Wm. Henry Thos.

SHARP Reg. Walter
SIMMONS Raymond Joffre
SIMMONS Wesley
SIMMONS Wilfred Hubert
 (D. 8.4.41)

TOOGOOD Maurice George
TOOGOOD Robert Charles Harvey
TRATT Edward George (D. 3.10.41)
TRATT Wallace Edward (D. 8.4.41)

VOWLES Edward James (D. 8.8.41)

WALL Matthew Frank
WASHER Leonard Oakley
WHEATON Daniel (D. 8.4.41)
WHITCOMBE A.
WHITCOMBE Jesse
WHITCOMBE Wm. George
WHITCOMBE Wm. Henry (D. 14.11.41)
WILKINS Geo
WILLCOX Douglas Rowland George
 (D. 18.6.41)
WILLCOX Wm. Geo. Arthur

GLASTONBURY RAILWAY HOME GUARD

Glastonbury Station, on the Somerset and Dorset Railway, was a hub of railway activity with substantial goods yards and platforms. A branch line linked Glastonbury with the G.W.R. at Wells. Goods arriving by train would be dispatched by railway staff. Wally Vincent was the carter whilst Reg Whitcombe, Ted Billett and Charlie Ham were lorry drivers. Ern Napper worked in the goods shed. 'Captain' Reg Cox was the headganger whilst Herbie Francis and Harold Hurd were ganger foreman and ganger respectively. Guy Parsons was the porter in charge of Ashcott Station, renowned for his breeding of budgerigars after the war.

Those featured overleaf were not the total complement of railway Home Guards. The Glastonbury Invasion War Book of 1944 quotes:

Available Resources as follows:
(a) Regular Troops none
(b) Home Guard, Two Platoons of approximately 75 men each
Approximately 25 per cent of the strength are classed as category II, and the whole number is liable to considerable alteration. There is also a Railway Unit of the Home Guard having a present strength of 37. They come under the Glastonbury Company if the Railways cease to function.

Railway employees at Glastonbury were 'list II' men, being part of the 22nd Devonshire (5th Southern Railway) Battalion Home Guard. In the event of invasion, whilst the other Home Guard units would go to their pre-planned positions, list II men would be required to operate the railway as long as possible.

After the initial rush to join the Home Guard, when invasion seemed imminent, numbers began to fall as, to the man in the street, the perceived threat seemed to diminish. Until 1942 it was possible for a Home Guard to resign subject to 14 days' notice. This was of concern to the Government and the poster reproduced here was an attempt to arrest the slide. This particular poster was displayed at Glastonbury Police Station.

(John Harris collection)

Two photographs showing members of **Glastonbury Railway Home Guard**. *(left) Back Row: Unknown; Cpl. Harold Hurd; Dennis Davis; Reg Glass; Ron Snook; Unknown; Jack Burge; L/Cpl. Ern Napper; Jack Richards*
Middle Row: Reg Whitcombe; Ted Billett; Bill Milton; George Emery; Gilbert Lee; Unknown; Unknown; Unknown (face out of shot)
Front Row: Mr. Cox; Charlie Ham; Fred Milton; 'Jug' Parsons; Fred Lester
(Alan Hammond collection)

(below) Back Row: Wally Vincent; Reg Whitcombe; Cpl. Harold Hurd; Unknown; Ted Billett; Unknown; L/Cpl. Ern Napper; Unknown
Front Row: L/Cpl. Herbie Francis; Unknown; Sgt. Guy Parsons; Reg Cox; Sgt. Bert Rodd; Les Carter; Unknown; Charlie Ham
(John Harris collection)

STREET COMPANY

COMMANDING OFFICER	Major L.A. Leavey	2ND IN COMMAND	Capt. George A. Pursey
	Capt. R. Peddie		(Mr. Bancroft Clark)
	Major E. Page, M.C.	ACTING INTELLIGENCE OFFR.	2nd Lt. A.T. Martin

With Glastonbury Platoon being elevated to Company status, various appointments and promotions changed the command structure of the original No. 3 Company from its 1940 configuration shown immediately below to that as detailed in the Street Invasion Committee notes of 17.3.44 to be found on p.128.

COMPANY COMMANDER	Major E. Page, M.C.	PLATOON COMMANDERS	
2ND IN COMMAND	Mr. Bancroft Clark	VILLAGE SECTIONS	Lt. Ronald Peddie, C.S.M. R.C. Taylor
LIAISON OFFICER	Capt. H.F. Scott Stokes	RESERVE PLATOON	Lt. G.A. Pursey
		GLASTONBURY PLATOON	Lt. G.H. Harland
		STREET PLATOON	Lt. J.B. Seager

NO. 1 (STREET) PLATOON

In early 1941 before the formation of other platoons in the Street Company area, Street platoon mustered some 133 men as detailed in the list below:

Platoon Commander: J.B. SEAGER	BAWN James Philip (Cpl.)	CAINES George James Medland	DANIELLS Jack Owen (D. 2.5.41)
	BENNETT Frank	CARTER Albert	DARE Wm. Sprague (D. 12.9.41)
ALLEN Wm. Geo.	*BLISS Philip Fredk. Henry	CASTLE Albert Edward	DAVIES George Henry Albert
*ANDERSON Charles Henry	BOND Harold Cecil	CHIFFERS Allan Kenneth	*DAVIES Hughes
ANDREWS Alfred Chas.	BOOTH Ernest (Cpl.)	CHIVERS Frank	DOWDEN Clifford Lionel
ANDREWS Ronald Alf. (C. 18.7.41)	BRIGHT R.A.	CHUBB Henry Wm.	DOWDEN Jack
	BROUGHTON Ernest	CHURCH Fred. George	DOWDEN Leslie
BANKS Clifford Geo. (C. 15.7.41)	BROUGHTON Horace Jack	(D. ?.?.41)	
BARNES Maurice Frank (Sgt.)	(C. 25.7.41)	COOPER Hedley Horton	EDWARDS Herbert Wm.
BARNES Vernon (C. 30.5.41)	BRYER Douglas Elwyn (C. 20.6.41)	*CORNELIUS Wm. Mather	ELLIS Fredk.
BARTLETT Frederick (D. 18.7.41)	BURBIDGE Hy. George (D. 1.8.41)	CROSSMAN Cecil Joseph	EMERY Stanley

FIELDING Jonas Arthur (D. 11.4.41)	KING Albert George (C. 1.2.41)	PERKINS Leslie Har.	*STRANGE John Helmdon St. Clair
FRANCIS Lionel Frederick (C. 20.6.41)	KINGTON Essington George (Sgt.)	POCOCK Stephen Ed.	*STREETEN Peter Garrett
*FRENCH Peter John Maurice Francis		POMPEY Harry	SUMMERHAYES Colin
	*LACEY Michael Blomfield	*PRITCHARD Jack Wm. Harman	SUMMERHAYES Maxwell
GILLETT Reginald Charles	LAMBERT Harold (C. 8.8.41)	*PROWSE William John	
(D. 18.7.41)	LAMBERT John Arthur	PURSEY Arthur Thos.	*TARGET Terence Loury Gore
GILROY Stephen	LANGDON Eli		TAYLOR Reginald Chas.
GODWIN Ronald Francis James	LAPHAM Edward Arthur	RAYES Basil Lewis (D. 15.8.41)	TERRELL Frank Cecil
GREEN George	*LAWSON Harry Campbell	READ C.S.	*THRELFALL John Forster
GRIFFITHS Harold Edward (C. 5.9.41)	LEADER Harold	REES James Edmund	TOLE Horace
	LE CALSI Charles R.J. (Cpl.)	RICE Albert Edwin	TRASK Walter
HANCOCK Wm. Wood (Cpl.)	LEE Leonard Gilbert	*RICKETTS Norman Ed.	TREWAVAS Stanley Julian
HANNAM Frank Leslie (Cpl.)	LEWIS Jack	ROSENBERG S.	TURNER Reginald
HARRIS Edward T.	LINHAM Ernest Chas.	RUSSELL Cecil Fred	
*HAWKER Harry Conrad Vaughan		RUSSELL Wm. George	VINING Leslie Arthur
HAWKINS Clifford (D. 11.4.41)	MARSH John Henry		VOWLES Ernest (D. 25.4.41)
HEATHFIELD Henry James	MARSH Leslie Cecil (D. 11.7.41)	SAMBELLS Walter Henry Charles	
HIGGINS Edwin Geo.	MILES Geo. Samuel	SAPSEAD Gilbert Chas. (Cpl.)	WARMAN Herbert William (J. 5.12.41)
HILL Ernest Francis	MILES Percival Leonard (Sgt.)	(D. 18.7.41)	WEBB William (D. 4.4.41)
HOOPER Edwin Chas. (C. 1.8.41)	MOORE Arthur Wm.	SAPSEAD Horace	WELLS Harold Geo.
HORSTEAD Wm. Charles		SELLICK Charles (D. 1.8.41)	WELLS Stanley Herbert
HOSKINS Arthur	NORRIS Wm. Lewis C.	SHARP Ewart Roland (D. 1.8.41)	WHITEHEAD Allan Percival
HOSKINS Ernest Glyn	NORTON Ronald Albert	SHEPHERD Eddie Norman	WHITEHEAD Raymond
		SHERWOOD Reginald F.	WOODBRIDGE Kenneth Clifford
INGERFIELD Ernest (D. 29.8.41)	PARISH Walter (Sgt.)	SKELTON Allan Noel (Cpl.)	WORGAN Joseph (Cpl.)
	PARKER Maurice Albert Wm.	STACEY Guy	
JEANES Reginald Henry (Cpl.)	PAULL Herbert Arthur	STEVENS Roland Thos.	[Those marked with an asterisk were
KENCHINGTON James John (Cpl.)	PAYNE Edwin	STOCKMAN Stanley Wm.	members of No.5 Platoon, see p.127]

No. 1 (Street) Platoon, c.1944.
Back Row: Horace Sapsead; Alf Andrews; Jack Marsh; Unknown; Harry Chubb; Tom Lockyer; Bill Searle; Unknown; Hedley Cooper
Second Row: Cpl. Hilton; Cpl. Hancock; Unknown; Reg Turner; Unknown; Harold Bond; George Pompey; Cpl. Bert Rice; Cpl. Jim Bawn
Third Row: Albury Griffen; Allan Chiffers; Bert Parker; Bert Carter; Lt. J.B. Seager (Platoon Officer); 2nd Lt. Charles Le Calsi (Platoon Commander); Sgt. Maurice Barnes; Unknown; Albert Castle; Bert Paull
Fourth Row: Unknown; George Pursey; Bill Norman; George Longley; Fred Chick; Jack Lambert; Alf Biffin; Unknown; Leslie Dowden; Unknown
Front Row: Noel Hares; Unknown; John Trott; Joe Hubert; Ed Paine; Unknown; Mr. Vowles; Edwin Payne. (Author's collection)

*A few more members of **No. 1 (Street) Platoon** pose for the cameraman.*
Back Row: No. 2 Maurice Albert William Parker
Front Row: Unknown; Unknown; Sgt. Maurice Frank Barnes; Cpl. James Philip Bawn; Herbert Arthur Paull
(Mrs. Pat Willcox collection)

With so many volunteers enrolling in the L.D.V., typing errors were bound to occur. Maurice Parker (*above*) was enrolled as Parker, Norris and E. Hughes-Davies, a pupil at Millfield School, was enrolled as Davies, Hughes.

No. 1 Platoon was comprised of residents of Street area. Many featured were in trade in the town. Harold Bond ran a cycle shop whilst Bert Paul was the local fishmonger. Corporal Hilton ran a chemist's shop in the town. Alf Andrews played right back for Street Football Club. George Pursey ran Pursey's Garage which was established in Walton in about 1934. Charles Ramsey James Le Calsi taught at the Board School. Bill Norman was in trade in Glastonbury as the local blacksmith. An early member, Clifford Lionel Dowden, was subsequently called up and captured by the Germans in Italy.

Tom Lockyer was a member of No. 1 Platoon. He recalled one hot summer's day early on in the war being put in charge of a detail of 20 men digging some form of weapon pit in Miles' Orchard off the Somerton Road. (Tom thinks he was left in charge because he was the only one who could handle the horse and cart that was borrowed from Herb Wall.)

The promise of a hot summer's day ... rising sun ... dew drying off the grass ... clear skies ...hard digging ... and not very far away *The Street Inn* beckoned. When the Platoon Officer returned to inspect the weapon pit he was met by a horse tethered to the hedge and shovels and picks abandoned in the partly dug hole. He waited. Finally some well-lubricated hole diggers were flushed out of *The Street Inn*. "Do you know?" Tom said, having recalled the story recently, "they never put me in charge again!"

However, Tom had the last laugh. In his young days he was a slim athletic youth, a fast runner and very agile. As a result he was made Captain Pursey's runner/guide.

During one night exercise the platoon was out on the moor in the region of Black Bridge. Tom was sent back to guide the rest of the Platoon up to the 'start line'. He recalls, "I led 'em across all the rhines I knew I could jump – 'twere funny standing there in the dark, hearing 'em falling into the water, cussin' and that, officers an' all". History does not record if Tom was replaced as a runner/guide after this incident.

NO. 2 (CLARKS FACTORY) PLATOON

This platoon was divided into several sections as detailed below:

<u>C.W.S. Tannery Section</u>

Section Commander: P. BARRY (Sgt.)

ASHFORD Harry	BUSH Eddie Frederick (C. 20.6.41)	LANFEAR Percival S. (J. 15.8.41)	THYER Bertram Charles (Cpl.)
BADMAN Sidney William	BUTLER Fredk. Charles (C. 20.6.41)	MARTIN Stanley	TOOP Arthur James (Cpl.)
BADMAN Wm. Frank	CARTER Jack Douglas (Cpl.)	MUNKTON Harold James (D. 30.5.41)	UNDERWOOD Donald
BARRY Kenneth T.	CHIFFERS Arthur Leonard	OLIVER J.A (C. 20.6.41)	UNDERWOOD Herbert John
BEST Geo. Victor (D. 30.5.41)	COOK Wm. Alb.	RAWLINGS Arthur W. (D. 20.5.41)	VOWLES Alan G. (C. 27.6.41)
BOWLES Alec Gordon (D. 15.8.41)	CROCKER Arthur James	SILVESTER Colin George	VOWLES John W.H.
BUSH Arthur George	HUMPHRIES Ronald K. (J. 24.10.41)	TAZWELL Stanley John	WHIPPEY Wm. Fred (C. 27.6.41)

Clark, Son & Morland Ltd. Section

Section Commander: G.E. ROBINS (Sgt.)

BIFFIN Edward Alfred	GENGE Eric (C. 20.6.41)	LENEY Fredk. John	VINCENT Edward Ramsey M.
BRYER Rowland Fred. Henry (Cpl.)	HAMLETT Wm.	PARSONS Harry Edward	WEBB Percival Hubert
CARTER Wallace	HAYES Derrick	RIXON Leonard Cecil (Cpl.)	WOOD Graham (D. 20.6.41)
FOURACRES Bert. James	LAMBERT Daniel	SYMES John Henry	WOODGATE Wilfred George (D. 25.4.41)

C. & J. Clark Ltd. Section

Section Commander: A.J. CHAFFEY (Sgt.) (D. no date)

ANDREWS Alb. Bevan	CHUBB Fred. Chas. (D. 11.7.41)	LISK Cyril Victor (D. 27.6.41)	TALBOT Bertram Harry (C. 29.8.41)
ANDREWS Frank (J. 31.10.41)	CURTIS Courtney Albert	LOVELL Arthur Claude	TASWELL Dennis Edward (C. 23.1.42)
BADMAN Robt. Ashton (C. 8.8.41)	DAVIES William	LOVELL Bert. John	TAYLOR Wm. John (D. 15.8.41)
BARTLETT Colin Arnold	DAVIS Wilfred John	LUKINS Douglas	TUXILL Fred. Herbert
BEALE Cecil Charles (Cpl.) (D. no date)	FISHER Edward Harry (C. 20.6.41)	MACKAY James Edward (Cpl.) (D. 23.1.42)	UNDERWOOD A.G. (Cpl.)
BERRY Stanley Frederick	GARE John H (C. 20.6.41)	MAINE Arthur Edwin	UNDERWOOD A.H
BLACKMAN Eric Alan (C. 11.7.41)	GLANDFIELD Percy Sterling	MARSH Ernest Wm	VOWLES Douglas William (C. 29.8.41)
BROUGHTON Doug. Hazel (C. 27.6.41)	GRAVES Alfred Leslie	MARSH Horace	VOWLES Reginald Carter (C. 29.8.41)
BROUGHTON Harold Edward	GRENTER Ronald	MARTIN Arthur Thos. (Cpl.)	WEBB Ernest Downton
BURGESS Mervyn Thomas (C. 11.7.41)	GRIFFIN Herbert Frank	MULLINS Maurice Henry (Cpl.)	WEBB Harold William
BURLETON Thos. Sylvester (C. 29.11.41)	HOCKEY Percy	OSMOND Gilbert Thomas	WEBB Oliver Oram (Cpl.)
CHAFFEY Donald Herbert (D. 23.1.42)	HOLLEY Percy Edgar (Cpl.)	PERRY Frederick Charles (Cpl.)	WELLS Arthur Leslie
	HYDE Albert Edward	POPLE Leslie	WELLS Samuel
	KING Herbert James	ROSS Lewis Cyril	WHIPPEY Harold James
	LEAVEY Lionel Alfred (Sgt.)	RYALL Avalon	
		STEVENS Dennis Arthur	

Avalon Leather Board Co. Ltd. Section

Section Commander: R.M. HARVEY (Sgt.)

BARNES Leo. (C. 4.7.41)	FEAR Nelson	MERRIOTT Henry J.	WALL Geo. Henry (Cpl.)
CLEMENT Robt. Claude	FISHER Albert Edward (Cpl.)	PETHERICK Ernest (D. no date)	WESTLAKE Austin John
CORNISH Cecil Gilbert	HUGHES Reg.	SUMMERS Herbert T.	WYATT Chas. Leslie
DURSTON Frank (D. 30.5.41)	MARSH Reg. F.R. (J. 13.6.41)		

A. Baily & Co. Ltd. Section

Section Commander: A.C. WEST (Sgt.)

BADMAN Alan Edward	HENNESSEY Wm. (J. 3.10.41)	KING Jack	MARSH C.
BAILEY Alb. Geo.	HINES J.	KING Percy Geo. (D. 2.5.41)	NASH Leonard
CLARE H.	HOLLOWAY Arthur Ernest (Cpl.) (C. 5.9.41)	LAMB Geo. Chas.	NASH Wm. Arthur (Cpl.)
DAVIES Austin (D. 2.5.41)		LOVELACE Wm. George	TUCKER E.J.V.

No. 2 (Clark's Factory) Platoon. *This photograph was located with the names of many of those featured written on the back. As the list was not complete the following names are the result of several lines of enquiry.*
Back Row: Mr. Hooper; George Carter; Henry J. Merriott; Cyril Victor Lisk; Unknown; Nelson Fear; Kenneth T. Barry; Cpl. Leonard Cecil Rixon; Colin George Silvester; Stephen Clark; Unknown; Gilbert Underwood; Derrick Hayes
Second Row: Tom Stone; Bert Ball; Fred Richards; Sam Wells; Tom Humphries; Colin Arnold Bartlett; Harold Edward Broughton; Unknown; Courtney Albert Curtis; Avalon Ryall; Unknown; Stan Martin
Third Row: Horace March; Cpl. Jack Douglas Carter; Albert Webb; Mr. Hooper; Bill Lewis; Victor Hooper; Harold Mills; Unknown; Unknown; Edward Moore; Arthur Edwin Maine
Front Row: Albert Coles; Bill Wilton; L/Cpl. Dick Ross; Unknown; Sgt. (later 2nd Lt.) Alan H. Underwood (Platoon Officer); Lt. Stanley F. Berry (Platoon Commander); Lt. Lionel Leavey; Sgt. Les Wells; Cpl. Douglas; Cpl. D. Lukins; L/Cpl. Harold Whippey; John 'Jack' Davis; Unknown
Mr. C. Troop was also a member of the Platoon but has not been identified in the photograph.
(C. & J. Clark Archive Department collection)

Alan Underwood and Leslie Graves were both employees of Clark's. Sadly Alan died in 2001 and Leslie the following year, but not before they had compiled a record of the events of the night of 7th-8th September 1940.

My name is Alan Underwood. I am 90 years old and live in Street. As I sit down to write this I am conscious of the fact that I am recording something which happened 58 years ago and, as far as I know, there is only one person alive who can verify these events.

I was a member of the Home Guard when it was first formed. In Street there were two platoons – No. 1 and No. 2. No. 1 was the Street Home Guard and No. 2 was Clark's Factory Home Guard. I was a private in the Factory Platoon.

In those very early days the rank and file consisted mainly of old soldiers of the First World War, personnel in reserved occupations working on war work, and younger men not yet old enough for the armed forces. In charge of our platoon was Captain Page of Ivythorn Manor and Mr. Bancroft Clark, a Director of C. & J. Clark of Street.

The main duty of No. 2 Platoon was to guard the factory premises, as there was a great deal of war work being done, particularly in the Mechanics Department and in the departments making flying boots, and later American Army boot repairs. Some of these departments worked round the clock, day and night. Later, of course, a great deal of factory space was taken over by Whiteheads Torpedo Works, a branch of the Weymouth factory.

The duties of members of our platoon, as well as ordinary training, involved spending one night a week from 10.00 p.m. to 6.00 a.m. on the factory premises. To that end we had a guard room with bunk beds in the old house of Mr. Frank Clark called Netherleigh, which adjoined the factory. Each night a section consisting of one Corporal and seven Privates would take two-hourly patrols of the perimeter of the factory.

I am not certain of the actual date, but early in 1940, after Dunkirk, the section on duty consisted of Corporal Oliver Whitehead and Privates Graves, Edwards, Glandfield, Mullins, myself and two others whose names I cannot recall (but they were all Street men). As far as I know only Leslie Graves and myself are still living, Leslie being 92 years old and myself 90.

On the night in question, Leslie and I were doing the 12.00-2.00 a.m patrol. Sometime during these hours we heard voices at the main factory entrance. We investigated and challenged two persons, who identified themselves as Captain Page and Mr. Bancroft Clark, our

Commanding Officers. They asked us who was in charge and we told them it was Corporal Whitehead, We were asked to find him and send him to Mr. Bancroft's office, which we did.

By this time, of course, we were all wondering what was happening and returned to the Guard Room to talk about it. After a while Corporal Whitehead returned, looking rather sick, and when we asked him what was afoot, he replied "it's started". We asked what had and were told that invasion was imminent and actually happening.

You can imagine what our thoughts were at that moment! Here were we, totally untrained men, who might at any time be up against highly-trained German Forces. After a while Corporal Whitehead was again summoned to the office. When he returned he asked if any of us had a motorcycle with us that evening. No one had, of course. When asked why a motorcycle was needed, we were told that three urgent dispatches had to be delivered to the Home Guard at Glastonbury Station, to the Officer-in-Charge at Meare and Westhay, and to the Officer-in-Charge at West Pennard. I told him that I had a Morris Eight car in the factory car park. This information was taken to the officers concerned.

I was sent for and given the three dispatches to deliver. I remember Captain Page saying to Mr. Bancroft Clark as I was about to leave the office: "You had better send another man with him as there is bound to be a lot of activity about tonight and he might be stopped". Private Glandfield was delegated for this job. He was told to take his rifle and accompany me. It was quite a dark night and we duly got started with No. 1 Dispatch for Glastonbury Station.

It must be remembered that in 1940 no uncovered lights were allowed on motor vehicles; side lights were covered with four layers of paper and it was compulsory to fit a metal cowl with slots to minimise the amount of light showing. We had to progress quite slowly because of this, but duly arrived at Glastonbury Station. It was all darkness, no light anywhere.

I parked outside and went onto the platform and tried all the doors of the rooms without success. I was just coming away when I heard the sound of a door being opened in a shed on the side of the main building. From it came two Home Guards quickly doing up their uniforms. They had evidently been bedded down somewhere. One was a Corporal. I made myself known and handed over the dispatch. He had to go back into the shed to be able to read it. After reading the dispatch he said that it stated that he was to get in touch with his Platoon Officer in Highbridge and acquaint him with the contents. He said this was not possible because he did not know where the officer lived in Highbridge. I suggested that he should telephone Highbridge Station – that was sure to be manned – to see if they could help him. With that I left him to sort it out.

We then drove to Westhay. I had been given the name and address of the Officer-in-Charge. I found it was on the main road out of Meare. On knocking on the door a light went on upstairs and a man came and unlocked the front door. I identified myself and handed over the dispatch. He read it and, except to thank me, made no comment. I then left. By this time it must have been about 2.00 a.m.

We then made our way to West Pennard Station. As at Glastonbury, it was all in darkness. I could see the rough outline of the station and a wire fence leading down to it. After groping my way along the fence, I must have made a noise as immediately a voice said: "Halt, who goes there?" I identified myself and was told to advance and be recognised.

I replied that this would be very difficult because of the darkness. The voice then said: "Hang on, I will shine my torch". This was done and I met the two Home Guards who were on duty at the station. I told them that I had an urgent message for the Officer-in-Charge of West Pennard Home Guard. I was told that he was the local Station Master and lived in the Station House adjoining. I made my way there and knocked on the front door. Presently a light went on upstairs and the door was opened by a man in a dressing gown carrying a candle. I told him who I was and my purpose and he asked me in. He produced a lamp and read the dispatch. He then asked me if I knew its contents and I replied that I did not. He said he did not know how he was going to carry out his instructions, as part of them was to get a Platoon mobilised and, if possible, equipped with rations for two days. I told him that I could not help and left. I returned to Street and reported to the Guard Room.

While I had been away there had been great activity there. Orders had been given to issue several outside village Platoons with any spare rifles and ammunition. These were normally kept in the Quartermaster's Stores in the factory at Street.

A word here about the rifles issued to all Home Guard Companies. Unlike the British Short Lee Enfield, they were American Springfields of First World War vintage. They differed in calibre, the ammunition being .300 instead of the .303 on British rifles. All this ammunition had to be sent from the States and was always in short supply.

In addition, we also had in the Stores at Street a reasonable supply of petrol bombs, known as Molotov Cocktails. It was claimed that these would put a tank out of action if delivered in the right place.

All these weapons and ammunition had been hurriedly got together and it had been decided that they should be issued immediately to selected outside Platoons. Mr. Bancroft Clark and Private Graves were responsible for this. At that time there was in the factory garage a large American car and this was used as transport. Later I was told by Private Graves that Platoons at Baltonsborough, Butleigh and Lydford had been visited and all the spare weapons and ammunition issued. Thet had then returned to Headquarters at Street at about 5.00 a.m.

We were left wondering what was to happen next. This turned out to be somewhat of an anticlimax, as at about 7.00 a.m. our Corporal was again summoned to the office and told by Captain Page that information received previously had been false and we were to keep what had happened that night strictly private.

After reading this, perhaps when you are next watching *Dad's Army* and the adventures of Captain Mainwaring on television (and nobody enjoys it more than I do), you will realise that there was also a very serious side to the Home Guard. Remember that tens of thousands of part-time soldiers from every town, village and hamlet in the country served in its ranks.

Just imagine what would have happened had the message received by the Commanding Officer been authentic. It would have meant that all branches of the Home Guard would have been involved in conflict against the highly-trained troops of the German invasion forces.

Truly, in the words of Winston Churchill, they would have been used to fight them on the beaches, in the towns and in the countryside. Remember the Home Guard motto – "to the last round, to the last man".

The message which Alan Underwood carried read as follows:

> 8th Sept. 1940 2.15 A.M.
> From O/C No. 3 Coy Glastonbury Bn. Home Guard
> To Section Leader S. & D.J. Rly Glastonbury Station
>
> Orders have been received that the Home Guard will "stand to" at 4.30 a.m. this morning.
> Your station guard will therefore remain on duty day and night until this order is cancelled.
> I think you should double your guard from 4.30 a.m. onwards and assemble at your Command post as many men as you have rifles for. You should make arrangements for all these men to be relieved and for them to get their meals.
> Warn all men to carry their Gas Masks.
> The information I have at present suggest that the trouble is not in our part of the country but all men should be warned to be particularly on the alert against parachute landings and enemy agents.
>
> Signed E. Page
> O/C No. 3 Coy
>
> N.B. Please acknowledge receipt of this to bearer by initialling the envelope and let me know if I can get you on the telephone day and night, and if so what number.
>
> Coy HQs. telephone Street 4.

An identical message was sent to West Pennard Station. This message was sent as a result of the code word 'Cromwell' being received at Company HQ at 22.37 hrs. The telephone log for the night of 7th-8th September 1940 gives an insight as to the activity that night that would be repeated throughout the kingdom.

22.37	'CROMWELL' *
(22.55	Air Raid warning)
23.05 approx.	Order from Col. Thoms' HQ Bridgwater: Company to assemble at Platoon Posts at 4.30 a.m.
23.23	Gen. Webber told Capt. MacDonnell (*sic*) of Wells Home Guard to advise O/C No. 3 Coy that activity not in our part of the country: but men to be collected and at posts at 4.30 a.m.: to look out for Parachute Troops.
23.30	O/C No. 3 Coy asked Gen. Webber re Barricades: Gen. Webber ordered patrols out but no barricades to be put across roads.

Sunday morning: 8th September 1940

01.00 approx.	Gen. Webber ordered barricades to be mounted to check traffic: help police in this duty.
02.15	Message from Jack Whitehead, Butleigh: Francis reported church bells ringing at Compton.** On enquiring from Section Leader, Compton, E.P. [Captain Page] informed that it had been a mistake and the ringing had been stopped. Francis of Butleigh so informed and asked to give B.C. [Mr. Bancroft Clark] message to warn all other villages against similar tomfoolery.
03.20	Harland reported police wished to withdraw from barricades and E.P. ordered him to call in his men since the police in any case would leave with red lamps.
03.23	Action confirmed by Adjutant, Battn. HQ. He also said he had no further information on the situation yet.
03.40	Rang up Powell of Meare and gave him orders for his Section and told him to be back at his house at 4.15 to meet B.C. for further instructions.
(03.50	'All Clear' siren)
04.45	Barry (*Rose and Portcullis*) rung up on behalf of Francis of Butleigh to report that his men are standing to and posts are manned.
04.52	Adjt. Bttn. HQ.: The General wishes Circular 29 of August 17th to be brought to the notice of all men in the Company forthwith. A Bttn. Regular troops have been held up many times when trying to pass through another Company area early this morning. Headquarters have no further information yet of general situation.
05.30	B.C. returned.
06.20	Gen. Webber ordered we may stand down at 7.30 – be ready to be called together at short notice.

* 48th Division Operational Instruction No. 12 of 17th July 1940 – CROMWELL

The code word CROMWELL will be sent when enemy landings by sea or air are considered to be imminent. On receipt of this code word, units will be at 1 hrs notice, the following steps being taken:

No officer or man to be absent from billets.
Transport to be packed as far as possible.
Troops to sleep with their equipment and weapons by their side.
All transport to be full of petrol.

** The ringing of church bells was only to be carried out if enemy troops were actually seen in the vicinity. The reader must remember that this furious activity took place less than four months after the formation of the Home Guard. The pressures on the Company Commander that night must have been immense, for, at the back of his mind must have been the pitiful amount of arms and ammunition at his disposal.

The weekly return to Battalion Commander at 16 Castle Street, Bridgwater, dated 1st August 1940, less than 6 weeks before, lists the equipment on charge.

Rifles, Ross .303"	100
.303" ammunition	895 rounds
Shotguns	8
Lethal Ball for shotguns	300 rounds
Buckshot	nil
Revolvers	4
.45" ammunition	nil
.22" ammunition	700 rounds
.22" rifles	nil
Denim suits	195
	(plus 55 odd trous. and 45 odd blous.)
Caps	205
Armlets	374
Field dressings	440
Steel helmets	nil

All this to be shared between 752 men!

By November 1941 the situation had improved somewhat as this return shows:

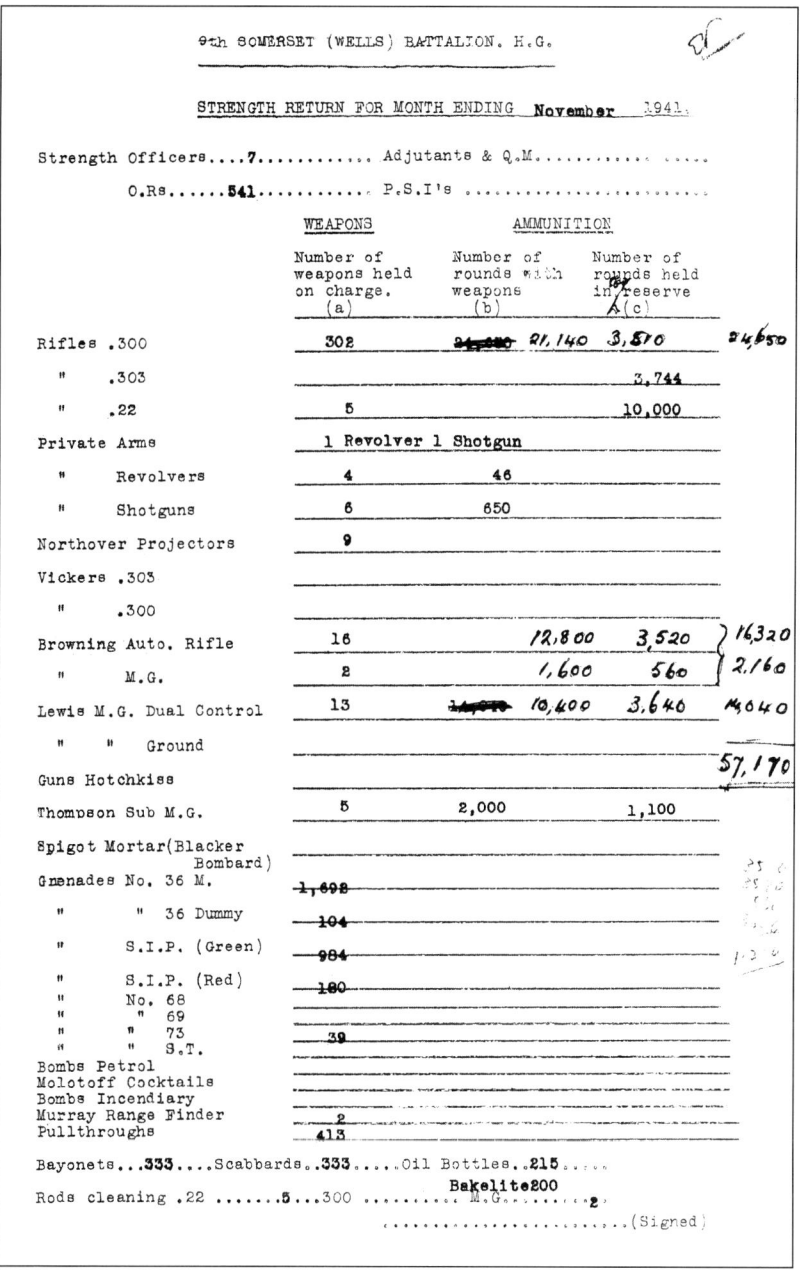

Even then Company Commanders were always looking for excuses to increase their armoury as the exchange of memos reproduced here shows:

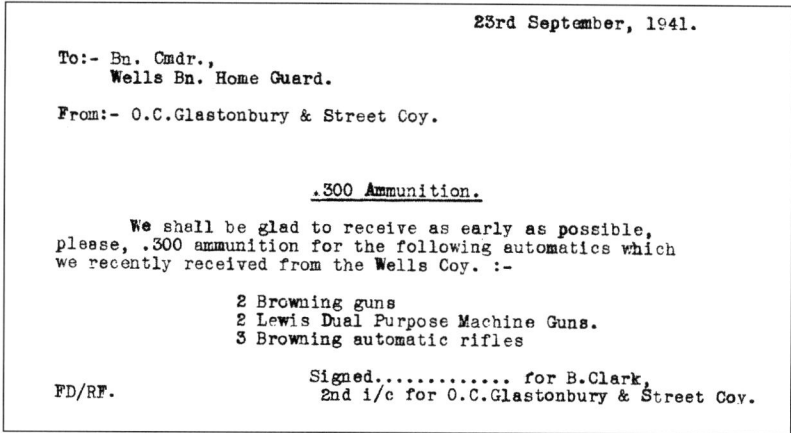

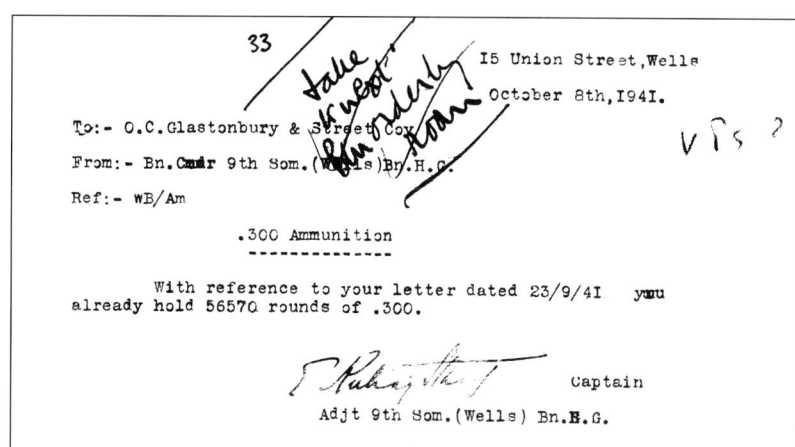

The night of 7th/8th September 1940 was remembered by the author's late father, John Wilson, who was at the time a 2nd Lieutenant in the Somerset Light Infantry, part of the 48th Division. That night he was attending a dance in Cullompton, Devon, when an ashen-faced runner arrived at the dance hall, saluted and said, "Cromwell, sir". A fellow officer, rather well into his cups, said, "Bloody good chap, bring him in and buy him a drink." Suddenly, the significance of the message sank in and all thoughts of merriment were abandoned and replaced with thoughts military. At the time 2nd Lieutenant Wilson's only personal weapon was a .32" smooth-bore revolver given to him by the vicar of Cullompton, such was the shortage of weapons. John remembers firing it once at a tree and missing!

NO. 3 PLATOON, NO. 9 (BALTONSBOROUGH) SECTION

The most easterly unit of Street Company, this section mustered some 50 men.

Baltonsborough Section

Section Commander: HUGH CHAMPION (Sgt.)

ACREMAN Fredk. George (D. 11.4.41)	BURGE Harold Frederick	BUTTLE Albert Edward (D. 11.4.41)	DUNKERTON Bert. Stanley
ATTWELL Henry John	BUSH Albert	BUTTLE John	DUNKERTON Wm. Leonard
BANWELL Stanley	BUSH Albert Isaac (Cpl.)	CARTER Maurice	DUREY Alfred Edward
BILLING Fredk. Walter (D. 11.4.41)	BUSH Douglas Harold	CHINNOCK Ernest Reginald	GARLAND Albert Frank (D. 11.4.41)
BILLING Reg. (D. 11.4.41)	BUSH Harry Raymond	CLAPP Dennis	GODFREY Harvey (D. 13.10.41)
BROWN Archibald William E.	BUSH Reginald George	COOK William	GOULD Arthur Edwin Samuel
		CORNICK William Thomas	GOULD Edwin G. (Cpl.)
		DAVIES John G.	GUY William

HARDING William (Scout Patrol)
   (transferred to Aux. Unit 4.4.41)
HIGDON Ed. Chas.
HOBBS Mervyn
HOLE Nelson
JENKINS Fred.
JENKINS Walter Henry
LONGMAN Wm. Martin (L/Cpl.)
MARSH Frank
MEATYARD Herb. Arthur
NICHOLAS Ernest Wm. (Cpl.)
NORRIS Cyril (D. 11.4.41)
PLUMLEY Sam. R.
PORTER Chas. J. (Cpl.)
PORTER George
SMITH W.A.
SOMERS Ronald
STEVENS Everett
STEVENS Kemp
WHITEHEAD H.J. (Scout Patrol)
   (transferred to Aux. Unit 4.4.41)
WILTON Ronald
WITHERILL Fred.

NO. 3 PLATOON, NO. 10 (BUTLEIGH) SECTION

Charles Lampert was a member of Butleigh Home Guard living in Quarry Lane. In 1940, when he was 41, he joined the L.D.V. having served in the First World War where he was wounded and taken prisoner at the Battle of Cambrai in 1917. Charles Lampert passed away several years ago but his son, R.G. Lampert, recalls some stories that his father told him.

Our Sergeant was Thomas Francis who lived at Higher Hill Farm. He used to bring me his 12-bore shotgun to take on night patrols. Initially we were issued with denim uniforms, it was only later on that khaki battledress arrived. Later I was promoted to Corporal and issued with a Sten gun. We used to parade at the British Legion Hut. Other members I recall were Stan Higgins, Charles Dyer, Arthur Earl and George Lock.

We had a rifle range close to the Hood Monument overlooking Compton Dundon. This was not only used by us but by American Troops stationed in the area. This range included a 'mock up' of a tank which was pulled across the range to provide a moving target.

This range was about 600 yards in length with butts at map ref. ST 501 331 and the 600 yard firing point at map ref. ST 495 334. It is shown on early 20th-century maps.

The late Lionel Crocker was another Butleigh resident. Young Robert George Lampert worked his apprenticeship with Lionel and would be regaled with Home Guard stories told by his father (also called Lionel) who had been in the Home Guard. Two remain fixed in his memory.

During the period when we were threatened with invasion an Army Colonel came to the Legion Hut to give a talk to Butleigh Home Guard on what they should do if German Paratroops were to land. The Colonel said that we must run to the nearest phone and report it to higher authority. My father stood up and said, "I will tell you, Sir, what I will do. I will shoot him if I can as if he gets to the ground he will be better equipped and I live ½ a mile from the nearest phone." "But", said the Colonel, "you will have to make out a report why you shot him." "That's easy," said my dad, "I only have to fire his weapon and say he was shot in self-defence."

On another occasion an exercise was being carried out and my dad was sent with two or three other men to the road junction above Butleigh Hospital where Higher Road meets the Marshalls Elm/Christian's Cross Road and detailed not to let anyone enter Higher Road unless they could identify themselves. A staff car arrived with an Officer of Staff Rank but when stopped would not show his identification. He told his driver to drive on but my dad stood his ground saying: "If you do we will open fire and stop you." The officer then showed his identification and was allowed to pass.

When the exercise was over the officer approached my dad and asked, "Would you really have fired if I had driven on?" "Oh! Yes," said dad, "have no fear, we would have stopped you."

Incidents such as this were not uncommon; many civilians were shot and killed by Home Guards. The author is aware of one incident in the 13th Battalion area where the only reason why the driver of a car was not shot was because the Home Guard could not release the safety catch on his rifle quickly enough in the dark before the motorist sped off.

Butleigh Section

Section Commander: T.W. FRANCIS (Sgt.)

BALL Cyril T. (Cpl.)
BALL F.C. (Scout Patrol)
   (transferred to Aux. Unit 4.4.41)
BARRY Leo. Geo. (C. 5.9.41)
BIRCH Albert
BIRCH Ernest
BIRCH Frank
BOBBETT Henry J.
BURICH William
BURROUGH Robert Chas.
   (Scout Patrol)
   (transferred to Aux. Unit 4.4.41)
COATES Robert
CROCKER Lionel Ernest (Cpl.)
DAVIS Alfred Edward
DAVIS Arthur Edward
DYER Charles
EARL Arthur
FORD Arthur Leslie
FORD Roy John
FORSEY Wilfred Albert
GANE John Robert
HAIMES Leonard Bond (Scout Patrol)
   (transferred to Aux. Unit 4.4.41)
HIGGINS Alf. Wm
HIGGINS Ronald
KILLEN Wm. Stan
KNIGHT Chas. Hy.
LAMPERT Chas. (L/Cpl.)
LAMPERT Herbert Wm. (C. 20.7.41)
LYE Ernest George
MARSH Hy. George
MARSH Leo. Percy
MASTERS Harold
PARKER Nelson Hugh
PIKE Leslie Grinter
PITMAN Harold Arthur
POPE C.P.
POPE Wm. Francis
RENDALL Charles
RENDALL Leonard
RIGGS J. (Cpl.)
RIGGS Ted.
SHORE Kenneth George
SMALL Joseph Henry James
STUDLEY Harold Edgar
TRASK J.
WHITCOMBE Philip
WILCOX George (Cpl.)

A mile or so to the west of Street lies the village of Walton. More than 30 villagers were enrolled in the Home Guard by 1941; they included those listed below. By 1944 Walton Section had become No. 7 Platoon.

Weekly drill took place in Walton Village Hall. Transport was provided by Mr. Evelyn Frampton who owned a Morris 12.

Walton Section

Section Commander: C. SWEET

ATYEO Harry T. (D. 29.11.41)	CULLIFORD Cyril Thomas	LOCKE Stanley	STACEY Frank
BIRD Ernest Colin	DAVIES Charles A.A (C. 4.7.41)	LOCKYER Leo. Albert (L/Cpl.)	STACEY James
BLACKBURN Chas. Ed (D. 27.6.41)	ELLIOTT Clifford Oliver S. (C. 20.7.41)	LOCKYER Wm. J.	TAYLOR John Hy.
BOWN Hy. Joseph		MARSH Ernest Frank	VOWLES Albert
BROUGHTON Arthur Ed. Geo.	FISHER George Ernest Chapman (Cpl.)	MARTIN James	VOWLES Chas. Alfred
COOMBES Herb. John	FISHER Jack	PERRY Bernard Leslie	WHITCOMBE Chas. Ernest
COOPERMAN	GOODEN Evelyn Frank	PERRY Vernon C. (Cpl.)	WHITCOMBE Met. John
CROSSMAN Albert Ed. (D. 29.8.41)	HOLMES Ernest G.	PITMAN Albert Ed.	WHITE Alexander Alfred
CROSSMAN George Henry	LESSEY Chas. Arthur	PITMAN Bertram F.	WHITE Evelyn Lewis
CROSSMAN Kenneth Vivian	LOCKE Hy. James (D. 15.8.41)	PURSEY Leo. Charles	WINSLADE Harold John (D. 29.8.41)

NO. 5 PLATOON

No. 5 Platoon was commanded by 2nd Lt. N.L. Barry Tait, a Physics teacher at Millfield School, recently invalided out of the regular army with the rank of Captain. Platoon Headquarters was at the school whilst Battle Headquarters was to be at Phelps Mill, in 2002 occupied by The Wessex Hotel. Platoon members were drawn from senior pupils at the school. David Ford, an ex-pupil now living at Pen Selwood, remembers the platoon being mustered, possibly in June 1944, to guard a Waco Glider which landed prematurely at Compton Dundon, the crew and passengers returning to camp leaving the glider full of stores. On other occasions the platoon helped to move vast quantities of military stores from dumps on the Mendips to Wells Railway Station.

> Norman Ricketts was a senior pupil at Millfield School in 1940. In a recent letter he recounted those early days of the Home Guard:
>
> My experience starts with the Local Defence Volunteers (L.D.V.). You will recognise that in those dangerous days just before the Dunkirk evacuation by the Royal Navy of the British Expeditionary Force and Allies wishing to continue the fight from Britain, there was an element of turmoil which was soon replaced by British tenacity and organisation but with a lack of weapons and equipment. The senior pupils at Millfield School immediately volunteered to play their part in the Defence of the Realm, probably being the first 'organised' unit in Street. Among our motley lot were an Indian Maharajah and his princely brother.
>
> The Millfield Contingent was young and ready since most had been in the Officer Training Corps (O.T.C.) and were therefore qualified for entry to the armed forces, having passed the requisite Certificate A required for a Platoon Commander. Thus they were already an integrated unit and took their role very seriously. No uniforms were issued; we had to rely on 'official' armbands (L.D.V.) and looked a rather motley lot. We drilled regularly at school and conducted attack and defence manoeuvres in the grounds amongst ourselves, being much admired by the younger pupils. Later we were issued with P14 rifles and limited ammunition; much older than the Lee-Enfield Mk3 with which we were already familiar. However, after a few 'sighters' on the range, we felt confident that we could put up a good show if called upon.
>
> As for duties, we assembled at the School House and then marched about 2½ miles to our observation point every night. This was located along the ridge above Compton Dundon. One weekend we were engaged with others on an exercise on King's Sedgemoor. Something must have happened because next time we became umpires.
>
> On the ridge, those off duty slept in a hut which was used by the local Golf Club. At dawn we marched back to school and a welcome breakfast, immediately followed by lessons. Communications were elementary but our duties followed strict military discipline and responsibility. We were never aware of an overall plan. However, orders concentrated on security. These stemmed from the concern of the authorities that the Dunkirk evacuation may have provided a conduit for the infiltration of spies and saboteurs bent on destabilising the United Kingdom with the help of 'sleepers' as was later to occur in Norway and German occupied territories. Therefore, vigilance was an important part of our orders. We were instructed to stop and identify the spasmodic traffic along the Marshalls Elm/Christian's Cross Road. On one occasion, in the small hours, we stopped an open sports car driven by an extremely attractive young lady, only to discover in the torchlight a passenger hiding under a rug – he turned out to be one of our younger masters! Discretion was respected.
>
> On leaving Millfield most of the Platoon members were commissioned into the Forces. My close friend and I were lucky to be commissioned into the Royal Marines as probationary 2nd Lieutenants. He eventually became the Colonel Commandant of the Royal Marines Depot at Deal. At the close of hostilities I was a Major R.M. on the personal staff of the Allied Naval Commander-in-Chief of the D-Day Invasion Force and, on occasion, in the company of the Supreme Commander, General Eisenhower. I was able to regale him with stories of the early days when we were in the L.D.V. and Britain stood alone. He enquired how we did this. I replied: "With the use of masterly inactivity". Years later when we met again, he asked: "Still practising masterly inactivity?"

NO. 7 PLATOON

No. 7 Platoon, commanded by 2nd Lt. W. Parish of Street, had its headquarters at Walton Rectory Coach House. Battle headquarters was to be a defended house in Walton, either The Coach House or The Old Rectory, Walton.

HOME GUARD SITUATION AS AT 17.3.44

An extract from The Street Invasion Committee War Book of this date shows just how much Street Home Guard had developed in less than four years.

A. <u>Regular troops</u>
None available on Action Stations. There are two camps in Street, one in Somerton Road and the other at Woods Batch, but they are used by troops for training. It is quite likely that most of the personnel in these camps would be sent elsewhere on Action Stations.

B. <u>Home Guard</u>
Coy Headquarters — Strode Lane
Battle HQ — Phelps Mill
O.C. Company — Major L.A. Leavey
2nd in Command — Capt. G.A. Pursey

Strength 3 platoons of approx. 200 all told with approx. 10% of the strength classified in Category II.

The details of all platoons in the Street Company area was as below:

No. 1 Platoon HQ — 51, High Street, Street
Battle HQ D.L. — Flemington's Bakery
Platoon Commander — Lt. Le Calsi
L.O. — Lt. J.B. Seager

No. 2 Platoon HQ — C. & J. Clark Factory, Street
Battle HQ (D.L.) — Phelps Mill
Platoon Commander — Lt. S.F. Berry
Platoon Officer — 2nd Lt. A.H. Underwood

No. 3 Platoon HQ — 'Elmleigh', Elmhurst Road
Battle HQ (D.H.) — Butleigh Court Estate Office
Alternative D.H. — Roods Farm, Butleigh
Platoon Commander — 2nd Lt. R.L. Potter

No. 9 Section Baltonsborough
HQ — Baltonsborough Cross
Battle HQ (D.H.) — Baltonsborough Cross
Alternative D.H. — Orchard Neville
Section Commander — Sgt. C. Porter

No. 10 Section Butleigh
HQ — Butleigh Court Estate Office
Battle HQ (D.H.) — Butleigh Court Estate Office
Alternative — Roods Farm, Butleigh
Section Commander — Sgt. C.T. Ball

No. 4 Platoon HQ — The Factory, Street
Battle HQ (D.L.) — No. 1, High Street
Platoon Commander — 2nd Lt. A. McTavish

No. 5 Platoon HQ — Millfield Street
Battle HQ (D.L.) — Phelps Mill, High Street
Platoon Officer — 2nd Lt. N.L. Barry Tait

No. 7 Platoon HQ — Walton Rectory Coach House
Battle HQ (D.H.) — Walton Rectory Coach House
Alternative — Old Rectory, Walton
Platoon Officer — 2nd Lt. W. Parish

Street Company's principal role by now was to deny the enemy the use of the roads at Street Cross, and the defended locality was sited near these crossroads. Outside *The Bear Hotel* the roadway was furnished with sockets to take 'hairpins', steel girders bent into a 'V', inverted with one leg placed vertically into a socket, the other leg, slightly longer, forming a strut.

Cover of the programme for the Stand Down Parade at Wells, 3rd December 1944.

13th Somerset (Axbridge) Battalion

HEADQUARTERS	Bromswald House, Axbridge
DATE FORMED	May 1943
COMMANDING OFFICER	Lt. Col. L.M. Stevens, D.S.O. (from 10.7.44)
	(Lt. Col. A.H. Yatman, D.S.O., D.L.)
2ND IN COMMAND	Major A.M. Henniker

H.Q. STAFF

A & Q OFFICER	Capt. J.R. Barnes, Gloucester Regt.
ADJUTANT	Capt. H.J. Ormerod, General List
AMMUNITION OFFICER	Lt. Arthur M. Ashford
CHAPLAIN	Rev. W.E.L. Houlden
GAS OFFICER	Lt. S.H. Hess
INTELLIGENCE OFFICER	Lt. Pickering
MEDICAL OFFICER	Major H.W.H. Holmes
SIGNALS OFFICER	Lt. G.V. Williams
WEAPON TRAINING OFFR.	Capt. E.J. Cornish

'C' (BURNHAM) COMPANY

COMMANDING OFFICER	Major E.F. Hobbs
	(Major L.M. Stevens)
2ND IN COMMAND	Capt. W.W. Tucker

Burnham Company's boundary extended northwards to the River Axe and eastwards to the villages of Mark, Chapel Allerton and Weare. The discovery of an original 1" War Department map indicates that Burnham Company was divided into 3 platoons: Burnham, Highbridge and East Brent.

Members of Burnham-on-Sea Platoon at Manor Gardens in 1944.
Back Row: Unknown; Mr. Law; Mr. Higgins; Mr. Coles; Mr. Holmes; Mr. Baker; N. Buncombe; Mr. Phelps; Mr. Giblett; Mr. Ward; Mr. Smith; Mr. Dredge; Mr. Crowther; Unknown; Unknown
Middle Row: Mr. Cox; Mr. Dunn; Mr. Browning; Mr. Brewer; Mr. Braybrook; Mr. Mitchell; Mr. Brawn; Mr. Fear; Mr. Marchent; Mr. Puddy; Mr. Marchent; Mr. Ansell; Mr. Cann; Mr. King; Mr. Turk; Unknown
Front Row: Cpl. J. Buncombe; Cpl. Litton; Sgt. King; Sgt. Fox; Cpl. Marsh; Lt. Williams; Major Holmes; Major (later Lt. Col.) Stevens; Lt. Pearce; Lt. Williams; C.S.M. Trott; Sgt. Burland; Sgt. Jenner; Sgt. Grimes

Messrs. Cox, Mitchell, Turk and Dredge were all employed by Wallbutton's Garage. Mr. King was a dental technician, Mr. Trott a barber and Mr. Phelps was a fishmonger.
(Mrs Margaret Young collection)

Brean Sands was used for grenade practice and occasionally accidents happened. Margaret Young, the daughter of Sgt. Fox, remembers her father returning one day suffering from shrapnel wounds to his head, caused when a grenade rolled back down a dune towards the thrower. Small pieces of shrapnel remained in his head for the rest of his life.

Rupert William Harris was a member of Brent Knoll Home Guard whose meeting place was the Parish Hall. Names that Rupert recalls are A. Lee, S. Williams, H. Clay, P. Day, J. Buckton, H. Waddon, D. Rollison and Mr. Saunders. N.C.O.s included Sgt. Challoner. *The Red Cow* skittle alley provided a .22" rifle range.

Guard duties included protecting Brent Knoll Pumping Station. During the build-up to D-Day Brent Knoll Home Guard, in conjunction with other platoons, patrolled the stretch of the G.W.R. from Brean Halt, adjacent to the Battalion Boundary, the River Axe, to Brent Knoll Station.

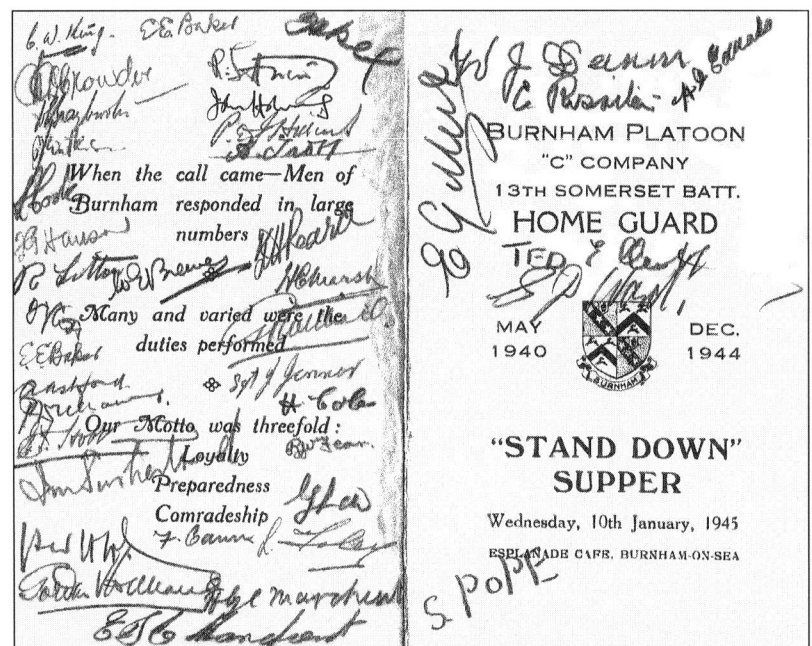

*(right) It was not until January 1945 that **Burnham Platoon** held their Stand Down Supper, with those present signing the programme.*

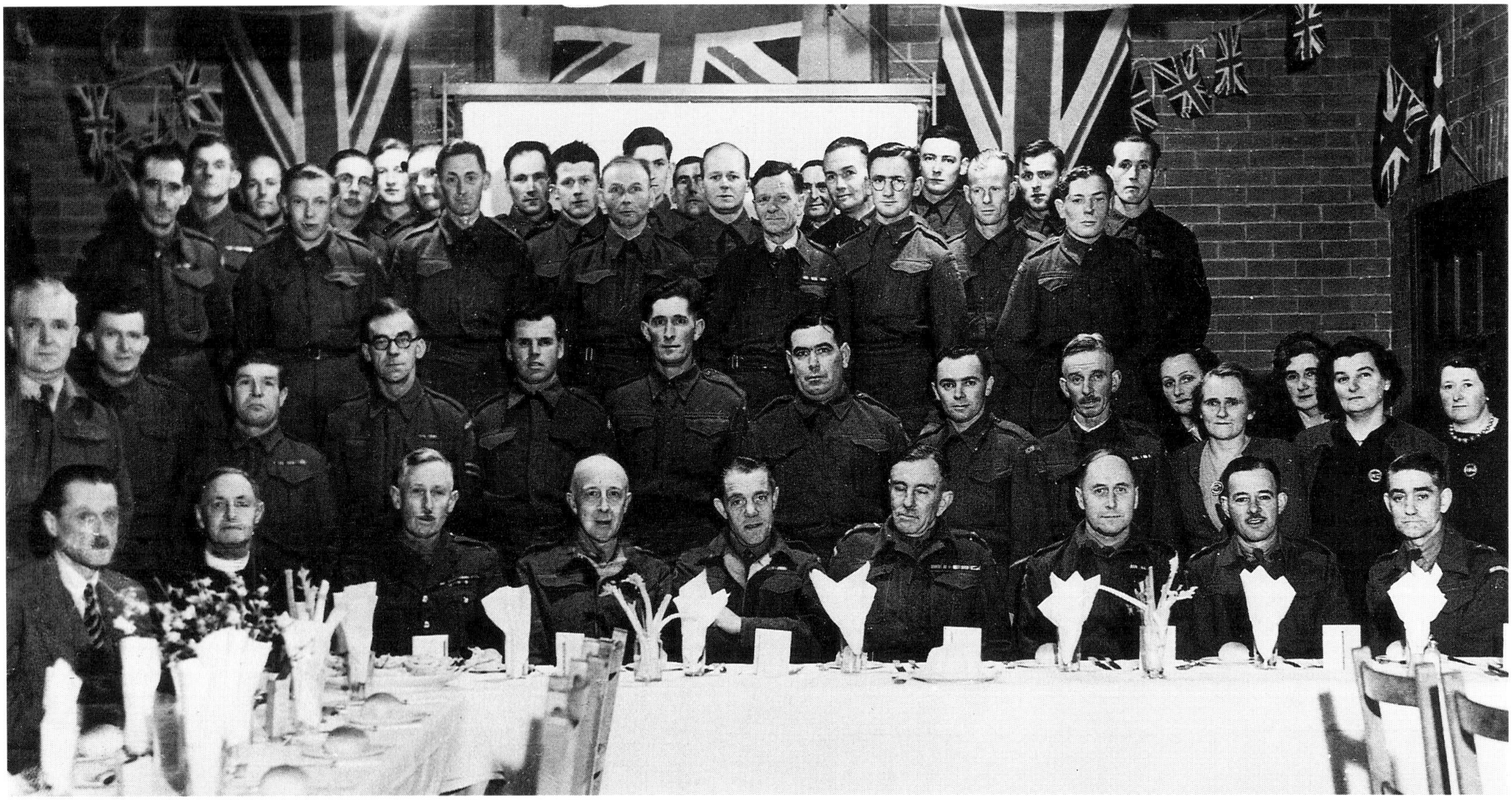

Berrow and Brean Home Guard Stand Down Supper on Saturday 2nd December 1944.
Group at the back: Lt. N. Dill; Sgt. Talbot*; Philip Frost; George Parsons; Norman Yates; S. Holland; Unknown; Bob Brimicombe; John Perrett; Gilbert Coggins; T. Westcott; Bill Collins; Jim Kerton; Henry Puddy; Sgt. Joe P. Foster*; Wally Chick; Q.M.S. Freke; Ben Harris; Michael Harris; E. Jones; Cpl. F.B. Welland; Ron Parsons; Cpl. Thompson
Row behind the guests: Capt. W.W. Tucker; L/Cpl. Linham*; Toby Smith*; Cpl. Frank Boobyer*; Philip Champion; Horace Pitty; Cpl. Herbert Chick*; Arthur Harris; Unknown; Unknown; Unknown; Unknown; Unknown; Unknown
Front Row (Guests): Mr. G.H. Furness; Revd. Williams; Mr. Holland; Capt. H.J. Ormerod; Major E.F. Hobbs; Lt. Col. Stevens; Major H.W.H. Holmes; Lt. Arthur M. Ashford; Lt. Pearce

* Many senior officers had fought in the First World War but those marked with an asterix were definitely WW1 veterans.
(Frank B. Welland collection)

Mark Home Guard at The Royal Clarence Hotel, Burnham on 3rd December 1944.
Back Row: Ray Tidball; Austin Cox; G. Whitting; Jack West; Don Puddy; Stan Coombes
Middle Row: W. Coleman; A. Dyer; S. Buncombe; Ern Tidball; Reg Puddy; G. Rice; Don Buncombe; Ted Cox; C. Starr
Front Row: Cpl. S. Salvidge; L/Cpl. M. Thomas; Cpl. Alb Wall; Sgt. S. Leigh; Lt. E. Tucker; Lt. C. Russell; Cpl. H. Haines; Cpl. John Matthews; Cpl. Bob Webber; Cpl. Ted Fisher
Robert Vigar is not featured in the photograph as he was working at home at Chestnut Farm, Vole Road. Also missing from the photograph is Dispatch Rider J. Wensley who used his own motorbike, Reg. No. CLJ 289, on Home Guard business.
(Robert G. Vigar collection)

Mark Home Guard's meeting place was the Assembly Rooms. Company stores were held at the Burnham Drill Hall (since demolished). N.C.O.s remembered by Robert Vigar included Sgts. House and G. Blaber. An observation point was established on the top of Mark Church Tower. Here the lookouts would amuse themselves by firing pebbles from a catapult onto the corrugated iron roofs below, much to the consternation of those beneath. The build-up to D-Day saw members of Mark Home Guard taking its share of guarding the railway through Highbridge.

*Men of **Burnham Home Guard** march along Victoria Street in December 1944.*
(Mrs June Thomas collection)

Highbridge Platoon taken outside The Royal Clarence Hotel in Burnham on 3rd December 1944.
Back Row: No. 9 Clifford Marsh
Middle Row: No. 2 Harry Major (haulage contractor); No. 7 Les Cook
Front Row: No. 2 Cpl. Gilbert Hector; No. 3 B. Luke; No. 6 Lt. Wilfred H. Porter
It is interesting to note the sign on the wall behind the group. There is no doubt that this photograph was taken at the same time as the one at the top of the page but why has the developer of the photograph obliterated the First Aid Party sign?
(Mrs. June Thomas collection)

Bob Rogers was a member of (No. 2 Section) Highbridge Platoon in 1940. Headquarters were at Highbridge Town Hall. Bob recalls the following details about the membership of the Home Guard.

COMMANDING OFFR.	Major E.F. Hobbs, Manager of Lloyds Bank		Pte. Hubert Pople, farmworker at Isleport Farm
			Pte. George Holt
PLATOON CDR.	Lt. Knapp, Assistant Manager Barclays Bank		Pte. Dicks, farmworker at Alstone Farm
			Pte. Joe Day
NO. 2 SECTION CDR.	Sgt. W.H. Porter, Home Grown Timber Manager, John Bland and Co. Ltd. (promoted to Lt. when Lt. Knapp joined Army)		Mr. Morris, evacuee from London
			Mr. Stevens (or Stephens)
			Les Smith
			Bob Rogers
	Sgt. Percy Hicks, Builder		Bill Chedgey, shunter on docks railway
	Pte. H. Tommy Cave, Builder's Clerk, W.J. Channing & Sons	NO. 1 SECTION	Buster Needs, baker, Huntspill Road

From a brief description it would appear that the Platoon's rifle range was on the south side of the Estuary of the River Brue, the back stop being the river bank, with the Danger Area the Estuary of the River Parrett.

HIGHBRIDGE LOCOMOTIVE WORKS HOME GUARD
22ND DEVONSHIRE (5TH SOUTHERN RAILWAY) BATTALION HOME GUARD

George Leonard Brooks joined the Somerset and Dorset Railway in 1925 aged 13. Names George recalls are Lt. Cecil Hill, Ron 'Chummy' Andrews, Bill May, Alan Jones and Fred Meaker.

S&D Locomotive Works Home Guard.
Ern Cook; Maurice Cook; George Wheadon; Victor Newman (Alan Hammond collection)

S&D Locomotive Works Home Guard.
Back Row: Frank Jones; Ern Cook; Harry Miller
Front Row: Maurice Cook; Tom Day; Wilf Rowden
This photograph also came from another source but with different names supplied.
Back row No. 3 was identified as Mark Hawkins, Front row No. 1 Bill May, No. 2 'Chummy' Andrews. Yet another source identifies Tom Bass in the back row with Harry Biffin centre front and Mark Hawkins to his left. With so many years passing since the photograph was taken such contradictions will occur.
(Alan Hammond collection)

S&D Locomotive Works Home Guard.
Again, uncertainty surrounds the names.
Back Row: No. 2 Mark Hawkins
Front Row: No. 1 Bill May; No. 2 'Chummy' Andrews
(Mrs. Sheila Tutt collection)

D' (WINSCOMBE) COMPANY

COMMANDING OFFICER   Major R.V. Weeks
2ND IN COMMAND   Capt. S.J. Mills

'D' (Winscombe) Company.
Back Row: Jack Seymour (gardener at Sidcot School); Doug Tucker (farmer); Tom Mansfield; Unknown; Frank Larder; Ted Hares (porter at Winscombe Station); Arthur Badman; George 'Lou' Day (quarryman at Sandford Quarry): Lyn Jakeway (haulier); William Farr; George Sheppard; Unknown; Norman Horsham; Jack Bailey; Unknown; Mr. Emery
Second Row: Bill Seabright; Ernest Charles Pople (builder); Wally Grant; Unknown; Dr. Veal (solicitor); Charlie Gower (builder and undertaker); Unknown; Mr. Daffern; Archie Shepstone; Reg Nigh; Clifford King; Mr. Hurn (chauffeur); 'Muddy' Morgan; Sam Langford; Harold Buncombe
Third Row: Sgt. Jack Lindsay (head gardener at Sidcot School); Sgt. Tom Cutler; Sgt. Neil Blower (foreman for Axbridge R.D.C.); Celia Rendell (W.V.S. and H.G. Auxiliary); Mrs Veal; Lt. George Whitcher (apple grower); Lt. Salter; Capt. S.J. Mills (Company 2 i/c); Lt. Champney (cider manufacturer); Doreen Venn (née Cooper, fruit and fish shop proprietor); Unknown; Sgt. Jack Lintern; Cpl. William Salter (gardener); Cpl. Lovell; Cpl. Percy Simms (gardener); Lou Newphry
Front Row: Phil Stephen; William 'Bill' Ferris (gardener at The Hall); Bill Bradford (postman); Walter Roe (postman); Burdon Besley; John Gatehouse; Albert 'Bert' White (strawberry punnet maker); Billy Milkins (coalman).
During the war some lecturers from a London Polytechnic were transferred to Sidcot School. Amongst them was a Mr. Simmons who may, with other staff members, be included in the 'unknowns' above. (Margaret Ballard collection via Roy Rice)

*Men of **Axbridge Home Guard** march through the town.* Leading the column is Sgt. Bill Kitley followed by Cpl. Jim Callow. Heading the file nearest the kerb is Dick Tanner followed by Frank Wilson and his brother Chris. No. 5 in the same file in front of the black door with the fanlight is Edmund Durston. Frank Payne (with moustache) leads the file nearest the camera. The second man behind him is Elton Nichols. At the rear of the file is Peter Urch.
  Of the civilians, on the extreme right is Olive Sherstone with Miss Francis on her right. On the extreme left of the photograph is Miss Macdonald followed by Bett Urch, sister of Peter.
(Trustees of King John's Hunting Lodge Museum collection)

To the south of Winscombe there existed a 19th-century rifle range using the rising ground of Wavening Down as a butt stop. After the introduction of the .303 rifle in the 1880s, the range was resited into Bourton Combe with the butts at approx. map ref. ST 411 556 and the firing point, now totally obliterated, some 200 yards to the east.

Cheddar Platoon, taken by Norman Heal outside the old Wansborough and Budgett paper mill situated at the bottom of Redcliff Street in 1944. This building later became the West of England Concrete Works. During the war it was owned by Mr. George Gilling.
Back Row: Ernest Packer; Mr. H. White; Mr. Difford; Mr. Douglas Gough; Ray Brice; Ron Dyke; Mr. Evans; Len Winter; Dick Lewis; Mr. Cosh; Mr. Pitman
Middle Row: Unknown; Reg Evans; Mr. Howard; Tim Hill; Unknown; Cyril Gregory; George Gilling; Aubrey Gough; Alf Varney
Front Row: L/Cpl. Bill Baker; L/Cpl. Fitzgeorge; L/Cpl. George Mansfield; L/Cpl. Bill Barber; Sgt. Garn Lewis; Lt. Gilbert Brown; Lt. Bernard Butcher; Sgt. Stan Chick; Cpl. Jimmy Foot; Cpl. Met Evans; L/Cpl. Farthing; Cpl. Reg Thatcher
(Richard Brown collection)

Mr. Pitman, Mr. H. White, Tim Hill and Met Evans were all market gardeners whilst Alf Varney was a strawberry grower. Mr. Difford was the local handyman. Douglas and Aubrey Gough worked for Axbridge Rural District Council whilst Mr. Farthing was the treasurer. Ray Brice was the local dairyman, Gilbert Brown owning Cheddar Valley Dairy Company at Rooksbridge. The farming community was represented by Ron Dyke and Reg Evans. Several Home Guard members were involved in quarrying, namely Mr. Evans and Bernard Butcher (Batscombe), and Reg Thatcher (Chelmscombe). Len Winter worked for Callow Lime Rock. Bread was supplied by Dick Lewis, Garn Lewis and Bill Baker. Mr. Cosh was employed by Bristol Water Works. J. Scorse and Co. employed Mr. Howard as a painter and decorator whilst Stan Chick was another painter and decorator. George Mansfield was employed as a general labourer. Bill Barber was a potter, producing items that were sold in local shops principally catering for the tourist. The kiln was situated in the old paper mill featured in the photograph above. This building also housed a cider works. Jimmy Foot was a local printer who had fought in France in WW1 with the King's Royal Rifles. After being wounded he was sent back to England, for a year in hospital to recover. His daughter remembers the Home Guard rifles being stored in a cupboard under the stairs at Cheddar Valley Press which Mr. Foot owned and where he lived. Better-off inhabitants could buy wireless sets and have them repaired at Cyril Gregory's shop which also provided an accumulator-charging service. Ernest Packer was at various times a farmworker, builder's labourer and concrete worker.

Cheddar Platoon in Bath Street.
Leading the column are Lt. Bernard Butcher and Lt. Gilbert Brown, behind them Sgt. Edson.
Column nearest camera: Sgt. Garn Lewis; L/Cpl. George Mansfield; Tim Hill; Unknown; Ernest Packer; Mr. Howard; Unknown; George Gilling; Unknown
Centre column: Unknown; Unknown; L/Cpl. Fitzgeorge; Unknown; Unknown; Unknown; Dick Lewis; Cyril Gregory; Len Winter
Column furthest from camera: Harold Starr; L/Cpl. Farthing; Mr. Cosh; Ray Brice; Unknown; Unknown; Reg Evans; Mr. Banbury
(Richard Brown collection)

(right) **Banwell Home Guard**.
Back Row: Sidney Steer; Raymond Daw; Stanley Harris; George Neads; Cpl. Bill Tabbrett; Donald Rains; David 'Dewey' Davies; Albert Clarke
Middle Row: Edgar Badman; John Clarke; L/Cpl. Ken Hunt; Ted Croaker; Morris Hembury; Ross Saint; Tom Lack; Frank Newton; Reg Rice; Unknown
Front Row: L/Cpl. Norman Bishop; L/Cpl. Eddie Evans; Frank Keate; Jim Cannon; Lt. Millard; Lt. Pat Channon; 2nd Lt. Jack Bradfield; Sgt. Leonard Jones; Bob Stabbins
Although unidentified, the man at the end of the middle row joined the Home Guard late in the war and lived next to the church gates. Jim Cannon was the manager of Sandford Quarry whilst Lt. Millard was manager of the Westminster Bank, Winscombe.
(Roy Rice collection)

(above) With Raymond Daw now sporting corporal's stripes, this photograph was probably taken some time after the one at the top of the page. With wet tarmac visible this may have been taken on 3rd December 1944 as rain fell over most parts of Somerset that day.
Back Row: Albert Clarke; Sidney Steer; Frank Newton; Tom Lack; Edgar Badman; Bob Stabbins; Morris Hembury; David 'Dewey' Davies
Front Row: L/Cpl. Norman Bishop; Cpl. Bill Tabbrett; Frank Keate; 2nd Lt. Jack Bradfield; Sgt. Leonard Jones; Cpl. Raymond Daw; L/Cpl. Eddie Evans.
(Roy Rice collection)

(right) Like so many villages on important routes, Banwell Home Guard planned to obstruct the main road as the drawing kindly reproduced by Roy Rice from an original in the John Keates collection shows.

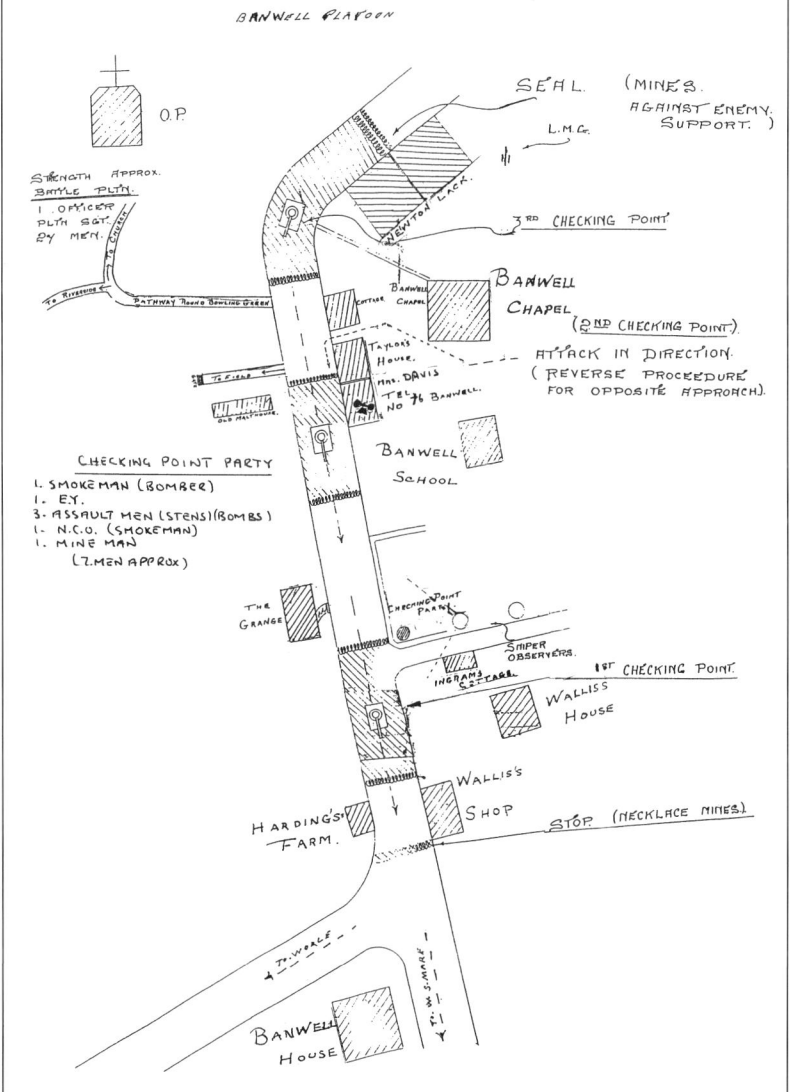

Joseph Councell Gibbs of Green Farm, Biddisham and Joe Comer of Manor Farm were veterans of The Great War. It was at Green Farm that a Home Guard unit was formed under the command of Lt. Gibbs, their numbers reaching about 30. Don Ham and Don Burbridge became dispatch riders as they both owned motorcycles.

For storage of ammunition a standard Nissen hut was built in the yard at Green Farm at map ref. ST 381 538. Demolished after the war, its base now forms the foundation of a greenhouse. A similar hut was built in the field adjacent to 'Hobbs Boat' at Lympsham.

With a shortage of weapons shotguns were carried by some of the men. Before 'lethal ball' ammunition could be fired it was necessary for the guns to be inspected. Joseph Gibbs' gun was sent to Bristol for examination and returned with a 'B' stamped behind the trigger guard, indicating it was approved for lethal ball.

Joseph's copy of the 5th Edition Ordnance Survey map of the area shows some interesting pencilled marks at various locations to the east of Biddisham. All are situated on roads, mostly leading either to Cheddar or to Wedmore, and appear to show the positions of road blocks or check points. Arrangements such as this would have been repeated throughout the County as a co-ordinated attempt to slow down invading forces.

In 1944 Joseph Gibbs' son Guy was a member of Taunton School O.T.C. On the morning of December 3rd 1944 preparations were well in hand for the Stand Down Parade of the Taunton Home Guard. Due to an oversight no military band was available to lead the column. At the eleventh hour Taunton School's O.T.C. Band stepped into the breach and lead the parade which terminated at Vivary Park. All proceeded well until the order, 'Pile drums' was given. The band had not been taught this drill but a creditable effort was made and passed without comment.

Roy Clapp recounts his memories of night-time guard duty. Ernest Popham was prone to snore so it became standard practice to put him on guard duty first, then send him home. At around 11.30, the rest of us were in our Guard hut when we heard Ernest's loud voice shouting: "Halt! Who goes there?". Silence. The challenge was repeated three times. Then: "Halt or I fire". Still silence. Ernest chambered a round. Coming up the A38 was a villager pushing her pram who had been visiting her parents. All was well, but when Ernest came off watch, he entered the hut, squeezed the trigger and the shot missed a fellow Home Guard by inches.

'E' (WRINGTON) COMPANY

COMMANDING OFFICER   Major R.F. Lyne
2ND IN COMMAND   Capt. G.W. Anson, M.B.E., M.C.

Officers and N.C.O.s of 'E' (Wrington) Company.
Back Row: Bill Organ; Sgt. Harry Wookey; Unknown; Unknown; Unknown; William Lane; Alfred Greenslade; Unknown; Unknown; Ernest Drew
Middle Row: Lt. A.R.S. Toothill; Unknown; Sgt. A.R. Millard; Sgt. A. Dicker; Sgt. W. Burns; Unknown; Sgt. A. Barnes; 2nd Lt. Tidman; Unknown; 2nd Lt. Frank Light; Lt. G.T. Meller; Unknown
Front Row: Lt. J.S. Frith; Capt. Wilfred Anson; Major R.F. Lyne; Dr. H.A. Bell; Lt. S.R. Jones
Transferred into the new 13th Battalion in May 1943 the caption suggests that the above photograph was taken before then.
(Roy Millard collection)

Fortunately a complete set of early enrolment cards has survived for members of Wrington Company when it was part of the 8th (Weston) Battalion. Salient details follow in the relevant sections.

Key: (T/F) – transferred   (C) – called up
         (R) – resigned   (D) – discharged

In some cases this is then followed by a date. It is not known if this is the actual date of leaving or the date when published in Part II orders. Occasionally a comment 'Part II' followed by a date has been pencilled on the card but no explanation of why the individual was mentioned in Part II Orders.

Blagdon Platoon.
Back Row: Dennis Clark; Reg Baber; George Lewis; Alfred James Greenslade; Charlie Durbin; Bert Pearce; Maurice Payne; Bert Hollier; Alfred Hemmens; Jack Brean
Second Row: A.W. Tripp?; Unknown; Bill Bush; L/Cpl. Bernard Downey; Sid Redgers; Charlie Chamberlain; Gilbert Morris; Ern Cole; L/Cpl. Frank Pearce (or Pearse); Jack Clark
Third Row: L/Cpl. Bert Buxton; Cpl. James Murphy; Sgt. Laurie Williamson; 2nd Lt. Francis Henry Light; Lt. Grahame Temple Meller; Sgt. Denvers; Sgt. Dennis Tricks; Cpl. Reg Jones; L/Cpl. Archie Kingman
Front Row: Glyn Stone; Dick Shipsey; Ted Crocker; Henry Hemmens; Charlie Marks; Arthur Cook; Len Coles; Jim Bush
The identification of Lt. Meller is based on the premise that he is the only Lieutenant listed in the nominal roll for Blagdon Platoon. He also appears in the previous photograph.
(Royal British Legion, Wrington Branch)

Blagdon Platoon's duties included guarding the dam at Blagdon Reservoir where a corrugated iron hut was used as a shelter for the picquet. It was the standard drill when coming off guard in the morning for the senior N.C.O. to ensure that all weapons were made safe. Yet again another accident during the procedure resulted in a hole being shot in the side of the hut.

One morning Dennis Tricks offered a lift in his car to a fellow Home Guard coming off-duty. As the passenger climbed into Sgt. Tricks's car his Sten gun was accidently fired resulting in a superficial wound to Sgt. Tricks. His request for a wound badge (as he had been on duty) was refused, Sgt. Tricks receiving a severe reprimand instead.

This was the second time that Sgt. Tricks had been disappointed. Having served in the First World War, he rightly expected to be given the rank of 2nd Lieutenant (Platoon Officer). However, he was passed over in favour of Francis Light, the village postmaster, as he possessed a telephone.

Alfred James Greenslade was an ex-naval officer with 22 years service. His military training caused him no difficulties in accepting orders from 19 year old Sgt. Kenneth Greenslade, his son.

Butcombe Section, Blagdon Platoon at Butcombe Court in November 1943.
Back Row: H. Hemmens; R.G. Gibbs; J. Clark; R.G. Bendall; A. Brailey
Middle Row: E. Crocker; A.J. Bendall; R. Maclaren; B. Patch; F. Day; J. Hemmens
Front Row: Cpl. A. Gibbs; Cpl. B.F. Somers; Sgt. R.S. Denvers; J.B. Hope-Simpson; L.A. Coles
Absent were A. Brean; A. Cook; D. Clark; C.E. Marks and M.G. Bendall
(Author's collection)

Butcombe Section Blagdon Platoon

Benjamin William Beardsworth
    (T/F 27.5.42)
Arthur James Bendall
Reginald Gay Bendall
Maurice George Bendall
Allen Brean (ex Redhill Section)

J.F. Clark
Leonard Alfred Coles
Charles Douglas Crocker
    (C. 3.3.42)
Edward James Crocker
Francis Edmund Cross

Kenneth Edmund James Cross
    (T/F Regular Army 1942)
Francis William Albert Day
Sgt. Rewforth Silvey Denvers
Cpl. Archibald James Gibbs
Bertram Frederick Somers

Edmund Michael Sharp
    (C. 17.11.41)
Kenneth John Tregidgo
Ronald Leslie Warford
    (T/F Regular Army 1942)

Village Section Blagdon Platoon

Reginald Arthur Baber
Cpl. Roland John Lere Boyd
L/Cpl. Charles Thomas Brunt
Roderick Campbell-Kaye
    (Pt. II 1942)
Arthur Chamberlain
Philip Sidney Cole (C. 1942)
Ernest George Coles
John William Filer (R. Feb. 1942)

William Leslie Filer
James Gilling
Wilfred Victor James Green
Alfred James Greenslade
L/Sgt. Kenneth James Greenslade
Robert James Gulliver
Alvan Henry Harris (C. 1942)
Frank Henry Hollier
L/Cpl. Reginald Beaman Jones

Archibald Joseph Kingman
George Arthur Joseph Lewis
2nd Lt. Francis Henry Light
Wilfred James Light (D. 21.4.42)
Daniel Reece Lovell
Arthur Raymond Lyons (C. 2.9.42)
Benjamin Watts Lyons
Lt. Grahame Temple Meller
Joseph George Henry Mitchell

Gilbert Charles Parsons
Robert Cecil Parsons
L/Cpl. Francis John Floyd Pearse
Edward James Russell
    (R., joined A.F.S.)
Cyril Randolph Mark Stevens
    (C. 11.9.42)
Dennis Norman Frederick Tricks
Cyril Tucker
Maurice Albion Villis (Joined up)

Water Works Section Blagdon Platoon

John Balch
Harold James Bath
Francis William Board
James Edward Bush
William John Bush
L/Cpl. Gilbert Buxton
Donald Clark
William Coles
Morris W. Collier

Frank Davis
Charles George Durbin
Edward Durbin
Frederick Fear (R. 21.2.41)
Frederick Flower
Reginald Arthur Filer (R. 20.9.42)
L/Cpl. Frederick Gregory
Archibald Beaumont Harris
John Howard Ladbrook (C. 22.7.42)

James Lewthwaite
Sidney Theodore Matthews
William George Monk
L/Cpl. James Borthwick Murdoch
Cpl. James Murphy
William Herbert Pearce
James Reginald George Pitman
    (R. 30.12.41)
Charles Henry Redgers

Sidney Thomas Redgers
Victor Sainsbury
Rowland Frank Skinner
    (R. 20.11.42)
Jonathon George Weaver
Ernest Charles John Westbrook
    (R. 30.12.41)
Sgt. John Williamson
Laurie Hunter Williamson

No. 1 CHURCHILL PLATOON

Roy Millard joined the Home Guard in 1942 aged 17. In 1943 he joined the Royal Marines. The operational role of the platoon was defined as follows:

(a)   to harass the enemy and destroy them in any attempt they make to pass or attack;

(b)   the aggressive defence of the Cross Roads at Churchill and destruction of the enemy if any attempt to use same is made.

Original notes dated September 1940, held by Roy, indicate that Churchill Platoon was originally part of 'D' Company whose headquarters was at The Assembly Rooms in Winscombe. Roy remembers being told that when the Army removed the Spigot Mortar located on The Batch opposite Dolberrow Warren it was found to be incorrectly sighted. Projectiles intended to strike the crossroads would have hit the school 100 yards away. Officers also included a 2nd Lt. Eveleigh who was the Signals Officer. He was over 70 years of age and would cycle from Weston-super-Mare with large flags strapped to his bicycle to give weekly instruction in Morse Code, semaphore and other signal topics. Practice in the summer was carried out on The Batch.

Members of No. 1 Section Churchill Platoon, based on Churchill:

L/Cpl. Albion Charles Coles
Sgt. Arthur Thomas Dicker
    (Platoon Sergeant)
Edmund Charles Haddrell
William Edwin Harry Hancock
Robert Dunnett Jackson
L/Cpl. Albert Edward Kington
Victor Clarence Newton
John Frank Parkin-Bell (C. 18.4.41)

Thomas Shorland Roynon
Douglas Stedman Small (C. 18.12.41)
Alfred James Taylor
2nd Lt. Alfred Roy Stanley Toothill
James Arthur Tyley
    (T/F Pioneer Corp.)
Clifford Charles Williams
Cpl. Edwin James Wookey
James William Wright

Members of No. 2 Section Churchill Platoon, based on Lower Langford:

Arthur John Badman
Cpl. Arthur Ernest Barnes
Francis Willard Board (R)
Clifford James Burdge
Sgt. William Burns
Frederick Joseph Corp
Donald Sidney Day

Cpl. Fred Hale
Wyndham Charles Hewlett
Charles P. Leydell Hibbard
Russell Percival Howell (T/F. 4.2.42)
James Stewart William Jones
John Henry London
Thomas William Yeeles

Members of No. 3 Section Churchill Platoon, based on Upper Langford:

Keith Wilfred Crabbe (R. 31.1.42)	Joseph George Lintern
Albert Frost	Edward George Norton
Kenneth Stanley Champion Frost	Sgt. King Edward Kitchener Plumley
Cpl. Frederick James Gilling	Frederick Ernest Pring (C. 18.12.41)
Samuel Grundy	Reginald John Rouse
Ronald Sidney Hill (R. 18.12.41)	Joseph Hilton Smith
Ivor Keel	Cpl. Robert Hilton Smith
Reginald Frank Keel	Richard Williams (R. 14.10.41)

Members of No. 4 Section Churchill Platoon, based on Burrington:

Reginald William Charles Young (R. 24.2.42)	Norman Kitchener Kirby (Pt. II 20.11.42, T/F 7th Batt.)
Francis William Batson	Reuben Martin (R. 24.2.42)
Sidney Joseph Bosley	Sgt. Arthur Raymond Millard
Arthur George Brooks	Herbert John Purnell
Arthur Francis Coles	Cpl. Charles Herbert Reason
Christopher Withington Harper	L/Cpl. Ernest P. Wilson
Wilfred Evan George Harvey	Frederick George Wookey
	Sgt. Henry Clement Wookey

No. 1 (Churchill) Platoon.
Back Row: Unknown; Roy W. Millard; Unknown; Unknown; C. Haddrell; Unknown; Unknown; E. Norton; T. Roynon; Unknown; Unknown; Unknown; Unknown
Second Row: F. Hale; Mr. Roe; R. Smith; L/Cpl. Albert Kington; Cpl. A. Coles; Unknown; Unknown; Unknown; Cpl. C. Reason; V. Bridges; A. Taylor; Unknown
Third Row: C. Hibbard; B. Legge; Unknown; J. Badman; V. Newton; H. Hancock; L/Cpl. E. Wilson; R. Lee; S. Westlake; H. Carpenter; Unknown; L/Cpl. C. Harper; Unknown; R. Seaton
Fourth Row: W. Hewlett; J. Purnell; Sgt. A.R. Millard; Sgt. W. Burns; Sgt. A. Dicker; Lt. S.R. Jones; 2nd Lt. A.R.S. Toothill; Sgt. H. Wookey; Sgt. A.E. Barnes; Sgt. R.D. Jackson, M.C.; Unknown; A. Chaplin
Front Row: Unknown; F. Wookey; Unknown; S. Bosley; Unknown; R. Small; D. Hedges; Unknown; Unknown
(Mrs. Jean Darby collection)

Shipham Section Churchill Platoon.
Back Row: George Thiery; Stanley Edward Harding; Charlie Barber; Bevis Sawtell; Gilbert Foord; Charles Hain?; Unknown
Second Row: Oliver Perkins; Ken Adams; Percy Foord; Percy Brooks; Harry Day; Eric Adams; Edmund 'Jack' Branch
Third Row: Rowland Day; L/Cpl. Peter Garrett; L/Cpl. Sidney 'Cecil' Fountain; Sgt. Jack Moss; Lt. Charles William Poulsford; Cpl. George Smith; Cpl. Hurt; Wally Watts; Frank Foord
Front Row: Ray Thomas; Mervyn Fountain; Colin Ford; Unknown; Charles Reason.
(Royal British Legion, Wrington Branch)

Peter Garrett, a 17-year-old schoolbnoy when the photograph was taken, recalls some details of Platoon members. Stanley Harding busied himself in the manufacture of Molotov Cocktails and the modification of 12-bore shotgun cartridges, either by pouring candle wax around the shot or by replacing it with somewhat larger lumps of lead. Jack Moss was landlord of *The Miners Arms*, Shipham, whilst George Smith owned Rowberrow Dump Garage, taking over from Foster Redfern who had become a P.O.W. of the Japanese. Eric Adams, although included in the Platoon photograph, had already left the Home Guard and joined the Army, as close examination of the photograph indicates his cap badge is not a Somerset Light Infantry one. Cpl. Hurt, it is believed, was a Regular Army instructor. Oliver Perkins was a local estate agent and auctioneer. Rowland Day was born in 1909. A serious motorbike accident when he was 21 nearly cost him a leg. Declared unfit for military service, he joined the Home Guard on 18th June 1940. Anthony Wade was called up on 4th February 1942, later joining the 2nd Battalion Duke of Cornwall's L.I. He was killed on 8th August 1944, aged just 21, and is buried in the Florence War Cemetery Plot 5, Row F, Grave 11.

In 1940 membership of Shipham Section included:

L/Cpl. Eric Adams	Edward George Fountain	Ernest Ronald Lenthall	Arthur Rowland Thomas
Kenneth Adams	Sidney Fountain	Gilbert Ronald Lenthall	Raymond Albert Thomas
Charles Henry Barber	Derrick Mark Garrett	Gilbert Lock	Anthony Philip Samuel Wade
Edmund Dury Branch	Peter Laurie Garrett	Sgt. John Lapthorne Moss	(C. 4.2.42)
Edward Victor Conibere (C. 11.9.42)	Charles George Hain (T/F Locking Airport H.G. about March 1941)	Lt. Charles William Pulsford	Roger Frederick James Wade
Ernest Henry Day		Joseph Francis Roper	Wallace George Watts (R. 1941)
Rowland Edward Day	Henry Roland Hares (C. 4.2.42)	Cpl. George Worsley Smith	Graham John White
Percy William Foord		Harold Spence	Kenneth Yarde (C. 1942)
		George William Thiery	L/Cpl. Edward Thomas Young

Brinsea Section Congresbury Platoon.
Back Row: A.J. Sydenham; Unknown; Herbert Norton; Unknown; Unknown; George Birch; Unknown; Unknown; Unknown; 'Major' J.S. Frith
Front Row: Unknown; Mr. Ackery; Cpl. Reg Edwards; Cpl. Harold Harvey; Sgt. Wilfred Cleverton (Managing Director of Cheddar Valley Egg Distribution); Unknown; Unknown; Unknown.
Sgt. Cleverton did not have a telephone and in the case of an emergency could only be contacted via his neighbour.
(Mrs. Jean Darby collection)

CONGRESBURY PLATOON

Brinsea Section

Walter John Ashford
Sgt. Wilfred Laurier Cleverdon
    (Section Leader)
Cpl. Reginald Ernest Edwards
    (Section 2nd In Command)

William Charles Edwards
Cpl. Melvin Howard Ellis
Charles Adrian Ford
Dennis Sidney Gill (C. 2.9.42)
John Ernest Golby (T/F 18.12.41)

Douglas Oliver Charles Hall
L/Cpl. Harold Edward Harvey
Richard Hendon (R. 1942)
Frank John Neath
Herbert Charles Norton

Eric Mervyn Pincott (Services no
    longer required 18.12.41)
Alfred Thomas Richards
Arthur A. Richards
William James Sparex (D. 11.9.42)
Albert Thatcher

Centre Section

Those listed below are again extracted from the card index. Of interest are the pencilled notes on the records for L/Cpl. Stephen S. Fairhurst and William A.C. Price, 'Transferred Special Section'. These two section members became members of a local Auxiliary Unit.

George Ormston Claridge
    (Section 2nd In Command)
William Henry Archibald Cockram
    (R. 29.12.41)
Samuel John Dyer
Stanley George Edwards

L/Cpl. Stephen Samuel Fairhurst
    (T. Special Section 20.1.42)
L/Cpl. Reginal Fisher
Lt. James Stratton Frith
    (Platoon Commander)
Percy Nunny Gill

Lionel Murlif Griffin
Anthony Edgar Jarman
    (Pt. II, 20.1.42)
William Edward Jones (R. 4.2.42)
Sgt. John Percival Jones
Norman John Martin
Walter Henry Palmer
Cpl. George Parsons (C. 8.7.42)
William Thomas Phippen
Kenneth John Pike
William John Pollitt (C. 12.3.42)

William Alfred Charles Price
    (T. Special Section 5.1.42)
Cpl. L.H. Robbins
Cpl. Archibald Stacey
2nd Lt. Albert James Sydenham
    (Section Leader)
John Henry Thomas
Albert Edgar Wheeler
Tom Wheeler (R. 29.12.41)

(left) Congresbury Platoon.
Back Row: none identified
Second Row: No. 13 Bill Phippen; No. 14 George Birch; No. 15 possibly Mr. Ackery
Third Row: Unknown; Cpl. Ellis; Cpl. Jack Hamblin; Unknown; Sgt. Wilfred Cleverton; Unknown; 'Major' J.S. Frith; A.J. Sydenham; Unknown; Unknown; Unknown; Mr. Gardiner; Unknown; Unknown; Harold Harvey; Reg Edwards
Front Row: No. 5 Mr. Hunt

'Major' Frith was the Platoon Commander with the rank of Lieutenant. The title 'Major' originated from his First World War rank. He lived at what is now The Cadbury Country Club. George Birch was a garage mechanic at Congresbury. Harold Harvey was also in trade in Congresbury as a coal merchant working out of the railway yard. Mr. Hunt worked at Sheppey's Flour Mill.
(Mrs. Jean Darby collection)

Hewish Section

Again no photograph has been found but the members were as follows:

Edwin John Banwell (C. 21.4.42)
Richard Champion
L/Cpl. James Sandys Cox
William Cox
Reginald Walton Curry

Bertram Neil Emerson
Herbert Frost (R. 24.2.42)
L/Cpl. Raymond Gardiner
Mervyn Leonard Hale
   (C. 18.12.41)

Sgt. George Edward Hancock
   (Section Leader)
Henry George Hewlett
Leslie Alexander Horler
   (Services no longer
   required 18.12.41)
Robert Jesse Jones
Harold King
Leslie John King

Edward James Reece Lutley
Sgt. Charles Richardson Oliver
Arthur William Parker
Percival Sidney Parker
Sidney Parker
George Poulsom
Leslie George Raines
Cpl. George Star
William Henry Watts

Wrington Road Section

Leonard William Atherton
Frederick Cornelius (T. 1942)
C.Q.M.S. Thomas Day
   (Company Quartermaster)
William Herbert Flint

Sgt. Walter Leonard Gardner
   (Platoon 2nd In Command
   and Quartermaster)
Graham Charles Griffiths
Trevor Hamlin (Pt. II, 14.10.41)

Cpl. William John E. Hamlin
   (Section 2nd In Command)
Aldwyn William Hiles
Frederick Hunt
James George Hunt (Pt. II, 14.10.41)

Sgt. William Walter Keel
   (Section Leader)
Montague Lane
Robert George Trapnell (C. 11.9.42)
Leonard Fred Tratt
Frederick James Wear

Wrington Road Section Congresbury Platoon.
With a Mr. Hunt identified, front row No. 3, and 'Major' J.S. Frith, back row No. 1, this photograph is thought to be that of Wrington Road Section. (Mrs. Shirley Grant collection)

No. 2 Section

Frederick William Foxall Page (H.M. Forces 17.2.42)

No. 4 Section
Clifford Albert Winter

The above two Sections were probably re-titled, a clerical error resulting in two one-man sections!

WRINGTON PLATOON

Just to the north of Lulsgate nestles the hamlet of Downside which was, in 1940, able to muster the following men to form a Section:

Cpl. Edwin John Newman Briffett
George Clifford Buncombe
   (R. 3.4.41)
Albert James Cleeves (R. 1.12.40)
George Henry Cleeves
Raymond John Cleeves
   (C. 4.2.42)

Robert Charles Cleeves
Sidney Francis Dyer
Alec George Febrey
   (Pt. II, February 1942)
Percy Harse
Walter Fred Holloway
Arthur Edward George Lock

Sgt. Charles Henry Lock
Frederick Silvester Lock
Philip Charles Lock
   (C. 8.7.43)
Stanley Christopher William Lock
   (R. 22.2.43)
Walter Lock

Arthur Marshall
Cpl. Frank Marshall
Walter Milton
Leslie John Pell
Frederick James Stokes
William Hopkin Stokes (C. 22.7.42)
James Young

Redhill Section Wrington Platoon in 1941.
Back Row: W. Andrews; R.J. Lowis; H. Rudeman or F. Harding; A. Ashley; Mr. Hemmings or Mr. Ellis; C. Kitchen; Mr. Stevens; Mr. Rugman
Middle Row: H. Fear; F. Bennett; H. Ogbourne; W. Perry; C. Harding; J. Banwell; G. Crocker; E. Goodenough; H. Vauden; J. Crocker
Front Row: H. Crocker; W. Brean; L/Cpl. J. Hucker; Cpl. C. Wilkins; Sgt. S. Bingham; 2nd Lt. Tidman; Cpl. S. Baldwin; L/Cpl. R. Banwell; L/Cpl. A. Crocker; T. Brean; Mr. Wyatt or Atherton
Absentees: E. Ashman; H. Ashman; Mr. Marshall; Mr. Stiles; Mr. Taylor; Mr. Throssell; Mr. White
The photograph was taken before Mr. Goodenough lost the sight of one eye when it was hit by an ejected cartridge case on Yoxter rifle range.
(Mrs. S. Crocker collection)

Redhill Section, 1941

Arthur Henry Ashley
Cpl. George Edward Baldwin
L/Cpl. Francis Raymond Banwell
Thomas John Banwell
Edwin Gibbs Berry (R. 24.2.42)
Duncan Henry Bingham
   (Pt. II, 31.7.42)
Cpl. Henry G. Bingham
Frederick Thomas Brean
   (R. 19.12.41)
Thomas Henry Brean
William Brean
Norman Edward Brean
Robert James Buxton
L/Cpl. Arthur Henry Crocker
Gilbert Crocker
Gordon Crocker
Henry Crocker
L/Cpl. Arthur John Hucker
Charles Edgar Kitchen
Robert James Lowis
D.R. Markland
   (T. 4.2.42)
Gilbert Marshall
Reginald James Ogbourne
   (R. 18.12.41)
Arthur William John Perry
John Henry Shepherd
L/Cpl. George Rowland Stevens
Arthur Eric Stiles
Sgt. Harold Tidman
Harold Arthur Vauden
Frank White
Edwin Sylvester Wilkins
   (C. 22.7.42)
L/Cpl. George Sylvester Wilkins

Alfred Hudson was born in Bristol and spent his youth growing up during the war and in a couple of letters written in 2001 he outlined his life then. His story was typical for many of the young rural generation of that time.

At the beginning of the war, at the age of 14, I was working near Wells. Later I moved to Redhill where I worked on three different farms. At Lye Pole Farm I was what you would call a farm boy. At the age of 16 when I was at Redhill I was getting around 17/6d (87½p) per week plus keep. I worked seven days a week, sometimes to 9 p.m. at hay-making time. The Redhill Home Guard's Headquarters was *The Redhill* Pub which still stands. I asked if I could join them and was accepted but being 16 I could not have a rifle, although I could train with them once a week. The officers and some others had been in The Great War.

Later in 1943 the airport at Redhill was being prepared for fighter planes. We trained in the woods overlooking the Weston Road and one job was to guard the new airport. It was often very foggy so many planes left, leaving a few to protect Bristol. I used to go from village to village on my push-bike which cost 30/- (£1.50). It was nice to be with older men because on the farms one would be working alone. Later I moved away from farming and went to Winford where I joined their Home Guard. Their meeting place was *The Prince of Waterloo*. It was here I was issued with my own rifle. We used to have enjoyable days out shooting on the range at Clevedon.

I can recall a job I had was hauling ash and cinders from hospital boiler rooms to Redhill airfield. We used to collect about 15 tons a day. It was thirsty work but cider was available at 4d per pint.

In June 1944 when I was 18 I left the Home Guard, being called up for Military Service. By the time I joined the Army I had been earning around £3.00 a week.

I left the Army in 1947 returning to my mother's home at 21, Caledonia Place, Clifton where I started work in a town earning about £5.00 per week. When I retired in 1991 I was earning £5.00 an hour.

Wrington Section

The home village of the Company Commander, Major R.F. Lyne who lived at Woodlands, and his 2nd i/c, Capt. G.W. Anson who resided at West Hay, Wrington Section mustered some 48 men of all ranks as listed below:

Capt. George Wilfred Anson	Francis George Corfield	Harold Frank Leigh	James Percival Roe (C. 12.3.42)
Malcolm Allinson Anson	Albert Edward Ivor George Corrick	Major Robert Francis Lyne	James Short
Stanley George Bailey	Sidney Hugh Cox	Roland Mark (R. 24.2.42)	William John Smith (R. 4.2.42)
Lt. Harold Alexander Bell	Clifford Crocker (C. 3.3.42)	Leonard Millard	L/Cpl. Harry Steer
Joseph Sidney Bird (T. 21.4.42)	Frederick Arthur Crook	Oliver John Millard	Ernest Tincknell (C. 18.2.41)
Robert Henry Brice (Pt. II, 4.2.42)	Cpl. Norman Alfred Day	Arthur Herbert Nipper (C. 12.3.42)	Ronald William Tincknell
Thomas Edward Brice	Thomas Meyrick Deakin	Cpl. Richard Kenneth Organ	William Tincknell
Thomas Ridgway Bridson	Cpl. John Frederick Dobson	2nd Lt. William Henry Organ	L/Cpl. Roy B. Tripp
L/Cpl. Douglas Harry Winden Chapman	Thomas Henry Ferris (C. 18.12.41)	Sgt. Edward Maurice Owens	Frank E. Vowles
Cpl. Thomas Cleeves	Lionel George Gunning	Arthur James Pickford (T/F 21.4.42)	Thomas Edgar Vowles
Gordon Percival Cockram	Arthur Reginald (or R.A.) Lewis	Richard Thomas Plumley	John Desmond Wills
Henry George Collins	(T/F Nailsea)	George Sidney Puddy (C. 31.7.42)	Cpl. Dubric Wood
			Edward John Wyatt

'H' (WEDMORE) COMPANY

COMMANDING OFFICER   Major E.J. Banwell, M.B.E.   2ND IN COMMAND   Capt. W. Bowles

Company Headquarters was initially in West Holme Farm, Wedmore, the home of Major Ernest Banwell. He was a veteran of the First World War where he served in the North Somerset Yeomanry. Later in the war, two prefabricated wooden huts were delivered to the farm and erected as one building in the garden of West Holme Farm to serve as Company Headquarters. Ian Banwell recalls that in about 1943 two Nissen huts, with doors at each end and a centre partition of 9" blocks laid on flat, were erected in the orchard behind West Holme Farm. These would have been storage sheds for munitions. Detailed instructions prepared at the time stated that explosives were to be stored at one end whilst inflammable materials were to be stored at the other, with a substantial wall separating the two storage areas.

Writing in 2001, Eric Kingston, who joined the Home Guard on 14th February 1941, remembers that the Wedmore Company comprised men from the villages of Wedmore, Blackford, Theale, Allerton and Weare. With a major route, the A38, running close by, duties included guarding the bridge over the River Axe where a road block was constructed. Men of Blackford, Theale and Wedmore were rostered to patrol the village of Wedmore during the hours of darkness. This would occur about once a fortnight.

Live firing practice took place on the range at Yoxter where facilities also existed for grenade practice. Although allowed to take his rifle home, it was not until he had passed a test that Eric was allowed to keep ammunition at home.

Wedmore Company Headquarters in 2000. (Author's collection)

Some weapons and general stores were held at Sgt. Edwin Wall's blacksmith's shop in the High Street, Blackford. Ammunition was stored at The Police Station in Church Street, Wedmore, since demolished. Blackford County Primary School was one of the locations used for evening drill.

On the evening of Saturday 7th September 1940, the night of the invasion scare, officers and N.C.O.s were gathering at West Holme Farm. Even the local vicar called to offer his assistance. Finding the house getting crowded Major Banwell asked the vicar to take some of the men to the cider store and give them a drink. Seeing two large barrels and one small one, the vicar drew a pint off the small barrel and handed it to the nearest man who took a large swig and immediately sprayed it out over the vicar – he had been served cider vinegar!

One Wedmore Home Guard observation post was on the Mudgley Road in a field known locally as Causlett where a bell tent was erected to provide shelter for the picket. One night, when Fred Cook was in charge of the observation post, Major Banwell decided to carry out a spot check and found them all fast asleep. Prodding one man with a bayonet Major Banwell hissed, "I am a German Paratrooper, do you know what to do?" "Yes, Sir," said the Home Guard, "I've just done it".

*A fine photograph of **Wedmore Company** taken by local photographer Charles Thomas Pitcher on Sunday December 3rd 1944.*

Back Row: Unknown; Unknown; Victor Davis (farmworker); Unknown; Ray Bethell (farmer); Unknown; Toby Kennedy (farmworker); Unknown; Harry Leigh (farmworker); Allan Cockayne; Jeff Cook; Unknown; Unknown; Eli Leigh (farmworker, brother of Harry); Unknown; L/Cpl. Stan Tincknell (worked for Sheldon's as a delivery driver); Unknown; George Wookey Duckett (farmer); Unknown; Unknown; Unknown; Unknown; Unknown; Unknown

Second Row: Unknown; Don Watts; John Duckett; George Banwell (farmer); Unknown; Reg Stitch (farmer); Walter Watts (farmworker); Albert Leigh (farmworker); Edward 'Ted' Amesbury (farmworker); L/Cpl. Eric Kingston (farmworker and thatcher); George Adams (farmworker); Unknown; Unknown; Cyril Rice (farmworker); Gilbert Dean (farmworker); Unknown; Henry Wheatley (worked for Wedmore Gas Works at the Lerburn); Walter Packer (farmworker); Albert Packer (farmworker, brother of Walter); Unknown; Unknown; Frank Pike (farmworker); Clarence Adams (baker's roundsman); Robert 'Bob' Nichols; Unknown; Unknown

Third Row: Sgt. Edwin Wall (blacksmith); Unknown; Unknown; Unknown; Albert Grimstead (farmworker); Unknown; Unknown; Wilfred Stowell (boot-maker); Unknown; Cpl. Frank Payne (market gardener); Unknown; Gus Millard; Unknown; Stanley Byrne (farmworker) or Donald Ham (agricultural contractor); Ray Hole; Unknown; Herbert Puddy (farmworker); Austin Fear; Unknown; Unknown; Unknown; Unknown; Unknown; Ivan Rice (worked at The Dairy as a cheesemaker, brother of Cyril Rice); Tom Denbee; George Harris; Unknown; Unknown; Bill Cattell; Rev. Daven Morris; Unknown; Ernest Tincknell (farmworker); George Arnold (farmworker); John Ham (farmworker); Unknown; Unknown; Ron Sully (farmworker); Henry Amesbury (farmworker); Cliff Fear (farmworker); Unknown; Unknown; Unknown; Jack Puddy (farmworker); Gilbert Harris (farmworker); Unknown

Fourth Row: Unknown; Cpl. Victor Stevens (road works supervisor); Unknown; Unknown; Unknown; Unknown; L/Cpl. James 'Jim' Clapp (shop-floor worker, R.A.F. Ordnance Factory, Bristol); Jack Binning; Unknown; Unknown; Unknown; Sgt. Sid Cook (gardener for a local solicitor); Unknown; Austin Champney; Capt. Bill Bowles, Company 2nd i/c; Major Ernest Banwell, Company Commander; Unknown; Unknown; Unknown; Sgt. Arnold Sugg; Sgt. Jim Callow; Unknown; Ernest Padfield; Unknown; Unknown; Unknown; Dick Tanner (quarryman); Bill Kerridge or Colston Brooks

Front Row: Unknown; Unknown; Unknown; William 'Bill' Larder (farmworker); Unknown; Unknown; Albert Roper (farmworker); Unknown; Randolph Duckett; Peter Urch; William Kitley (manager of an Egg Packing Station)

Ted Dean is missing from the photograph.

Whilst the above occupations were typical of a rural area, Henry Wheatley was a rather special 'one-man band', running Wedmore Gas Works at the Lerburn. His duties included changing gas mantles on the street lights.

(Mrs. Heather Banwell collection)

With so many men in the Wedmore Company, 135 of them being featured in the photograph above, accidents did happen from time to time. On one occasion Toby Kennedy, whilst preparing to go out on patrol, loaded his rifle, slammed the bolt shut, squeezed the trigger and promptly shot a hole through the ceiling of *The Lamb* Inn in Wedmore.

Two other members of the Home Guard are also remembered by their colleagues. On the humorous side, Ted Dean's party trick was to lie a man on the floor and lift him on to a table by grabbing his braces in his teeth.

Ray Hole, on the other hand, is remembered for his untimely death. At Stand Down, Home Guards were allowed to keep their clothing including their greatcoats. In the winter of 1946 or '47 he was chatting one day to Ian Banwell whilst standing by his tractor. Thirty minutes later he was dead, his army greatcoat having caught in the tractor power take-off, with fatal results.

South Somerset Group/Sector

HEADQUARTERS	Territorial Hall, Taunton (to 4.10.43)	H.Q. STAFF	
	6, Elm Grove, Taunton (after 4.10.43)	INTELLIGENCE OFFICER	Captain J.J. Aitkin, C.M.G., D.S.O., O.B.E.
DATE FORMED	21.10.40	LIAISON OFFICER	Major Broadmead
COMMANDING OFFICER	Col. C.L. Norman, D.S.O., M.V.O., D.L.		(Capt. T.E. Parker, M.C.)
2ND IN COMMAND	Lt. Col. B.C.H. Drew, C.M.G., C.V.O., C.B.E.	STAFF OFFICERS	Major C.D.G. Lyon, D.S.O., O.B.E.
	(Lt. Col. J.B. Taylor)		Captain H.I.R. Allfrey, D.S.O., M.C.
	(Lt. Col. C.F.W. Hughes, M.C.)		(Captain V.D.S. Williams)
			Capt. T.A. Bushell (Sector Signals Officer)

The South Somerset Group comprised the 1st (Minehead) Battalion, 2nd (Taunton) Battalion, 3rd (Yeovil) Battalion and 10th (Bridgwater) Battalion. In April 1943 the name was changed to South Somerset Sector. In the same year the 11th (Ilminster) Battalion and 12th (Somerton) Battalion were formed by detaching part of the 2nd (Taunton) and 3rd (Yeovil) Battalions respectively.

O/C SECTOR SIGNALS	Lt. A.N. Harries
TRANSPORT OFFICER	2nd Lt. L.J. Tolman
	(Lt. R.C. Unmack)
SECTION SECRETARY	Mrs. A. Downes
TRAINING OFFICER (attached)	Major Geary, The Buffs

(left) **South Somerset Sector HQ Staff**, *photographed in July 1944 at No. 6 Elm Grove, Taunton, which became Sector Headquarters on 4th October 1943.*
Back Row: Pte. Mogford; Cpl. Trim; Cpl. Paul; Cpl. Barrington
Middle Row: Cpl. Stanley Chedzoy; Sgt. (later 2nd Lt.) L.J. Tolman; Lt. (later Capt.) T.A. Bushell; Pte. Porter; Lt. A.N. Harries; L/Cpl. D. Hembrow; Cpl. Hold; Cpl. Fouracre
Front Row: Capt. H.R. Allfrey, D.S.O., M.C.; Major C.D.G. Lyon, D.S.O., O.B.E.; Lt. Col. B.C.H. Drew, C.M.G., C.V.O., C.B.E.; Colonel (Brigadier General retired) C.L. Norman, D.S.O., M.V.O., D.L. (Sector Commander); Mrs. A. Downes; Capt. J.J. Aitkin, C.M.G., D.S.O., O.B.E.; Major Broadmead
Sitting: Miss Joan Foster; Mrs. Wheeldown
(Donald Hembrow collection)

(right) **South Somerset Sector Dispatch Riders**.
Back Row: Cpl. Stanley Chedzoy; L/Cpl. Donald Hembrow; Cpl. Fouracre; Cpl. Paul
Front Row: Sgt. L.J. Tolman; Lt. A.N. Harries; Cpl. Hold
   Donald Hembrow joined the Home Guard in May 1943, subsequently joining the R.A.F. in July 1944 when these two photographs were taken. Although only a teenager at the time, he remembers being issued with a revolver when on duty as a dispatch rider attached to Sector Headquarters.
(Donald Hembrow collection)

1st Somerset (Minehead) Battalion

HEADQUARTERS	'Wyncote', Martlet Road, Minehead	AMMUNITION OFFICER	Lt. D.P. Hewett
DATE FORMED	May 1940	GAS OFFICER	Lt. R.C. Holden
COMMANDING OFFICER	Lt. Col. R.D. Alexander (from 13.9.42)	INTELLIGENCE OFFICER	Lt. W.H. Ashwin
	(Lt. Col. E.R. Clayton, C.M.G., D.S.O.)	LIAISON OFFICERS (Sector)	Lts. J.S.W. Arthur, Lt. H.J. Taylor, D.S.O.
2ND IN COMMAND	Major E.L.D. Ackland C.B., M.V.O.	(Military Report Centre)	2nd Lts. J.W. Rawle, M.C., A.C. Vowles
		(Minehead Invasion C'ttee)	Lt. E.H. Potter
H.Q. STAFF		(Watchet Invasion C'ttee)	Lt. W.D. Thomson
A & Q	Capt. H.S. Keynton, Somerset L.I.	MEDICAL OFFICER	Major W.T.P. Meade-King
ADJUTANT	Capt. P.E. Stanley, General List, Infantry	SIGNALS OFFICER	Lt. R. Kingsley Tayler

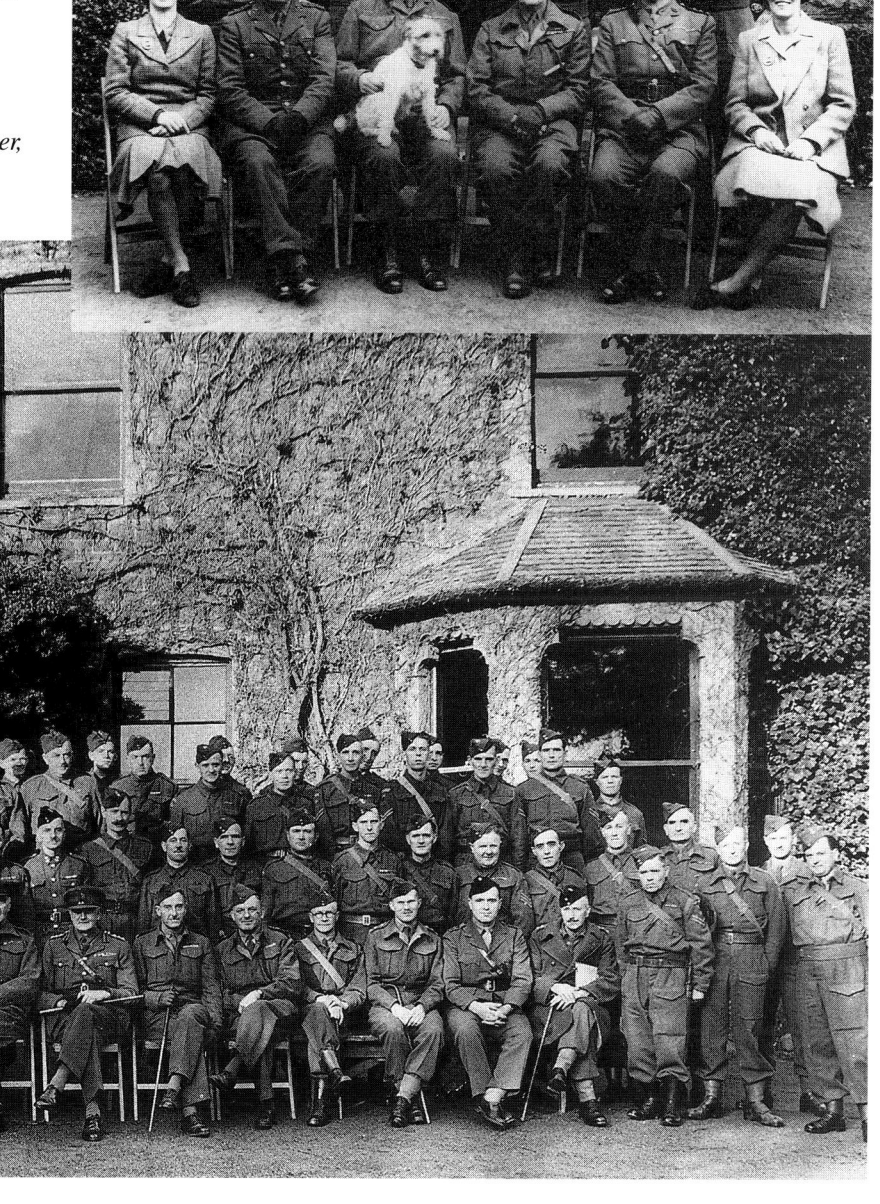

(right) **Headquarters Staff**, photographed at 'Wyncote', Martlet Road, Minehead. Both Mrs. Butter and Mrs. Kievill are wearing a brooch badge in plastic, which was intended to be worn on the left lapel, issued from July 1943 to 'Nominated Women'. This title was changed to 'Home Guard Auxiliaries' in July 1944. At Stand Down there were over 1,130 Home Guard Auxiliaries in the County Battalions.
Back Row: all unknown
Front Row: Mrs. M. Kievill; Capt. H.S. Keynton; Lt. Col. R.D. Alexander; Major E.L.D. Ackland, C.B., M.V.O.; Capt. P.E. Stanley; Mrs. M. Butter
(West Somerset Rural Life Museum collection)

(below) Another photograph taken at 'Wyncote'. Apart from Major E.M. Driver, No. 10 in the front row, no others appear to feature in other photographs.
(Mr. H. Gregory collection)

Officers of the 1st (Minehead) Battalion, *again photographed at 'Wyncote'. Note that the vegetation on the walls in the previous picture has been removed.*
Back Row: No. 9 Capt. Bill Parsons; No. 10 2nd Lt. A.C. Vowles;
  No. 11 Lt. Stoate; No. 12 Lt. W.F. Arthurs; No. 13 Lt. J.F. Clatworthy;
  No. 14 Lt. R. Moore
Middle Row: No. 1 Lt. R. Kingsley Tayler; No. 2 Lt. Stan Baker; No. 3
  Capt. Edwin Herbert Davis; No. 5 Lt. C.F. Thomas; No. 6 Lt. V.E. Danby;
  No. 8 2nd Lt. Bill D. Thomson; No. 9 Mr. Howe; No. 15 Charles Bartlett;
  No. 19 2nd Lt. Sidney Connett; No. 20 Mr. Hurford; No. 21 Mr. Laidlaw;
  No. 24 Major Sandford; No. 25 Mr. Bates; No. 27 Lt. H. Webber
Front Row: No. 2 Dr. J. Erskine-Collins; No. 4 Capt. G.F. Nuthall;
  No. 8 Major E.M. Driver; No. 10 Capt. H.S. Keynton;
  No. 11 Lt. Col. R.D. Alexander; No. 12 Major E.L.D. Ackland, C.B., M.V.O.;
  No. 13 Capt P.E. Stanley; No. 14 Capt. Parsons; No. 16 Major F.H. Norton;
  No. 17 Major W.T. Greswell; No. 19 Capt. Douglas C.H. Edwards, M.C.
(Author's collection)

NO. 1 (PORLOCK) COMPANY

COMMANDING OFFICER   Major H.P. Hewett   2nd IN COMMAND   Capt. B. Taylor, M.C.
                                     (Major R.D. Alexander)   (Capt. E.T. Bullen)

Porlock Company comprised four platoons, Porlock, Oare and Brendon, Selworthy and Wootton Courtenay. No photographs have been located of Oare and Brendon or Wootton Courtenay Platoons. It is known, however, that Capt. Hewett was officer i/c Wootton Courtenay Platoon.

Porlock Home Guard, *photographed in 1944 outside Court Place Farm (Platoon Headquarters).*
Back Row: Unknown; Bill Keal; Raymond Keal; Stan Hooper
  (Allerford); possibly Charlie Fox; Bill Thomas; Bill Thomas
  (senior); Bill Tame; Jeff Farrant; Tom Harris
Second Row: Reverend J.A. Smart; Jack Meade; George Hall;
  Cecil Westcott; Bill Chiswell; Patrick Joyce; Bert Tancock;
  Harry Rawle; Reg Huntley; Charlie Brooks
Third Row: Tom Sully; Bert 'Tacker' Gibbons; Alfie Keal;
  Sid Rawle; George Bushen; Vivian Langrish; Francis White;
  Clifford Barwick; Herbert Kingdon; Henry Webb
Fourth Row: Unknown; Arthur Ward; Jack Farmer; Ernest Sully;
  Fred Kent; Dudley Richards; Peter Leach; Sid Gibbons;
  Fred Middleton
Fifth Row: Sgt. Jim Wilson; Sgt. Sid Ferris; Sgt. Bill Yeandle;
  Sgt. Sid Bass; Sgt. Glascow; Sgt. Fred Willicombe
Front Row: Capt. Bill Parsons; Major Sandford; Lt. Hugh Webber.
  Born in 1896 Vivian Langrish was a well-known concert
  pianist and professor at the Royal Academy of Music, London,
  who rented a cottage from Major Roberts.
(Dennis Corner collection)

At the outbreak of war the late Hugh Webber, who attended King's College, Taunton from 1925-29, was directed into work of national importance in the form of timber production. This was due to a leg injury sustained whilst playing rugby which precluded him from conscription. He subsequently joined the Porlock Home Guard.

In a letter of 1993 he recalled a fatal accident at Holnicote when, whilst a local unit was being instructed by an N.C.O. of the Regulars on field stripping the Thompson sub-machine gun, a live round was accidentally chambered and fired, shooting Sgt. James Farmer of Stratford in the femoral artery. He also remembered an occasion when an unnamed unit was undergoing training with a Spigot Mortar in Porlock Recreation Field. Using a motorcycle leaning against a wall as a target, it was loaded with a drill round and 'fired'. Unfortunately the drill round was live with an inert warhead. A direct hit was scored on the motorbike, much to the fury of the owner and the utter amazement of the mortar team.

A potentially serious incident occurred during an all-night exercise involving an attack on an R.A.F. observer post on Porlock Hill by members of the local Home Guard units. Whilst the pre-exercise briefing was being carried out the rifles were piled, namely stacked in pyramids of three using the piling swivel attached to the fore ends of the rifles. Included in the stack of weapons was that of the local Home Guard Sentry. On completion, the rifles were recovered and the exercise commenced. A rapid halt was called to the exercise and all rifles examined when the sentry, patrolling his lonely beat, opened his bolt and noticed 'his' rifle was loaded with blank ammunition. This meant that one of the participants in the exercise had a rifle loaded with live ammunition, which could have led to fatal consequences.

Hugh Webber remembered that the Platoon, apart from having a Blacker Bombard, was issued with American P17 rifles, a Lewis machine gun, pistols and Sten guns. Grenade practice took place at Bossington Beach.

As with many Home Guard units scattered around the county it was necessary to establish a local rifle range. In the case of Porlock this was built at Crawter Hill, the firing point being at map ref. SS 892 455 and the butts at SS 892 454. Even now in winter-time, when the bracken has died back, it is still possible to see where the men of Porlock honed their musketry skills.

The first Company Commander, Lt. Col. R.D. Alexander lived at Doverhay House and it was here in his garden, at map ref. SS 887 466, that a specially built brick building was used for storing explosives.

Sentry duties were carried out at Pitt Combe Head, where a wooden hut was erected to provide shelter opposite the AA box on Porlock Hill. No doubt the sentry would have had a key to the box to summons assistance if needed. It was reported on one occasion in September 1940, that the sentry was startled by a fellow Home Guard arriving breathless at Pitt Combe Head stating that Germans had landed at a local beach but not to worry, they were sending another man up to help!

Porlock Weir Home Guard.
Back Row: Ernest Pollard; Alfred Cook; Arthur Lee; Victor Manley
Front Row: Cpl. Bruce Baldwin; George Garnish; Capt. Parsons; Sgt. Jack Roberts; Harry Pollard
(Dennis Corner collection)

Ernest Pollard, son of Harry, was employed as a gardener by Miss Wylde. Alf Cook, a First World War veteran, was Porlock Manor Estate's gamekeeper. His income was supplemented by gathering ferns which were dispatched to Billingsgate Fish Market on which fish were displayed. Arthur Lee was the local fisherman who also looked after Goodland's Coal Yard where the coal arrived by boat until the late 1950s. Victor Manley owned a store in Porlock Weir. He subsequently emigrated to Australia.

Bruce Baldwin was the chauffeur and general factotum for Mrs. Blathwayt of Porlock Manor Estate, the family seat being Dyrham Park, near Bath. George Garnish was a local farmworker, whilst mail was delivered by Capt. Parsons. The company quartermaster was Jack Roberts who was a local house painter. Meat was provided by Harry Pollard, the local butcher.

The Home Guard Stores were situated on the upper floor of what is now the Miles Tea Company Headquarters.

Selworthy Platoon at Holnicote Stables. Although this photograph was initially thought to be of either Holnicote Platoon or Porlock, a report of the Stand Down in the West Somerset Free Press states 'The Porlock Platoon before marching to Holnicote had a group photograph taken at their own assembly point, and the other three platoons (Oare and Brendon, Selworthy and Wootton Courtenay) joined them at Holnicote'. As no names are common to the Porlock Platoon photograph it is more likely that this is the Selworthy Platoon.

Back Row: Arthur Kingdon; Ted Rawlings; Jack Gould; Philip Moore; Harold Priscott; Alfie Starks; Arthur Moore; Wally Harding

Middle Row: George Davies; Reg Tame; Stafford Mills; Dick Creech; Eddie Keal; Bob Williams; Tom Farmer; Bill Tame; Leonard Bennett; Jack Farmer

Front Row: Mervyn Arscott; Ern Bellamy; Cpl. Sid Webber; Cpl. Bill Gunter; Sgt. Jack Kingdon; Tom Rawle; Sgt. Jack Crockford, M.M.; Tom Hill; Tony Hale; Percy Sedman; Clifford Choke

(Rod Farmer collection)

Sgt. Jack Crockford was a veteran of the Great War, joining up the day after war was declared. Geoffrey Holt remembers him as a fiercely brave man and a good shot. He was wounded facially at Loos in 1915, was subsequently promoted to Sergeant and received the Military Medal. Having committed some minor misdemeanour, 1919 saw him fighting in Mesopotamia in a punishment Battalion, as part of the multinational force supporting General Anton Denikin in his struggle against the Bolsheviks.

Born in Allerford in 1923, Ron Moore was a member of the Selworthy Home Guard whilst awaiting his call-up papers. Although not a member of the Home Guard for long, Ron was involved in night-time exercises. On one such occasion the Platoon had to approach North Hill, Minehead via Selworthy Combe. The unit carried all their equipment with them including their jars of cider and beer, the cider being supplied by Sgt. Bill Tucker of Tivington Farm. The following morning Ron remembers waking up at home covered in scratches and bruises but was unable to recollect how he got them – probably, he suggests, due to the influence of the cider!

Ron was subsequently called up and joined the Royal Navy. Whilst on anti-submarine duty Ron was aboard *H.M.S. Woodpecker*, a sloop of the Black Swan class, captained by Commander H.L. Pryce. The ship was torpedoed in mid-Atlantic on 23rd February 1944. Despite having her stern blown off, *H.M.S. Woodpecker* refused to sink immediately. She was taken in tow but some seven days later she capsized and was lost. Ron was rescued by a Canadian destroyer. It was not until after the war that Ron discovered that one of his rescuers was a Canadian cousin.

February 1945 saw Ron serving on *H.M.S. Lark*, a modified Black Swan class on which he had served during the D-Day landings. On the 17th of that month *Lark* was homeward bound from Murmansk to Greenock. Sailing off the Kola Inlet she attacked and sank U425. Later that day she was hit by a torpedo fired from U968. Again Ron's ship failed to sink and was subsequently beached at Murmansk, repaired by the Russians and re-commissioned as the *Neptun*. Whilst under tow prior to being beached, the tow rope parted and fouled the rescue ship's propeller. Russian records report that a Russian naval rating dived into the icy water and freed the propeller at the second attempt. One memory Ron will never forget of this incident was that of a fellow shipmate named Hardy being blown 30 feet into the air, still standing on a piece of deck. He fell into the water and was promptly picked up by a small Russian craft. (Ron was obviously fated. Of 11 Black Swan class ships and 20 modified Black Swan class ships only five were lost and Ron had to be on two of them!)

(right) Cpl. Sid Webber (left), a First World War veteran who worked at the Holnicote Estate, and Sgt. Jack Kingdon (right), another First World War veteran and second gardener at Holnicote House where five gardeners were employed, stand behind Ron Moore, then aged about 17. Ron Moore for a time was No. 5 gardener at Holnicote House. (Ron Moore collection)

NO. 2 (MINEHEAD) COMPANY

COMMANDING OFFICER   Major C. Cabe
(Major Edmund Murray Hill)

2ND IN COMMAND   Capt. C.A. Muirhead, C.I.E.
(Capt. S. Beckett)

(left) Major Edmund Murray Hill, 1891-1984.

Major Hill fought with the Somersets in the First World War and was wounded at Ypres, so seriously that his kit was 'shared out'. He subsequently spent 18 months in a Military Hospital being patched up and having the worst of the shrapnel removed, leaving 19 pieces visible on an X-ray which the surgeons decided to leave. As a result he received a war pension and was classed as unfit for service in 1939 when he was 48 years old. He joined the Home Guard, becoming the first officer to command No. 2 (Minehead) Company.

(above right) Private The Hon. Earl of Cromer, G.C.B., G.C.I.E., G.C.V.O., to the left of the table, presents Major Hill with an inscribed wrist watch on 8th February 1942 to mark the latter's relinquishing command to take up a Government appointment. Others in the photograph who have been identified are Tom Stewart, 2nd from right; Arthur Willis, 3rd from right; and Stan Beckett, 4th from right.

Major Hill died one month short of his 93rd birthday still carrying 19 pieces of shrapnel 'collected' 69 years previously. (both photographs Bridget Hill collection)

Geoffrey Holt joined the Home Guard as a messenger in August 1940. During the invasion scare in early September he spent several nights at North Road waiting for orders to cycle around Minehead and call out the Home Guard. His task would have been made easier by the letters 'HG' to be found outside volunteers' houses as Mrs. A. Newton, daughter of C.S.M. Colman, clearly remembers a large 'HG' painted on the pavement outside her father's home. It must be remembered that at this time not many homes possessed a telephone. Indeed in one platoon in the north of Somerset the platoon Sergeant could only be contacted in an emergency via his neighbour's telephone.

In the early Home Guard days Geoffrey remembers the unit was issued with Canadian .303 Ross Rifles, a weapon that had seen some service in the First World War but which was subsequently found to be unable to stand up to the rigours of the battlefield, being replaced in the Regular Army by the Rifle, Short, Magazine Lee Enfield. Other weapons recalled were the Blacker Bombard, Tommy gun, Browning Automatic Rifle and, unusually for a Home Guard unit, the Bakelite-bodied No. 69 Grenade. Geoffrey later left the Home Guard, together with his friend and fellow Home Guard member H.J. Blackwell, and both joined the R.A.F.

Writing in June 2001 Mr. Holt recalled his involvement with live firing:

The Minehead HG Rifle Range

The target was paced out at 200 yards from the bottom of the shingle bank due north of the harbour. A couple of sandbags provided our firing point. This 'range', if I can call it that, was used soon after we first received our excellent Ross rifles. I also used this range later when entrusted with a Browning Automatic Rifle. At the time I thought this was a recognition of my prowess with the Ross, but it did eventually dawn on me that the privilege of humping around the B.A.R.'s 17lbs was reserved for the callow and credulous.

The Blacker Bombard Ranges

It must be probable that I was assigned to the Blacker Bombard for similar reasons. My role in the four-man team was confined to fetching and carrying heavy components.

Our first firing took place in a field adjoining Middlecombe Combe, at map ref. SS 948 456, when I believe we succeeded in lobbing a bomb a distance of as much as 250 yards.

My second and last firing was on Porlock Marshes, map ref. SS 877 477, when we were put through our paces by a Training Wing detachment of the Gloucester Regiment. Our target was a bank of shingle on the far side of a cluster of little lagoons known as The Decoy. Our bomb, visible for most of its trajectory, was always going to fall alarmingly short – and did. We were not allowed a second shot.

(above) **Officers and Men of No. 2 (Minehead) Company**. This photograph was taken on 8th February 1942 to commemorate Major E.M. Hill's departure to take up a Government appointment. See the next page for the names of those identified. (Bridget Hill collection)

Stand Down Parade, Minehead, 3rd December 1944.
  Major E.M. Hill returned to Minehead for this parade and can be seen on the daïs wearing a trilby hat.
(Bridget Hill collection)

Key to photograph on previous page and names below

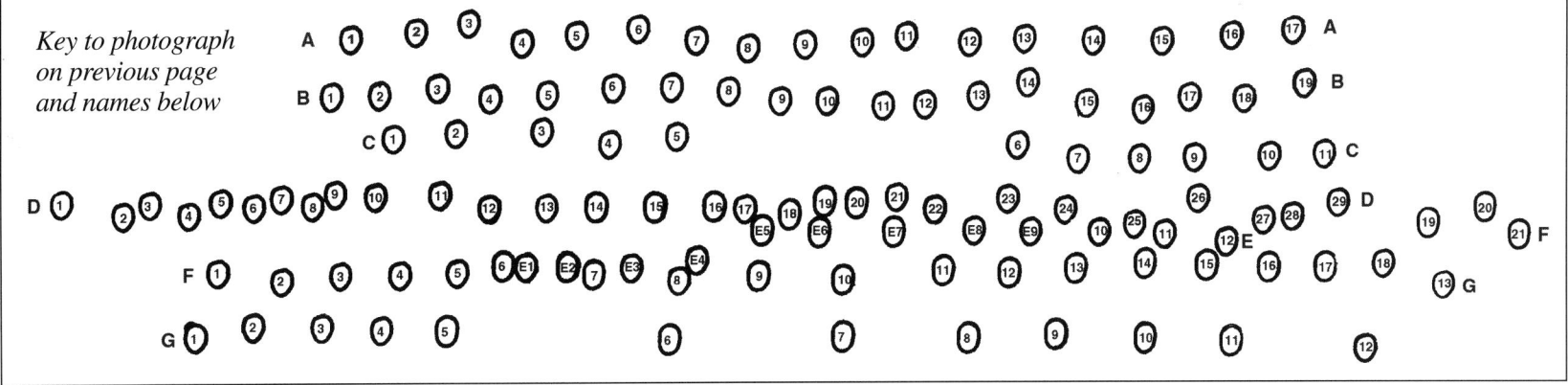

A1 F. Poole	B7 Clarence Venn	D3 ?Edgar Reed	F6 The Earl of Cromer
A2 Mr. Hills	B10 F. Goldsmith	D4 Hubert Killie	F7 Padre Lyddon
A6 Mr. Priscott	B13 Mr. Stone	D5 C. Foy	F8 Captain Cabe
A7 Geoffrey Holt	B14 Alfred Vowles	D7 Morty Cole	F9 Major E.M. Hill
A8 H.J. Blackwell	B16 A. Passmore	D12 Ron Horsey	F10 Stan Beckett
A13 D. Parker	B19 Harry Wells	D15 Mr. Baker	F11 Mr. Lofthouse
A14 G. Adams	(also possibly in this row are C. Brown;	D20 Maurice Jennings	F12 Company Sgt. Major Noah Atkins
A15 Vic Heard	Mr Coles; W. Martin and D. Williams)	D21 Mr. Webber	
A16 G. Coles			G1 Mr. Laidlaw
A17 Doug Parker	C2 ?Edgar Reed	E2 Mr. Meredith	G2 Charlie Bartlett
	C3 'Lofty' Amor	E5 George Catford	G3 P. Bach?
B1 Arthur Newton	C4 Mr. Chamberlain or Mr. Gubb	E12 M. Thomas	G4 Mr. Thale?
B4 Richard Hill	C8 W. Baker		G5 Mr. Hobbs?
B5 ?Mr. Thorne	C10 Mr. Needs	F1 Fred Mullis	G6 Mr. Willis
B6 Billy Martin	C11 Mr. Davis	F2 ?Mr. Thorne	G7 Mr. Stewart
		F3 T. Badcock	G8 R. Kingsley Tayler
		F4 Bill Corney	G9 Mr. Coleman
		F5 Ernest Potter	G10 Cyril Newcombe
			G11 McNally?
			G12 Reg Holmes
			G13 Fred Stevens

The first copy of this photograph was sent by Bridget Hill, daughter of the late E.M. Hill, Company Commander. An accompanying list identified many in the photograph. Further study raised several queries due to the fact that the 'troops' were not standing in straight lines. By this time Bridget Hill had died. Hopes were raised when a framed photograph was found in a Minehead loft with the names written on the back. However, again fate conspired against the author. Although some names had been written, those unidentified in some cases were not annotated at all. The number of names and unknowns did not add up to the total number featured. The names proffered above are the result of several lines of enquiry; in some cases a 'majority vote' has been taken as to identification. As with all photographs in this book the author would be pleased to receive additions and corrections.

(right) A Home Guard 'Armoured' Car, photographed in Bratton Lane, Minehead. This appears to be a genuine attempt to produce a mobile mount for a Lewis gun. What is certain, however, is that it is mounted on the body of a sports car which would be unable to support much weight of real armour. Perhaps the whole arrangement was for training purposes only. For a photograph of this vehicle in civilian guise see Somerset at War *by Mac Hawkins, page 131. It is believed that the vehicle may have belonged to Lt. Kingsley Tayler, the Company Signals Officer. It is a 1935 9-H.P. Singer Le Mans Sport, first registered in Bedfordshire on 13th March 1935. Standing on the right of the photograph with his left arm crooked is C.S.M. W. Colman.*
(by courtesy of The Tank Museum, Bovington)

NO. 3 (DUNSTER) COMPANY

COMMANDING OFFICER   Major E.S. Collier   2ND IN COMMAND   Capt. F.C. Butterfield
(Brigadier Thackeray, D.S.O., M.C.)   (Capt. R.R.L. Johnson)

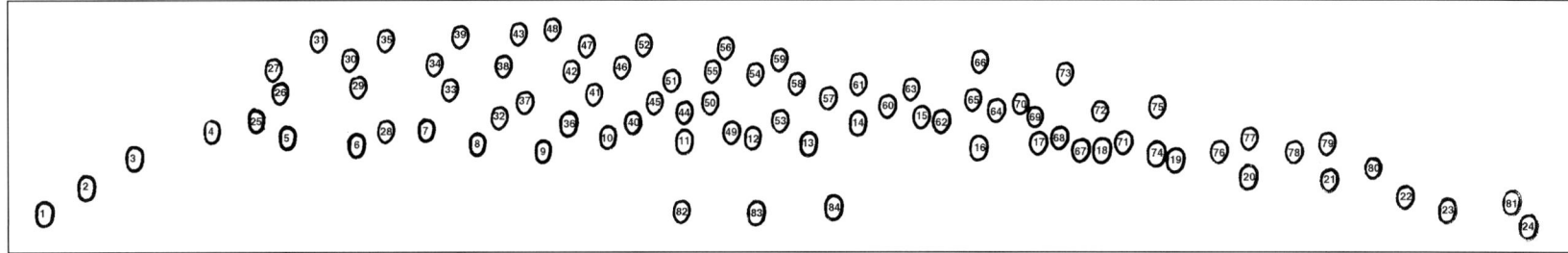

Officers and Men of No.3 (Dunster) Company. *(Key: WX = Wheddon Cross Platoon Members; T = Timberscombe Platoon Members) (Author's collection)*

1 Cpl. Bert Stevens WX	15 Sgt. Reed (Watchet Paper Mills employee)	34 Mr. Chapman or Walter Gregory T	62 ?Clifford Rowe (Crown Estates worker)
2 Bill Bawler	16 ?Sgt. Jimmy Parsons (garage worker)	35 Bert Gunter (farmworker)	63 Harry Simons (shepherd)
3 Cpl. James Jefferies T	17 Sgt. Fred Webber	36 L/Cpl. Harold Gill	65 Mr. Storey (railway ganger)
4 Cpl. Charlie Baldwin (head gardener for Luttrell family)	19 ?Cpl. Scudamore	37 Arthur Ladd	66 Kenneth Heard WX
5 Joe Williams (electricity company worker)	20 William George Storey	38 Ernie Ray WX	67 Dudley Parsons (bus driver)
6 Raymond Escott (baker's roundsman)	21 Cyril Copp	40 Ron May	71 ?Ossie Gould
7 Jim Downer (nurseryman)	22 Fred Norman	43 Colin Potter (baker)	73 Frank Chaplin
8 Carl Meddick	23 Jesse Woodberry (baker)	46 Ted Griffiths or Robert Young Barr (farmer)	75 Preston Thomas WX
9 L/Cpl. Donald Vaulter	24 ?Dick Scudamore (AA patrolman)	47 Lionel Besley	77 Reg Ayres WX
11 Cpl. Tommy Winter	27 Colin Watts (stonemason)	51 Ken Radford (farmworker)	78 ?Walter Gregory (gardener)
12 Sgt. Butterfield (gamekeeper)	30 Mr. Elford	56 Fred Luxton WX	79 Ron Slader WX
13 Sgt. Harold Down (butcher)	31 Tom Thrush (grocery roundsman)	57 Jack Jones (goods driver)	82 ?Brig. Thackeray
14 Sgt. Elton Bates (tomato farmer)	32 Tom Bryant (bus conductor)	60 Mr. Ridley	83 ?Capt. Reg Johnson (farmer)
	33 Stan Ladd/Dudley Huxtable WX	61 Arthur Webber	84 ?Capt. F.C. Butterfield or Lt. Col. E.R.Clayton

This photograph was one of the first to be lent to the author, the names coming from various sources. Later, other photos of smaller groups, often of far greater quality, were lent with many faces identified. During the preparation of this book several discrepancies have come to light whilst cross-checking names and photos. In this case doubt even exists as to the correct identification of the three senior officers in the front row. Traditionally these would have been the Company 2nd in Command, the Company Commander, and possibly the Battalion Commander. As with all the photographs in the book the author would welcome any additional identification and corrections.

As in the case of the Minehead Company photograph memories have faded with the passage of time and a few contradictions have occurred, in which case both names have been included. Whilst a contemporary report of the Stand Down indicates that the Company comprised men from Timberscombe, Wheddon Cross, Carhampton and Old Cleeve, company members also came from Wootton Courtenay and Dunster.

Penny Woods was used for grenade practice. One of the observation points was the Giant's Chair at Grabbist Hill where the boredom of the lookouts was relieved by the consumption of a considerable amount of scrumpy.

In 1942 Dunster Company comprised 4 officers and 161 other ranks, armed with 140 rifles and 9 light machine guns with a total ammunition holding of 13,000 rounds.

Lt. R. Kingsley Tayler was a well-known photographer in Minehead. He was also the Battalion Signals Officer. The majority of the photographs of Minehead Battalion shown here were taken by him but unfortunately they were not captioned. Accordingly the titles of photographs on the following pages are sometimes vague, often having been added many years later.

Men of Dunster Home Guard.
Back Row: Bill Baker; L/Cpl. Carl Meddick; Donald Vaulter; Unknown; Unknown; L/Cpl. 'Pop' Storey
Middle Row: Cpl. Jim Jefferies; Cpl. J. Williams; Cpl. Ray Escott; Cpl. Jim Downer; Unknown; Cpl. Tommy Winter; Cpl. Jim Parsons; Cpl. Scudamore; Unknown; Cpl. Charlie Baldwin; Bert Stevens; Unknown
Seated: Sgt. Clifford Rowe; Sgt. Harold Down; Sgt. Butterfield; Sgt. Reed; Sgt. Elton Bates; Fred Webber
The location for this photograph is Castle Drive outside the stables, now the National Trust shop. Not all photographs taken at this location were executed at the same time as the vegetation over the porch and ivy growing up a tree behind will testify.
(Charles Parsons collection)

In 1940 Charles Parsons was a member of the Dunster Home Guard. Other names he can recall were Captains Johnson and Bates, Jack Jones and Bob Thomas. Duties included guarding Loxhole Bridge and patrolling Dunster Beach which was also used for rifle practice. Butter Cross Quarry reverberated to the blast of hand grenades on practice days. In August-September 1940, during the invasion 'scare', lookouts were posted on Grabbist Hill. In 1941 Charles Parsons left the Home Guard and was called up, joining the Royal Electrical and Mechanical Engineers.

Dunster Home Guard in 1943.
Back Row: Ossie Gould; Gerald Sully; Stan Ladd; Bert Davy; Jimmy Copp; Chris Champion
Middle Row: Reg Vaulter; Roy Sully; Jack Jones; Charlie Welsh; George Needs; Fred Hunt
Front Row: L/Cpl. Harold Gill; Cpl. Don Vaulter; Cpl. Clifford Rowe; Sgt. Tommy Winter; L/Cpl. Ken Radford; Mr. White
At least two different Marks of Sten guns are visible in the front row.
(West Somerset Rural Life Museum collection)

(left) **Dunster Home Guard**, photographed by Kingsley Tayler.
Back Row: Clifford Ell; G. Maidment; F. Elliott; A. Ladd
Middle Row: A. Sully; W. Morris; Robert Greenslade; Bob Atkins; J. Webber
Front Row: Cpl. E. Radford; Sgt. Jim Parsons; L/Cpl. W. Storey
Cpl. E. Radford appears to be holding a Mk II Sten gun whilst Messrs. Parsons and Storey have the earlier Mk I* introduced at the end of 1941.
(Phil Parkman collection)

(right) Sgt. W. Lloyd was a member of Dunster Company, joining on 22nd June 1940, and obviously devoted much time and effort to the Home Guard as this certificate indicates. By June 1942 he had been promoted to Sergeant and by December 1944 he had obtained the rank of Lieutenant.
(Mrs. Joyce Lloyd collection)

(left) **Dunster Home Guard** Skittles Team.
Back Row: Sgt. Tommy Winter; Jack Jones; Jim Wilkins; Roy Sully; Ken Radford; Sgt. Jim Parsons
Front Row: Sgt. Clifford Rowe; Bob Atkins; Robert Greenslade
Bob Atkins ran The New Inn, Dunster, now known as The Stag's Head. It was thought that the photograph was taken at The New Inn but subsequent information revealed that the team had been photographed outside the Beagle Kennels across the drive from Dunster Castle stables. The building to the right is still standing but the run on the extreme right of the photograph has disappeared as have the palisade gates, leaving just the hinge pins in the stone pillars. Jim Wilkins, in the fireman's uniform, was the Luttrell family's shepherd.
(Charles Parsons collection)

(right) **Carhampton Home Guard**.
Back Row: George Downer Snr.; Frank Passmore; Bert Gunter; Bill Middleton; Sid Williams; Frank Salter; Arthur Laramy
Middle Row: Arthur Taylor; George Downer Jnr.; Gordon Farmer; Eric Pearce; Mr. Ridley; Henry Pugsley
Front Row: Cpl. Jim Downer; Cpl. Harry Simons; Sgt. Joe Williams; Cpl. Joe Stephenson
Other members not featured but associated with Carhampton Home Guard were Mr. Bates, Mr. Fenwick, Capt. Reg Johnston, Colin Potter, Thomas Thrush, John Tozer, Colin Watts, Raymond Escott, Mr. Tidly, and Mr. Reed.
(Philip Laramy collection)

(left) **Carhampton Home Guard** outside Sherrin's Garage. Taken on the main Minehead to Taunton road, one would cringe at the thought of safely marching a body of men along the road these days.
Left to Right: Lionel Besley; Joe Williams; Bert Gunter; George Paski; Arthur Laramy; Unknown (between Arthur Laramy and head of petrol pump); Bill Middleton; Henry Pugsley; Unknown (in front of Esso pump); Unknown; Bill Thrush; Clifford Yeandle; Harry Lewis; Unknown (immediately behind Harry Lewis); Harry Simons; Stan Winter; Jim Downer; Joe Stephenson
(Philip Laramy collection)

(right) **Carhampton Home Guard**, photographed outside Sherrin's Garage, Carhampton. The road to Minehead seems little more than a country lane!
Cpl. Harry Simons; Clifford Yeandle; George Paski; Lionel Besley; Arthur Laramy; Colin Watts; Bert Gunter; Billy Middleton
(Norman Lewis collection)

(left) **Carhampton Home Guard** 'On Parade', outside Sherrin's Garage, Carhampton built in the style typical of the 1920s-1930s. This is an unfortunate photograph in as much as many on parade have their faces concealed by others, making identification impossible. Taking the parade is an unidentifiable person, possibly Mr. Butterfield, and Mr. Elton Bates. On parade are, from left to right: Joe Stephenson; Stanley Winter; Jim Downer; Eric Pearce; Walter Griffiths; George Downer (son of Jim Downer); Harry Simons; Harry Lewis; Unknown (small portion of face visible); William Thrush; Unknown; Frank Salter; Unknown (rim of helmet visible); Reginald Bindon; Unknown (helmet and part of face visible); Frank Griffiths; Stanley Webber; Unknown (nose visible); Unknown; Unknown (possibly Robert Young Barr); Unknown (helmet visible); Lionel Besley (extreme right-hand side of photograph)
(Norman Lewis collection)

(right) **Timberscombe Home Guard**.
Back Row: Arthur Smith; Bill Priscott; Cuthbert Perry; Walter Pope; Archie Dyer; Ken Grabham; Ted Griffiths
Middle Row: Leslie Bishop; Dudley Parsons; Jack Heywood; Tom Alford; Walter Poole; Alf Bowles
Front Row: Cpl. Bert Stevens; Sgt. Major Herbert Gregory; Sgt. Charlie Baldwin.
Dudley Parsons, Cuthbert Perry, Archie Dyer and Bert Stevens were all Wootton Courtenay residents whilst Bill Priscott, Ken Grabham and Herbert Gregory were from Timberscombe. Occupations were varied. Bill Priscott and Archie Dyer were farmworkers, as was Leslie Bishop who worked at Oaktrow, whilst Bert Stevens farmed at Harwood. Ken Grabham worked at Cowbridge Saw Mills. Village footwear was looked after by Ted Griffiths, the local boot repairer. On the horticultural side, Herbert Gregory was head gardener to Lady Ryder of Knowle, Charlie Baldwin was a gardener at Dunster Castle, whilst Tom Alford was also employed as a gardener. Home Guard evening parades at Timberscombe were held in a barn at 'Duddings', now a holiday cottage complex.
(Dudley Parsons collection)

Dudley Parsons, who celebrated his 95th birthday in September 2003, was a Special Constable when war was declared, receiving 1/6d per week 'Boot Money'. He was employed by Mr. W.G. Burnell, the proprietor of the garage in Wootton Courtenay, having started work there in 1928. As Mr. Burnell had 14-, 20- and 32-seater coaches he was employed to transport the local Home Guard units to various locations. Dudley Parsons, one of his drivers, had his plans for joining the R.A.F. 'scuppered' by Mr. Burnell who successfully retained Mr. Parsons under the 'reserved occupation' rule. Dudley remembers as a driver being issued with a Sten gun which fitted neatly down the side of the driver's seat. Rifle practice was carried out on the range at Dunster Castle Deer Park.

(right) **Wheddon Cross Home Guard**.
Back Row: John Bawden; Bert Farrant; Sidney
   Western; Ron Slader; Tom Bawden; Reg Ayres;
   Sidney Webber
Front Row: Arthur Webber; Cpl. Wilf Weston;
   Sgt. Joe Barwick; Lt. Nichols; Sgt. Fred Webber;
   Cpl. Fred Norman; Cpl. Jack Taylor
This photograph appears to be taken towards the end of the war. Four chevrons can be seen on the right sleeve of the battledress of those in the front row, awarded for four years of good conduct. Although awarded annually, troops were wary of sewing these on their battledress, as a missing chevron would signify to all and sundry that some misdemeanour had been committed. Photographs taken in 1944 show a plethora of troops proudly showing four chevrons.
(Mrs. Eileen Webber collection)

(left) Army Council Instruction 491 of 7th April 1941 introduced Proficiency Badges for all members of the Home Guard who had served below the rank of Sergeant for a minimum of three months. To be entitled to wear the one-inch red felt square, to be worn with one corner uppermost on the lower part of the right sleeve of the battledress blouse, the candidate had to answer questions on general knowledge, the rifle and one of the following topics: Automatic Weapons, Field Works, Map Reading and, if employed as an instructor, to be able to give satisfactory instruction on selected subjects. The certificate awarded to Private A.J. Webber of Wheddon Cross bears the signatures of Lt. Col. R.D. Alexander, Battalion Commander, Capt. P.E. Stanley, and Lt. H.E. Davis.

(below) **Wheddon Cross Home Guard**. (Mrs. Eileen Webber collection)
Back Row: Preston Thomas; Harold Short; Frank Chaplin; Ron Slader;
   Ned Fowler; Fred Luxton; Arthur Webber
Middle Row: Ken Heard; Jack Bale; Reg Ayres; Harold Heard;
   Sidney Western; Johnny Upham
Front Row: L/Cpl. William Hill; Cpl. Sidney Webber; Cpl. John Taylor;
   Sgt. George Goacher; Sgt. Fred Webber; Cpl. Joe Barwick;
   L/Cpl. Wilf Western; L/Cpl. Fred Norman
Fred Webber is holding a .45" Thompson SMG Model 28 AC with a 50-round magazine and Cutts compensator, a weapon favoured by American gangsters of the 1920s and 30s. Most were later withdrawn and replaced by the Sten gun.

NO. 4 (WILLITON) COMPANY

COMMANDING OFFICER   Major W.T. Greswell
(Major J.R. Hutchinson, D.S.O.)
2ND IN COMMAND   Capt. W.C. Hurley

Williton Home Guard, *photographed at Stand Down.*
Back Row: Bill Upham; Jimmy Burnell (farmworker from Doniford); Unknown; Bill Coles; Bob Trebble (local council worker and HG First Aid N.C.O.); Percy Hembrow (general factotum at Williton Workhouse); Bill Squibbs; Mr. Williams; Unknown; Dick Maddocks (coalman); Charlie Jenkins (tailor)
Middle Row: Leslie Sweetland; Bert Sully; Lionel George Doble (farmworker); Mr. House; Bill Sully; Clifford Bray (shoemaker); Bill Scott (chauffeur); George May (farmworker); Tommy Webber; Arthur Sully (GWR delivery man at Watchet); Jimmy Hawkins (farmworker from Doniford); Stan 'Sniffer' Hunt (shoemaker)
Front Row: Mr. Stone; L/Cpl. Walt Hole (photographer); Cpl. Alf Stockwell; Cpl. Morris Bryne (WWI veteran); Sgt. Bill Court (WWI veteran, printer at The West Somerset Free Press*); 2nd Lt. Sidney Connett (Station Master); Lt. Jack H. Bissell (farmer); Major W.T. Greswell; Sgt. Russell G. Cox (member of the family which owned* The West Somerset Free Press*); Sgt. Laity Gliddon (agricultural engineer); L/Cpl. Harry Davis (farmworker from Sampford Brett); Mr. Bulpin*
Others known to have been members of the Platoon were N. Coles; J. Court; J. Sully; L. Webber; Sgt. Bill Gardiner; Sgt. Hunt; Cpl. Byrne and Cpl. Bryant
(Norman Coles collection)

The Williton Home Guard operated its own full-bore rifle range in Pigeon Field, Williton, which was also used by Regular Army units. Sgt. H.J. Cox used to collect the 'range fee' in the form of .303 ammunition. This presented the Home Guard with a problem. As the they were issued with P17 rifles in .300 calibre, Sgt. Cox then had to borrow .303 rifles so that the Home Guard could 'spend' its income.

This range was also used for the firing of Lewis machine guns. Norman Coles, who joined the Home Guard at the age of 16, recalls that regular parades were held on Tuesday and Thursday evenings with a Church parade on Sunday mornings. 'Keen types' spent Sunday afternoons improving their shooting skills, sometimes shooting a 'falling plate' competition. Falling plate competitions involved shooting at a group of approximately 10" square metal plates standing in front of the butt stop. The competition was won by the team which was the first to knock down their plates. This was highly dangerous as far as ricochets were concerned. On official War Department ranges the butt marking party were required to take cover indoors during such competitions.

On one occasion Sgt. Gardiner detailed Norman to take the Lewis gun home, strip it and clean it. How times have changed. The sight of a young lad walking home through Williton carrying a machine gun these days would have the local population in a panic. During the following parade Sgt. Gardiner asked Mr. Coles about the whereabouts of the gun. "In the sack over my shoulder, Sergeant", was the reply. Young Mr. Coles had managed to strip and clean the gun but couldn't re-assemble it!

For small-bore rifle practice an indoor range was used which was attached to the Mens' Club in Long Street, Williton.

Apart from the P17 rifles already mentioned, Williton Company armoury included Sten guns, Spigot Mortars and Browning Automatic Rifles. In 1942, the 4 officers and 267 other ranks possessed 150 rifles and 7,500 rounds of ammunition in addition to ten light machine guns and 7,000 rounds of ammunition.

As with many Home Guard units, Williton had its war-wounded members. Sgt. Hunt, who had lost an arm in the previous conflict, was issued with a revolver. One section of the Williton Company was comprised of older men which permitted smart marching albeit at a slightly slower pace.

In Williton the Company had a Nissen hut for storage purposes. This was situated between the Church and Orchard Mill. Mr. Coles can clearly recall that Sgt. Major Bill Venn had the use of a small army car.

One exercise Norman remembered was when the Williton Home Guard was detailed to carry out a night attack on the BBC Transmitting Station at Washford. One member, who we shall call Joe, arrived late on his bicycle at the start line, and found the Home Guard had moved off. Cycling to the transmitting station he enquired of the sentries on duty if the Home Guard had arrived and was promptly captured. Meanwhile, Williton Home Guard ploughed on across fields, hedges and ditches carrying ladders to scale the palisade fence which still surrounds the site today.

Whilst this was going on Joe was being 'entertained' at the Radio Station. By the time the fence had been scaled and the Radio Station successfully captured, Joe was in such a state of intoxication that he was unable to cycle home.

On some occasions night time exercises were timed to finish at day break with beer and sandwiches at the Girls' Friendly Society Hall behind Williton Post Office. Williton Company was part of the 1st Minehead Battalion and on one occasion a live firing exercise was carried out at Porlock. Williton scored the highest points for shooting but the Officer Commanding, Lt. Col. R.D. Alexander, awarded the competition to Porlock Company because they appeared more soldierly. Lt. Col. Alexander was a Porlock man!

Extract from *The West Somerset Free Press*, December 1944

Home Guard's Keenness Praised

The 'Stand down' parade of the Williton Company, at Williton, on Sunday last, was attended by a muster of 186 from the five platoons which made up the Company. The fall-in at 11 o'clock was in the yard of the Railway Hotel, the Platoons being:

Williton, O.C.; Lt. J. Bissell and Lt. S.C. Connett; Watchet O.C.; Lt. V.E. Danby and Lt. W.D. Thomson; Stogumber O.C.; Lt. H.E. Davis and Lt. C.F. Thomas; Bicknoller O.C.; Lt. J. Millard; Crowcombe O.C.; Lt. S.S.W. Baker. The C.O., Major W.T. Greswell, was present while the assembly was taking place under the direction of C.S.M. E. Stevens. When this had been completed, to the tune of 'Sure and Steady', played by the Watchet Silver Band (Bandmaster A. Wedlake at their head), the parade moved off, led by Captain W.C. Hurley. The march was an outstanding credit to the training the Company had received, and when the parade had completed the arranged itinerary, and re-entered Fore Street by way of Bank Street, Admiral E.L.D. Ackland, C.B., M.V.O. (2nd in Command of the Battalion) was waiting in front of the Rural District Council Offices to take the salute. In company with him were Mrs. Sadler, Mrs. W.T. Greswell, Major Greswell, Lt. Col. J.R. Hutchinson, D.S.O., Major M. Geary, Lt. Taylor, Lt. R.J. Bird, Dr. J. Erskine-Collins (M.O. of the Company), Mr. A.T. Love, Staff Sgt. W.J.D. Venn, D.C.M., Mrs. Venn and P.S. A.C. Coombs (representing the Chief Constable of Somerset). The order "Eyes right!" rang out as each Platoon Commander came abreast ...

WATCHET PLATOON

PLATOON COMMANDER   Lt. Victor Emmanuel Danby   2ND IN COMMAND   2nd Lt. W.D. Thomson

*This photograph of the commanders and senior company officers of **Watchet Platoon**, taken by Henry Hole, was sent to the Commander Watchet Platoon, Lt. V.E. Danby, by the O.C. No. 4 Company with the greeting: "Wishing you a Merry Xmas and Happy Memories".*
Back Row: Ernest Stevens; Unknown; Sgt. Major W. 'Bill' J.D. Venn, S.L.I.; Mrs. Beryl Venn; Cyril Thomas; Margaret Blanchflower; Maude Trebble; 2nd Lt. W. 'Bill' Thomson; Unknown; Stan Baker
Front Row: 2nd Lt. Sidney Connett; Lt. Jack H. Bissell; Lt. Victor E. Danby; Capt. W. 'Bill' C. Hurley; Major W.T. Greswell; Lt. Col. E.R. Clayton, C.M.G., D.S.O.; Dr. J. Erskine-Collins (Company M.O.); Capt. Edwin Herbert Davis (Company Adjutant)
(Alec Danby collection)

*With greatcoats now removed, members of **Watchet Platoon** pose with their Company Commander and fellow Platoon members.*
Back Row: Les Wedlake; Ivor Prole; Frederick Warren; Bill Watts; Stan Amies; Hubert Wescott; Arthur Salmon; Len Eveleigh
Middle Row: Cyril Western; Harold Webber; Jack Clavey; Jack Bartlett; L/Cpl. Stan Duddridge; Jimmy Lee; Ron Prole; Basil Bindon; James Bryant
Front Row: Billy Lee; Cpl. Tom Bulpin; Sgt. George Willicombe; Lt. V.E. Danby; Major W.T. Greswell; Sgt. Major W.J.D. Venn, S.L.I.; 2nd Lt. W.D. Thomson; Sgt. Joe Hunt; Cpl. Walter Bulpin
(Alec Danby collection)

After Anthony Eden's appeal on the wireless for volunteers to join the Local Defence Volunteers, some 40 men presented themselves at the local Police Station. They were subsequently informed that their services would not be required as "the Military were protecting Watchet". As a result of representations to the appropriate quarters by Mr. W.J.E. Lee, a meeting was held at the British Legion Hall on Monday 10th June 1940 at which Mr. W.C. Hurley, who had taken a leading part in forming a section at Williton, gave an address. As a result it was decided to form a section at Watchet and Mr. V.E. Danby was unanimously elected section leader. Mr. W.J.E. Lee undertook to assist in clerical duties. The first enrolments took place on 12th June and some 21 men enrolled on that day including Mr. W.D. Thomson who accepted the post of 2nd in command.

8th July 1940 was a red letter day for the Watchet L.D.V. Two Ross Rifles and nine Short Lee Enfield rifles arrived and were issued to certain platoon members who, interestingly, were also issued with a few items of clothing. Eleven rifles between 77 men! A few others were issued with odd items left over, such was the shortage of equipment.

By June 1941 the status of the unit had changed to Platoon and the following N.C.O.s were in post:

Platoon Sgt.	H.C. Joslin
No. 1 Section	Sgt. R.H. Prole, Cpl. W.H. Bulpin, L/Cpl. G.H. Pope
No. 2 Section	Sgt. L.L. Morgan
No. 3 Section	Sgt. G. Willicombe, Cpl. T.W. Bond, L/Cpl. J.A. Bartlett
No. 4 Section	Sgt. F. Willicombe, Cpl. C. Bishop, L/Cpl. T.W. Bulpin
Reserve Section	Sgt. W. Prole, Cpl. J.W. Hunt
Orderly Room	Sgt. W.J.E. Lee

By Stand Down the following had been members of Watchet Platoon, many only whilst awaiting their call-up papers. Names preceded by an asterix are of men who answered Anthony Eden's call and joined the L.D.V. Later military careers, where known, and other remarks are given in brackets.

In June/July 1940 Messrs. A.W. Salmon, H.R.G. Allen, E.J. Bacon, A.J. Binding, S. Binding, E.W. Headford, T. Norman and C. Webber were formed into a squad for Paper Mills duties, presumably to guard the works at night.

* ACKLAND Walter Fredk. Geo.(South Coast Defence 1915, Scout)
  ALDERMAN John
* ALLEN Harold Richd. Geo. (R. AVC (T.A.); struck off 9.8.41)
* ALLEN Harold Stanley
  AMIES Stanley
* ANDREWS Edward Percy (Transferred to Special Section 9/42;
    reinstated 31.12.42)
  ATTIWELL Fredk. Redvers (Enrolled 29.9.42)
* BACON Ernest John (1/1st West Somerset Yeo. and 12th Somerset L.I.)
  BACON Walter Sidney
  BALE Albert (Joined H.M. Forces 12.8.41)
  BALE Thomas (Enrolled 8.7.42; discharged 18.2.43)
* BARTLETT John Arthur, L/Cpl. (7 years Coldstream Guards;
    resigned and rejoined 8.7.42)
  BEDFORD Henry Edward (Enrolled 10.6.41)
* BINDING Albert John (Middlesex, Suffolk and Northants Regiments)
  BINDING Arthur (1st V Bn. Somerset L.I.; resigned 30.6.41)
  BINDING Robert John (Enrolled H.G. 27.9.41)
  BINDING Sidney Arthur (Somerset L.I., France 1915-1918)
  BINDING William Henry (Transferred)
  BINDON Basil Chas. Sparks (Member of A.T.C.)
* BINDON Ernest (1/4th Somerset L.I., India and Mespotamia 1914-1919;
    resigned 30.6.41)
* BISHOP Clifford, Cpl.
* BLACKMORE Alfred John (2 years in R.A.F.;
    transferred to Washford Section)
* BOND Transvaal Wm., Cpl. (Dorset Regiment)
  BOSLEY Lawrence Stuart
  BOSLEY Geoffrey
* BOWDEN Wm. Thomas (Joined R.A.S.C.)
  BOYS Ernest Edward
  BOYS Ernest Lewis (R.F.A., France 1915-1919; enrolled H.G. 23.8.43)
  BROWNING Reginald John
  BROWNING Robert (Enrolled H.G. 10.8.41)
* BROWNSEY Chas. Levi (Kings (Liverpool) Regiment and R.A.F.;
    discharged on medical grounds 20.8.42)
  BRYANT Alfred Lionel (Enrolled H.G. 6.10.42)
  BRYANT James, L/Cpl.(Royal Navy)

* BULPIN Thomas Wm., Cpl.
* BULPIN Walter Henry
* BULPIN Wm. Henry, Cpl. (1st BN. Somerset L.I.)
* BULPIN Wm. John
  BULPIN Wm. John (Joined Royal Engineers)
* BURGE Richard Henry (Joined Admiralty Police)
  BURNETT Wilfred George
  CHAMBRE Eric Chris A. (Joined R.A.F. 19.3.42)
  CHIDGEY Fredk. Shewan (1st V.B. Somerset L.I.;
    transferred from B.B.C. Platoon 29.8.42)
  CHILCOTT Francis (Joined Royal Navy 5.8.42)
* CHUBB Philip (M.G. Corps)
* CLAVEY Douglas Hy. John
  COLES Herbert (Somerset L.I., India 1914-1919; resigned 28.6.41)
* COX Frederick Percival (Bristol University OTC)
* DANBY Victor Emmanuel, Lt. (1st Bn. Somerset L.I., France 1914)
* DANE Wm. Herbt. (R.A.S.C. (M.T.) 1918)
* DAVIDGE Albert Leslie (R.N.V.R., R.N.D., H.L.I. (70% disabled))
  DAY Francis James (G.W.R. Section H.G.)
* DUDDRIDGE Ernest J.H. (Egypt and Palestine 1915-1919)
  DUDDRIDGE Jesse Manning
* DUDDRIDGE Stanley, L/Cpl.
* DYTE Wallace
* EDWARDS Arthur Jas. (Joined R.A.F.;
    killed in action whilst flying with 51 squadron R.A.F.V.R. 26.7.43
    aged 29; buried Bergen-Op-Zoom War Cemetery, Netherlands)
  EDWARDS Saml. Victor (Enrolled 29.10.42)
* EVANS Gwyn Elwyn
* EVELEIGH Leonard, Cpl.
* GARDNER Herbert William
  GARDNER Redvers Donald (Enrolled 26.1.43)
* GARDNER Walter John (Somerset L.I. (Mil. [Foot] Police))
  GAYTON Eric John (Transferred from 4th Bn. Wilts H.G. 1.10.42;
    transferred to 10th Bn. Somerset H.G. 9.6.43)
  GILES Thomas (Enrolled 26.9.42)
  GOOSTREY John Dickinson (R.A. (A.A.) 1922-28, enrolled 29.5.42)
* GREENSLADE Walter Lancelot (Sea Scout (Coast watching);
    joined R.A.F. 22.11.41)
  GREGORY Thomas Foster
* GRIFFITHS William Albert
  GROVES Arthur John Morgan (Enrolled 8.7.42)
  HAYWARD Eric Reg. (Enrolled 13.6.41; R.A.S.C., attached to Wiltshire
    Regiment 1941; discharged from Army because of defective sight)
* HEADFORD Ernest William
* HOLE Ivor Charles (Transferred to Special Section September 1942)
* HOOPER Leonard
  HOPKINS Rees
  HOUSE Oliver Walter (Enrolled 6.1.42)
* HOUSE Wm. Wallace (Joined ??? 30.4.42 – ??? possibly refers to
    Special Section)
  HUNT Joseph Walter, Sgt. (Somerset L.I.; G.W.R. Section H.G.)
* HUNT Reginald John
* JONES Alfred James
  JOSLIN Henry Codd Sgt. (Worcestershire Regiment 1917-1926;
    transferred to Cardiff H.G. on leaving Watchet 8.8.41)
  KEMP Wm. Leslie (Enrolled 8.7.42)
  KEMPSTER Charles Henry (Enrolled 20.6.42)

* KIRBY Elias, Sgt. (R.A.; transferred to Special Section September 1942)
LANGDON Leslie George (Enrolled 25.5.42; discharged from H.G. 20.8.42 on joining the Army)
LANGDON W.T. (Transferred from B.B.C. Platoon 29.8.42)
* LEE Willie John Eames, Drill Rm. Sgt. (1st V.B. Somerset L.I.; compulsorily retired on account of age (72) 25.10.42; awarded Certificate of Service in New Year's Honours 1942)
* LEONARD Arthur Thos. (Joined Royal Engineers)
LEY Ernest Robert (1st V Bn. Somerset L.I.; enrolled 5.5.41; left the district December 1941)
LLOYD Norton D. (Enrolled 5.2.42; joined R.N. 2.4.42)
MILES Wm. (Transferred from 7th Devon Battn. 1.9.42)
* MILTON Herbert (1/5 & 1/4 Somersets 1914-19; enrolled 16.2.43)
* MORGAN Lewis Lawrence, Sgt. (Royal Tank Corps)
MURPHY Kevin Maurice (Enrolled 10.4.42; joined R.A.F. 4.3.43)
NEALE John (Enrolled 12.7.41)
NEALE Richard (Enrolled 10.6.41)
* NICHOLAS Cyril Keen (Enrolled 8.7.42)
* NICHOLAS Edwin John
NICHOLAS James Wolsey
NICHOLS Roland (Joined Royal Navy 29.10.42)
NORMAN Edgar Maurice
* NORMAN Geoffrey Wm. F. (Joined Army 20.5.43)
NORMAN Harold (Joined R.A.C. 15.1.42)
* NORMAN Russell Clifford (Joined R.A.F.)
* NORMAN Thomas
* ODAM William George (Called up for Civil Work)
PAYNE Henry Arthur (Western Front 1914-18; G.W.R. Section)
* PEARCE Robert James (1st Bn. G.I.P. Railway Regiment (India); Chaplain to the Forces (R.A.R.O.) 1929-1937, Non Combatant (First Aid))
PEPPIN Cecil James (Enrolled 26.1.43)
POPE George Henry, L/Cpl. (5th Bn. Somerset L.I.)
POPE John Alfred (Enrolled 8.7.42)
PROLE Arthur Henry (Joined Royal Navy 10.2.43)
* PROLE Ernest William (Great War Russian relief force)
PROLE Ivor John (Enrolled 7.1.42)
* PROLE Ronald Henry, Sgt. (Duke of Cornwall's L.I. and Devonshire Rgt.)
PROLE William, Sgt. (Russian Expeditionary Force 1919)
* PUGSLEY Dennis George (R.A.F. (deferred service))
PUTT Frederick Raymond (Enrolled 23.6.42; joined R.N. 26.1.43)
* ROLLINGS John Alfred
* SALMON Arthur Wm. (Transferred from Williton Platoon)
SHARP Albert Thomas
* SHORT Frances Edwin
* SOBEY Stanley Hume (Joined R.A.S.C. 12.8.41)
STACEY Alexander (Enrolled 8.12.42)
STOATE Richard
* STONE Raymond George
SUCHLEY Louis Wm. (Enrolled 11.2.41)
* SULLY Rufus Sidney
SULLY Wm. James (Somerset L.I.)
* THOMSON Wm. Danskin, 2nd Lt. (7th Black Watch)
TIPLER Ronald Herbt. (Enrolled 26.5.42; joined Somerset L.I. 18.6.42)
TUDBALL Arthur Wm., L/Cpl. (G.W.R. Section)
WARREN Fredk. Wm. John (Enrolled 26.1.43)
WATTS Stanley (Enrolled 3.4.42)
WATTS Wm. John (Enrolled 29.5.42)
WEBBER Albert Jas. (Joined Pioneer Corps 17.7.41)
WEBBER Arthur Thomas (Enrolled 6.5.41, joined Royal Marines 5.8.41; killed in action 17.8.44 aged 33; buried La Délivrande War Cemetery, Douvres, Calvados, France)
WEBBER Charles (R.A.S.C. 1916 - 1920)
WEBBER Harold Edward (Enrolled 29.9.42)
WEBBER Henry George (Enrolled 27.3.42)
WEBBER Wm. John (Enrolled 26.1.43)
WEDLAKE Alfred Leslie (Enrolled 12.8.43)
WELLS Percival Thomas (Enrolled 14.5.41)
WESCOTT Hubert John (Enrolled 12.6.41)
* WESTERN Cyril Herbert (Enrolled 11.3.43; formerly in H.G. from 26.6.40 to 19.5.41)
* WHITE Wallace J.H.
WILKINS Leonard Jas.
* WILLIAMS Arthur James (1st Bn. Somerset L.I.)
WILLIAMS Percy (Enrolled 29.9.42)
* WILLICOMBE Fredk. Herbt., Sgt. (Somerset L.I., Mesopotamia)
WILLICOMBE George, Sgt. (Somerset L.I., Burma and India 1914-1919)
WILLICOMBE James Fredk. (Joined Royal Navy (F.A.A.) 28.4.42)

Not all of the above conducted themselves in accordance with military discipline as the letter below shows.

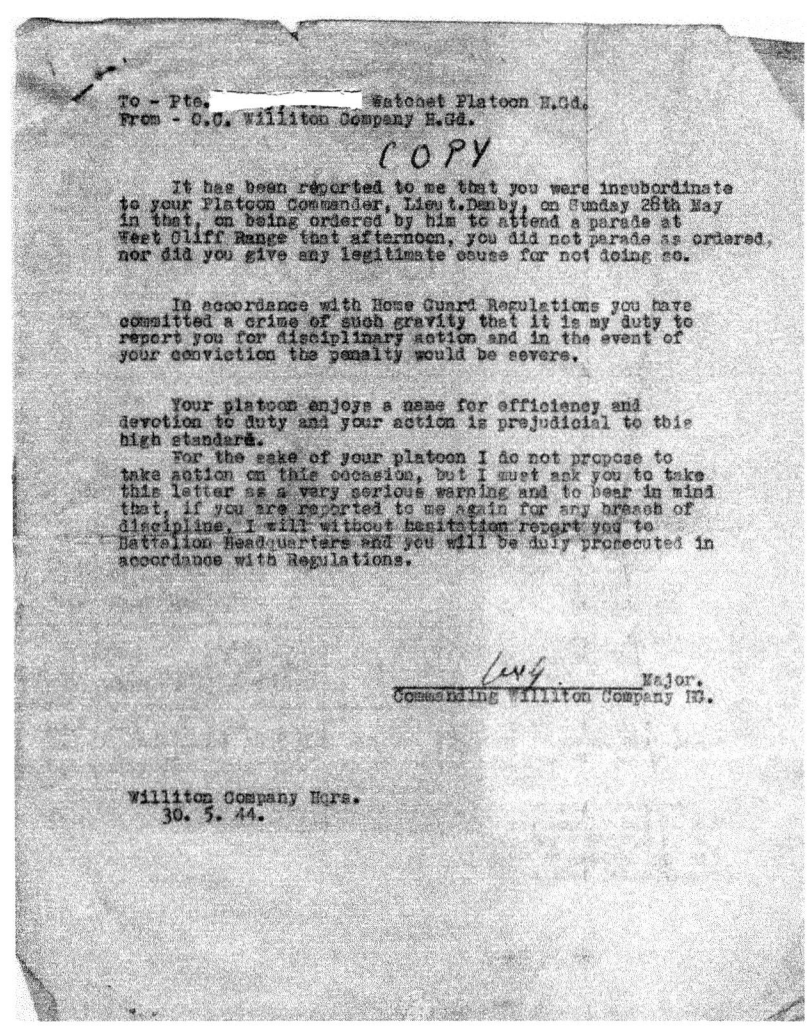

The rifle range mentioned in the letter was constructed at Daws Castle, Cleeve Hill, Watchet. The range was inspected by Supt. S.C. Edwards of Dunster Police on 22nd October 1940. With the butts at map ref. ST 060 432 and the firing point at ST 062 433 approached by a cliff path, the range was declared to have provided proper precautions to safeguard the public. Subsequently approved by the military, the range was opened on 8th July 1941. Sten gun and grenade practice was carried out nearby. The final use of the range was for the disposal of Molotov Cocktails and Self Igniting Phosphorus grenades at the end of 1944.

The war-time map reproduced below shows the dispositions of the Home Guard. To this has been added further information kindly provided by Alec Danby, son of the Platoon Commander.

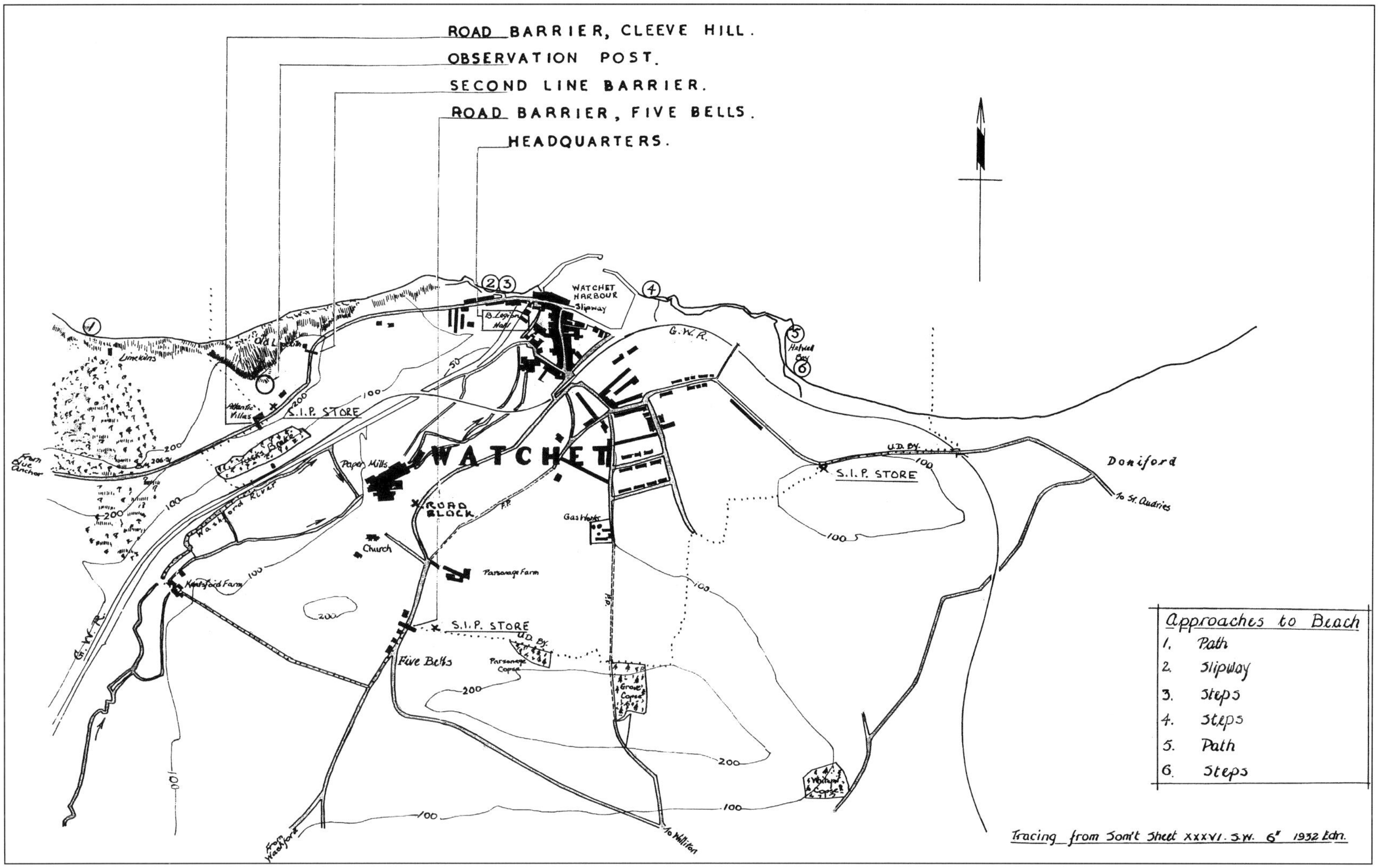

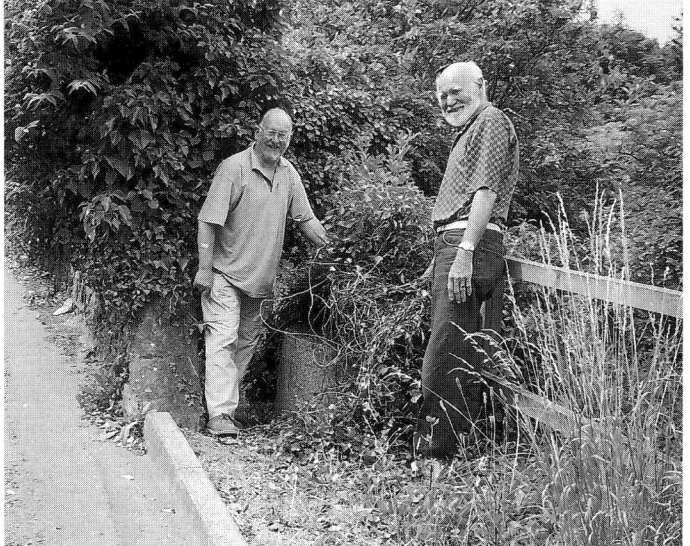

(left) Alec Danby and Nigel Swinburn stand by a concrete cylinder in July 2003, one remaining of five intended to obstruct Brendon Road, now forgotten opposite No. 39, watching over traffic and the passing years. The high wall once continued down towards the harbour but for a small gap where the five cylinders would have been rolled out by the Home Guard. On the opposite side of the road, at a site now occupied by the driveway to No. 39, there was an access track to farmland. This track was furnished with pre-formed sockets to accept a road block, possibly of the 'hairpin' type. (Author's collection)

WATCHET PLATOON,
HOME GUARD.
---oOo---
STAND-DOWN Dinner
at
British Restaurant,
Watchet.
Saturday, January 6th.
at 7 p.m.
Tickets: 2/6 each.

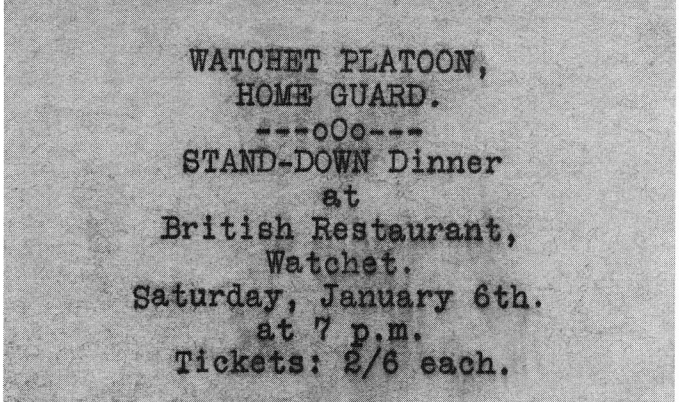

```
WATCHET PLATOON, HOME GUARD
(Williton Co., 1st Somerset (Dunster) Bn.)
―――――
ORDERS for the week ending Sunday, July 6th, 1941:―

    Ordly/Sergt.  -  -  H. C. Joslin

Parades at H.Q.―TUESDAY and THURSDAY, at 19 hrs.
                SUNDAY, at 10 hrs.
        FRIDAY, n.c.o.'s class at 19.15 hrs.

NOTE.―Further Recruits, particularly young men of 17 and upwards,
    will be welcome.  Names should be given to the officers
    or n.c.o.'s belonging to the Platoon.

    (Signed),
                                      Platoon Commander
```

BBC Washford Home Guard with a handsome trophy won by their small-bore rifle team.
Back Row: Bill Coomer; John Gilman; Archie Cubbon; 'Jock' Crawford (engine room mechanic); Unknown; Unknown; Unknown; Unknown
Seated: L/Cpl. Rigg; Cpl. Bert Sparkes; Sgt. Sutherland Reed; Lt. R.J. Bird (engineer-in-charge); Sgt. Bob Lyne (assistant engineer-in-charge); Cpl. Ray Bryant (station clerk); L/Cpl. Joe Neal
Front: Unknown; Nobby Clarke; Mr. Cridland; possibly Mr. Viara

Little further is known of this unit. Close examination shows that the cap badges are that of the Somerset Light Infantry and that the shoulder flash indicates that these men were part of the 1st (Minehead) Battalion. Interestingly, coastal defence plans of April 1942 drawn up to counter a seaborne invasion record that the BBC (Washford) Platoon together with Bicknoller Platoon, Williton Platoon and Watchet Platoon would come under the command of O.C., 8 L.A.A. Practice Camp Watchet.
(by courtesy of Washford Radio Museum)

(right) **Stogumber Civic Group**.
On the steps: Unknown; Stanley Dennett; Unknown
Standing: Lesley Hyatt; Unknown; Arthur Gulliver; John Hutchins; Sgt. Sid Bennett; Leonard Chidgey; Ernie Stevens; Unknown; Unknown; William Yendell; Nichol Red; Jack Hill; Ted Stevens; Unknown
(Sgt. Major Ernie Stevens has been suggested but badges of rank are that of a lieutenant and the officer is carrying a pistol in a leather holster)
Sitting: Jack Hayes; Mr. Fevre; Rev. A. Couch; Mrs. Bladderwick; Miss Maddocks; Mrs. Marden; Mr. Baker; Dr. Atkinson; Col. Hutchinson; Cyril Thomas; Jim Brewer; William Hill. *(Richard Denôt collection)*

(above) **Stogumber Platoon**, *from an original photograph priced at 1/6d.*
Back Row: Morris Bryant; Unknown; Arthur Gulliver; Clifford Tremlett; Jeff Hayes; Bernard Routley; Unknown; William Hill (or Alf Chidgey)
Second Row: Unknown; Unknown; Frank Bishop; Unknown; Unknown; Unknown; Arthur Burnett; Unknown; Jack Bishop; Chris Clarke; Unknown; Jack Hayes; ?Jack Davies; ?Arthur Banbury
Third Row: Jim Nation; Roger Hutchins; Jack Hill; Unknown; ?Ernie Hayes; Tom Summerfield; Rex Howe; Jack Redwood; Unknown; Sam Gadd; Unknown; Percy Alan; Bill Summerfield; Jeff Sellick; Bob Summerfield
Fourth Row: Unknown; Unknown; Fred Bailey; ?Jack Davies; Unknown; Unknown; Sgt. Sid Bennett; Sgt. Major Ernie Stevens; Col. J.R. Hutchinson, D.S.O.; Sgt. Major Davies; Major W.T. Greswell; Lt. Cyril F. Thomas; Sgt. Ted Stevens; Percy Bryant; Leslie Hyatt; William 'Shaver' Yendell; ?Ernie Hayes; Bill Lewis
Front Row: Harold Balman; Jimmy Brewer; Unknown; Frank Hayes (or B. Hayes); L/Cpl. Jim Horsey; L/Cpl. Percy Watts; L/Cpl. Arthur Routley; L/Cpl. Bill Burge.
Two other members of the Home Guard, Fred 'Daisy' Bryant and Stan Dennett, have not been identified or are not 'on parade'. (Richard Denôt collection)

Crowcombe Platoon.
Sitting Left to Right: William H.P. Parsons; L/Cpl. James Henson; Cpl. William H.E. Conibeare; Sgt. Stanley S.W. Baker; Sgt. (Capt.) C.H.W. Malet; Lt. (Lt. Col.) A. Hewlett; Sgt. H. Jim Merson; Sgt. William Tuckfield; L/Cpl. P.C. Crane; A.G. Hall
Standing: William C. Payne; Herbert Herniman; E.H. Coleman; L/Cpl. George H. Touchins; Leslie Ames; William C. Chidley; S.R. Baker; K.D. Harrison; Richard A. Cooper; Woolstan G. Smith; Dennis R. Webber
Top Row: S. Harold Smith; Arthur Cavil; R.J. Tarr; Bert Durrant; G. 'Philip' Langdon
This is one of the few photographs that was contemporaneously captioned. It is interesting to note that it refers to the 1st (Dunster) Battalion. On 3rd August 1943 Dunster Battalion was renamed Minehead Battalion.
(Wilfred F. Chidley collection)

The Quantock Hills have been quarried for centuries and the following Home Guard members worked on the hills: William Parsons (Triscombe); William Conibeare, William Tuckfield, Bert Durrant and Philip Langdon. James Henson farmed at Flaxpool Farm whilst William Chidley, Woolstan Smith and Dennis Webber were also involved in agriculture. Stanley Baker was the local haulage contractor. Military expertise was provided by C.H.W. Mallet, A. Hewlett and Richard Cooper, all being ex-army. Jim Merson was a local chauffeur/handyman. A.G. Hall was the estate agent for Crowcombe Court whilst E.H. Coleman was employed as the gardener. S.R. Baker was also on the staff of Crowcombe Court, dying of T.B. at an early age. Halsway Manor employed William Payne and George Touchins as gardeners. Herbert Herniman was the local postman, also working at Crowcombe Court as a gardener. Leslie Ames was employed on highways maintenance whilst Arthur Cavil worked at the concrete works located at Crowcombe Station.

Home Guard dispatch riders often used their own machines and Crowcombe was no exception, William Parson's machine sporting an 'A.A.' badge in addition to the obligatory headlight blackout mask.

Observation duties were carried out at Willett Tower whilst Crowcombe Village Hall was used for meetings. Mrs. Phyllis Herniman remembers a Home Guard store shed being built in a field at Crowcombe over the garden hedge of 'Sunnyside' and to the south-east of Hagleys Green, approximately at map ref. ST 137 366. This has long since gone.

During December 1944 and in the following months many Home Guard units held Stand Down dinners, Crowcombe Platoon holding theirs on Saturday 3rd February 1945 as the programme (*right*) shows.

```
1st.  SOMERSET  BATTALION  H.G.

      C R O W C O M B E   P L A T O O N.

              ---ooo0ooo---

               STAND - DOWN

               D I N N E R.

The School,                   Saturday,
CROWCOMBE.                    Feb.  3rd.  1945.

                 -oOo-

               T O A S T S

  Chairman.........Major  W.T.  CRESWELL.

               ------

"THE KING"................The   CHAIRMAN.

"HOME GUARD"..............Capt. W.G. HURLEY.
       Response - Lt. H. DAVIS.
"CROWCOMBE PLATOON"..........The  CHAIRMAN.
       Response - Lt. S.S.W. BAKER.
"VISITORS & THE LADIES"......Sgt. H.J. MERSON.
       Response - Dr. B.M. YOUNG.

--------ooooo0ooooo---------

               A R T I S T E S.

       THE  TAUNTON  ENTERTAINERS
```

NO. 5 (WIVELISCOMBE) COMPANY

COMMANDING OFFICER   Major E.M. Driver   2ND IN COMMAND   Capt. G.F. Nuthall
                                  (Lt. Col. A.S. Capper, D.S.O.)

(above) **Officers and N.C.O.s of No.5 (Wiveliscombe) Company including Brendon Hill Platoon.** *The photograph was taken on Wiveliscombe Football Field by Kingsley Tayler.*
Back Row: L/Cpl. Jack Sharland; Bob Wyatt; George Bradner; L/Cpl. Ern Lee; L/Cpl. Harvey; L/Cpl. John Thomas; Unknown; Unknown; Alf Cross; 'Ganger' Hawkins; L/Cpl. Maybely Byrde; A.J. 'Bert' Calloway; Fred Webber; Unknown; Unknown; Unknown; Frank Pulsford; Arthur Shepherd; Unknown; Cyril Warman
Middle Row: Sgt. Jack Loosemore; Donald Pulson; Cyril Edmunds; Cpl. Jimmy Watts; Unknown; Unknown; Hubert Baker; Mr. Hutchins; Bert Lewis; E.B.D. Hall; Bert Hall; Unknown; Unknown; Sid Pulsford; Unknown; Unknown; Cyril Berry; George N. Frankham
Front Row: Sgt. Jack or Walt Jacobs; Unknown; Unknown; Fred Besley; Sgt. Tom Thorne; Sgt. Bill Brown; Frank Marle or Morle; Unknown; Lt. Ted Burston; Capt. G.F. Nuthall; Major E.M. Driver; Unknown; Mr. Dulborough; Lt. Chris Shapland; Sgt. Sealey; Hubert Dascombe; Unknown; Unknown; Sgt. Bert Yandle
The photograph includes Lt. Ted Burston and Lt. Chris Shapland of Milverton Platoon.

    Company duties included guarding Venn Cross railway tunnel and viaduct. Full-bore rifle practice was undertaken at Whitefield Quarries, Langley whilst The White Harp, Milverton, provided facilities for small-bore shooting. (Bert Calloway collection)

(left) Stanley Shopland, who lived at Huish Cleeve, Huish Moor, was a member of No. 2 Platoon Huish Champflower before joining the 55th Field Regiment Royal Artillery in 1943, aged 27. Headquarters of the Platoon was Combe End House, Huish Champflower. For guard duties a wooden hut was erected at Flint Cross some 1,000 yards to the north-west. Stanley remembers four members of the Home Guard were on duty each night with a frequency of one duty per week. Whilst most would have walked or cycled to their lonely vigil, L/Cpl. Shopland rode his B.S.A. motorcycle. During the war he possessed two machines, registration nos. EYA 513 and CYA 168, which he also used for carrying dispatches on Home Guard exercises.
(Stanley Shopland collection)

Pencilled notes taken by L/Cpl. Shopland at various meetings have survived. One extract covers the arrangements made in the event of invasion. It would appear that on the receipt of the code word 'Cromwell' Sgt. Billinger would alert E. Holland, J. Broom, F.G. Bear and R. Muxworthy. On the ringing of the church bells these four would call out the rest of the platoon as follows:

E.F. Holland having rung the church bell, would warn R. Grabham.
R. Grabham would warn M.W. Gadd.
M.W. Gadd would warn L/Cpl. Shopland, S.J. Hunt and W. Willis.
R. Grabham, having warned K. Dear, D. Chapman, W. Hill and S. Willmott, would proceed to Flint Cross.
W. Willis would warn E. Headon, A. Lock, Mr. Tout, Mr. Yeatons and K. Norman.
E. Holland would warn J. Norman and Cpl. S. Holland.
F.G. Bear would warn L/Cpl. E. Broom, S. Clapp and H. Nicholls.
Mr. Coles would be contacted from the Flint Cross post.

On being called out all troops would proceed to 'Combe End', Platoon Headquarters, as soon as possible. These details have been included as it must cover nearly all platoon members, many of whom would be included in the Wiveliscombe photograph.

On the night of 7th/8th September 1940 the church bells *were* rung and one can only imagine what the platoon's thoughts were on being called out 'for real'.

Milverton Home Guard, *photographed at The Old School, Milverton by R. Kingsley Tayler (note the netball hoop on the wall).*
Back Row: Henry Hart; Unknown; Harold Winter; Unknown; Walter Lang; Bill Locke; Dick Wyatt; John Ackland-Troyt; Lionel Hayes; Bill Gardener; Unknown; Arthur Venton; Jack Rowen; Harold Blue; Harold Rowen (brother of Jack); Jack Besley; Frank Sulley; Harold Wyatt; G. Prole; Jack Hope
Middle Row: Bunny Wyatt; Albert Raffel; Unknown; Jack Kingdom; Jack Goss; Don Noble; Bill Mead; Bill Rowe; Cliff ?; Tommy Shephard?; Jack Perry; Geoff Gill; Burt Smith; John Tarr; Ike Westcott; Sid Grabham; Cliff Nutt; Tommy Shephard?; Harold Tarr; Ern Tooze
Front Row: L/Cpl. Bill Hawkins; L/Cpl. Alf Cross; L/Cpl. Ern Lee; L/Cpl. John Thomas; L/Cpl. Jack Sharland; L/Cpl. George Bradner; L/Cpl. Maybely Byrde; Sgt. Jack Loosemore; Sgt. Harry Sealey; Lt. Chris Shapland; Lt. Ted Burston; Sgt. Bert Yandle; Sgt. Jack or Walt Jacobs; Cpl. Donald Pulson; Cpl. Cyril Edmunds; Cpl. Jimmy Watts; L/Cpl. Harvey; L/Cpl. Bob Wyatt
Missing from the photograph are Bert Winter, Harry Winter, Jack Stone, Eddie Barter and Ernest Parkman.

Ted Burston ran Milverton Post Office with his wife who also operated the manual telephone exchange. After serving in WW1 Ern Lee became a Milverton butcher, Bill Hawkins being the other Milverton butcher. Bob Wyatt was tragically killed when a tree fell on him in the 1950s.

Milverton rifle range was situated to the north of Milverton Station where it was possible to shoot up to 300 yards. Grenade practise took place at Castle Wood, Wiveliscombe. In addition to the usual range of Home Guard weapons, Milverton also boasted a Boys anti-tank rifle. (Author's collection)

NO. 6 (DULVERTON) COMPANY

COMMANDING OFFICER   Major Reginald Charles Nelder
2ND IN COMMAND   Capt. C.H. Abbott

Reginald Charles Nelder 1892-1977

Reginald Charles Nelder was born at *The Carnarvon Arms*, Brushford in 1892. He completed his education at Taunton School in 1908. Being interested in farming, which at that stage was in depression, he was sent by his father to a distant relative in Canada to try his luck there. He found temporary work on farms, travelling through Canada. Finally he teamed up with George Boulton when they acquired Exmoor Ranch – a half-section (320-acre) prairie homesteading ranch in Alberta, west of Calgary.

Farming at that time was very tough and difficult. After George and Reginald had built their shack, Reginald sent for one of his sisters from *The Carnarvon Arms* to keep house for them.

At the outbreak of the Great War Reginald Nelder was keen to enlist which he did after George Boulton had married Miss Nelder in order to retain title to the property. Joining the Canadian cavalry his riding skills came to notice and he was promoted to Sergeant Instructor in the Fort Garry Horse. His continual application for a posting to France, where he could see some action, was finally accepted. He was sent overseas in charge of a troop under the condition that he would drop his stripes on arrival in France. R.C. Nelder took part in one of the last 'drawn swords' cavalry charges of the Great War.

In about 1918 he returned to Canada only to see much of the ranch stock lost in the drought of 1921 or '22. Friction had also built up between himself and his brother-in-law. Relief was at hand when his father asked him to return to Brushford and take over the running of *The Carnarvon Arms* which he did, much improving the hotel in the process.

At the outbreak of the Second World War, now aged 47, Reginald Nelder again sought a role in which he could serve his country but his application to join the Special Constabulary was turned down as he was a licensee of a hotel.

On the formation of the Home Guard he found himself nominated for the post of Company Commander of the Dulverton Company by persons unknown. Obviously his military experience and first-hand knowledge of the countryside around Dulverton gained from hunting had not gone unnoticed. He was highly thought of, more so than many retired ex-military men who did (and still do) populate rural areas.

Major Nelder put all his efforts into the Home Guard with assistance from Roland Pertwee, a well-known dramatic author and actor whose career started before the First World War and which was still flourishing in 1940. Roland was succeeded by Hardy Abbott of Dulverton. Together they forged Dulverton Company into an efficient fighting force as the following photograph shows. (Roland was, incidentally the first cousin, once removed, of Bill Pertwee, who played the part of Mr. Hodges, the A.R.P. Warden in *Dad's Army*.)

The Nelder family contributed to the war effort in other ways, as the programme below shows, where more than half of the concert party came from the ranks of the Nelder family. Originally the concert party entertained the guests staying at *The Carnarvon Arms* but in the war it also gave performances in the nearby small towns and villages including Brushford and Dulverton, usually to raise money for the British Red Cross.

After the war, Major Nelder returned to farming, this time in Moretonhampstead, Devon and finally kept the Post Office at Meare, near Glastonbury. He retired to Wilmington in Devon where he died in 1977 aged 85.

The author is indebted to Robin Nelder, son of Major Nelder, for the above notes. During the war he was a pupil at Blundells School and at the age of 17 became his father's personal runner in the Home Guard.

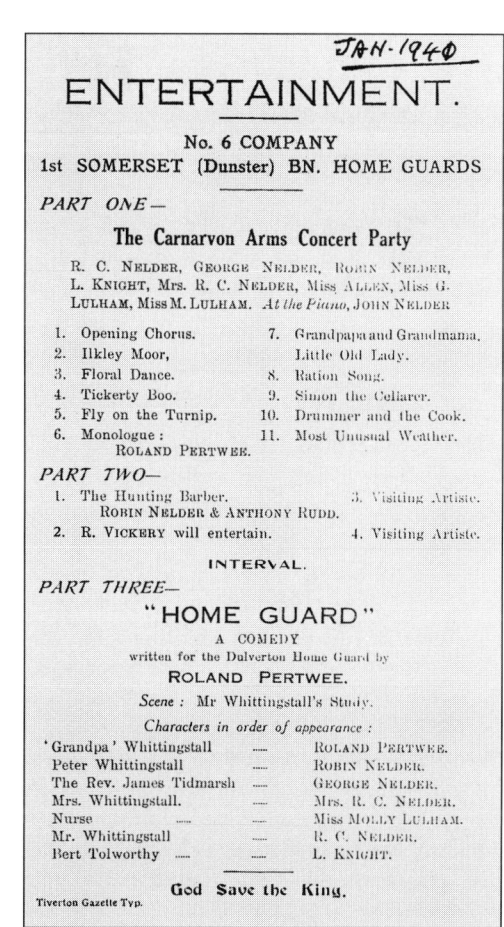

Officers and Men of No. 6 (Dulverton) Company, taken on 3rd December 1944 in the Town Square, Dulverton. A press report for the day states:
"In a fortunate hold up of the weather the Company fell in at the H.Q. of the Platoon at 2.30 p.m. and headed by the Dulverton Silver Band under their bandmaster Mr. F.R. Loosemore, Major N.C. Nelder, the Company Commander, led his men in order of platoons to the saluting base opposite the Company H.Q. in the High Street ..."

Dulverton Company comprised five platoons, Bridgetown, Brushford, Dulverton, Skilgate and King's Brompton, also known as Brompton Regis. To date no photograph of Dulverton Platoon has been located although no doubt Mr. Kingsley Tayler was very busy that day photographing the various units in the Minehead Battalion. An original copy of the photograph above was marked 2/6 (12½p), a not inconsiderable sum in those days when one considers a pint of beer was about 1/- (5p).

Those who have been identified include the following:
Front Rank, from left to right: K. Bawden or Bernard Bolsom; Lt. J. Howe (Dulverton Platoon); Lt. E.C. Mylne (Brushford Platoon); Major R.C. Nelder (Company Commander); Lt. J. Parsons (King's Brompton Platoon); Lt. A.A. Thomas (Skilgate Platoon); Lt. Bert Bawden (Bridgetown Platoon);
Second Rank, from the left: behind K. Bawden or Bernard Bolsom, with the moustache, is Mr. Philpott and to his left is A. Cozens or Mr. Lazrath; two further along is Phil Farmer with the tall Ron German behind him; behind Lt. Parsons is Bill Stone and on his left is H.J. Martin.
Others in the photograph include Mr. Chilcot, Eddie Tarr, G. Land (a local butcher, standing on the pavement behind the troops); Mr. Darch, William Harvey, Fred Tout (leaning out of the window of his bicycle and fishing tackle shop on the right), Jack Quartley and, in the dark raincoat and leaning against the window of Fred Tout's shop, Mrs. Chilcot. (Phil Parkman collection)

Bridgetown Platoon, taken outside Exmoor House in Dulverton, as with many of the Platoon photographs that follow.
Back Row: William Norman; Cyril Hole; Clifford Gunter; Mr. Skinner; Frank Quick; Ron Hayward; Dai Jones; Stanley Ferris
Front Row: Charlie Vaulter; Rev. Roberts (vicar of Exton); Cpl. Jack Quartly; L/Cpl. Percy Stephens; Sgt. Godfrey; Lt. Bert Bawden; L/Cpl. Charlie Gunter; Cpl. Soaper; Charlie Farmer.
Missing from the photograph is Jack Stevens.
  William Norman and Percy Stevens were farmers, Percy Stevens farming Red Door Farm with his father. Roy Hayward and Stanley Ferris were farmworkers. Whilst not engaged on Home Guard duties, Clifford Gunter worked on the Miltons Estate. The local millers, James Phillips and Sons, employed Cyril Hole.
(Mrs. Lily Westcott collection)

Bridgetown Platoon, which also covered Exton, used the village hall at Bridgetown for their meetings. A rifle range at Shircombe Farm, owned by Wilfred and Hubert Davey, was used by members of the Dulverton Company. Mr. White of Shircombe Farm, writing in November 2001 recalls:

The target area was a banked pit now disappeared due to a track being taken along the hedge line. The firing area was a small level area fenced off with oak rails and posts which have all but disappeared. The firing area will still be there, under Knapkindham, part of the Miltons Estate and the target was in Shircombe Farm. [From a map supplied by Mr. White, the firing point would have been at map ref. SS 931 317 whilst the targets would be at map ref. SS 932 317.]

Christopher Everard, who was a young boy during the war, recalls that the local Home Guard Platoon had a shelter at Miltons Quarry at map ref. SS 923 323 whilst behind *The Rock Inn* now known as 'Badgers Holt', at map ref. SS 925 332, there existed two further huts, one of them brick-built. After the war a quantity of small arms ammunition was found nearby. It must be said that at this spot the road was bordered by a steep bank on one side and the river on the other, an ideal 'nodal point' where the Home Guard could delay an enemy advance up the valley road, possibly with the help of a Spigot Mortar.

At Higher Week, two sheds remain which were the accommodation blocks for Canadian soldiers manning a searchlight, the hard standing visible on the south side of the track at map ref. SS 912 333. Every Thursday these troops were permitted to have a bath at Miltons but were ordered by the lady of the house to use a separate bath mat! Exercises were held between the Home Guard and the Canadians based on attack and defence of the area around Miltons.

At South Hill, map ref. SS 893 321, the U.S. Army carried out tank training, ramps being built against hedge banks to enable tanks to cross. A camp was set up with U.S. troops instructed to draw water from the Kent River to acclimatise them to drinking stream water. Slit trenches were also dug at map ref. SS 907 332 in an area known as Summer Way.

Brushford Platoon.
Back Row: George Shire; Unknown; Kempton Baker; Michael Burns; Tom 'Squeaker' Sharp; Unknown; Unknown; Bert Crook; Unknown; Unknown; Roland Hill; Barry Hodge; Unknown
Middle Row: Arthur Pike; Mr. Rice; Unknown; Ray Saunders; Unknown; Bill Hayes; Reg Buckingham; John Summers; Unknown; Lionel Maddock; Jack Aplin; Bill Venn
Front Row: Unknown; Charles Hutter; Cpl. Jack Parfitt; Cpl. Brewer; Sgt. Bill Harvey; Sgt. Arthur Smallridge; Lt. Mylne; Sgt. Ern Crossman; Sgt. Jack Thomas; Unknown; Unknown; L/Cpl. Robin Nelder; Cyril Adams; Unknown
It is believed that Arthur Smallridge was a signalman at Dulverton Station.
(Mrs. Margaret Hall collection)

The following poem, penned by Mrs. Edith May Nelder, wife of the Company Commander, gives some insight into Brushford Platoon activities.

The Song of the Brushford Home Guard
(to the tune of Old Farmer Giles)

1. 'Tis hatten on six years since they called on we –
With our rifles and shot guns – the old L.D.V.
But Churchill renamed us the Home Guard quite soon,
And here's to the lads of the Brushford Platoon.
    Ritorel – itorel – itorel itay
They worked us at all times and all without pay
To keep watch for jerries by night and by day
    Ritorel – itorel – itorel itay.

2. Oh, this is the song of the Brushford Home Guard,
Who paraded each Sunday out there in the yard –
Our gallant Commanders their names we must fill in,
Messrs. Pertwee & Littlewood & Harrison & Milne.
    Ritorel – itorel – itorel itay
We learnt all our drill in the new-fangled way
With our greasy old rifles from far U.S.A.
    Ritorel – itorel – itorel itay.

3. Who drilled the recruits and who marked on the range?
And sometimes stood beers if they had any change,
Who inspected our rifles and all that was on us? –
Sergeants Smallridge & Crossman & Harvey & Thomas.
    Ritorel – itorel – itorel itay
They took us out shooting to Shercombe one day
And us beat up King's Brompton in our usual way
    Ritorel – itorel – itorel itay.

4. One fine Sunday morning the battle was on,
'Twas Brushford Platoon against old Dulverton.
Their fine mobile column they thought was so good,
Us ambushed 'em proper from out Allers Wood.
    Ritorel – itorel – itorel itay
They argled and bargled but us won the day
For we caught 'em napping – whate'er they may say –
    Ritorel – itorel – itorel itay.

5. They sent us new weapons, agen and agen,
Tommy Gun – Northover, Lewis and Sten,
And anti-tank rifles, and one called a Barr –
But us liked the Carnarvon one better by far.
    Ritorel – itorel – itorel itay
Us fired Blacker Bombards down Musey Park Way
And beat up the Searchlights another fine day
    Ritorel – itorel – itorel itay.

6. They took us out bombing way down Bowden's Bottom, –
If there'd been Jerries there, we'd have sure to have got 'em –
We startled the jackdaws who fled from their perch
And frightened the good folk a-singing to Church –
    Ritorel – itorel – itorel itay
In contests for shooting we soon made our way,
They gave cups for prizes, and us pinched all they,
    Ritorel – itorel – itorel itay.

7. And then came the stand down and our work was done –
And us never had one bloomin shot at the hun,
But us frightened 'em proper – so they dursn't come,
And that's how the Home Guardsman's victory was won,
    Ritorel – itorel – itorel itay
We're back at our jobs in the same dull old way –
And now us push prams or dig tetties all day,
    Ritorel – itorel – itorel itay

King's Brompton Platoon, *photographed at Brompton Regis School, by R. Kingsley Tayler. The price is written on the back as 'big 2/6d small 9d'.*
Back Row: Ray Stevens; Ted Davey; Ron Thomas; Ern Howe; John Hayes; Bill Williams; William Yerbury; Bob Hole; Hubert Davey
Middle Row: Herbert Tooze; Hedley Norman; Eddie Lock; Harold Hayes; Harry Evett; Richard Gale; J. Hurcock; Arthur Hole; Tom Salter; Gordon Hayes; George Snell
Front Row: L/Cpl. George Heywood; L/Cpl. Edward Colman; Cpl. Wilfred Davey; Sgt. Jim Vaulter; Lt. John Parsons; Sgt. Sid Gibbs; Cpl. Charlie Snell; L/Cpl. Leslie Norman; L/Cpl. Bill Lock
(Ray Stevens collection)

Brompton Regis Spigot Mortar Section.
Ray Stevens; Leslie Hole; L/Cpl. Bill Lock; Sgt. Sid Gibbs;
Hubert Davey; Richard Gale; Harry Evett and Arthur Hole
The stores and Spigot Mortar were kept in an outbuilding together with the 'bombs' at The George Inn in Brompton Regis. As with the previous photograph, it was taken at Brompton Regis School by R. Kingsley Tayler.

Ray Stevens recalled in September 2000 that, for training purposes, the Spigot Mortar was fired diagonally across a field at Nicholls Farm, Brompton Regis owned by John Hayes Snr. Grenade practice was carried out at Brocks Bridge, Exebridge.
(Ray Stevens collection)

(right) **Skilgate Platoon**, again outside Exmoor House, Dulverton.
Back Row: Mr. Curtis; Herbert Andrews; Jim Norman; Russell Muxworthy; K. Gibbs; Unknown; Victor or William Norman; Bill Perriott; Fred Muxworthy; Phil Parkman; Mr. Gibbs
Middle Row: Sid Lock; Jack Lee; Bill Delve; Reg Evans; Bill Cording; Frank Heywood; Gilbert Evans; George Nation; Ron Maunder; Alfred Saunders; Ern Pinkham
Front Row: L/Cpl. Wilfred Gibbs; L/Cpl. Walter Chubb; Sgt. Hubert John Martin; Lt. A.A. Thomas; Cpl. Sid Veysey; L/Cpl. Thomas Douglas Ayre; L/Cpl. Bill Muxworthy; L/Cpl. George Gibbs
The original photograph, again taken by R. Kingsley Tayler, was captioned on the back 'Upton/Skilgate Platoon'. 'Skilgate Platoon' is a more accurate title. There is a distinct possibility that this photograph was taken at the time of the Home Guard Stand Down.
(Mrs. Vera Ayre collection)

This platoon was made up of people from Brompton Regis, Upton, Skilgate and Bury. Mr. Evans of Moorhouse Farm, Upton states that in the early days a Colonel Whitmore of Frogwell Farm, Skilgate and Mr. Thomas of Withywine Farm, Morebath were both appointed to form a local 'army' from the above villages. Training was carried out on Haddon Hill on Sundays. Indoor training was carried out at Upton Vicarage.

Initially they were armed with their own shotguns but one night Colonel Whitmore and Mr. Thomas arrived on Mr. Evans's doorstep, handed him a rifle and ammunition and, as he had never used a rifle before, showed him how to load it. He was then told to get up on the hill within half an hour and look out for German Paratroops. As he owned a car he was given a petrol allowance as it was used for picking up other Home Guard members to take them to training. A field at Helebridge was used as a rifle range and hand grenade practice was carried out in an old quarry. One day members of the Home Guard were travelling to a training venue by bus when one soldier, who had forgotten he had fitted his bayonet on his rifle during the journey, stood up to get off the bus and promptly punctured the roof.

NO. 7 (EXMOOR) COMPANY

COMMANDING OFFICER   Major F.H. Norton   2ND IN COMMAND   Capt. Douglas C.H. Edwards, M.C.

Exmoor Company was the smallest of the companies forming the Minehead Battalion and comprised 4 officers and 116 other ranks. Their armoury (in 1942) included 85 rifles with 4,000 rounds of ammunition and 7 light machine guns with 5,000 rounds.

(left) **No. 7 (Exmoor) Company Senior Officers**.
Standing: Lt. F.J. Maggs (Company Dispatch Rider); Lt. W.P. Arthurs (Adjutant); Lt. J.F. Clatworthy; Lt. R. Moore
Seated: Major F.H. Norton; Capt. D.C.H. Edwards, M.C.
  Lt. J.F. Clatworthy, whose home was at West Water Farm, Withypool, was the officer i/c Withypool Platoon; Sgt. Major W. Mullins, an ex-Somerset Light Infantry Officer, was the commander of Winsford Platoon and Sgt. Jack Vinnell commanded the Simonsbath Platoon. It is believed that he was on the staff of a girls' school that was evacuated to 'Diana Lodge', Simonsbath, now the Simonsbath House Hotel. *(Percy E.H. Bawden collection)*

(below) **Exford Platoon** at Exmoor Stores, Exford.
Left to Right: Cpl. Reg Toogood; Sid Ridd; Lt. Bob Moore; Sgt. Alec Meadows; Sgt. Percy Bawden; L/Cpl. Jim Steer; Bill Carey; Bill Winzer; Ken Bawden; Sid Carey; Herb Steer; Ken Crook; Frank James; Tom James; Geoff Tucker; Ernie Criddle; L/Cpl. Peter Steer; L/Cpl. Gordon Williams; Dick Marley; Frank Ford; John Cressey; George Winzer; Bob Moule; Eddie Philips
John Cressey was originally a member of the Home Guard but at the time of the photograph he was in the army. Eddie Philips' 'uniform' is explained by the fact that he was a new recruit and was waiting to be kitted out. Fred Balmond and Fred Lock were also members of the Platoon. *(Percy E.H. Bawden collection)*

(below) 'Somewhere on Exmoor', a photograph taken by R. Kingsley Tayler of George Curtis of Withypool with his wireless set No. 38. *(Percy E.H. Bawden collection)*

Percy Bawden, in a letter of April 2002, recalls the location of several local ranges. A rifle range was built near Westwater Farm, Withypool in a valley south of Worth Farm on a north-south axis centred on map ref. SS 843 331. Exford Platoon had their own range at Curr Cleeve. The frames for the two targets here were of an unusual design. Situated on the south side of the River Exe, with the firing points set at 100, 200 and 300 yards to the north of the river, the targets were arranged vertically above each other with an axle at the junction of the two frames. This allowed for one target to be 'patched' whilst the other one was exposed for the next shot. The iron work was constructed by Dick Steer of Exford whilst the woodwork was carried out by his neighbour, Herbert Steer, another branch of the Steer family. A field telephone linking the firing point to the butts completed the facilities. As with most wartime ranges they never survived long enough to be plotted on O.S. maps but the shots would have crossed the river at about map ref. SS 865 364.

Practice with grenades with their large danger area was carried out in quarries at Kitnor Heath, 1½ miles to the north-east of Exford.

In about 1976 roadworkers had a nasty surprise when a considerable amount of explosives was uncovered in Exford. A contemporary press report listed 14 nitroglycerine anti-tank missiles with badly corroded caps, 56 Molotov Cocktails, hand grenades, detonators, three blocks of T.N.T. and practice mortar bombs; all appear to have been disposed of by the local Home Guard. However, Major Douglas Edwards, who was 81 when the discovery was made, was reported as saying: "I don't remember anything of this sort". The find was made close to the site of a Home Guard hut.

Percy Bawden remembers a Nissen hut that existed in the Auction Field which was used for the storage of targets, practice grenades and the platoon Northover Projector. He recalls the find and believes that the Regular Army disposed of their surplus ammunition in the time honoured way of simply burying it. A photogaph taken at the time of discovery would indicate that the practice mortar bombs were in fact Spigot Mortar projectiles – which it is thought were unlikely to have been used by the Regular Army. We shall never know who was responsible or how many other 'embarrassing' stores were buried in quiet locations at the end of hostilities.

After the war, members of the local Home Guard formed the Exmoor Rifle Club which ran for about five years, the rifles being bought from the National Rifle Association. As in the war years, the rifle range at Filleigh was used.

Raymond Rich of Timberscombe was originally a member of the Home Guard at North Molton but transferred to the Simonsbath Platoon on moving home. This photograph of him was taken next to the Old School at Simonsbath, the building in the background having subsequently been demolished. The Beer Family who ran The Exford Forest Hotel possessed some six horses, one of which was lent to Raymond, the remainder of the horses being provided by their riders. Initially Raymond was issued with a rifle but after training this was replaced by a Sten gun. Raymond can recall others in the platoon, namely Cpl. Harry Bond, Joe Jones, Harry Prout, F. Coward and Dick Rowle. Meetings were held in the Tea Rooms at the hotel. (Raymond Rich collection)

Post Office Staff, Minehead, photographed outside Minehead Post Office.
Back Row: Mr. Stoate; Unknown; Unknown; Mr. House; Unknown; David Lloyde; Douglas Bryant
Middle Row: Mr. Nation; Unknown; Unknown; Mr. Ford; Mr. May; Wilf Mason; Mr. Double; Clem Williams; Unknown; Unknown; Mr. Bart Naylor
Front Row: Mr. Reed; Cpl. Agers; Unknown; Unknown; L/Cpl. Moore; Mr. Baggett or Mr. Puttock
These Post Office employees were members of 'D' Company, 15th Gloucester (Post Office) Battalion based at Taunton, which had a section at Minehead. The people unidentified could well have been Taunton-based employees. In the event of invasion Minehead-based staff would have come under the Command of the 1st (Minehead) Battalion. Messrs. Stoate, House, Lloyde and Reed were all engineers, responsible for the installation of telephones; Mr. Naylor was their supervisor. Mr. Agers was the local inspector and Mr. Moore was the chief mechanic responsible for Post Office vehicle maintenance. Messrs. Bryant, May and Williams were all local postmen. (Dennis Williams collection)

Geoff Griffiths of Creech St. Michael, Taunton was a member of the Post Office staff based at Taunton. Their commanding officer was Major Harrison assisted by Lt. Martin and Sgt. Len Gibbs. Duties included guarding Bathpool Bridge and the G.P.O. repeater station in Hamilton Road. In addition to the usual weaponry Geoff remembers them having a Boys anti-tank rifle. Annual camps were held at Portishead Radio Station. On one exercise Bill Pincott was standing next to a slab of gun-cotton when for some inexplicable reason it 'went off', covering his face and glasses with mud and cow dung. Terrified, Bill rushed around the field screaming, "I'm blind, I'm blind". His sight was rapidly restored with the aid of a piece of rag. On another occasion an incident happened which many platoons seemed to have experienced at some stage. Sgt. Gibbs was demonstrating loading a rifle and 'easing springs' when he closed the bolt on a live round and shot a hole in the ceiling.

David Lloyde, seen in the photograph on the previous page, later became a 'Bevin Boy'. By mid 1943, 36,000 miners had left for better-paid work, leaving an estimated 40,000 shortfall. Despite several appeals, even to headmasters of relevant schools, matters did not improve. In December 1943 Ernest Bevin, Minister of Labour, devised a scheme to make up the shortfall.

Every month, for 20 months, Mr. Bevin's secretary placed the digits 0-9 in a hat and drew out two. All men whose National Service Registration Number ended with either digit were directed, without exception, into the coalmining industry. Those who refused either faced a heavy fine or possible imprisonment. Pay was about £3-10-0d, from which £1-5-0d was deducted for accommodation which took the form of hostels similar to army camps, or billets.

After four weeks of training the men commenced work in nearby collieries. Two weeks later they began their work with seasoned miners below ground. For many boys who came from middle-class or upper-class homes this was a real culture shock; many had never really got their hands dirty before.

The last of the 47,859 Bevin boys were demobbed in 1948. A vital part of the war effort, these conscripts received no recognition for their services to the nation, no medal, no demob suit, no paid leave or official thanks until May 1995 when they belatedly received official recognition. In November 1995 they took their place for the first time in the Remembrance Sunday Service held at The Cenotaph in Whitehall, with representatives of other organisations who had contributed to final victory.

DEVON HOME GUARDS NEAR WITHYPOOL

Hanging in *The Sportsman's Inn*, Sandyway, near Withypool, is a set of three photographs of the local Home Guard. Although photographed in Somerset these are Devon troops. The author is indebted to David Sewell of Photoscene, South Molton, Hector Delbridge, Herb Green and Archie Little of Rooksmead, Exford, for supplying the information below.

*(above) Lt. B.F. Chichester of the **4th (Devonshire) Battalion Home Guard**.*
(left) Back Row: A. Hutchins, farmer, Higher Ball, Twitchen; L/Cpl. W. Hutchins, farmer, Easter Ball, Twitchen; S. Jarman, farmworker, Blindwell, Twitchen; W. Rashly, farmworker, Twitchen; E.G. Thorne, farmer, Sindercombe, Twitchen; S. Little, farmer, Lower Sherdon, Sandyway; J. Bray, farmer, Butery Heasly Mill; F. Gardner, bus driver, Bridge End, Molland
Front Row: L/Cpl. J. Carter, landlord of The Sportsman's Inn; *Sgt. W. Westcott, farmer, Willingford, Sandyway; Lt. Chichester, Whitcott Farm, Twitchen; Cpl. J. Sankins, farmer, Woolcombe, Sandyway; L/Cpl. L. Carter, farmer, Litton, Sandyway; L/Cpl. A. Little, farmer, Barkham, Sandyway*
Sitting cross-legged: Johnny Bray, Butery Heasly Mill

Lt. Chichester and his men having no doubt sampled some Somerset Hospitality, mount up to return to Devon, some 200 yards away!
From left to right: Lt. Chichester;
  A. Hutchins; L/Cpl. A. Little;
  Sgt. W. Westcott; S. Little;
  L/Cpl. J. Carter; Cpl. Sankins;
  E.G. Thorne; S. Jarman;
  L/Cpl. W. Hutchins; W. Rashly;
  L/Cpl. L. Carter; J. Bray;
  Johnny Bray
Note that some men are carrying Sten guns and all are wearing puttees.

Devon Home Guard at Jubilee Inn, *West Anstey*
The author is indebted to Paul and Lynne Wraight and customers of Jubilee Inn for providing the following information. Although not Somerset Home Guards, with so many names kindly supplied the opportunity has been taken to preserve these for posterity.
Back Row: No. 1 Reg Down; No. 2 Mr. Rolle;
  No. 3 Percy Sowden; No. 4 Mr. Marshall;
  No. 11 Mr. Gough
Second Row: Unknown; Herby Dascombe;
  Mr. Bucknell; Eddie Bullard; Mr. Coleman;
  Unknown; Unknown; Frank Spencer;
  possibly Mr. Tackle; Unknown; Unknown
Third Row: Unknown; Cpl. Tom Crossman;
  Cpl. John Carter; Cpl. Reg Vellacott;
  Cpl. Herbert Harris; Major Farquhar;
  Unknown; Unknown; Cpl. Fred Frayne;
  L/Cpl. Albert Tackle; L/Cpl. Albert Spencer
Front Row: Maurice Follett; Herbert Tapp;
  Herbie Follett; George Nicholl; Fred
  Venner; Cecil Crudge; Mr. Chiplin;
  Kenneth Gudge; Bill Southwood
Others in this unit were Mr. Poole, Wilf Hill and Fred Golf. With the passing of the years it has not been possible to confirm if they are featured in the photograph or not.

  The area of operations of this unit covered West Anstey, East Anstey and Knowstone.

  Close inspection of the photograph shows a mixture of rifles, some with cup dischargers, Sten guns (two patterns) and a Browning Automatic Rifle.
(Mrs. Helen A'Brooke collection)

2nd Somerset (Taunton) Battalion

HEADQUARTERS	No. 11 Hammett Street, Taunton. Territorial Hall, Taunton (from 19.6.42)	ADJUTANT	Capt. H. Willis (The Queen's Royal Regiment)
DATE FORMED	June 1940	ASSISTANT A & Q	Lt. G.F. Mellor
COMMANDING OFFICER	Lt. Col. H.F.L. Hilton-Green, D.S.O., M.C. (from 15.12.42) (Lt. Col. L.A. Jones Mortimer)	CAMOUFLAGE OFFICER AMMUNITION OFFICER	Lt. L.C. Brooks (Lt. H.C. Skeens) Lt. C.E.M. Ellison, M.C.
2ND IN COMMAND	Major A.D.N. Merriman, D.S.O. (Brig-General C.L. Norman, M.V.O., D.S.O., D.L.) (Brig-General H.R. Done, C.M.G., D.S.O.) (Major R. Benson) (Major J.H. Lipscombe)	GAS OFFICER INTELLIGENCE OFFICER LIAISON OFFICER TO INVASION COMMITTEE MILITARY INFO. OFFICER SIGNALS OFFICER	Lt. H.J. Potter Lt. W.A. Kingdom Lt. Barrington Moore Capt. C.A. Matterson Lt. A.H. Chandler (Lt. J.D. Bevan) Lt. T.A. Bushell
H.Q. STAFF A & Q	Capt. A.H. Blake (The Queen's Royal Regiment) Capt. Trotman (S.L.I.)	TRANSPORT OFFICER WEAPONS TRAINING OFF'R	Lt. G.F. Duthie Capt. J.R. Roberts Lt. A. Rattray, M.C.

'A' (TAUNTON SOUTH) COMPANY

COMMANDING OFFICER	Major R.F. Drew M.B.E. (Major C.E.M. Ellison M.C.) (Lt. Col. G.P. Clarke T.D.)	2nd IN COMMAND	Capt. C.T. Pitcher (Capt. E.B. Mitford M.C.) (Capt. A.S. Turier)

'A' (Taunton South) Company, photographed at the Territorial Drill Hall at Shuttern, Taunton, most likely on 3rd December 1944. Many faces are recognisable from other photographs, including the following:

Back Row, No. 13: L. Herman; 2nd Row, No. 10: Cpl. W. Sparrow; 3rd Row, No. 1: Major Hargreaves; 4th Row, 3rd from right: Alec Lord; 5th Row, No. 8: 2nd Lt. Edmonds; No. 10: Lt. Frederick Cousins

'A' Company Home Guard Intelligence Section.
Donald S. Pascoe of Taunton was a member of 'A' Company Intelligence Section. These photographs from his family album indicate that camps were held at Bickham Manor near Minehead, a large country house still occupied by the Dru family.

Left and right: Sixty years separate these two photographs. Bickham Manor, photographed by the author, stands unchanged whilst the stone arched bridge has given way to a more utilitarian structure.

Below: Members of **'A' Company Intelligence Section** take a rest in the walled garden of Bickham Manor. Sitting in the foreground is an unidentified Lieutenant, possibly Lt. W.A. Kingdom, Battalion Intelligence Officer. (Sylvia Wickenden collection)

Sadly another uncaptioned photograph, possibly taken on 3rd December 1944. What is certain is that the clergyman is the Rev. Davies, Rector of Heathfield and Halse during WW2. Whilst the photograph on the left was taken at the T.A. Centre, this one appears to have been taken at Jellalabad Barracks and may be of Home Guard Commanders, as close examination reveals precious few 'young' faces.

Members of 'A' Company.
A very fine photograph by H. Stainer of Bridge Street, Taunton which was contemporaneously autographed by those featured including Mr. Lord of Van Heusen and Mr. Wickenden. Some Old Boys of Huish's Grammar School, Taunton will no doubt remember Mr. Wickenden. Having served in the First World War and later in Ireland during 'The Troubles', he became a teacher of history at Huish's. Keen on local history he wrote a book on the history of Taunton published shortly before the war. His other interests included the wildlife on the Quantock Hills. On one occasion shortly after the war he had a lucky escape when he was attacked by an enraged buck deer, severing ligaments in his left hand when he attempted to escape by climbing a tree. This left him with a permanent injury to his hand.
Back Row: W. Paterson; J.A. Lord; W.W. Cook; L.J. Hime; W.G. Pring
Front Row: L/Cpl. C.E. Brayley; H.J. Wickenden; Sgt. C.J. Sweet; W. Luscombe
(Sylvia Wickenden collection)

Throughout the county the Home Guard mounted guard over places of strategic importance or established observation posts at vantage points. Accommodation varied from cottages to tents. One unit near Bruton rested in a hollowed out haystack. After their night-time vigil, they would return home to have a quick shave, breakfast and go off to their civilian occupations. There were times when men literally fell asleep at their workbench, such was their exhausted state.

Members of No. 2 Platoon 'A' Company in their hut at the entrance to Blagdon Reservoir. In the top bunk is Peter Watkin with Jim Berry in the bottom one. Corporal Bill Phippen is at the table. The label on the large box above the oil lamp reads 'No. 2 Guard danger TNT'. Note the small can used to collect milk from the local farm for the guards' tea. Not all milk was procured in such an honest fashion.

A farmer at Portfield near Langport could not understand why a particular cow was 'dry' every morning. The local Home Guard picket would quietly hand milk it during the night! (Peter Watkin collection)

On one occasion No. 2 Platoon made the local press much to their embarrassment as the cutting (right) shows. Subsequently an inquiry was held and the Home Guard (believed to be Jack Huxtable) was commended on his marksmanship.

Home Guard circles in the West are recounting with amusement the experience of one of their number when on night duty recently in the neighbourhood of a reservoir. It seems that this particular section, and no doubt others, had been warned of the possible crash landing of a German bomber believed to have been hit by anti-aircraft gunfire near a coastal town.

There was also the possibility that the Nazi crew might be forced to bail-out by parachute. Consequently all Home Guard men were ordered to keep a sharp look-out. The zealous H.G., of whom the story is related, saw approaching through the mist what appeared to be the figure of a stalwart night raider. Twice he challenged and received no reply. A third time he called on the intruder, to halt. Again there was no response, and as the figure continued to advance he rapidly discharged his rifle in the direction of the "enemy."

To the consternation of the H.G. and his comrades, who were quickly on the scene, it was then discovered that the cause of the alarm was nothing more formidable than a grey horse. The animal, by some mischance, had strayed in search of fodder to the vicinity of the reservoir, and in consequence became a fatality, for the H.G.'s aim proved deadly.

The owner, a well-known farmer, is seeking compensation, I understand. However, after an inquiry, the Home Guard was exonerated from blame, and in consequence a tricky problem has arisen. Will the Army authorities admit the farmer's claim or must he suffer the loss of an animal valued at 60 guineas? A problem not very amusing for the horse's owner, but a story that the Home Guard love to relate.

Members of No. 2 Platoon included Cpls. Bill Phippen, Stan Manners and Geoff Fooks. 'Other ranks' included Bill Dawe, Trevor Pratt, Norman Long, Bert Smith, John Meikle, Dennis Attrill, Jack Major, Bill Ham, Tom Millard, Peter Chapman, Bob Jury, Tom Hull, J. Rowsell, Derrick Hender, Peter Shapland of A.C. Mole, Accountants, Jack Laverock, Bill Quick, Kenneth Tong, Don Power of Power's Grocers, High Street and Reg Walsh, chef at a small pie shop in Station Road. Bill Spiller, an employee of Avimo, was the platoon messenger whilst Tom Millard busied himself in the Quartermaster's stores at Mary Street.

Dennis Grinter, writing in 1994, recalls an incident which occurred 50 years earlier:

In 1944, as a 16-year-old member of Huish's Grammar School Army Cadets, I was attached with several other cadets to the South Somerset Sector, Headquarters Signal Section of the Home Guard at the Territorial Drill Hall, Taunton. We regularly attended for duty on Sunday mornings and some evenings, taking messages on the switchboard and line-laying work to gun sites on the outskirts of Taunton. One Sunday morning in the spring of 1944 I arrived on my cycle at the T.A. Centre when I saw a truck with the Signal Section on board speeding into Westgate Street. On seeing me the truck stopped and I was dragged on board leaving my cycle in the road. There was great excitement as it had been reported that someone had cut the telephone wires at White Ball Tunnel near Wellington. This railway tunnel was guarded at one end by the Devonshire Regiment and at the other end by the Somerset Home Guard. We proceeded at great speed to the tunnel entrance and started to walk through to investigate the cut lines when we were informed the emergency was over.

I often wonder whether we were involved in an act of sabotage, as we were led to believe, or whether it was merely another Sunday exercise.

Sadly Dennis Grinter passed away in 1996 never knowing the truth behind the 'panic'.

Taken at the same time as the photograph below, this could be captioned 'Officers and N.C.O.s of No. 3 Platoon' as it features two sergeants and a 1st and 2nd lieutenant in the front row, Lt. Cousins in the back row centre and, on the left, Cpl. Dilliston. (Brian Dennis collection)

No. 3 Platoon, *July 1943.*
Back Row: No. 2 Maurice Kenner
Middle Row: No. 1 Cpl. Dilliston;
  No. 2 possibly Mr. Bealey;
  No. 10 Mr. Gould; No. 11 Mr. Tolley
Front Row: No. 6 Lt. Frederick George
  Cousins; No. 9 L/Cpl. Hawkins
(Maurice Kenner collection)

Gas Works Home Guard.
Back Row: W. Bennett; W. Tancock; Mr. Palmer; Mr. Troake; S. Cort; Unknown; Unknown; Unknown; F. Bragg
Second Row: Unknown; Unknown; Cpl. W. Saunders; Unknown; L/Cpl. T. Starkes; Unknown; Unknown; Unknown; Unknown; Cpl. J. King
Third Row: Cpl. W. Bale; L/Cpl. T. Sellick; L/Cpl. H. Rayson; Unknown; Unknown; Unknown; Unknown; Unknown; Unknown or Stan Bale
Front Row: Unknown; Sgt. Thompson; Sgt. S. Bale; Sgt. W. Puffet; Lt. Frederick Cousins (Platoon Commander); Lt. Fred Fudge; Sgt. Sadler; Sgt. Hosegood; Unknown; Cpl. Bill Underhill
The following employees of the Gas Works were Members of the Home Guard, the first five all gas fitters, joining in the days of the L.D.V.:
W.H. Bale; S.H. Bale; F. Fudge; W. Underhill; J. King; J. Stone (fitter); F. Bragg (labourer mains); T. Bragg (welder mains); W. Tancock (electric foreman); W. Bennett (paint sprayer); G. Yard; C. Cornish; D. Boak; T. Starkes (fitters); T. West; Mr. Palmer (apprentice fitter); D. Sheldon (storeman) and Mr. Troake.

In the first row Mr. Thompson was the Manager of Briggs Shoes, W. Puffet managed Somerwest, Lt. Cousins was the Company Secretary of Whites Collar Factory, Mr. Sadler was a local schoolmaster whilst Mr. Hosegood was the local manager of the TSB.

With Lt. Cousins identified in this photograph, the one at the bottom of the previous page, contemporaneously captioned 'No. 3 Platoon', and in the group photograph on page 180, it is more than likely that The Gas Works Home Guard was part of No. 3 Platoon 'A' Company. (Author's collection)

Edward Frank Dunn was a member of No. 3 Platoon. Shortly after he had joined, the recruits were assembled at North Town School for training. It was suddenly realised that no rifles were available for arms drill. The recruits were told to go to houses in Wood Street, at that time not one of the 'better' parts of Taunton, and borrow brooms to act as rifles. All went well until the end of the parade when it was time to return the brooms. "Not my broom, my broom had more bristles", and similar phrases were shouted up and down Wood Street when an attempt was made to return them to their rightful owners.

(left) **Members of No. 3 Platoon** *pose for the camera.*
Back Row: No. 3 Mr. Tolley; No. 5 Reginald Hoskins;
   No. 9 Cpl. Gold
Middle Row: No. 5 Unknown (worked for Spiller and Webber);
   No. 6 Mr. Pascoe; No. 7 Maurice Kenner
Front Row: No. 3 Unknown (worked for Hatcher's Furnishing);
   No. 7 Sgt. Dilliston
(Maurice Kenner collection)

(right) No. 4 (Bishops Hull) Platoon.
Back Row: George Wide; Arnold Lynas; L/Cpl. Frank Biffin;
   Unknown; L/Cpl. Bill Carrow; Unknown; Unknown; Bill Weaver;
   Unknown; Unknown
Middle Row: Unknown; Unknown; Mr. Manning; Unknown;
   Mr. Bradbeer; 'Teddy' Bonner; Mr. Huntley; Major Hargreaves;
   Unknown; Mr. Watts; Unknown; Unknown; Bill Guppy; Ben Gready
Front Row: Cpl. Arthur Weaver; Mr. Whiting; Lt. Rupert Yates;
   Sgt. Pollard; Cpl. Unwin; Cpl. Chalker; Cpl. Phillips.
An original print belonging to Frank Biffin was contemporaneously inscribed on the back 'No. 4 Platoon A Company Nov. 44'. Other negatives are held at Taunton Library but they are of smaller groups featuring people in the above photograph.
(Freda Evans collection)

The *Country Life* Miniature Rifle Competition

Country Life Magazine had sponsored this competition since 1941. The first stage was to find a team to represent their Battalion. This was shot at 25 yards range with open or aperture sights. No slings, rests or sand bags were permitted but the prone position was allowed. The winning team of eight in each Battalion then shot a 36" x 23" landscape target which had four marked objectives in the form of 1½" circles which were only visible to the team leader using glasses or a telescope who then had to allocate and define one target to each shooting pair who were allocated 3 rounds each. A hit on the 1½" circle counted for 8 points, a shot within a 2½" circle scored 5 points. The winning team held the Challenge Trophy for one year and each member of the team was presented with a commemorative medal. It was intended that the trophy was to be offered annually as long as the Home Guard remained in being.

In 1944 the competition was won by the 45th West Riding 'B' Company No. 7 Platoon with a perfect score of 192. Somerset Home Guard teams took part in the competition and their scores were as follows:

3rd (Yeovil) Battalion, Crewkerne Company, No. 1 Platoon	joint 4th	score 183
1st (Minehead) Battalion, Williton Company, No. 3 Platoon	joint 12th	score 177
6th (Admiralty) Battalion, 'C' Company, No. 11 Platoon	joint 46th	score 156
2nd (Taunton) Battalion, No. 4 (Bishops Hull) Platoon	joint 129th	score 126
4th (Frome) Battalion, 'A' Company, No. 4 (Stratton) Platoon	joint 186th	score 110
8th (Weston-super-Mare) Battalion, 'A' Company, No. 6 Platoon	joint 238th	score 77

The 'wooden spoon' was won by 2nd North Riding Battalion, 'B' Company, No. 6 Platoon who came 254th with a score of 49.

(right) **No. 5 Platoon**.
Back Row: W. Shute; George Williams; C. Palterman; Stan Garland; J. Hopkins; Unknown; Unknown; Unknown; L. Heman
Middle Row: L. Chedzoy; Alec Lord; Unknown; Unknown; C. Cooke; Unknown; Arthur Woodrow
Front Row: Cpl. Sparrow; Sgt. R. Manning; Sgt. Medhurst; Lt. Gaine (Platoon Commander); Lt. Edmonds (Platoon 2nd in Command); Jim McHardy; Johnny Holden; J. Mitchell

No. 5 Platoon trained at King's College under the watchful eye of Lt. Edmonds, ex Somerset Light Infantry, who also trained the college cadets. The Platoon included staff of the Van Heusen Factory. One of the night-time duties of the Platoon was to guard the Avimo Factory which was at the time next to Taunton Railway Station.
(L. 'Jim' McHardy collection)

(left) **No. 5 Platoon** *at The Blue Ball, Triscombe in 1943. Left to right: Unknown; Unknown; Sgt. Major Edmonds; Sgt. Medhurst; Lt. Stott; Unknown; Sgt. Pook; Unknown (Leslie Berry collection).*

(right) Home Guards occupied their Sunday mornings with route marches, usually finishing at a local pub. Here members of **No. 5 Platoon** *happily pose for the cameraman. Perhaps the location explains their happy state, it being outside* The Rising Sun *in Bagborough, the building in the background being 'Bashford's Farmhouse' which still exists, albeit with a new tile roof.*
Front Row: Unknown; L. Berry; Unknown; Mr. Jordan; Unknown; Unknown; Mr. Edney; Mr. Chant
Back Row: No. 3 (with glasses) Mr. Lord
(Leslie Berry collection)

'A Day on the Ranges'.

(left) This photograph is believed to show members of **No. 5 Platoon** at what was initially an unknown location. Several years after the photograph was discovered, the author read a report by Capt. T.A. Bushell describing a shoot in Williton where the troops "marched past the church into a field that was about 500 yards wide by ½ mile long where a trench at the butts had been cut out of solid rock". This proved to be land owned by Orchard Wyndham Estates and the author was kindly given permission to enter the field in the summer of 2000 to confirm the site. Note an unidentified N.C.O. shooting left handed! Both men are firing .303" rifles.
(L. 'Jim' McHardy collection)

(below left) Although the two pine trees remain in the background, nothing is left of the firing points. Sheep graze peacefully where once the fields echoed to the crack of service rifles and the rattle of Lewis machine guns.
(Author's collectiona)

(above) Under the watchful eye of their sergeant, bolts are removed and left in the grass whilst bores are given a thorough clean out. Note the band painted around the fore end of the rifle to the right of the picture, to distinguish weapons firing the American .300" rimless round to those firing the British .303" rimmed round.
(L. 'Jim' McHardy collection)

(left) Believed to have been taken at Pigeon Field, Williton, this shows members of the **2nd (Taunton) Battalion Home Guard**, probably a rifle team. In the front row can be seen Sgt. (Later Lt.) Frederick Cousins at No. 3, with Sgt. Puffet at No. 5. On 8th October 1916 Sgt. Cousins was promoted to W.O. Class II, Regimental Master Sgt. in the West Somerset Yeomanry. On 16th July 1918 he was promoted to 2nd Lt. An extremely proficient shot, he continued his shooting into the 1960s, often competing at Bisley.
(Brian Dennis collection)

Van Heusen Collars Home Guard, part of No. 5 Platoon, 'A' Company, photographed on 4th November 1940 outside the factory in Victoria Street, Taunton.
Back Row: Stan Cox (Chief Engineer); Mr. Dunlop (Works Manager); Mr. Indemaur; Mr. Sobers; P. Glanville; Mr. Stokes; Jimmy Holden (Director); Unknown; F. Walton; Cliff Wakely; Harry Curry; Bill Williams; Walter Hordle; Unknown but possibly Lionel Pole
Second Row: Vic Glanville; A.E. Smith; J. Fox; H. Saunders; L. Heman; Mr. Jones; Mr. Rivington; L. Hort; Bill Rowsell; Alfred Sparrow; D. Russell
Third Row: R. Greed; E. Silvester; J. Singleton; Charlie Coles; Sgt. Pook; H. Hartley; Unknown; Sgt. Stott; Sgt. W. Hartley; Bill Curry; Cpl. Alec Lord (Under Manager); Edgar Pook; Mr. Pilgrim
Front Row: Les Jones; Les Titcombe; Ken Betty; S. White; Fred Dimon; C. Hill; Jesse Jones. (J. Singleton collection)

John Denham, in a letter of 2002, recounted his memories as a member of the Avimo Works Platoon.

Being an Avimo apprentice in the early 1940s, I was directed to join the factory Home Guard Platoon on its formation.

As with many units in those early days there was little equipment available. The appeal in the U.K. and to our overseas Empire and friends brought forth a variety of weapons. The Avimo Platoon received some of these weapons, sporting rifles, pistols and shotguns.

To make these weapons resemble some sort of military order slings were required. Leather belting as used for transmission in the machine shop became the sling and the necessary swivels were made in the tool room. My 'own' weapon was a sporting rifle which came from Canada – I think it was .310" or .320" bore with a lever cocking mechanism. I was issued with five rounds of ammunition and allowed to keep the weapon and ammunition at home in Greenway Road.

I fired the weapon once at the butts located somewhere beyond Vivary Park (Ash Meadows). The only casualty it ever inflicted was a rat which got into my house – beaten to death with the butt.

We trained one evening per week under Drill Sergeant Wheeler who was the gate commissionaire during the day. In his earlier years he had been a regular soldier serving in Palestine and India. Mr. Douglas, an army Captain from the First World War, who was from the works administration office became our commander. Air Commodore Drew became our commanding officer.

The platoon had its small-bore range in the Fuselage Department at the factory in Herbert Street. Field craft was practised on the recreation ground at Leslie Avenue, usually on a Sunday morning.

As with other Taunton-based units, guard duties centred on the White Ball Tunnel on the main Paddington-Penzance line. Sleeping accommodation was in a bell tent supplied by the army. Fortunately this was only about once a month. We also took part in defence schemes with the Regular Army, placing the steel 'hairpin' tank obstacles in the road at the junction of Greenway Road and Kingston Road, the headquarters for these exercises being *The Cherry Tree Pub*.

The platoon eventually had a Blacker Bombard for which Avimo made a mobile carriage. Flame Fougasse was installed at the foot of Rumwell Hill in the wall opposite *The Rumwell Inn* whilst machine gun posts were established at the cemetery end of the town.

As the war progressed women replaced the younger men in the factory and the strength of the platoon diminished.

'B' (BISHOPS LYDEARD) COMPANY

COMMANDING OFFICER   Major V. Batchelor D.S.O.   2ND IN COMMAND   Capt. Cedric E. Hedderwick
(Major A.G. Arbuthnot C.M.G., D.S.O.)   (Capt. P. Spence)

Bishops Lydeard Platoon, *photographed at Bishops Lydeard House in 1944.*
Back Row: Sid Gillard; Rupert Stone; George Hellard; Cyril Coles; Tom Sealy; Jack Sedgebeer; Frank Poole
Second Row: Bill Saunders; Albert Simons; Cecil Meade; Lou Venton; Harold Collard; Maurice Mead; Walt Coggins; Arthur Simons; George Knight
Third Row: Frank Cavill; Bill Tooze; Bert Greedy; Walt Eason; Bob Cook; Albert Thorne; Walter Purchase; Fred Milton; Jim Milton
Fourth Row: Q.M.S. Harry Woollen; Cpl. Reg Stone; L/Cpl. Jeff Bawden; L/Cpl. Ted Shattock; L/Cpl. Fred Tooze; Cpl. Jim Gay; L/Cpl. Jack Adams; L/Cpl. Ron White; Harry Bew
Fifth Row: Cpl. Gilbert; Cpl. Alan Morris; Sgt. Dick Tuffin; Lt. Reg Jennings; Lt. Ulick Huntington; Sgt. Lionel Cornish; Sgt. John Reed; Cpl. Claud Snell; Cpl. Jack Cornish
Front Row: Ralph Shattock; Frank Boon; Don Besley; Bob Power; Stan Shorney; George Sedgebeer; Percy Parker
(Walter Purchase collection)

At the outbreak of war Walter Purchase was living at Sutton Montis. One evening, when milking, he was visited by a retired Colonel who lived next door. "You have a shotgun", he said, "I suggest you get up to Cadbury Castle one and a half hours before sunrise and look out for paratroops." Later a shepherd's hut was erected and the lookouts stayed all night.

On moving to the area he joined Bishops Lydeard Platoon. As he owned a B.S.A. Blue Star Junior motorcycle, registration no. YD 7485, he became a dispatch rider, resisting the army's insistence that his pride and joy should be painted camouflage green. One day, when riding his motorcycle on military business, Walter was passing a lorry when a swinging chain caught on the fore end of his rifle, pulling him off his machine. A local resident, Mr. Armitage, took pity on Walter and lent him a .455 revolver to replace the rifle.

On the subject of accidents, the reader may wonder the reason for George Knight appearing in the photograph heavily bandaged whilst Fred Milton is sporting a black eye. According to Walter, George and Fred had had a serious accident one night on an exercise – they suffered a head-on collision whilst cycling in opposite directions.

Bishops Lydeard Platoon had the use of two rifle ranges. Just to the west of Lydeard House, in an area of waste ground, a small-bore range was established. It was at this site that a typical Nissen storage hut was built. For full-bore shooting, a field next to *The Rising Sun*, Bagborough, was used.

One day at the range at Bagborough, Walter borrowed a rifle from a platoon member. Close inspection, prior to firing, revealed a piece of 4 x 2 cleaning cloth stuck in the barrel. "Don't worry," said the owner, casually, "the first round will blow the cloth clear." Fortunately for all concerned, the rifle was returned to the armourer to be cleared.

Pte. Ralph Shattock of Bishops Lydeard was selected, together with G.H. Forrester and H.G. Redstone, to represent the 2nd (Taunton) Battalion Home Guard at the Stand Down parade in London which took place on 3rd December 1944.

Employees of Watts House Estate, Bishops Lydeard.
Back Row: W. Whitmore (maintenance electrician); Cpl. H.R. Tuffin (head gardener); R. Wiscombe (estate carpenter); Cpl. Milton (dairyman); L/Cpl. A. Simmons (gardener)
Front Row: F. James (chauffeur/mechanic); S. Burgess (butler); Sir Gerald Boles; Cpl. 'Capt.' R. Kitson (agent); A. Sheppard (groom)
Two other estate employees, Bill Rogers and Mr. Hobbs, the estate plumber, would probably have been in this Home Guard unit.
Sir Gerald Boles was killed towards the end of the war when an ammunition ship blew up in Bari Harbour. Reference is made to this in an autobiographical book by Alan Whicker. Captain Kitson held and used the rank of Captain from his days in the Royal Flying Corps during the First World War. However, this was not recognised by the Home Guard, the 'Captain' having to settle for two stripes.
During the war Watts House became home to boys of Connaught House School, Weymouth, run by Mr. R. Hoyle. *(D. Tuffin collection)*

(right) **No. 3 (Lydeard St. Lawrence) Platoon.**
Back Row: Ernie Coles; Unknown; Unknown; Fred Baker; Cecil Tarr; Unknown; Unknown; Arthur Flood
Second Row: Dennis Willis; R.T. Merlin Waygood; Gordon Waygood; John Crang; Ray Lock; Tom Thresher; Unknown; Phil Stone; Charlie Burnett; Bill King; Cpl. Bill Cook; Fred Darlow
Third Row: Jack Hill; Walt Flood; Cpl. Ted Symonds; Percy Burnett; Charles Davis; L/Cpl. Bill Sully; Cpl. George Honeybun; L/Cpl. Wally Taylor; Harry Baker; Trugg Rich or Sid Chiplin
Front Row: Cpl. Eli Pike; Sgt. Fred Sweet; Unknown; Major V. Batchelor; Lt. Mark Day; Unknown; Major Spence; Sgt. Ernie Triggol; Cpl. Bill Woods
The inclusion of Major Batchelor in this photograph would certainly indicate that this unit formed part of Bishops Lydeard Company, because those featured were living in Combe Florey, Lydeard St. Lawrence and Bagborough. Sgt. Fred Sweet was the landlord of The Rising Sun. *(Merlin Waygood collection)*

A field next to Stout Lane, West Bagborough, was used as a rifle range. For grenade practice Lydeard St. Lawrence Park was chosen. It was here that E.G. 'Ted' Pike, a Home Guard member until 17.12.42, nearly lost his life in a typical accident. The Home Guards were waiting their turn to throw grenades from the trench when the man in front of Ted, having pulled the pin, dropped his grenade. Fortunately, the grenade was fitted with a seven second fuse which gave Ted time to pick it up and throw it clear. The detail suffered no serious injuries apart from being covered with flying dirt and stones as the grenade exploded just over the parapet.

On 4th May 1941 Lydeard Platoon was detailed to guard a Heinkel 111 which had crashed near Crowcombe Railway Station. Ted and comrades had been on duty for about 1½ hours when one of the Heinkel's crew appeared saying, "Ze bomb, ze bomb". They followed him into the wood and found a landmine hanging from a tree by its parachute, 18 inches off the ground.

*Part of **No.5 Platoon, the men of West Monkton Home Guard**, pose for the camera.*
Back Row: Ken Dunn; Harry Rogers; Frank Curtis; Perce Martin; Fred Baker; Arthur Atkins; Les Parker; Dick Dollings (face hidden); Mr. Lever
Second Row: Sgt. Knight; Roy Bishop; L/Cpl. Archie Richards; Bill Price; Joe Cavill or Les Hooper or Fred Hooper or Sid Batten; Sgt. Jack Innocent; Ted Gange; Bill Kerswell; Dick Hooper; Fred Blackmore; Lt. C.E. Hedderwick; Bill Porter; Toby Reading; Mr. Lee; Ron Strickland
Front Row: Bill Burnett; Jeff Clute; Mr. Zeisburger; Bob Baker; Bert Reynolds or Bert Richards; Bob Burnett; Jim Keitch; George Hooper

Captain Hedderwick was 2nd in Command of Bishops Lydeard Company at Stand Down. It would appear that this photograph was taken whilst he was still a lieutenant. In the 1950s Cedric Hedderwick was involved in the reforming of the Home Guard which was instigated to counter the perceived threat from the communist block. He subsequently became secretary of the 9th Somerset (Home Guard) Rifle Club which is still extant. The author remembers him in the mid-1960s when his features had remained unchanged since the photograph was taken 20 years previously. It has recently been suggested by a club member that Major Hedderwick only rejoined the Home Guard to ensure that the 9th Somerset (Home Guard) Rifle Club would have ready access to ammunition for their sport! (Jim F. Aish collection)

With much of Europe in ruins after nearly six years of conflict and the continent awash with displaced persons, the thought of another conflict was not at the forethought of contemporary thinking. However, unfolding events soon gave cause for concern. In 1947 it was discovered that the Russians had obtained secrets concerning the atomic bomb. 1948 saw the blockade of Berlin, an overt attempt to drive the British, French and Americans out of the city which stood in the Soviet zone of East Germany. In 1949, on the other side of the world, Chinese Communist troops entered Peking forcing Chaing Kai-Shek's retirement. In February 1950 Russia and China announced that they had formed a common united front against the world. In June of the same year Communist troops invaded South Korea, precipitating the Korean War.

Concern at home was expressed by the military and politicians that a Soviet attack from captured forward bases in Europe was feasible. The attack, it was believed, would be preceded by air raids and an airborne invasion which would be assisted by help from within the United Kingdom in the form of Communist-led rioters. Without the catalyst of 1940 when the Germans were advancing rapidly through France, the debate on resurrecting the Home Guard rumbled on until the end of 1951 when the Home Guard was born once again.

From the very beginning, recruitment was slow and dogged by apathy. By the autumn of 1952 it was apparent that the projected numbers of Home Guard volunteers would never be attained, despite many further attempts to increase recruitment. In December 1955 the Home Guard was stood down and at the end of July 1957 it ceased to exist, having become obsolete as a result of technical advances in modern warfare.

Men of Creech St. Michael, part of No. 5 Platoon, assemble in the grounds of Creech Vicarage.
Back Row: H. Pollard; Bill Hunt; Mac Marchant; Harold Wyatt; Mr. Cornwell; Robert Wheadon; Tristram Foxwell; Norman Drew; FrEddie Jewell; Ron Welch
Middle Row: Mr. Cornwell; A. Mitchell; William Cruwys; Fred Hunt; George Sandford; 'Toosey' Hooper; Lance Coombes; Jack Taylor; Ivor Brooks; Harold Thomas; Jim Wadham
Front Row: L/Cpl. Jack Sweeting; L/Cpl. Reub Bauler; L/Cpl. Perce Brookes; Cpl. 'Cubby' Bishop; Sgt. S. Sweeting; Lt. Fisher; Sgt. Ron Smith; Cpl. Len Mitchell; L/Cpl. Claude Wyatt; L/Cpl. John or Brian Wakeley
(Ron Smith collection)

```
VERY CONFIDENTIAL.

No.1.   By canal bridge over river. Partly facing paper mills.
        Has loose stone 'buttresses' and brushwood on top.
        Old canal is here on arches: where these are exposed
        their fronts are filled by masonry walls arranged for
        defence.

No.2.   Built into masonry of canal and approached by arch under
        canal. Field of fire very restricted but this point is
        obviously intended to cover road block by railway arch.
        Some young trees here require cutting down to 4 ft. level
        as they obstruct field of fire.   Forward view obstructed by
                                          railway embankment.

No.3.   By the side of railway. Concrete is tarred and chimney
        has been erected on top to resemble railwaymen's hut.
        Good field of fire here.

No.4.   Canal still above ground level. This point shews concrete
        construction but has been paint camouflaged. Field
        of fire forward obstructed by bushes and trees which should
        be lowered.
                            bridge over
No.5.   Between 4 and 5 is             canal bed protected by
        tank blocks.
        No 5 has same appearance as No.4. Only field of fire at
        present is up and down canal bed. Embrasures do not
        permit space below point to be covered.   Forward view
                                                  entirely obscured.

No.6.   Between 5 and 6 is declivity in canal banks protected by
        four large cubic concrete blocks;
        No.6, same appearance as 4 and 5: paint camouflage with
        brushwood on top.
           Straw
No.7.   Haystack alongside road. Excellent field of fire all round.
        Nearby is bridge over canal bed with tank traps.  From 7 to
        8 keep cottage and wind pump on right.

No.8.   Old barn, excellently contrived. Field of fire at present
        hampered by foliage. To reach 8 from church climb five-barred
        gate due E. from green              and proceed straight ahea
No.9. Straw Haystack in isolated position with excellent field of fire.
        To approach by night follow hedge N.E.from No.8. crossing
        four barred gap in hedge and then three barred gap in hedge.
        Turn along third hedge, approx 100 yards left.
```

Headquarters for these men was in a cottage in the grounds of Creech St. Michael Vicarage. Later on in the war Lt. Fisher was replaced by Lt. Norman, Sgt. Sweeting being promoted to 2nd Lieutenant.

With Creech village centred on a river, canal, railway and road it was heavily fortified, forming part of the Taunton Stop Line (see the map on the next page). The observation point was located at Worthy Hill, shelter being provided in the form of a bathing hut 'borrowed' from the canal bank.

The map, reproduced by kind permission of The Somerset Archive and Record Service, shows Creech St. Michael in late 1940 with the positions of pillboxes and other defensive works. The squares with a dot inside indicate dummy pillboxes, whilst barbed wire and anti-tank cubes are represented by a crossed line and squares respectively.

On the left is a typewritten list of camouflage details and fields of fire for the various pillboxes.

One incident recalled by Ron Smith was when the Section's first Lewis gun arrived at The Old Vicarage, Creech St. Michael. This was the home of Capt. Percy who was instrumental in forming a section of Creech men. Capt. Percy's son, like most boys, was very inquisitive about the large box arriving. It was not long before, as the report goes, he managed to assemble the gun and fire it indoors!

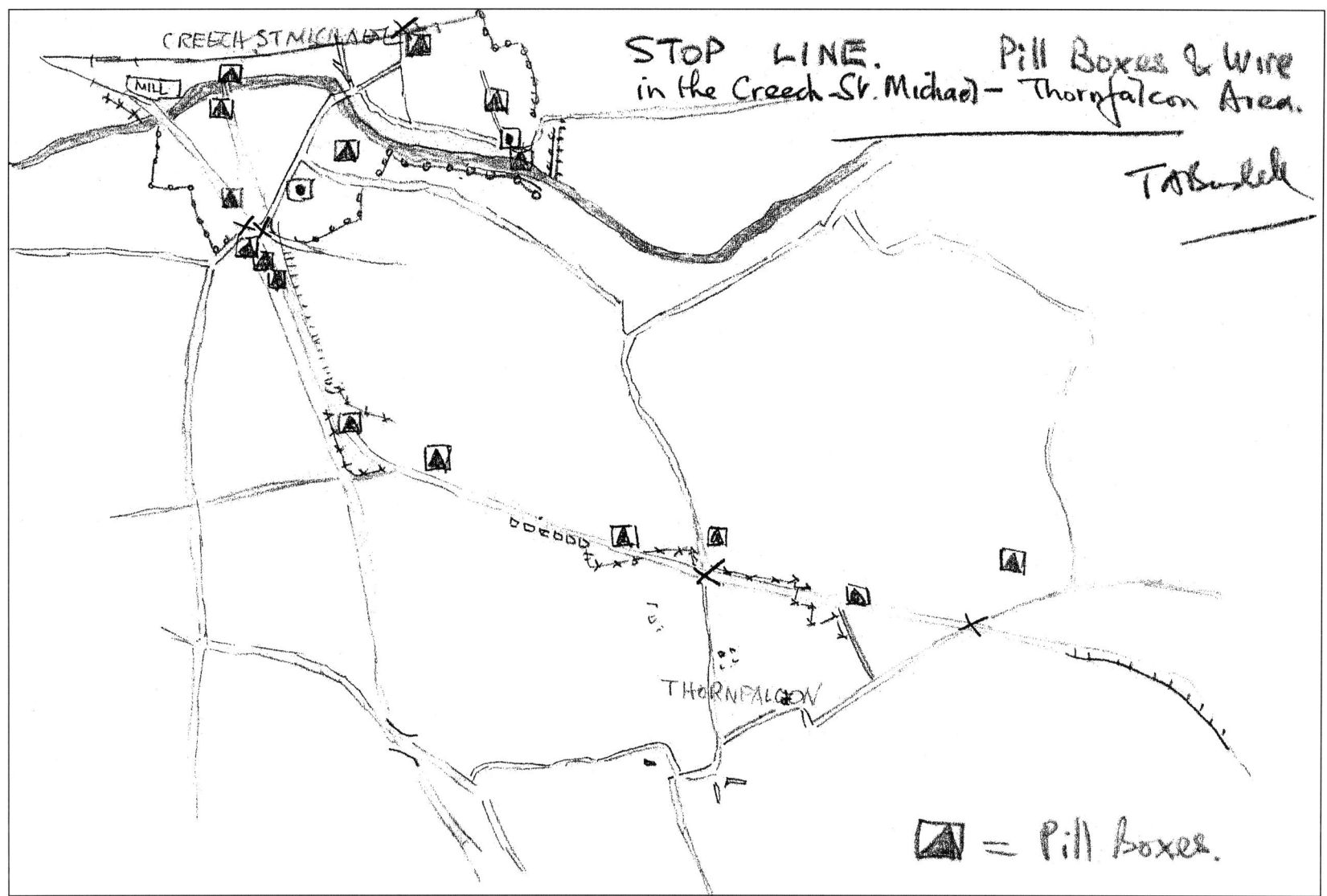

Thomas John 'Basher' Hunt taught English and History at Huish's Grammar School, Taunton. He joined the L.D.V., becoming one of two squad commanders in the Cheddon Fitzpaine Section, Mr. Hind being the other. The Section Commander was Mr. Mortimer-White, a farmer from Nerrols Farm who later left to join the local Auxiliary Unit. He was replaced by Mr. Ken Norman from Gotton. In 1941, in addition to his Home Guard duties, Thomas joined 1568 Flight A.T.C. which he ran until 1945, based at his school.

Home Guard parades were held either at Rowford School or at Upper Cheddon Farm, the home of Mr. Musgrave, where the Home Guard store was situated. Sunday mornings were reserved for training which was often followed by patrols around the Parish, getting to know the lie of the land. Unusually for a Home Guard unit the parade was not dismissed at a public house but at a cider-producing farm (Cheddon had no public houses by order of the Portman family of Hestercombe House who owned most of the parish). It was expected by the 'other ranks' that the N.C.O.s would buy the drinks.

In the long summer of 1940, one role of the Home Guard was to look out for German parachutists. Cpl. Hunt, armed with a Zulu Club and a pair of field glasses borrowed from his mother-in-law would cycle the 2½ miles to Volis Cross just before sunrise to carry out this duty.

In the same year a removable road block was set up on Volis Hill with the intention of obstructing German troops who might land in the hills from advancing into the valley. One story, oft recounted, was the number of false hill starts performed by Saturday night revellers having been stopped in their cars by the Home Guard. This road block was, it is believed, manned all night. Later on, a horse-box was provided as a shelter by Ken Norman for those who formed an all-night picket from this spot. Conditions were later improved when the box was replaced by a chicken house.

With timber taken from a derelict cottage in Rowford donated by Lady Portman, Cpl. Hunt, after several hours work in a sand-pit at Pitcher's Hill, constructed two knife-rest barriers. Some time later the Cheddon Section took part in an exercise with regular troops and Cpl. Hunt's knife rests were duly deployed. The first 'enemy' vehicle, a Universal Carrier, drove straight through the barrier without even slowing down. The tattered remains of Cpl. Hunt's handiwork were thrown unceremoniously over the hedge and were never replaced.

With the passing of so many years there remains precious little evidence of field works constructed by the Home Guard, but from conversations held between Thomas Hunt, his son David and others including Mr. Bob Mead, who was the sergeant in charge of Cheddon Section in 1944, the following is known.

Kingston St. Mary Home Guard established a checking point at the lower end of Beech Copse on the road to Buncombe at map ref. ST 214 308. Here a Flame Fougasse was sited on the west side of the road in a small quarry which would have effectively blocked the road whilst anyone attempting to escape the conflagration would have been fired upon by a Spigot Mortar situated in another quarry on the east side of the road. It was here that a Nissen hut was built in which the bombs were stored. Abandoned knife rests were recalled by David Hunt still lying in the quarry to the west of the road in the 1950s. One of the platoon's other Observation Posts was about 330 yards to the north of Beacons Close at map ref. ST 228 304. This position also boasted slit trenches. As the war progressed, this position was abandoned but not until after it was believed a field telephone connection was made. Another communication point was at Miss Metcalf's home at Beacons Close where a G.P.O. telephone existed, a rarity in rural areas during the war.

A wartime map showing the boundary of 'Q' Company 10th (Bridgwater) Battalion also indicated that Defended Houses existed at the centre of Kingston St. Mary and near West Monkton at map ref. ST 254 278.

Rifle practice took place at Happy Valley (Gadd's Bottom) at map ref. ST 233 292 whilst grenade practice was undertaken in the West Monkton Quarry.

KINGSTON HOME GUARD
STAND DOWN DINNER, FEBRUARY 9th, 1945.

"THE BATTLE OF BUNCOMBE HILL."

THIS is the Post that we built.

THIS is the Knife Rest and Dannert wire,
The Glass Bottle bombs and the Fougasse fire,
And the Bombard guns, weighing several tons,
All cunningly placed to destroy the Huns
Who attack the Post that we built.

THIS is the Section Commander, East,
Whose hair turned grey and whose weight decreased,
With sleepless nights as he planned the sites,
And worked out his schemes for the ' all-in ' fights,
With the Bombard guns, weighing several tons,
So cunningly placed to destroy the Huns,
And defend the Post that we built.

THIS is the terrible drenching rain,
Which drove in torrents across the plain,
And started early and never ceased,
And soaked the Section Commander, East,
And flooded the sites so carefully planned
And frequently changed by the High Command ;
The sites of the trenches, and O.Ps. and guns,
And other devices for beating the Huns
Who attack the Post that we built.

THIS is the Home Guard, all forlorn,
Who manned the Post in the early dawn,
And got their clothes all tattered and torn,
And were feeling wet and weary and worn,
And deeply regretted the day they were born,
As they stood in the terrible drenching rain
Which drove in torrents across the plain,
And washed out the Section from Cheddon Fitzpaine ;
And poured down the neck of Sergeant East,
Whose hair turned grey and whose weight decreased,
As he waded about in the muddy sites,
And the " last man " trenches for " last man " fights,
Which he'd carefully planned in the sleepless nights
The sites of the guns, weighing several tons,
So cleverly placed to destroy the Huns
And defend the Post that we built.

THIS is the senior N.C.O.,
Who said he would very much like to know
Why on earth the line of defence was laid
So far from the place where the beer is made !

And this is Corporal Nicholson,
Who said that By Gum ! they would see some fun !
For his Bombard platform was not fixed level,
And the gun and the crew would be blown to the devil !

And this is a Corporal called Stonex,
Who said they would break their blinking necks
If they had to flit, in marching kit,
Through a blinking slippery bramble pit !

And these are the junior N.C.Os.,
Who'd had nothing to eat since—goodness knows !
They were losing weight, they were growing thinner,
And they (blue pencil) wanted their (blue pencil) dinner !

SHORT INTERVAL, during which the weather cleared and the junior N.C.Os. each put on two stone in weight.

THESE are the monstrous German tanks
Which tried to attack them upon the flanks,
And swaggered along down Buncombe Hill
Where all was peaceful and very still.
" Die Englisch was fled ! Heil Hitler ! Hoch !
Die Englisch run vay !—But vat a shock !
Die cowardly Englisch der road haf block ! "

Then a sheet of flame from the Fougasse came,
And that was the start of a wonderful game ;
For a Northover shell, from Lance-Corporal Bell,
Knocked the first of these German tanks to hell ;
And a Bombard gun got the second one
With a bulls-eye from Corporal Nicholson.

The other tanks stopped, and the crews jumped out,
But the Section Commander gave a shout,
And the brave Home Guards, all ages and ranks,
Popped up like rabbits from hedges and banks,
The stout, the slim, the short, the tall,
Every man who could run or walk or crawl ;
The slim, the stout, the tall, the short,
They handled their weapons as they'd been taught
From their earliest days, of Bailey, of Eaton,
When all the world said that England's beaten ;
And with rifle and Browning, with Lewis and Sten,
They shot up the Germans again and again ;
And when they had shot every round they had got,
They threw their grenades and they wiped out the lot.

THIS is the famous Village Hall,
Where the food is good, and there's room for all,
And the Home Guards, Kingston, Section D,
Are celebrating their victory ;
With songs and cider and barley brew,
And tales of the things which they did do,
And tales of the Bosches which they did kill
In the terrible Battle of Buncombe Hill,
When they smashed the ugly German tanks
Which tried to attack them upon the flanks,
And laid the Nazis out in rows
In spite of complaints from the N.C.Os.

They were not forlorn, nor weary and worn,
And no longer regretted the day they were born,
But merry and bright, all shaven and shorn,
They banged on the tables and blew the horn,
And the Section Commander was not careworn,
Nor lay awake till the crack of dawn,
As he worked out his plans with a sigh and a yawn ;
But he felt like the cock which crowed in the morn,
For they'd wiped out the nasty Nazi spawn
Who attacked the POST THAT WE BUILT !

A. C. P.

(right) **Heathfield Home Guard**.
Back Row: Victor Henry Babb; Ernest William Lock; Clement Charles Matthews; Richard John Smith; George William Swain; Gordon Summers
Front Row: L/Cpl. Leslie Cornish; L/Cpl. John 'Jack' Bodger; Sgt. (later 2nd Lt.) Charles John Thomson; Thomas William Bodger; Colin George Thomson
The above photograph was taken outside the garage at Manor Farm, Charles Thomson's home.
(Margaret Bromwich collection)

(below) Although much has been written about the pitiful amount of equipment the Home Guard possessed at the beginning of the war, this list shows the considerable amount of stores issued, signed and accounted for by the Home Guard members later on. This is by no means a comprehensive list. The poem on the next page comes from a book entitled Home Guard Rhymes, written by Lt. A.H. Watkins with drawings by Lt. Col. J.C.T. Willis, R.E. Many other items are listed which would have been issued to Thomas Bodger and his pals.

T. W. BODGER		
Trousers Denim	3	T W Bodger returned
Blouse Denim	4	T W Bodger returned
Hat ✓	6 7/8	T W Bodger ✓
Armlet ✓		T W Bodger returned
Boots ✓	7	T W Bodger ✓
Cap Badge ✓		T W Bodger ✓
Belt ✓		T W Bodger ✓
G. Coat ✓	5	T W Bodger ✓
H. sack ✓		T W Bodger ✓
Legging ✓	1	T W Bodger ✓
Gloves ✓		T W Bodger ✓
Steel Helmet ✓		T W Bodger ✓
Blouse ✓		T W Bodger ✓
Trousers ✓		T W Bodger ✓
Resp. Holder ✓		T W Bodger returned
6 Eye Shield ✓		T W Bodger ✓
Water Bottle ✓		T W Bodger ✓
Respirator ✓		T W Bodger ✓

'C' (TAUNTON NORTH) COMPANY

COMMANDING OFFICER	Major E.B. Mitford, M.C.
2ND IN COMMAND	Capt. J.D. Bevan
	(Capt. C.W. Glade-Wright, M.C.)

No further information on this Company has been discovered but it is possible that the two photographs on the last page of the book show this Company. Below is a ticket for a 'C' Company Smoking Concert. These concerts, whilst not strictly for men only, did involve the singing of more risqué songs, with comedians to match.

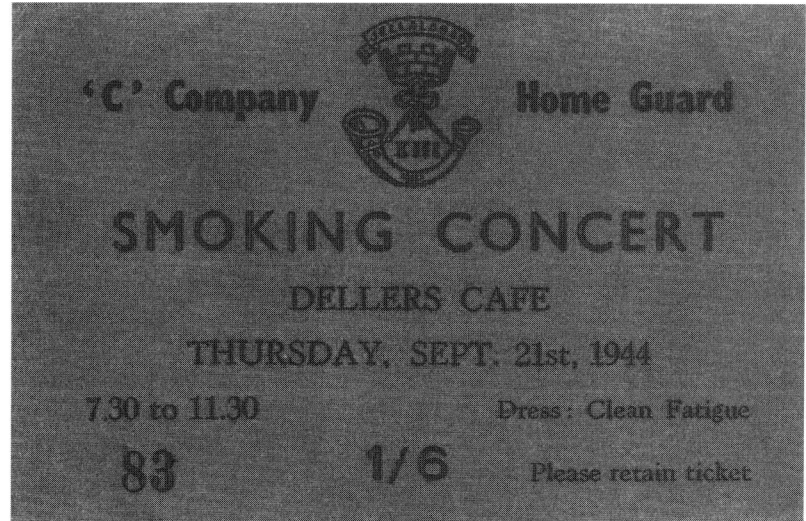

The Tragic Mystery of Corporal Plum

Wherever a group of men is seen –
Gallant Home Guardsmen, sturdy and keen –
At the village pub, or in the canteen,
You will hear them discuss, with visage glum,
What they conjecture might have become
Of their gallant old comrade Corporal Plum.
This really remarkable, tragical mystery
Has, until now, been muffled in history.
Now the Security Officer gives his consent,
I can give you the dope on the whole sad event.

Plum, an old soldier, manly and tall,
Was one of the first to answer the call
(Made some of the slackers look a bit small).
Soon all the neighbours turned out to see
Plum marching homeward as proud as could be,
With his manly arm labelled 'L.D.V.'
He attended parades, and he worked very hard.
Mr. Churchill altered the name to 'Home Guard'.
Then, in overalls, denim, we meet our old chum,
Henceforth to be known as Corporal Plum.

Then things began to move with an urge;
From the Quarter Bloke's store we saw Plum emerge
Bravely arrayed in Battle-dress, serge.
Then a cap, F.S., was the next to appear
Perfectly poised upon his right ear.
Boots, ankle, pairs one, and Anklets, leather
(Useful things these in the dirty weather),
And a nice leather belt to hold him together
Dressing, field, one, Ointment A.G.,
A packet of Eyeshields containing three.
Then he found they hadn't done with him yet;
There was Rifle and Bayonet, and Frog, bayonet.
Then, on parade, a few minutes later,
The R.S.M. said, "Where's your Respirator?"

After every parade he called up at the store
And they loaded him up with something more:
Kept sticking bits on from his head to his feet,
Till, at last, they made him a soldier complete.
'Twas his own idea that he'd look a bit bolder
With one of those lanyard things over his shoulder.

Then Mrs. Plum's task was entered upon:
Titles, shoulder, Home Guard, she had
　to sew on,
Flashes and Numerals, Stripes, and
　so on.
She complained, though she had
　been a most dutiful wife,
"This sewing on bits is the plague
　of my life.
I don't understand, but it seems
　to me
They're making you look like
　a Christmas Tree.
Isn't there anything else you
　can cadge?"
"Yes, there's Conduct Stripes and Proficiency Badge."

"*This sewing on bits is the plague of my life*"

They gave him a Greatcoat, then called him back;
They'd forgotten to give him a Haversack.
Still they got on with the jolly old game;
Bottle, water, one and Carrier for same;
Tin, mess, one; Gloves, worsted, one pair,
And then they decided while he was there
To fill up the few remaining spaces
With Webbing Equipment, Sleeve, Pouches and Braces.
He tried to make his escape, but, alas!
They dished him out a Cape Anti-Gas.
"Sixty-nine items," said the Quarter,
　"I make it."
Plum manfully murmured,
　"O.K. – we can take it."
Bravely, he shouldered the
　mountainous pack.
It was too much. Alas and
　Alack!
You remember the tale of
　the camel's back?
He could not support one
　little bit more;
That Cape Anti-gas was the
　very last straw.

He staggered away down the
　roadway dark,
And just as he reached the gates
　of the park –
Some twenty minutes, I suppose,
　had elapsed –
There came the end. Our hero
　collapsed!
He was lulled to his rest by
　the evening breeze
As the chestnut leaves
　fluttered from fading trees.

"*Sixty-nine items," said the Quarter, "I make it. . . .*"

The following morning the milkman found,
As he started out on his early round,
A sort of a new and peculiar mound
The leaves did not entirely conceal
A bundle of rags, and some bits of steel.
The milkman thought, "I suppose some chump
Has been and started a Salvage Dump;
I'll do MY bit," and in generous style,
He added three milk bottles to the pile.

Soon round the village the rumour ran.
Somebody brought an old petrol can,
Then pots and kettles, and saucepans galore,
Frying-pans, bottles, more and still more,
Some bits of old bikes, and a motor tyre,
Quickly the dump rose higher and higher.
And so it went on until, one Friday,
The Mayor, driving by, said: "That looks untidy."
He told the Council the very next day
To come and carry the whole lot away.

Tom Brown and Bill Jones had the job to do,
And both worked like heroes, trusty and true,
With just one stop – for a pint of bitter –
They toiled all day removing the litter.
And not until the last load was shifted
Was the veil of the mystery lifted.
Then, with the evening sun sinking down,
Came an agonized cry from Thomas Brown:
"Lor, lumme! You come and look here, Bill Jones;
Here's a blooming skull, and some human remains!"

'E' (BLAGDON HILL) COMPANY

COMMANDING OFFICER   Major C.T.G. Walmesley D.S.O., M.C., T.D.
                               Capt. L.W. Withinshaw,
                                   (Churchstanton Independent Platoon)

*Although uncaptioned this is believed to be a photograph of **Blagdon Hill Company**. Residents of Staplehay, Blagdon, Angersleigh and Pitminster have been identified. The photograph was taken at Fullwood Farm.*
Back Row: No. 2 Cyril Day; No. 3 Leslie Day; No. 5 Clem Warner; No. 9 Don Stutt; No. 15 Jack Cozens; No. 17 Ray Langdon; No. 19 Roy Day
Middle Row: No. 2 Sam Smith; No. 4 Bert Sleep; No. 5 Bob Fouracre; No. 6 Mr. Virgin; No. 13 Bill Warren; No. 21 Cpl. Charles Mutter
Front Row: No. 1 Major R.J.K. Mott; No. 2 Mr. Gibb; No. 6 Fred Alibone; No. 7 Fred Davey or Bill Hamblin; No. 8 Fred Pavey; No. 9 Jim Davey; No. 11 Mr. Osmond; No. 12 Ted Hunt; No. 13 Dick Groves; No. 15 Charlie Ford; No. 17 Gerald Long; No. 18 Jack Goldworthy; No. 19 Reg Male; No. 20 Tom Jackson; No. 22 Arthur Elkington; No. 25 Herb Reed; No. 26 George Langdon; No. 27 Major Walmesley

Other members of the Home Guard, but not identified in the photograph, included: Eddie Bond, A. Bond, Walter Collard, Ron Day and Ray Davis.
Shortly before the war Charles Mutter's home was provided with an inside flush toilet, making the outside privy redundant. However, Charles found the 'void' under the wooden seat ideal for storing his sten gun ammunition. For added security the gun was not kept with the ammunition; it was hidden in the kitchen copper!
(Mrs. Sheila Smith collection)

Blagdon and Pitminster N.C.O.s.
Back Row: No. 5 Cpl. Herb Reed; No. 6 Cpl. Charles Mutter
Front Row: No. 1 Sgt. George Langdon; No. 3 Major R.J.K. Mott;
  No. 4 possibly Major C.T.G. Walmesley D.S.O., M.C., T.D.
Close examination of the Major's medal ribbons shows, in addition to campaign ribbons of long ago, a D.S.O. and M.C., which suggests that it is Major C.T.G. Walmesley.
(Mrs. Audrey Hoyle collection)

Men of Blagdon Home Guard.
Back Row: No. 1 Unknown; No. 2 Gerald Long; No. 3 Bob Fouracre;
  No. 4 Mr. Virgin; No. 5 Unknown; No. 6 Unknown; No. 7 Ted Hunt
Front Row: Unknown; Mr. Gibb; Unknown; Don Stutt; Unknown
(Mrs. Sheila Smith collection)

Pitminster Home Guard.
Back Row: Joe Warren; Bill Warren; Roy Day; Mike Challice; Tommy Jackson; Bob Millen
Front Row: Herb Derman; Herb Reed; George Langdon; Ray Langdon; Jack Cousins
(The White Hart, Pitminster)

The reservoir at Quants, south of Taunton, not yet completed, was used for the firing of Spigot Mortar and for grenade practice. The area was also used by American troops for firing the bazooka anti-tank weapon. On some occasions ordnance would fail to explode and would not be disposed of correctly, but merely abandoned. One day in June 1944 some local children were playing in the area when one such abandoned projectile was disturbed with tragic consequences. Young Freddie Jones, George Jones, Margaret Ann Jones and Reginald William Phillips lie buried in the churchyard of St. Michael's Church, Angersleigh.

Churchstanton Independent Platoon comprised many more members than those featured left. The author is indebted to Mr. Jeffrey Berry for supplying the following names of known Platoon Members:

Sgt. Jim Cook, Leonard Ackland, Alfred Chard, Leonard Braddick, John Hannaford, Albert Sparkes, James Panton, Bill Berry, Bill Thomas, Bob Lye, Bill Bradford, Reg Berry, Howard Cross, Walter Cross, Major Lubbick, Percy Hayes, Harold Dommett, Albert Andrews, Bill Trim, James Trim, Charlie Jenkins, Ern Perry, Maurice Sparks, William Stowell, Sgt. Edwin Cottey, Jack Lyons, Walter Shire.

The Rev. Arthur Humphries and Nelson Webb were both stretcher bearers.

The Commanding Officer, Capt. Withinshaw, resided at Feltham where a rifle range was established. On some occasions training was taken by Sgt. Pettifer of the Somerset Light Infantry. Not all the correct drills were remembered. One night Albert Sparkes was severely reprimanded by 2nd Lt. Elkins. Instead of issuing the challenge, "Halt! Who goes there?", as Lt. Elkins approached he said, "Who's that?" Such was the casual attitude sometimes adopted.

Not all challenges were ineffectual. Sam Spiller was returning from Honiton one night when he failed to stop at a Home Guard checkpoint. H. Rosewell and his detachment promptly opened fire. Fortunately they only had shotguns and the only damage was to Sam's car, which then stopped.

Churchstanton Independent Platoon, *photographed outside Churchstanton Village Hall in 1944.*
Back Row: E. Perry; W. Grabham; H. Rosewell; V. Norrish; H. Shire
Middle Row: R. Shire; J. Payne; G. Rosewell; G. Rich; W. Stowell
Front Row: H. Venn; L/Cpl. G. Crabb; Cpl. T. Peters; 2nd Lt. Elkins;
   L/Cpl. J. Verdun Pitman; L/Cpl. C. Hayes; A. Venn.
Note the four years' good conduct stripes on 2nd Lt. Elkins' sleeve.
(Jill Cresswell-Higgs collection)

'F' (WELLINGTON) COMPANY

COMMANDING OFFICER	Major Leo G. 'Pukka' Dawe T.D. (Art Master at Wellington School)	STAFF OFFICER	Capt. O.S. 'Oscar' Hughes (Junior House Master at Wellington School)
2ND IN COMMAND	Capt. T. Fox		

No. 1 Platoon 'F' (Wellington) Company, *photographed on the school field of Wellington School in 1944.*
Back Row: No. 1 E. Eastment; No. 4 F. Taylor;
   No. 12 Cpl. M.I. Dick
Middle Row: No. 2 Cpl. Tregaskis;
   No. 3 Cpl. R.J. Saunders; No. 6 R. Warren;
   No. 8 L/Cpl. W.F. Hinds; No. 10 A. Winterton
Front Row: No. 3 Cpl. R.J. Authers;
   No. 4 Sgt. E. Prideaux; No. 5 Sgt. B.L. Haddon;
   No. 6 Sgt. T. Stenhouse; No. 7 Lt. E. Hookway;
   No. 8 Capt. O.S. Hughes; No. 9 Sgt. L. Prideaux;
   No. 12 Cpl. Harold Cousins
(John Hookway collection)

In a letter of May 2003, John Hookway, the son of Lt. Hookway, kindly included the following information taken from the Platoon Roll, dated 21.12.1941:

Section 1
Sgt. T. 'Jock' Stenhouse (? foreman, Fox Bros. & Co. Ltd., Tonedale)
Squad 1
Cpl. S. 'Sam' Purchase (Landlord of *The Dolphin Inn*)
Cpl. W. Waygood
Vol. E.W. Bowerman
Vol. J. Giles
Vol. F. Hockey
Vol. P. Dollin
Vol. J. Green
Squad 2
Cpl. R.J. 'Reg' Sanders (proprietor of an ironmongery shop in town centre, issued with a Browning Automatic Rifle)
Vol. E. 'Ern' Eastment
Vol. T. 'Tosh' Tregaskis (hairdresser in North Street)
Vol. C. Parr
Vol. F. 'Frank' Langham (? accountant, Fox. Bros.)
Vol. S.F. Phillips
Vol. W.S. Hutton

Section 2
Cpl. E. 'Ernest' Prideaux for administration
Squad 3
Cpl. E. 'Ernest' Prideaux (? gamekeeper)
Vol. J. Jordan (? painter and decorator)
Vol. S. Jordan
Vol. S. Rowlands
Vol. N. Trembath
Vol. H. Northam
Cpl. R.C. 'Reg' Dunn (shoe repairer in North Street)
Squad 4
Cpl. T. Antrobus
Vol. F. Taylor (? agricultural worker)
Vol. J. Lane
Vol. S. Southcott
Vol. H. Ling
Vol. R.T. Rugg
Vol. H. Perry (worked at Fox Bros.)

Section 3
Sgt. B.L. 'Baldwin' Haddon (bank manager)
Squad 5
Cpl. R.T. 'Reg' Authers (butcher in South Street)
Vol. F.L. Chick
Vol. R. Blackmore
Vol. W. Giles
Vol. E. Sparkes
Vol. R. 'Reg' Warren
Vol. N.F. Tidball
Squad 6
Cpl. H.W. 'Harold' Cousins (? fishmonger)
Vol. W. Are
Vol. W. Alford
Vol. W. Porter
Vol. R.J. Donovan
Vol. S.K. Kinnersley (? bank clerk)
Vol. H. Waygood

Attached Platoon HQ
Cpl. H. Male (no regular duties)
Vol. Hicks (medical orderly)

Attached Coy HQ – will answer for duties and guards when duties permit
Actg. Cpl. W.F. 'Porky' Hinds (Messing) (pork butcher in North Street)
Actg. Cpl. D.E. Griffin (Intelligence) (proprietor of a clothing manufacturer)
L/Cpl. F. 'Frank' Lee-Michel (Intelligence) (solicitor)
Vol. T.J. Ball (recommended for Transport Section)
   [It is not clear if the above roll was compiled for guard and other duties, or for tactical organisation; it was probably for the latter.]

Platoon Comd.
Lt. Ernest ('Basil') Hookway (Company Secretary of Fox Bros. & Co. Ltd.)

In further correspondence John Hookway added the following notes:

The Spigot Mortar practice range was, as near as I can remember, adjacent to a rifle range to the north of Wellington Monument firing up into Three Ponds Copse (map ref. ST 133 181). It could well have been just to one side or other of the Rifle Range so as to miss the butts. I can't remember what the target was, if indeed there was one. It was for demonstration rather than training on the weapon, although 'F' Wellington Company, which was static, might well have had Blacker Bombards on their strength. The bombs ricocheted most spectacularly up into the copse, but were only inert rounds.

With the build up to D-Day, 'vulnerable points' (VP) such as major road and rail bridges, which included Beam Bridge, would have been guarded, and the following list, dated 18th April 1944, indicates how many members of No. 1 Platoon were rostered to have some sleepless nights. No doubt many of them are featured in the Platoon photograph on the previous page.

NO.1.PLATOON.

GUARDS FOR V.P.

GROUP 1.	GROUP 2.
Sergt. Dunn R.C.	Sergt. Prideaux E.
L/C. Eastment E.	L/C. Bowerman E.
Pte. Phillips S.F.	Pte. Perry H.
Pte. Dyer C.	Pte. Perry E.
Pte. Dollin P.	Pte. Russell
Pte. Giles J.	Pte. Northam H.
Pte. Langham F.	Pte. Milton G.
Pte. Tregaskis T.	Pte. Alway B.T.S.
Pte. Deacon C.	Pte. Lock T.F.

GROUP 3.	GROUP 4.
Cpl. Dick M.I.	Cpl. Goldsworthy H.
Cpl. Authers	Cpl. Ware A.
Pte. Giles W.	Pte. Cornish G.
Pte. Chick L.	Pte. Porter W.
Pte. Sparks E.	Pte. Alford W.
Pte. Warren R.	Pte. Reed R.
Pte. Winterton A.	Pte. Fox W.
Pte. Slade H.	Pte. Burnett
Pte. Parminter H.	Pte. Quick R.

SPARES. Cpls. Sanders R, Cousins H, L/C. Kinnersley S.
EXCUSED. Ptes. Taylor F, Adams H, Burston H, Spiller.
TO H.Q.GUARD. Ptes. Donovan R. J.O'. Jordan S. Jordan J, Rowland S.

To mount and inspect nightly.   Lt. E. Hookway
                                Sergt. Stenhouse T.
                                Sergt. Haddon B.L.

.... Lt.
OC No.1 Platoon

18th April 1944

Terry Hake, writing from Australia in 1995, recalled his time in the Wellington Home Guard. The photograph below shows members of the Hake Family.

Back Row: Terry Hake, sister Muriel, brother Claude and father Samuel James Hake
Front Row: sister Aileen with her son Allan and, on the right, Mrs. Hake with Aileen's daughter Pat
(Terry Hake collection)

Summer 1940

The news steadily unfolding, via newspaper and radio, was horrific. That our men had been recovered for the most part from Dunkirk was outweighed by the loss of equipment, and morale, both in the Forces and on the Home Front.

To all intents and purposes our island was no longer impregnable. No longer could we regard ourselves immune to the war. The call came over the air, and in the papers, for all able-bodied men to register for Local Defence Volunteer duty at once. Everyone became involved overnight, and a rush to join this civilian army ensued. Unfortunately, few instructions were given as to where one had to go for this. My father, an ex-senior N.C.O. from the earlier war, took the bull by the horns, as it were, and after approaching the Officer in Command of the local Officer Training Corps at Wellington School was ably assisted by the school's Sgt. Major in organising the drawing up of a number of evening parades a week, on the parade ground, for the purposes of getting the names of volunteers and training with the school's rifles. The fact that these rifles were for training only with portions of bores drilled out and firing pins missing was sadly spoken about with the assembly of men. which in any case outnumbered the number of weapons.

Some weeks later our first uniforms arrived in the shape of khaki-coloured brassards with L.D.V. stamped on. I can remember distinctly my own embarrassment at putting this on for the first time. When I looked around I could see others faces reflecting the thought, 'Is this all?'

In the meantime order started to come to life, and we were divided into platoons (sans rifles). One platoon had the job of waiting around at the newly established H.Q., the ex-Drill Hall in Wellington, for reports to arrive via bicycle or whatever from those on patrol elsewhere. No. 2 Platoon, of which I was a member, consisted of those considered active, in the sense that we had bikes and local knowledge. We, like the other Platoon, had our own shotguns, or nothing, and were given jobs consistent with our bicycle ownership. In my case, together with one other person, this consisted of a dawn patrol on the hills. We were given a stretch of a mile or so, and arriving before dawn were to look out for parachutists and other mundane things. This patrol started an hour or two before sun-up and ended an hour after. It was taken for granted that any German effort would take advantage of the early hours. This timing allowed for a stalk over the common for a brace of rabbits to take home for the pot as well as to be on time for work.

Parachutists

It was considered that the Invasion would be preceded by an attack by these elite troops to hold ground inland, prior to the Beach Landing. Some instructions included the importance of wearing the brassard at all times since this might stop one from being shot, if captured. Other more readily received instructions gave a summary of the weapons these blokes would be carrying and how to use them if you were lucky enough to shoot one with your shotgun. Heady stuff indeed for us to mull over on patrol.

On other nights we were placed on duty on railway bridges or pumping stations, and halted all who wished to pass with a yelled challenge of "Halt! Who goes there?", having to receive "Friend" in reply. (God knows what would have happened if a voice had replied with any other answer.) Then, with the order "Advance friend and be recognised," the person would slowly make his or her way into your dimmed flashlight for inspection. No instruction came my way as to what to do with anyone considered suspicious. Its effect I suppose was slowly to bring Britain's precarious position to the front of people's minds as no other way could have.

On other nights we had to parade in small contingents of six, below Rockwell Green Water Tower. Then, after the production of notepaper and pencil, four of us climbed to the top, with two below, to act as messengers to the rifle platoon, in case we observed Paras. The messages from above were considered too hard to hear in windy conditions so a rigid wire was pulled from top to bottom and a Heath Robinson message bottle strung from this to the ground.

I am, of course, aware that all of this is laughable now but it was far from that then. Consider the fact that almost overnight some one and a half million men volunteered for the L.D.V. Some with local knowledge, and armed with their own shotguns, would have to be taken into consideration by an invading force. Although it may seem puny now, in those days to drop Paras into virtually undefended countryside presents a somewhat different situation with the thought of people determined to fill you up with No. 5 shot lurking in the hedgerows.

Together with this, of course, as the months drew on our untrained force was now at least partly-trained, with all members equipped with rifles, machine guns and in some rare instances sub-machine guns of which I became a proud possessor. My gaining the distinction of a stripe and the unit's sole possessor, came about after a competition between us at a shooting match. By some stroke of good luck not only had we received the Tommy gun, but a rare thing indeed, a large number of .45" rounds to go with it. Now everyone wanted that gun, and after some deliberation it was decided that the one most proficient with it would have it. On the Sunday morning a large number turned up for testing at the Butts to the south of Wellington, each issued with 25 rounds and each took his turn. The 'thing', as soon as you touched the trigger, took off as though demented, firing up and to the right and some near misses took place. After seeing this happen, when it was my turn I gripped it like it was alive, and aiming deliberately slightly to the left of the target stitched it through the middle as neat as in a Cagney film. A halt then to make running repairs and then single shots at the German on a stick with a man running along backwards and forwards in the trench of the butts, holding our mock bloke well above his head. We then had to fire single and five-shot bursts at him. I won the competition and the gun was my pride and joy until I joined the R.A.F.

However, before all this, our shotguns had to be handed in for inspection by an Armourer to see if they were safe to fire 'Lethal Ammo'. This lethal stuff consisted of normal-looking 12g cartridges but instead of containing shot they held three massive wedge-shaped interlocking chunks of lead. These, after leaving the barrel, slowly divided until after a short distance they presented a lethal ten-foot group, either of which, according to father, who had used them in the First World War, could kill an elephant. Our guns, mostly now stamped under the breech as 'unsuitable for Lethal', were duly returned to us. Thank goodness, since nothing weakens a man more than to have no weapon in hand. My shotgun came back stamped as 'suitable right barrel only'. The reason for this was, of course, that it had a cylinder for the right barrel, and choke for the left, it being obvious that the lethal stuff would burst the barrel if fired through the choked bore. We then waited for this ammo to arrive; it never did.

The arming and distribution of uniforms and boots happened during the winter months, after the possibility of invasion had receded until the following spring. We were renamed 'Home Guard' and army N.C.O.s arrived on the parade ground one Saturday morning. They hammered us into some semblance of order and then we were marched singly before a Sergeant Major who sourly took our names. After getting us to turn around and bend over he uttered a series of grunts and numbers for his clerk to take down, asked us for our boot size, and off we were marched. To our surprise, by the following weekend our stuff turned up, all labelled for each individual, and all fitting, more or less. With this, our respect for the Army increased somewhat. Our turnout the next week left a little to be desired from my father's point of view, and people who were wearing a collar and tie with the uniform rapidly took them off. Some exchanges took place between the one with overlarge battle dress, and the one with too small. A lecture from The Boss on who could wear a tie and who could not was followed with the requirement to salute Officers from now on when in uniform. How to salute and wear the headgear followed, so that before long, passing each other after parade resulted in a salute with a very uncomplimentary statement regarding one's ancestry, all with the ultimate in good humour, of course.

P17 rifles arrived in transit chests holding 10 weapons with the serial numbers stencilled on the outside. (Author's collection)

Rifles turned up covered in a mass of hard grease in which they had been packed in America at the end of the First World War. They took hours of cleaning; the grease had to be removed with boiling water and then the hot bores would sweat from the heat, and had to be pulled through over the next day or two. The rifles were from various manufacturers, Remingtons etc., but all to the same specification. The ammunition was different to English and in short supply initially, each of us only getting five rounds. Its calibre was .300 against our .303 and in addition was rimless. To have a rifle other than a shotgun in hand gave the Home Guard a great boost and now probably made us seem at last worthwhile, and a force to be reckoned with.

We also received a couple of old First World War Lewis machine guns. These were carried on drills and route marches with the number two carrying huge magazine pans alongside. The proud gunners were selected for this job, since they had used them in the war before. These old chaps carried them for hours without complaint, changing shoulders from time to time. I forget the weight, about 25lbs from memory, and after lifting one, was glad I had my smaller edition to carry.

I must relate this true episode, though. On one of our Sunday fitness cross-country marches an aircraft crossed our front, very low, which was easily seen to be German. We took cover as the plane passed again overhead and on. As a result of this, new orders came into effect about having a go at these if in range with a lecture on aiming off and leading the plane in order to have some remote chance of hitting it. One of our worthy machine gunners piped up and asked if he was included in this and was told, "Yes, of course". Some two weeks later on an exercise we were undergoing with another platoon, we were placed in trenches overlooking a valley. Each was lectured by his N.C.O. on his field of fire etc., and the exercise took place with us all firing, or strictly speaking making appropriate noises off and on to simulate firing. When this exercise ended, my father got us all together, and told us a few home truths fairly letting us have it about our lack of commitment. Up pipes the Machine Gunner and says, "But I didn't forget", and whipping off the drum from his Lewis proudly showed us the fact that it was fully loaded. My Father looked at him and said, "Did you have the drum on through the exercise?" "Yes, Sir, never forgot what you told us about the plane, always be ready." My Father said, "And did you have it cocked, with one up the spout?" "Oh yes, but I had my safety on though." No-one had much to say after this since we were acting at the time with him up in the front aiming his machine gun at the on-coming infantry, and yelling, "rat, tat, tat" like a dervish with his gun traversing from left to right. Just how little it would have taken for him to slip the safety forward by accident was obvious to us all. All ended well and the colour returned to my father's face later. The gunner had to strip his weapon every time for inspection from then on, and if we knew we were going to exercise against his gun later, we would all queue up to inspect it before moving off. This applied to his number two as well, his ammo pans also being scrutinised. This was done and received in good humour but we all knew there was a filled magazine somewhere in the gear. So much then for memory of the gradual emergence of a reasonable force. As for its intentions, let it never be forgotten that we meant business from the word go. No derring-do stuff, just try landing within range or where we lay in ambush. Any Para would have been killed without doubt or compassion. Any one of us would have used his weapons despite all odds as long as we lasted.

The 'Boys' Anti-Tank Rifle

This dreadful weapon came our way, with a number of rounds, during the early days. As far as we could find out it was useless as an anti-anything. It should, if it hit a light tank at the right angle, penetrate and ricochet around inside killing all and sundry. The main drawback was the need to hit at right angles, in a soft spot which we were told was the floor of the tank, or the driver's visor. This lead to some serious questions, for instance, "On which side of a German Tank does the driver sit?" "They drive on the other side of the road, don't they?" Then again, how do you hit the bottom of a tank at a right angle?

The weapon itself looked like a larger-than-life .303 rifle. It was twice as long, and had a bore like a drain. The shells ('rounds' seems the wrong description) were about eight inches long and the calibre, which escapes me, about half an inch. A huge steel-cored bullet topped this fearsome looking cartridge case.

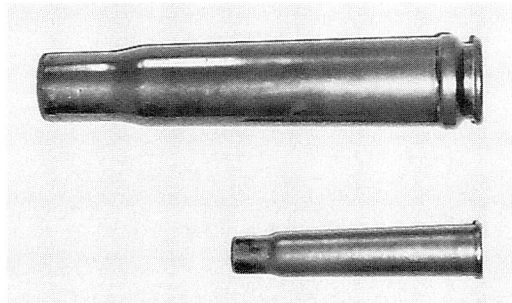

An example of a cartridge case for the .55" Boys Anti-Tank rifle and the standard .303" rifle cartridge case, showing the vast difference in size. (Author's collection)

Instructions for holding and firing this weapon came via an Army Sergeant whose first heartening words were: "Wouldn't catch me firing it". He then, at the firing butts, got the biggest and the most gormless looking bloke to demonstrate – me, of course. Everyone told me it wouldn't hurt, damned if I knew how they knew that, but on my trying to hand over the reins nobody else seemed keen so the Sergeant showed me how to lie down with my body in line with the weapon. No traditional prone position with this thing; just lie in line, keep your feet together and dig them in the ground if possible. "Steel shoulder straps over and under the shoulder, butt to be pulled in very tight and aim, over open sights, with the same sights for 300 yds as for 50," our Sergeant cheerfully waffles on. "It's a powerful gun this one, OK who is going to act as number two?" First we had heard of a number two: "what does he do, load?" " No, he lies across your shoulders to help with the recoil." A big bloke was selected and duly lay in the prescribed position. "Right away, back everyone and you can now load." Same bolt action as a rifle and one of the rounds is inserted. Sergeant says: "Aim at the sheet of plate, and fire when ready", before retiring to a safe spot. I pulled the butt into my shoulder, asked the huge weight above if he was all right, and squeezed the trigger. Seemed like minutes afterwards we picked ourselves up from a huddle, and sorted out the weapon now lying facing the rear. "See now why it's only single shot, can't you," says the Sergeant, coming into sight again. Well, a look at the target sheet of steel; there was an impressive dent in the middle, and a groove cut out to the edge of the sheet but no penetration. It had been placed at right angles too, so we didn't think much of the gun's tank-stopping ability after this. The Sergeant carefully repositioned the sheet and suggested that I now hit it again at the same point. My shoulder started to regain its feeling, having felt like someone had hit it with a sledgehammer. I suggested it was only fair to allow someone else to take it on. No volunteers, and everyone kicking the ground at this. He detailed a large, older bloke for it this time, and the number two not being around, another number two. Same routine and I carefully watched the recoil. Blokes went ass over head, gun flew up in the air, and I felt for the bloke's shoulder. Trouble was he missed the sheet altogether. No one would have anything to do with the thing now, and we were dismissed only after the Sergeant gave us some delightful memories of broken shoulders and a reluctance even on the part of regulars to fire it. Our anti-tank weapon stayed in the armoury as the powers that be came to the conclusion that no Tank Commander is going to stay idly watching a couple of idiots aiming this, waiting for him to present his weak underside, or point out where the driver's visor was. Thank goodness for that. But strangely enough, I was to see it and fire it again, in the R.A.F., when we had to do a survival course with the Durhams, of all people.

An extract from a wartime training manual, dated 1942, states:

"Weight 36lbs, calibre .55", total length 5'4". Penetration .91" of armour at 100 yards at right angles, 14" of brick wall or 10" shingle in a sand bag." With a muzzle velocity of 3,250 feet per second, no wonder troops were wary of the weapon's recoil.

Home Guard with 2-Pounder Anti-Tank Gun.
The caption on the photograph merely says 'Wellington'. Despite an appeal for information run by the Wellington Weekly News *in December 2000 no response was forthcoming. However, as a result of a further appeal, the site has been positively identified as Wellington School sports field, but who are the Home Guards posing with the gun?*

The gun featured is a British Two-Pounder which was formally approved on 1st January 1936. With a 360° traverse, a muzzle velocity of 2650 feet/second and capable of penetrating 1⅜" of armour at 1000 yards at 30°, it was the best anti-tank gun in the world. However, by 1939, it was beginning to reach the end of its useful life. Nonetheless, it remained in production until 1941. Some pillboxes in Somerset were designed and constructed to accommodate the gun. In late 1943 it was issued to some Home Guard Units, but weighing some 18cwt, one can imagine elderly Home Guards struggling with such a bulky piece of equipment.
(Freda Evans collection)

Oake and Nynehead Home Guard.
Back Row: Unknown; Unknown; Jack Hawkins; Roy Hartnell; Mr. Broom; Unknown; Unknown; Tom Hutchins; Fred Pulman; Edward Stevens; Jim Floyd
Middle Row: Cpl. Sid Jones; Tom Lock or Mr. Hutchins; Henry Dunn; Reg Marks; Bill Winter; Bob Winter; Harold Sharland; Bill Pavey; Charles Tarr; Cyril Cornish; L/Cpl. Leslie Stone
Front Row: Cpl. Bill Radford; Sgt. L. Sparks; Sgt. The Rev. Rees Davies; Lt. R.B. Hankey; Sgt. H. Elston; Cpl. F. Bickham; Unknown
(John Sparks collection)

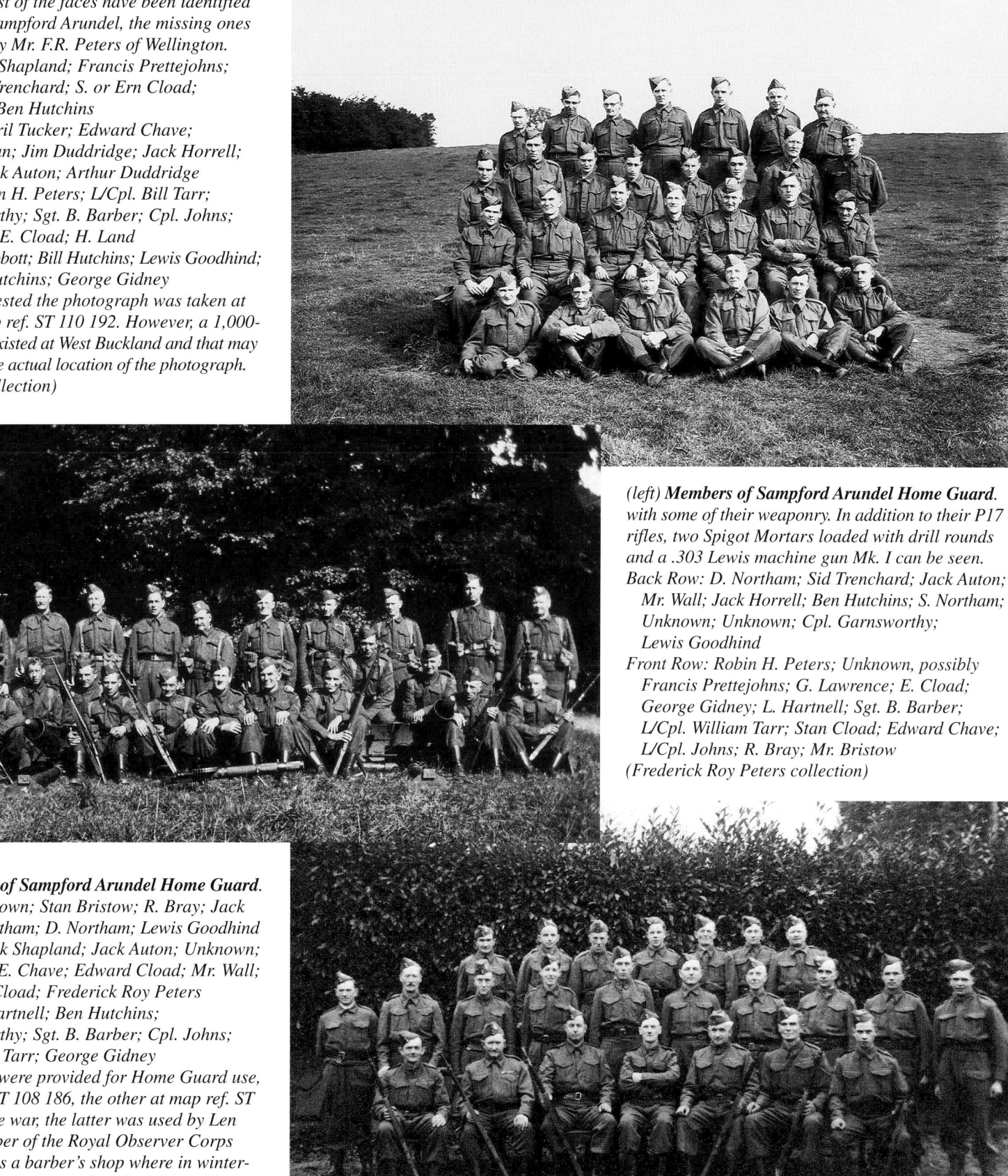

(right) **Members of Sampford Arundel Home Guard**. This photograph also hangs in Sampford Arundel Village Hall. Most of the faces have been identified by residents of Sampford Arundel, the missing ones being provided by Mr. F.R. Peters of Wellington.
Back Row: Jack Shapland; Francis Prettejohns; Len Hill; Sid Trenchard; S. or Ern Cload; Stan Bristow; Ben Hutchins
Second Row: Cyril Tucker; Edward Chave; David Trevelyan; Jim Duddridge; Jack Horrell; John Rich; Jack Auton; Arthur Duddridge
Third Row: Robin H. Peters; L/Cpl. Bill Tarr; Cpl. Garnsworthy; Sgt. B. Barber; Cpl. Johns; L/Cpl. Stan or E. Cload; H. Land
Front Row: W. Abbott; Bill Hutchins; Lewis Goodhind; Mr. Wall; J. Hutchins; George Gidney
It has been suggested the photograph was taken at Stoney Stile, map ref. ST 110 192. However, a 1,000-yard rifle range existed at West Buckland and that may well have been the actual location of the photograph.
(Freda Evans collection)

(left) **Members of Sampford Arundel Home Guard**. with some of their weaponry. In addition to their P17 rifles, two Spigot Mortars loaded with drill rounds and a .303 Lewis machine gun Mk. I can be seen.
Back Row: D. Northam; Sid Trenchard; Jack Auton; Mr. Wall; Jack Horrell; Ben Hutchins; S. Northam; Unknown; Unknown; Cpl. Garnsworthy; Lewis Goodhind
Front Row: Robin H. Peters; Unknown, possibly Francis Prettejohns; G. Lawrence; E. Cload; George Gidney; L. Hartnell; Sgt. B. Barber; L/Cpl. William Tarr; Stan Cload; Edward Chave; L/Cpl. Johns; R. Bray; Mr. Bristow
(Frederick Roy Peters collection)

(right) **Members of Sampford Arundel Home Guard**.
Back Row: Unknown; Stan Bristow; R. Bray; Jack Horrell; S. Northam; D. Northam; Lewis Goodhind
Middle Row: Jack Shapland; Jack Auton; Unknown; Ken Hellings; E. Chave; Edward Cload; Mr. Wall; E. Pike; Stan Cload; Frederick Roy Peters
Front Row: L. Hartnell; Ben Hutchins; Cpl. Garnsworthy; Sgt. B. Barber; Cpl. Johns; L/Cpl. William Tarr; George Gidney
Two Nissen huts were provided for Home Guard use, one at map ref. ST 108 186, the other at map ref. ST 112 186. After the war, the latter was used by Len Hellings, a member of the Royal Observer Corps during the war, as a barber's shop where in wintertime he would manage to cut hair by lamplight.
(Frederick Roy Peters collection)

(above) **Bradford-on-Tone Home Guard**.
Back Row: A. Underhill; P. Underhill; E. Braddick; S. Bowie; A. Comer; B. Edwards;
  F. Warren; C. Webber; B. Hodge; Robert (Bob) Symons
Middle Row: L/Cpl. William Perrot; Cpl. Tom Berry; Sgt. Henry Roberts;
  C.S.M. Lewis Johnson; Lt. Col. H.F.L. Hilton-Green D.S.O., M.C.; Sgt. Jack Symons;
  Cpl. Tom Sydenham; Cpl. William (Bill) Hill; L/Cpl. Arthur Lucas
Front Row: William Symons; C. Braddick; Abraham Shire
  Other Members of the Bradford Home Guard included J. Roberts, S. Jenkins, Major
Parker, J. Batten, Den Clist, P. Nickerson. After the formation of the Home Guard,
Glen Line, part of the Ocean Shipping Line, evacuated to Upcott Hall, Bishops Hull.
Many of the staff joined Bradford Home Guard. Lieutenant Henry Charles Jefferies,
an accountant with Glen Line, succeeded Lt. Col Hilton-Green as Commander.
(Bob Symons collection)

*(right) William Symons, aged 100, with his nephew Bob Symons, both former members of the
Bradford-on-Tone Home Guard, photographed by the author in early 2004.*

The Home Guard was responsible for manning road blocks at Three Bridges and Bradford Bridge where an old horse-drawn fire pump filled with sand bags was used. At one stage during the war, the railway bridge on the Oake road was guarded at night where the off-duty guards would sleep in a hut by the railway line.

Home Guard meetings were held at Bradford-on-Tone Village Hall. Stores were kept at Bradford Court Stables where an outdoor .22 rifle range was built. At some stage a Nissen hut was built north-west of Lower Stoford Cottages in an orchard. This building was still standing in 1993 when the photograph (*right*) was taken. By the summer of 2002 the building had deteriorated further. How long before a piece of history finally succumbs to neglect?

(Brian Emmett collection)

***Wellington Members of the 2133 Motor Transport Company**. Although not coming under the command of the local Home Guard Commander, the picture has been included here as the members were Wellington residents. The background suggests that the photograph was taken in Wells, probably at their Final Parade on 10th December 1944.*
Back Row: No. 1 W. Gwyther; Nos. 2-4 Unknown; No. 5 E. Pike; Nos. 6-7 Unknown; No. 8 P. Hockey
Middle Row: Nos. 1-2 Unknown; No. 3 T. Jefferies; No. 4 Unknown; No. 5 J. Lane; No. 6 Unknown; No. 7 J. Auton
Front Row: No. 1 Cpl. E. Johnson; Nos. 2-3 Unknown; No. 4 possibly Mr. Kerslake; No. 5 J. Underhill; No. 6 Lt. W.G. Radford; No. 7 Mr. F. Colman; No. 8 Mr. W. Green; No. 9 Mr. A. Luxton; No. 10 Sgt. H.K. Radford.
(Bill Radford collection)

Lt. Radford was the son of the owner of Radford Brothers Ltd., local hauliers, and had been a member of the Royal Horse Artillery. His brother, Sgt. H.K. Radford was also in the unit, using his own 350c.c. BSA motorcycle on Home Guard business. Bill Radford, son of H.K. Radford, recalled the Home Guard practising convoy drill using bicycles, with the leading and last 'vehicle' carrying the respective flag. He also remembers the late Major E.M. Snow of the Wellington Company recalling an incident during the war when intelligence had been received that German Paratroops had landed at White Ball Tunnel. The local Home Guard unit had turned out and went to defend the tunnel with rifles and five rounds of ammunition between the whole company!

'G' (STOKE ST. MARY) COMPANY

COMMANDING OFFICER   Major G.F. Waterworth, D.S.O.
                                  (Major J.B. Glencross, D.S.O.)
                                  (Major F.C.P. Williams-Freeman, D.S.O.)
2ND IN COMMAND   Capt. K.H.O'R. Sadgrove

(right) **No. 2 Platoon**, photographed at Orchard Portman Saw Mills in April 1943.
Back Row: F. Foster; F. Hoare; Unknown; Mr. Stapleford; A. Allen
Second Row: Ted Matravers; George Garland; Unknown; Unknown, but possibly Mr. Hilliard; H. Shattock
Third Row: F.A. Brice; A. Counsell; G. Baker; P. Greed; B. Morse; Unknown; Unknown
Fourth Row: Mr. Venn; H. Ellett; P. Drew; Unknown; W. Vile; H. Bond; Jim Cozens; Bill Board; Mr. Spiller; G. Rawle
Front Row: Sgt. Roy Drew; Sgt. A. Budden; Lt. A. Villar; Capt. M. Cole; 2nd Lt. F. Lock or B. Murray; Sgt. G. Burt; Cpl. W. Callow; L/Cpl. S. Coles
(F. Brice collection)

(left) **Ruishton, Henlade and Thornfalcon Home Guard**, photographed at The Nag's Head, Thornfalcon in 1944.
Back Row: Mr. Taylor; Ron Stevens; Mr. Coles; Bill Derrick; Cyril Webber; Sid Bosley; Walter Hussey; Gilbert Potter; Harold Heywood
Second Row: Clifford Rowsell; Jim Stevens; Ernest Bowey; Mr. Blaney; Bert Beer; Bill Stenson; Courtney Webber; Bill Hitchcott
Third Row: Cpl. Bendal; Frank Hunt; Theo Ling; Ernie Webber; Tom Pinney; Fred Hussey; Douglas Hewings; Ted Bowditch; Cpl. Dennis Coles
Front Row: Cpl. Charlie Fyfield; Cpl. Zelley; Sgt. Walter Wood; Sgt. Eddie Hunt; Lt. Clarke; Lt. Payne; Sgt. George Briers; Cpl. Clifford Vickery; Cpl. Roland Gordge; Cpl. Leslie Matravers.
(Ernie Webber collection)

    Both Jim and Ron Stevens worked at Manor Farm, Thornfalcon, which was owned by fellow Home Guard Harold Heywood. Cyril Webber was another farmer, working at Stoke Hill Farm whilst Bill Hitchcott worked at Ash Farm, Thornfalcon. Frank Hunt and George Briers were both residents of Henlade, Frank being a wood and stone carver whilst George was a local nurseryman. Henlade House employed Charlie Fyfield as a gardener and general handyman. Other Platoon Members included Messrs. Baker, Blackmore, Bray, Matravers, Perkins and Sandford.
    Eddie Hunt was the local thatcher, living at Thornfalcon. Up to the 1960s the main Taunton-Ilminster road at Thornfalcon was a narrow single-carriage road, the section between *The Nag's Head* and Mattocks Tree Hill passing through a deep tree-lined cutting. On the opposite side of the road to *The Nag's Head* was a carpenter's shop occupied by Leslie Matravers. In the 1960s this section of road was 'improved', sweeping away Leslie's place of work. Other buildings nearby included Harry Stevens's blacksmith's shop situated in the yard behind *The Nag's Head*. Harry joined the L.D.V. in 1940, but died in June 1941 before this photograph was taken. Another omission from the photograph is Jack Matravers, a brother of Leslie, who left the Home Guard due to hearing difficulties, and spent the remainder of the war in a team salvaging crashed aircraft. A concrete floor slab at map ref. ST 283 232, close to a copse, is all that remains of the Home Guard storage shed.

In a letter written in 2001, George Stokes of Henlade recalled his experience of Home Guard activities:

One night in the summer of 1940 Harry Stevens was detailed to carry out observation duties from Thorn Hill with another member of the L.D.V. but found his companion was not available. He contacted me asking if I would be the second man on watch and as my mother was running *The Nag's Head* at the time to bring up a flagon of beer. On my arrival Harry outlined his defence plan for Thorn Hill. In the event of German Paratroops landing he would hold them at bay with his shotgun, give me the key to the local A.A. box and I would run across the field to the box and ring (platoon) headquarters for assistance.

George never joined the Home Guard but served on H.M. Submarines, including the unlucky *Sportsman*, which had been bombed by the Americans before he joined her. After George left the submarine it was lost with all hands in a diving accident.

Home Guard instructions dated November 1943 credit the Shotgun as an effective man-killing short-range weapon with three types of shot issued: S.G., L.G. and Lethal Ball. With a maximum effective range of 40 yards it was considered ideal for night patrols and ambushes. Illustrated are examples of 12-bore W.D. cartridges together with an early LDV armband worn by the author's uncle at Porton Down Germ Warfare Centre. (Author's collection)

'H' (G.W.R. TAUNTON) COMPANY

COMMANDING OFFICER	Major P.H. Spence, M.B.E.
2ND IN COMMAND	Capt. J.R. Gardner
	(Capt. F.L. Lambert)
COMMANDING LIGHT AA TROOP	Capt. C.G. Connett

Alec Bowditch, writing in December 1994, recorded his memories of the early days of the Home Guard:

In May 1940, when Anthony Eden made a public appeal for a civilian force to be formed, I was aged 19½ and employed by the Great Western Railway as a Lad Messenger. The G.W.R., realising that it had many strategic points to be guarded, immediately sent out its own call for railwaymen to come forward and form its own L.D.V. In common with many rail centres, a company was formed at Taunton, the foot drill being taught by the 'old sweats' of World War 1. I had two brothers who were 17 and 16 years older than me and we all went along to the Railway Engineers' Department at Obridge to commence our training. After a few evenings of foot drill we were sent out to patrol railway bridges at dusk and dawn to look out for German Paratroops. Initially we were not armed but after a period of a month or so we were handed a .45" Webley revolver and *two* rounds of ammunition. I spent several evenings and early mornings in the company of three others patrolling the Staplegrove Railway Bridge. We used to argue whose turn it was to carry the pistol and what we should do if we did see any paratroops. There was a real possibility of this happening and we took our duties very seriously.

Patrolling was interrupted at times by two of us, in turn, paying a visit to Taunton West Signal Box, situated quite near to Staplegrove Bridge. The signalman on duty would allow us to brew up on his stove. On cold nights it was nice to have a warm in front of his stove. On duty one evening at Station Bridge in Kingston Road, a passenger guard coming off duty said to me: "If you want to see a sight go up to the Up Main Platform and see the train which has just arrived from Plymouth". On going to the platform I was amazed to see a train with many of its windows smashed, with 'Jolly Jack Tars' in the corridors. The occupants of the train were French Sailors who had mutinied on board their vessels in Devonport because the British Fleet had fired at and sunk some of their vessels in North Africa. There was an awful lot of blood around, and fighting was still in progress as the train went on its way. Not many people in Taunton ever knew of that incident as censorship, for obvious reasons, was very tight.

'H' (G.W.R. Taunton) Company.
Back Two Rows: No. 4 Ern Webb (platelayer); No. 5 D. Cundy; No. 8 A. Miller; No. 9 A. Jones; No. 10 T. Wilcox; No. 17 V. Churchill; No. 20 G. Wilkinson; No. 22 J. Anon
Second Row: No. 3 J. Hoare
Third Row: No. 1 H. Blackmore; No. 4 C. Wadham;
Fourth Row: No. 1 T. Strickland; No. 5 (standing to right of Sgt. below) F. Waygood; No. 8 Bill Bond (Goods Dept.)
Fifth Row: No. 2 S. Woodley; No. 7 Sgt. H. Berry; No. 9 T. Bridgwater; No. 10 Mr. Coles; No. 13 Mr. Vickery; No. 15 G. Cross; No. 16 D. Staples
Front Row: No. 1 Sgt. Bert Trott (Engineers Dept.); No. 3 Sgt. Major J. Vellacott (Traffic Dept.); No. 6 Lt. Alec Keitch (Traffic Dept.); No. 7 Lt. H. Dryden (Engineers Dept.); No. 8 Capt. J.R. Gardner (Exeter D.G.M.O.); No. 9 Major Spence; No. 10 Capt. C.G. Connett (Goods Dept.); No. 11 Lt. Harold Potter (Goods Dept.); No. 16 Sgt. Rosewarne
Major Spence was awarded the M.B.E. (Military Division) in recognition of outstanding services to the Home Guard. He was assistant to the Divisional Engineer, Taunton.
(Author's collection)

'H' Company Tug-of-War Team.
Front Row: No. 4 Alec Keitch; No. 5 Harry Dryden; No. 6 Jack Vellacott.
Behind Alec Keitch, wearing a shirt and tie, is Harold Potter. Other members of the team included T. Strickland, J. Heenan, H. Blackmore, P. Short and T. Orrell (trainer).
(Author's collection)

*Taken at Obridge, Taunton, with the houses in Priorswood Road visible in the background, **N.C.O.s of 'H' Company** pose for the camera. Many faces are recognisable from the photograph on the left. Those identified include, in the front row, No. 3 Sgt. H. Berry and No. 6 Sgt. Major J. Vellacott.*
(Leslie Berry collection)

In addition to those identified in the preceding three photographs, the following railway employees are also known to have been members of the Home Guard in Taunton, although the list is not exhaustive: Messrs. T. Prosser, F. Wyatt, W. Overton, W. Burford, Sweetland, E. Webber and J. Dommett.

***Taunton members of the 2133 Motor Transport Company** pose outside The Deanery, Wells on the day of their Final Parade. Unlike other Home Guard Units, the Somerset M.T. Column paraded on 10th December 1944. Before the service at Wells Cathedral the column were drawn up on the Market Square. After the service the column paraded on the Cathedral Green. After a rendition of The National Anthem the column was dismissed and passed into history.*
Left to right: No. 3 T. Lock (from Ash Priors; worked for W.J. King); No. 5 Mr. Stone (Bishops Lydeard); No. 6 Mr. Jones (Taunton); No. 10 Cpl. Bowerman (Taunton); No. 11 Mr. Venton (Bishops Lydeard); No. 12 Sgt. Trim (Taunton); No. 15 Capt. Ridler (Taunton; owned Express Garage); No. 19 Mr. Hodge (Bishops Lydeard); No. 21 Bert Cavill (Bishops Lydeard; worked for W.J. King); No. 22 Mr. Tucker (Taunton); No. 23 Cpl. Frank Knight (Bishops Lydeard)
In front row: No. 1 Cpl. Sully (Bishops Lydeard); No. 2 Mr. A. Rowlands
(Frank Knight collection)

Hydrographic Supplies Establishment Home Guard.
Back Row: Sidney Supman; John Forsdyke; Horace Boyer; Ken Arnold; A. Martin; Fred Williams; Jack Goodhall; Mr. Garland; Eric Gilles; Unknown; G. Faulkner; Harry Carey or Harold Groves; Les Roberts; Unknown; J. Townsend; Unknown; Unknown

Second Row: R.E. Clark; Keith Jolly; Jeff Willey; Unknown; Van Stratton; 'Ginger' Parker; Arthur Ginnings; Richard Wellstead; Fred Leamon; Frank Pavey; Unknown; Bill Warner; Bert Windsbrow; Don Barham; Rex Searle

Seated: Unknown; Cpl. Hutchinson Jnr.; Cpl. Len Welland; Sgt. Gazlet; Tom Rivett; Mr. C. Towsey (Superintendent); Lt. Greenwood; Major E.B. Mitford; Bill Elston; Sgt. Bill Dodd; Sgt. John Hutchinson; Cpl. Frank Halse; Cpl. Ted Cooper; Cpl. Phil Cook; Cpl. John Allsop

Front Row: Stan Leavey; Unknown; Unknown; Unknown; Unknown; W. Brassington; Unknown; Unknown

Other Members of this Home Guard unit included Sgt. Kelland, 2nd Lt. Green, George Huddle, A. Clay, G. Henderson, V. Leavey, R. Balls, S. Payne, R. Sears, and P. Fletcher.

Eight of the group were veterans of the First World War. Pte. Hemmingshaw lectured on German uniforms and how to deal with a prisoner. L/Cpl. Johnson lectured on unarmed combat. Camouflage was the subject of Lt. Brooks and Sgt. Cottrell, whilst aircraft recognition was covered by Cpl. Cooper. Lt. Hatcher, R.M., lectured on discipline. Close examination of the photograph shows that the Somerset L.I. cap badge is being worn. Later the Admiralty Home Guard became part of the 15th Gloucestershire (Post Office) Battalion. As with other units, guard duties were carried out at strategic places; in this case Bathpool Railway Bridge was guarded by The Admiralty Home Guard.
(by kind permission of the Hydrographic Office, D.S.A., Taunton)

3rd Somerset (Yeovil) Battalion

HEADQUARTERS	11, Summerlands Preston Road, Yeovil	INTELLIGENCE OFFICER	Lt. C.R. Hayward
DATE FORMED	May 1940		Lt. R.J. Willcox
COMMANDING OFFICER	Lt. Col. G.H.A. Ing, C.M.G., D.S.O., D.L.	KINEMA OFFICER	Lt. R.H. Etchells
2ND IN COMMAND	Major H.C.C. Batten, D.S.O.	LIAISON OFFICER	Lt. D.C. Boles
	(Major C.G.S. Hodgson, M.C.)	MEDICAL OFFICERS	Major F.G. Parker
H.Q. STAFF			(Major F. Barlow)
A & Q	Capt. F.W. Simkins, Somerset Light Infantry		Capt. A.W. Duncan
ADJUTANT	Capt. L. Beazley, The Buffs	MESSING OFFICER	2nd Lt. J.A. Jones
AMMUNITION OFFICER	2nd Lt. A.L. Pavey	SIGNALS OFFICER	Lt. M.D. Stirling

YEOVIL BOROUGH COMPANY

COMMANDING OFFICER	Major H.C.E. Oliver, M.C.	2ND IN COMMAND	Capt. H.T. Whittaker
	(Major H.C.C. Batten, D.S.O.)		(Capt. W.C. Noble)

Officers of Yeovil Company with Col. H.C.C. Batten, D.S.O..
Back Row: 2nd Lt. Crouch; 2nd Lt. Maurice Stirling; 2nd Lt. John Snell; Lt. John Pittard; 2nd Lt. Douglas Pittard; 2nd Lt. Bilby; 2nd Lt. Vic Ball
Front Row: Lt. Way, M.M.; Capt. W.C. Noble, M.C.; Major H.C.E. Oliver, M.C.; Col. H.C.C. Batten, D.S.O.; Capt. H.T. Whittaker; Lt. Rawlins; Lt. C. Snell.

Whilst H.C.C. Batten is often referred to as Colonel Batten, Capt. Bushell's report in the C.R.O. lists him as a major as does The Army List. In the above photograph the crown and two pips, signifying a man of the rank of colonel, are not visible. A major's crown could well be being worn, hidden by the fold in the epaulette.
(Museum of South Somerset collection)

No. 1 Platoon Yeovil Borough Home Guard.
Back Row: Unknown; Sidney Leonard Drew; Unknown; Unknown; Unknown; Unknown; Mr. Warren; Mr. Hodder; Mr. Stevens; Unknown; Ernie Lobb; Mr. Penfold; Aldred 'Sam' Peach
Middle Row: Unknown; Mr. Gosney; Les Trion; Unknown; Unknown; L/Cpl. Chilcott; Unknown; Mr. Fry; L/Cpl. Drayton; L/Cpl. Harry Woolacott; Mr. Stradling; Mr. Elliott; Cpl. Harry Jones
Front Row: Unknown; Cpl. Hall; Cpl. Jack Cook; Sgt. Banfield; Sgt. Rogers; Lt. Rawlins; Capt. Noble; 2nd Lt. Douglas Pittard; Sgt. Doe; Sgt. Lock; Unknown; Unknown

Captain Noble was a schoolmaster at Huish Boys' School, Yeovil which stood on the site of what is now a Tesco supermarket. Sidney Drew spent his whole working life in the employ of Mr. Newman of Key's Farm, Dorchester Road. Sgt. Doe attempted to join the army on three occasions but as an electrician with the local electricity company it was decided that he could better serve the war effort by remaining at his job.
(Harry Woolacott collection)

Barwick and Stoford Section No. 1 Platoon.
Back Row: Mr. Elliott; Mr. Gosney; Sidney Leonard Drew; Aldred 'Sam' Peach
Middle Row: Unknown; Unknown; Mr. Fry; Mr. Warren; Mr. Stradling; Mr. Penfold
Front Row: L/Cpl. Harry Woolacott; Cpl. Jack Cook; Sgt. Rogers; Sgt. Doe; Cpl. Hall; L/Cpl. Chilcott
(Harry Woolacott collection)

Harry Woolacott joined the Home Guard on 2nd October 1941. His platoon's duties included guarding Summerhouse Reservoir, Yeovil Hospital, Aplin and Barrett's factory and the telephone exchange. In addition to the usual Home Guard weapons, Yeovil Company possessed a Smith gun, officially known as Ordnance, Smooth Bore 3" Mk. I on Carriage 3" Mk. I. This was an interesting piece of equipment, first appearing in mid-1941 and named after its inventor, Mr. Smith of Trianco Engineering Company. Weighing just over 600lbs and capable of being towed by a 9 H.P. motor car it could fire an 8lb High Explosive shell some 500 yards. When firing a hollow charge anti-tank bomb it could penetrate 2½" of armour at maximum range. (It is believed this was the first ever gun-fired hollow charge shell to see service in the British Army. The principle is still applied today.) Attempts to improve the Smith gun came to nothing. The smooth-bore barrel could not withstand increased chamber pressures and the gun was declared obsolete in December 1945. For a photograph of this weapon and limber see p.250.

*An unknown section of **No. 1 Platoon**.*
Taken at the same time and location as the previous photograph, some members of his section have been identified by Ernie Lobb.
Back Row: Unknown; Les Trion; Unknown; Mr. Hodder; Mr. Stevens; Unknown; Ernie Lobb
Front Row: Cpl. Harry Jones; Unknown; Sgt. Lock; Unknown; Unknown; L/Cpl. Drayton
(Ernie Lobb collection)

When engaged on fire-watching duties Ernie would take up his post on the roof of the bank at the top of Silver Street in Yeovil with nothing but a rope to abseil down in the case of emergency. Other nights were spent guarding Whistle Bridge where the Dorchester Road passes over the Waterloo-Exeter railway line. Here, before starting their duty, the section would have a fry-up in their little hut by the light of candles, the rations being 'supplied' by Aplin and Barrett, Creamery Proprietors of Yeovil. Afterwards they would patrol in pairs, finding time for a quiet 'Woodbine' leaning on a gate listening to the nightingales. Here was a time for contemplation looking at the stars, wondering if tonight death and destruction would come from above in the guise of *Fallschirmjäger*.

No. 4 Platoon Yeovil Borough Home Guard.
Back Row: No. 2 Ron Mitchell; No. 6 Mr. Buttle; No. 14 Reg Quinton
Middle Row: No. 4 Bill Quarterman; No. 10 Frank Pike; No. 11 Kenneth 'Ben' Pike; No. 15 Stan Abbott; No. 17 Donald McKenn; No. 18 Clifford Reeves
Front Row: No. 1 L/Cpl. George Day; No. 7 Capt. George Way; No. 8 possibly Sgt. Thompson; No. 10 Cpl. Ted Thorne
The photograph was taken at the back of Mr. Moore's garden at 'Far End', Higher Kingston, now the site of Yeovil Hospital. Mr. Moore was a partner in Watts, Moore and Bradford, a local firm of solicitors. Sgt. Turner was another member of this unit but he has not been identified in this photograph. 'Other ranks' included Bob Daskford, A. Axe and 'Cyril'.
(Graham Quinton collection)

Private Kenneth Pike recalls the Company Sergeant was Ted Thorne, and one other N.CO. remembered was Corporal George Day.

Section duties included guarding Summerhouse Reservoir where the duty included turning the water off at night and on again on stand down in the morning.

One moonlit night the section heard the droning of a single aircraft. Cyril, an expert on aircraft recognition, soon spotted a lone Heinkel flying amongst the barrage balloons. A shout to the resting members of the picket resulted in Cpl. Day rushing out into the moonlight wearing only longjohns and carrying his Tommy gun. "Where is the b.....d?" "Coming through, now!", shouted Cyril. Immediately Cpl. Day opened fire, emptying his magazine with the result that 20 rounds of precious ammunition were expended and the Heinkel continued flying serenely onwards on a south-westerly course. At 0545 hrs. the guard stood down and dispersed. With the cycle replaced in the shed and his rifle hidden under the stairs, Ken Pike proceeded to fill a kettle. Alas, no water. In the excitement of the night no one had remembered to turn the water back on! On with greatcoat, cycle clips and off to Sgt. Thorne's home to collect the keys for the reservoir and restore the water supply.

That was not the end of the affair. The following Wednesday an enquiry chaired by Major H.C.C. Batten at The Drill Hall was convened to discover why a Home Guard section charged with guarding a reservoir against saboteurs should take upon itself to fire at an enemy plane. The final comment by Major Batten amidst much laughter was: "Damned dangerous, could have killed a cow in Barwick Park".

Not all training was carried out around Yeovil. Ken remembers one particular week-end training camp held at Bickham Manor, Timberscombe. Under instruction from Lt. Pittard, the platoon was firing grenades from their rifles, the back stop being a quarry face. For a time all went well, the grenades exploding with a satisfactory 'bang', a few clearing the backstop and exploding out of sight. After some time, a halt was called to the proceedings. Suddenly a voice cried out from afar and a person carrying a sickle appeared over the ridge.

"Oi hope ye don't moind waiting vor a while whilst I do finish cutting this yer gorse up yer only 'tis growing out onto the Golf Course." "Anyone hurt?", called Lt. Pittard. "Not as Oi can see but there be a vew holes and such on the Golf Course." A count indicated seven grenades had cleared the ridge.

Ken Grabham of Timberscombe confirmed the incident, having been told about it by Jack Haywood of Slade Farm who had been working the fields at the time. The nine-hole Golf Course was situated just before Couple Cross at map ref. SS 951 387, extending north-eastwards.

Fields around Timberscombe were also used for firing the Spigot Mortar with inert rounds, as firing with live warheads was restricted to a few special sites in Somerset. The target was a stretched hessian sheet. However, many rounds were fired too low, missing the target and ploughing neat furrows across the farmer's field, resulting in a confrontation between the landowner and the Home Guard Commander. This was resolved amicably when the farmer's palm was crossed with silver.

It was not only the Home Guard who suffered embarrassing incidents. In the early stages of the war, several types of flame weapons utilising the destructive power of petrol were devised. One type was the Flame Fougasse. Essentially it involved up to four 45-gallon drums filled with an inflammable mixture, typically 40% petrol and 60% gas oil. These were concealed at suitable locations by the sides of roads and detonated remotely with the intention of enveloping the 'target' in a fireball. One day members of the Home Guard were collected in army lorries and transported to a disused quarry off the A303 at Camel Hill to see a demonstration of this weapon by the Royal Engineers. The six trucks were parked up and the spectators ushered to a safe spot. On detonation there was an almighty explosion and a spectacular fireball burst out in front of the audience. Unfortunately, the transport had not been parked far enough away. Four of the vehicles suffered scorched paintwork, cracked windscreens and burnt tyres. Prompt action by the Royal Engineers prevented further damage. Ken Pike never saw another demonstration.

As with many other towns, roads were prepared to receive steel rails of various designs to prevent the passing of enemy vehicles. It is known that one such arrangement existed in Yeovil at the junction of Sherborne Road and Middle Street. The steel rails were stored at the edge of the road on a site now occupied by a BMW dealership.

Francis 'Frank' Gay was another member of the 3rd Yeovil Battalion, joining the L.D.V. in 1940 aged 17. On 16th December 1941 he joined the R.A.F. being demobbed in 1946. Names Frank Gay recalls are Sgt (i/c Training) Bill Burge, his son Billy Burge and veterans of WW1, Fred Taylor and Bert Denman. Duties included guarding the pumphouses at Summerhouse and Vagg Hills and the Telephone Exchange in Clarence Street.

For local shoots a range was used between Over Compton and Great Lyde Farm. The targets were at map ref. ST 580 177 whilst the furthest firing point was at map ref. ST 579 173.

Alan Cornelius remembers the local Home Guard Unit and has kindly allowed the following to be extracted from his memoirs:

Of course, it wasn't originally called the Home Guard. Anthony Eden's broadcast on 14th May, called for Local Defence Volunteers and it was Winston Churchill who some months later changed the name of a force that was to grow to over one and a half million men. At first the only 'uniform' to be issued consisted of a brassard printed with the initials L.D.V., followed a month or so later by HOME GUARD. At least it put an end to the 'Look, Duck and Vanish' gibe of those who hadn't signed up. When, many years later, I unpicked my mother's stitching on the brassard, I found a printed crown above the legend ROYAL MAIL showing that the only means of identification available in those first desperate days, were armbands originally for use by G.P.O. 'Christmas Postmen' that had been reprinted L.D.V. Towards the end of summer 1940 the first ill-fitting denim overalls were issued but regular battledress did not become available until well on into the New Year. The Army was still suffering from the shortages of Dunkirk including weapons. All the stories that were thought to be apocryphal, were all too desperately true for the first squads who went 'on watch' during the hours of darkness while Operation 'Sealion' was still very much in the mind of Ober Kommando der Wehrmacht. As expected in a rural area, all manner of shotguns were to hand; one in the East Coker Armoury bore the

Jack Cornelius on his 1927 250cc. Ariel Colt. He was a member of the East Coker Platoon from 1940 until he joined the Royal Signals in 1942. He was designated Company Dispatch Rider and his sleeve badge is shown above. He would also have worn a blue and white brassard over his special issue short greatcoat. (Alan Cornelius collection)

engraved inscription that it had once belonged to W.G. Grace! Many schemes were devised to make the shot more effective than that normally used in 12- or 16-bore cartridges. In some cases the lead shot was removed, covered with melted candle wax and replaced in the cartridge case. Others melted down the lead itself and produced a 'ball' round that would just as likely have killed the defender as any enemy foolish enough to have come into range. Stout sticks, hammers and ancient swords were also taken for personal protection but what use they would have been against a Mauser automatic is doubtful. I have a picture of my father with a Zulu War Martini-Henry which I later found had had its firing pin removed and a saw cut through the breech. At least they were not called upon to defend their own lives as well as those of their kith and kin with the infamous pikes. The first consignment of United States P17 .300 Rifles arrived towards the end of July, still covered in the heavy brown grease that had been used to preserve them after the end of the First World War. Even after they had been meticulously cleaned and 'pulled through', on the kitchen table, the smell persisted for months. Only ten rounds of live ammunition could be spared from the 50 that came with each weapon and so training was effected with dummy clips and wooden bullets. There were no 'live' rounds available for target practice. Defence against attack by motorised units was provided by the 'Flame Fougasse', mines installed where the roadway was narrow and inclined. Three or four tar barrels filled with oil, lime and petrol with a small explosive charge were to be fired from a secret position by a brave Home Guard when he saw the enemy vehicles approaching the ambush. Two local sites were at Pincushion Corner and at Furzy Knapp. Years later I found a barrel from this latter site, riddled with Sten gun bullets when they were de-activated by a frustrated squad of Home Guards after the danger of invasion had passed.

The East Coker Platoon was part of the 3rd (Yeovil) Battalion and at its peak numbered between 70 and 80 men. For the first nine months, there was no commissioning of officers and hence no officially recognised rank higher than 'Private' in the Regular Army. This was put on a more orthodox basis in February 1941 when, as well as commissioned officers, N.C.O.s were also named. However the rank of 'Volunteer' was retained in place of 'Private' until later when men registered for National Service could be directed to serve in the force. In command was Fred Gilley, the village milk roundsman, later to be given the army rank of Captain. I'm sure he must have had First World War experience although no one ever spelt it out in detail. Certainly all the N.C.O.s were 'old sweats'. Cecil Pulman, Billy Best, Fred Ackerman, Bert Langdon and Fred Abbott had done their time in the trenches, mostly with the Somerset Light Infantry. Cecil Drake was a veteran of the Boer War, being a cavalry officer when young Winston Churchill was a mere newspaper reporter. There was then a significant generation gap compared to the young men still awaiting call-up. My brother Jack, Kingsley Rendell and Roy Cutler were soon to join the regular Army, Navy and Air Force respectively and there were many others. As the war progressed, the call-up age came down to 18 and three at least of these younger recruits, Alan Thompson, Eric Coombes and Alan Whetham, were later to be killed 'on active service'. Duties were organised on a seven-day watch rota with pairs doing two hours on and four (later six) hours off. Times of watches varied with the seasons but they were typically from nine in the evening until five o'clock the following morning. In the early days the 'Watch Room' was the waiting room at Sutton Bingham Station, on the Waterloo to Exeter railway. As well as the bridge near the station, regular inspection of the Netherton Bridge was also required, causing some misgivings among the younger and more impressionable recruits when tales of the gruesome murder of Constable Cox were recalled by the older hands. By the spring of 1941 a concrete 'Watcher Post' had been built on the ridge overlooking the spread of country towards Corscombe and the heights of Toller Down. It was much colder and damper than the railway waiting room and those on watch were glad to return to the comfort of the 'Legion Room' in the *New Inn* yard. There were also regular parades, notably on Sunday mornings, and an organised programme of small arms training was soon in place, first with the

U.S. rifles or the few Lee-Enfields still about and then with the 'Woolworth's Tommy-Gun', the Mark 1 Sten Automatic. After the earliest Molotov Cocktails and phosphorus-filled medicine bottles (76 SIP), a whole new menu of explosive grenades began to be issued to Home Guard units and, as well as the WW1 'Mills Bomb', now renamed the 36 grenade, there were the 68 (anti-tank rifle cup-discharged), 69 (bakelite/stun), 73 ('Thermos/Woolworth'), 74 (Sticky Bomb) and 75 (Hawkins), to be lectured about and practised with, at almost any old stone quarry where the risk of accidental injury to passers-by was minimal, but usually it was the one alongside the railway at Sutton Bingham. My father became the Company 'Bombing and Demolition Instructor' and 10 years after his death, 40 years after the end of the war, a block of fulminate of mercury fuses and one inch gun-cotton primers had to be de-activated by the local Army Bomb Squad when they were found in the collapsing garage where he had privied them away. There were also many new special weapons such as the Blacker Bombard Spigot Mortar, the Smith gun and Northover Projector and, as time went by, sufficient rounds to allow for practice shoots at Yeovil Junction or the 'County' ranges. Cpl. Bob Oaksford was in charge of the 'Blacker' and recalls such a practice exercise when, with his young assistant Ray Dodge and WW1 veteran Bert Langdon, they were on the 'Sigwells' range and given explicit instructions to 'aim over' the target so that it remained *in situ* for the next group. Bob said that unfortunately he did not hear this part of the order and consequently Ray and Bert 'laid' the practice shot directly at the target. The effect was dramatic and saw the steel-sided vehicle smashed to pieces with the result that all practice for the day was abandoned. By the spring of 1941, however, the imminent threat of invasion began to recede and the initial enthusiasm was replaced by reluctant acceptance that someone had to 'mind the shop' while our frontline troops engaged in offensive operations in North Africa. By 1942 men in deferred occupations were obliged to serve in the Home Guard as part of their National Service and some of the amateur spirit went out of Britain's largest ever non-professional army. Bob Oaksford tells the tale of 'Tiffer' Purchase who was persuaded by his more worldly-wise fellow farmworker Archie Neville to 'test' his gas mask in the farm stable. "B'aint no bloody good," said Tiffer, "the'se can still smell the horse farts."

I became eligible to join on my 17th birthday in May 1944, although I was a member of the Army Cadet Force. I was already attached to the 3rd (Yeovil) Battalion and had turned out as a Runner/Messenger on a number of 'Invasion Exercises'. My actual service, however, was to be very short-lived. After the D-Day landings had been secured and the risk of a counter-invasion was no longer a threat, regular parades ceased and all Home Guard units were first stood down on 6th September, parades after that date being voluntary. They held their final Parade on Sunday 3rd December 1944, culminating in a Grand March Past of the 3rd Battalion through the streets of Yeovil. The entire organisation was officially disbanded on 31st December 1945.

Residents of Yeovil watch a 'Wings for Victory' Parade, c.1942-'43. Such Parades were held during the war to boost the war effort.
Left hand column (front to back): Pte. Wallbridge; Pte. Gordon Matthews; Cpl. Crouch (i/c bugles)
Centre column: No. 1 Pte. F. Down
Right hand column: No. 6 Eric Day
(Fred Down collection)

Yeovil Borough Platoons *are drawn up outside Elim Church. Nearest to the camera is Lt. Wray, M.M., but who are the others? With the reflections on the road surface the date could well be 3rd December 1944.*
(Museum of South Somerset, Yeovil)

Again with a wet road the photograph could have been taken at the same time as the one above. The lad on the right is obviously more prepared for inclement weather than those on the left. Note the 'S' sign fixed on the hotel wall, indicating the location of a public air-raid shelter. Only Mr. Grunhill on the bass drum and Lt. Noble leading the centre column of troops have been identified.
(Museum of South Somerset, Yeovil)

(left) ***'Q' Section No. 5 Platoon***. *Members of Yeovil Home Guard gather around a 2-pdr. anti-tank gun. It is not certain if this is a gun 'on charge' or one brought by a Home Guard Travelling Wing. A similar weapon is also featured in the Wellington and Bruton Home Guard photographs.*
Back Row: Mr. Nutland; Mr. Andrews; Unknown
Middle Row: Sgt. J. Collins; J. Pilton; Mr. Denmead; Mr. B. Thorne; Mr. McConnell; Unknown; Unknown; Mr. J. Wilson; Unknown; Mr. P. Moon; Cpl. E. Ball; 2nd Lt. John Snell
Front Row: Unknown; R. Sinnick; Steve Eason (sitting)
John Snell was the son of Charles Snell, founder of Palmer Snell, auctioneers and estate agents.
(Museum of South Somerset, Yeovil)

(below) The Rice Family of East Coker. Brothers Charlie, Eddie and Dick Rice pose for the camera with their father, who is standing between Charlie and Eddie. Close examination shows Charlie wearing pattern '37 webbing gaiters. Although some Home Guards were issued with such gaiters, it is probable that Charlie was on leave from the army.
(Gerald Smith collection)

(above) ***East Coker Platoon***. *Although undated, this photograph may well have been taken on 3rd December 1944. On this day the Yeovil Company attended a thanksgiving service at the Gaumont Cinema, Yeovil, it being the largest venue available. Leading the Platoon and saluting is Lt. Graham Lock. Other faces recognised by Mr. Dunning are:*
Left-hand column: No. 6 Fred Clayton
Centre column: No. 3 Ern Baker, No. 5 E. Dunning, No. 8 John Dunning.
A copy of this photograph hangs in East Coker Village Hall.
(Jack Cornelius collection)

(right) **Rimpton Home Guard**.
A rather faded photograph of bombing practice over a line, in this case a clothes line!
From left to right: Selwyn Wadman; Unknown; G. Darch; Harold Sibley; Unknown; Unknown; Harold Cresse; M. Brownsey; Unknown; T. Hancock; Rowland Morgan
(Mrs. B. Darch collection)

(left) **N.C.O.s of Rimpton Home Guard**.
Back Row: Selwyn Wadman; Harold Sibley
Front Row: Harold Cressey; Charles Baker; Rowland Morgan; Unknown

Selwyn Wadman farmed with his brother and father at Marston Magna. Harold Sibley's brother was the signalman killed when Castle Cary Station was bombed. Harold Cressey was a farmworker whilst Charles Baker was a smallholder. Other Home Guard members included Stanley Apsey and Gerald Urwick who was remembered as being Officer i/c Marston Magna and Rimpton.
(Jack Cornelius collection)

QUEEN CAMEL HOME GUARD

Whilst no photograph of Queen Camel Home Guard has been found, the following information has kindly been supplied by Jeff Biggin. One of the earliest officers of the unit was Captain R.B. Moore, a veteran of the First World War. He passed away during the war and was succeeded by Mr. Marples who used his home, Eyewell House, as the headquarters.

Grenade practice with drill grenades was carried out at Johnson Park, Yeovil. The rifle range at Sutton Montis was shared with Sparkford Home Guard or possibly Rimpton Home Guard's range at Woodhouse. At Sigwells, to the north of Corton Denham, it is believed that another range existed on the opposite side of Corton Ridge to Woodhouse. (Unless locations have been confused, three ranges seem to have existed close to each other.)

ILCHESTER COMPANY

| COMMANDING OFFICER | Major F.C. Marples
(Lt. Col. A.L.B. Anderson)
(Brig. Gen. E.J.F. Vaughan, C.M.G., D.S.O.)
(Yeovil District Company) | 2ND IN COMMAND | Capt. H.R. Henry
(Col. F.G.E. Lumb, C.B., D.S.O., M.C.)
(Yeovil District Company) |

Lt. Col. Arthur Louis Brunker 'Ginger' Anderson had spent nearly 30 years military service in India, with spells during the First World War in the trenches in France and Belgium and in Mesopotamia, where he was severely wounded.

He reached the maximum age for retirement in October 1939, was transferred to the Indian Army Reserve and returned to live in the house which he and his wife had earlier bought, at Limington, in Somerset. He supposed that he would immediately be recalled for active service, but his war wounds and a lifetime in India (together with a suspect heart) meant that he was thought better employed in rallying the defence of Somerset.

The following notes are taken verbatim from his own autobiographical manuscript since they refer precisely to the Somerset Home Guard:

"While awaiting possible employment under the War Office: Raised and took command of Ilchester and District Platoon Local Defence Volunteers (L.D.V.) 250 strong May 1940 and when 3rd Somerset Home Guard came into being took over Yeovil District Company representing 36 villages six platoons. 1941-1944 Limington. Gazetted 2nd in Command 7th Battalion Home Guard 1952-1956 Castle Cary."

His son continues:

As far as I can recall, the strain of the early years of WW2 on my father's health had been very considerable. By the time he returned from India in 1939 the family were already living in Limington House and he was several times summoned to Millbank by heart specialists. Though never told, I sensed that the reports were always gloomy.

My own recollections of the early days of the Second World War are vivid. The family had returned from India in the spring of 1937; my father joined us in London just before the Coronation and I well remember his taking my younger brother and me to meet the members of the Indian Cavalry contingent encamped in Hyde Park and sampling pieces of their *chapatis*. My parents then rented a house for the summer in South Dorset whilst house-hunting. I was by then aged nine and in September 1937 was packed off to a prep school north of Oxford. The decision to purchase Limington House – in very rural Somerset and far from any nasty airfields – was taken and, leaving me to spend holidays with friends near Stoke-sub-Hamdon, the rest of the family returned to India. Since my father's retirement was close, my mother, brother and sister returned home for the summer of 1938 and following the Munich crisis I remember the exodus of the considerable number of German and Austrian diplomats' sons from my prep school and the excitement of seeing a large air-raid shelter being built – and the subsequent disappointment because it was not until late in 1940 that there was an excuse for us to spend a few nights in it.

My father returned home virtually as war was declared but Limington seemed a pretty dull place during the holidays, though I do remember crossing the weir to Yeovilton to watch the first bulldozers and graders I had ever seen, beginning to level the ground for the new naval airfield. (Of course, no one at Limington could understand why the Royal Navy could possibly want to venture so far inland. We were having tea in the nursery when the buzz came up from the servants' hall via a housemaid that all was explained – they were going to dam the River Yeo between Limington and Yeovilton (which floods in winter anyway) so that the Navy could land their seaplanes!)

By the beginning of my summer holidays in late July 1940 matters had hotted up considerably. No sooner had I been fetched from Pen Mill station than I was told to get changed and lend a hand in the field not far from the front of the house. There was an old concrete block there on which had once been mounted an engine for a water pump. Round it were several men and stacks of wooden crates of empty beer bottles. Their task was the manufacture of Molotov Cocktails and I was soon usefully employed holding a funnel whilst the mixture was poured. I saw very little of my father during those holidays but before going back to school towards the end of September, I recall walking with him up the road to the right-angle bend between Lower Draycott and Draycott Farm where he had chaps digging a large hole in the bank to seat a 'fougasse' – an improvised mortar made from an oildrum charged with oil and pitch to be exploded in the face of the leading enemy tank as it came round the corner. This was sited at map ref. ST 548 215.

I think it was in the Easter holidays of 1941 that I helped to distribute the newly arrived .300 rifles from America – each was painted with a red band round the handguard to distinguish it from the British .303 rifle. The coach house at Limington had become a veritable arsenal which included stocks of 'slug' cartridges for 12-bore shotguns, each loaded with nine pea-sized lead pellets which, early on, were about all the L.D.V. had for slaying Germans. The family car, a bull-nosed Morris, became the 'platoon truck'. I also recall the arrival of a consignment of Thompson sub-machine guns, being given a quick lesson on how to strip and assemble them and then bicycling round in the evening to various cottages in the area and giving a demonstration on the kitchen table before handing each one over. I also remember a 'Blacker Bombard', a primitive anti-tank Spigot Mortar, being tested against the aforementioned concrete block with singularly little effect.

During the early years of the War, the L.D.V./Home Guard kept watch on the top of the Limington church tower every night for German parachute landings – two men on the top and the remainder of the guard sleeping below in the ringers' gallery. It is only quite recently that the staples taking the string which connected those above to a small hand-bell in the gallery were removed from the masonry. Because of the waste of manpower my father was much annoyed that the gallant watchers insisted that they must have two men on top of the tower because they did not fancy overlooking the graveyard alone!

Of course, church bells were only to be rung as a signal that the Germans were in the vicinity. I believe that a few church bells were rung when there was a false alarm, but my father was very careful never to allow this to happen in his area.

In hindsight it may seem an unkind comment, but I know that after a lifetime of active service with highly-trained professional soldiers, my father found it a near impossible task to train the Home Guard up to the standard to which he was used. He could expect bravery from several if the occasion arose, but the reliability of some of his 'troops' was a source of constant concern and I believe that it was this that brought on his serious heart attack in 1941. In a much reduced manner he continued his service with the Home Guard until 1956. He died in 1984, aged 95 after an earlier life packed with interest, danger and excitement – and was always only too thankful that he had not been called upon to lead the Somerset Home Guard into action!

NO. 2 SECTION. NO. 2 PLATOON.
ILCHESTER COMPANY HOME GUARD.

Top Row—B. M. Morgan, J. Sweet, R. J. Eason, R. J. Mitchem, F. R. Ingram, A. Savidge, J. C. Moores.
Middle Row—A. G. Higgins, H. G. Pond, J. Tilley, F. L. White, F. Guppy, R. Knight, V. J. Laver, A. J. Hill, W. G. Hodge.
Bottom Row—N. G. Cook, L/Cpl. Collings, Cpl. A. E. Robbins, Sgt. G. W. Haines, 2nd/Lt. G. F. C. Warry, Cpl. W. Tuck, L/Cpl. A. A. Patten, C. F. Lewis, R. O. Plenty.
Absent: Sgt. R. B. Brooks, L/Cpl. W. C. S. Pickford, L. R. Banfield, N. P. R. Cornish, W. F. Marsh, R. J. Maunder, E. J. Pickford, F. Woodruff.

The above photograph was taken outside Thorne Coffin House and includes men from Chilthorne Domer.

Mr. W.F. Marsh, a member of No. 2 Section, remembers that two local rifle ranges were used, one at Tintinhull and one at Yeovil Marsh. The Yeovil Marsh Range was in existence before 1890 and had firing points up to 600 yards in increments of 100 yards in addition to 350- and 550-yard firing points. It was during the Second World War that it was decided to provide a trench for the target-markers to provide protection whilst shooting was in progress. After much digging the trench was established. Overnight it filled with water and was abandoned. The markers returned to their old shelters, large trees nearby. It was observed that the posteriors of the larger Home Guards extended alarmingly beyond the 'shelter' of the trunks!

(left) **Ilchester Home Guard**, including men from the villages of Limington and Yeovilton.
Back Row: Cyril Freestone; Bob White; Unknown; Reg Banfield; Jim Eades; Wally Wills; Arthur Bond; Maurice Gillard; Roy Wetherall
Second Row: John Denning; Gerald Masters; Alfie Wigmore; Bob Beaton; Harry Smart; Henry Clark; Unknown; Joe Bethel; Tony Parsons; Jack Wetherall
Third Row: Bill Brake; Mr. Wigmore; Unknown; Harold Evans; Ron Stevens; Cecil Raymont; Mr. West; William Evans; Fred Hubbard
Fourth Row: L/Cpl. Fred Pickford; L/Cpl. Charlie Brock; Cpl. Wills; Cpl. Tewkesbury; Sgt. Walter Vincent; Sgt. Hermann Rasmussen; Cpl. Bert Evans; Cpl. Lord; L/Cpl. Frank Stephens
Fifth Row: George Gard; Mr. E. Barnes; Bernard Starke; Cliff Raymont; Albert Wigmore; Unknown; Ron Last; Unknown
Front Row: Arthur Holland; Jack May; Unknown; Ernie Cake; Sammy Burt; John Miller; Wilf Cox; Fred Masters; Jack Little
(Myrtle Parsons collection)

(below) Men of **Ilchester Home Guard** parade at Castle Farm on 6th June 1943. Sadly the original of this photograph has been lost and the only copy is in two sections.

Main photograph
Extreme left: Sgt. Tewkesbury
Front Row: Charlie Brock (local butcher); Mr. Lord; G. Clark (farmer); Clifford Raymont (farmer); Ronald Stephens; Cecil Raymont (farmer); Unknown; Unknown
Standing behind Cecil is Harry Smart and behind him stands Wilf Cox.

Small photograph
Extreme right: Lt. Boxall; next to him, Walter Vincent.

Close examination of the photograph shows Mr. Lord is carrying a Thompson sub-machine gun whilst Charlie Brock, Henry Clark and Clifford Raymont have Browning Automatic Rifles. Apparently, there was considerable squabbling over who should have the Thompson and the B.A.R.s. A training poster for the Browning is shown on the right.
(Gerry Masters collection)

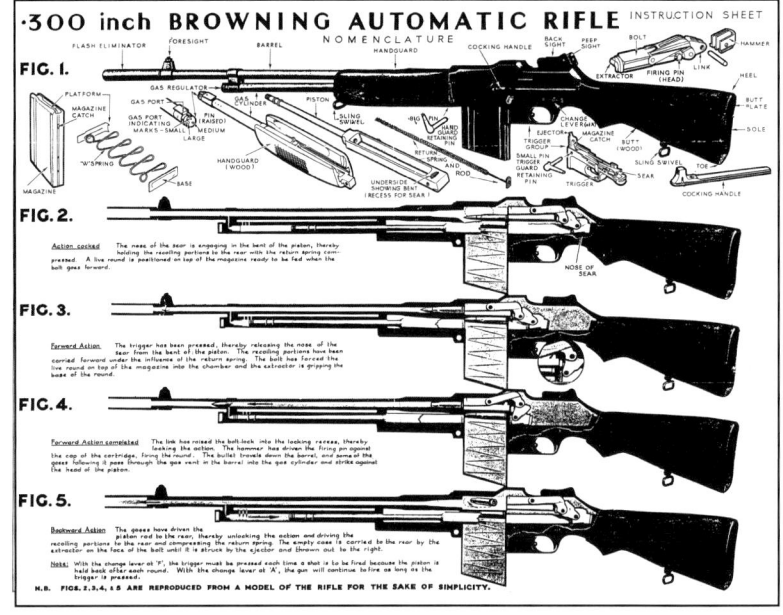

HAMDON COMPANY

COMMANDING OFFICER   Major W.F.Q. Shouldham
2ND IN COMMAND   Capt. F. Gilley

Despite numerous appeals, not a single photograph of Hamdon Company has been forthcoming, although the following are known to have been members of the unit at Stoke under Ham: Ted Broome, Lionel Little, Eric F.C. White and Sgts. W. Gillman and F. White (father of Eric White) who was a member of the Falklands Defence Force during the First World War.

> Ken Rogers, the son of Sgt Major Rogers, joined the L.D.V. on the first day at Montacute. His commander was a Mr. Ewens of 1, Townsend. He recalls the following incident.
>
> On the night of 7th September 1940, Sgt. Major Rogers and his son were setting out for observation duty at Batemoor when the church bells rang out, the signal for 'enemy in the vicinity'. Shortly after, Mrs. Rogers heard two shots followed by silence and was convinced her husband and son had been killed! This was not the case. The night of 7th/8th September was a time of great nervousness and many shots were fired at the imaginary enemy.
>
> Home Guards were turned out in accordance with a pre-planned programme. One volunteer, having spent the evening at Platoon HQ, *The Phelips Arms*, ran to take post in his prepared position behind a stone wall backed by a holly hedge. On approaching, he tripped and fell full-length into his weapon pit. This is believed to have been the first Home Guard 'casualty' at Montacute.

One trench position that has been confirmed was at the entrance to Montacute House. This covered the roads from Stoke sub Hamdon and the village square. Many other defensive positions would have been dug but no record has been found. The local .22 rifle range was in the Old Quarry at Batemoor Barn approximately at map ref. ST 489 164.

Pte. A.H. Carey joined the Home Guard on 6th September 1941 and served until Stand Down on 31st December 1944. His Certificate of Proficiency, dated 23rd February 1944 and covering general knowledge; use of the rifle, M Grenades and Spigot Mortars; battlecraft; and map-reading, is reproduced on the right.

> Charles Benjamin Arthur Ford of West Chinnock was a member of Hamdon Company from the first day of formation of the L.D.V. He writes:
>
> As soon as the call was made nationally my father Arthur Ford and myself registered as volunteers at the Local Recruiting Centre. I remember in the early days having to use pick helves for rifle drill which was carried out under the watchful eye of full-time instructors and staff from local army camps. As time progressed we were eventually issued with battledress, black gaiters, rifles and all the other equipment needed to turn us into real soldiers. Other platoon equipment included a Lewis gun, Mills Grenades, No. 74 Sticky Bombs (for attacking armour), Cup dischargers whereby our rifles could be converted to fire Mills Grenades or the 68 anti-tank grenade, and Sten guns.
>
> Our rifle range and grenade range was at Bagnell Farm, Little Norton, at map ref. ST 491 146 and Sundays were reserved for practice here.
>
> Our Observation Post, which was used for looking out for paratroop landings, was off East Lane, opposite the public footpath to Burrows Hill, 'tucked' into the corner of a field at map ref. ST 470 130. Access was off a track that ran to Higher Farm, known as Ashay Track. Postwar farm improvements involved removal of hedges and Ashay Track. However, the hut occupied by the Home Guard when not on lookout duty survived the war and was bought by my father. It was approx. 8' x 10' with a ridged roof fitted with two 2-tier bunks and built by the well-known firm Harry Hebditch of Martock. It survived for many years.
>
> The platoon's Blacker Bombard weapon pit was situated at Snails Hill at map ref. ST 461 132 above Snails Hill Cottage and covered the road leading into the village. Access to this position was by means of a five-barred gate off the road to the left of Rose Cottage and into high ground behind the cottages.
>
> The machine gun crew were 'mobile' to the extent that they were positioned where the commander thought they would be most effective, co-operating with other neighbouring platoons.

The Village Hall was used as a Drill Hall, for weekly meetings, drill exercises, lectures etc. and Battle Drill and Instruction, as well as occasional Saturday Night Dances run by the Home Guard.

The Armoury as far as I can remember was under the control of Major Coke at Norton sub Hamdon.

The two village Public Houses were used to pass on information to personnel, the one in the centre of the village called *The New Inn* and the one at the bottom of the village called *The Half Moon*. *The New Inn* was only a Beer and Cider House, but *The Half Moon* was fully licensed. *The Half Moon* was the more popular, because it was much larger and it contained an area outside the pub that could be used as an assembly area, a drill area and dismissal area. There were other organisations in the village to help the War Effort and the Public Houses were always the scene of much activity, involving Forces personnel on leave, the searchlight personnel and, later on, the Americans.

There was a section specially trained to operate the Blacker Bombard. I remember the team to man the machine gun as my father, Cpl. Arthur Ford, who was No. 1, I was the No. 2 and Ken Day was No. 3.

Activities

Our main activities consisted of Foot Drill, Rifle Drill, Drill Parades through the village, Church Parades, Parades with neighbouring villages and towns, Lectures on Mill Grenades, Sticky Bombs etc. and practice in their use; machine gun lectures and practice, Blacker Bombard lectures, practice and combined Battle Exercises with neighbouring Units. Lectures were carried out by Regular Army Instructors. I remember that on a couple of occasions the Regular Army organised Mock Attacks on our defences, accompanied with Regular Army 'umpires' to analyse and control activities. Claims and counter-claims as to who fired the first effective shots and whether Armoured Fighting Vehicles had been knocked out or not would rumble on long after the exercises ceased.

There were many amusing happenings during the course of our training and activities. One incident in particular springs to mind. At the outset we were detailed for Watch Duty and kept to the rota to take our tour of duty on watch at the Watch Post. I was a member of a four-man crew with Godfrey Chant, Fred Langdon and Wilfred Langdon. If anyone was unable to take their turn on the night as detailed a stand-in would be provided. One night in mid-summer 1942 our crew were due to take their turn of Watch Duty. Fred Langdon was unable to attend so the Reverend Gerald Stubbs was detailed to take his place, volunteering to do the first Watch of the night. The vicar always turned up with his little bag of sandwiches and a flask of tea or coffee. Wilfred Langdon was a great practical joker and came up with the idea that it would be a great joke if we helped ourselves to the tea or coffee and refilled his flask with lemonade from Wilfred's flask. It was agreed that we should play this joke on the vicar seeing as he was a very friendly and jolly person and Godfrey would finally give him a hot drink from his flask. On completion of his watch the vicar returned and went to his flask for a hot drink. He started to pour the contents of the flask into his cup and immediately said: "This is cold water". He blamed his wife for failing to fill his flask properly, went outside and poured out the contents of his flask. Godfrey then gave him a hot drink from his flask.

We never divulged what had actually happened and often wondered what was the sequel to confronting his wife over the contents of his flask. We shared the joke for many years.

Members of West and Middle Chinnock Platoon Hamdon Company:

Major Coke (retired soldier)
2nd Lt. Southcombe (glove manufacturer)
Sgt. Alfred Radford (retired farmer, former Sgt. Major, Dorsetshire Rgt.)
Sgt. Walter Clarke (farmer, Higher Farm, Middle Chinnock)
Cpl. Arthur Ford (farm craftsman, First World War veteran)
L/Cpl. Carol Shire (apprentice engineer, Westland Aircraft Ltd, Yeovil)
L/Cpl. Godfrey Chant (village baker in West Chinnock)
Reverend Gerald Stubbs (vicar of Middle Chinnock)
Pte. Charles Ford (apprentice engineer, Westland Aircraft Ltd, Yeovil)
Pte. John Marks (farmer, Lower farm, Middle Chinnock)
Pte. Wilfred Langdon (farmworker, Bow Mills)
Pte. Kenneth White (engineer, Westland Aircraft Ltd, Yeovil)
Pte. Ernest Larcombe (farmworker, Manor Farm, Chiselborough)
Pte. Harold Fry (farmworker)
Pte. Jim Doble (farmworker, Manor Farm, West Chinnock)
Pte. Kenneth Day (glover/engineer, Westland Aircraft Ltd, Yeovil)
Pte. George Lacy (farmworker, Manor Farm, West Chinnock)
Pte. Cecil Lacy (tent erector, Paulls, Martock)
Pte. Jack Hawkins (tent erector, Paulls, Martock)
Pte. Alfred Young (farmworker, Manor Farm, West Chinnock)
Pte. Fred Langdon (farmworker, Higher Farm, Middle Chinnock)
Pte. George Mines (evacuee, labourer)
Pte. Alfred Gould (council worker, Yeovil)
Pte. Charles Gould (Bakelite worker, Merriott Mouldings)
Pte. Charles Axe (farmworker, Lower Farm, Middle Chinnock)

***Martock and Bower Hinton Home Guard**, taken outside Bower Hinton Congregational Chapel. The same photograph appeared in* Martock Memories *written by Roy Maber and was published with the names of those featured but not in order of appearance. Even with the assumption that the man in the clerical collar is the Reverend Malliphant it has been impossible to reconcile the list. There are 53 names listed below the photograph and 53 faces but the names given for the individual rows do not tally with the numbers in each row. Only Walter Palmer (second row from the back, No. 2) has been positively identified. Whilst no doubt exists as to Martock being in the 3rd (Yeovil) Battalion it has not been possible to confirm its parent Company.*
(Patrick Palmer collection)

Back row: C. Jeanes, D. Elliott, W. Vaughan, P. Davies, R. Gaylard, F. Lock, H. Gummer, T. Strickland, W. Satherley, R. Steed, R. Dunford, W. Acourt, L. Farnham. 2nd row: Bowditch, W. Palmer, J. Maunder, C. Underwood, C. Morey, G. Warner, F. Brown, L. Lock, J. Williams, A. Mattock, E. Fishlock, A. Keetch S. Dabinett, D. White. 3rd row: C. Beaton, G. Gaylard, S. Davis, H. Gaylard, R. Rogers, P. Gaylard. 4th row: R. Dunford, F. Ashford, L. Davies, R. White, W. Stone, H. Bush, G. Best, S. Dyer, A. Land, A. Fishlock, A. Reid, Capt. Sperway, Rev. Malliphant. Front row: H. Perrett, Branston, Bradford, E. Parsons, H. Ford, A. Dyer, B. Gaylard.

(right) No doubt exists as to the duties expected of the men in the defence of their homeland. Note "Pinnacle, Martock (for final stand if driven back)" – shades of Rorke's Drift.

(below) Thomas James Mayled was a railway employee at Martock Station and a member of the Home Guard, living at Ash. The note below is self-explanatory.

```
              OUTLINE OF PROBLEM
              ------------------

1.  Enemies probable attack from the South West.

2.  Possible Parachute or Glider landings.

Vital Points.  PETHERTON BRIDGE (FOSSEWAY) to TINTINHULL FORTS.
               PARRETT WORKS BRIDGE
               LONG LOAD BRIDGE
               GAWBRIDGE
               PINNACLE, MARTOCK (for final stand if driven back).

Intention.     (a) To deny enemy use of FOSSEWAY from the PETHERTON
                   BRIDGE to TINTINHULL FORTS.

               (b) To prevent enemy by-passing FOSSEWAY by turning
                   north and coming through Platoon Area by way of
                   SOUTH PETHERTON.

          NO. 1. BATTLE PLATOON. (BOWER HINTON SECTION)

TASKS.  To hold or delay enemy troops and A.F.Vs. at PETHERTON BRIDGE,
        FOSSEWAY and RINGWELL HILL, in conjunction with STOKE SECTION
        and PETHERTON PLATOON.

        To patrol RIVER PARRETT in Battle Platoon Area, and observe
        from the top of CRIPPLE HILL.

        To retire, if necessary, down RINGWELL HILL to SPARROWS CORNER,
        or along FOSSEWAY to CARTGATE, to re-inforce defenders there.

          NO. 2. BATTLE PLATOON. (MARTOCK SECTION)

TASKS.  To deny enemy use of PARRETT WORKS BRIDGE.

        If necessary to retire, to fall back to HURST BOW.

        To mount guards on HATCHES near PARRETT WORKS BRIDGE.

        To prevent their destruction in order that water level may
        be maintained as an anti-tank obstacle.

        To defend HURST BOW and roads leading thereto.

        To have Mobile Battle Squad of 8 - 10 men in reserve at
        HURST BOW to re-inforce No. 1 Battle Platoon.
```

Martock and District invasion instructions to the Home Guard (extract).

GREAT WESTERN RAILWAY.

Traffic Department,
13 MAY 1944 Date.   Martock Station.

HOME GUARD.   MUSTERING IN EMERGENCY.

This is to certify that **T. J. Mayled**, a member of the Company's Staff enrolled in the 3rd (Yeovil) Somerset Battalion. Home Guard, will, in an emergency, be required to carry on with his railway duties until the Company release him, in order that the Company may be in a position to operate the Railway, and is, therefore, in List ii (vide Home Guard Regulation 6c).

LT. COL.
No. 3 SOMERSET (YEOVIL) BN. H.G.

Chief, District or Divisional Officer.
Divisional Superintendent

CREWKERNE COMPANY

COMMANDING OFFICER   Major A.E.L. Craven
                                (Major J.H. Blake)
2ND IN COMMAND   Capt. A.T. Frampton

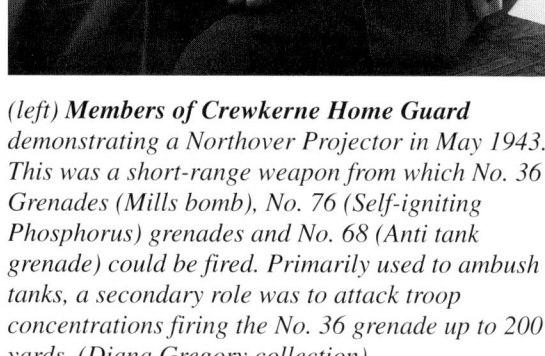

(right) 2nd Lt. A.E.L. Craven, c.1915.
Like so many of his contemporaries, Eric Craven was involved in the ghastly fighting of the trenches in the First World War. After an engagement a few weeks after this fine photograph was taken the body of 2nd Lt. Craven was discovered and it was assumed that he was dead, having suffered a massive wound to his right shoulder. Fortunately, close examination revealed a spark of life and he was taken to hospital after which he spent many months convalescing. Due to his injuries he had to learn to do everything left-handed. The trauma also left him with a permanent stammer. Whilst commanding Crewkerne Company, he lived at the family home of Clapton Court, near Crewkerne. Eric Craven died at the age of 94. (Diana Gregory collection)

(left) **Members of Crewkerne Home Guard** *demonstrating a Northover Projector in May 1943. This was a short-range weapon from which No. 36 Grenades (Mills bomb), No. 76 (Self-igniting Phosphorus) grenades and No. 68 (Anti tank grenade) could be fired. Primarily used to ambush tanks, a secondary role was to attack troop concentrations firing the No. 36 grenade up to 200 yards. (Diana Gregory collection)*

(right) Major A.E.L. Craven and Pte. Aldridge at Clapton Court. Built in the 17th century, Clapton Court was part of a network of some 500 properties taking part in the 'Lady Ryder Scheme' which had its beginnings in the 1914-18 War. Its official name was 'The Dominion and Allied Services Hospitality Scheme'. This scheme made it possible for households to provide hospitality for officers of the Air Forces of Australia, New Zealand, South Africa and Canada. Here they became members of the host families where they could enjoy their leave in convivial surroundings. Where possible the service personnel were allocated to hosts who had similar interests. Many who could not provide sleeping accommodation contributed by providing meals and taking their guests to social functions. During the War some 99,568 visits took place nationally. Clapton Court did its bit, some 600 service men passing through its portals. The Craven family album is full of images of young men enjoying the hospitality at Clapton Court. Sadly, so many of the young smiling faces failed to return to their homeland. (Diana Gregory collection)

(left) **The Fortescue Cup**.
Apart from Major Craven, holding The Fortescue Cup, only Mr. Dickinson, front row No. 6, has been identified. Crewkerne Home Guard benefited from a 600-yard rifle range on their doorstep, close to Crewkerne Station. The butts were situated at map ref. ST 436 079 with the firing point at ST 440 083. Note a pair of Lewis machine guns .303" Mk. I. These were brought into Army service in October 1915. (Diana Gregory collection)

(right) A Carrier at Clapton Court.
This small boy's dream has come true! Master Jonathan Craven standing in a Bren Gun Carrier on the drive at Clapton Court. Note the civilian number plate HMC 129. The 'Carrier, Bren, No. 2 Mk. I' was issued to infantry battalions in 1938 and was produced in several variants being 'stood down' in 1960. This one appears to be occupied by a member of the Black Watch.
(Diana Gregory collection)

(left) **Members of Crewkerne Company** *march through the town on 3rd December 1944. Note the static water tank to the left of the picture. There were two in Crewkerne, one outside the Victoria Hall and a second one behind the War Memorial on the Oval of Remembrance in Severalls Park Avenue. For public safety, chain link fencing was fitted across the top of these tanks. On one occasion 'Rosie', a local girl who was very popular with troops billeted in Crewkerne, found herself in the company of three 'admirers' who took exception to being 'two-timed'. They intended to throw Rosie unceremoniously into the water tank but she promptly bounced off the chain link into the road!*
(Diana Gregory collection)

Merriott Platoon.
Back Row: Unknown; Unknown; Unknown; Jack Shiner; Cecil Langdon; Bert Mitchell (tall man placed in back row); Norman Pittard; Bill Hooper; Ernie Watts; Unknown; Unknown; Fred Hawker; Reg Smith
Second Row: Unknown; Unknown; Unknown; Unknown; Ernie Osborne; Thomas Shiner; Bill Samways; A. Osborne; Unknown; Unknown; Unknown; Unknown; Leonard Paull
Third Row: Wilf Lawrence; Unknown; Unknown; Harry Pattemore; Unknown (partly hidden); Unknown; Edwin Swain; Unknown; Oliver Farr; Unknown; Unknown; Percy Hutchins
Fourth Row: Unknown; Harry Lawrence; Unknown; Unknown; Norman Cannon; Major A.E.L. Craven (Company Commander); Lt. Southcombe (Platoon Commander); Sgt. G. Cable; William Napper; Unknown; Unknown; Sgt. Harry Elswood
Front Row: Unknown; Unknown; Unknown; Unknown; Unknown; Percy Lacey; Unknown; Dennis or Andrew Dodge; Unknown
Edwin Swain subsequently joined the Pioneer Corps, serving in France whilst Jack Shiner joined the R.A.S.C., having worked in Merriott as a baker. Reg Smith worked for the farmers Webb and Sons. Young master Dodge initially joined the Army Cadets. After service with the Home Guard, Alan Robinson joined the Royal Navy. Lt. Southcombe left his business of glovemakers and joined the R.A.F., Colonel Watkins taking over command.
(Mrs. Gwen De Winter collection)

Initially Merriott Platoon met at the bakery next to the rear of the Co-op. Later the platoon moved to a bakery at the junction of Lower Street and Tail Mill Lane. The Platoon H.Q. was Merriott House, Lower Street, Merriott. Transport was provided by lorries loaned by the London and Central Meat Company. Grenade practice was carried out at Bagnell Farm, south-east of Norton.

Frank Sadler, a boy at the time, recalls his father, F.H. Sadler being arrested by the Merriott Home Guard as a suspected spy when reporting for work at Merriott Mouldings shortly after being evacuated from London – presumably on the basis of a strange face with a non-West Country accent. Frank remembers playing with his father's rifle and pointing it at his mother. Frank suspects that the ensuing fuss was due not to the fact that he could have shot his mother, as the rifle was found to be loaded, but that it was the only round of ammunition his father had.

In the recreation field in Merriott two big huts were erected for Italian P.O.W.s. No doubt the Italians would have worked on local farms.

Whilst the modern perception is of the Home Guard being comprised of men who rushed to volunteer in May 1940, this was not the situation as the war progressed. Because of falling numbers of volunteers, The National Service Bill, outlined on 4th December 1941, was introduced to direct unmarried women between the ages of 20 and 30 years of age, with few exceptions, into the police, fire and armed services. In addition, the age of call up for men was lowered to $18^1/_2$ years, with an increase in the upper age limit to 50. As the Home Guard was deemed to be part of the Armed Forces, men could be directed into the Home Guard in areas where it was considered to be under-manned. Boys aged 16 were also to be encouraged to become Home Guard Cadets. It is possible that it was at this stage that the designation for conscripted 'other ranks' became 'private' whereas their predecessors had proudly rejoiced in the title of 'volunteer'.

George Case of Merriott received the following communication which required him to enrol in his local Home Guard Unit.

MINISTRY OF LABOUR AND NATIONAL SERVICE

DEFENCE (HOME GUARD) REGULATIONS, 1940

Direction to enrol in the Home Guard.

To: *George D. W. Base,* *Church Street*
South View Broadway *Crewkerne*
Merriott

14.10.42 (Date)

In pursuance of Regulation 3(1) of the Defence (Home Guard) Regulations, 1940, I, the undersigned, a National Service Officer within the meaning of the Defence (General) Regulations, 1939, do hereby direct you to enrol in the Home Guard and for that purpose to present yourself at *The Drill Hall Crewkerne* (place) on *Sunday 25 October 1942* (date) at *11 a.m.* (time).

[signature]
National Service Officer.

NOTE 1.—Any person failing to comply with a direction under the Defence (Home Guard) Regulations, 1940, is liable on summary conviction to imprisonment for a term not exceeding three months or to a fine not exceeding £100 or both such imprisonment and such fine. There are heavier penalties for conviction on indictment.

NOTE 2.—Any person desiring to apply for the withdrawal or modification of a direction on the ground that it would be an exceptional hardship if he were required to enrol in the Home Guard, may do so by making an application to the National Service Officer on the appropriate form which may be obtained from the Local Office of the Ministry of Labour and National Service. Such application must be made within four days of the giving of the direction. If such an application is made within the period stated, the person to whom the direction to enrol is issued may regard the direction as suspended until a further communication is received from the National Service Officer.

E.D.447.

Wt. 47704/8038 300M. 3-42 C.N.&Co.Ltd. 749 (7180)

Roger Baker recalls the following wartime activities at Tail Mill, Merriott.

In the 1930s my grandfather and father managed a business in Osnaburgh Street, London, manufacturing various components for the automotive industry. With the approach of war, production switched to parts for aircraft and barrage balloons in particular. Of significant importance were the 16- and 32-way bomb selector mechanisms eventually fitted to all heavy bombers. These enabled bomb aimers to select particular bombs for specific targets. Also manufactured were a number of aircraft instruments including altimeters and quick release mechanisms for barrage balloons. Eventually, the War Ministry issued an ultimatum to relocate to a 'safe' area or lose the business. The specified safe area was west of a line drawn from Weymouth to Bristol for, "as you know old chap, they have not got any bombers capable of reaching that area!". My father found an old mill complex near Merriott which just about lay in the safe area and most of the manufacturing was shifted to Tail Mill. The mill complex, about 40 acres of fields and a few cottages, was purchased for under £2,000. The first German bombing raid into the area missed the mill building by about a mile.

That raid alerted the top people in Whitehall who then insisted that steps be taken to secure the area. So a sentry box was placed on the approach lane to the factory. The sentry controlled a barrier and his instructions were that only those with official passes could enter. The managing director (George Wheway who lived near Broadwindsor) arrived one day at the barrier. The sentry, who up till then had been working in the factory, asked for his pass. Wheway had forgotten it and try as he might to get the sentry to lift the barrier –"You know me old chap, I manage the place, etc." – he had, in the end, to return home to get it.

The raid also meant the installation of a Lewis gun on top of the main mill building. The 'gunner' chosen to man it was a First World War veteran whose eyes were past their best, as was his health. It was all he could do actually to climb up inside the building to the gun platform mounted on the roof.

One day he heard a plane, couldn't find his glasses, so let fly in every direction until the gun jammed. Terrified at the low dives the plane kept making, the poor chap decided to call it a day and seek safety on the ground but while clambering down he met the M.D. clambering up. "What the bloody hell are you doing?", he asked. "Just letting that Jerry know we mean business," replied the gunner. "That 'Jerry' happened to be flying a Spitfire," roared the M.D. Apparently, if the R.A.F. were fired on by friendly fire, they dispatched a high-ranking officer to make a full enquiry. This duly happened and a worried M.D. lectured the driver detailed to meet the officer at Yeovil Junction on the absolute necessity to find out all he could about the person – his likes and dislikes. The driver did very well and quietly told the M.D. that venison and cider would work wonders. So they did, for the report "was unable to apportion blame and another visit would be necessary to investigate this matter further". There were at least five more visits and they only stopped when war ended – the matter remains unresolved to this day.

The factory was also asked to raise a Home Guard which was readily supported. However, exercises were not very successful until all the girls in the finishing shop – about 100 – offered to act as the enemy; exercises had to be rearranged to Saturday nights!

Battalion Headquarters was at Ilminster and all serious exercises involved men from Ilminster Company. One such exercise, towards the end of the war, created much head-scratching at Merriott, for Ilminster had acquired an ancient tank and the exercise involved Ilminster trying to capture the factory. How do we stop the tank? The night duly arrived and Ilminster set off to Lopen Head to take the road to Merriott. The tank was leading the way and going flat out in the lane from Lopen Head towards the S bend before the village of Lopen. Suddenly chaos – the tank had gone straight on at the S bend, burying itself and its gun in the bank – baffled Ilminster Home Guard were all captured and daylight revealed Merriott's secret weapon – a tarpaulin. This had been stretched across the road between the high banks and dropped over the tank so the driver could not see where he was going.

Ilminster got their own back. Apparently a cottage next to the factory was for sale and Ilminster Home Guard (so the story goes) 'persuaded' the occupants to co-operate with them. No one queried a removals lorry arriving to 'move' the occupants and even the sentry did not smell a rat – that is until the back of the lorry was opened and out poured the entire Home Guard capturing the sentry, the M.D. and the factory.

North Perrott Platoon in Spring 1943.
Back Row: Don Willmott; Mr. Ferguson; Billy Wills; Edgar Beames; Archie Culpitt; Ken Bartlett
Second Row: R. Beaumont; Leslie Parkman; Unknown but believed was a farmhand for Harry Collins; Cecil Purchase; Jim Bromfield; Gordon Lemon; Len Brown; B. Mason; Stan Gear; Tony Wilson; E. Wallis; Lindley Burton; S. or Charlie Meech
Third Row: Reg Rodford; Tony Brunt; Bob Draper; L/Cpl. Charlie Pike; Cpl. Arthur Peach; Sgt. Sam Rodford; Lt. Bill Grundy; Major Hayward; Sgt. Godfrey Raper; Sgt. Frank Manning; Sgt. Tony Champion; Cpl. Ralph Trask; Cpl. Harry Collins; Keith Leighton
Sitting on the grass: John Leamon; Leslie Cox; T. Mickleburgh; Vernon Bromfield
(Raymond Bromfield collection)

Major Hayward was the Platoon's first commander but had to retire through ill health.

Feltonfleet School, which evacuated to North Perrott from Cobham, provided three members of the Platoon: Tony Wilson, Tony Champion and Keith Leighton, the school's Headmaster.

The White House at Haselbury Plucknett was one of the local 'watering holes', which also possessed a small-bore rifle range. Note the fine trophy in the photograph.

S.I.P. Grenades were on issue to North Perrott Platoon. Notoriously dangerous, one mishap resulted in Sam Rodford and two or three other platoon members suffering burns to their faces and hands when an S.I.P. Grenade was accidentally broken.

Raymond Bromfield joined the Home Guard as a Cadet in March 1944. This was when he was 16 years of age when he had to register for War Service and join either the Air Training Corps or the Cadets or be directed to employment for the War Effort.

A shepherd's hut overlooking the London and South Western Railway at Downclose Farm was used as a shelter for the picket.

WESTLANDS COMPANY

COMMANDING OFFICER   Major B. de la Perrelle   2ND IN COMMAND   Capt. G.R. Turner

No. 3 Platoon Westlands Company.
Back Row: Bob Walker; F. Folkard; J. Perrott; Unknown; Basil M.C.Garvey; Malgwyn Edwards; Unknown; G. Penny; Tony Williams; Vic Gardner
Second Row: Unknown; Unknown; J. Brown or Johnny Sacker; Ernie Hoskins; Unknown; Mr. Legg; Eric Ebsworth; Mr. Curtis; Jack Straw; W. Cousins
Third Row: Cpl. J. Atkins; Unknown; Sgt. Frank Pape; Sgt. L. Wiscomb (Platoon Sergeant); Lt. Paley; 2nd Lt. Ted Gibbons; Sgt. Collard; Sgt. Bob Collie; John Edgeley; Cpl. Bill Williams
Front Row: L/Cpl. Doug Willis; C. Ellen; L/Cpl. F. Nash or L/Cpl. Lane; Tony R. Yates; Unknown; Mr. White; A. White; John Bush; B. Tetlow; Dennis Lea
(Fred Ballam collection)

Originally No. 3 Platoon was numbered No. 4. When the Company was reorganised, the men from two small platoons transferred to those remaining which were renumbered 1 to 3. Apart from these platoons there was a small bomb disposal unit which was formed to deal with small unexploded devices.

Anti-aircraft defence consisted of quad-mounted anti-aircraft machine guns emplaced in pits close to a pillbox. The entrances to the factory from the airfield were obstructed with knife rests protected by small-arms fire from a nearby pillbox constructed on the factory side of the fence.

Officers and Sergeants of Westlands Company.
Back Row: Sgt. Jones; Sgt. Loman; Sgt. Powell; Unknown; Mr. Le Lohe; Sgt. Abbott; Sgt. Vickers; Sgt. Gardner; Unknown
Second Row: Unknown; Sgt. Pape; Sgt. Collie; Sgt. Petley; Sgt. Pilkington; Unknown; Sgt. Watts; Sgt. Baker; Sgt. Hockey; Unknown; Sgt. Spilsbury; Unknown
Third Row: Sgt. Chappel; Lt. E. Frost; Mr. Dodge; Capt. G.R. Turner; Major B. de la Perrelle; Mr. Bex; Mr. Harrison; Mr. Seymore; Mr. Rowlands; Unknown
Front Row: Mr. Paley; Mr. Gibbons; Mr. Meadon; Mr. Wilmont; Unknown; Mr. Dowsett; Mr. Clayton
Both these photographs were taken in front of the erecting shop which on one occasion was peppered with shrapnel during an air raid.
From the composition of the photograph the back and second rows are undoubtedly composed of Sergeants. In the third row, with the exception of the first and last and the two senior officers, all others appear to be first or second lieutenants, as is the first row. Note Mr. Dowsett's 'Wings'.
(Wyndham Rowlands collection)

In January 1938 Ted Frost joined Westlands at Yeovil as a jig and tool draughtsman. At the outbreak of war Ted was about to join the Royal Electrical and Mechanical Engineers but his call-up was deferred on account of his work. At the formation of the L.D.V. Ted immediately enrolled. As it was thought necessary for the company to form their own bomb-disposal unit, a call went out for volunteers. Ted offered his services and in one day was promoted from Volunteer to Lieutenant. Our new Lieutenant's first experience of bomb disposal was when some bombs were dropped near the gasometer which was situated close to where Lysander Road now exists. At least one bomb failed to detonate and Lt. Frost, in the absence of any formal procedure, attached a slab of gun cotton to the bomb. Retiring to a safe distance, the bomb was destroyed, as was part of the factory roof when the bomb-casing fell through it.

Shortly after this unfortunate incident Ted Frost was sent to Melksham to attend a bomb disposal course run by the Royal Engineers. Returning as a trained B.D. Officer and subsequently sporting a red fabric flash in the shape of a bomb on his sleeve, Lt. Frost and his team got down to the work of bomb disposal, dealing with about six during the war. Their work was not confined to Westlands because the unit covered a radius of about 10 miles from Yeovil. One bomb disposed of by Ted and his unit was at Stoke sub Hamdon.

Lt. Frost's fiancée, Rosina Norris, also worked at Westlands and she remembered the day when a lone Heinkel strafed the drawing office, puncturing the roof in several places. Members of the factory Home Guard just had time to fire a few rounds off from their quadruple machine gun but surprise was on the side of the attacker and he made good his escape.

Another incident had far more serious repercussions. It was normal procedure at Westlands for female staff to be allowed to leave for lunch five minutes before the men. One day just as the ladies emerged from their work place a bomb fell on the car park with fatal results. The administration block still bears the scars to this day.

Unusually for Home Guard units Ted remembers that he was issued with a Short Lee Enfield rifle which he became very fond of, hiding it in his office after the war in the hope that he would be able to keep it!

Interestingly, rifle practice took place in Birds Quarry next to the *Lime Kiln Inn*, Long Sutton. Redvers Burt, a member of Long Sutton Home Guard thinks this may have been an isolated incident as local Home Guard units either shot at Curry Rivel or at Paradise, Langport where the facilities were better. Back at the Westlands factory a .22 rifle range existed at the Sports Club which is still in use today.

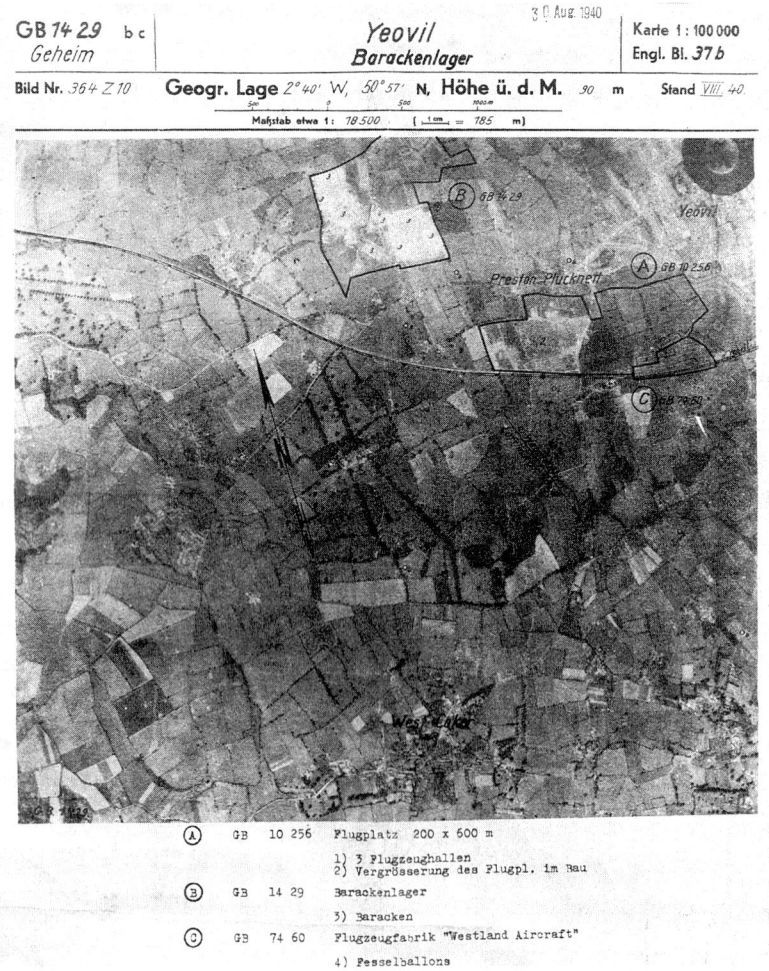

(above) Luftwaffe aerial photograph of Westlands Works
(Wyndham Rowlands collection)

Westlands B.D.U. proudly show off one of their successes. The pick head carries the letters B.D.U., no doubt an attempt to keep 'tabs' on their equipment. Only Peter Brown, No. 3, has been identified. Others in the 10-man unit included Mr. Giles and 'Sapper' Knapper who due to his deafness, was unable to carry out certain B.D. duties. The bomb featured is a 50kg S.C. (thin-walled) fitted usually with a type 28 fuse which incorporated a short delay, ideal for a raid on a factory complex. A Heinkel 111 could carry up to 32 of these bombs. Not all B.D.U. members survived the war. Over 100 lost their lives in the line of duty.
(Ted Frost collection)

HERON COMPANY

COMMANDING OFFICER   Capt. L.E. Atkinson
(Major D.G. Paterson)

COMMANDING OFFICER
LT. ANTI-AIRCRAFT TROOP   Lt. A.S. Wilmott

Members of Heron Company, comprising civilians working at Yeovilton. Only one has been identified – Jock Tolleith, sitting in the third row from the back, No. 6.
(Gerry Masters collection)

Auxiliary Unit at Yeovil Police Station.
Back Row: Unknown; Thomas David Oxenbury; John Robert Hillier; Unknown; George Hutchins
Middle Row: John Denning; Unknown; Unknown; Unknown; Glyde Scammell; Unknown; Unknown; Frederick George Hughes
Front Row: Arthur Frank Whetham; Dennis George Ford; John Jones; Nigel Leonard Palmer; Lt. Eric George Loader; William Bramwell Martin; Sgt. William Henry Austin Whetham; Unknown; Unknown
Lt. Eric Loader was a farmer of Podimore; John Denning a farmer of Draycott near Limington and Bob Hillier from Hainbury Mill Farm, Ilchester. The Podimore Boys' hideout was in a wood at Annis Hill, West Camel.
(Gerry Masters collection)

The organisation and history of the Auxiliary Units merits a book of its own. Having carried out their basic training in the Home Guard, the members quietly absented themselves from overt defence of the realm. In the event of any invasion they would have 'gone to ground' in small groups, surfacing to cause damage and disruption to the enemy in tip-and-run raids. Their combat life expectancy would not have been very long and if captured they could not expect to receive protection under the Geneva Convention.

Bradford Abbas Home Guard, *photographed outside the Village Hall in about 1942. Although Bradford Abbas is in Dorset this photograph and information has been included for the sake of posterity.*
Back Row: Fred Gale; Charlie Percy; F. Upshall; W. Blackmore; Bob Hooper; Ern Smith; Charlie Dewberry; Cecil Smith; Charlie Smith; Austin Coomes; Unknown
Second Row: Reg Jenkins; Wyatt White; J. Chant; Unknown; Unknown; Tom Gosney; Unknown; Charlie Fowler; Sid Parker; Harry Gillham; Unknown
Third Row: Unknown; Cyril Ring; T. Mellish; Mr. Day; Jock Little; Lt. Turnbull; 2nd Lt. Dunster; Sgt. Bert Woodman; Cpl. Whiting; L/Cpl. Bill Gale; L/Cpl. Frank Smith
Front Row: Fred Cleal or Reg Parker; Bill Lucas; Bill Pauley; P. Baywell; Arthur Bowditch; Bert Garrett; Mr. Meaker; Mr. L.T. Gosney; Unknown
Other platoon members were W. Hurford, T. Weller, E. Bridle, G. Cox, Doug Frampton, Mr. Osborne, Mr. Rand and Mr. Dowding.
(Arthur Bowditch collection)

Platoon Headquarters was at Ruskin House. The Platoon's rifle range was at Oborne near Sherborne. Before his death in 2002 Arthur Bowditch was able to provide civilian occupations for a few of the platoon members: Cecil Smith worked at Wyke Farm, Fred Jenkins was a local baker. Mr. Day was the Headmaster at Bradford Abbas School and Frank Smith ran Bradford Abbas Post Office.

Arthur Bowditch spent his early years in Dorset working as a builder's labourer, before turning his hand to agriculture. He was involved in the building of the cottages erected in memory of the Tolpuddle Martyrs. In his twilight years he would attend the annual meeting organised by the T.U.C., being the sole survivor of the original building team. His name is commemorated on the memorial stone that was erected at the cottages but which is now stored in the archives at T.U.C. Headquarters. Arthur died in 2002, aged 90, having spent some 70 years farming in Somerset and Dorset, providing for his wife and three children. Before he died, Arthur always maintained that he was the only one in his unit trusted to throw grenades, the reason being he was the only one able to throw them far enough with accuracy. (Instructions for the No. 36 grenade stipulated that they had to be thrown from behind cover, the danger area being in excess of 300 yards from the point of burst!)

Yeovil Platoon 'D' Company, 15th Gloucester (Post Office) Battalion *in 1944.*
Middle Row: No. 1 Ted Rossiter; No. 4 Donald McLean
(Peter Rossiter collection)

10th Somerset (Bridgwater) Battalion

HEADQUARTERS	Drill Hall, Bridgwater
DATE FORMED	October 1940
COMMANDING OFFICER	Lt. Col. R. Chamberlin, O.B.E.
2ND IN COMMAND	Major B.M. Fox
	(Major H.W.A. Collum, D.S.O.)
	(Major N.W.B.B. Thoms, C.B.E., D.S.O., M.C.)

H.Q. STAFF

A & Q	Capt. W.A.L. Pardoe, General List
ADJUTANT	Capt. D.G. Avery, General List
AMMUNITION OFFICER	Capt. C.C. Harris
ASSISTANT ADJUTANT	Capt. M. Barnett
GAS OFFICER	Lt. J.R. Banfield
INTELLIGENCE OFFICER	Lt. N.J.S. Leggatt
	(Lt. C.C. Trenchard)
LIAISON OFFICER (Sector)	Lt. The Lord St. Audries
	Lt. H.G. Haggett
(Military Information Centre)	Lt. G. Rees
	2nd Lt. R. Varney
MEDICAL OFFICERS	Major O.J. Bollon
	Major G.L. Lyon Smith
SIGNALS OFFICER	Lt. R.N. Shaw
	(Lt. F. Purves)
	2nd Lt. Austin
TRANSPORT OFFICER	Lt. P. Gill
WEAPONS TRAINING OFFR.	Lt. A. Aitkenhead

Officers of 10th Somerset (Bridgwater) Battalion Home Guard.
Back Row: 2nd Lt. H. Poole; 2nd Lt. G. Stratton; Lt. W.J. England; 2nd Lt. F.A. Branston; 2nd Lt. J.C. Ford; 2nd Lt. L.F. Curtis; 2nd Lt. E.R. Gregory; Lt. G.C. Woodhouse; Lt. P.H. Bradbury; Lt. A. Biddiscombe; Lt. W.A.L. Pardoe; 2nd Lt. G.R. Mather; 2nd Lt. H. Whitcombe; 2nd Lt. A.G. Broughton
Second Row: 2nd Lt. B. Leicester; 2nd Lt. G.F. Vowles; 2nd Lt. G.H. Hobbs; 2nd Lt. R. Meade; Lt. V.E. Gumbrell; Lt. F. Greenhalgh; 2nd Lt. W.I.E. Lane; Lt. J. Moon; 2nd Lt. W.H. Pollard; 2nd Lt. E.H. Pearce; Lt. E. Wills; Lt. B.R. Broughton; Lt. G.C. Furze; Lt. W.A. Carne-Williams; 2nd Lt. N.A. Smith; Lt. W.M.T. Parsons
Third Row: 2nd Lt. C.L. Durston; 2nd Lt. J.C. Pardoe; Capt. G.S. James; Capt. W.D. Hay; Capt. C.C. Harris; 2nd Lt. H.G. Haggett; Lt. A. Aitkenhead; Lt. W.R. Pettitt; 2nd Lt. J.R. Banfield; Capt. A.H. Jones; Capt. E.F. Sherwood; 2nd Lt. C.G.V.M. Wardell; 2nd Lt. R.S. Graham; 2nd Lt. J.H. Vale; Lt. J. de C. Pook; Capt. A.C. Birt; 2nd Lt. H.L. Shepherd
Fourth Row: Lt. The Lord St. Audries; Major B.M. Fox; Major R.C. Seymour; Major G.L. Lyon Smith; Capt. M. Barnett; Major H.W.A. Collum, D.S.O. (2nd i/c Btn.); Lt. Col. R. Chamberlain, O.B.E. (Commanding Officer); Capt. D.G. Avery; Major W.H. Tamlyn, M.C.; Major G. Christopher; Major R.M. Phelips; Lt. C.C. Trenchard; Lt. A.J.D. Crawford; 2nd Lt. A.E. Porter; Lt. W.J. Greener
Front Row: 2nd Lt. G.F. Ballance; 2nd Lt. P. Chidgey; 2nd Lt. A.G.C. Powell; 2nd Lt. R. Varney; 2nd Lt. F. Moverley; 2nd Lt. C.G. Collis; 2nd Lt. M. Vinnicombe; 2nd Lt. G. Brimson; 2nd Lt. J.H. Dosson; Lt. R.M. Rowley
The photograph was taken before the Sergeants in the front row had received their 2nd Lieutenant's 'pip'.

At the end of the war Lt. Col. Chamberlin continued to serve his community, as a Justice of the Peace and as Mayor. In December 1944 one William Stephen Briffett appeared in front of him charged with stealing a Savoy cabbage valued at 6d. He was found guilty and sentenced to one month's hard labour. (Author's collection)

QUANTOCK COMPANY

COMMANDING OFFICER   Major R.C. Seymour
                                      (Major The Lord St. Audries)

2ND IN COMMAND   Capt. W.D. Hay
                                        (Capt. G.L. Lyon-Smith)

Phillip George Stockham was a member of Bridgwater Battalion from 2.9.1942 to Stand Down. Many years after the war he bought a silver-plated tankard from a local jumble sale which he subsequently stored in his attic. One can only reflect on this sad postscript to a man who, as the Battalion Training Officer and later Adjutant, gave so much to the Home Guard, yet within a few years this token of esteem found its way to a jumble sale, unwanted and unloved. (Author's collection)

Nether Stowey Platoon.
Back Row: Arthur Bryant; Ed Rich; Jack Chidgey; Sid Knight; Harry Wilkins; Bill Cavill; Albert Venn; Gerald Wyatt; John Bellringer; Fred Stockham; Sid Villis; Jack Routley; Bill Chilcott; Norman Chilcott
Middle Row: E. Baker; Sidney Wooley; Frank Cousins; Bill Wyatt; Peter Vowles; Jack Trout; Phil Lewis; Raymond Palmer; William Villis; Cecil Day; Ed Salvage; Jim Palmer; Ted Ackland; William Trickey; Tom Ham; John Prowse
Front Row: L/Cpl. Tom Moore; L/Cpl. Joe Villis; Cpl. Jack Cruise; Sgt. Ted Lane; Sgt. Ernest Taylor; Sgt. William Tucker; C.S.M. Harry Prowse; Lt. Dirom Crawford; Staff Sgt. Charles Groves; Q.S.M. Walter Ware; Sgt. Jack Down; Sgt. Frank White; L/Cpl. Peter White; L/Cpl. George Wyatt; L/Cpl. Harold Palmer

The above photograph was taken in July 1944, during Jim Palmer's embarkation leave, he being a member of the Home Guard from March '43 until he was called up on 4th April '44. With most Home Guards in civilian employment several members are not featured including Fred Dare, Ken Payne and Bert Stacey, Ken Payne being busy on the day killing pigs. Also not featured is young Tom Ware, a member of the A.T.C. who served as a runner.
(Fred Stockham collection)

The Platoon's local rifle range was situated in Cannington Park, rifles being a mixture of Remington and Winchester P17s. Peter White, aged 16 in 1940, and one of the younger members of the platoon, remembers the unit also possessed Sten guns, Tommy guns, a Lewis machine gun and a Browning automatic rifle. Small-bore shooting and grenade practice took place locally in Park Quarry. In winter evenings the small-bore range in *The Rose and Crown* was used, run by Home Guard Charles Groves, whose cellar doubled as the armoury. Stores were kept in S. Whare's Saddlery, Lime Street. whilst explosives were stored in a Nissen hut.

In the early days of the war lookouts were posted at Quantock Farm and Stowey Mount, the guards cycling to their posts.

Lt. Crawford, a member of the Crawford's Biscuit family, lived outside Nether Stowey where he employed Bill Wyatt as his chauffeur. Recently it has been reported that Lt. Crawford, considering his home of strategic importance, painted the walls in disruptive paint. If only a photograph had been taken.

> Joe Villis recalls an incident when he was attending a camp at Watchet. The Platoon N.C.O.s were being drilled under the watchful eye of a Regular Sergeant Major. With the cruelty that only Sergeant Majors possess the Home Guards were being marched towards the cliff top with all ears waiting for the command, 'About turn'. Onwards they marched until, when they were only about four yards from the cliff top, Sgt. White called out: "For God's sake say something even if it's only 'Goodbye'".

Cannington Platoon.
Back Row: Gordon Conibeare; Alf Conibeare; Bill Conibeare; Harold Haywood; Unknown; Unknown; Henry Gardiner; Mr. Pearce; Edward Venner; Unknown; Unknown; Unknown; Unknown; Unknown
Second Row: Albert Bartholomew; Unknown; Unknown; William Evans; Unknown; Unknown; Arthur Hurley; Unknown; Unknown; Unknown; Unknown; Herbert Venner; Wilf Venner
Third Row: Unknown; L/Cpl. Bill Burland; Unknown; L/Cpl. Geoffrey Duckham; Gerald Gough; Herbert Pople; L/Cpl. H. Brown; Metford Pople; Mr. Fudge; Unknown; George Bishop; Unknown; Unknown; Albert Lee
Front Row: Unknown; Unknown; Unknown; Sgt. Cornish; Sgt. Ackland; Sgt. Showbrook; Sgt. Quartley; Lt. Furze; Lt. Shephard; Edward Bridgman; Cpl. Goodman; Sgt. Somers; Unknown; Cpl. Brown; Les Pople

Edward Bridgman ran The Globe *Public House during the war, having previously been a Sgt. Instructor (P.E.) in the 18th Hussars. Herbert Venner remembered that he worked the Platoon extremely hard. L/Cpl. Brown was the organist at Durleigh Church whilst Mr. Pearce was a farmer at Steart. Sgt. Somers, previously in the Royal Navy, was i/c Combwich section with Cpl. Brown as his No. 2. Subsequently Sgt. Somers was awarded the M.B.E. for services rendered to the Home Guard. Lt. Furze, the Platoon Commander, worked at Cannington Institute.*

For shooting practice the obsolete Cannington range was used. By 1942 conditions improved when the Cannington Quarry was made available.

The Platoon Nissen hut was at approximate map ref. ST 255 397, the site now having been built over during extension work at Cannington College. (Herbert Venner collection)

Stogursey Platoon, photographed in 1944.
Back Row: Unknown; Unknown; Unknown; Unknown; Charlie Burge; Bob Burge; Gordon Sparkes; Horace Rich; Unknown; Frank Knox; Unknown; Harold Pearce; Sam Rich; Mervyn Payne; Stanley Cridge
Second Row: Unknown; Phil Perrot; Burt Victor Chilcott; Eric Buller; Jim Chilcott; F. Stone; Cpl. Jack Tarr; Cpl. Frank Coles; L/Cpl. Gerald Newberry; Edward Shepherd (WW1 veteran); Clement Govett; Unknown; Mr. Stepney; Unknown
Third Row: Tommy Chilcott; Unknown; Cpl. Jim House; Cpl. Cyril Scott; Sgt. Joe Jones; Sgt. Alvin Triggol; 2nd Lt. Percy Chidgey; Lt. Jim Crosby; Sgt. Tom Westcombe (baker and farmer); Sgt. Jack Burge; Unknown; Unknown; Sgt. Norman Jones; Sgt. Bob Ridler-Rowe; Unknown; T. Chilcott
Front Row: Billy Gunningham; Sid Buller; Unknown; Unknown; Donald Willicombe; Stanley Gunningham; Jim Lukins; John Newton; Unknown; Unknown; Unknown; Unknown; Mr. Perrot; Unknown; Unknown

Interestingly only six members appear to be wearing campaign ribbons. The initial rush to enrol in the Home Guard in 1940 resulted in many decorated ex-WW1 veterans enrolling. As the war progressed these old soldiers retired, and thus military experience was reduced. By 1943 the average age of members nationally was about 30 and less than 7% were World War 1 veterans.
(Clara Pearce collection)

Members of Stogursey Platoon in the grounds of The Ackland Hood Arms.
Back Row: Clement Govett; L/Cpl. Jack Burge; Gordon Jones; William Bax; Harold Pearce; Cpl. Tom Hole; Bill Sulley
Front Row: Cpl. Norman Jones; Basil Jones; Sgt. Burt Hole; L/Cpl. Joe Jones; Rupert Hern

All of those above lived in the parish of Stogursey. Jack Tarr, Lester Tarr, and Harold Pearce's duties included patrolling the lonely shore line between Stolford and Shurton. Lester used his own horse whilst Harold and Jack would share Harold's horse 'Molly'. The Platoon was issued with at least one Vickers machine gun which Harold Pearce kept at Stolford Farm. On the beach at Stolford an empty cottage, one of a group of three known as Chapel Cottages (pronounced locally as 'Chippel') was used as a patrol centre. This photograph was taken earlier than the previous one as Joe Jones is still a Lance Corporal.
(Clara Pearce collection)

*Other members of **Stogursey Platoon**, no doubt taken at the same time as the photograph on the left. Some 19 faces wait to be identified. (Michael Chamberlin collection)*

The author is indebted to Clive Knox for the following information provided by his father Frank.

A large field abutting the shore west of Hinkley Point Power Station, centred on map ref. ST 195 460, is known locally as Landing Ground. During the war the area was obstructed with timber to prevent it being used as a landing strip. It is not known if the name comes from that period or earlier as at the south-east corner of this field is a wood known as Air Force Covert.

To the south of Landing Ground, at the end of a track at map ref. ST 197 454, the local Home Guard occupied a hut. Prefabricated, it was unlike the standard Nissen hut, being constructed of flat sheets of corrugated iron on a timber frame lined with asbestos sheets. It was approximately 10' long by 6' wide and 7' to the eaves of the gabled roof. One door and one window were provided. Removed to Stogursey in the 1950s for re-use as a store shed, it was then refurbished as a changing hut for the tennis court before finally succumbing to the years in the 1990s.

The beach at Shurton Bars was not backed by any cliffs and was thought to be an ideal landing spot. Stakes and barbed wire were erected to block the beach exit. During the war American Troops were stationed in small Nissen hut encampments at West Kilton Farm and at Alfoxton Park.

(below) **Spaxton Platoon**, *taken at Spaxton Court Farm, home of Lt. Woodhouse.*
Back Row: Tom Fackrell; Horace Porter; Reg Speed; Bob Chidgey; Leslie Stevens; Geoff Burland; R. Attwater; Stephen Harris; Bill Roe; Metford Jeanes
Second Row: Peter Thorne; Percy Parsons; T. Fackrell; Leslie Horn; Wilfred Small; Harold Snook; Ted Saunders; Mr. Todham; Ern Hawkins; Fred Mildon; Jim Lewis; Fred Smaldon
Third Row: Jack Porter; John Bird; Tom Jenkins; Unknown; Frank Bryant; Gilbert Thorne; Jack Cavill; Jim Greed; Unknown; Unknown; Unknown; J. Jenkins; Unknown; Bill Webber; Fred Waterman
Front Row: Frank Jeanes; Cpl. Albert Jeanes; Cpl. Jack Waterman; Sgt. Jim Rood; Sgt. Jack Mildon; Sgt. Victor Hook; Lt. Geoffrey Woodhouse; 2nd Lt. Jack Dosson; Sgt. Ken Kinnersley; Cpl. Ern Bishop; Cpl. G. Bacon; Cpl. Ern Sparks; Bert Harris
Other platoon members included Dennis Bawdon who served between 29.3.42 and 31.12.44. He remembers that practice with the Platoon's Spigot Mortar took place in Cannington Quarry.
(Bert Harris collection)

Fred Waterman was the proprietor of Waterman's Buses whilst Tom Jenkins was another bus operator. The story goes that Tom would use his bus on a Wednesday morning to take pigs to Bridgwater Market, returning to collect two-legged passengers who paid for the privilege of travelling in what had been an ersatz cattle truck earlier in the day.

A one inch to the mile War Department map shows a 'defended home' in Bush Lane, Spaxton which was also Platoon Headquarters. It is known that a weapon pit was dug in the corner of the field on the south side of Bush Lane covering the lane from Spaxton to Hawkridge, together with a trench dug in the front garden of the cottages facing Bush Lane. In addition there was a Home Guard store in the field to the south of Bush Lane which was just standing in the 1990s. Today it has been totally demolished. Perhaps it was here that explosives in the form of No. 75 Hawkins Mines were stored ready to block the road. A chance comment in 1999 resulted in the location of a removable road block constructed of three rows of steel rails placed in pre-formed sockets just to the east of the Bush Lane junction.

(right) What the enemy failed to do but time has achieved. The remains of the Home Guard store in the 1990s showing the interior partition that would have separated inflammable munitions from explosives.

Members of North Newton and Moorland Section *parade at Impen's Farm in North Newton. Heading the left-hand column is Sgt. Porter; the second column is led by Alfred Farthing. In the third column, from front to back, are Mr. Osmond, Reg Burrows and Dennis Collard. Third from right is Dicky Lock followed by Sgt. Sellick; and on the extreme right is Geoffrey Broughton.*

In 1971 it was discovered that this Home Guard unit had £6 in the 'kitty' which was spent on premium bonds. It is not known if their numbers ever came up!

Geoffrey Thomson was a member of Huntworth Platoon, joining in May 1940. Other members he recalls were Ben Gibbs, Ken Moote and his brother, C.E. Devas (an officer who resigned early on, due to health reasons), Geoffrey Broughton, John Norman and Messrs. Keirle, Gill, Higgins and Baird. Lt. W.A. Carne-Williams was the Platoon Commander. The Platoon was split into three sections: Huntworth Section under Sgt. Higgins; North Newton, commanded by Sgt. (later 2nd Lt.) Geoffrey Broughton; and Moorland Section, commanded by Sgt. Addicott. (Geoffrey Broughton collection)

Writing in October 1992 Mr. Thomson added:

I heard of the formation of the L.D.V. on the wireless one evening. The next day, before going to work, I went to the Police Station in Dampiet Street to enrol. (There were still separate police forces for the Borough and the County.) The constable there didn't know any more than I did but made a note of my name.

In due course I received an L.D.V. brassard and five or six of us mounted guard to watch for parachutists at Huntworth Park. We did duty in pairs, one shift from sunset to 1.00 am, the next till sunrise. We only had shotguns at first – the others all had their own, being farmworkers. There was John Norman, the farmer, with three or four of his men and a couple of other farmers.

Later we received .300 rifles, denim suits, leather gaiters and boots. We were attached to a unit based at North Newton whose officer was Lt. Carne-Williams of Batts House, North Newton. He was the manager of Starkey's Brewery in Northgate, Bridgwater.

One day Lt. Carne-Williams discovered I had hidden talents – I could read, write and add up. He therefore made me his quartermaster sergeant, in which capacity I had the difficult job of fitting everyone with proper uniforms when these were issued shortly afterwards.

Our little group at Huntworth was under Sgt. Higgins, the gardener at Huntworth House, a First World War veteran and a very good instructor. Occasionally we went to North Newton where we were drilled in proper military fashion by other WW1 veterans but without success. Once or twice they actually tried to make us march at Light Infantry pace.

North Newton Section.
Back Row: No. 6 Alfred Farthing
Middle Row: none identified
Front Row: Unknown; Unknown; Cpl. Parker; Sgt. Sellick; Lt. W.A. Carne-Williams; Sgt. (later 2nd Lt.) Geoffrey Broughton; Unknown; Cpl. Finnemore; Richard Lock
(Geoffrey Broughton collection)

(below) When the memo of 16th December 1940 was written, North Petherton and Huntworth Platoons formed part of Sedgemoor Company. In early 1941 the above platoons were transferred to No. 5 (Bridgwater) Company. This presented certain administrative problems and the platoons were subsequently transferred to Quantock Company.

```
To O.C. Bridgwater Bn. H.G.                SG/TC/ITC-103
From South Group Comdr. H.G.
----------------------------

     Subject:- Home Guard Course at I.T.C., Taunton.

                December 2nd. - 7th. 1940.

     The following report from the O.C., I.T.C., Som. L.I. has
been received, and is forwarded for your information and any
necessary action:-

"Sgt. B. Broughton.    No previous service - benefited considerably
                       by the Course but requires a little more
                       instruction before making an instructor.
                       Worked hard and learnt a good deal."
```

C. L. Norman

Copy for

```
                                        J.G.124/40
                        HEADQUARTERS
                                    BATT.
                                            THE
                                                BRIDGWATER
To:-    Lieut. Broughton.               10 Oct. 44.


Dear Broughton,

        I have just received a cheque from Col. Alexander, of
the Minehead Battalion H.Gd. with the intimation that you have
been successful in obtaining a second in the "Master-at-Arms"
Competition.
        I would like to congratulate you very sincerely on
your achievement, which has brought credit to the Battalion.

                                Yours truly,
```

POLDEN COMPANY

COMMANDING OFFICER   Major W.J. Greener
(Major G.S. James)
(Major B.M. Fox)
(Major E.F. Browning, M.C.)
(Major C.H. Greenhill)

Pawlett Platoon.
Back Row: Percy Smith; F.J. Wynn; E. Chidgey; Mr. Riddell; W. Parkhouse; Eddie Reasons; William Powell; D. Difford; J. Poole
Middle Row: Mr. Claverly; Albert Hembury; E. Harwood; George Reasons; V. Avery; Sid Mayled; Lambert Allen; Mr. Cox; P. Stockham; Maurice Small
Front Row: G. Porter; Fred Ash; Sgt. W. Baker; Sgt. Reg Sandy; 2nd Lt. H. Whitcombe; Lt. Shepherd; Sgt. Major F. Hamlin; Sgt. E. Nutt; Cpl. Wilf Norman; L/Cpl. Bert Holley
Mr. Parkhouse ran the Ilex Stores in West Huntspill, whilst Sid Mayled and Lambert Allen worked for W.J. Thyer, agricultural implement agents who were subsequently incorporated into Kellands. 2nd Lt. Whitcombe ran the garage midway between Pawlett and West Huntspill, and Lt. Shepherd was the Manager at Lloyds Bank in Highbridge.
(F.J. Wynn collection)

Although its location is unknown, evidence of the existence of a Home Guard hut comes from the records of the Bridgwater and District Electricity Supply and Traction Co. for 1942, stating that the account for the Pawlett Home Guard Hut was overdue by £2-3-1d.

Pawlett and West Huntspill Home Guard and A.R.P.
Back Row: Percy Smith; F. Wynn; E. Chidgey; Mr. Riddell; W. Parkhouse; Eddie Parsons; William Powell; D. Difford; J. Poole; Maurice Small
Second Row: Mr. Claverly; G. Porter; Albert Hembury; E. Harwood; George Reasons; V. Avery; Sid Mayled; L. Allen; Mr. Cox; P. Stockham
Third Row: Mrs. Joan Long (née Kick); Doris Staples; Miss Buncombe; Mr. C. Haggett; Miss Buncombe; Fred Ash; Sgt. W. Baker; Sgt. Reg Sandy; 2nd Lt. H. Whitcombe; Unknown; Lt. H. Shepherd; Sgt. Major F. Hamlin; Sgt. E. Nutt; Cpl. Wilf Norman; L/Cpl. Bert Holley; Mr. Cliff Wilkins; Mrs. Gulliver; Mr. Webb; Beryl Peters; Mrs. Lowndes; Miss Webb
Front Row (messengers and A.R.P. personnel): Sam Chilcott; Jim Edwards; Unknown; Unknown; Leslie Gulliver; Unknown; Unknown; Mr. Gulliver; Cecil Fry
(Charles H. Connolly collection)

Cossington and Bawdrip Platoon.
Back Row: Ivor Williams; Stan Hembury; Ted Nurden; Walt Dyer; Bill Millener; Maurice Shorney; Tom Porter; Pete Bradford
Middle Row: L/Cpl. Bill Tucker; L/Cpl. Cyril Fisher; Clifford Sparkes; Stan Braddick; Fred Cross; Harry Mead; Harry Gilbert or Reg White; Eric Taghill; Wyndham Walker; Arthur Marsh; Jack Field
Front Row: D/R Harry Aldridge; Cpl. Harry Woodrow; Cpl. Raymond Haggett; 2nd Lt. Jack Berry; 2nd Lt. Clifford Durston; Sgt. Bill Burston; Cpl. John Burston; Cpl. Brown; Cpl. Ray Alford
Sitting: Jack Braddick; L/Cpl. Reg Mogg; Jack Gardiner; Sam Gardiner
(Mrs. Margaret Alice Mogg collection)

Eric Westman was a member of the local Home Guard unit. He remembers:

On the night of 7th September 1940 [the occasion when the code word 'Cromwell' was passed down the chain of command indicating conditions suitable for invasion] we all congregated in the woods by the bungalow/lodge at the entrance to Knowle Hall just to the north of the King's Sedgemoor Drain. There seemed to be no plan, I remember; we just huddled in the trees with no idea of what was going on. During the night a jug of tea was brought over from *The Silver Fish* and early in the morning we were told we could go, and off we went to our jobs.

South of *The Silver Fish* the A39 crossed over the Somerset and Dorset Railway. Here, concrete cubes and cylinders were installed on each side of the road. The road was prepared for spider mines by boring 7"-diameter holes in the road and fitting them with metal lids. In the event of any imminent attack the holes would be charged with mines. I remember some 10,000 holes had been drilled in the roads in Somerset to accept these mines. Sadly the holes were drilled for Mk I mines which, by the time the holes were drilled, had been superseded by Mk II which were larger and therefore would not operate in the Mk I hole!

On the A39, just past *The Knowle Inn* at Bawdrip, a Flame Fougasse was dug in the left-hand bank as the road rose up towards Woolavington. The site is now occupied by new houses.

Meetings were held one evening a week in Bawdrip Village Hall, next to the S&D Railway Halt. It was lit by oil lamps hanging from the low ceiling. Meetings were also held here on a Sunday after which we would repair to *The Knowle Inn*. In the early days we carried out lookout duties at Bawdrip, close to a property occupied by Miss Jelf. Our armament was a double-barrelled 12-bore shotgun. During the day the gun and ammunition were hidden in the wooden lagging of Miss Jelf's domestic water pump. In the evening the gun would be collected by the Home Guard lookouts who would then walk through the garden into a field where a 15-foot square area was fenced off, surrounding an 8' x 6' shed, which became the sentries' shelter for the night.

After several months we abandoned our garden-shed lookout on the hill (I realise now it was the borrowed bicycle shed of the middle-aged spinster headmistress of the village school, 'Duckie' Heal). We eventually spent our night duties based in a small store outhouse in the grounds of *The Silver Fish*. It was equipped with a stove, lantern and blackout curtains and became oppressively hot and full of cigarette smoke, but we were glad to sit in it after patrolling the road on cold, wet wintry nights. Bawdrip Hall was also abandoned in favour of the former dining-hall of *The Silver Fish* where training continued. I remember a 'drill' grenade which was regularly used to practice inserting the detonator set. Later, when we benefited from instruction from a Regular Army Sergeant we discovered that the grenade was not a drill one, but still charged with explosive.

Over many months various weapons arrived including an ex-aircraft .300 Lewis gun that would overheat and jam if fired for too long. Later a .303 Mk I Lewis gun arrived together with water-cooled Vickers and Browning machine guns, Tommy guns, Spigot Mortars, Northover Projectors, Sten guns and S.I.P. grenades. Rifles initially were .303 Ross Rifles, followed by .300 Springfields. Large weapons were kept at *The Silver Fish* but individuals took smaller weapons home with them, including Lewis guns.

My memories of the very early dates are pretty acute as it was all a novelty – I had never been out in the middle of the night before, but the later times were tedious and I don't remember much about them. We had meetings two evenings a week plus Sunday mornings, and occasional 'manoeuvres'. On top of that we worked very long hours on war work and had to do night firewatching at the factory as well. We were all dreadfully tired and many fell asleep on duty.

My former headmaster was a military-mad man who had served in WW1. He once gave me a very severe caning for missing rugby practice. One Sunday morning, the Home Guard had a 'manoeuvre' in which we had to defend our positions at Knowle against invading Home Guards from, I think, Stawell. Inside the end of the woods near *The Knowle Inn* I captured an invader crawling through the undergrowth. When he stood up I recognised him as my former headmaster. He was a puckish little man with disguising leafy twigs sticking out from his steel helmet, and in the setting of the woods looked just like 'Jack the Green'. He was not at all pleased at being captured by his former errant pupil.

As we had no dummy ammunition (and precious little real), whilst on manoeuvres we 'clicked' the triggers of our rifles to indicate we had fired at a foe. On one manoeuvre, invading Chedzoy, I think, one of our men 'clicked' his rifle and claimed to have 'shot' a member of the other side. But this man claimed to have 'clicked' first; there ensued a fierce argument and the umpire had to intervene to prevent them from coming to blows.

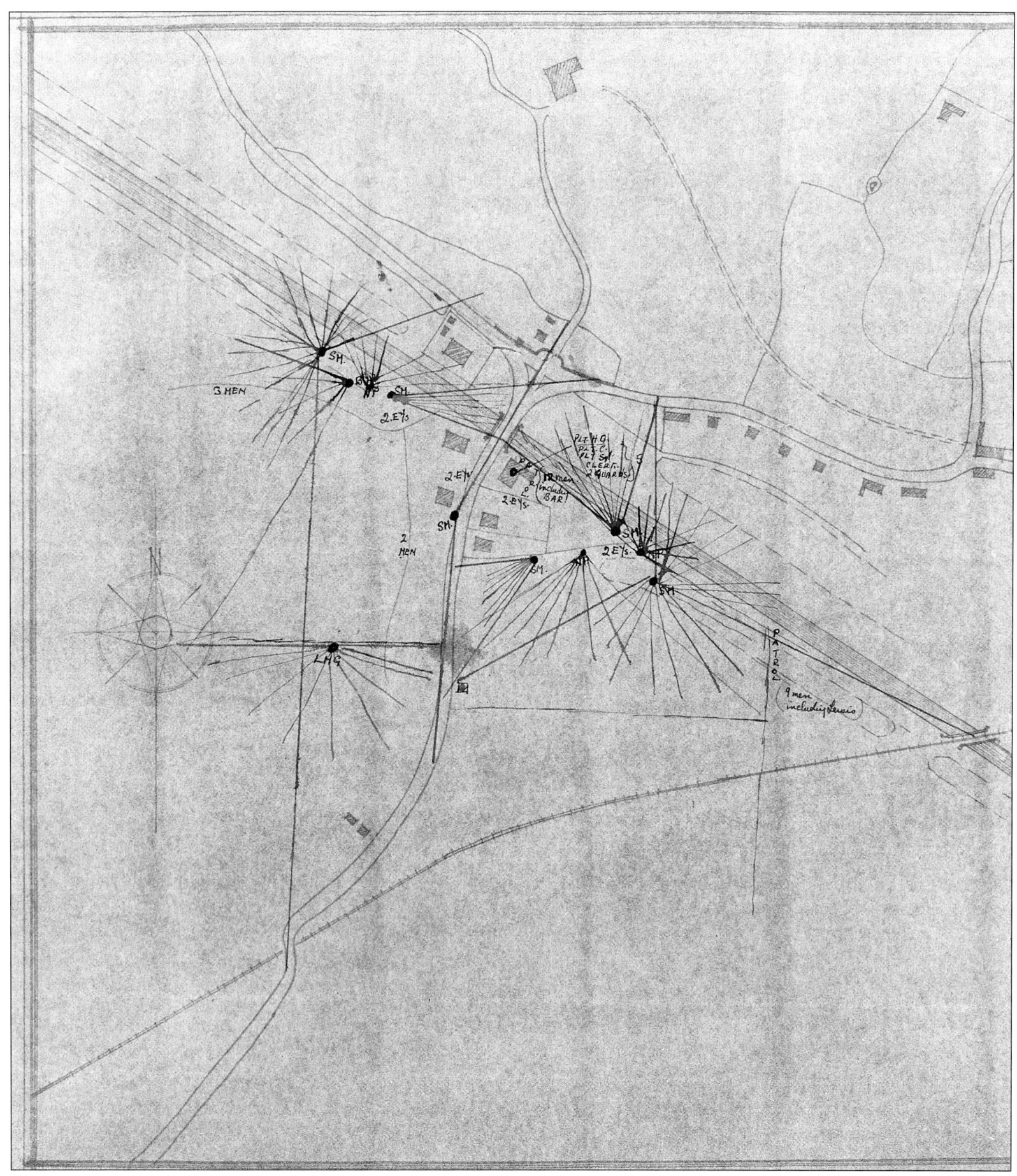

(left) One of the few defence plans to have survived. Here plans have been made for the defence of the Nodal Point at The Silver Fish *on the Bridgwater-Street road where the A39 crosses the King's Sedgemoor Drain.*

Notes attached to the plan show that 74 men would have fought and died in order to prevent the enemy advance. The weapons listed are six Spigot Mortars (18 men), three Northover Projectors (6 men), two Light machine guns (6 men), six E.Y. rifles (10 men) and one B.H. (2 men). The meaning of the abbreviation B.H. is uncertain. Possibly, in view of its location, it could have been a Browning machine gun, emplaced to give protection to the Spigot Mortar and Northover Projector teams. (Author's collection)

PURITON HOME GUARD

By its size Puriton would no doubt have had at least its own Home Guard Section but detailed information has not been forthcoming. However, David Howe of Puriton was a member of this unit and recalls that their rifle range was situated in a quarry to the south of the village at map ref. ST 307 411. The Observation Post was on the ridge to the south where a 'steam roller' hut to the north of Ashen Covert provided shelter. Meetings took place in the village hall on Thursday evenings and Sunday mornings. The hall was also used for keeping stores.

Burtle Platoon.
Left to right: Walter Clark; Nelson Moxey; Norman Moxey; Frank Lee; Hubert 'Taffy' Rice; Charlie Sandford; Alan Moxey Jnr.; Victor Leigh; Ralph Pollard; Alan Moxey Snr.; Sgt. Wilfred Parsons; Ray Court; Ivor Bell; Lt. J. de C. Pook (Platoon Commander); Alfred Hynam; Sgt. Roland Norris; Tom Willis; Walter Cook; Edward Cox; Charles Tratt; Arnold Tucker; Victor Pollard; Bill Vowles; Unknown

It has been suggested that the existence of the signpost indicates an early photograph. However, work to remove signposts and direction indicators nationally commenced on Wednesday 29th May 1940, two weeks after the formation of the L.D.V. – hardly time for the L.D.V. to receive even their brassards. It is more likely that this photograph was taken in 1944 when the invasion threat was over and signs were being replaced. In June 1943 the government had announced that signposts could be replaced in most rural areas. (Eileen Moxey collection)

Lt. Pook's notes have survived the years and included an attendance list of members for the four weeks up to 2.5.43 which has been reproduced below, together with subsequent additions of their civilian occupations where known:

Sgt. Wilfred Parsons (railway); Sgt. Norris (*The First and Last* Public House); Cpl. W.F. Lee; Pte. Tratt; A. Moxey; T. Fisher; J. Fewings (farmer, Robins Lane); Ivor Bell (farmer, Burtle Road); Moxey; A.J. Norris; Francis Fisher; Cpl. N.R. Moxey (*The Railway Inn*); Pte. Norman A. Moxey; Len Hayes (farmer, Burtle Road); Freddie Coombes; Ern Gillard (farmworker); William Vowles (porter at Edington and signalman at Shapwick Stations); E. Grant; Harry Moxey (farmer, opposite *Burtle Inn*); Reg Thyer; B. Tidball; R. Gillard (lorry driver); Vic Tidball; F. Vowles; Cpl. Norris; Pte. T. Willis; Vic Pollard; Ralph Pollard (farmer, Robins Lane); E. Cox; Charlie Sandford; J. Tyler; Cpl. Harry Sweetland (signalman); H. Rice; V. Cook; A.E. Trynan; E. Millett; W. Clarke; M. Watts; A.F. Pollard; A.W. Smith and R. Cox

Lt. Pook's notes also show that even a desolate spot such as Burtle was part of an overall defence plan. Estimated platoon strength was 39 with help from 9 members of the 22nd Division. Deployment was to have been as follows:

H.Q.	Station Master's Office or Station Farm
Lt. J. de C. Pook	
Sgt. W. Parsons	
Cpl. Sweetland (i/c First Aid)	
Pte. S. Tyler	Clerical duties
Pte. A.F. Pollard, Pte. A.W. Smith	Cooks – Railway Hotel or Field Kitchen at Station Farm
Pte. T. Willis, Pte. R. Thyer	Motorcycle D.R.s, one at Company H.Q., Woolavington and one at Platoon H.Q.
Guides: Pte. R.R. Cox	at Post Office
Pte. V. Tidball	alternately
and one from 22nd Division.	

South Post
Cpl. W. Cox	Commander
Pte. L. Hayes (later replaced by Cpl. A.J. Norris)	L.M.G. in 'Sunnyside', second window from road first floor
V. Pollard, I. Bell	Machine Gunners
Pte. F. Vowles, Pte. Fisher, R. Pollard	E.Y. Rifle
and one from 22nd Division	

East Post
Cpl. A.C. Norris	Commander
L/Cpl. W.F. Lee, Pte. J. Fewings, Pte. C. Sandford, B. Tidball	Browning Automatic Rifle
3 men	Northover Projector
2 men and 2 from 22nd Division	Northwest Post
8 men and 2 from 22nd Division	Spigot Mortar
5 men and 3 from 22nd Division	Mobile and Reserve

Subsequent notes show that the South Post was moved to "North of the Canal in Station Yard".

'Sunnyside' was to be the location of the Lewis gun, but where was 'Sunnyside'? No properties exist of that name now but a chance remark revealed it was the cottage just to the south of the Railway Level Crossing.

In addition Mobile Reserve was to provide two men for the observation point in the Railway Hut. Lt. Pook's mention of men from the 22nd Division refers to members of the Railway Home Guard, the 22nd Devonshire (5th S.R.) Battalion Home Guard.

'Sunnyside', probably in the 1960s. It was from the upstairs bedroom window that the brave men of Burtle Platoon, probably surrounded and outnumbered, would have poured withering fire on the enemy advancing across the moor from Edington until ammunition ran out. Mrs. Fry, née Gillard, remembers as a girl living in 'Sunnyside' being told never to go in the cupboard under the stairs – probably the home of the platoon's machine gun and ammunition. Note Edington Junction Station's canopy on the left of the shot. For an evocative photograph of the station see Alan Hammond's Heart of the Somerset & Dorset Railway. *(Mike Fry collection)*

(left) Private Charles Tratt and, on the right, his son-in-law Nelson Rufus Moxey. (Eileen Moxey collection)

Burtle Home Guard held a Stand Down Dance which raised £50.00 for The Red Cross Prisoner of War Fund. It was to be some nine months after the Stand Down of the Home Guard before the war ended and P.O.W.s in the Far East were released.

The eastern flank of Polden Company was protected by East Polden Platoon under the command of Lt. H. Poole of Council House, Ashcott. His 2nd in command was 2nd Lt. L. Hall. Their defended locality was *The Piper's Inn* at grid ref. 5877576 (this appears to be a typing error; the more likely reference being 877576).

Donald Board was a member of Lt. J. de C. Pook's platoon, living at Chilton Polden. Names that come to mind in the Home Guard are the local vicar, the Revd. A. Young, Major Wardell, Ralph Board, E.J. Pike, F. Cox, J. Jamieson, Mr. Hibberd and Mr. Stone. Sergeants Timbrell and Lawrence were the N.C.O.s. The observation post for the unit was the tower at The Priory, Chilton Polden, just to the north of the A39. Their rifle ranges were at *The White Hart*, Chilton Polden and at Cossington Quarry, now filled in. Their grenade range was at Socombe Hill, Edington.

In September 1943 Donald joined the R.A.F. where he trained as a flight engineer. In August 1944 he was posted to No. 419 (The Moose) Squadron Royal Canadian Air Force based at Middleton St. George, Doncaster, flying Halifax Bombers. Donald was the only Englishman in his crew. On the night of 20th-21st January 1945 he was returning from a raid on Magdeburg, his ninth operation, when JD420, VE-D, his plane, was hit by flack above Oldenburg. The navigator was killed outright, the pilot was wounded and lost the use of his right arm and the bomb-aimer was also wounded.

The aircraft was considerably damaged on the port wing. Two engines and the radio were wrecked together with, Don suspects, the escape dinghy. In the pitch dark Don and his crew, apart from the navigator, baled out and landed safely. After capture and a three day journey in cattle trucks Don arrived at Stalag IV B. Liberated by the Russians on 20th April 1945, Don arrived home in time to celebrate his 27th birthday on 22nd May. Not all Bomber Command aircrew were so lucky; more than 50,000 were killed on operations.

Eric Solomon was an employee of Wilts United Dairies at Bason Bridge, East Huntspill. The factory had its own Home Guard Section which guarded the factory railway sidings and the bridges over the River Brue. Section members included W. Salvidge, G. Hector, L. Skuse and E. Perkins. Their N.C.O. was Sgt. G. Vowles whilst the senior officer was a Captain Greener. In the Bridgwater Battalion a Lt. W.J. Greener is identified whilst the last C/O of Polden Company is a Major W.J. Greener. No doubt Eric's section was part of Polden Company.

When vast quantities of grease-encrusted American P17 rifles arrived many Home Guards spent hours cleaning the grease off. Not so with the Wilts United Dairies section. The rifles were placed in the Sterilising Room steam cages – the result, spotless rifles in double-quick time.

NO. 5 (BRIDGWATER) COMPANY

COMMANDING OFFICER	Major W.H. Tamlyn, M.B.E., M.C.
2ND IN COMMAND	Capt. J.W. Moon
	(Capt. A.H. Jones)
COMPANY QUARTERMASTER	Capt. M. Barnett
	Lt. H.S. Pole
INTELLIGENCE OFFICER	Lt. W.H. Pollard
LIAISON OFFICER	Lt. W.I.E. Lane, M.C.

Officers of No. 5 Bridgwater Company.
Back Row: Lt. W.H. Pollard (builder); 2nd Lt. P.S. Huggins (No. 2 Platoon) (jeweller); 2nd Lt. H. Pitman (No. 1 Platoon); Lt. F. Greenhalgh (No. 9 Platoon)
Middle Row: Lt. S.V. Hardiman (No. 3 Platoon); Lt. G. Brimson (No. 4 Platoon); Lt. W.I.E. Lane, M.C. (gentlemen's outfitter); Lt. E.H. Pearce (No. 3 Platoon, owner of Bridgwater Motor Company); Lt. H.S. Pole; 2nd Lt. M. Vinnicombe (No. 5 Platoon)
Front Row: Lt. P.H. Bradbury, M.C. (No. 6 Platoon); Capt. J.W. Moon (optician); Major W.H. Tamlyn, M.C.; Lt. E. Wills (No. 2 Platoon, owner of Kingsley Art Furniture); Lt. A. Biddiscombe, M.M. (No. 4 Platoon, furniture shop proprietor)
(Michael Chamberlin collection)

Identified in Major Tamlyn's book, Stand Easy, *as **Sergeants of Bridgwater Company**, 1943.*
Back Row: No. 12 Sgt. John 'Jack' Lock
Middle Row: No. 1 Mr. Harold Hawkes; No. 6 Sgt. Sidney Owen;
  No. 13 Sgt. S. Hardiman
Front Row: No. 1 Sgt. Phil Huggins; No. 3 Sgt. Bob Bryant; No. 4 C.S.M.
  H.T. Harvey; No. 5 C.S.M. Harold Paling; No. 6 Major Tamlyn;
  No. 7 Capt. A.H. Jones; No. 8 Colour-Sergeant Leonard F. Hutchins
Harold Hawkes, a resident of Barclay Street, Bridgwater, was torpedoed in the First World War, spending seven days in an open boat. (Philip Owen collection)

When the above photograph appeared in the *Bridgwater Mercury*, Patrick Harvey contacted the author as follows:

C.S.M. H.T. Harvey was my father, living at 184, Bath Road. In WW1 he was a R.N. Writer. At the time the photograph was taken he was about 47 years old and a commercial traveller for Allison's Flour which I think made exercises quite strenuous for him. As a five- or six-year-old I can recall him removing his army boots and his feet being all bloody after some route march. People who look on the Home Guard as a bit of a joke have no idea how dedicated some of these chaps were.

After the War C.S.M. Harold Paling's marching days were not over as he was selected to march in the Queen's Coronation Parade.

Sergeant Sidney Owen, born in 1892, moved from London to Bridgwater with Hobson's Aircraft Components Ltd., whose premises were later occupied by Bridgwater Motor Company. A new Platoon, No. 9, was raised from Hobson's employees. Other No. 9 N.C.O.s included Q.M.S. W.R. Spiffle, Sgt. F.J. Hinds and Sgt. W.A. Francis.

On Sunday 16th May 1943 the Home Guard throughout the United Kingdom celebrated the completion of its third year. Bridgwater Battalion held its Anniversary Parade which included a march past of all the companies, the salute being taken by Major General G.M. Lindsay, C.B., C.M.G., D.S.O. A series of photographs was taken of the march past, and copies of these were mounted in the personal photograph album of Lt. Col. Chamberlin. The author is indebted to his son Michael, for permission to reproduce them. Unfortunately, they were not captioned but three of the series are reproduced here. The appearance of Smith guns in the photograph on the right suggest that this may well be part of Headquarters Company.

Two of the series of photographs showing the march past of two of the platoons of **Bridgwater Battalion** *on 16th May 1943. (Michael Chamberlin collection)*

No. 1 Platoon Bridgwater Company. Only some of those in the 5th Row have been identified. They are as follows: No. 8 Lt. J.W. Moon; No. 9 Lt. W.I.E. Lane, M.C.; No. 10 C.S.M. H.T. Harvey and No. 13 Sgt. R. Bryant.
   The following were also officers of the platoon: 2nd Lt. V.E. Gumbrell, 2nd Lt. H.W. Van Trump and 2nd Lt. H. Pitman.

The Platoon Quartermaster Sergeant was E.J. Sloman. Other sergeants at Stand Down were W. Bradford, R. Bryant, W.J. Hurford, C.E. Holman, P. Nosworthy, H. Pollard, H.V. Sharkey and M.G. Sharkey.
(Patrick Harvey collection)

No. 1 Platoon, led by Lt. W.I.E. Lane, marches over the Town Bridge in Bridgwater. Unlike other photographs taken in the town the men are unarmed. Could this be a V.E. or V.J. Parade?
(Author's collection)

No. 2 Platoon Bridgwater Company. Those who have been identified are listed by the numbers on the key to the right, including their occupations where these are known.
No. 5 Jack Adams; No. 7 F.J. Ashman (gravedigger); No. 14 L.B. Addicott; No. 20 Reg Marker; No. 22 R.T. Woolaway; No. 36 Walter Rugg (withy worker); No. 41 Harry Cooze (hairdresser); No. 42 C. Perry; No. 43 Stan (or Jack) Lock; No. 44 L/Cpl. Robert Lee (printer); No. 48 Bill Hobbs; No. 49 Mr. Gaylor; No. 50 Andrew Kelly; No. 51 Ernie Pitman; No. 52 H.V.A. Rowles;

The original Platoon Roll for late 1942 has survived together with the platoon's proposed deployment in case of attack:

NO. 1 SECTION	NO. 2 SECTION	NO. 3 SECTION		NO. 4 SECTION
Sgt. HUGGINS, P.S.	Sgt. ROOKE, S.J.	Sgt. RABJOHNS, F.G.	PAYNE, F.J.	Sgt. LOCK, J.
Sgt. VARNEY, R.	Sgt. LEE, W.R.	Sgt. PITMAN, E.W.	PROSSER, L.W.	Sgt. HAWKINS, H.
Cpl. ADDICOTT, L.B.	BAILEY, S.B.	Cpl. WINTER, B.	DAY, E.	L/Cpl. BAKER, R.J.G.
Cpl. KELLY, A.M.	COWARD, S.W.	L/Cpl. WINTER B.	MITCHELL, N.	BROOM, D.
L/Cpl. STEER, P.W.	CROKER, W.H.	Vol. RYCROFT, G.	STOODLEY, C.H.	BROOM, E.G.
Vol. DICKENSON, H.	GAYLOR, A.E.	OWENS, T.J.	SPRANKLING, E.R.	DANDO, J.T.
CHILVERS, W.	GAYLOR, H.G.	RAWLINSON, E.	WOOLAWAY, R.T.	DAVIES, F.R.
BEECHEY, E.T.	GUIAS, C.F.	ROWLES, R.	HESMER, D.	FARRANCE, H.W.
HOWELL, C.N.	HAGGETT, W.A.	CULVERWELL, R.	PAISEY, J.J.	GARDENER, J.
CROMPTON, R.	HODGES, R.V.	DYER, W.	HESMER, D.	Cpl. HOBBS, W.J.
ASHMAN, F.J.	HOLDERNESS, G.	WILLIAMS, C.A.E.	HURFORD, F.J.	LEWIS, L.A.
ASHMAN H.F.	HOLMAN, K.	RUGG, W.J.	NEWBURY, R.J.	MARKER, R.C.D.
ROGERS, W.R.	HUTCHINGS, L.F.	BAKER, R.E.	CORNISH, W.	RAWLE, D.V.
LOCK, S.	STUART, N.	SHARKEY, W.J.	BELL, K.G.	SAUNDERS, G.
GRAY, L.	Cpl. PERCY, F.	HAM, P.R.	COLLIER, J.	SCONE, R.A.G.
DAY, R.	PERRY, C.	PROSSER, H.J.	DAVEY, C.R.	SCOTT, F.R.
BOWYER, H.J.	PRING, R.	PROSSER, C.H.	ESCOTT, C.R.	SEALEY, D.D.G.
DART, R.C.	ROSE, R.A.	SPENDER, M.D.T.	HOBBS, D.H.W.	BELL, H.G.
FERNIE, J.	ROWLES, H.V.A.	COLEMAN, C.	JAMES, CLIFFORD	SHAPTER, S.E.
ROWLES, W.T.	SPOORS, J.	PALMER, R.C.B.	KEARLE, E.J.	THORNE, W.J.
STONE, F.	WALTER, C.J.	FINCH, N.R.	STOODLEY, CHAS.	WARREN, E.L.
BURNETT, G.H.	Sgt. WARNER, G.H.C.	REDMAN, C.E.	STOODLEY, C.H.	BELL, K.
WHITE, E.N.	WEBBER, W.L.	BAILEY, L.J.	DAY, R.D.	WARREN, G.
CHIVERS, J.H.	NORMAN, S.	GREEN, K.	SALISBURY, W.T.	LETHAM, D.
HEAVERY, B.J.	BERRY	HOOPER, K.M.	RENDLE, G.	BAKER, D.W.J.
MORGAN, F.	CROUCH, E.J.	PERKS, A.C.	FACEY, R.	SETTER, H.J.
BAKER, R.F.	BOTTLE, H.A.	STONE, H.		SYMONDS, W.J.
HARRIES, R.F.	KENDLE, N.C.			SEARLE, H.
	DAY, R.			CREEDY, D.
				STOODLEY, C.H.
				STOODLEY, CHAS.

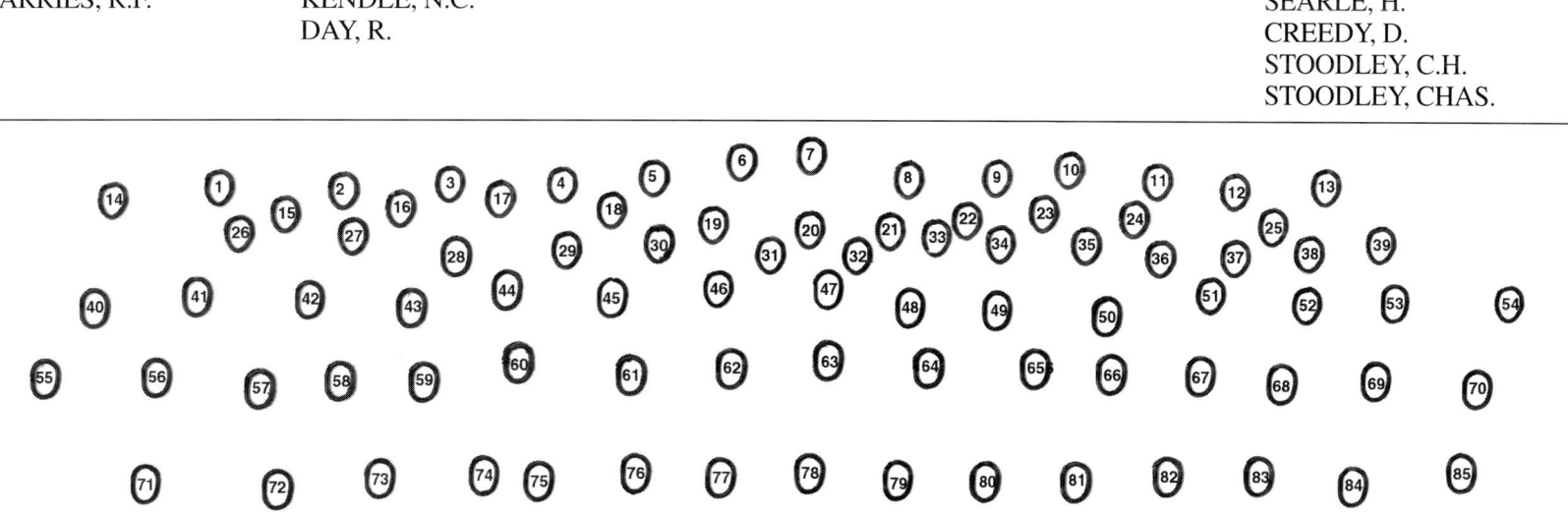

Key to photograph on previous page and names below

No. 57 Sgt. Jack Lock; No. 60 C.S.M. T. Davey (employed at the Royal Ordnance Factory, Puriton); No. 61 Lt. Edward Wills; No. 62 Major W.H. Tamlyn (auctioneer); No. 63 Lt. Col. R. Chamberlin (owner of Quantock Preserving Company); No. 64 Capt. Arthur H. Jones (accountant);

No. 65 Lt. E.R. Gregory (accountant); No. 67 Sgt. (later 2nd Lt.) P.S. Huggins; No. 75 H.W. Farrance; No. 77 Mr. Bond; No. 81 Mr. Horseman (schoolmaster)
(Brian Wills collection)

The disposition of the four Sections and individual responsibilities were listed as follows:

BRISTOL ROAD LOCALITY – NOS. 1 AND 3 SECTIONS

Patrolmen and Bombers
Cpl. Winter
Vols. Howell
       S. Lock
       White

Northover Gun
Redman
D. Hesmer

Vickers Gun
Sgt. Rabjohns
L/Cpl. B. Winter
Vol. Sprankling
     R.C. Palmer
     Chilvers
     E.N. White
     F. Hurford

Pill Box
Lewis Gun
Sgt. Pitman
Vol. Perks
     Cornish
     Hooper
     Day
Riflemen Rycroft
         Coleman
         Woolaway
         H.F. Ashman

Leggar Road – Browning Gun
Cpl. Addicott
Vol. Ham
     Dickenson
     Dart
     Mitchell
     Green

Castlefields – Pill Box 'A' Post
Vol. Sharkey
     Rogers
     E. Hesmer
     Bowyer

Lewis Gun – 'B' Post
Sgt. Varney
Vol. Owens
     Finch
     C. Williams
     F.G. Ashman
     H.T. Rowles

'C' Post
L/Cpl. Steer
Vol. Crompton
     R. Day
     F. Stone

DRAWBRIDGE LOCALITY – NOS. 2 AND 4 SECTIONS

Drawbridge Locality
No. 1 Post - Lewis Guns
L/Cpl. H.G. Gaylor
Vol. Holman
Vol. Norman
Vol. Haggett
Vol. Hodges
Vol. A.E. Gaylor

Barhams Yard – Browning Gun
Cpl. Hobbs
Vol. Rose
Vol. Croker
Vol. Rowles
Vol. Spoors
Vol. Chas. Stoodley

Outside Post - Browning Gun
Cpl. Percy
Vol. Perry
Vol. Bailey
Vol. Pring
Vol. Coward
Vol. W.L. Webber.
     F.R. Scott
     D. Letham

Clink Post – Lewis Gun
Cpl. Baker
Vol. Marker
Vol. E. Warren
Vol. Baker
Vol. Gardener
Vol. Thorne
Vol. Farrance

C.F. Guias – Post Runner

Lt. Wills's notes also included some 70 men held in reserve including R. Culverwell and C.R. Escott who were listed as dispatch riders.

No. 2 Platoon Bridgwater Company, probably taken in December 1944.
Back Row: No. 1 Thurston Walter Patten (plumber); No. 2 Cecil Parker (joined Somerset L.I.); No. 3 Ernie Wegg, (Manager of Bridgwater Gas Light Co. shop in High Street); No. 4 Reginald Baker (storeman for Thompsons Ironmongers); No. 7 Raymond George Beard (worked for Bristol Wire Ropes); No. 8 Mr. W.J. Sharkey, (council drains and sewage worker); No. 9 H.V.A. Rowles; No. 11 Bert Bailey (employed by Thompsons Ironmongers); No. 12 Bertie Cecil Hill (painter and decorator)
Second Row: No. 2 Mr. R.T. Woolaway; No. 4 Mr. Gaylor; No. 5 Andrew Kelly (owner of the tea kiosk on the Town Bridge); No. 6 Ernie Pitman; No. 8 Mr. C. Perry; No. 9 Mr. Dando; No. 10 Bill Hobbs (ran dry cleaners on West Key)
Third Row: No. 1 Sgt. Bill Lee (printer); No. 2 Sgt. A.T. Escott, (grocer in Victoria Road); No. 3 Sgt. Len B. Addicott (employed by Thompsons Ironmongers); No. 4 Sgt. J. Lock (service engineer for Winkworths); No. 5 2nd Lt. P.S. Huggins (jeweller in St. Mary Street); No. 6 Lt. E. Wills; No. 8 Sgt. Bert Winter (worked at Quantock Preserves); No. 10 Cpl. Arthur Wilson; No. 11 Edgar Warren (solicitors' clerk)
Front Row: No. 1 Stan or Jack Lock; No. 4 L/Cpl. William Thorne (withy worker in West Street)
Other N.C.O.s were Sgts. D. Broom, H.G. Bell, C. Percy and F.G. Rabjohns. (Michael Chamberlin collection)

Ralph Scorey, born on 21st September 1924, had been a pupil at a London nautical college and was one of many children evacuated to Bridgwater. He eventually found lodgings in Kendale Road with Mr. Street, a Bridgwater butcher and his family. Having been less than honest about his age (Ralph being only 15) he was accepted into No. 2 Platoon. His memories were typical of many of those who joined in the early days, night-time guard duties at the local reservoir, sharing one rifle and having no uniform. In 1941, aged 17, Ralph joined the Merchant Navy, serving on Eagle Oil Tankers. He was torpedoed twice and spent a considerable part of the war in Barbados and Atlanta, U.S.A., waiting for his ships to be made seaworthy. Marrying his ex-landlord's daughter in 1951, Ralph spent his lifetime in the Merchant Navy. He passed away in the early 1990s. In his possessions were found a fine studio photograph of himself aged about 16 (*right*), resplendent in his Home Guard uniform, together with an invitation to a Christmas get-together and greetings card, both composed by Lt. Edward Wills, his Platoon Commander.

(all items from Rosemary Oram collection)

HOME GUARD.
No. 5 Bridgwater Company.
No. 2 Platoon.

Men of No. 2 Platoon,
   Your Platoon Officers send you—
   CHRISTMAS GREETINGS.

The best Message we can send you is that spoken by His Majesty the King:—

   "Put into your task, whatever it may be, all the courage and purpose of which you are capable.
   Keep your hearts proud and your resolve unshaken.
   Let us go forward to the task as one man, a smile on our lips, and our heads held high and with God's help we shall not fail."
                                    May, 1940.

We hope the coming year will bring us an honourable Peace but, should Duty call us, let us make at least one resolve to attend regularly and make ourselves fully efficient.
   IT IS OUR DUTY !
Keep your Hearts Proud—We are proud of you.
   Yours sincerely,
EDWARD WILLS,   ::   E. R. GREGORY,
   O/C.   Asst. O/C.
                                    CHRISTMAS, 1940.

HOME GUARD
No. 5 Bridgwater Company.
No. 2 Platoon.

Men of No. 2 Platoon,
   On Wednesday, 18th December, 1940, we are having a Social Evening at the Westover School.
   There will be Music, Games, Dancing, Refreshments and Cigarettes. Commencing 7 p.m. Admission Free.
   We hope every member of the Platoon will attend and bring one friend (either sex) but no children.
   Pack up your troubles for a few hours and have a care-free evening. Uniform to be worn.
                         Yours faithfully,
                              EDWARD WILLS,
                                    O/C No. 2 Platoon.

(right) 16th May 1943 and Lt. W.R. Pettitt leads his men past the saluting base in Bridgwater High Street. Note the Spigot Mortars lined up and the Browning machine gun behind. The salute is being taken by Major General G.M. Lindsay, C.B., C.M.G, D.S.O., the Deputy Regional Commissioner. After the six Companies marched past, the Battalion was formed up and a demonstration of all weapons was given in Bridgwater Fairfield. Lt. W.R. Pettitt was the manager of The National Provincial Bank at 23, Fore Street from 1942-1960, living above the bank in a flat which even boasted a garden.

Mr. Pettitt's son Michael remembers a large pike being kept behind the dining room door. This was not the only weapon on the premises. Apart from Lt. Pettitt's service revolver, he kept another pistol in his drawer in the manager's office! (Michael Pettitt collection)

(left) No doubt the reader would have heard of reference to the Home Guard pikes. Apart from an issue in 1942 consisting of redundant bayonets welded onto steel tubes, promptly hidden by the Quartermasters, 1940 saw the issue of genuine War Department pikes to Home Guard units. On the Stand Down of Bridgwater Battalion in 1944 some found their way into private hands and the photograph below shows Lt. Col Chamberlin's granddaughter with such a weapon. Measuring 5' 11" long, complete with a W.D. stamp, it looks a fearsome weapon. (Author's collection)

(right) Taken by the same photographer as above, another platoon marches past. Close examination shows a metal disc resembling a coolie hat between the daïs and the drum. This is one of the wheels of a Smith gun, a weapon with which Bridgwater Battalion was issued. The gun would be turned on its side before firing so that one wheel served as a turntable, the other wheel providing some overhead protection for the crew. (Michael Pettitt collection)

Reg Marker joined No. 2 Platoon in 1941. His fellow privates included F. Davies, E. Warren, W. Thorne, E. Lewis, H. Lewis, G. Harris and G. Gibbs, the Platoon Scout. Sgt. Lock and Cpl. Hobbs were platoon N.C.O.s. Guard duties, carried out twice a week, included guarding Bridgwater Telephone Exchange and Durleigh Reservoir. At the time Reg lived at his parents' home at 24, Chilton Street where the section Lewis gun was kept under his bed. A lodger and fellow platoon member at No. 24 was Mr. Davies who worked at the Royal Ordnance Factory in Puriton. He was the No. 2 on the Lewis gun. One memory Reg will never forget was the exhortation not to waste ammunition. This was at a time when only five rounds per rifle were available and precious little more for the Lewis gun whose magazine capacity was 47 or 97 rounds, depending on its pattern.

In July 1942 Reg joined the Royal Marines. After basic training in England including a spell on *H.M.S. Raven* at Southampton Airport, he was posted to Ceylon with 11 Detachment R.M. He was then sent as part of the defence force to the Cocos Islands which had already suffered air raids from the Japanese ensconced on nearby Christmas Island. Fortunately for Reg, who at one time was on an island ½ mile x 500 yards, there was no invasion.

No. 3 Platoon in 1945. Only a few faces have been identified, as follows:
Third Row: No. 2 L/Cpl. C.E. King
Front Row: No. 1 Cpl. Harry J. Day; No. 6 Lt. E.H. Pearce; No. 7 Lt. S.V. Hardiman; No. 8 Sgt. E.H. Chalk

George Lush was a butcher and slaughterman for Ellicot, Bridgwater Butchers. Sadly, he passed away at the age of 52. Harry Day was a leather merchant with premises in Court Street, Bridgwater. During the war he sold considerable quantities of leather to Italian prisoners of war who made them into items such as handbags which they could sell or barter.

Other Platoon officers at various stages were Lt. D.G. Avery, Lt. K.B. Williams and Lt. R.M. Rowley.

Other N.C.O.s included Q.M.S. A.W. Beavan, Sgts. F. Betty, H. Bold, H.W. Crocker, S.F. Evans, H. Sparkes, B. Turner, A.H. Tratham and F.W. Welsh.
(Mrs. W.M. Pearce collection)

1942 and a triumphant **'A' Section No. 3 Platoon** display their trophies. The blackboard reads:
  10th Som (Bridgwater) Home Guard
  1942
  Rifle Competition Cup Winners
  'A' Section No. 3 Platoon
  Ptes R. Young, M. Rainey, R. King, E. Tilley,
  Cpl. C.T. Husband, Sgt. S. Hardiman, L/Cpl. C.E. King,
  Sgt. E.H. Chalk
  (Section Leader)
(William Husband collection)

3rd December 1944. A fine photograph of part of the Stand Down Parade at Bridgwater. The original photograph was endorsed by hand: "3rd Dec. **1944 Dispatch Riders 10th Som. Batt. Bridgwater Home Guard** at Bridgwater Stand Down Parade March Past at saluting base High Street Field Marshal Birdwood K.G.B. etc. taking the salute".
Front: Colour Sgt. R. Escott
Second Row: L/Cpl. Culverwell, L/Cpl. Jack Chappell, L/Cpl. Gardiner
Third Row: D/R Bryant, D/R Davy, D/R Farthing
Fourth Row: D/R Hancock
Fifth Row: D/R Humphreys, D/R Bradford, D/R Pope
Back Row: Sgt. Fred Sweet
(Gerald Escott collection)

(below) A fine line up of dispatch riders. Left to right are R. Escott or Mr. Ridgemount, Fred Sweet, Jack Chappell, Bob Bryant, Wally Humphreys and Mervyn Farthing.

One day the Battalion 2nd in Command Major Collum was talking to the dispatch riders in their garage in Chandos Street. Turning to Sgt. Escott he enquired: "Could you take me to Crowcombe Gate?" "Yes, sir", said Sgt. Escott, "now?" "No need", said the Major, "just testing". It was just as well he was "just testing" for as soon as he was out of earshot Sgt. Escott asked one of the other D.R.s: "Where the b….. hell is that?"

Bob Bryant was the machine shop foreman at Trojan Works, Colley Lane, which later became Wellworthy's. He was a keen motorcyclist taking part in London to Land's End trials.
(Mrs. Bowyer/Fred Sweet collection)

(above) Bridgwater dispatch riders relax at Langport rifle range. The only faces recognised are Fred Sweet, middle row right, and L/Cpl. C.E. King, front row right-hand side. Langport rifle range was built in the 19th century, realigned before the Second World War and still in use in the 21st century by the Naval Air Command and civilian rifle clubs. In addition to the Home Guard, thousands of conscripts and National Servicemen have fired their weapons here before departing to the four corners of the globe.
(Fred Sweet collection)

No. 6 (British Cellophane) Platoon.
Back Row: Ernie Moyse; Jim Talbot; Ivor Kingston; Bill Knight; Mr. Male; Unknown; Unknown; Len Kelly; Terry Sparkes; W. Kingston; Len Duddridge; Unknown; Jack Andrews; Charles Maunder; Arthur Collins
Second Row: Mr. Farrer; W. Stevens; J. Denman; Unknown; Unknown; Unknown; Sam Thomas; Unknown; Roy Bryant; Unknown; Unknown; Phil Shannon; Bill Budd; Mr. Chilcott
Third Row: Unknown; Sgt. C. Cottrell; Unknown; Sgt. Maurice Vinnicombe; Lt. Bradbury; Sgt. Bert Squires; Sgt. Stan Williams; Cpl. Ted Cave; Cpl. Tom Picton
Front Row: Jim Gower; L/Cpl. Ron Spearing; Cpl. M. Hooper; Cpl. M. Jarvis; Cpl. Jack Bodley; L/Cpl. S. Burge; Unknown
(Author's collection)

One occasion Charles Maunder remembers was when two Home Guards were returning very early in the morning from a night-time bridge guard in 1944. With the town deserted, they decided at the entrance to The Arcade in the High Street, to take a pot shot at the weather vane on the top of the steeple of St. Mary's Church. They then ran down the arcade, out of sight. Nothing was mentioned and no reports were received of a shot being fired in the town. Some 40 years later the steeple was being renovated and the local paper reported that two bullet holes were found in the weather vane, wondering how they got there. So did the Home Guards as they had only fired one shot!

The Platoon's armoury and stores was situated at Sydenham Manor, seen in the background of the photograph above. Weapons included Ross rifles, a Lewis machine gun and Sten guns, which replaced the one Tommy gun and a Spigot Mortar. .22 rifles were also available for target practice which took place on a range built in the grounds of the Manor which also provided space for a grenade practice range. The Platoon met on a regular basis two evenings per week in the evening plus a Sunday morning march down through the town to the T.A. Drill Hall for a Company muster.

*This photograph of **No. 6 Platoon** marching through Bridgwater, probably in the summer of 1943 was supplied by Charles Maunder. He joined the Home Guard on 7th May 1941 aged 17 and served until 31.12.44 when he left as a Lance Corporal. In 1945 he was called up and served as a Petty Officer in the Royal Navy.*
(Charles Maunder collection)

NO. 6 (SEDGEMOOR) COMPANY

COMMANDING OFFICER   Major R.M. Phelips   2ND IN COMMAND   Capt. E.F. Sherwood

*With no caption but with Major R.M. Phelips and Capt. Sherwood identified, this photograph could well be of members of **No. 6 (Sedgemoor) Company** whose battle headquarters was on the outskirts of Middlezoy. A visit to Greinton in the summer of 2003 confirmed that the photographer was standing on a hedge bank at map ref. ST 409 370 looking south towards West Town Farm. See below for the names of those identified. (Ann Meade collection)*

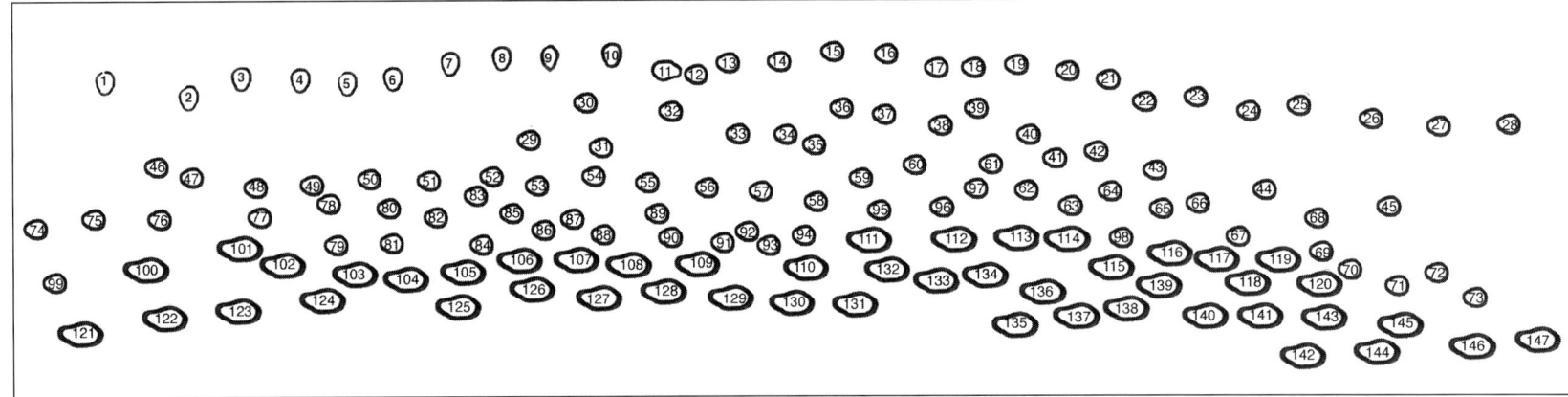

1. Charlie White	65-86. Unknown	110. Bert Peppard	131. Major Phelips
2. Unknown	87. Mr. Lowe	111-112. Unknown	(Commanding Officer)
3. Cecil May	88. Cecil Bown	113. C.S.M. C. Hall	132. Unknown
4-14. Unknown	89. Unknown	114. Mr. Musgrave	133. Lt. Col. Chamberlin
15. Norman John Burrow	90. Eddie Kidner	115. Henry Fry	(Battalion C/O)
16-31. Unknown	91. Horace Gillard	116-117. Unknown	134. Alfie Arnold
32. Mr. May (twin of No. 3)	92-97. Unknown	118. Fred Lock	135. Col. Collum
33. Mr. Keirle	98. R. Summers	119-120. Unknown	136. Unknown
34-39. Unknown	99-100. Unknown	121. Fred Sellick	137. Major Lyon Smith
40. Ted Groves	101. Bill Groves	122. Jim Pocock	(Battalion M.O.)
41. Leslie Groves	102. Unknown	123. Sidney Bawden or Mr. Bond	138. Unknown
42-46. Unknown	103. Frank Priddle	124. Unknown	139. Jack Gillard
47. Bill Tucker	104. Jack Churchill	125. C.Q.M.S. Murdock	140-141. Unknown
48-53. Unknown	105. Sidney Boobyer	126. Cpl. Jack Duddridge	142. Sgt. Howard Stafford
54. George Langford	106. Leonard Bagg	127. Sgt. Charles Lovibond	143-144. Unknown
55-62. Unknown	107. Roy Davey	128. Lt. William Lang	145. J. Hazel
63. Bert Gillard	108. Unknown	129. 2nd Lt. Victor Gumbrell	146. Unknown
64. Harry Burrows	109. Leonard Read	130. Capt. Sherwood	147. Mr. Pittey

MIDDLEZOY HOME GUARD

Although no photograph exists of members of Middlezoy Home Guard their initials are still recorded by their coat hooks at their wartime meeting place consisting of a room in the loft of a barn. Originally the loft had been converted for members of the Regular Army using boarding produced by sawing poplar trees felled at Westonzoyland Airfield. Never used as intended, the local Home Guard moved in. Photographed in May 2002, the initials of the following members were still visible by their coat hooks: Sgt. Charles Lovibond, Sgt. Stanley Atyeo, Cpl. Jack Duddridge, Cpl. Frank Pearce, Sgt. Howard Stafford, Harold Atyeo, L/Cpl. Ernest Bawden, Maurice Bown, Wesley Dorse, Alvin Dorse, Graham Dorse, Howard Davis (Dispatch Rider), Jack Davis, William Head, William 'Bill' Keirl, Wallace Martin, William Short. The Platoon Commander was Lt. Meade of Greinton who succeeded Lt. Jefferies of Othery on the latter's death. The Spigot Mortar was kept at Lt. Meade's farm. The Platoon stores were located in a Nissen hut in the south-east corner of a minor road junction at map ref. ST 379 337. This was not far from their rifle range at Sandpits Lane and the battle headquarters.

Platoon duties included assisting Regular Troops to man the searchlight on Knowleyards Hill and, with other platoons, to guard the railway bridge at Lyng. Vast quantities of barbed wire were stored at a local farm for constructing road blocks; never used, it was finally disposed of in the early 1990s.

(left) Bill Keirl, one of the members of Middlezoy Home Guard, poses by Sgt. Charles Lovibond's coat-hook. 58 years has elapsed since this coat-hook was used for what it was intended. (Author's collection)

(above) Cast in solid rubber and painted red, this is a practice No. 76 S.I.P. Grenade which would have been fired from the Platoon's Northover Projector. (Author's collection)

Parchey Platoon *photographed on Chedzoy Rectory Lawn in May 1944.*
Back Row: Privates W.H. Collard; G. Butt; E. Brooks; H. Overd; E. Triggol; F. Tucker; C. Cary; L. Gigg; A. Lockyer; H. Baker; D. Morse; H. Hill; F.G. Stone
Middle Row: Privates E. Clapp; W. Davies; M. Sullivan; L. Pinchen; W. Morgan; E. Hucker; G. House; L. Butcher; Herbert Ashford; F.C. Stone; A. Baker; G.C. Stone; A. Davies; F. Prowle
Front Row: L/Cpl. Chappel; Cpl. Stone; Cpl. Lampert; Sgt. Pomeroy; C.S.M. Timbrell; Lt. Fowler; Sgt. Guntripp; Sgt. Hanham; Cpl. B. Stokes; Cpl. Hooper; Cpl. S. Gigg
Sitting: Cadet Newton; Private H. Collard; Cadet Stokes

Close examination of the photograph shows Private E. Clapp is missing a thumb. This was caused when a shotgun barrel failed.
(Manor Inn collection)

Although close to Bridgwater, Parchey Platoon was part of Polden Company. Mr. Herbert Ashford was a member of the Platoon and recalls the Platoon manning a road block where the Chedzoy-Stawell road crossed over the King's Sedgemoor Drain. A weapon pit was dug here, perhaps for the Platoon's Northover Projector. The bridge was also prepared for demolition. Just to the west of the bridge a Flame Fougasse or Flame Trap was installed to further harass the invaders' advance.

BURROWBRIDGE HOME GUARD

Mr. L.W. Musgrave joined the Home Guard in 1940 as a member of Burrowbridge Platoon, Sedgemoor Company, whose area extended as far west as Lyng where a section of the Platoon was located. Stores were kept at Lyng Farm near the school whilst the armoury was situated at Aller Moor Pumping Station. Other members included Don Gillard, Frank Boobyer, Jack Gillard, Fred Lock, Jack Churchill, Jim Pocock, Fred Cox, Bill Watts and Roy Davey.

Platoon Commander was Lt. W. England with 2nd Lt. Houghton as his 2nd in command. Platoon Sergeant was Sgt. L.W. Musgrave. Sgt. H. Phillips was one of the section commanders whilst Cpls. Dyer, Pocock, Burrows and Cattle were other Platoon N.C.O.s.

A check-point was manned on Parrett Bridge whilst nearby Burrow Mump provided an ideal vantage point for 360-degree observation.

With few crossing points of the River Parrett between its estuary and its confluence with the River Tone, the bridge at Burrowbridge was of significant importance. A position was selected for a Vickers heavy machine gun on the slopes of Burrow Mump to cover the road from Taunton, firing on 'fixed lines'. A hut was also built at Burrow Mump for weapons instruction. This replaced an Anderson shelter in Mr. Musgrave's garden which had itself replaced the pumping station as a storage dump for ammunition and explosives.

Regular inspections by senior officers were quite common, the 'Top Brass' having a soft spot for the First World War veterans. On one occasion Burrowbridge Platoon was being inspected by the Battalion 2nd in Command. As he passed each man he was heard to ask: "How long have you been in, my man?" One of the 'other ranks' replied, "Since the creation, Sir!" Sgt. Musgrave heard a voice mutter, "He's older than Adam!"

WESTONZOYLAND PLATOON

Whilst no photograph has been found, Mr. E.W. Bury has kindly provided the following names of Platoon members: Cyril Aldridge, Ernest Allen, Howard Branfield, Sgt. Jack Brown, Eric Bury, Roland Bury, Jack Elworthy, Raymond Evans, Bert Gilbert, Leslie Heard, A. Lock, Ernest Mortimer, Sidney Mortimer, Ted Palmer, Sgt. Cecil Pitman, Denis Pople, Clem Reed, Ivor Reed, Ted Richards, Percy Rosewell, Cpl. Percy Spraggs, Percy Winslade. Robert Selway and the May twins are also known to have been members.

Mr. Bury was the Platoon's dispatch rider, using his own motorcycle. Before rifles were issued he had to make do with his own 12-bore shotgun for which he was issued with 'lethal ball' cartridges. Platoon Commander was Mr. Gumbrill – no doubt Lt. V.E. Gumbrell. Platoon duties included guarding the Railway Bridge at East Lyng – a duty shared with other platoons. Transport was provided to take the men to their posts in the form of a local coal lorry. Use was made of the training area at Greinton where Sidney Mortimer had a lucky escape when he accidentally dropped a live grenade. Quick-thinking by a Regular Sergeant and no doubt a seven-second fuse saved the day as there was time to pick up the grenade and throw it away.

Robert Heard was another member of the Platoon, serving as a messenger from 1943 to 1944. He adds:

"The meeting room was the Wesleyan School Room in Standards Road. Platoon members included H. Winn, E. Richards, O. Ling, M. Winn, V. London, Sgt. Bawden. The Platoon also had the use of an old double-decker bus which provided a shelter for the Home Guard at Lake Wall, watching across the wind-swept expanse of the Weston Level."

Not all Westonzoyland Home Guards survived the war. Cyril John Edwards Oldridge was called up and served in the 2nd Battalion The Devonshire Regiment. June 1944 saw him fighting in Normandy but his fight was to be short-lived when he lost his life on 8th June 1944, aged just 19. He was subsequently awarded a posthumous Military Medal. He lies at rest in Bayeux War Cemetery, plot 10, row H, grave 17.

Ralph Baker was a member of the Home Guard unit based at Stawell where they met at a room in The Grange. Other members were Wilfred Phillips, Walter Webber, Dick Hillman, Mr. Davis, Mr. White, Henry and John Stabbins, Robert Graham, Fred Vernon. N.C.O.s included Sgt. Phillips and L/Cpl. Baker. It is believed that members of this unit also included Moorlinch men. Their patrol area extended as far west as Parchey Bridge.

NO. 7 (ROYAL ORDNANCE FACTORY) COMPANY

COMMANDING OFFICER	Major G. Christopher	2ND IN COMMAND	Capt. J.C. Ford

*On the right are two photographs of **R.O.F. Company**. In the upper one, members pose outside the factory canteen. Only two have been identified. These are Sgt. Elijah Albert Gibbs, fourth row No. 10 (sitting cross legged) and Bernard Arthur Wilfred Fox, third row No. 11 (sitting). Sgt. Elijah Albert Gibbs was a Londoner who moved to work at R.O.F. Puriton during the war.*
(Author's collection)

A better quality photograph has enabled a few faces to be identified. Front Row: No. 6 Capt. J.C. Ford; No. 8 Lt. Col. R. Chamberlin; No 9 Major G. Christopher
The photograph was taken outside R.O.F. Puriton. Note a section of the perimeter palisade fence behind the Sergeant on the extreme right-hand side and factory buildings behind. This fence extended around the entire perimeter of the works and incorporated specially-designed pillboxes to provide enfilade fire along the outside of the fence line.
(Martin Bell collection)

NO. 8 (HEADQUARTERS) COMPANY

COMMANDING OFFICER   Major A.H. Jones   2ND IN COMMAND   Capt. W.R. Pettitt
(Major N.W.B.B. Thoms, C.B.E., D.S.O., M.C.)   (Capt. C.C. Harris)
(Major G.L. Lyon Smith)

No. 8 Headquarters Company. The only officer identified is that of Major G.L. Lyon Smith who was the first Commanding Officer of Headquarters Company. Nobody has been identified in the two back rows; others include the following:

Third Row: No. 1 D/R Jack Chappell; No. 2 D/R Mervyn Farthing; No. 21 D/R Wally Humphreys (bricklayer from Stogursey)
Fourth Row: No. 10 Major G.L. Lyon Smith; No. 15 Sgt. King
Front Row: No. 7 L/Cpl. Horace Stacey (carpenter)
(Author's collection)

2148 INDEPENDENT MOTOR TRANSPORT PLATOON

Originally the Motor Transport Platoon was part of Headquarters Company but on formation of Home Guard Motor Transport Units in 1942 it was taken out of the Battalion.

M.T. Platoons were formed to transport stores and ammunition. The members generally had access to vehicles, either their own or their employer's. This is exemplified by the employment details given below for the Bridgwater men featured in the next photograph. Most were either self-employed or worked in the transport industries. Lt. Rendle worked for Anderson and Wall whilst his 2nd in Command, 2nd Lt. Coles, owned a saw sharpening business in Ashleigh Avenue. Mr. Hamblyn drove for Combwich and District Farmers whilst Cyril Ridgment owned his own bus company comprising two vehicles. He subsequently sold his business to Western National and drove for them where he worked with Fred Harris. Len Wynn worked for Bridgwater U.D.C. on refuse collection, and Ben Lyon owned his own haulage business, employing Noah Godwin. Bown's Transport employed Fred Blake. Another well-known Bridgwater firm, G.T. Hodge, Corn Merchants, was owned by Rodney Hodge. G.C.J. Lush was a local butcher/slaughterman working for Ellicots. He lived with his wife and seven children in Chilton Street.

Jim Standerwick was a member of the family which owned J. Standerwick and Sons, builders of Taunton Road. The war saw a massive building programme undertaken throughout Somerset and local companies 'did their bit'. Jesse Carver, who worked for Wynns, coal merchants of Polden Street, was involved in hauling sand and other building materials from Dunball to Dunkerswell where an airfield was being built. By the time Jesse's fully laden lorry had ground its way up Blagdon Hill, to the south of Taunton, the radiator would be boiling merrily. A stop was needed here to enable the crew and vehicle to cool down. Invariably an impromptu game of football would follow, using Noah's bowler hat.

The Platoon's pride and joy was not a vehicle but a Bren gun Mk. I. It was the only unit to possess such an up-to-date weapon (introduced in 1937) in Bridgwater, which may explain its prominence in the photograph.

2148 Independent Motor Transport Platoon, *photographed at Eastover School, the Platoon's Headquarters.*

The framed photograph was presented to 2nd Lt. N.C. Rendle by the unit on the latter relinquishing command in September 1943. As a result of a 'tip-off' it was found languishing in a bric-à-brac shop in Dunster. Publicity provided by *The Bridgwater Mercury* resulted in the following names being supplied.

Back Row: Cyril Thomas Ridgment; Mr. Hamblyn; Unknown; Gilbert Cyril John 'George' Lush; Unknown; Jim Standerwick; Unknown; Jesse Edwin Carver; Owen Hughes; Len Wynn

Middle Row: Fred Harris; Unknown; Graham Rendle; Ben Lyon; Harold Redman; Unknown; A.H. Chard; George Burge; Bill Hancock; Noah Godwin; Ernest Buttle

Front Row: Unknown; Lionel George Palmer; Cpl. Harold Haydon; Sgt. Rodney Hodge; 2nd Lt. Coles; Lt. N.C. Rendle; Sgt. Jack Seymour; Tom Gardiner; Fred Blake; Tom Searle; Mr. Chedzoy

Close inspection of the photograph shows Graham Rendle's youthful features. This is explained as Graham lied about his age in order to enlist in the M.T. Platoon.

(Author's collection)

11th Somerset (Ilminster) Battalion

HEADQUARTERS Butts Farm, Ilminster
DATE FORMED April 1943
COMMANDING OFFICER Lt. Col. Thomas Washington-Metcalfe
2ND IN COMMAND Major J. Duke

H.Q. STAFF
A & Q OFFICER Capt. William H. Beeston, General List
ADJUTANT Capt. C.H. Moore, General List
AMMUNITION OFFICER Lt. L.G.H. Freeman
CAMOUFLAGE OFFICER Lt. Hugh Skeens
GAS OFFICER Lt. W.T. Gibson, O.B.E.
INTELLIGENCE OFFICER Capt. D.C. Maclean
LIAISON OFFICER 2nd Lt. W. Gundry (Police)
MEDICAL OFFICER Major F.R. Daniel
PHYSICAL TRAINING OFFR. Lt. F.T. Lawson
SIGNALS OFFICER Lt. H.H. Smith
TRANSPORT OFFICER 2nd Lt. W.H. Painter
WEAPONS TRAINING OFFR. 2nd Lt. L.J. Harris

Lt. Col. T. Washington Metcalfe
(Elizabeth Browning collection)

(above) **Headquarters Staff of the 11th Somerset (Ilminster) Battalion.**
Back Row: Lt. Lindole Hawkins; Unknown; Unknown; Sam Marshalsea
Middle Row: Unknown; Donald Maclean; Unknown; Unknown; Lt. Hugh Skeens; Capt. W.H. Beeston
Front Row: Mrs. Mary G. Beeston; Major J. Duke; Lt. Col. T. Washington Metcalfe; 2nd Lt. W. Gundry; Unknown
Hugh Skeen was well-suited to be the Battalion Camouflage Officer as he taught art at Ilminster Grammar School.
(Heritage of The Isle Trust collection)

On behalf of myself, this Headquarters, and the Battalion generally I wish most cordially to thank those ladies who have so enthusiastically served in the signal section, as telephonists, clerks, or in whatsoever capacity. The keenness they have displayed and the high standard they have reached in comparatively so short a time are most gratifying. Their attendance has been exemplary. They have indeed proved most valuable auxiliaries during the days of crisis, and may be assured that their work receives the very great appreciation it deserves. So, in view of the possible early disbandment of the Home Guard, I thank you one and all, and wish you all good luck.

Thomas Metcalfe
Lt. Col.
Comdg. 11th Somerset
(Ilminster) Bn. Home Guard

(left) The memo sent to Home Guard Auxiliaries by Thomas Washington-Metcalfe was instigated by a sudden announcement on the wireless on 6th September 1944 that all future Home Guard parades would be voluntary and operational duties were being suspended.
(Penelope Trott collection)

'A' (NORTH CURRY) COMPANY

COMMANDING OFFICER   Major L.J. Hembrow

2ND IN COMMAND   Capt. W.M. Yeo
(Capt. H.T. Copinger Hill, M.C.)

North Curry Platoon.
Back Row: H. Gridley; Charles Perry; J. Perry; J. Duke; H. Stevens; Edwin 'Ted' David; R. Loveridge; P. Wakley; F. Denman; H. Stenson; G. Stone; H. Bowey or R. Geanes
Second Row: B. Gridley; C.W. Dare; Jack Richards; A. Jeanes; Roy Barrington; E. Foster; Martin Derham; Dan Coate; W. Snook; J. (or P.) Sutton; Tom Spearing
Third Row: V. Pipe; Tom Wembridge; L/Cpl. F. Lewis; T. Harris; Ron Lane; Jack Garwell; A. (or H.) Derham; John Pine; Reg Lane; W. Wyatt; T. Priddle
Front Row: Cpl. C. Totterdell; Cpl. E. Bartram; Cpl. A.W. May; Sgt. J. Snook; Sgt. Edmund Duke; Lt. J.C. Peard; Sgt. F. Paull; Cpl. A. Bellringer; Cpl. R. (or D.) Hebditch; Cpl. S. Allen; Cpl. Cuthbert Duke or Cpl. Channing.
This photograph was taken in 1943 or earlier as Ted David and his wife Hazel, moved to Wearne, Langport, in that year, where he promptly joined Langport Home Guard. (Author's collection)

Parts of the earthworks of the Taunton-Chard Canal and Taunton-Chard Railway were incorporated into the Taunton Stop Line which ran from Bridgwater to Seaton through Wrantage. It was at this location that Ted David remembers practice sessions being carried out with a Spigot Mortar. Fortunately, no mishaps occurred unlike a Regular Army detachment nearby. Here, on the east side of the road, a concrete 6-pounder gun emplacement was built on top of the canal embankment facing west. On firing a practice round the shot passed clean through the roof of a nearby farmhouse!

(right) Ted David, featured in the photograph above, was a member of Knapp Section where he was responsible for the Lewis gun. He is shown here in 2002 standing by a row of anti-tank cubes built at the foot of the west side of the canal embankment at Wrantage. (Author's collection)

Stoke St. Gregory Platoon.
Back Row: L. Venn; E. Staple; B. Broom; B. Hembrow; B. David; F. Chedzoy; L. Chedzoy; F. Hembrow; E. Garland
Second Row: F. Hembrow; H. Adams; C. Keirle; D. House; L/Cpl. F. Chedzoy; Cpl. C. Doster; G. Hearn; Cpl. M. Garland; V. Boobyer; F. Stokes; S. Dare
Third Row: W. Dunell; A. Slade; C. Yarde; H. Cox; M. Morris; F. Coate; P. Peach; F. Duddridge; F. Champion; W. Musgrave
Fourth Row: S. Davie; A. Chedzoy; Sgt. A. Nicholas; 2nd Lt. P. Coate; Lt. P. Woodland; Sgt. G. Patten; L/Cpl. F. Frampton; M. Patten; S. Boobyer
Front Row: B. Hubbard; I. Keirle; C. Musgrove; L/Cpl. R. Staple; R. Boobyer; E. Chedzoy; V. Musgrove; J. Doster
As with many Home Guard Platoons, Stoke St. Gregory Platoon had a stores hut. This was at Meare Green at map ref. ST 337 264 on the north side of the road.
(The Rose and Crown, Woodhill, collection)

Arthur Yard joined Hatch Beauchamp unit on 18.7.42. He recalls that during the build up to D-Day, platoon duties included guarding the section of the main G.W.R. railway in the vicinity of Bull Place Farm on the minor road between Stoke St. Gregory and Stathe. To get to their post a cattle-truck was borrowed from either Mr. Patten or Mr. Badge. For shelter a bell tent was erected in the railway cutting. Food, in the form of milk and sandwiches, was provided by the farmer's wife at Bull Place Farm.

Church Parades took place at Curry Mallet Church under the command of Captain Yeo. On one occasion he was forced to miss the church parade. Whilst drilling the men in front of the church before the service he took two smart steps backwards and promptly fell into a muddy ditch!

Hatch Beauchamp Platoon
photographed outside Hatch Court.
Back Row: D. Beak; A. Woods; H. Manning; B. Bailey; N. Perry; E. Priddle; L. Groves; A. Meare; P. Cottell; S. Priddle
Second Row: Arthur Woods; Unknown; A. Yard; L. Perry; A. Newis; L/Cpl. F. Cousin; Unknown; L/Cpl. R. Coles; J. Dare; Unknown; F. Doble
Front Row: P. Matravers; Unknown; Cpl. D. Meare; Sgt. B. Oram; Capt. Fowler; Sgt. Baller; Cpl. Dibble; L/Cpl. F. Matravers; B. Bowey
While it is not known how many of the nine repeated surnames in the top photograph were related to each other, it is known that the photograph on the right shows three sets of brothers. These were members of the Perry, Priddle and Woods families.
(Arthur Charles Yard collection)

'B' (SOUTH PETHERTON) COMPANY

COMMANDING OFFICER   Major R.W. Beacham, M.C., O.B.E.
2ND IN COMMAND   Capt. A.W. Portal

(left) Lt. Col. Robert William Beacham, painted in Cairo in 1908. He had a long and varied career in the British Army. (Mrs. Bobye Hawes collection)

(right) Captain Andrew Wallace Portal in 1945. He served in the First World War in the Royal West Surrey Regiment but within five months was wounded in the leg and sent back to England. (Barnaby Portal collection)

An extract from the *11th General Operational Idea of 11th Somerset Home Guard* runs as follows:

> There is a strong mobile force, principally cyclists furnished by the South Petherton Company, designed primarily for harassing the enemy and raiding his transport or harbours. This force has singularly proved its value in large-scale exercises against regular troops.

South Petherton Company's area extended westwards as far as Ilton and would have included the parishes of Stocklinch, Shepton Beauchamp, Seavington St. Michael, Seavington St. Mary, Barrington and possibly Puckington. No other records have been found regarding the membership of South Petherton Company except that a Corporal Farr of South Petherton Company took part in the Stand Down Parade in London on 3rd December 1944.

South Petherton Home Guard paraded in a field just to the south of the village at map ref. ST 431 161. Just to the north-east a Nissen hut was erected at Coles House in the north-east corner of a field at map ref. ST 435 163. Two other huts were also erected at map ref. ST 442 166; their purpose is uncertain.

(left) **Ilton Platoon**, *photographed outside Drakes Farm.*
Back Row: Alan May (steam-roller driver); Harold Trott (farmworker); Fred Brice (farmworker); Sid Falkner (farmworker); Sam Crabb; Vince Perrin; Jack Crabb (farmworker); Reg Trott (greenhouse worker); 'Young' Vic Warfield (farmworker); Arthur Bond (farmworker)
Front Row: John Tancock (teacher); L/Cpl. Dick Cox (mould maker); Cpl. Tom Horsey (farmer); Sgt. Newman (licensee of Wyndham Arms*); Lt. Fred Warfield (farmer and milkman); Cpl. Vic Offer (farmer); Cpl. Don Baker (racehorse groom and farmworker); 'Old' Vic Warfield*

The local Commander was remembered by Arthur Bond as Sgt. Newman.

One duty carried out by Ilton Home Guard, presumably on the build up to D-Day, was to patrol the section of the Taunton-Chard Railway between Rowland's Crossing and Beer Crocombe. As a 'treat' the members of the section were taken for an aeroplane flight from Ilton, probably the first time they had ever been airborne. Most of them had to use a bucket thoughtfully provided by the crew. (Mrs. Marjorie Trott collection)

'C' (ILMINSTER) COMPANY

COMMANDING OFFICER   Major J.C. Davie   2ND IN COMMAND   Capt. R.W. Manderson

Ilminster Home Guard, c.1941.
Back Row: No. 2 Lindole Hawkins
Second Row: No. 4 Preb. Gerald Hickman
Third Row: No. 3 2nd Lt. Sheppard
Fourth Row: No. 5 Lt. Rose;
    No. 7 Capt. Donald Maclean
Front Row: No. 1 Capt. W. Gundry;
    No. 2 possibly Major A.C.G. Luther;
    No. 5 Major Duke;
    No. 6 Lt. Col. Thomas Washington-Metcalfe; No. 7 Capt. W.H. Beeston;
    No. 8 Major J.C. Davie
(Elizabeth Browning (née Beeston) collection)

In September 1993 Elizabeth Browning, daughter of Captain W.H. Beeston, recalled her memories of living in Ilminster during the war:

My father joined the L.D.V. immediately on its inception, but later re-enlisted in the Somerset Light Infantry in which he had served in World War 1. He was seconded to the Ilminster Home Guard as Administration and Quartermaster Officer. I remember Captain, later Major, Duke was a solicitor who lived in North Street and Major, later Lt. Col., Metcalfe resided at New Wood at the top of New Road. Thomas Washington Metcalfe was the author of some seven novels and several works of non-fiction including *A Country Bloke's Chronicle*.

In the early days volunteers were really armed with pitchforks. I remember a little group of them manning a bridge on a Sunday afternoon when there was an invasion alert. To my amazement a girl friend and I were allowed to go for a walk, regardless of the possible danger!

For years we had in our house one or two rather beautifully-turned wooden bottles, used for practice in throwing 'Molotov Cocktails' *(see right)*. The genuine articles were, I believe, hidden in caches in the ditches alongside roads leading to the town.

The first HQ was in the premises of a former hairdresser on the corner of Silver Street opposite the Doctor's Surgery. Later the move was made to the house shown in the photograph.

Ilminster was surrounded by an anti-tank ditch with wooden bridges at intervals to provide access for farm vehicles.

(Author's collection)

On 9th September 1939 The Duke of Gloucester's Appeal for the Red Cross and St. John Fund was launched. One of the special appeals was the 'Penny a Week Fund' which raised over £20 million, one third of all the money collected for the Appeal. One method of collection was by volunteer collectors carrying out a weekly house-to-house collection. Even this was regulated by the Government – the *House to House Collections Act* of 1940 required doorstop collectors to wear an identity badge. Mrs. M.G. Beeston, in addition to being a Home Guard Auxiliary, was a supporter of the Red Cross, spending one long evening every week collecting one penny from each household in the East Street area of Ilminster. Her service as a Home Guard auxiliary was acknowledged by the certificate reproduced right.

The Defences of Ilminster in 1940. Not only an anti-tank ditch but pill-boxes, barbed wire and road blocks were all constructed either as part of the defences of the Taunton Stop Line or to convert Ilminster into an anti-tank island. Positions 32-33, 36-40 and 43 were to be manned by sections of the Regular Army whilst the Home Guard was stationed at 34, 35, 41 and 42. The pillbox situated between 32 and 33 was to be manned by a detachment from the reserve section of the Home Guard.
(reproduced by kind permission of the Somerset Archive & Record Service)

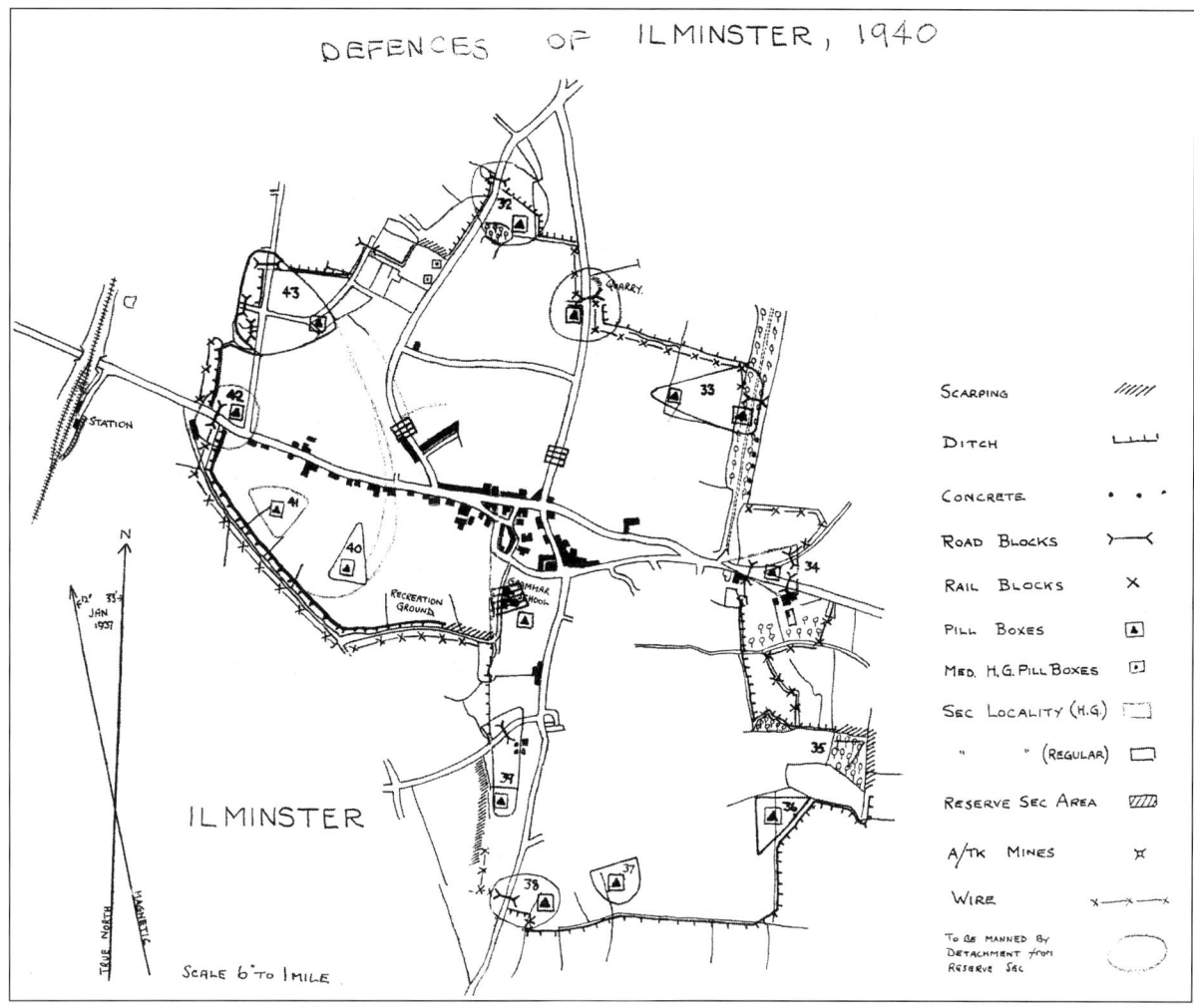

I have received The King's command to express His Majesty's appreciation of the loyal service given voluntarily to her country in a time of grievous danger by

M. G. BEESTON.

as a Woman Home Guard Auxiliary.

The War Office, London.

Secretary of State for War

(below) Captain Beeston and Lt. H.H. Smith outside Battalion Headquarters, Butts Farm, on 24th September 1944. By then, Home Guard operational duties had been suspended and attendance at parades was purely voluntary. It was to be just three months before the Ilminster Home Guard, together with the Home Guard throughout the land, faded into history. (Elizabeth Browning (née Beeston) collection)

*No. 1 (**Station Road and Winterhay**) Platoon in 1944.*
Back Row: Phil Holley; P. Irish; Unknown
Second Row: Bill Close, Cyril Baker; Mr. Hooper or Frank Bulgin; Les Tutcher; Ernie Loveless; Percy Rogers; Ern Turner
Third Row: Bill Wakeham; Unknown; L/Cpl. Ernie Chubb; Cpl. Lindole Hawkins; Herbie Trott
Front Row: Cpl. Lionel Roy; Sgt. Potts; 2nd Lt. Sheppard; Major J.C. Davie (Platoon Commander); Lt. Rose; Sgt. Barrington; Unknown
(Heritage of The Isle Trust collection)

The above photograph belies the total strength of the platoon. In 1942 it was '65 other ranks'. Weapons on charge were 40 rifles, 1 Lewis gun, 3 dual-purpose Lewis guns, 4 Browning Automatic Rifles, 12 Sten guns, 1 Browning medium machine gun, 2 Northover Projectors and 2 Spigot Mortars.

Lt. Rose was not an Ilminster man; he was a teacher from London evacuated with his school.

John Pearce was a very young member of Ilminster Company in 1944. Born in 1932 he was a boy messenger at Horton. The local Home Guard unit had a Nissen hut in a field beside *The Lamb Inn* in Horton. Mr. Groves, the landlord, was the local 'commander' together with a Mr. Tarr, a local farmer. John remembers his mother, bearing in mind his tender age, forbidding him to go outside the village on Home Guard business in case he got lost!

Anthony Clifford Parsons was a member of the Broadway Home Guard until he left and joined the Royal Navy on 18th February 1941. Although only a member for a short time, Anthony remembers that the Platoon Commander was a Lt. Halliday. Duties included manning a road block near *The Lamb Inn* at Horton Cross during the invasion scare. Drill was carried out in the yard of *The Bell Inn* at Broadway.

*N.C.O.s of No. 3 (**Whitelackington/Kingstone**) Platoon.*
Back Row: Cpl. Ned Gudge; Cpl. Tom Rocket; Cpl. Nelson Bragge; Unknown; Cpl. Barnes
Front Row: Sgt. Frank Plyer; 2nd Lt. E. Robert Gummer; Lt. H.E. Madge (farmer at Whitelackington Farm); Sgt. Rex Harvey; Sgt. Harry Woodland

An original copy of this photograph is endorsed on the back 'To Sgt. Woodland with best wishes for Christmas and New Year from H.E. Madge Lt. O/C No. 3 Platoon'. The photograph of Lt. Madge's platoon at the bottom of the next page is typical of so many photographs taken of the Home Guard. With so many members in full-time civilian employment, often regularly working a six-day week or involved in agriculture where their attendance would have been seven days, it proved extremely difficult to assemble a full unit for a formal photograph, especially at the time of Stand Down in December when the days were so short. No. 3 Platoon comprised some 45 'other ranks' armed with 35 rifles, 1 Lewis gun, 2 dual-purpose Lewis guns, 4 B.A.R.s, 8 Sten guns, 2 Northover Projectors and 2 Spigot Mortars.
(Mrs. Cynthia Lane collection)

(right) **Dowlish Wake Section No. 10 Platoon**.
Back Row: Ned Gudge; Cpl. Barnes; T. Rocket; Unknown; Unknown; Unknown
Second Row: Sgt. Frank Plyer; Unknown; Unknown; Unknown; Cpl. Nelson Bragge; Mr. Trott; Unknown
Third Row: Sgt. Harry Woodland; Rex Harvey; Unknown; Unknown; Unknown; Eddie Baker; Unknown; Unknown
Front Row: Unknown; Mr. England; Unknown; Unknown; Unknown; Major J.C. Davie; Lt. Rose; Lt. Hubert E. Madge; 2nd Lt. Sheppard; 2nd Lt. E. Robert Gummer
(all three photographs John Scott collection)

(below) Charlie Gudge, P. Rowley, Will Parsons, Percy Larcome, George Sumption, Eddie Scott, Charles Singleton and Fred England pose for Hubert Madge with Mr. Scott's Morris Cowley outside *The Castle Inn*. In addition to their rifles this section is armed with what appears to be a Savage-Lewis Aircraft machine gun, Model 1918. This weapon, with a 97-round magazine, was known as the Lewis Mk. III and issued to the Home Guard in 1940.

No. 10 Platoon's strength was some 80 other ranks under the command at one stage of Lt. R.A.L. Cole. The Platoon covered the area to the south of Ilminster, including Dowlish Wake. Weapons included 16 rifles, 8 dual-purpose Lewis guns, 15 Sten guns, 2 Northover Projectors and 2 Spigot Mortars.

Cyril Lane was a member of the Dowlish Wake Home Guard and remembers Lt. Hubert E. Madge as the Platoon Commander. His farm at Whitelackington was used as the Platoon Stores whilst a hut was erected at Kingstone Farm. Although long since gone, it is believed to be of the standard Nissen hut style and would have been used for munitions. In the early stages of the war an observation point was established on the top of Kingstone Church where a telephone was provided for the lookouts.

(right) **No. 3 (Whitelackington/Kingstone) Platoon**.
Back Row: George Smith; Percy Rowley; Mr. Pike; Mr. Symes; Charlie Gudge; Harold Rocket; Frank Phelps; Sid Smith
Second Row: Charlie Faulkner; Mr. Strawbridge; F. Summerhay; Mr. England; Tom Hill, Bill Smith; H. Harris; Mr. Choak
Third Row: Sid Doble; Mr. Pearce; Tom Coleman or Mr. Hansford; Cyril Cox; Reg Hill; Mr. Gillingham; A. Cox; W. Parsons
Front Row: Cpl. R. Barnes; Cpl. Frank Plyer; Sgt. Rex Harvey; Lt. Hubert Madge; Bob Gummer; Cpl. Harry Woodland; Tommy Rocket; Ned Gudge

Charlie Gudge recalled the Platoon's meeting place was *The Castle Inn*, Kingstone, whilst weapons were stored at a house next door to *The Frog and Slate* pub in Ilminster. Other Platoon members were Percy Larcome, George Sumption and their N.C.O. Guy Thompson. It is believed Wilfred Vile was another member. The .22 rifle range at *The Castle Inn* was used by the platoon whilst grenade practice was carried out at Long Pond.

(right) The Ammunition Store in Ilminster. Whilst Nissen huts of various sizes were the usual method of storing explosive and inflammable stores, Ilminster Home Guard appear to have also used a 'one off'. Constructed of pre-cast concrete panels with a steel door (now missing), it survives some 60 years later, still showing traces of its disruptive camouflage paint. (Author's collection)

Small arms ammunition allowances for Ilminster platoons were as follows. Each rifleman would carry 40 of the 60 rounds allocated. B.A.R. teams would carry 550 rounds of the 800 allocated for each gun. Those issued with Sten guns would carry some 100 rounds with 50 rounds per gun in reserve. No. 1 Platoon's Browning medium machine gun crew would have to struggle with some 850 rounds.

D' (CHARD TOWN) COMPANY

COMMANDING OFFICER	Major L.P. Townsend,
	(Major S. Smith, O.B.E.)
	(Major E.D. Browne, O.B.E., J.P., C.C.)
2ND IN COMMAND	Capt. J. Gurdon, M.C.

(above) Although uncaptioned it is believed those depicted are members of **'D' Company**. *The photograph was taken before August 1941 as by then Leslie Beasley, a local optician and jeweller, had joined the Royal Navy, not returning home until almost five years later. Although details of the area of operations of this unit are not known, members of one section featured above, including Rex Rogers, Sgt. John Stevens and Clifford Mear, patrolled the ridge by* The Wind Whistle Inn.

Back Row: No. 6 F. Dobson (bakery employee at Crimchard); No. 20 Rex Rogers (took over Wreath Farm from his father who then worked Sunshine Cider Mills); No. 21 Clifford Mear (farmer)

Middle Row: No. 2 B. Woodland; No. 4 Mr. Strawbridge (gamekeeper); No. 6 Roy Rogers; No. 8 Leslie Broad (estate agent); No. 14 John Pownall (joint Managing Director of Phoenix Co. of Chard)

Front Row: No. 3 L/Cpl. (later Sgt.) Morton (WWI veteran, commercial traveller); No. 6 Sgt. E. Marriot (worked at Jarman's Nurseries, Snowdon); No. 8 Lt. Harold Owen Taylor; No. 9 Lt. Ernest George 'Johnny' Townsend; No. 10 Lt. G. Gillingham (manufacturer of artificial limbs); No. 11 Sgt. John Stevens; No. 12 Sgt. Leslie Beasley
(Penelope Trott collection)

(left) **Members of 'D' (Chard Town) Company** *at their Drill Hall in Furnham Road.*

Back Row: Ernest Hopgood; Charlie Corley; Ivor Bettridge; William Hill; Douglas Hounsell; Harold Gollop; Charles Dickson; Unknown; Lesley Wellington; Unknown; Unknown; Mr. Holland; Ken Bidgood; Unknown; Jack Chick

Second Row: Charlie Bowditch; Michael Parsley; Douglas Benjafield; Donald Eastwood; Mervyn Howells; Wilfred Hobbs; Douglas Bennett; Ronald White; Wilfred Turner; Ivor Powell; Gordon Pierce; Tim Tucker; Arthur Penfold; Bert Connett; Jim Trenchard

Third Row: William Rainbow; Raymond Skinner; Vernon Franklin; Gordon Bright; Alfie Garwood; Edward White; Percy Hounsell; Mr. Brown; Albert Wallford; Ernie Brown; Cyril Wood; Jim Matthews; Mr. Hake; Tom Martindale; Les Dowell

Fourth Row: Clifford Gale; Walter Pattimore; George Huish; Wilf Morecombe; Stewart Hutchins; Unknown; Alec Long; Bill Long; Jim Galpin; William Plyer; George Adams; Len Boyland; Ben Pavey; Les Long; Fred Berry; Les Brown

Fifth Row: Cpl. Jack White; Cpl. Jack Fowler; Cpl. Harold Cork; Sgt. Arthur Woodland; Sgt. Henry Long; Sgt. Edward Huish; Sgt. Reg Evans; Lt. Arthur Hill; Capt. Jeff Gillingham; 2nd Lt. Arthur Bewell; Quartermaster Brodrick; Sgt. Jack Tratt; Sgt. Wyatt; Cpl. Arthur Barnaby; Cpl. Reuben Long; Cpl. Albert Gollop

Front Row: Dick Harvey; Arthur Whitehead; Fred Derby; Jack Stacey; Jack White; Jesse Huish; Doug Curwood; Charles Phippen
(John Scott collection)

(Derrick Warren collection)

Derrick Warren joined the Chard Home Guard in 1941, aged 17. The photograph shows Derrick aged 17 or 18 with his personal weapon, a Browning Automatic Rifle which he kept at home under his bed.

Derrick remembers once being called out to search for a German airman when his plane was shot down near Wambrook. The parachute of one of the crew members failed to open. His impression on the soft ground was about a foot deep.

Other duties remembered were manning a look-out post in the vicinity of Hornsbury Mill where the silence of the night was broken only by the song of a nightingale.

In 1942 Derrick left the Home Guard and joined the Royal Corps of Signals.

The Home Guard rifle-range had existed for many years before the War and was situated at Foxdon Hill. Here it was possible to shoot distances up to 600 yards. The targets were at map ref. ST 307 095 whilst the 600-yard firing point was at map ref. ST 311 099. The area around Foxdon Hill saw considerable activity according to Richard 'Dick' Masters who was a Home Guard runner at the time. Just to the north-west of the targets, in Hale's Copse, S.I.P. Grenades were stored. Unfortunately, these were discovered by schoolboys whose curiosity got the better of them. Two boys were injured when the glass containers were broken and the phosphorus contents ignited.

To the south-east of the targets an old stone pit was used on one occasion for detonating unexploded German bombs dropped at Crimchard. 140 yards to the east of this spot an area at map ref. ST 308 094 was used to demonstrate Flame Fougasse. Dick remembers that the grass took four years to grow back. Finally, a large chalk pit at map ref. ST 309 095 was used to demonstrate newly issued weapons which included Northover Projectors and the No. 74 Sticky Bomb.

Dick recalls that a Flame Fougasse was installed at Snowdon Hill on the A30 at map ref. ST 309 089 with its junction with Gipsy Lane. Derrick Warren remembers this spot well as throughout one long weekend exercise he was detailed to guard it. More enjoyable was the demonstration of the Spigot Mortar firing high-explosive rounds in a half-completed reservoir at Blagdon to the south of Taunton at map ref. ST 201 172. One Spigot Mortar practice did not go as planned. The propelling charge was faulty and the bomb just cleared the muzzle of the mortar. Panic followed until it was realised that the bomb was fitted with an impact fuse.

E' (CHARD RURAL) COMPANY

COMMANDING OFFICER   Major A.C.G. Luther
2ND IN COMMAND   Capt. E.H. Lowe

A press report of December 1944 listed the following platoons and commanders as part of 'E' (Chard Rural) Company:

Buckland St. Mary	Lt. J.C. Pringle
Combe St. Nicholas	Lt. Scott Hopkins
South Chard	Lt. W. White
No. 2 Winsham	Lt. C. Grant-Davie

*Home Guard at Tatworth, part of **South Chard Platoon**.*
Back Row: Percy Down; Edgar Down; Mr. Collins; Jack Stonham; Charlie Stonham; Frank Buller; Jim Hallett; Bob Love; Mr. Restorick
Middle Row: Albie Hallett; possibly Mr. Hoare; Harold Land; Mickey Scott
Front Row: 'Bunny' Harris; Mr. Chubb; possibly Mr. Scott; Mr. Passmore
(Ron Farley collection)

No. 2 (Winsham) Platoon.
Back Row: Sidney Lawrence; George Nichols; George Martin; Jim Evans; Charles 'Mumbler' Phelps; Mr. Shannon; Mr. Tubbs; Eddie Partridge; Roy Loveridge; Jack Ewins; Graham Strawbridge; Charles Phelps, Snr.; Fred Meech
Middle Row: Wilfred 'Buffy' Beer; Ralph Doore; Arthur Sibley; Andy Long; Leslie Morgan; Courtney Newton; Cyril Sawyer; Reg Singleton; Jack Horsey; George Pennecard; Les Rowe; Ernest Knott; Fred Butler; Ern Forsey
Front Row: Cpl. Sidney Creech; Cpl. Alfred Phelps; Sgt. Harry Chubb; Gilbert Lacey; possibly Major A.C.G. Luther; Lt. Col. T. Washington-Metcalfe; Capt. 'Johnny' Hall; Lt. C. Grant-Davie; Lt. Ray Wheaton; Dick Powell; Mr. Davidson; Mr. Froud; Cpl. Leslie Griffen (Christopher Beer collection)

The map below, reproduced from an original owned by Robert Coates, shows a section of the Taunton Stop Line which extended from Bridgwater to Seaton.

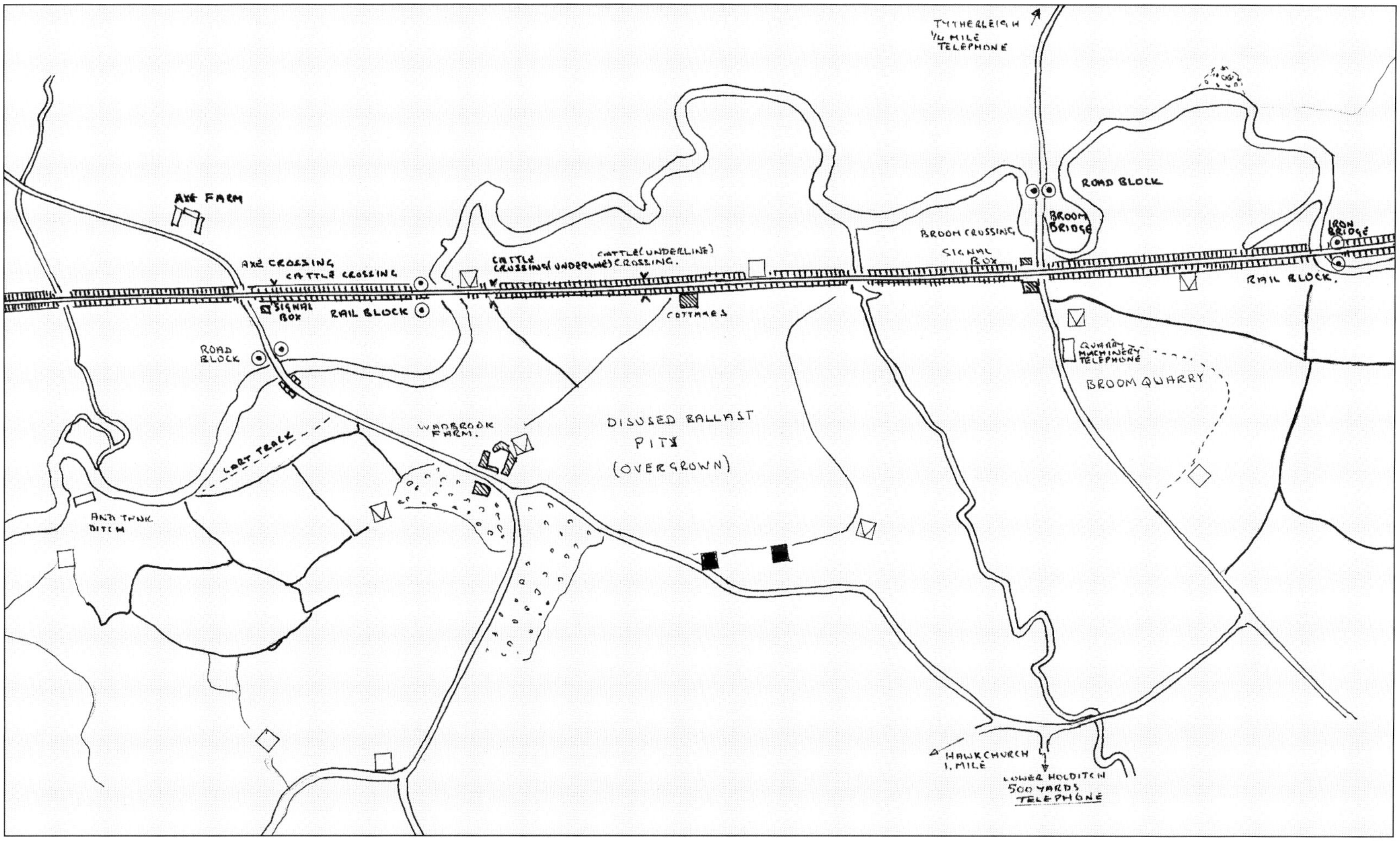

12th Somerset (Somerton) Battalion

HEADQUARTERS	Coombe Hill House, Keinton Mandeville	AMMUNITION OFFICER	Lt. W.S.V. Seager
DATE FORMED	February 1943	ASSISTANT ADMIN. OFFR.	Lt. E.A. Bray, O.B.E., M.C.
COMMANDING OFFICER	Lt. Col. Sir C.E. Walker, Bt., D.S.O., M.C.	GAS OFFICER	Lt. W. Tindall
2ND IN COMMAND	Major P.E. Prince, D.S.O.	INTELLIGENCE OFFICER	Lt. J.R. Davis
		LIAISON OFFICERS	Lt. A.G. Hammond (Police)
H.Q. STAFF			2nd Lt. L.G. Lavington Evans (Sector)
A & Q OFFICER	Capt. W.E. Jones, General List	MEDICAL OFFICERS	Major J.L. Glover
ADJUTANT	Capt. E.W. Archer, M.C., Durham Light Infantry		Capt. G.A.F. Quinnell
		SIGNALS OFFICER	Lt. A.L. Freke

CURRY RIVEL COMPANY

COMMANDING OFFICER Major C.G.S. Barnes   2ND IN COMMAND Capt. H. Hoskings

*Major C.G.S. Barnes poses with the men of **Curry Rivel Platoon**.*
Back Row: Charlie Dabinett; Cecil Langford; Unknown; Unknown; Unknown; Ken Priddle; Bill Richards; Cecil Harwood; Archie Lock; Unknown; Unknown; Bill Langford; Bruce Martin
Second Row: Ernie Barnard; Unknown; Unknown; Unknown; Reg Cousins (landlord of the King William Public House); Claude Sturgeon; Unknown; Unknown; Unknown; Unknown; Stan Harwood
Front Row: L/Cpl. Charlie Langford; Gerry Trott (farmer); Cpl. A. Bailey; George Millard; Unknown; Dr. Glover (local G.P.); Major C.G.S. Barnes; Capt. H. Hoskings (ran a building company); Unknown; Unknown; Cpl. Jim or Reg Simmonds; Cpl. Percy Lock; Cpl. George Hartland; Unknown; Cpl. Len Baker; Mr. Perry

Missing from the photograph or not identified are two members of the Gullidge family, Jim Barnard, Mr. Tilley, Bert Treasure, two members of the Wood family, Bill Webb, Tommy Priddle, Mr. Dabinett of Dyers Road and possibly Bob Trim. Other Home Guard members included Bert Knap, Bert Salway, Harold Boobyer and his brother, Albert Dare, Bill Weaver, Jack Langford, Hubert Burge, Frank Lombard, Cpls. William Langford and Cook. Colonel Findley was also involved in the Home Guard but his placement is unknown.
(Mrs. Amelia Langford collection)

The fields below Burton Pynsent Monument were used as a small arms range, using the scarp face below the Monument as a back stop. For several years after the war Spigot Mortar rounds were being ploughed out of the field. During shooting practice, it was normal to place a lookout at the base of the Monument. However, on one occasion, the lookout was somewhat startled when a ricochet struck the plinth next to him. Another rifle range used by the Platoon was at Somerton Erleigh. In the early days The Round House at the top of Red Hill served as an observation point.

Burton Pynsent, the home of the Company Commander Major Barnes, possessed a range of outbuildings which were used for the storage of small arms, ammunition and general stores. Spigot Mortar bombs and S.I.P. grenades were kept at the Monument.

Raymond Langford joined the Royal Engineers in 1939 and was discharged, injured, in 1941. He subsequently joined the Home Guard but in 1944 he left to drive workers to the Royal Ordnance Factory, Puriton. One morning, visibility was made difficult not only by blackouts on the vehicle but by heavy fog. Reaching a road junction, Ray could not see his way out safely so the steward dismounted and, unable to see or hear traffic, shouted, "O.K., Ray". Ray promptly put his foot down and sped off to Puriton 15 miles away, leaving the steward behind. Next morning's greeting was unrepeatable.

Curry Rivel Home Guard. *The original photograph was endorsed 'Taken at Heale House, Curry Rivel (HQ) 1943'. Whilst the background is the same as in the previous photograph it is unlikely the date is the same unless Major Barnes has borrowed Capt. Hoskings's gloves!*

Back Row: Henry 'Rocky' Richards; Bill Webb; Joe Gullidge; Maurice Harwood; Ken Priddle; Cecil Langford; Len Baker; Mr. Marchetti; Percy Lock

Second Row: Mr. Chubb or Stan Harwood; Bill 'Brassy' Barnard; Bill Langford; Charlie Langford; George Hartland; Frank Bown

Front Row: Unknown; Sgt. Jim Simmonds; Cpl. A. Bailey; George Millard; Unknown (but remembered as a Somerset L.I. instructor); Capt. Hoskings; Major C.G.S. Barnes; Unknown; Unknown (both regulars from the Somerset L.I.); Sgt. Frank Stroud; Sgt. Tommy Scott

(Frank Bown collection)

*(above) With Major Barnes and Major McEvoy both in the photograph this appears to be a photograph of men from **Curry Rivel (CR) and Langport (L) Companies**, including men from Muchelney (M) and Drayton (D).*
Back Row: No. 3 Ernie Bonning (L); No. 5 George Hartland;
   No 7 D.J. Webber (L); No. 10 Percy Lock (D); No. 12 Ken Priddle;
   No 17 Richard or Claude Sturgeon; No. 18 Len Baker (L)
Second Row: No. 6 Cecil Langford (CR); No. 13 Robert Trim (M); No. 18 Mr. Perry
Third Row: No. 1 Tom Scott; No. 2 Roy Jones; No. 5 Tom Norris;
   No. 6 Frank Parris; No. 7 Tom Salt; No 8 Capt. H. Hoskings (CR);
   No. 9 Major C.J.S. Barnes (CR); No. 10 Major R.J. McEvoy (L); No. 11 Capt. H.G. Jefferies (L); No. 12 Lt. W. Loman (L); No. 14 Ashton Knight (L)
Front Row: No. 3 Henry 'Rocky' Richards (CR); No. 8 Charles Langford;
   No. 10 Bill 'Brassy' Barnard
(Jeffrey Lock collection)

Members of Curry Rivel and Langport Companies.
Back Row: No. 5 Robert Trim;
Extreme left: Tom Scott (with white arm band) and, next to him, Len Baker
Standing in group of four, front centre; No. 1 Tom Norris; No. 3 Tom Salt
Sitting on the log, front right: No. 1 Percy Lock (D); No. 5 Cecil Langford (CR);
   No. 6 Ken Priddle
Standing in front, far right: No. 1 Ashton Knight (L); No. 2 Henry 'Rocky' Richards (CR); No. 3 Mr. Male (CR). *(Jeffrey Lock collection)*

No. 2 (Kingsbury Episcopi) Platoon in 1943.
Back Row: L/Cpl. Bert Talbot (Kingsbury Episcopi Silver Band Bandmaster); Herbie Lock; John Hebditch; Walter Lock (WW1 veteran); Maurice Packe (baker); Fred Lock; Unknown; Unknown; Bob Mounter; Len Duck; Jack Smith; Bob Martin; Norman Paull; Unknown; Fred Hallett
Middle Row: Will Bradford (standing); Bert Gillett; Mick Follett; Ben Oaten; Jeff Derby; Jack Mounter; Arthur Brake; Albert Brake (father and son); Ron Talbot; Cpl. Fred Reed; Harry 'Henny' Lock; Len Stuckey; Bob Duck; Unknown; Ern Duck; Charlie Elliott (standing)
Front Row: Cpl. Fred Russ; Cpl. Headley Savage; Cpl. Don Thomas (teacher); Cpl. Leonard Jacobs; Sgt. Frank Jennings; 2nd Lt. Frank Parris; Lt. Tom Salt; Sgt. Major Tom Norris (ex-Regular Army, one of the 'Old Contemptibles'); Bert Hodder (stonemason); Sgt. Charlie Russ; Charlie Watts; Will Mounter; Herb Westlake; Percy Clarke; Ken Duck; Harry Lock (standing)
Other members of the Platoon included Lewis Male, Joseph Hebditch, Fred Paull, Cpl. Cecil Legg, Ted Elliott, Bert Bradford, Percy Satterly, Walter Townsend, Mr. Quantock and Will Grinter. Bill Stone also served in the Platoon, having won a D.C.M. in 1917 at Zeebrugge.
(Mrs. Peggy Best collection)

The Platoon stores were held in a Nissen hut at Home Farm, Kingsbury Episcopi. In the early days a lookout for parachutists was undertaken on the top of Burrow Hill. As it was an extremely exposed site, an Austin car body was carried up to provide protection for the lookouts. It was probably from here that Ben Stone once reported "2 Parachutists landing at Westmoor". The parachutists turned out to be swans. Other later duties included guarding the Railway Viaduct at Langport in conjunction with other platoons.

At Manor Farm the roof of the cow stall was surmounted by a sandbagged gun emplacement to cover the road from Martock. It is believed that Cecil Legg kept the Platoon's Spigot Mortar at the Milk Depot in Thorney Halt.

At West Lambrook, members of the Home Guard under Sgt. Charles Russ had a Spigot Mortar position established on the west side of the New Cross-West Lambrook Road facing south at map ref. ST 414 188.

Charlie Elliott remembers a day on the rifle range at Burton Pynsent, when a stray dog entered the target area during the shoot. Major Barnes gave the order: "Shoot the b.....". but either the Platoon were dog lovers or their shooting was bad, as the dog rushed off unscathed.

> Lanc.Cpl. Hebditch's Section - by sawdust heap in R.Frys ground
> Objective - by W.Talbots mangold-cave (by the alotments)
> umpire Mr Parris
>
> Section III. Section Leader - Sgt. Oliver.
> also. Cpl Burrows, Cpl. Jacobs, Cpl Lock. F.
> Lanc.Cpl Savage & Men
>
> At 19.00 hours today the Drayton Searchlight reported a lowflying Ju. troopcarrier dropping 6 parachute troops over the center of Westmoor & at 19.30 hours the policeman came rushing into H.Q. to say that 6 Germans were digging-in just behind W.Talbots mangold cave looking from Sidney Furbers across the alotments. They are dressed in disguise wearing Home Guard overcoats & forage caps; one was seen carrying a bose concern which might be a wireless set or ammo.
>
> I want you to capture at least one prisoner alive & the wireless set if possible, the remainder if they will not surrender must be destroyed.
>
> You will send out one N.C.O. & 3 men in the recky patrol at 20.30 hours unarmed & stripped down to the battle dress, they must be back at 21.00 hrs. This will be my battle H.Q. & you will post one N.C.O. & 5 men as sentries 15 yds from this spot, they will wear great-coats & forage caps & be armed with rifles & stens. The remainder will form the fighting patrol & will set out at 21.10 hrs from here. Any questions P.T.O.
>
> When the enemy is captured or if the whistle sounds first (at 21.50 hrs) report at this spot
>
> The wireless set is represented by the white flag which will be 15 yd from the nearest sentry
>
> The recky must not try to capture enemy

Above are reproduced undated notes covering an exercise involving members of Kingsbury Platoon. These were designed to present the local unit with a typical scenario they might meet. Such exercises would only have been held after the threat of immediate invasion had passed; in the summer of 1940 such a task would have been beyond the remit of the L.D.V./Home Guard.
(John Hebditch collection)

> Subject Travelling Wing
> To O.C. No 2 Platoon.
>
> Movements Order
>
> Parades Tuesday 11 Jan 2000 hrs KINGWESTON HOUSE PARK
>   Map Ref. 965 520
>   Wednesday 12 " 2000 hrs " " "
>   Thursday 13 " 2000 hrs Queens Inn KEINTON MANDEVILLE
>   Map Ref 985 520.
>   Friday 14 " 2000 hrs " " "
>   Sunday 16 " 1100 hrs KINGWESTON HOUSE PARK.
>
> On Tuesday 11 Jan. Curry Rivel 'bo will rendezvous at KINGWESTON PARK GATE 965 320 at 1935 prompt.
>
> The Sunday Parade will commence at 1100 prompt until 1300 hrs. Lunch 13 00
>   Demonstration 1330 - 1500.
>   Haversack rations will be brought on the Sunday.
>
> Dress Tuesday Wednesday & Sunday.
>   Battle order. Arms, Steel helmets, Respirators
>   Thursday & Friday Clean fatigue
>   Students should bring note books & pencils to all parades.

Having carried out their day's work, Home Guards would have been expected to attend courses run by the Home Guard Travelling Wing, who covered the whole of the country giving various demonstrations on weapons and tactics.

Note that the map references are based on the Cassini Military Grid. Before publication of the 6th edition 1" Ordnance Survey series, maps were not produced with the now well-known 1km-square grid; the military authorities therefore overprinted O.S. maps with their own grid which did not correspond to the subsequent civilian grid. The writer of the above notes had not obviously 'got to grips' with these map references. Curry Rivel Company would find themselves at Sutton Bingham, Yeovil if they had motored to 965320.
(John Hebditch collection)

Fivehead Home Guard.
Back Row: Fred Cullen; Bob Dyke; Bert Yarde;
  Unknown; Unknown; Charlie Pester;
  Unknown; Jack Chedzoy; Reg Yarde
Middle Row: Frank Amor; Jim Burge;
  Unknown; Ray Cornell; Unknown;
  Unknown; Unknown
Front Row: Cpl. Tom Marshall; Fred
  Wembridge; R.C. Lamb; Alfie Male;
  Lt. Dunkling; Sgt. Sid Miller; Bill Yarde;
  Edgar Milton; Unknown (lived at Isle Abbotts)
(Mrs. Dorothy Lloyd collection)

(right) **Hambridge Home Guard**.
Back Row: R. Marsh (builder); Peter Keech
  (labourer); Bill Whaites (builder); Stan
  Woodland (farmer); Bill Harvey (labourer);
  R. Taylor (labourer)
Middle Row: Fred Lambert (brewery worker);
  Ern Whaites (builder for Hoskins);
  D. Franklin (lorry driver) or Mr. Chard;
  Jack Chard (farm labourer); C. Cable
  (lorry driver) or Mr. Glover; Charlie Showers
  (worked on Bowdens Farm); T. Allen (builder)
Front Row: Bert Adams (gardener at
  Earnshill House); L/Cpl. Doug Duck (farmer);
  Cpl. Harold Grey (gardener at Earnshill
  House); Sgt. Eddie Priddle (farmer);
  Lt. Dunkling; Cpl. Hobbs; Cpl. Frank Payne
  (brewery worker); Cpl. Morris Salway
  (brewery worker)
(Arthur Welch collection)

Other Home Guard members included Harry Gillard and sons, Theo Dabinett and Cpl. George Willey, M.M. In the First World War George was shot through the mouth, losing several teeth. He was also a 'King's Corporal', a rank bestowed on the battlefield that can only be rescinded by the Monarch. This was explained to the Company Commander, Major Barnes, when his order to Cpl. Willey to remove his stripes, earned in the previous conflict, was refused. This is the explanation why Cpl. Willey does not appear in any Home Guard photograph. Major Barnes did not have authority over Cpl. Willey's stripes but he had control over who was in the photographs. Charlie Showers was once reprimanded for his shooting on the Langport Rifle Range, having taken several 'pot shots' at magpies, using his service rifle.

The Langport-Hambridge road crossed the River Isle by a small hamstone bridge and it was here that the road was prepared to accept a road block. A few score yards on the Langport side of the bridge was the Hambridge Brewery. Information suggests that a Blacker Bombard was kept at the Brewery to provide covering fire for the road block.

LANGPORT COMPANY

COMMANDING OFFICER   Major R.J. McEvoy   2ND IN COMMAND   Capt. H.G. Jefferies

Officers and N.C.O.s of Langport Company.
Individual's platoons or sections are given as follows, where known: L – Langport Platoon; HH – High Ham Section;
LS – Long Sutton Platoon; A – Aller Section.
Back Row: Unknown; Bill Wainwright; Harry Willmott (worked for Kelways, Wearne); Charlie Scriven (farmworker from Low Ham); Fred Cox (farmer – LS); Redvers Burt (farmworker – LS); Harry Crocker (farmer – HH); Reg Suter (farmworker – LS)
Second Row: 'General' Lewis (farmworker); Dennis Lock (farmer); Hubert Cox (farmworker – LS); Ashton Knight (builder – L); Fred Cornelius (insurance agent – L); Ted Pavey (worked for Yeo Bros. and Paull – L); Bruce Cox (farmer from Low Ham); Ernie Walters (mechanic from Wearne)
Third Row: Ray Reading (forestry worker from Low Ham); Wally Mitchell (farmer – A); Jack Cullen (works foreman from Pitney); Ted Lockyer (farmer at Bere); Fred Parker (local electricity employee – L); Albert Cullen (War Agricultural Committee – HH); Jack Squire (insurance agent – LS); Harold Martin (council employee); Albert Jones
Front Row: Bert Davis (local electricity company manager – L); Fred Clark (worked for Matthew and Scales – HH); Bill Loman (worked at Ilminster Station – L); Capt. H.G. Jefferies (headmaster – L); Major R.J. McEvoy (worked for Matthews and Scales – L); Eddie Martin (rating officer – L); Les Hector (painter and decorator – L); Charles Burt (farmworker – LS); W. Rouse (photographer – L)
Charles Burt, father of Redvers, served in the Hampshires in World War 1 and lost his Corporal's stripes – twice!

George Cox was a member of the Langport Platoon, joining it when it was in its infancy. Weapons were stored, he remembers, at Langport Grammar School together with the Spigot Mortar. Langport, situated on one of the few downstream crossings of the River Parrett, would have played a vital role in the defence of this nodal point. A Flame Fougasse was built into the edge of the main Langport-Taunton Road near its junction with Frog Lane; the bridge over the river was either prepared for demolition or modified to accept rails or spider mines. Don remembers an exercise held between Langport Home Guard (the defenders) and a Guards unit. The Platoon's Spigot Mortar was emplaced to the east of the river, upstream of the bridge, whilst the Platoon waited. In the 'battle' that followed Langport managed to remove the track from an 'enemy' Universal Carrier by thrusting a scaffolding pole between the track and sprocket. The driver was not amused.

The Flame Fougasse mentioned above was not the only one in the Company Area. Ted David recalls that on the north side of the Aller-Langport road at map ref. ST. 419 282 (west side of the hedge) there lurked another one waiting for the enemy who never came. Records recently discovered show that a third one was installed at Huish Episcopi on the Muchelney Road at ST 426 265.

George Cox remembered Ashton Knight as regularly being late on parade. On one occasion whilst 'easing springs' on his rifle, Ashton shot a hole through the ceiling of the Platoon Headquarters. He was soundly reprimanded by Major McEvoy. Apologising profusely Ashton repeated the drill and promptly shot a hole through the floor.

It may have been the same exercise that Don Webber, a Platoon member, recalls, amongst other incidents, in a recent letter:

During the night of a three-day exercise carried out in February 1943, being the Company Dispatch Rider, I was conveying messages between H.Q. Langport and a base at Huish. Pte. Henry Adams was pillion rider, many aircraft were overhead, as we were travelling over the railway bridge at Garden City on 13.2.43 when two of the planes collided overhead and the falling débris fortunately missed us. The Wellington, No. BL 460, came down at Kingsbury Episcopi and the pilot was safe. The Halifax, W1182, crashed in pieces in the flooded moorland. I believe Home Guard Dick Vearncombe was a witness and there were no survivors. On the last day of the exercise I was loader in the Spigot Mortar team, dug in and camouflaged at Baulk Yard to the left of the river bridge. In the afternoon the armoured vehicles came round the corner above the station. We fired a dummy round and the smoke gave our position away. The enemy infantry were soon upon us and threw a thunder flash. The umpire declared us all dead.

During the same exercise Cpl. Ashton Knight was seen walking down the road opposite *The Dolphin Hotel*. He was accosted by one of the enemy who was heard to say: "You are not dead", and struck Cpl. Knight across the face with his rifle, causing a damaged and bloody nose.

On 20th April 1944 security restrictions were enforced and on 24th April operational orders for the defence of the railways came into effect.

Langport Home Guard mounted guard at our side of the tunnel and at the ventilation shaft with communication links between guard posts. I was on duty for two days during which a minor case of sabotage occurred – telephone wires were cut.

We were informed that a convict had escaped and was dressed in a Home Guard Sergeant's uniform and we were told to be on the alert.

There was a dogfight overhead, tracer bullets criss-crossed the sky travelling down the searchlight beams, extinguishing two. Bullets also zipped through the hedge close to our guard hut and personnel including Cpl. Knight sent out a search party, with no results.

(right) Lt. Loman with the **N.C.O.s of Langport Platoon**, photographed outside the Old Grammar School, Langport.
Back Row: L/Cpl. Bill Wainwright; L/Cpl. Crumb;
 L/Cpl. R. Jotcham; L/Cpl. Hale
Middle Row: L/Cpl. John Jotcham; Cpl. Ashton Knight;
 Cpl. Lou Churchill; Cpl. Ted Pavey
Front Row: Cpl. Harold Martin; Sgt. Fred Parker; Lt. Bill Loman;
 Cpl. Albert Jones
(Mrs. Hazel Jotcham collection)

(left) **Men of Langport Platoon** in October 1944. This plate was contemporaneously inscribed by the photographer, W. Rouse, a member of Langport Company.
Back Row: Pte. Coe; Pte. Cox; Pte. Lampert; Pte. Hussey;
 L/Cpl. Hale; Pte. Childs; Pte. Adams; Pte. Tovey
Second Row: L/Cpl. Wainwright; Pte. Webber; L/Cpl. J. Jotcham;
 L/Cpl. Crumb; Pte. Badman; Pte. F. Smith; Pte. Vile;
 Pte. A. Smith; Pte. Langford; Pte. Dimond; Cpl. Davey;
 L/Cpl. R. Jotcham
Front Row: Cpl. Churchill; Cpl. Jones; Sgt. Parker; Lt. Loman;
 Maj. McEvoy; C.S.M. Davies; Cpl. Martin; Cpl. Knight
(Freddie Vile collection)

Members of Aller Home Guard pose outside Mr. Jackson's office at the Aller Dairy.
Back Row: Dennis Harvey; Bill Peppard; Ray Mitchell; George Peppard; Mr. Napier
Front Row: Warburton 'Warry' Mitchell; Ted Lockyer; John Lockyer; Stuart 'John' Jackson;
No doubt exists as to their identification as the photograph was contemporaneously captioned. Ray Mitchell was in the Royal Navy and was on leave when the photograph was taken. In the 1980s when Ted Lockyer's home was being renovated, a considerable amount of 9mm Sten gun ammunition was found hidden on a wallplate in the roof.
(Miss Evelyn Jackson collection)

(below) **Part of Langport Company, High Ham Home Guard** parade outside the Village Hall.
Back Row: Ray Reading; Hubert Priddle; Norman Crossman; Jack Cullen; Maurice Gould; Harry Johnson; Albert Cullen; Maurice Hurd; Jeff Oram; Ted Gould; Austin Lavis
Middle Row: Vigar Webb; Charlie Scriven; Bill Richards; Sid Vigar; Sid Langford; Henry Vigar; Ed Brooks
Front Row: Ron Tapscott; David Coombes; Sgt. Fred Clark; Henry Crocker; Ken Duddridge; Percy Windsor; Gordon Vigar; Sid Shepherd

Whilst the quality of the photograph precludes correct identification of rank, it is known that Fred Clark was a Sergeant. Early meetings were held in the garage of the cottage by the green. Later the more spacious village hall was used. With the threat of invasion imminent in the summer of 1940, High Ham Home Guard kept a night-time vigil over the countryside looking towards Pitney from a hut erected close to High Ham Windmill. Turn Hill, presented to the National Trust in memory of a young man who fell in The Great War, was also used as an observation point.
(Author's collection)

Long Sutton Home Guard, *photographed behind* The Devonshire Arms.
Back Row: Albert J. Lewis; Fred Thomas; Percy Shire; George Watts; Fred Small; Bill Lock
Middle Row: William Warner; Percy Parsons; William Curtis; W. Edwards; William Burt; J. Rendall; Albert Vigar; Charles Bennett
Front Row: L/Cpl. Redvers Charles Burt; Cpl. Hube Cox; Q.M.S. Charles Burt; Mr. Elmer; L/Cpl. R. Suter; L/Cpl. Fred Cox
Albert Lewis, Percy Shire, William Warner, William Burt, Hube Cox, Charles Bennett, Redvers Burt, Charles Burt and R. Suter were all farmworkers whilst George Watts, Percy Parsons, Fred Cox, Fred Small and Albert Vigar were local farmers. William Curtis was a woodworker for Harry Hebditch at Martock. Mr. Elmer was the licensee of The Devonshire Arms, *the skittle alley of which was used for Home Guard purposes and Mr. Elmer's inclusion in the photograph was by means of saying "Thank you".*
(Redvers Burt collection)

The following were also members of the Platoon: Samuel Mitchell, Bert Pope, Charles Sheppard, George Bennett, Edward Burt, Allan Burt, George Aldworth (all farmworkers), Ronald Bryant, Charlie Vaux (both sons of farmers), Charles Cheeseman (a retired Colonel and Platoon Lieutenant), Joseph Cox (Dispatch Rider) and Jack Squire (the local Pearl Insurance agent).

As with many platoons, Long Sutton possessed a Spigot Mortar. Two 'Harry Hebditch' pig huts were purchased for storage of this weapon. One was sited in the corner of an orchard in Long Sutton at map ref. ST 469 251 whilst the other was erected in a small copse at map ref. ST 469 248 overlooking the Long Load river bridge.

One of the duties of Long Sutton Platoon, in conjunction with Langport and High Ham Home Guards, was to guard the western portal of the Somerton tunnel and the ventilation shaft on Somerton Hill. For the convenience of the guards, huts were erected at both spots.

For carrying out this duty the men were paid about two shillings (10p) a night which could last up to ten hours. During the day a detachment of the Coldstream Guards protected the tunnel. No sleeping in wooden huts for them, they were billeted in *The Devonshire Arms*.

Army instructions clearly laid down the procedure to be adopted by sentries guarding installations. Should no response be given to the initial challenge it was to be repeated. If this was also ignored the sentry was authorised, in certain circumstances to open fire. This was in the mind of an officer on one occasion carrying out his night-time rounds of the sentries. He heard the first challenge but was concerned to hear the challenge repeated (the sentry having failed to hear his response of "friend" to the first one). Realising that the next thing he would receive was a shot, he cried out at the top of his voice: "Say something, man". Fortunately the words "advance one" were heard and no fatal shot was fired.

SOMERTON COMPANY

COMMANDING OFFICER	Major H.M. Clowes	COMPANY HEADQUARTERS	Montclefe House
2ND IN COMMAND	Capt. R.N. Chudleigh	BATTLE HEADQUARTERS	Montclefe House (D.L.)

Somerton Company comprised three Platoons and a mobile reserve as detailed below:

Somerton Platoon
O.C. Platoon   Lt. W.J. Hawker
Headquarters   Montclefe House
Battle Headquarters   Montclefe House

Compton Dundon Platoon
O.C. Platoon   Lt. R.J. Luffman
Headquarters   Village Hall, Compton Dundon
Battle Headquarters   Montclefe House

Kingsdon Platoon
O.C. Platoon   2nd Lt. T.G. Badelow
Headquarters   Reading Room, Kingsdon
Battle Headquarters   The Lodge, Kingsdon House

Mobile Reserve
O.C. Platoon   2nd Lt. G.W. Pangbourne
Headquarters   Kirkham House, Somerton
Battle Headquarters   Tithe Barn, Somerton

Somerton Home Guard, photographed outside Somerton Church.
Back Row: Jim Hawker (War Agricultural Committee); Roy Haines (farmer); Arthur Sweet (carpenter); Jack Burt (War Agricultural Committee); Fred Escott (farmworker); Bill Squires (employee of Somerton Radio Station); Eric Matthews (milkman); John Hewson (farmer); Mr. Searle (Stationmaster at Somerton Station); Arthur Fevin (River Board employee); Les Miles (farmworker); Bill Haskett (blacksmith); Bert Deacon (farmworker)
Middle Row: Fred Gooding (G.W.R. permanent way worker); Arthur Beacon (employed by Cow and Gate); Albert Pittard (quarryman); Ted Burfitt; Bill Kiddle (local council employee); Fred Beacon (farmworker); Jack Gooding (farmworker); Arthur Childs (gardener); Reg Spiller (farmer); Don Paramore (engineer); Charlie Lawrence (farmworker); Mr. Westlake; Norman Glover (farmworker); Gerald Newbury (War Agricultural Committee); Roger Barker (carpenter); Roly Wainwright (gardener)
Front Row: Jack Bond (chemist); Mr. Teagle; Charlie Goddard (smallholder); Lt. Bill Hawker (saddler); Major H.M. Clowes (barrister); Capt. R.N. Chudleigh; Lt. Gerald Pembourne; Bill Burfitt (farmworker); Tim Buckland (baker); Ron Bennett (farmworker)
(Ron Bennett collection)

Unidentified members of the Home Guard march through Somerton. The member nearest the camera is carrying a Sten gun.
(Redvers Burt collection)

CHARLTON COMPANY

COMMANDING OFFICER   Major W.G.A. Freke   2ND IN COMMAND   Capt. F.B. Hardinge

Members of Charlton Mackrell Company pose outside The Quarry Inn *in Keinton Mandeville.*

First Floor Windows: A. Locke; Philip Cabble; Percy Eades; George Davey; Jeff Dabinett; Doug Denning; William Davey; George Small; Ed Hodges; Stan Hodges

Back Row: George Arthur; Edgar Weeks; Bill Hallett; Don Atyeo; Unknown; Bernard Willcox; Stan Jeffrey; Perce Alford; Unknown; George Thresh; John Burton; Jim Crab; Ted Dayment; Wilf Crab; Bill Burton

Second Row: Bob Hodges; Fred Ingram; Unknown; Unknown; Unknown; Mr. Baker; John George; George Feltham; Unknown; Robert Willcox; Unknown; Unknown; Unknown; Arthur Hellings; George Reeves; Charlie Jefferies; Frank Phillips; Unknown; Henry Burton

Third Row: Unknown; Walter Perry; Joe Boyce; Fred Hodges; Unknown; Bert Sealey; Jim Hunt; Ralph Atyeo; Edric Atyeo; Harold Croom; Stan Pullen; Unknown; Arthur Burton; Arthur Crang; Sid Dyer; Cecil Crang; Henry Gibbs; Alec Whitehead; George Gibbs; Unknown; Jack Pickford; Unknown

Fourth Row: Unknown; Unknown; John Escott; Unknown; Maurice Board; Unknown; Perce Sevior; Maurice Davey; Mr. Dykes (head gardener, Coombe Hill House); Charles Hart; Stan Comer (blacksmith); Unknown; Ray Bailey; Cecil Coates; Sam Langford; Ken Southway; Richard Corp; Brian Paddock; Arthur Lambert; Arthur Coate; Harry Parker; Unknown; Unknown; Walter Croom; Percy Burton or George Warren; Jack James; Ken Spearing; Harry Mogg; Bill Hodges; Fred Willmott; Unknown; Chris Pickford; Eddie Cox; George Hanham; Reg Davey

Front Row: Mrs. Violet Griffin (née Webb); Mrs. Cox; Mrs. Bryant; Mrs. Cathleen Cross (née Cox); Sgt. William Paddock; Sgt. Harry Paul; Lt. Alan Freke; Lt. William Seager; Lt. Wilf Hasell; Capt. F.B. Hardinge; Major William G.A. Freke; Lt. George Stoodley; Lt. Harry Cabble; Sgt. Ralph Maggs; Sgt. Lukins; Sgt. Jack Wines; Sgt. George Warry; Mrs. Freke; Mrs. Ingram; Mrs. Feltham; Mrs. Doris Maggs

Sitting on the groundsheet: Sgt. Mogg; W.O. Alfred Ingram

(H. Burton collection)

(left) Opposite Battalion Headquarters in Keinton Mandeville stands the remains of a typical Home Guard stone house at map ref. ST 551 316. Regulations covering such buildings stated that:

A combined store house may be used provided that

The explosive portion is completely divided from the inflammable portion by a fire-proof sandbag, concrete or brick partition at least 9" thick and,

Explosives do not exceed 500lbs

Inflammables do not exceed 100 gallons

Separate access is provided to each portion

This particular building, with doors at both ends, shows no signs of a central partition, suggesting that its interior wall was built of sandbags. The doors appear to be postwar replacements. (Author's collection)

(right) **Members of Keinton Mandeville and Barton St. David Platoon (Battalion HQ Platoon).**
Back Row: Reg Davey; William Davey; John Escott; Perce Sevior; Bill Vining; George Davey
Front Row: L/Cpl. Jack Vining; L/Cpl. Maurice Davey; Sgt. Mogg; Charlie Hart; Lt. Harry Cabble (Officer Commanding Platoon); Doug Denning; L/Cpl. Ern Cook
One can only guess at the significance of the trophy!
(William Davey collection)

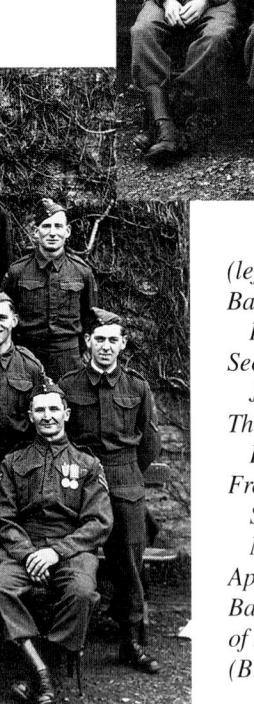

(left) **Charlton Section Charlton Platoon.**
Back Row: Bob Hodges; Jack Wiltshire; Bert Sealey; Mr. Baker; Fred Ingram
Second Row: Maurice Board; Walter Perry; Brian Paddock; Jim Hunt; Harold Croom; William Hallett; Ralph Atyeo
Third Row: Fred Hodges; George Arthur; Edric Atyeo; Walter Croom; Percy Eades; Cyril Eades; George Small; L/Cpl. Stanley Hodges
Front Row: Cpl. Edward Hodges; Sgt. William Paddock; Lt. William Seager; Lt. George H. Stoodley (Officer Commanding Platoon); Mrs. Ingram; W.O. Alfred Ingram; Cpl. Harry Mogg
Apart from Bert Sealey and William Seager, who both worked at Barham's Quarry, nothing else is known of the civilian occupations of members of this section.
(Brian Paddock collection)

Static and Battle Headquarters for Charlton Platoon was Charlton House, Charlton Mackrell.

Brian Paddock joined Charlton Section in May 1943 and left in December 1944 to join The Royal Artillery. He recalls the following facts:

Charlton Mackrell Reading Room was the section meeting place. Ammunition was stored in a steel hut at Barham's Quarry whose manager was Lt. William Seager. The road through Charlton Mackrell was protected by two 'pillboxes', most likely to have been sandbagged emplacements constructed at each end of the village. The one at the northern end of the village was situated at the bend in the road by Charlton Court facing up the road to Christian's Cross whilst the one at the southern end was again situated on the west side of the road opposite the lane to Charlton Adam looking towards Lytes Cary. It was known locally as Stepp'n' Stones.

The rifle range was situated on Snap Hill, the site of the near fatal accident involving Harry Paul, described on p.292.

Lydford Members of the Babcary-with-Lydford Platoon.
Back Row: Gerald Phillips; Harry Hallett; Norman Hawkins; Joe Thrush; Stan Jeffrey; Frank Phillips; Alec Whitehead; Stanley Phillips; Ivor James; Ken Spearing; George Warren
Middle Row: Don Richards or Len Dunn; Charles Jefferies; Chris Pickford; Cecil Bacon; Cliff Shepherd; Jim Boyes; Perce Alford; Ken Parham; Bill Brown; Bernard Willcocks; Jack Pickford; Unknown (worked at Park Farm)
Front Row: Cathleen Cross; Cpl. Charles Meade Kidd; Sgt. Jack Wines; 2nd Lt. Ralph Maggs (Platoon Officer); Unknown; C.S.M. Stoodley; Cpl. Jack James; Cpl. Reg Helps; Mrs. Doris Maggs
(John Maggs collection)

(left) **Babcary Members of the Babcary-with-Lydford Platoon.**
Back Row: Reg Bisgrove; Cecil Crang; Henry Gibbs; George Gibbs
Second Row: Arthur Burton; Sidney Dyer; George Feltham; Fred Hooper; John Burton; Jim Crab; Ted Dayment; William Burton
Third Row: Arthur Crang; Bill Hooper; Stan Pullen; Bill Hodges; Arthur Hellings; Bill Venner; Henry Burton
Front Row: Mrs. Bryant; Sgt. Percy Burton; Mrs. Feltham; Lt. Alan Freke; Major William Freke; Lt. Wilf Hasell (Officer Commanding Platoon); Sgt. George Warry; Mrs. Freke; Cpl. George Reeves
Other members included S. Cannon, Mr. Jenner, H. Bisgrove, E. Bisgrove, Ted Damon, G. Thorn and D. Pelton.
(George Reeves collection)

Babcary Home Guard's 'home' was Babcary School. *The Red Lion* provided facilities for shooting .22 rifles. The firing point was in a garage whilst the targets were in a pig sty. The cellars of Kingweston House provided another site for a small-bore range, whilst the range at Snap Hill was used for service rifles.

At Foddington a searchlight battery manned by the regulars was guarded by the Home Guard. George Reeves recalls on more than one occasion the accommodation huts sited in a nearby orchard were 'shot up' by German planes on their way home from raids in the north.

Battle Headquarters for Babcary with Lydford Platoon was the Lydford Cross Roads map ref. 004 519, whilst static headquarters was Standerwick Farm, the home of Wilf Hasell.

Keinton Mandeville Platoon Small-bore Rifle Team. Although not captioned, the title was suggested by the late Sam Langford. The photograph was taken to commemorate Keinton Mandeville Platoon's success in a competition which took place at The Cross Keys Public House.
Back Row: L/Cpl. Cecil Coates; Sam Langford; L/Cpl. Art Lambert; Harry Parker; L/Cpl. Eddie Cox
Front Row: Raymond Bailey; Capt. Hardinge; Sgt. Harry Paul; Lt. Harry Cabble; Cpl. Fred Willmott
(Raymond Bailey collection)

Harry Paul was a local undertaker who was lucky not to meet his Maker prematurely when he was struck in the chest by a ricocheting bullet on the Snap Hill range. He was taken to the doctor's at Somerton, proclaimed fit and discharged.

The Snap Hill Rifle Range was built solely for the Home Guard. It was sited on the north side of the Keinton Mandeville-Somerton Road. The firing point, according to the late Sam Langford, was approximately at map ref. ST 515 297 whilst the butts were at map ref. ST 515 298. Passing the site today, nothing appears to remain of the range. However, a visit in April 2003 revealed the rotted stump of a flagstaff close to the butts (*below*).

This range lies approximately one mile to the east of the site of a much larger 1,000-yard range which existed in the 1890s. When the G.W.R. was built through Somerton, the range was truncated and could not be used for its full length. However, it appears to have survived, being shown on early maps of the 20th century.

Part of the Platoon's duties in 1944 was to guard Skew Bridge where the Great Western Railway crossed over the Keinton Mandeville-Somerton Road. A wooden hut was erected in the field to the north-east of the bridge to provide shelter for resting pickets. This was a commodious shelter complete with a stove. Unfortunately, this proved too comfortable on one occasion when the picket, coming off their turn on a cold night, was unable to gain access, their comrades preferring playing cards to sentry duty. They were soon 'smoked out' when a wet sack was stuffed down the stove pipe.

Sam Langford, well known after the war for his beekeeping, joined the Home Guard in 1941 as a member of the Headquarters Platoon whose meeting place was Keinton Mandeville Village Hut, destroyed by fire in 1992. Possessing a Triumph Speed Twin motorcycle he was used as a dispatch rider. Writing in the 1990s he recalled some of his experiences:

(Author's collection)

> The officer in charge of Somerton Company reported Charlton Mackrell Company for failing to man their post at Skew Bridge one night. During the build-up to D-Day in 1944, Philip Cabble and I were on guard duty there. In the early hours of the morning, after a hot night, a car approached very slowly from the Somerton direction. We took post, one on each side of the road. When the car reached us we jumped out and commanded the driver to stop. As both windows were down rifle muzzles were pressed each side of the driver's neck. The driver turned out to be 'our friend' the C.O. of Somerton Company who had previously reported our fellow Home Guards. He was suitably impressed.
>
> Shortly before D-Day the Home Guard from Cornwall to Salisbury Plain was mustered as Guards Units were staging an exercise along an unknown route. Charlton Mackrell Company was deployed behind walls and hedges armed with all kinds of 'soft' missiles. Being a D.R. my duty was to patrol as far west as Snap Hill and look out for any convoys leaving Somerton, return and report without being captured. Eventually a convoy of military vehicles was seen leaving Somerton. Charlton Mackrell Company were alerted and waited. As the vehicles drove rapidly through Keinton they were 'ambushed'. Alas, it turned out to be an American Unit who received a good pasting from our soft missiles. They were not amused to be covered in all sorts of débris. Our real 'target' travelled via Langport and Podimore, unaware of the surprise that was waiting for them.

CASTLE CARY COMPANY

COMMANDING OFFICER   Major H.B. Clark, O.B.E., M.C.   2ND IN COMMAND   Capt. W.A. Osborn

***North Cadbury, Woolston, Galhampton, Yarlington, Sparkford and Weston Bampfylde Home Guard**. Whilst no names were provided with the photograph, many faces appear in the one below. Both photographs were taken outside* The Sparkford Inn, *the lower one in 1944, the upper one a little earlier the same year, as the shrubs have not grown up the left-hand window. (Kenneth Alway collection)*

***'B' Platoon Castle Cary Company**, comprising men from West Cadbury, Woolston, Galhampton and Yarlington.*
Back Row: A.M. Troakes; G.J. Walter; W.E. Pitman; M.G. Alway; J.H. Alway; W.J. Dyer; E.J. Candy; W.C. Kempster; E.C. Ryall
Second Row: G.H. Elford; A.H. Day; F.W. Cook; G. Clothier; G. Griffin; A.G. Apsey; I.T. Pitman; L/Cpl. E.H. Davis; L/Cpl. H.R. Miller; G. Marshall; C.J. Cocks; L/Cpl. J.S. Chamberlain; P.C. Clothier; R.E. Stickland; L/Cpl. G.J. Bartlett; A.M. Herman; G. Raymond; H.W. Chalker; B. Fox; E.J. Whitehead; R.D. Bartlett; H.W. Snook
Third Row: W.J. Beach; Cpl. E.W. Parker; Cpl. S. Osborne; Cpl. F. Sparey; Cpl. R.J. Hunt; Sgt. L.T. Bartlett; Sgt. L. Davis; Lt. W.A. Osborn; Lt. C.G. Wills; Sgt. W. Heath; Cpl. S. Paynter; Cpl. R.W. Hockey; Cpl. L. Buckley; Cpl. T. House; A.H. Cox
Front Row: C. House; H. Sparey; F. Windsor; R.F. Mitchell; K. Davis; L.W. Snook; S.A. Newport; A.B.C. Rendell; L. Henderson; E.S. Brain; G.A. Higgins.
(Kenneth Alway collection)

Sparkford and Weston Bampfylde Home Guard.
Back Row: G. Fowler; J. Dyke; Mr. Mitchell; R. Hobbs; Mr. Chivers; D. Cluet; H. Hoskins; R. Payne; J. Edwards; J. Coleman; C. Alexander; Unknown
Second Row: D. Stevens; J. Morrison; Unknown; F. Hedditch; R. Perry; Mr. Osborne; H. Lane; F. Reeves; B. Bishop; D. Green; T. Perry
Front Row: Mr. House; M. Toop; J. Sugg; R. Brooks; F. Pomeroy; A. Budgell; C. Penny; H. Lintern
(The Sparkford Inn)

Barrow Section, Castle Cary Home Guard.
Back Row: Tom Goodland; Les Marsh; George Shipper; Alec Powell; Donald Carpenter; Vivian Marsh; Eddie Dauncey; Claude Lawrence; Ambrose Lawrence; Nat Higgins; Jack Wake; Bill Shire
Front Row: Ern Goodland; L/Cpl. Rev. John Wright; Cpl. Percy Bowyer; Lt. Carr; Cpl. Jim Miles; L/Cpl. Charlie Coward
Missing from the photograph is Sgt. Carpenter.
(Les Marsh collection)

Les Marsh joined the Home Guard in 1941 aged 16 and recalls the Headquarters of the Company being at Castle Cary Drill Hall. As with all units at the beginning of the war a lookout for parachutists was kept at North Barrow. As the build-up for D-Day progressed, Barrow Section guarded the railway bridge at the end of Dimmer Lane.

Private Marsh's proudest moment was shooting for his marksman's badge at Hadspen Range in the presence of the Company Commander. He successfully shot a 5 round 4" group at 200 yards, receiving Major Clark's congratulations. (This standard of shooting required Les to prevent the muzzle of his rifle moving by less than the thickness of a postcard off the centre of the target with ordinary iron sights, no mean feat.) Les believes there were only two members of the Castle Cary Home Guard who received this award.

Castle Cary's last Home Guard Parade outside The Britannia Hotel. *The above title was written on the back of the original photograph with the date 11th September 1944. On 6th September an announcement had been made on the wireless that Home Guard parades would in the future be voluntary. It would be another three months before Castle Cary Home Guard took part in their final parade on 3rd December 1944, again in the rain!*
(Castle Cary and Ansford Living History Group collection)

BRUTON COMPANY

COMMANDING OFFICER   Major F.F. Whitfield
2ND IN COMMAND   Capt. J.E.S. Jones

Wyke Champflower Platoon, photographed at King's School, Bruton.
Back Row: W. Shepherd; K. Golledge; John Hall; John Tapp; Roy Hatcher; Norman Isgrove
Middle Row: Sgt. Major Bill Lucas; Capt. J.E.S. Jones; Cpl. Bruce Clothier; Ted Shepherd
Front Row: Sgt. Bill Moxham; Lt. Bob Snell; Cpl. Dan Clothier; Geoff Norman; Leonard Adams
Note the Marksman's badge on Geoff Norman's sleeve. Other Platoon members included C. Richards, B. Snadden, K. Hatcher, E. James and Sgt. W. Garland.
(Roy Hatcher collection)

Weston Broadway was a member of Pitcombe and Shepton Montague Home Guard, part of Bruton Company. Names recalled by Weston are T. Russ, B. James, K. Moger and L. Arnold. Weapons were stored at Cole Manor whilst stores were kept at *The Blue Ball*, Bruton.

Roy Hatcher was a member of Wyke Champflower Platoon, part of Bruton Company. The unit included men from the villages of Wyke Champflower and Lamyatt. The commander was Lt. Bob Snell, a farmer from Wyke Champflower. Capt. Jack Jones was one of the other officers, his civilian occupation being the owner of the animal feed mill in Bruton.

A pre-war 5-target range was used at Lower Hadspen. The targets were at map ref. ST 656 332 with the 600-yard firing point at map ref. ST 661 334. In addition to rifle and sten gun practice the range was used for the throwing of No. 73 anti-tank grenade and the No. 74 sticky bomb. Grenade practice took place on Creech Hill. The Lower Hadspen range was also used by local Army Units. A visit to the range in November 2001 revealed nothing of the range had survived apart from some 1"-thick slabs of steel now used as drain covers. The butts and firing points had been totally flattened, filled in and an orchard planted. Small-bore shooting was undertaken on the indoor range at Kings School, Bruton.

In the early years of the Home Guard a night-time watch for paratroops was undertaken from local hilltops. Creech Hill to the north-west of Bruton was one of the vantage points used, a wooden hut being erected to provide some protection for the sentries during their lonely vigil. At Higher Hadspen a hollowed out haystack to the south-west of Stump Cross was also used as a shelter in the early days. Locations guarded included Black Hole where the Somerset and Dorset Railway crossed over the Great Western Railway and also where the G.W.R. crossed over the A359, where a small wooden hut was provided. During the war there was a searchlight unit based at Wyke Champflower on the left-hand side of the Bruton-Wyke Champflower road. The Nissen huts, located at map ref. ST 670 349, remained on site until the 1990s. During the war local Home Guards were always assured of a welcome mug of tea here.

Great Western trains passing through Bruton gave the Home Guard the opportunity to practise aiming at a moving target. Unfortunately, on one occasion, a volunteer who we shall call Reg G. of Lamyatt had a loaded rifle and fired at a passing train. The shot fortunately went 'high'. However, his actions had not gone unnoticed by those in authority and he was subsequently requested to leave the Home Guard.

On a lighter note a well-practised two-man drill involved 'falling in' at Bruton before marching off with the platoon and smartly 'falling out' into a deep ditch when the column was under way. Time was then spent in a local hostelry before waiting in the ditch to rejoin the returning column. Problems arose if either the column varied its return route to Bruton or the absentees were asked what they had learnt from the evening's exercise.

(left) Major F.F. Whitfield poses with some of his men in October 1944.
Back Row: Frank Sly; Mr. Chamberlain
Middle Row: Dick Cox; Major Whitfield; Capt. Jack Jones; Walt Tyndall; Mr. Catley
Front Row: Sgt. Bill Oram; Jim Hoskins; Cpl. Stan Vincent
(Bruton Museum)

(right) **Members of Bruton Home Guard** *with a 2-pounder Anti-Tank Gun.*
Back Row: H. Fowler; Unknown; Cecil Travis or Travers
Middle Row: B. Creed; T. Pearce
Front Row: Ted Payne; W. Tyndall; Stan Vincent
Jim Hoskins, featured in the previous photograph, confirms that this photograph was taken on the playing field at King's School, Bruton. The photographer was standing with his back to the railway line and with the local church out of shot to his right.
(Bruton Museum)

(above) The epitome of the Home Guard. Viv Marsh stands outside his home at Dimmer.
(Les Marsh collection)

Bruton Home Guard, *photographed on the playing field at King's School, Bruton.*
Back Row: Sgt. Major William Lucas; Weston Broadway; Albert Stone; Mr. Sargeson; George Martin; William Bendle
Front Row: Eric Hansford; Cpl. Walter Cox; Sgt. Lane; Lt. Reg Bullock; Sgt. William Mills; Cpl. Arthur Biggs; Reg Elliott
Both Sgt. Lane and Reg Bullock were teachers at Sexey's School, Bruton.
(Miss Freda Sarah Elliott collection)

MILBORNE PORT COMPANY

COMMANDING OFFICER   Major B.B. Dyke   2ND IN COMMAND   Capt. Hector G. Southcombe

'A' Platoon Milborne Port Company.
Back Row: L/Cpl. George Batten; Mr. Button; Mr. Dungey; Mr. Crossley; Albert Mitchell; Eddie Masters; Ossie Masters; Bert Guppy; Mr. Mitchell; Bill Biddiscombe; L/Cpl. Donald L. King
Second Row: Mr. Durrant; Stan Hannam; Stan Dowding; Len West; Lionel Raison; John Waltham; Mr. Hallett; Alan Brown; L/Cpl. Arthur Higgins; L/Cpl. Archie Scammell
Third Row: L/Cpl. Bill Weller; Mr. Thompson; Eric Frost; Ted Tuck; Lionel Grimes; Richard Waltham; Percy Hallett; Mr. Marsh; Frank Stanier; Mr. Clases
Fourth Row: Cpl. George Heritage; Cpl. Alec Davis; Cpl. Harry Smith; Sgt. Bert Snook; Capt. Hector G. Southcombe; Major B.B. Dyke; Lt. John Buck; Lt. Fred Roun; ?Sgt. Bernie Ham; ?Sgt. Percy Durrant; ?Cpl. Hugh 'Litty' Cabell; ?Cpl. Charlie Lamb
Front Row: Sid White (Légion d'Honneur); Mr. Lewis; Aubrey Chant; Bill Hide or Mr. Lane; Bill Cooper; Bert Cook
(D.L. King collection)

Information received from Mr. D.L. King shortly before his death provides the following details. Henstridge and Yenston villages formed 'B' Platoon whilst Charlton Horethorne and Corton Denham formed 'C' Platoon. Company armoury and stores were situated at Dyke's Glove Factory, Milborne Port. Guard duties included: 1940-42, parachutist night patrol, railway line and bridge patrols; 1942-43, relief night-time guard at the local searchlight battery. In addition to using Sherborne Territorial Drill Hall for small-bore shooting, the company built their own outdoor range at Vartenham Hill, Milborne Port. Interestingly, Mr. King clearly remembered all the .300" rifle ammunition that had been issued for their rifles and light machine guns being recalled as a large amount all over the country had been found to be faulty, causing some accidents.

Sutton Montis/Corton Denham Home Guard.
Back Row: F. Cleal; D. Lock; J. Maidment; C. Lock; E. Snook; C. Kynaston; R. Kynaston; J. Foot; R. White; J. Rendell
Second Row: L. Rendell; W. Garrett; W. Maidment; E. Coward; F. Penny; Jack Doddington; V. Coles; W. Andrews; G. Thompson
Third Row: G. Foot; Mr. Stephens; J. Groves; W. Chant; R. Lamb; W. Davis; C. Lamb; L/Cpl. D. Creed; F. Mead; G. Pritchard
Front Row: Cpl. T. Watts; Cpl. C. Partridge; Sgt. H. Lamb; Capt. H.G. Southcombe; Major B.B. Dyke; Lt. F. Paul; Sgt. D. Crofts; Cpl. F. Lucas; Cpl. J. Bartlett; Cpl. G. Spencer
(Mrs. M.J. Hughes collection)

Mr. C.W. Jones of Wincanton remembers the following:

The Platoon rifle range was at Sutton Montis where the back stop was the high ground of Cadbury Castle. Other elevated positions at Sigwells and Charlton provided good vantage points for lookouts. In addition to their personal weapons two ambush sites were selected for Flame Fougasse. The first was on the road from Charlton Horethorne to Wincanton on the left of Charlton Hill a few yards before the summit at ST 671 242. The second was on the Charlton Horethorne to Milborne Port road, "on the crossroads after the Crescent Buildings", at ST 673 211. Another ambush site was at Blackford Hollow on the road leaving the old A303 down to Blackford which had very deep banks. Flame Fougasse was not installed here.

One exercise involved ambushing a Guards Armoured unit as it passed through the area. The Home Guard were issued with chalk bombs. To make things more 'interesting', Sgt. Jones, remembering an old WW1 trick, mixed creosote and pig manure, pouring the mixture into old bottles. These were then placed into old stockings or socks. The attack on the armoured vehicles went to plan. Unfortunately, two Home Guards were captured. The 'enemy' then took them for a ride of about eight miles leaving them on the roadside to walk home. Milking started late that day.

Members of an unknown platoon, **Milborne Port Company**, photographed at Stand Down. Letters in brackets indicate the members' home villages:
CH=Charlton Horethorne; BK=Blackford; CP=Compton Pauncefoot.
Back Row: J. Collis (CH); W. Bundy (BK); L/Cpl. L. Wilton (CP); C. Clothier (CH); E. Wingham (CH); W. Lucas (CP); W. Dewfall (CH); Unknown; T. Hodges (CH); E. Bond (CH)
Second Row: S. Williams (CH); F. Perry (CH); J. Swain (CH); Unknown; Mr. Shoemark; C. Newport (CP); K. Ashman (CH); E. Starks (CH); J. Richards (BK)
Third Row: L. Warr (CH); F. Newport (CP); W. Newport (CP); J. Parker (CH); Mr. Cross (CH); W. Moorse (CH); T. Miller (CH); S. Shergold (CH); H. Axe (CH); Mr. Tilly
Front Row: Cpl. Dibben (CH); Cpl. R. Harris (CH); Cpl. New (CH); Sgt. H. Silk (CH); Capt. Southcombe; Major Dyke; Lt. J. Parsons; Sgt. W. Jones (CP); Cpl. C. Norris (CP); Cpl. W. Dewberry (CP)
(C.W. Jones collection)

WINCANTON COMPANY

COMMANDING OFFICER   Major A.C. Clark   2ND IN COMMAND   Capt. L.E. Agar

Wincanton Home Guard.
Back Row: J. Frazer; H. Crocker; W. Hookings; F. James; S. Stott; D. Coggan; S. Mullin; Harry Small; L. Eves; R. Arnold; E. Bargery; Percy Brixey
Second Row: Cpl. J. Thompson; H. Bristol; N. Trim; J. Tucker; M. Bastable; T. Hibberd; D. Dike; J. Brown; B. Keen; T. Buckingham; D. Clarke; S. Candy; J. Arnold; Cpl. T. Webb
Third Row: W. Hurst; W. Blow; D. Higgins; F. Doe; J. Haskett; G. Biles; F. Andrews; F. Dunston; R. Hibberd; D. Keen; J. White; F. Wyatt; B. Taylor; K. Leach
Front Row: Cpl. M. Hamblin; Sgt. V. Webb; Sgt. F. Hayter; Sgt. D. Dunford; Sgt. Major E. Bargery; Lt. W. Parsons; Major A.C. Clark; Capt. L.E. Agar; 2nd Lt. E. Hibberd; Sgt. S. Talbot; Sgt. W. Street; Sgt. J. Maddox
(Reginald Hibberd collection)

2nd Lt. E.P. Hibberd was a member of Wincanton Platoon whose Headquarters was at the Wesleyan Church Hall. The Platoon possessed the usual array of Home Guard weapons. Sten gun practice took place at Windmill Farm, Stowell, the highest part of the village where, in the early days a wooden hut, complete with stove, was erected for the look-out picket. Duties also included guarding Templecombe Station and Wincanton Telephone Exchange. Lt. Parsons and Lt. Hibberd inspected the guard on alternate nights between 11.00 and midnight.

On at least one weekend Battalion officers met at Burton Pynsent House, Curry Rivel (the home of Major Barnes, the Commander of Curry Rivel Company) for an officers' meeting.

Two exercises remembered by Lt. Hibberd were when Wincanton Home Guard travelled to Taunton to take the part of an attacking force, and the night-time exercise at Lydford-on-Fosse when Lt. Hibberd and his men became hopelessly lost. (The reader should be aware that during the war village signs were removed or obliterated, station name boards painted out, signposts removed, in fact anything that would indicate to an attacker his location. This, together with the blackout, must have contributed to Lt. Hibberd's predicament.)

One Sunday the Platoon travelled to Corton Denham to see a demonstration of the Spigot Mortar. Lt. Hibberd's impression was that it was "an awesome weapon and dangerous for one and all". (In fact, at an early demonstration, the future President De Gaulle of France nearly became the first casualty.)

Reginald Hibberd was a private in the Home Guard, joining on 19th January 1942. His guard duties included patrolling the area around Hawker's Bridge, Wincanton Station and the Town Hall. Wincanton Laundry provided a billet for the off-duty guards.

One incident Reg remembered was when Wincanton Town Clock was 'accidentally' shot whilst loading and unloading practice was taking place.

*As the sun sets slowly in the west, men of **Wincanton Home Guard** proudly march down Wincanton High Street, past* The Dolphin. *(Mrs. Alice Brixey collection)*

North Cheriton, Maperton and Holton Home Guard in 1944.
Back Row: C. Snook; Reginald Lloyd; Lloyd McCreadie; Col. D.R. Edwards; R. McCreadie; H. Avery; Mr. House; A. Polden; Vic Watts
Middle Row: L/Cpl. W. Martin; Cpl. W. Banting; Sgt. Baker; Sir Digby Lawson; Sgt. C. Dunford; Cpl. W. Newman; Cpl. W. Paull; L/Cpl. Collins
Front Row: B. Butcher; M. Hughes; L/Cpl. A. Cole; J. Rowden; Unknown
Col. D.R. Edwards and Mr. Baker, who was a Company Sergeant-Major, had both served in the First World War.
Note the beehives in the background; honey was an important source of sweetener during the war. (Dick Bell collection)

Pen Selwood Home Guard, taken at The Rectory.
Back Row: Pte. Norman Candy; Pte. Frank Coffin; Pte. Stanley Candy
Front Row: L/Cpl. Cecil Arnold; Pte. Gilbert Mathews; Cpl. Dick Bennet
   Other members included Q.M.S. Jack Peake, Pte. Derek Catley, Pte. Stanley Trim, Pte. Sidney Chandler, Pte. Jack Coffin, Sgt. Douglas Hamblin, Pte. Jack Chaplin, Pte. Mervyn Bastable and Pte. Leslie Moldram.
(David Ford collection)

The Pen Selwood Unit comprised between 10 and 12 men. Part of Wincanton Company, they initially shared in the guarding of vital points in Wincanton town including the area around Hawker's Bridge using the laundry (later Martin Dodge's premises) as a guardroom.

Periodic checks were carried out on traffic on the A303 at Hunters Lodge where the unit used an outhouse as their shelter. Weapon pits were dug on the opposite side of the road providing a good field of fire westwards along the A303. These pits finally disappeared when the A303 was improved. Once the threat of invasion had gone the unit was relieved of these duties but training continued once a week in 'The Hut' in Pen Selwood. The Platoon had its own rifle range at Marsh Lane in a field opposite Marsh Cottage, the home of Quartermaster Sergeant Jack Peake. It has been reported that Q.M.S. Peake used a local marsh to keep some 'ammunition' cool. This was probably the No. 76 S.I.P. grenade and Q.M.S. Peake could not risk the aftermath of an accidental breakage. A grenade range was established in a sand pit next to Long Lane, right on the Somerset/Dorset border.

This information and the accompanying photograph have been taken from *Pen Selwood Remembers* by kind permission of David Ford.

***Templecombe Home Guard**, 1944.*
Back Row: Albie Newman; Reg Newman (both farmers); Jim Hatchley (employee of Cow & Gate); Sid Brown (labourer); Len Lewis; Jim Hawkins (farmer); Vic Whitlock; Doug Maybee (farmworker)
Middle Row: Peter Sherston (estate agent); Dick King (labourer); Fred Bennett (farmer); Bob Collins; Bill Collins; Unknown; Dick Bennett (farmer); Ivor King (employee of Cow & Gate); Dick Bennett; C. Hawkins; Alex Appleby (shoe repairer)
Front Row: Cpl. Charlie Hoare (asst. manager of the Co-op); Sgt. J. Dukes (landlord of The Royal Hotel); Unknown; Lt. George Polly (farmer); Major A.C. Clark; Capt. L.E. Agar; Unknown; Sgt. Hazard (farmer); Unknown; Cpl. Saywell (carpenter)

Most of the above names are the result of the combined efforts of four former members of the Home Guard; even then no one after all these years identified their Company Commander and only one identified his 2nd in Command! (John Hawkins collection)

***Members of the 22nd Devon (5th Southern Railway) Battalion Home Guard Rifle Team**. The team had taken part in The Home Guard Inter Battalion Competition on 16th May 1942. They were reasonably successful in the competition, coming 4th overall with a score of 695. As the finals were shot in London it is possible that the photograph was taken there. Sixth from the left is Mr. Fred Rendle who was born in 1896 and joined the Railway aged 13. The First World War saw him in France as a member of the Railway Operating Division. During the Second World War he was employed as head shunter at Templecombe (S.R.) Station.*

Templecombe Railway Station Staff had their own rifle club with an outdoor range in Westwood on the edge of Templecombe.
(Michael Rendle collection)

Somerset Home Guard Motor Transport Column

COLUMN HEADQUARTERS	23, High Street, Wells	COMMANDING OFFICER	Lt. Col. N.S.M. Durnford
DATE FORMED	February 1944	ADJUTANT AND Q.M.	Capt. R.C. Lancaster, M.C., R.A.S.C.

NO. 2133 MOTOR TRANSPORT COMPANY

HEADQUARTERS	Territorial Hall, Taunton	COMMANDING OFFICER	Major C.W. Glade-Wright, M.C. (Major C.H. Burns, V.D.)
(For a photograph of Wellington members see p.207, and of Taunton members see p. 211)		2ND IN COMMAND	Capt. C.N. Ridler

NO. 2134 MOTOR TRANSPORT COMPANY

HEADQUARTERS	Lamb Hotel, Frome		
COMMANDING OFFICER	Major A.W. Evemy (Major N.S.M. Durnford)	2ND IN COMMAND	Capt. H. Frampton (possibly Capt. A.W. Evemy)

Other officers of this Company included: Capt. A. James, Lieut. H.G. Moulden, Lieut. E. Paul and Lieut. H.F. Hutt

(above) **No. 2134 Motor Transport Company**, photographed in Frome
Back Row: No. 7 Jim Hillier; No. 9 G. Symons; No. 10 Les Chantler; No. 11 Ivan Turner
Second Row: No. 11 Frank Craddock; No. 13 Ted Starling; No. 19 Frank Perkins; No. 21 Ron Beacham; No. 24 Reg Beacham
Third Row: No. 4 Tom Gale; No. 13 Jack Duck; No. 25 Sid Bodman; No. 27 C. Smith; No. 31 C. Doel
Front Row: No. 4 Jack Lambert; No. 8 Cpl. Albert Samuel Leat; No. 19 Capt. Horace Hutt; No. 32 Jack Rabbetts
All the above were employees of W. and E. Evemy of Chantry, Frome, except for Cpl. Albert Leat who was a bus driver and Capt. Horace Hutt who was a photographer for the Western Daily Press.

(right) Only Cpl. Albert Leat, front row No. 9, has been identified in this photograph, probably taken in Bath. (David Leat collection)

Horace Hutt, seen above as a lieutenant sporting his Somerset Home Guard Motor Transport shoulder title, was a photographer with the Western Daily Press *and the following photographs are the result of his daughter, Mrs. Doreen Weeks, preserving his glass negatives. (Mrs. Doreen Weeks collection)*

(above) Lt. (later Capt.) H.F. Hutt poses with one of his sections. The corporal, No. 8 in the front row, is wearing four years' good conduct stripes and a dispatch rider's badge.
(Mrs. Doreen Weeks collection)

Motor Transport Columns in Somerset came under Southern Command Home Forces and as such wore a black and yellow shoulder title incorporating five stars, the Southern Cross. This was sanctioned in February 1943. Affiliated to the Royal Army Serve Corps, some Motor Transport units wore the arm of service stripes of the R.A.S.C., a blue and yellow diagonal flash. Some Motor Transport Commanders also requested R.A.S.C. cap badges but this was apparently never allowed.

(above and right) Two more Section photographs of M.T. Troops taken at the same location, as yet unidentified. (Mrs. Doreen Weeks collection)

2136 INDEPENDENT MOTOR COACH PLATOON

HEADQUARTERS	Bristol Tramways and and Carriage Co. Ltd., Lawrence Hill Depot, Bristol
COMMANDING OFFICER	Capt. C.D. Jenkins

No photographs have been located for this unit.

Postscript

During a visit to the Somerset Archive & Record Service in Taunton, the two photographs reproduced here were discovered. There was no indication as to the date, location or identity of the subjects. However, it is likely that they were taken on 3rd December 1944 at the T.A. Centre and Jellalabad Barracks, Taunton, respectively and may feature members of 'C' Company 2nd (Taunton) Battalion Home Guard. The author would appreciate hearing from anyone who can confirm the above facts, identify anyone featured or provide any other information on the Somerset Home Guard which can be recorded for posterity.

The Lamentable Fate of Sergeant Bloggs

Henry Augustus Adolphus Bloggs
Was on of the "Old Contemptible" dogs.
He'd served at Mons, Neuve Chapelle and "Wipers".
And by very good fortune avoided the snipers.
He had managed to come back fit and well,
Unscathed by bayonet, bullet, or shell.
Having settled all international quarrels
He came back, as I said, to rest on his laurels.
With three bits of ribbon upon his chest
He felt quite entitled to take his rest.
He was sometimes heard in the village pub,
At the British Legion, or down at the club,
To break out in somewhat fiery orations
On what he thought of the "League of Nations",
But, on the whole, was quite willing to cease
All kinds of scrapping, and live at peace.

A full score of years had passed away,
Henry Augustus Bloggs had grown grey;
He'd lost quite a bit of his youthful vigour,
And gained, quite a bit, in his manly figure,
But his heart was as sound, and his spirit as keen
As it was in the days of Nineteen Fourteen.
When for reasons which I'll not attempt to explain,
The trouble with Jerry broke out once again.
When Henry came forward once more to assist,
They scornfully called him "too old" to enlist.
He chafed and he fretted – and he found life damned hard,
Till opportunity came to join the "Home Guard".

There we find Henry, once more in his glory,
Telling what's known as "the old, old story"
To an awe-stricken audience in the canteen.
He told what he knew, and what he had seen,
What he had done, and where he had been;
And if he did not entirely adhere to the truth,
His words carried weight, and encouraged the youth.
Promotion was rapid, and remarkably soon,
He became Sergeant Bloggs, of the A.1 Platoon.

And now I shall tell you, in some trepidation,
How the valiant Sergeant was lost to the Nation.
At the darkest hour ere the dawn of the day
The Sergeant was wending his homeward way;
He crossed the road, and with local knowledge,
Followed the footpath skirting the College;
He passed the cross-road, and, sad 'tis to say,
Forgot they had taken the railings away
(Of course they replaced them the very next day).
Not more than a yard could he see beyond,
And quickly was up to his knees in the pond.
He stumbled, and floundered, lost track of the edge,
His feet were enmeshed in the tangling sedge.
(I wouldn't suggest that the Sergeant was 'tight';
You'll remember I said, 'Twas a very dark night.)
He fought and he struggled, fast losing ground.
The Coroner's verdict was simply "Found drowned".

Should occasion arise to necessitate
Your passing that way an hour that is late,
You will hear a sort of a plaintive howl;
Some say it comes from the water-fowl;
But those who know better, you and I,
Recognize well the drowning man's cry.
We can't help him now, however stout-hearted,
But we *can* pay a tribute to the departed,
And in rain, or in snowstorm, or thickest of fogs,
Give our hero the greeting "Good night, Sergeant Bloggs".

Two cartoons drawn by L.P. Merchant of No. 6 Platoon, Ilchester Company, 3rd Somerset (Yeovil) Battalion. The Christmas greeting on the right is from Major Eric Craven, the Commanding Officer of Crewkerne Company. (by permission of Crewkerne Museum)

The King's Broadcast to the Home Guard
Sunday 3rd December 1944

Over four years ago, in May 1940, our country was in mortal danger. The most powerful army the world had ever seen had forced its way to within a few miles of our coast. From day to day we were threatened with invasion.

In those days our Army had been gravely weakened. A call went out for men to enrol themselves in a new citizen army, the Local Defence Volunteers, ready to use whatever weapons could be found and to stand against the invader in every village and every town. Throughout Britain and Northern Ireland the nation answered that summons, as free men will always answer when freedom is in danger. From fields and hills, from factories and mills, from shops and offices, men of every age and every calling came forward to train themselves for battle. Almost overnight, a new force came into being, a force which had little equipment but was mighty in courage and determination.

In July 1940, the Local Defence Volunteers became the Home Guard. During those four years of continuing anxiety that civilian army grew in strength; under the competent administration of the Territorial Army Associations, it soon became a well-equipped and capable force, able to take over many duties from regular soldiers preparing to go overseas. I believe it is the voluntary spirit which has always made the Home Guard so splendid and so powerful a comradeship of arms. The hope that this comradeship will long endure was strong in me this afternoon while many thousands of you marched past me in one of the most impressive and memorable parades that I have ever seen.

For most of you – and, I must add, for your wives too – your service in the Home Guard has not been easy. I know what it has meant, especially for older men. Some of you have stood for many hours on the gun sites, in desolate fields, or wind-swept beaches. Many of you, after a long and hard day's work, scarcely had time for food before you changed into uniform for the evening parade. Some of you had to bicycle for long distances to the drill hall or the rifle range.

It was well known to the enemy that if he came to any part of our land he would meet determined opposition, at every point in his advance, from men who had good weapons, and, better still, knew how to use them. In that way the existence of the Home Guard helped much to ward off the danger of invasion. Then, too, our plans for campaigns in many parts of the world depended on our having a great citizen force to help in the defence of the homeland. As anti-aircraft and coastal gunners, sentries at vulnerable points, units for dealing with unexploded bombs, and in many other ways, the Home Guard have played a full part in the defence of their country. Many will remember with special gratitude the unsparing help given to the Civil Defence Services in days and nights of terror and destruction.

But you have gained something for yourselves. You have discovered in yourselves new capabilities. You have found how men from all kinds of homes and many different occupations can work together in a great cause, and how happy they can be with each other. That is a memory and a knowledge which may help us all in the many peace-time problems that we shall have to tackle before long.

I am very proud of what the Home Guard has done and I give my heartfelt thanks to you all. Officers, non-commissioned officers, and men, you have served your country with a steadfast devotion. I know that your country will not forget that service.

A Special Army Order was issued to the Home Guard, with the folowing message from the King, on 3rd December 1944

For more than four years you have borne a heavy burden. Most of you have been engaged for long hours in work necessary to the prosecution of the war or to maintaining the healthful life of the nation; and you have given a great portion of the time which should have been your own to learning the skilled work of the soldier. By this patient, ungrudging effort you have built and maintained a force able to play an essential part in the defence of our threatened soil and liberty.

I have long wished to see you relieved of this burden; but it would have been a betrayal of all we owe to our fathers and our sons if any step had been taken which might have imperilled our country's safety. Till very recently, a slackening of our defences might have encouraged the enemy to launch a desperate blow which could grievously have damaged us and weakened the power of our own assault. Now, at last, the splendid resolution and endurance of the allied armies have thrust back that danger from our coasts. At last I can say that you have fulfilled your charge.

The Home Guard has reached the end of its long tour of duty under arms. But I know that your devotion to our land, your comradeship, your power to work your hardest at the end of the longest day will discover new outlets for patriotic service in time of peace.

History will say that your share in the greatest of all our struggles for freedom was a vitally important one. You have given your service without thought of reward. You have earned in full measure your country's gratitude.

George R.I., Colonel-in-Chief

Appendix A

Flame Fougasse and Flame Trap

The Flame Fougasse and Flame Trap both employed drums or barrels containing an inflammable mixture, typically of petrol and gas oil although other ingredients including creosote were used. They were sited close to roadways where vehicles would be forced to slow down or stop, either because of the road layout or obstructions such as road blocks. Both types were intended to envelope vehicles in a massive conflagration which would set fire to exposed flammable components of transport or suffocate the crews of armoured fighting vehicles.

The Flame Fougasse was based on drums being concealed close to the roadway and several designs were produced to suit different situations.

1) Totally enclosed
Here, as the name suggests, the drums, up to a maximum of four, were laid on their side with one end facing the roadway. (Some evidence suggests that an angle of 30° to the line of approach and at a spot where the vehicles approach up an incline was more effective.) The individual drums were fitted with a detonating charge on the end remote from the roadway and the whole installation was covered with earth, the end facing the road having thinner cover. Electric cables were run from the drums back to a suitable firing point. Care was taken to separate the drums to prevent sympathetic detonation.

2) Tunnelled
Where conditions were favourable, i.e. where the road passed through a cutting, drums were installed in blind tunnels, the detonating charge being placed in a small pocket at the end of the excavation. On completion the entrance to the tunnel was lightly backfilled.

3) Open ended
This was similar to the totally enclosed arrangement except that the roadside end of the drum was lightly camouflaged with local vegetation.

All the above installations suffered from one drawback. The drums were installed with their detonation charges which, unless care was taken, could suffer from damp and could not be easily replaced. (It was found by the Royal Engineers, who were responsible for the installations, that a ½lb Lyle's Golden Syrup tin provided a suitable damp-proof enclosure.)

With the inherent danger of leaving some 140 gallons of highly inflammable liquid with detonating charges permanently fitted, a fourth pattern of fougasse was employed.

4) The safety fougasse
This entailed installing a vertical pipe leading from the back of the drum through the top covering of earth to ground level. This enabled the detonating charge to be inserted when tactical conditions dictated.

Flame Traps were simpler to install than the fougasse but paid the price with reduced accuracy. Two types were developed.

1) Demigasse
This entailed placing the drum at a suitable site at the edge of the road painted to resemble those left behind by highway workers. Filled with the same mixture as the fougasse, it was carefully placed over a buried detonating charge. Fired remotely, it would then somersault through the air spewing blazing petrol in all directions.

2) Hedgehopper
Similar to the above, drums were stood on their end over a charge and canted towards the roadway. These were concealed behind cover, such as walls. The effect was similar to the Demigasse.

O.S. map references of known Flame Fougasse and Flame Trap sites in Somerset. All map references are prefixed by ST.

2ND (TAUNTON) BATTALION

Taunton Company
098 187   227 234
210 243   232 259
211 262   243 263
221 238

Blagdon Hill Company
184 172   210 121
202 204   210 202

Bishops Lydeard Company
160 303   213 309
172 307   253 288

Wellington Company
099 191   145 189
110 193   153 192
127 217   192 231
143 212

3RD (YEOVIL) BATTALION

Crewkerne Company
415 067   443 106
422 120   444 082
426 095   453 084
433 106   454 124
433 128   461 110
436 096   463 083
437 087   469 089

Yeovil Borough Company
536 190   552 144
539 144   554 170
546 161   556 169
547 164   565 156
550 170   565 166
551 146   579 158

Yeovil District Company
463 208   526 235
464 159   530 134
470 171   530 223
472 182   535 255
475 157   543 230
486 174   546 250
496 194   548 215
497 205   552 118
503 133   557 243
507 162   572 200
508 191   597 252
510 135
520 225
523 220
523 237

10TH (BRIDGWATER) BATTALION

Bridgwater Company
307 385   315 381
314 381

Polden Company
339 400   348 412
348 376   387 383

Sedgemoor Company
358 305

Chard Town Company
333 103

11TH (ILMINSTER) BATTALION

Chard Rural Company
281 095   360 086
290 135   371 065
309 089   378 061
325 056   379 057

North Curry Company
297 227   300 207
340 230

Ilminster Company
329 149   347 150
368 134   335 150
351 130   373 140
340 132

12TH (SOMERTON) BATTALION

Curry Rivel Company
339 231   393 211
417 190

Langport Company
411 266   418 283
426 265

Wincanton Company
680 256   703 232
692 248   711 218

Milborne Port Company
653 220   674 249
666 183   692 180
670 242   702 189
673 210   715 198

Somerton Company
476 286   495 281
486 281   498 283

Appendix B

A Matter of Interpretation

With the demise of Fox Bros. of Wellington, probably best known for their spiral-weave puttees worn by troops throughout the Empire, steps were taken to preserve the company archives before the factory site was redeveloped. A large-scale map of the area round Wellington was found pinned to a wall in a dusty office. After taking out many multi-coloured pins to facilitate its removal, a handwritten legend was noticed which read:

HQs – green	Fougasses – plain
OPs – blue	B. Bombard – pink
OPs (combined) – orange	Harassing points – red

On this map had been marked the battle deployment of 'F' Company of the 2nd (Taunton) Battalion but one swift action resulted in the information being lost for ever. Not lost, however, was the boundary of the Company which, as expected, followed county and parish boundaries. The map references for the pin holes are listed here in the hope that information may subsequently be forthcoming from other sources. At *The Crown Inn* in Rumwell and at Cox's Corner in Wellington, the significance of a pin hole has been confirmed as a result of correspondence to the author; these marked the site of Flame Fougasses. Recently the significance of another pin hole, at Bradford-on-Tone, has been confirmed by a former employee of Avimo as the site of slit trenches. Interestingly, 'F' Company included the parish of Bishops Hull. This was later transferred to Taunton, the platoon becoming No. 4 Platoon 'A' Company.

Map references of the pin holes:

County of Devon, outside 'F' Company Boundary:
ST 012 238   ST 052 194   ST 062 185   ST 078 165   ST 162 131
ST 025 242   ST 059 187   ST 064 186   ST 083 165   ST 196 104
ST 042 203   ST 061 186   ST 068 191   ST 108 150

County of Somerset, within 'F' Company Boundary:
ST 042 215   ST 092 187   ST 115 193   ST 145 190   ST 172 229
ST 044 238   ST 096 189   ST 116 192   ST 150 244   ST 173 205
ST 062 238   ST 098 190   ST 122 223   ST 151 193   ST 174 204
ST 064 239   ST 099 212   ST 128 217   ST 151 202   ST 174 229
ST 065 241   ST 100 193   ST 129 203   ST 151 234   ST 175 202
ST 069 214   ST 104 227   ST 136 202   ST 152 192   ST 176 228
ST 071 215   ST 106 197   ST 136 204   ST 165 246   ST 179 120
ST 077 228   ST 106 227   ST 141 228   ST 172 180   ST 179 141
ST 077 232   ST 107 185   ST 142 211   ST 172 204   ST 192 231
ST 080 201   ST 109 194   ST 145 192   ST 172 218   ST 198 238

County of Somerset, in Wiveliscombe Company area, all apparently Observation Posts:
ST 059 271   ST 066 280   ST 103 255   ST 106 282   ST 109 279

The following three locations, on the outskirts of Taunton, would have been transferred to Taunton Battalion sometime before 1944.
ST 206 242   ST 204 247   ST 204 248

Two pinholes, ST 208 285 ST 210 284, located in open countryside just in the parish of Kingston St. Mary outside 'F' Company's Boundary, as well as others in the original map, may be red herrings!

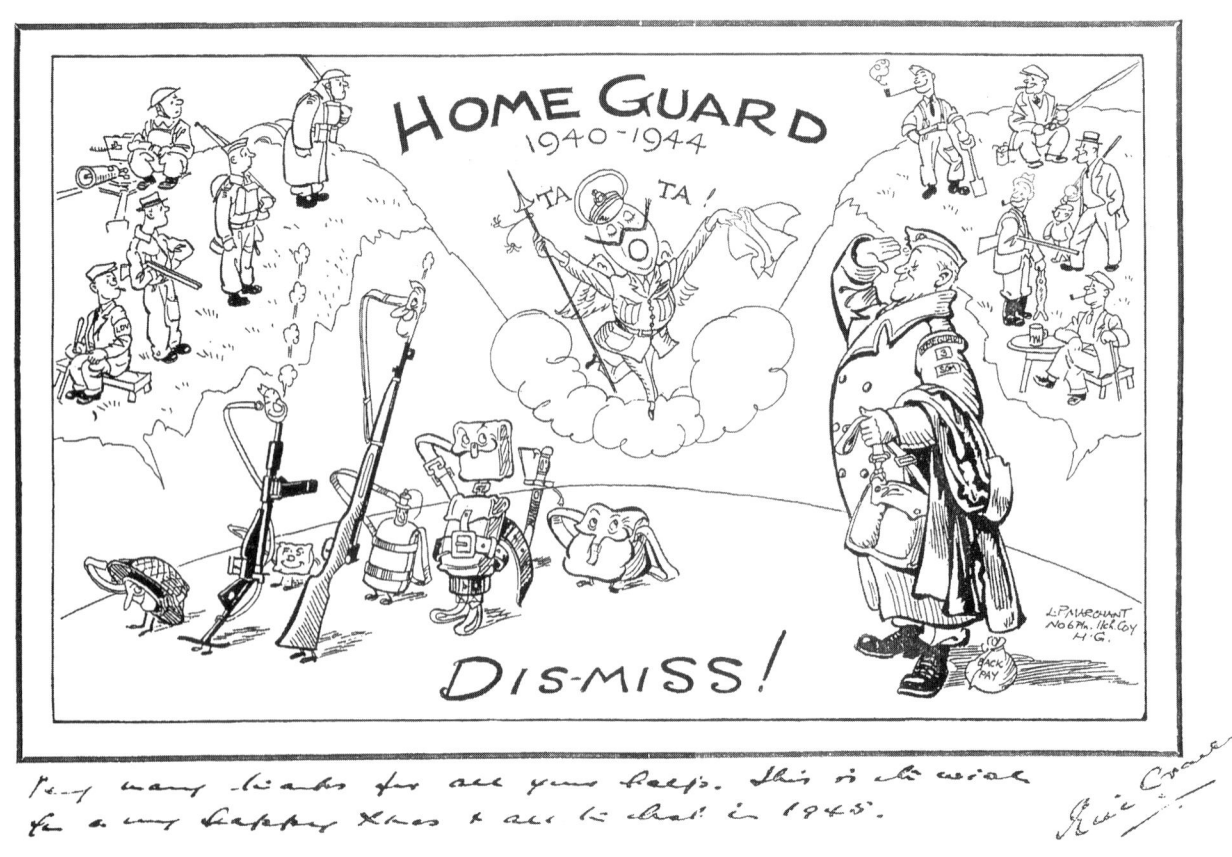

Index

This Index is arranged by Sector and then by Battalion, as in the book. Where a person has been identified in a photograph by their surname only, then only one entry is given for that surname, regardless of how many times the surname occurs, before entries for others with the same surname but with initials or first names. Thus the order is:
Smith
Smith, T.G.M.
Smith, Tom

As some identifications are by surname only it is possible that the same person could have more than one entry. Rank has been ignored as this sometimes varies between photographs.

North Somerset Sector

Allan, A.W. 9
Gooder, K.P. 9
Gould, A.J. 9
Henshaw, R.R. 9
Incledon-Webber, A.B. 9
Ingram, A.J. 9
Priestley, Mrs. 9
Rogers, G.H. 9
Stancombe, A.M. 9
Strutt, G.St.J. 9

4th (Frome) Battalion

Abel, W.T. 32
Ackerman, Fred
Adams, S.F. 9
Alford, Godfrey 29, 32
Allcott, L. 10, 14
Allen, Dick 25
Allen, Harry 25
Allen, Herb 25
Allen, Maurice 25
Anderson, Andy 12
Andrews, Harold 20, 21
Appleby, Bill 26, 27
Armstrong 10, 14
Armstrong, J.B.T. 9
Arnold 10
Arnold, Jeff 13
Arnold, Steve 12
Arnold, W.E. 13
Ashman, K. 33
Ashman, Ken 12
Ashman, W.F.T. 32
Attwood, Vic 29
Axon 10
Ayres 17

Badder 10, 14
Badder, E.H. 9, 16
Badder, L.A.C. 15, 16
Baily, E.C.R. 10
Baker, Charlie 12, 23
Ballantyne, Jock 12
Baldwin, Stan 13
Ball, Art 26
Ballam 16
Banfield, G. 29
Banton, S.A. 17
Barnes, Jim 23
Barnett, Arthur 'Snowy' 32
Barnett, Jack 29, 32
Barnett, Sid 29, 32
Barter 10
Bartlett, Cecil 'Mick' 19
Beauchamp, I.F.H.
Belcham 10
Belfield, Ted 25
Bennett 16
Bennett, Sam 10, 14
Benwell. Terry 23
Berry, C. 32
Berry, S.H. 19
Berryman P. 32
Berryman, S. 29
Bevan, Len 29, 32
Bicheno, Jim 12
Billing, Arthur 25
Billing, H.A. 24
Blacker 19
Bodman, L.W.T. 32
Bond 17
Bounton, Alf 13
Bourne 22
Bown, Nelson 29
Bracey 10
Bradley, Frank 19
Bradshaw 19
Bratten, Ron 20, 21
Brend, Philip 9, 10
Brewer, Lionel 28, 29
Brimble, Reg 23
Brittain, Jack 28, 32
Britten, Charlie 33
Britten, David 21, 22
Britten, H.E.M. 32
Britten, K.R. 32
Britton, A.C. 28, 29
Bromwell, Albert 29
Brooks, Oliver 19
Brown, Harold 22
Browning, L. 29
Bruzas 10
Bryant 29
Bryant, Harry 25
Bryant, Herbert 25
Bryant, Will 25
Bull 10
Bull, H.J. 15, 16
Burge, Roy 10, 14
Burnett, R. 29
Burr, Cecil 29
Burr, Gerry 30
Burt, J.F. 10, 14, 15, 16, 17, 18
Butcher, Bill
Butcher, Len 12
Butler 10
Butler, H. 17
Butt, V. 29
Button 10, 14

Calderwood, Jack 13
Candy, A.G.J. 32
Candy, Robin 33
Cannon, James Harris 13
Caple 10, 14
Carew, Sam 25
Carpenter 10
Carpenter, Beresford
Carpenter, Chris 22
Carter, Bill 26
Challenger, Reg 29
Chapman, Cyril 26, 27
Chapman, H.G. 32
Chapman, Noel 23
Charlton, Ernest 22
Charlton, Les 29
Chivers 10, 14
Chivers, Ernie 33
Churchill 10
Churchman 10
Churchman, A.G. 15
Clack, Reg 12, 13
Clark, L.A. 32
Clarke, Len 12
Clarke, Les 12
Clarke, 'Nobby' 33
Clerihew, C.F.P. 22
Clothier, Harold
Clough, Alex 12
Coates, Tom 13
Cobb 28, 30
Cobb, Tom 12
Colbourn, L. 29, 30
Coleman 10
Colman 10
Colyer, Ted 12
Conibear, Monty 19
Connock, Royston 26
Cook, Hector 13
Coombs, Arthur 22
Cooper, A.B. 27
Corbin 14
Cornish 10
Coward, E. 10
Cox 20
Cox, Bill 31
Cox, Charles 22
Cox, Gilbert 22
Cox, J.E. 32
Cox, James 22
Cox, Jeffrey 22
Cox, Sam 25
Cox, Tommy 10, 16
Crago, Jack 25
Craig 22
Cross 10, 14
Crowe 10
Cruttwell, Stephen 10, 14
Cullen, C. 29

Dainton, C.H. 9
Dale, Fred 15
Daniel 32
Dark, Herbert 10, 14
Davage 10
Davey, Raymond 29, 30
Davies 32
Davis 10
Day, C.E. 32

Day, H.F. 32
Defazio, Tony 13
Derrick, G. 29
Dew, Alf 27
Dew, Bert 26, 27
Diamond, Bill 29
Disney, Walter 12
Doble, Jim 25
Dodimead, Maurice 33
Domesa, Jim 23
Down, Arthur 25
Duck, L. 32
Dudd, Jim 25
Dudden, Powell 29
Dukes, H.G. 24
Dunford, Doug 25
Dunford, E.R. 17
Durbin, Harry 28
Durnford 10, 14
Durnford, Dick 25
Dyer, C. 10, 14
Dyke, E.S. 24
Dyke, Jack 22

East, Bert 13
Eavis, Joe 26
Edwards 10, 14, 16
Edwards, A. 17
Edwards, Bert 22
Edwards, Jesse 33
Ellis 10, 14, 15
Ellis, E.J. 17
Elmer, Bill 20, 21
Emery, Bert 29
Emery, R. 32
England, David 25
Ensor, F.C.C. 9, 10
Erswell, A.J. 32
Evans, A.G.P. 9
Evans, Bill 12
Evans, D.H. 32
Evans, W.H. 32
Evemy, W. 17

Feasey, Bob 12
Feaver, Bill 25
Feltham, Bill 29, 32
Firth, Charles 22
Fleming, Doug 26
Flower, Bill 29, 30
Flower, Jack 29
Ford 10
Ford, Ernie 13
Ford, S.H. 24
Ford, Tom 30
Foster, T.T. 9, 10
Fowler, Fred 19
Foxwell, Harry 30
Foxwell, W. 32
Frampton, H. 17
Francis, Percy 29
Francis, Walt 29
Frank 19
Franks 26
Franks, A.E. 10, 15, 16
Franks, R.K. 24
Fricker, Bill 29
Fry, S.W. 19, 28
Fuller, E. 29

Fuller, Fred 12

Gardiner 23
Gardiner, Ted 25
Garman, John 10
George, Charlie 17
George, John 25
Gibbons, William 21, 22
Gifford, Eddie 25
Gifford, Harry 25
Giles, Ted 20, 21
Gilham, John 29, 32
Gill, Dick 29
Gilson, Arthur 29, 31, 32
Gilson, D. 29
Gilson, Gilb 29, 32
Gilson, Jack 29, 32
Gilson, Wyndham 28
Gleed, Norman 12
Glover 10
Glover, John 9, 10, 14, 18
Goater, Bert 12
Godfrey, Claude 29
Golledge, F.T. 24
Golledge, G.T. 24
Golledge, H.N. 24
Gould, Jack 22
Gould, John 25
Goverd, Reg 25
Green, Alec 26, 27
Green, F. 17
Greenway, Bennett 28, 33
Griffen, F.
Griffin, J. 32
Griggs, E. 29

Haines 15
Haines, 'Butcher' 25
Hall, Bill 19
Harding, Archie 33
Harding, Doug 12
Harding, H.R. 17
Harding, L. 32
Hares 10, 14
Harris, Eddie 26, 27
Harris, Jack 26, 27
Harrison, N. 24
Hartnell, Fred 25
Haskell, Archie 10, 14, 16
Hatcher, Len 25
Hawke 22
Hawker 10
Hawkins, Charlie 23
Hayter, Bill 12
Hayward 26
Hayward, Basil 12
Haywood, L. 9, 10, 14, 16, 18
Head, Jack 33
Herridge, Reg 19
Heywood 24
Hibbs 32
Hicks, Fred 25
Hill, C. 22
Hill, Edwin 29
Hill, Kenneth 25
Hill, Morris 29
Hill, Percy 25
Hiller, Fred 19
Hillier 30

311

Hillier, Frank 19
Hillier, Gordon 22
Hillier, Jack 20
Hillman, Fred 22
Hinge, Sid 12
Hiscox, A.J. 32
Hiscox, W. 29
Hoare, Jim 25
Hockey, Cyril 29, 31
Hockey, Perce 29
Holroyd, C.I.P. 9, 10, 18
Horler 14
Horler, Les 12
Horner, Jack 13
Horseman, W.J. 17
Hoskins, Len 33
Howarth, John 12
Howlett, Bill 19
Howlett, Charlie 19
Howlett, Fred 20, 21
Hucker, K. 10
Hughes, Arthur 19
Hughes, Sid 12
Hugo, Johnny 13
Humphries, Darlow 10, 15, 16
Hutchins, Thomas 25

Isaacs, D. 29

James, A.C. 27
James, Frank 33
James, Harold 33
James, Howard 33
James, R.C. 10, 14, 16
Jelly, E. 32
Johnson 10, 14
Johnson, W.B. 17
Joyce, Charlie 25
Joyce, Maureen 16

Kennedy, D. 10
Kennedy, Don 13
Kent, Archie 25
Kent, Ted 25
Kerton, Len 30
King 10
King, E.E. 32
King, H.E. 32
Knee, Percy 10, 14, 17
Knight 10, 15

Lake, George 10, 14, 16
Lambert 10, 14, 17
Lambert, Bill 29
Lambert, J. 10
Lambert, K. 10
Lambert 'Shotter' 29
Lambert, Walter 29, 30
Lane, Stan 33
Lapham 10, 14
Lawrence 10
Ledbury 10, 14
Leonard, Mick 26
Lester, Hedley 25
Lewis, E.R. 24
Lewis, Eric 10, 14, 15, 16
Lillicrap, Arthur 13
Lillicrap, Frank 12
Lintern, Jack

Loan, Jim 12
Lodge, Ron 33
Look 24
Look, R.N. 24
Longman, Edward 22
Longman, H.R. 24
Longman, J.K. 24
Loring, E.J. 19
Lovelock, C. 29
Lovell, Bill 29
Luff, F. 24
Lye, I.H. 24

McDonald 14, 17
Macey, George 23
McLeod, W.J. 24
Malonski 33
Marklew, George 20, 21
Maidment, John 25
March, W.J. 32
Marks, Bob 29
Marsh, B. 17
Martin 10, 14, 16
Martin, V.W. 15, 16
Massey, Edgar 29
Massey, Fred 21, 22
Massey, 'Jumbo' 29
Matthews 10
Matthews, Steve 12
Matthews, Theo 25
May, Fred 22
Mead, Bill 13
Mears, Charlie 31
Melhuish, B. 32
Melville 25
Mencam 32
Merrifield, J.P. 9, 14
Midgley, E. 10, 17
Miell, Frank 26
Miller, D. 29, 32
Miller, Ron 12
Milsom 10, 14
Mondrell, George
Moody, Austin 25
Moody Reg 25
Moody, P.W. 24
Moon, L.A. 32
Moore, Henry 33
Moore, John 33
Moore, John 'Jumbo' 28
Moore, W.W.T. 28
Moore, Walter 33
Morgan, Fred 26, 27
Morgrove, W.H. 24
Moxey, Viv 25
Murray, Ron 12

Napier, 'Squire' Walter
Newport 10, 14, 25
Newport, Bill 25
Newton, Stan 13
Noaks, William 22
Norman, Fred 25
Nurse, Alan 25

Oliver, George 25
Oman, Ben 13

Padfield, Fred 26, 27

Padfield, Harold 33
Padfield, Hubert 29, 32
Padfield, Leslie 29, 31, 32
Padfield, Thomas 22
Paget, Charlie 33
Pain 10
Painter 10
Painter, H.E. 17
Palmer, Eddie 13
Paradise, W.J. 32
Parfitt 10
Parfitt, Alec 29
Parfitt, Frank 29
Parfitt, Fred 29
Parfitt, Ron 29
Parker, George 25
Parker, Frank Walter 10
Parker, K.J. 24
Passey, Reg 32
Paterson, Pat 13
Pearce, Fred 33
Pearse, George 25
Penny, Stan 13
Perkins, A. 29
Perkins, Gerald 33
Perkins, Thomas 31
Perry, L. 22
Pibworth, Robert Frank 12
Pickford, R.J. 15, 17
Plumley, Gerald 26
Potts, L.T. 32
Price, Hamilton 28, 30
Priddle, Fred 21, 22
Pritchard 10
Proost, Henry 13
Purnell, Lance 29, 32
Purnell, Tom 29

Quartley, W,W, 17

Rabbits, Edgar 25
Rabbits, Tom 25
Rabbits, Walt 25
Radway, C.B. 24
Ragbourne 10
Ragbourne, David 10
Ragbourne, Peggy 16
Raikes, Alan 25
Raikes, Harry 33
Raikes, Reg 25
Rayes, Jim 25
Rayner, Reg 20, 21
Read, Harry 13
Read, Nelson F. 9, 10, 16
Read, Reg 25
Reakes, George 25
Reakes, Mike 29
Reakes, W.E. 32
Redman, Ron 12
Reeves, F. 32
Reeves, Mick 32
Reeves, Reg 29
Reynolds 10, 15
Richards, Joe 19
Riggs, Ern 25
Robbins, Bill 33
Robbins, E.S. 9
Robbins, J. 10, 14
Robbins, Jim 13

Robinson, Bert 12
Rodgers, Gus 26
Rogers, Jim 27
Rogers, Roy 25
Rolls, Bob 29
Rose, George 17
Ross, Bill 13
Rossiter 10
Rossiter, Dennis 29
Rossiter, Herbert 29
Rowe 14, 16
Rowsell, Stanley 23
Ruegg, L. 9
Rymes, Bert 26

Sainsbury 10, 14, 16
Salmon, Ken 20
Salvidge, Ted 33
Sannigar, Bill 13
Saunders, H.O. 32
Scammells, W.H. 10, 16
Scarbrough, Arthur 12
Scutts, A.H. 24, 25
Searle, Fred 32
Searle, Les 12
Seviour, Albert
Seviour, Herbie
Seviour, Silvester
Shears, Harold 22
Shears, Stanley 22
Sheet, T. 10
Sheppard, F.G. 9, 16
Shore, Richard 20, 21
Silcocks, A. 10
Simmonds, Ernie 12
Singer 10, 14
Singer, G. 10
Skirton, Bert 28, 31, 32
Skirton, Maurice 29, 31, 32
Smith 16
Smith, Edgar 29
Smith, George 13
Snook, Hewart 29, 30
Spencer, Huntley G. 9,18, 21,25
Spering, Jim 23
Spicer, Ken 12
Spirrell, Walter
Spital 10
Standing, John 12
Starr, Archie 20, 21
Starr, Laurie 20, 21
Starr, Ted 20, 21
Staunton 33
Steeds, Bob 29, 32
Stent, Reg 10, 15, 16
Stevens, Terry 13
Stewart, G. 10
Stewart, Sid 12
Stewart, Vic 12
Stock, E.T. 32
Stockwell, Frank 26, 27
Stockwell, Frank (Jnr.) 26
Stone 9, 15, 27
Stone, B.M. 10
Stone, Norman 25
Sullivan, S.J. 24
Swain, D. 29
Swift, Eric 33
Syrup 29

Taeffe-Finn, P. 9, 28, 30
Tapscott, H. 29
Taylor, Fred 25
Taylor, G.
Taylor, H. 29
Taylor, Herbie 20
Taylor, Ken 10
Taylor, Percy 33
Taylor, R.W. 24
Thatcher, A.J.B. 22
Thompson, Gibb 9
Thorn, Bertram 22
Thorner, Frank 29
Thorner, Nelson 29
Thorner, Tony 29
Thorning, Alan 12
Tilley, Ford 26
Totterdale 10
Trayfoot, Basil 13
Treasure, Cyril 33
Treasure, David 29
Treasure, Francis R.J. 16
Treasure, Gordon 29
Treasure, Len 29
Treasure, Ted 29
Trim, A.C. 24
Trim, E.J. 32
Trim, E.V. 32
Trippick, P. 32
Trippick Reg 29, 32
Trivett, George 10, 16
Tucker, A. 32
Tucker, Harold 29, 31, 32
Tucker, Henry 29, 31, 32
Tucker, O.S.A. 32
Tucker, R. 29
Turner, Charlie 12
Turner, Frank 29

Upshall, Bill 25

Valentine, Jock 13
Vallis, R.W.H. 9, 10, 14, 16, 17, 18
Valton, P.A. 9, 10, 14, 17
Vaux, E.F. 24
Veasey, George 22
Veasey, Gilbert 22
Vernon, W, 17
Vince, Bill 19
Vincent, L. 29
Vining, F.H. 32
Vranch, H.T. 16

Waldron, Arthur 12
Waldron, Fred 13
Walker, G. 9
Walls, Richard
Walters 29
Walton 10, 14, 15
Walwin, Roy 10, 14
Wareham, George 20, 21
Warren, Cecil 25
Watch, Maurice 26
Watts, Maurice 17
Watts, Richard
Webb, Ivan 29, 31
Weeks, A. 32
Weeks, Ern 20, 21

Weldon, Jim
Wells, Bill 29, 31
Whalley 10
Wheeler, Bernard 9, 10, 16
Wheeler, Bob 33
Wheeler, Leslie 12
Wheeler, P.G. 32
White 10, 14
White, 'Chalkie' 10
White, Geoff 10
White, Ken 25
White, Tom 24
Whitehead, Bert 25
Whitmarsh, J.E. 32
Whitemore, Fred 25
Whitemore, Les 25
Whiting 15
Wickham, L.J. 32
Wilcox, M.A. 24
Wilkins 10
Wilkins, Bill 29, 31
Wilkins, Desmond 29, 30
Wilkins, L. 29
Williams, Bill 29
Williams, Geoff 26
Williams, Ted 29
Wiltshire, Claud 25
Wiltshire, George 22
Wiltshire, Gilbert 22
Wiltshire, John 22
Wiltshire, Reginald 22
Windsor, George 27
Wines 10
Winterbourne 10
Winters, Harry 33
Wisdom 28
Witcombe, Henry 29, 32
Witcombe, J. 32
Witcombe, P. 29
Withey, F.M. 32
Withy 10, 14
Woodhouse, Len 22
Woods 10, 14
Woods, Bob 'Bubble' 12
Woods, Ted 20
Woodward, Henry 12
Woolley, Bill 25
Woolley, Jim 25
Wren 10, 14
Wright, Donald 17

Yeoman, Arthur 25
Yeoman, T.N. 24
York 10
York, Edwin 'Pop' 15, 16
Young 33
Young, Bill 33

5th (Bath City) Battalion

Adams, George 48, 49
Adams, Lou 48, 49
Allard, Fred 48
Allen, R.G. 46
Anderson, Dick 43
Anderson, Sam 44
Arlett, George 48
Arnold, Fred 35

Ash, W.G. 46
Axford, A.H. 34

Bachell, Charlie 46
Baggs, William 48
Bailey, Bert 43
Bailey, Maurice 42
Bailey, Ted 43
Baker, F.H. 50
Baker, L.E.C. 34
Ball, Arthur 49
Bally, Leonard George 49
Bampfylde, Valdimir Austin 42
Banks, George 38, 39
Banks, Gordon 38
Barber, Harold 48, 49
Barber, John 'Jack' 48, 49
Barber, Paul 49
Barratt, Jack
Barrett, George 42
Barry, Harold Walter 50
Bartram, Bert 44
Bartram, Fred (Jnr.) 44
Bartram, Fred (Snr.) 44
Bath, Alfred 36
Bath, Leslie 36
Batt, Haddon 44
Bax, Bill 42
Bean, Ron 49
Beazer, J. 46
Bell 42
Bendall 45
Bennett, J.B. 34
Biggs, Harry J. 42
Bilsdon, Peter 49
Birdwood, Lord William 34
Black, A.Stuart 35
Blanchard, Chris or Phil 36
Bolomue, Arthur 48
Bond, C. 44
Bond, George 40
Boschi, E.J. 34
Brennan, Joe 42
Bridle. J.F.K. 50
Brockliss, F.L 46
Brooks, A. 44
Brooks, Fred 49
Brooks, Ray 35
Brown, Arthur 46
Brown, Bert 40, 41, 42
Brown, Charles 49
Brown, Douglas 48
Brown, E. 42
Brown, 'Pop' 46
Brown, S.W. 46
Budge, Ernest 44
Buffrey, Ern 49
Bullock, Edward 49
Buoy, Arthur Reginald 43
Burden, A.H. 46
Burden, Walter 42
Burnell 44
Butcher, David 35
Butler, Bill 42

Cahill, P.H. 36
Cambourne, Roy 36
Cambourne, Reg 36
Campbell, A. 44

Candy, Tony 35
Cannings, Bob 49
Carpenter, Brian 42
Carpenter, Earl 44
Carter 43
Cartman 40, 42
Castle, T.J. 40
Cavill 34
Chapman, Albert 49
Chapman, H.C. 46
Chave, Alec 43
Chick, Bert 42
Chick, H.S. 42
Chivers, Ernie 40
Chivers, Jack 48
Churchill, R. 46
Churchill, W.H. 46
Clancy 38
Clark 40
Clem, Dennis 49
Clewer, E.G. 46
Clothier, Robert 49
Cockle, V.H. 46
Cockle, W. 46
Cole, Crozier 39
Coles 38, 39
Coles, George 49
Coles, W. 46
Collett, P.R. 46
Collins 40
Compton, Jimmy 46
Cook, A. 44
Cook, C. 44
Cook, Charlie 44
Cook, Ray 35
Cook, Tony 43
Cooke, D.R. 46
Cottle, George 44
Cottle, Vic 46
Cox, Albert H. 42
Cox, Alfred 40, 44
Crocker, Charlie 49
Croon, Herbert Francis 35
Cross, Ernie 49
Cross, G. 38
Cross, Ted 48
Crump, S. 44
Cryer, Gerry F. 49
Curtis, W.A. 40
Cutler 42
Cutter, Stan 46

Dafforn, Dicky 35
Dale, Bob 43
Dancey, Hubert 45
Daniels, Dennis 36
Daniels, Len 36
Date, Peter 42
Dauncey, F. 44
David, Henry 37
Davis 46
Davis, Bert 43
Davis, Charlie 44
Davis, T.A. 40
Davis, Ted 42, 43
Day A.O. 34, 36
Day, Reg 42
de Ridder, L.E. 34
Dennis, Harry 44

Densley, W. 44
Doubleday, H. 40, 42
Dowding, A. 44
Dowding, Dick 35
Duck, Francis Edward 48
Dyer, Sid 42

Eastmont, Eddie
Ebdon, Bill 48
Edwards, W. 44
Elley, W. 38
Ellis, C.W.
Emery, Dennis 49
Epps, Fred 48
Evans, W. 44
Every, Thomas 49
Evry, Tommy 44

Farrant, H.J. 46
Fear, Albert William Stephen 48
Feasy, Bert 35
Fellows, Reg 49
Field, R.T. 34
Fish, T.C. 46
Fishlock, Albert 49
Fletcher, Norman 43
Fletcher, Ron 43
Flower, 'Con' Ernest W. 42
Folland, L. 44
Follom, E. 46
Ford, Robert 49
Forsey, Bert 44
Fortt, N.H. 48
Frankcom, Jack 49
Franklin, Dick 42
Franklyn 49
Franklyn, V. 42
Freeman, Fred 38, 39
Frost, E. 44

Gage, Leonard William 46
Gage, Louis 46
Garret, Jack 49
Gay 46
Gay, Jack 43
Gay, W. 44
Gibbs, Ted 36
Giles 44
Glynne-Jones, R.R. 40
Godwin 36
Godwin, Fred 44
Godwin, H.A. 46
Golledge, AS. 49
Gordon, C. 35
Gould, A.J. 34
Gouldstone, P.J. 46
Grath, L.M.P. 42
Gray, Jim 46
Gray, Norman 42
Gray, W. 46
Green, Frank 35
Green, Richard 35
Greening, A.H. 50
Greenslade, Les 36
Griffin, John Turner 36
Griffith, W.R. 45
Griffiths, A.F.E. 46
Gunning, Archie 48, 49
Gunning, Tom 49

Hake, Harold Reginald Scott 48
Hallett, Fred 42
Hallett, Roy
Hallett, Sam 40
Ham 44
Hamilton 38
Hancock, Ern 44
Hancock, J. 46
Hancock, Reg 35
Hancock, Ron 44
Hapgood, Bob 43
Hardick, Roy 42
Harding, Bert 44, 48
Harding, Bill
Harding, Dennis 44
Harding, Ivor 42
Harding, Jeff 44
Harding, Laurie 44
Harding, Len 42
Harding, Stan 44
Harris, Cyril 34
Harris, J.W. 46
Harris, Jack 43
Harris, V. 44
Hart, E.J. 36
Hart, Hewitt 36, 38
Hart, William 38, 39
Hartland, V.G. 46
Hartley, Ken 49
Hawker, Bill 44
Hawker, J.E. 46
Hawker, Len 44
Hawkes, Fred 43
Hayward, Stan 49
Headley 36
Hefferman, Ted 48
Hemmings, J. 44
Heron, J.B. 34, 47
Hervin, Walter 44
Hill, Ern 44
Hilleard, Stan 48
Hills, Jack 49
Hilton, Thomas 49
Hobbs, Reg 40
Hodder, Jim 46
Hodges, R.G. 49
Hodgkinson, T.J. 47
Holbrook 42
Holden, Douglas 48, 49
Holden, Ralph 48
Hole, R.D. 45
Holloway, J.W. 40, 42
Holmes, Vic 49
Holton, Harold 40, 44
Hone 40, 43
Hooper, H.J. 50
Hooper, Ralph 48, 49
Hopkins, M. 47
Hoskill, Bill 46
Hovey, George 34
Howell, H.M. 34, 45
Hughes, F.D. 46
Hughes, George 43
Hughes, Tommy 48
Hulance, Herbert 42, 49
Hunt 46
Hunt, Jim 40, 41
Hunt, L. 40
Hunt, V.F. 46

Huntley, W.M. 36
Hurd, Percy 48, 49

Iley, Reg 49
Ingram, Norman 46

James, Harry 44
Jefferies 36
Jefferies, Fred 48, 49
Johnson, W. 46
Jones, Rex 34
Jones, William 43
Kernery, K.F. 46
Kettlety, E.E. 44
Kettlety, F. 44
King 48
King, Arthur James 48, 49
King, Gordon 49
King, Jack 44
King, Robert 49
Knott, Fred

Lambert, J.C. 47
Lane, Bob 42
Lane, Peter 42
Lane W. 49
Lanning, Gordon Pearce 47
Lavington, G.E. 46
Lavington, K.J. 46
Lavington, T.E. 46
Lee, William 49
Legg, Alfie 42
Legg, John 34
Legg, Ron 34
Leverton, S. 34
Lewis, George 40
Lewis, Ron 49
Lewis, W. 34
Lewis, W.H. 46
Llewellyn, A. 40, 44
Lodder, A.E. 46
Lodge 35
Lovegrove, J. 42
Lovell, Frank 44
Lovell, Ted 44
Lyles, W.M.H. 46

Macdonnell, M.S. 34
McDougall 43
McKeag, R.H. 40
McNamara 38
McNamara, Clem 38, 39
Maggs, A. 44
Maidment, Bill 35
Maidment, H. 44
Makin, Harry 46
Mantle, William 49
Marchant 36
Marle, S. 34
Maslen, A. 44
Maslen, Charlie 35
Maslen, Sidney 49
Matthews, George 46
Matthews 38, 39
Mays, Herbert 35
Meader, Fred 49
Mealand, H.A. 34
Meddick, Dennis 42
Meddick, Roy 42

Mellor, N. 46
Merchant, Reg 36
Merritt 38
Midgley 38
Miles, Len 40, 41
Mines, Fred 38, 39
Mitchell, D.A. 34
Mitchell, Roy 46
Moger, W. 34
Mole, F. 46
Morgan, Les 46
Morris 40
Morris, George 40
Morris, R. 44
Morrison, R. 44
Morton, N. 34
Moss, Arnie 44
Moss, Walter 44
Mottram 35
Mulcock, F.H. 46
Mullins, Bert 42
Mullins, Ron 42
Myson, Pete 35

Newman, W.W. 50
Nicholls, Eddie 36
Nicholls, Les 44
Norris, C.F. 46
Norris, Ken 'Spider' 48, 49
Nowell, Philip 40

Oatley, Maurice Gordon 39
Oram 36

Page 36
Painter, John 36
Pakenham, A. 36
Palmer, H. 44
Parmee, C.C. 45
Parratt, J. 44
Parsons, Bill 43
Paton, R. 50
Payne, Norman 43
Peach, Fred 42
Pearce, Roy 49
Pegler, H. 46
Perkins, A. 44
Perry, S. 44
Pickford, Henry Charles 37
Pike, D.A. 34
Player, George 42
Player, Harold 35
Player, Reg 35
Plummer, Gerald 40
Pocock, Alan 42
Pocock, D. 44
Pollard, E.H. 46
Pollard, K.H. 46
Pooley 34
Prewer 40
Prosser 42
Punter, Tommy 35
Purnell, Bobby 42

Quinn, George 49

Radcliff, E.F. 34
Rawlings, C. 44
Rawlings, Stan 44

Reed, Albert 48, 49
Reynolds, R. 46
Reynolds, Wilf 44
Rhymes, Charlie 38, 39
Rich, Aubrey 44
Rich, Gerald 35
Rich, Ron 44
Rich, Stan 44
Richardson 34
Ricketts, H. 38
Ricketts, Harry 43
Roberts, V.G. 34
Rogers, A. 44
Rogers, E. 44
Rogers, Guy H. 34
Rogers, R. 44
Room, Bert 38, 39, 49
Room, Les 38, 39
Rose, Fred 42
Rosenburg, Len 42
Rosenburg, Norman 49
Rowe, Geoff 42
Rowett, Arthur 48
Rowlands, Vernon 44
Russell, Roy F. 42

Salter, Des 42
Sartain, George 36
Saunders, Ken 34
Sawyer, Bill 42
Scott, G.D. 47
Seal 48
Sellick, F. 44
Selman, A.T. 34
Shackell, Malcolm 37
Shailes, Hubert William 43
Sharpe, Cyril 34
Shawcross 42
Shearn, Ronald 48, 49
Shepherd, Selwyn 36
Sheppard, W.H. 45
Skrine 44
Slater, A.E. 46
Small, H.F. 46
Smith, A. 44
Smith, Jack (Jnr.) 43
Smith, Jack (Snr.) 43
Smith, P. 44
Smith, Tom 42
Staddon, G. 46
Stanton, George 40
Stebbings, L. 44
Stephens, Ken 36
Stephenson, E.F. 46
Stevens, C. 44
Stewart, K. 35
Stoffels, Eric 35
Stockdale, H. 44
Stokes, Fred 35
Stott, George 49
Stride, Bert 40
Stride, Bill 42
Strutt, G.St.J. 34
Symonds 44
Symonds, Jack 49

Taylor, David 44
Taylor, L.R.E.W. 34
Temlett, Arthur 40

Thomas Dai 42
Thurgar, S. 44
Thyer, Walter 46
Tidball, Arthur 49
Tidball, Dick 48
Tosseano, William 49
Tovey, Arthur 43
Treble, A.S.P. 46
Trim, Theo 42
Trott, Norman Stanley 49
Tucker, Edwin 'Ted' 48, 49
Tucker, Gudge 35
Tucker, W.E. 48
Tuckwell, Tony 43
Tugwell, Ernie 46

Venn, Bill 44
Vernon, L.D. 46
Vernon, Les 44
Vezey, E. 44
Vines, W. 44

Waldon, J.H. 46
Waldon, Sid Henry 46
Waldron, Henry 49
Walker, Len 44
Waller, F.E. 46
Walters, G. 46
Ward, Harold 48
Ward, W. 46
Watson, Herbert 44
Webb, Randolph 49
Wells, L. 44
West, Len 48, 49
Westcombe, Bart 48
Weston, Ernest 48
Weston, Walter 49
Whatley, Bert 43
Wheatley 38, 39
Wheeler 40
Wheeler, P. 44
Whitcombe, Reg 49
White, Bill 35
White, Bob 34
White, Fred 45
White, Jack (Newton St. Loe) 43
White, Jack (Stothert and Pitt) 49
White, Norman 49
White, Ray 43
Wiles, William 49
Willavoys 44
Williams 38
Williams, Bill 49
Williams, Edwin Curtis 40
Williams, John 34
Willis, F.W. 34
Woodward, Charles 48
Wotton, E. 44
Wright, Bill 43
Wyatt 44
Yewlands, Bill 40, 42
Young, M.G. 46

6th (Bath Admiralty) Btn.

Akers, S. 55
Allan, A.W. 51
Anderson 55

Armstrong, A.N. 58, 59
Ashfield, Arthur George 58
Attolls 55
Aves, L.A. 51, 58, 59

Baker, N.W.S. 58
Baldery, S.L. 58
Banham, H. 58
Banks 53
Barker, J. 55
Bartlett 53
Beaven, W. 55
Bennet, R.W. 58
Bennett, H. 55
Bennett, J.B. 51
Benzing, S. 51, 53
Bevan 54
Birchby, H.W. 51
Blair, J. 58, 59
Blake, Dougie 55
Blanchard, Jackie 55
Bolton, L.G.
Botting 55
Bradbury, F. 51
Bright 53
Brockway, G. 55
Brooker 53
Brown, W.C. 51, 53, 54, 55
Burch, Eric 53, 55
Burrows, D. 53

Canavan, J.O'B. 56, 58, 59
Cannon 55
Carter, P.F. 58
Chandler, Alexander Bertram 56
Clacton, E. 53
Cooper 56
Cotten, C.H.
Cowan-Dickie, W.E. 52, 53
Cracknell, W. 55
Craig 53
Creighton, R. 53
Curry, W.W. 58

Davis, L.A.W. 51
Dear, G.J. 51, 52
Digby, R. 55
Dwane, E. 58, 59

Elliott, Steve V. 54, 55
Elliston, B.R. 51
Emmerson, W.F.E. 58
Evans 54
Evans, E.R. 59

Farr, A.L. 51
Fell, A.Jimmy 53, 54, 55
Field 53
Fielder, Hughie 55
Fisher, A. 59
Fisher, C. 51, 53
Ford 53
Fradd, K. 55
Francis 55
Francis, D. 55
Fraser, I. 55
Freeman, N. 53
Frith, R. 53
Futcher 55

Gates, C.J. 58
Gill, Matt 55
Gilmour (née Griffin), Joan 52
Gooder, K.P. 51
Gothard, S.A. 51, 55
Grant, S.O. 51
Gray 53
Griffiths, Tommy 53, 55

Hackett, William 53, 55
Hales, Maurice 55
Hall, Charlie 51, 53
Hambly 53
Hands 56
Harrington, Edmund Lynn 51, 52
Hassett, W. 55
Hawke, S. 55
Hawkes, Aubrey 55
Hayden 55
Hayes 56
Hedger, Frank 55
Hender 55
Henderson, N.B. 51
Heward, R.A.D. 58
Holford or Hulford, E. 53, 55
Howard 51
Hughes 55
Hunt, C.I. 53
Hutchings, G.R.M. 58, 59

Iles, Roy 56

Jackson, H. 55
James, A.P. 58
James, N.J.Jeffery, Derek 55
Jermy, F.N. 58
Johns, J. 55
Judson, R.M.B. 58, 59
Jury, Alf 53, 55

Kingdon 54
Kitchener 55

Lamerton, Horace 53, 54, 55
Lamswood, R. 53, 55
Leonard, T.T.J. 52
Lester 56
Lewis, Arthur Samuel Bailey 55
Light 53
Longhurst, H.L. 51
Lynch 55
Lynham, L.F. 51, 52

McCall 54
McDermot 55
Marsh, W. 55
Marshall 56
Masters, H. 58
May 53
Merrett, C. 55
Miller, Bill 55, 56
Miller, K.L. 51
Mitchell, D.A. 51
Mogg 56
Moore, R. 55
Moorse, L.F. 52
Morgan, A.P. 58
Morrison, D.C. 51, 53, 54
Moss, C.Geoffrey 51, 52, 53

Murphy, Jack 53, 55

Neal 55
Neate, E.J. 52

Ovenden, Eddie 53, 55
Overy, H. 51, 53
Owens, H.H. 52

Palmer, Harold 51, 53, 55
Parr, Norman 55
Partridge, R.A. 58
Pascoe, William H. 54, 55
Patterson 51, 53
Phillips, Ivor McG. 58, 59
Phillips, P.A.N. 55
Phillips, S.F. 58
Pope, T.F. 58
Poulson, P. 55
Powell 55
Powlesland, G.T. 51, 53
Probst 56
Pusey, L.M. 58

Rawlings, Les 56
Reeds, R.N. 58
Rees, H.D. 58
Reeves, G.W.F. 55
Richmond, W.A. 51
Ridlington, A.C. 53, 55
Roscorla, E. 58
Rounthwaite, J.M. 51
Rowe, F. 55
Russell, Jack 51, 53, 54, 55
Ryan, P.J. 51, 52

Sargent, Ted 56
Saunter, S.R.G. 58
Shapter 53
Shephard, Norman E. 58, 59
Sidell, Ken 53, 55
Simpson, A. 51
Slater, M. 55
Slator 55
Smart 55
Smith 53
Smith, Aubrey 56
Smith, W. 51
Smith, Wally 55
Spearman, J.G. 51, 56, 58, 59
Stanworth, G. 55
Starks 55
Steane, E.A. 58, 59
Stevenson, D.F. 58
Sugrue 55
Sutherland 55
Sweetman 53
Sykes, W. 5

Tack 54
Thomas 53, 55
Trevis 55
Tutt, Bill 55

Vieyra, Bernard Eugens 55
Vivian 55

Waller 54
Watkins, George 56

Watts, C.F. 52
Weeks, A. 51, 53
Wemys, G. 55
Whalebone, Jackie 53, 55
Whitaker, C.J.O. 51
White 55
White, E. 58
Wickins, Frank 55
Williams, B. 51, 53
Williams, P.T. 51
Williams, W. 55
Woodley 53

Yates, T. 55

7th (Long Ashton) Btn.

Abbott, Lionel 63
Adams, L.F. 74
Aish, Fred 78
Almond, Kitty 67
Andrew, Bill 66
Ashford, D.G. 61
Ashley, Bill 62
Ashley, Edward 62
Ashman, Frank 71
Aston, Stan 67
Atkins, Oliver 64
Atlay, T.R. 74, 75, 76
Atlay, Tom 75, 76
Aulman 78

Baber, H. 81
Baber, L. 81
Bailey, Jim 63
Baker, A. 64
Baker, J.D.G. 61
Baker, Len 80
Ball 78
Banks 64
Banwell, Harry 73
Barnes 65
Barnes, S. 78
Bates, Jack 62
Bax, A. or H. 72, 73
Beacham, Ernest 62
Beal, George 64
Bennett, J.S. 60
Bennett, Reg 64
Barry, Fred 65
Bell, William 'Dinger' 72, 73
Berg, Norman 67
Berry, Lawrence 65
Berry, W.E. 61
Bessant, Bert 73
Bettles 69
Bewen, J. 73
Biggs, Henry 65
Bird, Cyril 65
Birdwood, Lord William 66
Blacker, C. 81
Blackmore, F. 69
Blake, Edward 73
Blannin, M. 81
Blanning, Thomas Walter 63, 64
Boddey, H.S. 74
Body, H. 81
Bond, George 79, 80

Bond, W.M. 62
Boucher, J.F. 85
Boulter, Ben 75
Boulton, G. 65
Boulton, L. 65
Bourne, H. 62
Bourton, C. 64
Bourton, L. 64
Bowen, J. 'Ted' 72
Bown, Bert 79
Bown, Esme 67
Bown, G. 62
Boxall 78
Boyd, E. 81
Boyd, F. 81
Boyes, H.C. 60
Branch, J. 81
Brawn, William 79, 80
Bray, Reg 71
Brice, Bob 75
Bridges, Cecil 65
Briggs, J.P.T. 62
Brimble, Albert 71
Brimble, Reg 62
Brimble, Stan 62
Briscoe, Peter A. 63, 64
Broadhurst, Geoffrey 71
Brock, Ivan 80
Brodie, G.R. 68
Brodie, M.E. 62
Brookhouse-Richards 78
Brooks, Fred 64
Brooks, G.C. 85
Brooks, Jim 67
Brown 78
Brown, J.P. 73
Brown, Jo 64
Brown, Maurice (Stanton Drew) 62
Brown, Maurice (Tickenham) 72
Brown, Walt 64
Bryne 78
Buckland, H.W. 79
Budgett, J.H.M. 61, 85
Bunker, L.J.C. 62
Burdge, J. 81
Burge, Fred 64
Burlingham, Archie 71
Bush 73
Bushell, T.A. 60
Butt, John 67
Buxton, C.A. 68, 69
Bye, Leslie 72, 73

Cainey, Harvey 79, 80
Caldwell, Jack 78
Callow, Wilfred 64
Campbell-Smith, A. 62
Canter, Wallace 72
Cantor, Fred 71
Cardew, P.G. 74
Carey, Gilbert 78
Carter, B. 64
Cathcart 62
Catherall, Dennis 64
Chaffe, J.L. 68, 69, 73
Challenger, Arthur 75
Chapman 78
Chapman, E.A. 79
Chapman, Harry 79, 80

Chapman, Seward 'Sonny' 67
Chappel, Frank 75
Chappel, Tom 71
Chapple, Stan 70
Cheston, H.L. 66
Chick, F. 74, 78
Chivers, Arthur 64
Chivers, Bertram 63
Chivers, Cliff 63
Chivers, Joe 64
Chivers, L. 64
Chivers, P. 64
Chivers, P.R. 79
Chivers, Ronnie 'Pinky' 64
Christie, G. 68, 69
Churches, James 79, 80
Churchill, Ken 64
Clark, Bill 70
Clark, G.F. 62
Clark, Hubert 79
Clark, Sidney 79
Clarke, C.C. 74, 78
Clarke, P.H.F. 85
Clarke, Roland 79, 80
Cleverley, G. 69
Clift, E. 81
Cockbaine, E.R. 60
Coles 70
Coles, Graham 73
Coles, N. 62
Coles, Tom 67
Collyer, F.C. 63, 64
Cooke, Frank 81, 82
Cook, R.V.C. 74
Cooke, Edward 79, 80
Coombs 78
Cooper 64
Cooper, Ben 71
Court, Edward 78
Cousins, R.D. 68
Cox 78
Cox, Francis George 79, 80
Cox, R. 78
Coxon, J. 63
Crabtree, H.S. 61, 66, 85
Crane, Aubrey 72
Crease, Jack 75, 76
Cridland, T. 69
Cripps, Harry 78
Crisp, S.D. 68, 69
Crowlie, H.C. 60, 61
Curl (or Currell), Norman 82
Cunliffe, E. 69
Curtis, E.L. 60, 67
Curtis, E.W. 63
Curtis, Ted 65

Dagger 79
Dale, Tom 75
Dallimore, F. 69
Davies, Fred 'Butch' 83
Davies, Ray 67
Davis, Peter 75
Davis, W. Twiston 74
Day, B. 73
Day, Frank 72
Deacy, Fred 75
Derrick, E. 69
Derrick, William 82, 83, 84

Derriman, J.I. 62
Dickenson, R. 66
Dickinson 67
Didlick, L.A. 66
Dobson, W.E. 63
Dominey, H.F. 62
Dommett, J.A. 74
Drake, George 82
Drewett, H. 74, 78
Duffy, D.T. 61
Dunlop, M.K. 83
Dunn, Arthur 73
Durant, Jack 78
Durbin, Bill 69
Durbin, Harold 82
Durbin, J. 78
Durston, William or Tom 72, 73
Dyer, Edwin 72, 73
Dyer, Gerald 65
Dyer, Rob 65
Dyer, Sam 70

Eberle, G.S.J.F. 66
Edwards, Clifford 67
Edwards, P.R. 68
Ekless, Stuart 67
Elliott, Rev. Norman 61, 83
Ellis, Reg 69
Elton, Roy H. 83, 84
Elver, E. 63
Elverd, Bill 'Fishy' 78
Endicott 78
Eshelby, A.D. 62, 63
Evans, Tom 75
Ewins, Reg 69
Ewins, Stanley 69
Exten, Charlie 64

Farndon, H. 69
Farrant 78
Farrant, D.P. 66
Farrell, J.A. 61
Farrow, F. 81
Farrow, G. 81
Fenton, Eric J.M. 63, 65
Filer, Fred 62
Fisher, Norman 71
Fletcher 69
Flower, Alex 80
Flower, L. 63
Floyd 78
Footman, J.W.F. 61
Forbes, Gordon 71
Ford 64
Ford, H. 78
Ford, Reg 68, 69
Forse, W.C. 79
Fowler, Bert 75
Frake, Jimmy 71
Francis, Charles 72, 73
Francis, Michael 79, 80
Fraser, H.A.H. 60, 62, 63
Fray, G.C. 62
French, Bert 75
Frost, W.J. 62
Fussell, George 72, 73

Gallop, George 78
Gallop, Ken 63

Galloway, Stewart 75
Gerrish, N.D. 62
Gillard 64
Gilling, Jack 73
Glide, N.C.H. 61
Goddard, B. 69
Godwin, B. 69
Godwin, C.K. 62
Goodbody, W.S. 61
Goodliffe 78
Gove, J.H. 66
Gray, J.E. 60
Gregory 65
Griffiths, Jack 73
Grigg, Bill 70
Grundy, H.N. 60, 74
Guest, Cecil 68
Gunson, R.S. 66
Guest, Cecil 70
Gunter, W. 65
Guy, Basil 82

Hack, D. 69
Hack, F. or M. 69
Haines, E. 68, 70, 72
Haines, R. 81
Hale, Clifford or Len 75
Hamilton, R.J. 66
Hammond 84
Hammond, Wilfred 72
Hampton, Esme 67
Hancock, Harry 68
Hancock, Thomas H. 79, 81, 82
Hand, A.W. 68, 70
Hand, Doug 70
Hanney, L. 64
Hanson 69
Harding, F. 62
Harding, J.J. 74
Hardwicke, C.E. 60
Harrington, 'Sonner' 64
Harris, Bert 79
Harris, F. 81
Harris, G. 81
Harris, Jim 79
Harris, Philip 75
Harris, R.E.B. 61
Harris, Sam 71
Harrison, C.T. Hudson 60
Harvey, Jack 62
Harvey, M. 81
Hasell, Bill 79
Hasell, Jeff 79
Haskins, Bert 79, 80
Hasnip, Bob 71
Havell, C.C.W. 74
Hawker, Albert 67
Hawkins 62
Hawkins, Ken 62
Hayes, R.A. 78
Hayman, Gordon 67
Hayward, Archie 64
Hebert, A. 79
Hewish, Harold 62
Hicks 78
Hillman, Alfie 64
Hills, Cecil 78
Hippisley 75
Hoare, J.G. 79

Hobbs, C. 64
Hobbs, Edgar 78
Hobbs, Robert 78
Hoddell, R.J. 68
Hodges, F.L. 66
Hodgson, I. 81
Holder, B.J.A. 66
Holder, Victor 'Neppy' 67
Hollyman, Walter George 70
Horler, George 79
Horlick, C.J. 62
Horsey, G. 68
Houghton, T. 69
Howard 71
Howe, Percy 62
Howell, Don 75
Hudson, Bert 62
Hughes, F.W.F. 79
Hume, Dennis 75
Hunt 78
Hunt, L.J. 60
Hurdle, George 73
Hussey, Tom 70
Hutton, J.McA. 68, 70, 72
Hyde 78

I'Anson, M. 68
Ives, John 67
Izzard, Alfie 'Pop' 71

James, G.E. 62
James, Jimmy 67
James, W. 73
Jarman 64
Jarrett, George 68, 69
Jarrett, Ronald 66
Jeanes, O.J. 78
Jefferies, Arthur 80
Jefferies, G. 73
Jenkins 75
Jenkins, Doreen 67
Jenkins, E.S. 83
Jennings, Edward 81, 82
Jesser-Coope, J.C. 60, 74
Johnson, Ivor 67
Jones 70
Jones, W.A. 61, 85
Jones, W.S. 66

Kathro, D.J. 63
Kelland, A. 78
Kempster, Fred 73
Kettlewell, H.W. 63
Kettlewell, N.H. 60
King, E.M. 81
King, G. 81
King, H.D. 79
Kingman 64
Kirkwood, D. 62
Kitchen, E.G.Gidley 69
Knight, R.J. 61
Knight, S.W. Donald 63, 65
Knott, John W. 'Bill' 63
Knowland, Reg 66

Lanaton, H.A. 68
Lane, George 79, 80
Lane, Ron 67
Latham, R. 68

Latimer, W. 60
Laver, Joe 68
Leach, Eric 82
Learoyd, H.E. 62
Leman, Frederic Baring 60, 74, 78
Lenaton, G. 74
Lewis, Fred 63
Lindsey, Alan 72, 73
Lister, A.N. 60
Llewellyn, Cliff 78
Llewellyn, G. 78
Lloyd, 'Gomer' 71
Lock, H.G. 66
Lodge, Frank 65
Long, Fred 78
Love, F.R.C. 60
Lovell, Wally 63
Lucas, G.C. 68
Luckwell 78
Luke, Bert 67
Luxton, Jim 78
Lyons, J. 81
Lyons, L. 81

McCornick, J.E. 66
MacGregor, J. 61, 83
Maggs, R. 81
Maggs, Tom 67
Maine, Charlie 78
Mainstone, A.H. 61, 84
Major, Harold 75
Manley, Len 75
Marks, Cyril 68
Marlowe, Martin 75
Marsden 78
Marsh, Charlie 68, 69
Marsh, Jack 79
Marsh, R.W. 61
Marshall, Fred G. 70
Marshall, Jack or Harry 75
Masters, Reg 72, 73
Maynard, C. 79
Maynard, Frank 75
Mayo, S.W.I. 79, 80
Meek, Norman 65
Melville, James L.S. 63
Melvin, R.W.M. 61
Membry, A.J. 62
Mereweather, A.V. 83
Mereweather, W.D. 83
Miall, A.J.B. 63
Middlemass, G. de S.H. 68
Miles, H.W. 60
Mitchard, Fred 65
Mogg, R. 69
Moore, Alf 75
Moorhouse, Jim 73
Morgan, A.G. 61
Morgan, Jack 70
Morris, W. 62
Morrish, John 72
Morrish, Sid 71
Mortimer, Harry 69, 72
Morton, D. 72, 73
Morton, F.D.B. 68
Moses, C. 73
Moses, Vernon 72
Moss, Bill 70
Moss, F.H. 79

Mounter, G. 66
Moxham, Ernest 65
Mumford, W.R. 74
Murison, J.H. 63

Neate, J. 78
Neath, Cecil 75
Neath, Walter 75
Newman 78
Newton 75
Newton, Alvin 68
Nicholls 77
Nichols, Albert 70, 71
Nock, V.E.W. 66
Norris, Charlie 67
Norman, Lestor 80
Norton, Ern 75
Nutman 78

O'Connell, Edward 'Kingy' 67
Oldham, Fred 63
Olive, D. 72, 73
Orchard, Tom 64
Organ, A.J. 66
Osmond 79

Packard, J.L. 66, 67
Packham, Bill 65
Padfield, M. 64
Paget, A.G.C. 62
Palmer 62
Palmer, Fred 67
Palmer, Gilbert 62
Palmer, H.F. 62
Pane, George 78
Paramore, W.J. 61
Parfitt, C. 64
Park, E.C. 83
Parker, Harold 78
Parsons, A.M. 74, 78
Parsons, Charlie 75
Parsons, Cyril 75
Parsons, H.C. 66, 67
Parsons, Reg 67
Partington, F.W. 62
Patch, Jim 79
Payne, David 65
Payne, Herbert 65
Payne, Seward 82
Peacock, Fred 67
Pearce, Albert 75
Pearce, M.F. 78
Peck, Sid 71
Pembury, F. 61, 83
Penney, Arthur 62
Penny, K. 73
Penny, W. 73
Pepler, Victor 68, 69
Parry, Arthur 79
Pembury, F. 83
Perkins, Alfred 79, 80
Perry, George 79
Perry, Roy 79
Perry, Wilf 63
Pierce, Tom 79
Pippit 78
Pippit, G. 78
Pitts, Reg 75
Plumley 69

Popham, George C. 61, 83
Powell 70
Powell, A.W. 62
Power, Bill 62
Pragnell, Mervyn 62
Price, 'Trixey' 75
Pritchard, Lewis G. 63
Pugh, Rev. J. 69
Purnell, Roy 65
Pym, A. 62
Pym, Harry 71

Rainford, R.C. 79
Read, Nelson 79, 80
Ready, J. 78
Reakes 84
Redwood 64
Reed, Robin 78
Reeves, Fred E. 63, 68, 71
Rex, H.S. 61
Rhymes, Jack 65
Richards, G.E.A. 62
Richardson, John 66
Rickards, Roy 72
Ridge, G. 78
Robbins, Ernest 66
Roberts, Gordon 'Podge' 72, 73
Robertson, D.N. 85
Rogers, George 67
Rogers, V. 64
Rogers, W.A. 79
Rowles, Arthur 'Sonner' 67
Roynon, T. 68, 69
Ryder, J. 78
Ryder, Richard 79

Sage, Bill 79
Sage, Roly 64
Sage, V. 64
Santer, Richard 73
Satchel, Jack 80
Saunders, K.S. 60
Savage, Bert 75
Savory, Albert 67
Savory, E.M. 61, 85
Savory, J.H. 61, 85
Sawkins, D.J.N. 68
Scammell, W.S. 62
Scarff, J.G.R. 61, 85
Scott, A.B. 63, 79
Scribbins, Ernie 71
Sellick, Iris 67
Selman, William 72, 73
Selvey, A.T. 67
Selvey, Arthur 67
Selvey, Ken 67
Selwood 70
Seward, W. 81
Sharman 64
Shaw, A. 74, 78
Shearn, Edward 'Teddy' 65
Shearn, H.C. 63, 64
Shears, H. 78
Shepherd, Hector 78
Shepherd, Reg 67
Sheppard, V. 81
Sherbourne, Donovan 64
Short, Arthur 75
Sibley, C.E. 85

Simmons, Donald 82
Simmons, Raymond George 80
Simmons, Wilfred Joseph 68, 72, 73, 79, 81, 82
Simms, Hilary 75
Simms, Ken 75
Skinner 67
Skinner, Harry 67
Smailes, F.C.
Smallman 78
Smallman, F.G. 74
Smart, Wally 62
Smith, A.G. 68, 70, 72
Smith, Arthur 81, 82
Smith, Bill 75
Smith, F. 73
Smith, G. 65
Smith, L. 83
Smith, Les 63
Smith, S.F. 79
Snelling 64
Southway, A.W. 61
Spear, Reg 67
Speed, Ron 64
Spencer, E. 68, 69
Sperring, George 65
Spinks, G.T. 61
Spratt, Gordon 75
Stacey, G.W. 61
Stallard, Francis 79, 80
Staple, K. 73
Stephens (or Stevens), M.E. 68
Stephenson 79
Stevens, Farnham 62
Stevenson, R.L. 79
Stewart, R. 60
Stidard, P.J. 66
Stock, Graham 64
Stock, J. 78
Stokes, B. 78
Stokes, Bill 78
Stokes, Len 78
Stone, Malcolm 75, 76
Strange, B. 85
Strange, Jesse 75
Strickland, Fred 70
Strickland, Ray 71
Stuart-Low, W.C. 66, 85
Stuckey, Frank 75
Summerell, Ernest 'Nung' 72, 73
Summerell, Oliver 72
Summerell, William 72, 73
Summers, Vic 68, 69
Sutton, N.G. 62
Sykes, C.M. 72
Symes, George 80
Symes, M.F. 79, 81
Symons, Jim 75

Tancock 63
Tavener, Charles 72, 73
Taylor 78
Taylor, Bill 71
Tebbutt, Geoffrey Norman 66
Teek, Glyn 64
Tennant, F.W. 62
Terrell, F.J. 63, 79
Thatcher, H. 63
Thayer, Iris 67

Thistlewaite, J. 60, 63, 79
Thomas, Alan 70
Thomas, H.G.S. 62
Thompson, J.S. 61
Thorne, A.E. 61
Thornet, Leonard 79, 80
Tiley, L.H. 68
Tiley, Len 72, 73
Todd, C.C. 79
Tovey, Norman 62
Townsend, M. 73
Treasure 64
Tredinnick, Reg 69
Trendell 79
Trigg, Ivor 72, 73
Trimm, James 79
Trott, Albert 78
Trott, Frank 75
Trott, Harry 75
Trussler, C.W. 62
Tucker, fred 82
Tucker, Harry 71
Tucker, Ken 67
Tuckey, E.C. 74, 78
Turner, R.G. 68
Tweedie, Sir Hugh J. 60, 66, 74, 78, 84
Tyte, Arthur 79, 81, 82

Udall, E.H. 78

Vaughan, F.D. 63
Venn, F.A. 62
Viney, Alan 75, 76
Virgo, Jack 73
Vowles, Cyril 64
Vowles, Edward George 68, 69

Wade, Les 67
Waite 78
Waite, Bill 71
Walker, Fred 70
Walker, Patrick 79
Wall, Lionel 64
Wallace, T. 60, 61
Wallis, John 71
Walters 65
Walters, C.F.H. 66
Warburton, Brian 76
Ware, Oliver 79
Wareham, Seward 82
Warford, P. 81
Watkins, Stanley 75
Waygood, Tom 75
Weaver, E.A. 68
Weaver, George 79, 80
Weaver, Len 80
Weaver, Reg 80
Weaver, Ted 68, 69
Webb, Albert 70
Webb, Stanley 71
Webber, Walt 78
Wedlake, Gilbert 79, 80
Wedlake, Herbert 79, 80
Wedlake, Kenneth 79, 80
Weeks, Bill 78
Weeks, Clifford 64
Weeks, Jonah 83
Weeks, Maurice 82, 83

Weeks, R. 81
Weeks, W. 81
Weir, G.M. 62
Wells, Ray 64
Wells, Rex 64
West, G.H. 63
West, H. 64
Weston, Vivian 79, 80
Whitehead, Tony 64
Whiting, W.S. 60, 63, 79
Whitting, Gruff 71
Wilkins, Herbert 72
Wilkins, J.H.A. 79
Wilkinson, E.H. 61
Williams 78
Williams, Arthur 68, 69, 72
Williams, E. 63
Williams, Frank H. 66
Wills, P.S. 79
Wilson 79, 80
Winfield, C. 83
Winstone, Edwin 62
Withers, L. 73
Woollard, R. 69
Wood, Cissie 67
Wood, George 78
Wood, J.L.R. 61
Woodall, B. 'Topper' 64
Woodall, N. 64
Woodland, B.L. 63
Woodward, R. 72, 73
Wyatt, F. 81
Wyatt, S. 81

Yates, Arthur 80
Young 78
Young, Charles 73
Young, H. 78
Young, John 62
Young, Newman 71
Young, Richard 73
Young, Walt 78

8th (Weston) Battalion

Ackland, Horace 96
Adams, Bob 98
Alford, Herbert 88
Amesbury, E. 87, 88, 89
Amesbury, W. 87, 88, 89
Apps 94
Ardin 101
Arlotte, F. 98
Atkins, P. 88, 93
Atkinson 86, 89, 95

Bailey, Alan 87
Bailey, Ralph 87
Bains 100
Baker, E. 92
Ball, S. 98
Banwell, Peter 87, 89
Banwell, Stan 93, 95
Barker, L. 86
Bartlett, Bill 100
Bass, Colin 101
Bateman 87
Beacham 96

Beamish, C.C. 92
Berkley, E.C. 88, 89, 92
Bird, 'Dickie' 101
Blackmore, F. 98
Blanning, L. 98
Blunt, W. 92
Bonning, S.L. 95
Briggs 88
Brown, F.S. 91, 92
Brown, J.K. 102
Bruce, A.W.A. 86
Budd, Jack 97
Budden, Ivor 94
Burrows 92, 96

Carpenter, Les 98
Chaplin, Ellis 96
Chaplin, Peter 96
Chidgey, Jim 100
Clark, N.M. 92
Clark, Sidney 91, 92
Clarke 88
Cole 91
Coles 87, 88
Coles, R. 98
Coles, W.J. 98
Cook, Norman 87
Cornish, Bill 98
Council 88
Courtenay-Smith, J.D. 92
Coward, D.R. 92
Coward, Rex 91, 93
Crandon, Metford 94
Crawford, William H. 91, 92
Culling, Alderman P. 87

Dare, M. 98
Dauncey, E.L. 86
Davidson 91
Davidson, H. 92
Davidson, M.N. 92
Davies, Barry 94
Davies, J.C. 92
Davies, J.H. 92
Davis 87, 88
Dawes, S.C. 97
Day, L. 98
Dicker, Terry 87
Dimoline, V.E. 86
Dobbins 101
Doule 87, 88
Drakeford 92
Drew, J. 98
Driver, Len 91
Dudley 88, 89
Durston, Clifford 94, 95
Durston, George 95
Durston, Kenneth John 94, 95
Durston, Reginald 94, 95
Dyer, H. 98

Earls, Paddy 101
Edwards 91
Eveleigh, W.L. 86

Fear, Arthur 88
Fear, Bert
Foy, W. 92
Francis, A.J. 92

Franklin, G.A. 92
Freeman, Ron 97
Fry, E.V. 92

Gallop, Sid 87, 88, 89, 93, 95, 102
Gamblain, C.C. 91, 92
Gamblain, Fred 91, 93
Gamblain, Jack 100
Gardner, John 94
Geary, J. 91, 92
George, L. 98
George, Lawton H. 86
Georgy, M.E. 86
Gibbs 88, 89
Gill, Henry 87
Gill, N. 92
Goodman 88, 89
Goodman, Edgar 94
Goodwin, Tommy 102
Gore, Jack 94
Gray 86
Greedy, Cliff 91, 93
Grenough, Charles 97
Grey, Charles 97
Griffiths, Len 96

Hack, Jack 96
Hammond 100
Hanniker, A. 86
Harris 98, 99, 100
Harris, George 94
Harris, W. 92
Harvey, Ronald 94
Hayes 92
Hess 89
Hess, H. 98
Heybern 88, 89
Hill, John 100
Hiscocks, John 87
Holt 91, 93
Holt, F.C. 92
Holt, J.D. 92
Hook, F. 98
Hooper, A.W. 86
Hope, R. 92
Hosbons, S.R. 86
Huff, W. 'Bill' J. 88, 89, 93, 95, 102
Hunt, Reg 96
Hussey, T. 92
Hutchins, Jack 96
Hutton, T. 92
Hynd, A. 98

James, R.W. 92
Jay 91, 93
Jenkins, E. 92
Jenkins, R. 101
Johns 88
Johns, Jack 98
Jones, Pryser 100
Jones, Ray 87
Judd, W.B. 92

Kemps, R.H.S. 98
Kerton, Fred 94
King, Maurice 96
Kingsbury, Wilf 96
Knight 97
Knight, Harry 96

Lake 91
Lane 91
Langfield, A.G.L. 102
Langford, G. 92
Ling, Arthur 94
Ling, Walter 94
Lock, George 88
Lovell, E.C. 98
Lovell, H. 98
Macdonald, J. 91, 92
MacNaughton-Wright, M. 92
Marshall, G. 98
Martin, J. 98
Mason, Ted 98
Mathewson, Ernest 96
Matthews, F.W. 91
Matthews, W.A. 92
Matthews, W.E. 92
Maxted, Ron 98
May, O. 98
Merrick, Mornington 88
Mew, J. 98
Millard, Bob 94
Millard, Clifford 95
Miller 88
Millier, Bert 95
Milton, G. 91, 92, 102
Minifie, David R. 91, 92
Minifie, W. 92
Mitchell, E. 98
Morgan, Dai 98, 100
Morris, David 96

Nicholls, Percy C. 86, 88, 93
Noakes, W.C. 86

O'Connell, Patrick Dominic 97, 98
Ormerod, H.J. 98
Osborne, W. 'Bill' 87, 88, 93, 95
Owen, R. 92

Palk, T.F. 91, 92, 93
Palmer 91
Palmer, Reg 96
Parrett, P.J. 86, 87
Parsons 91, 93
Pearce 91
Pennycott, H.S. 98
Perkins 89
Perks, William 96
Perriman, Norman 98-100
Phillips, Frank 96
Philpott, A.E. 86, 88, 89
Philputt 95
Phippen, Harry 96
Pickett, Stan H. 91, 92
Poole, 'George' 98
Pope 96
Pope, Gordon 96
Pople, E.C. 92
Popham 87, 88, 102
Prewitt, Percy 96
Price, Monty 88, 93, 95

Raines, Jack Crocker 97
Reakes, E. 92
Reed 86, 88, 89
Reed, A. 92
Reeves 100

Reynolds, F. 98
Robins, F.W. 86, 87
Robins, W. 91, 92
Robinson, P.S. 92
Rogers 96
Rooke 87, 88
Rush, H.J.W. 98

Sainsbury 95
Salt, Reg 97
Sansom, W.H. 92
Say, Bob 94
Scotchmer, Dick 94
Sewell-Grant, H.C. 86
Sheather, Frederick William 101
Sheppard, Jim 100
Simpson, F.W. 92
Singleton, Harold 97
Smart, E. 92
Smith, Bert 96
Smith, Bill 97
Smith, J.C. 92
Smith, R.M. 95
Snelgrove, D. 98
Snelgrove, G. 98
Snell, B. 98
Stanier, E. 98
Staples, Stan 91
Starr, Tim 96
Stuckey, W. 98

Taylor, Jack 100
Thoday, John 91, 92
Thomas 100
Thomas, C. 100
Thompson, H.A. 92
Thorpe, R. 92
Thyer, Jack 96
Tibbetts, H.A. 86
Trego 96
Trego, Kenneth 87
Trevelyan, E.T. 86
Trevor 86, 91
Trowbridge, Len.F. 92, 93
Turner, F.C. 92
Turner, Lawrie 88

Upham, Jim 91
Usher 91

Varder, Les T. 91, 92, 93
Venn, Len 96
Vickery 91
Vickery, R.A. 102
Vinning, Jack 96
Vinson, J.W. 97
Vowles, L.R. 92

Walker, C.J. 86
Walker, J.C. 95
Wall, J.C. 92
Wallace 92
Walters, R.S.L. 91, 92
Ware, D.W. 97
Watkins, Jack 96
Watts, Maurice 102
Webb, G.W. 92
Webber, Jack 91
Weber, D. 98

Weeks 92
Wheatley, H. 98
White, George 96
White, J. 98
Whyte, Derek 100
Williams, A.O. 86
Williams, E. 92
Williams, Fred 96
Williams, S. 98
Williams, Walt 96
Willingham, F. 92
Willingham, G.E. 92
Wilmot, A.M. 95
Wilson 88, 89
Wiltshire, Bert 94
Wood, George 86, 87
Woolacott, Frank 94
Wride, Jack 96
Wright, R.A.C. 86
Wright, W. 91, 92

Yaldwin 94
Yatman, A.H. 86

9th (Wells) Battalion

Acreman, Frederick George 125
Addicott 105
Ainsworth, R.M. 103
Alderman, J. 113
Allen, A.O. 113
Allen, E.J. 113
Allen, Percival James 114
Allen, R.J. 117
Allen, William George 118
Anderson, Charles Henry 118
Andrews, Albert Bevan 121
Andrews, Alfred Charles 118, 119, 120
Andrews, Frnk 121
Andrews, Harold S. 114
Andrews, Ronald Alfred 118
Ashford, Harry 120
Attwell, Henry John 125
Attwood, Edward 114
Atwell, Wilfred 114
Atyeo, Harry T. 127

Badman, Alan Edward 121
Badman, Robert Ashton 121
Badman, Sidney William 120
Badman, William Frank 120
Bailey, Albert George 121
Baker 106
Baker, Arthur Noel 117
Baker, Dennis R. 117
Baker, G.C. 113
Baker, G.W. 113
Baker, George 106
Baker, George Thomas 117
Baker, John W. 117
Baker, John William 117
Baker, L. 113
Baker, Leonard Frank 116
Baker, Leslie Arthur 116
Baker, R.H. 114
Ball, C.F. 110
Ball, Cyril T. 126, 128

Ball, F.C. 126
Ball, S.C. 113
Banks, Clifford George 118
Banwell, Stanley 125
Barnard, William 103, 105, 107
Barnes, Leo 121
Barnes, Maurice F. 118, 119, 120
Barnes, Vernon 118
Barnstaple, L.H. 114
Barry, Kenneth T. 120, 122
Barry, Leonard George 126
Barry, O.W. 104
Barry, P. 120, 124
Bartlett, Colin Arnold 121, 122
Bartlett, Frederick 118
Bartlett, J.C. 113
Battle, F. 110, 113
Baulch, Plassy 114
Bawn, James Philip 118, 119, 120
Beacham, E.E. 110
Beacham W.L. 110
Beale, Cecil Charles 121
Bell, M.C.W. 117
Bengefield 104
Bennett, Frank 118
Berry, Stanley F. 121, 122, 128
Best, George Victor 120
Biffin, Edward Alfred 119, 121
Billett, Ted 117, 118
Billing, Frederick Walter 125
Billing, Reginald 125
Birch, Albert 126
Birch, Ernest 126
Birch, Frank 126
Bird, Ernest Colin 127
Bird, G.R. 113
Bishop 113
Bishop, K. 110
Black, J.A. 113
Blackburn, Charles Edward 127
Blackman, Eric Alan 121
Bliss, Philip Frederick Henry 118
Blythman, Thomas Powell 114
Bobbett, Henry J. 126
Bond, Harold Cecil 118, 119, 120
Bowles, Alec Gordon 120
Bown, Henry Joseph 127
Bown, I.L. 110
Bown, M.H. 110
Bown, Metford Arthur 116
Bown, Kenneth Philip 114
Brake, Alexander Frederick 114
Brass, Albert Edward 114
Brewer, Ivor Headly Frank 114
Bright, R.A. 118
Broughton, Arthur Edward G. 127
Broughton, Douglas Hazel 121
Broughton, Ernest 118
Broughton, Harold Edward 122
Broughton, Horace Jack 118
Brown, A.L. 114
Brown, Archibald William 125
Brown, Charles 114
Brown, G.G. 113
Browning, Herb 114
Bryer, Rowland Frederick H. 121
Bryer, Douglas Elwyn 118
Buckingham, Claud Irish 114
Burbidge, Henry George 118

Burden, Thomas 114
Burge, Harold Frederick 125
Burge, Jack 118
Burgess, Mervyn Thomas 121
Burich, William 126
Burkin, R.K. 114
Burleton, Thomas Sylvester 121
Burridge, Jesse 117
Burrough, Robert Charles 126
Burrow, Charles George 114
Burt, William Robert Norman 114
Burton, Ronald 117
Bush, Albert 125
Bush, Albert Isaac 125
Bush, Arthur George 120
Bush, Douglas Harold 125
Bush, Eddie Frederick 120
Bush, Harry Raymond 125
Bush Reginald George 125
Butterfield, E. 108
Buttle, Albert Edward 125
Buttle, John 125

Caines, George James Medland 118
Caines, S. 105
Canniford, William John 114
Carey 108
Carter, Albert 118, 119
Carter, C.A. 110
Carter, E.H.C. 116
Carter George 122
Carter, Frank 114
Carter, Harry 114
Carter, Jack Douglas 120, 122
Carter, Les 118
Carter, Maurice 125
Carter, Wallace 121
Castle, Albert Edward 118, 119
Chaffey, A.J. 121
Chaffey, Donald Herbert 121
Chamberlain 105
Champion, Hugh 125
Champion, W.A. 114
Chapman, Gilbert 114
Chapman, Reginald Henry 114
Chappell, R. 110
Chard, A.I. 113
Chard, R.A. 113
Chauncy, Edward St. Martin B. 114
Chick, Fred 119
Chiffers, Allan Kenneth 118, 119
Chiffers, Arthur Leonard 120
Chinnock, Ernest Reginald 125
Chislett, Henry 114
Chivers, Edward 114
Chivers, Frank 118
Chivers, R.V. 114
Christopher, Alfred 114
Chubb, Frederick Charles 121
Chubb, Henry William 118, 119
Church, A. 110
Church, Frederick George 118
Church, G.M. 113
Church, V.H. 113
Churches, Joseph Edward 114
Clare, H. 121
Clapp, Dennie 125
Clark, Bancroft 118, 122-4
Clark, George 114

Clark, Harry 114, 116
Clark, Stephen 122
Clarke, J. 105
Clarke, Robert John Samuel 114
Clavey 110
Clement, Robert Claude 121
Coates, Robert 126
Coleman 108
Colenutt, Dennis Ronald 114
Coles, Albert 122
Collins 104
Cook, Bert 106
Cook, Gilbert 108
Cook, Stan 106
Cook, William 125
Cook, William Albert 120
Coombes, Herbert John 127
Coombs, Oliver C. 114
Cooper, Edgar 'Eddie' C. 115, 116
Cooper, George Edward 116
Cooper, Hedley Horton 118, 119
Cooper, Walter Horace 116
Cooperman 127
Cornelius, William Mather 118
Cornick, William Thomas 125
Cornish, Cecil 121
Cox 118
Cox, Bertie John 114
Cox, Ernest Gerald 114
Cox, Stanlet Bertie 114
Cox, Reg 117, 118
Cox, Richard 117
Cox, Thomas 116
Cox, William Frank 114
Cox, William James 114
Crane, James 117
Crane, William Henry 117
Crease, E. Max 104, 107
Creed, Roy Stanley Carey 116
Cressy, F.W. 108
Crocker Arthur James 120
Crocker, Duncan 114
Crocker, Lionel Ernest 126
Crockett, A. 110
Crockett, W. 110
Crossey, William Harold 117
Crossman, Albert Edward 127
Crossman, Cecil Joseph 118
Crossman, George Henry 127
Crossman, Kenneth Vivian 127
Culliford, Cyril Thomas 127
Culliford, Herbert 114
Culling, G.J. 104
Cunans, T.G. 108
Curle, Edward George 117
Curtis, Courtney Albert 121, 122

Dalley 108
Dallimore, G. 110
Dallimore, W. 109
Daniells, Jack Owen 118
Dare, William Sprague 118
Davies, Austin 121
Davies, Charles A.A. 127
Davies, George Henry Albert 118
Davies, John G. 125
Davies, William 121
Davis, Alfred Edward 126
Davis, Arthur Edward 126

Davis, Clifford Henry 114
Davis, Dennis 118
Davis, Ernest Ewin 114
Davis, Harold 114
Davis, John 'Jack' 122
Davis, Wilfred John 121
Day, Ernest Reginald 116
de Kremer, M. 113
Dean, Jack Loftus 114
Difford, Abram 117
Difford, Herbert John 117
Dodge, William Alfred 114
Donley Leonard C. 114
Dors, L. 110
Douglas 122
Douglas-Dufresne, E. 109, 110
Dowden, Clifford Lionel 118
Dowden, Jack 118
Dowden, Leslie 118, 119, 120
Dowden, Wallace 114
Dowdney, Francis Cecil 114
Downer, Robert West 117
Doyle, George Arthur 114
Doyle, Walter J. 114
Draper, Richard Jack 114
Driver, C.E. 117
Duck, Jack W. 109, 113
Dunford, F. 113
Dunkerton, Bert Stanley 125
Dunkerton, William Leonard 125
Dunthorn, Leslie R. 114
Dupuy, W. 105
Durey, Alfred Edward 125
Durston, F. 114
Durston, Frank 121
Dyer, Charles 126
Dyer, George 114
Dyer, William Samuel 114
Dyer, Wilfred 114
Dyke, Bob 109, 113
Dyke, Henry 109, 113
Dyke, R. 113
Dymond, John 114

Earl, Arthur 126
Edwards 106, 122
Edwards, Herbert William 118
Elliott, Clifford Oliver S. 127
Ellis, Frederick 118
Emery, George 118
Emery, Stanley 118
England, William Thomas 114
Eyking, Van 106

Fall, Bert 122
Faulk 105
Fear, Clifford Edward 114
Fear, Dennis Reginald John 117
Fear, Edward 116
Fear, Harold Aubrey James 117
Fear, Nelson 121, 122
Field, Derrick Bertram 114
Field, L.R. 114
Fielding, Jonas Arthur 119
Fisher, Albert Edward 121
Fisher, Edward Harry 121
Fisher, George Ernest Chapman 127
Flemington, Alan 114
Fooks, George Bertrand 114

Ford, A. 113
Ford, Arthur Leslie 126
Ford, C. 113
Ford, David 127
Ford, H. 113
Ford, Roy John 126
Forsey, Wilfred Albert 126
Foster, Frederick C.R. 117
Fouracres, Arthur 114
Fouracres, Bert James 121
Francis, Herbie 117, 118
Francis, Lionel Frederick 119
Francis, Thomas W. 124, 126
Franks, Reginald Stewart 117
Fraser, Stanley 114
French, Peter John Maurice 119
Friend, Arthur J. 114
Friend, William 'Bill' 115, 116
Friend, Walter G. 114
Fudge, Stan 104
Fussell, Albert Edward 114

Gaines, Sam 106
Gallop, Percy Alfred 105
Gane, Edwin Charles 114
Gane, John Robert 126
Gane, Walter 116
Gare, John H. 121
Garland, Albert Frank 125
Garland, Edward 'Ted' W. 115, 116
Garthwaite, William Brian 116
Genge, Eric 121
Gerrish, Harry 105
Gibbon-Pimlett, J. 113
Gifford, Albert James 114
Gifford, George 115, 116
Gifford, Wallace 115, 116
Gilbert, T.V. 114
Gill, Alfred George 114
Gillett, Reginald Charles 119
Gilroy, Stephen 119
Gilson, Raymond Gordon 109, 110
Ginn, A,W, 114
Ginn, Nathaniel 114
Glandfield, Percy S. 121, 122-3
Glass, Gordon H. 103, 107
Glass, Reg 118
Goddard, Ernest John 114
Godfrey, Harvey D. 125
Godwin, Ronald Francis James 119
Gooden, Evelyn Frank 127
Gould, Arthur Edwin Samuel 125
Gould, Edwin G. 125
Gould, Lewis James 114
Graves, Alfred Leslie 121, 122-3
Green, B. 109
Green, C. 113
Green, Dennie 114
Green, George 119
Green, Harry 114
Green, H.L. 113
Green, Percy Ernest Thomas 114
Green, Robert Green, H.L. 113
Grenter, Ronald 121
Griffen, Albury 119
Griffin, Herbert Frank 121
Griffiths, Harold Edward 119
Grunsell, Charles Stuart 114
Guildford, Claude C.L. 115, 116

Guise, Stanley J. 106
Gunning, Roly 106
Guy, C. 109, 110
Guy, O. 110
Guy, William 125

Haimes, Leonard Bond 126
Haimes, S.A. 114
Hale, David 108
Hallett, Frederick J. 114
Hallett, John 114
Ham, Charlie 117, 118
Hamlett, William 121
Hancock, William Wood 119
Hannam, Frank Leslie 119
Harding, W.G. 113
Harding, W.H.J. 108
Harding, William 126
Hare, Noel 119
Hargreaves 106
Harland, G.H. 114, 118
Harris, E.C. 113
Harris, Edward T. 119
Harvey, R.M. 121
Harwood, Sylvester G. 104, 106, 107
Hasell, W. 113
Hatch, Arthur John Louis 114
Hawker, Harry Conrad V. 119
Hawkins, Clifford 119
Hawkins, J.E. 110
Hawkins, W.H. 110
Hayes, Derrick 121, 122
Hayes, Ivor John 117
Heal, Horace George 116
Heal, Leslie John 113, 114
Heal, Roy Bertram 114
Heal, S. 113
Heal, W.J. 113
Heathfield, Henry James 119
Helliker, Bertram Henry 114
Hembury, John 'Jack' A.W. 115, 116
Hennessey, John 114
Hennessey, William 121
Hewish, J.E. 113
Hicks 105
Hicks, E. John 109, 110, 111, 113
Hicks, Frank 109, 110
Higdon, Albert Edward 116
Higdon, Edward Charles 126
Higgins, Alfred William 126
Higgins, Edwin George 119
Higgins, Ronald 126
Higgins, Stan 126
Hill, Ernest Francis 119
Hill, Frederick Walter 116
Hillard, H. 113
Hillier, M.W. 110
Hilton 119, 120
Hines, J. 121
Hippisley, W.H.J. 114
Hitchcock, James Vincent 114
Hobbs, Mervyn 126
Hockey, Percy 121
Holbrow, Bernard T, 114
Holcombe, Bill 106
Hole, Nelson 126
Hole, Percy A. 104, 105, 106, 107
Holley, Ern 104
Holley, Kenneth 104

319

Holley, Percy Edgar 121
Hollinshead, H. 105
Holloway, Arthur Ernest 121
Holloway, Ernest Philip 114
Holloway, John Henry 114
Holmes, Ernest G. 127
Hood, Frederick William 114
Hooper 122
Hooper, Edwin Charles 119
Hooper, Victor 122
Horsey, Arthur Tom 105
Horstead, William Charles 119
Hoskins, Arthur 119
Hoskins, Ernest Glyn 119
Hoskins, Sid 106
Howe, Fergus Henry 114
Howell, O. 113
Hubert, Joe 119
Hughes, F.R. 117
Hughes, Reginald 121
Hughes-Davies, E. 118, 120
Huish, Jack 108
Hulin, S. 113
Humphries, Ronald K. 120
Humphries, S. 113
Humphries, Tom 122
Hurd, Harold 117, 118
Huxter, Roland Charles D. 114
Hyde, Albert Edward 121

Ingerfield, Ernest 119

Jackson, James 117
James 105
James, G. 113
James, Martin 114
James, William 109, 110
Jeanes, Reginald Henry 119
Jefferies, H.W. 114
Jenkins, Fred 126
Jenkins, Walter Henry 126
Johnson, A.G. 104

Keeling, E. 103
Keen, H. 109, 113
Keen, J. 113
Kenchington, James John 119
Kent H.H. 116
Kent, Joseph H. 115, 116
Killen, William Stan 126
Kilmerster, W. 113
King, Albert George 119
King, Herbert James 121
King, Horace John 114
King, Jack 121
King, Percy George 121
King, S. 113
Kington, Essington George 119
Klinge, V.H.E. 104
Knight, Francis William 114
Knight, Charles Henry 126

Lacey, John William 114
Lacey, Peter James 114
Lacey, Michael Blomfield 119
Lamb, George Charles 121
Lambert, Daniel 121
Lambert, Harold 119
Lampert, Charles 126

Lampert, Herbert William 126
Lane, G. 113
Lane, G.J.S. 108
Lanfear, Percival S. 120
Langdon, Eli 119
Langdon, Oliver George 114
Lapham Edward Arthur 119
Lawson, Harry Campbell 119
Le Calsi, Charles R.J. 119, 120, 128
Leader, Harold 119
Leavey, Lionel Alfred 118, 121, 122
Lee, Gilbert 118
Lee, Leonard Gilbert 119
Lee, Leonard Percy 114
Legge, James Victor 114
Leney, Frederick John 121
Lessey, Charles Arthur 127
Lester, Fred 118
Lewis, Bill 122
Lewis, Jack 119
Linham, Ernest Charles 119
Linham, Ralph Stanley 114
Lisk, Cyril Victor 121, 122
Lock, George 126
Lockyer, Tom 119, 120
Locke, Henry James 127
Locke, Stanley 127
Lockyer, Leonard Albert 127
Lockyer, William J, 127
Longley, George 119
Longman, William Martin 126
Lonsdale, Edwin 117
Lovelace, William George 121
Lovell, Arthur Claude 121
Lovell, Bert John 121
Loxton, H. 105, 106
Loxton, S. 105
Lukins 104
Lukins, Douglas 121, 122
Lunnon, H.C. 108
Lush, F. 105
Lye, Ernest George 126

McDonnell, James 103, 107, 122
Mackay, James Edward 121
McTavish, L.A. 128
Maddaford, William 115
Maine, Arthur Edwin 121, 122
Malcolm, W.H. 113
Mantle, W.C. 110
Mantle, W.T. 110
Mapstone, Horace James 115
Marsden, G.C. 104
Marsh, C. 121
Marsh, Ernest Frank 127
Marsh, Ernest William 121
Marsh, Frank 126
Marsh, Henry George 126
Marsh, Horace 121, 122
Marsh, John Henry 119
Marsh, Leonard Percy 126
Marsh, Leslie Cecil 119
Marsh, Reginald F.R. 121
Martin, A.G. 117
Martin, Arthur Thomas 118, 121
Martin, Ivor 117
Martin, James 127
Martin, Stanley 120, 122
Martin, William 117

Masters, Harold 126
Masters, Jack 108
Masters, Robert 115
Mattock, Arthur W.F. 115
Mattock, Stanley Thomas 115
Maybury, F. 105
Meatyard, Herbert Arthur 126
Melmoth, Horace Joseph 115
Melrose, T.R.G. 103
Merchant, Fred 104
Merrifield, Henry Richard 'Dick' 115, 116
Merriott, Henry J. 121, 122
Micklewhite, Jack 105
Miles, George Samuel 119
Miles, Percival Leonard 119
Miles, William Charles 115
Miller, George 116
Miller, J. 105
Miller, Jack 115, 116
Miller, John Henry 115
Mills, Harold 122
Milton, Bill 118
Milton, Fred 118
Milton, H.C.F. 117
Mitchell, E. 113
Mitchell, F. 113
Moore 108
Moore, Arthur William 119
Moore, Edward 122
Mosley, D. 105
Moule, Lancelot 115
Moxley, Edward Horace 117
Mullett, Ern 109, 113
Mullins, George Arthur John 115
Mullins, Maurice Henry 121, 122
Mullins, Walter 115
Mundy, Edward Overton 115
Munkton, Harold James 120

Napper, D.C. 115
Napper, Ern 117, 118
Nash, Leonard 121
Nash, Leslie John 115
Nash, William Arthur 121
Nicholas, Ernest William 126
Nineham, H. 113
Norman, Bill 119, 120
Norris, C. 110
Norris, Cyril 126
Norris, L. 110
Norris, 'Pop' 106
Norris, William Lewis C. 119
Norton, Ronald Albert 119
Nurse, Leslie John 115

Oatley, S. 113
Oliver, J.A. 120
Ollis, A.L. 110
Osmond, Gilbert Thomas 121

Packer, A.G. 108
Packer, Charlie R. 109, 113
Page, E. 118, 122-4
Paine, Ed 119
Palmer, B.R. 113
Palmer, Stanley Fitz-James 115
Parfitt, H.B. 110
Parish, Walter 119, 128

Parker 104
Parker, Maurice Albert W. 119, 120
Parker, Nelson Hugh 126
Parsons, Albert Edward 115
Parsons, Eric William 115
Parsons, Geoffrey 117
Parsons, Guy 118
Parsons, Harry Edward 121
Parsons, 'Jug' 118
Pattison, Stuart Arthur 116
Paull, Herbert Arthur 119, 120
Payne, Arthur H. 109, 113
Payne, Edwin 119
Payne, K. 113
Payne, Lewis Albin 115
Payne, O. 113
Payne, R. 113
Pearce, G.H. 110
Pearce, Allan John 115
Pearce, Eric Robert 115
Pearce, Reginald 115
Pearce, Walt 104, 106
Peddie, Ronald 118
Perkins, Leslie Harold 119
Perry, Bernard Leslie 127
Perry, Frederick Charles 121
Perry, H. 110
Perry, Vernon C. 127
Petheram, Alfred 'Alfie' Ed. H. 115, 116
Petherick, Ernest 121
Phelps, Albert Henry 116
Phelps, Herbert Frank 116
Pike, Leslie Grinter 126
Pinnegar, T.K. 115
Pirkins, E. 110
Pitman, Albert Edward 127
Pitman, Bertram F. 127
Pitman, F. 113
Pitman, Harold Arthur 126
Pitman, Wilf 106
Plumley, Samuel R. 126
Pocock, Stephen Edward 119
Pointing, D. 104
Pompey, George 119
Pompey, Harry 119
Pope, C.P. 126
Pope, William Francis 126
Popham, John Thomas 115
Pople, Leslie 121
Porch, M.P. 115
Porter, Charles J. 126, 128
Porter, George 126
Potter, R.L. 128
Powell, A.W. 108
Powell, G.C. 110
Powell, T.J.H. 117, 124
Prettyman, Alfonso 115
Prior, R. 113
Pritchard, Jack William Harman 119
Prowse, William John 119
Pullin, H.G. 113
Pursey, Arthur Thomas 119
Pursey, George A. 118, 119, 120
Pursey, Leonard Charles 127

Radford, A. 105
Randall, R. 110

Randall, W. 113
Ravenhill, G. 105
Rawlings, Arthur W. 120
Rayes, Basil Lewis 119
Read, C.S. 119
Reakes, J. 106
Redman, Wilfred George 117
Reed, Arthur George 117
Rees, James Edmund 119
Rendall, Charles 126
Rendall, Leonard 126
Rendell, Thomas John 115
Reynolds, H.E. 109
Reynolds, R.E. 109
Rice, Albert Edwin 119
Rice, George 115
Rice, Hartnell 115
Richards, Fred 122
Richards, Jack 118
Ricketts, Norman Edward 119, 127
Ridout, Alfred James 115
Ridout, Sid 115
Riggs, J. 126
Riggs, Ted 126
Ritchie, Alexander John 115, 117
Rixon, Leonard Cecil 121, 122
Roberts, C.W. 110
Robins, Dennis Cecil 115
Robins, G.E. 121
Rodd, Bert 118
Rogers 104
Rogers, J.W. 110
Rogers, R.G. 110
Rogers, W. 110
Rogers, W.H. 113
Rogers, William Joseph Edward 117
Rolls, C. 110
Rood, Frederick William 115
Rood, Vernon 117
Rose, E.C.L. 108
Rosenberg, S. 119
Ross, Dick 122
Ross, Lewis Cyril 121
Rowsell, Albert Henry 115
Russell, Cecil Fred 119
Russell Clifton Henry 115
Russell, Jack 109
Russell, Stan 113
Russell, William George 119
Russell, William Henry Thomas 117
Ryall, Avalon 121, 122

Sambells, Walter Henry Charles 119
Sapsead, Gilbert Charles 119
Sapsead, Horace 119
Sartin, Gordon Dennis George 115
Sartin, William George 115
Saxby, B. 104
Scott, Fred 104
Seager, J.B. 118, 119, 128
Sealey, Arthur E. 108, 110
Searle, Bill 119
Sellick, Charles 119
Selway, Len J. 115, 116
Selway, Lionel 115, 116
Shadwell, Alfred Farr 116
Sharp, Albert Hamilton 115
Sharp, Ewart Roland 119
Sharp, Reginald Walter 117

Shenton, Jeff 115
Shepherd, Eddie Norman 119
Sherwood, Reginald F. 119
Shore, Kenneth George 126
Short, Leonard Robert 115
Short, Walter Robert 115
Silvester, Colin George 120, 122
Simmons, Raymond Joffre 117
Simmons, W. 113
Simmons, Wesley 117
Simmons, Wilfred Hubert 117
Skelton, Allan Noel 119
Small, Jeffrey Nelson 115
Small, Joseph Henry James 126
Smith, George Henry 115
Smith Kenneth Robert 115
Smith, W.A. 126
Snell, Wyatt 115
Snook, Herbert Richard 115
Snook, Ron 118
Somers, Ronald 126
Southwell, H.E. 104, 105
Sparkes, Aston 109, 113
Sparkes, H. Payne, O. 113
Sparks, A. Payne, O. 113
Spearing, Norman 104
Speed, A.R. 113
Speed, E.J. 113
Speed, N.F. 113
Speed, O. 110
Squire, Frederick John
Stacey, Frank 127
Stacey, Guy 119
Stacey, James 127
Stancombe, A.M. 114
Stanton, E. 110
Stanton, G. 110
Stevens, Dennis Arthur 121
Stevens, Roland Thomas 119
Stevens, Everett 126
Stevens, Kemp 126
Stock, R.J. 113
Stockman, Stanley William 119
Stokes 104
Stokes, H.F. Scott 103, 118
Stone, Tom 122
Stoodley, Robert Arthur 115
Stotesbury, J.S. 103
Stott 106
Strange, John Helmdon St. Clair 119
Streeten, Peter Garrett 119
Studley, Harold Edgar 126
Summerhayes, Colin 119
Summerhayes, Maxwell 119
Summers, Herbert T. 121
Swain, H. 105
Sweet, C. 127
Sweet, Percy 116
Symes, John Henry 121

Tait, N.L. Barry 127, 128
Talbot, Bertram Harry 121
Target, Terence Loury Gore 119
Taswell, Dennis Edward 121
Taunton, G. 103
Taylor 108
Taylor, Allan Henry 115
Taylor, Frank 115

Taylor, John Henry 127
Taylor, Leslie Samuel Charles 115
Taylor, Reginald Charles 119
Taylor, William John 121
Tazwell, Stanley John 120
Terrell, Frank Cecil 119
Thayer, John 109, 110
Thomas, Frederick William 115
Thomas, W.I. 113
Threlfall, John Forster 119
Thyer, A.G. 115
Thyer, Bertram Charles 120
Tincknell, Reginald F. 115
Tole, Horace 119
Toogood, Maurice George 117
Toogood, Robert Charles H. 117
Toop, Arthur James 120
Towler, R.D. 110
Townhill, Peter Wilham 115
Trask, J. 126
Trask, Walter 119
Tratt, Edward George 117
Tratt, Wallace Edward 117
Trewavas, Stanley Julian 119
Trickey 108
Troop, C. 122
Trott, John 119
Tucker, Allan Wilfred 115
Tucker, D. 113
Tucker, E.J.V. 121
Tucker, H. 113
Tucker, Richard Henry 115
Tucker Wilfred Harry 115
Turner, Ernest 115
Turner, Henry John 115
Turner, Reginald 119
Tuxill, Frederick Herbert 121

Underwood, A.G. 121
Underwood, Alan H. 121, 122, 122-4, 128
Underwood, Donald 120
Underwood, Gilbert 122
Underwood, Herbert John 120
Uphill, R. 110

Veale, John Edwin 116
Vickery, Albert Bruce 116
Vickery, Reginald Mark 116
Vincent, Edward Ramsey 121
Vincent, Wally 117, 118
Vining, Leslie Arthur 119
Vinnell, F.H. 104
Vowles, Albert 127
Vowles, Charles Alfred 127
Vowles, Alan G. 120
Vowles, Douglas William 121
Vowles, Edward James 117
Vowles, Ernest 119
Vowles, Frank Harry 116
Vowles, John W.H. 120
Vowles, Reginald Carter 121

Walker, Rev. H.L. 108
Wall, George Henry 121
Wall, Matthew Frank 117
Wall, William 116
Walters, Godfrey James 116
Wareham, Ollie 109, 110

Warman, Herbert William 119
Warner, N.S. 103
Washer, Leonard Oakley 117
Wason, Arthur C. Daniel 115
Weatherill, Reginald Owen 115
Weaver, B. 110
Weaver, J.R. 110
Webb, Albert 122
Webb, Ernest Downton 121
Webb, Harold William 121
Webb, Oliver Oram 121
Webb, Percival Hubert 121
Webb, William 119
Webb, William James 115
Webber, A.B. Incledon 114, 124
Weeks, A. 110
Weeks, A.T. 113
Weeks, D. 113
Weeks, H.R. 113
Weeks, L. 113
Wellman, Alfred George 115
Wells, Arthur Leslie 121, 122
Wells, Harold George 119
Wells, Samuel 121, 122
Wells, Stanley Herbert 119
West, A.C. 121
West, William L. 115
Westaway, W. 110
Westlake, Austin John 121
Weston, Ronald 109, 110
Weston, William 109, 110
Wheaton, Daniel 117
Whippey, Harold James 121, 122
Whippey, William Fred 120
Whitcombe, A. 117
Whitcombe, Charles Ernest 127
Whitcombe, Jesse 117
Whitcombe, Met. John 127
Whitcombe, Philip 126
Whitcombe, Reg 117, 118
Whitcombe, William George 117
Whitcombe, William Henry 117
White, Alexander Alfred 127
White, Bill 104
White, Evelyn Lewis 127
White, Frank 104
White, P. Wellstood 103
Whitehead, Allan Percival 119
Whitehead, F.S. 115
Whitehead, H.J. 126
Whitehead, Jack 122
Whitehead, Louis Frederick 116
Whitehead, Oliver 122-3
Whitehead, Raymond 119
Whitehead, Robert 115
Whitfield, F. 113
Whiting, Jack 106
Wilcox, George 126
Wilkins, George 117
Willcox, Douglas Rowland G. 117
Willcox, William George A. 117
Williams, Cyril John B. 115
Williams, W. 113
Willis, A. 110
Wills, Henry 115
Wilson, John 125
Wilton, Bill 122
Wilton, Ronald 126
Winslade, Harold John 127

Winter, Maurice J. 109, 113
Witherill, Frederick 126
Withey, J. 113
Witney, Frank 115
Wood, Graham 121
Woodbridge, Kenneth Clifford 119
Woodgate, Wilfred George 121
Woods, Hubert 115
Worgan, Joseph 119
Wyatt, Charles Leslie 121
Wynne, Leonard Percy 115

Yeatman, I.V. 103
Young, Ern 109, 113

13th (Axbridge) Btn.

Ackery 141
Adams, Clarence 145
Adams, Eric 140
Adams, George 145
Adams, Kenneth 140
Amesbury, Edward 'Ted' 145
Andrews, Ron 'Chummy' 132
Andrews, W. 144
Ansell 129
Anson, George Wilfred 136, 144
Anson, Malcolm Allinson 144
Ashford, Arthur M. 129, 130
Ashford, Walter John 141
Ashley, Arthur Henry 143
Ashman, E. 143
Ashman, H. 143
Atherton, Leonard William 142, 143

Baber, Reginald Arthur 137, 138
Badman, Arthur John 133, 138, 139
Badman, Edgar 135
Bailey, Jack 133
Bailey, Stanley George 144
Baker 129
Baker, Bill 134
Balch, John 138
Baldwin, George Edward 143
Baldwin, S. 143
Banbury 134
Banwell, Edwin John 142
Banwell, Ernest 144, 145
Banwell, Francis Raymond 143
Banwell, George 145
Banwell, Thomas John 143
Barber, Bill 134
Barber, Charles Henry 140
Barnes, Arthur Ernest 136, 138, 139
Barnes, J.R. 129
Bass, Tom 132
Bath, Harold James 138
Batson, Francis William 139
Beardsworth, Benjamin W. 138
Bell, Harold Alexander 136, 144
Bendall, Arthur James 137, 138
Bendall, Maurice George 137, 138
Bendall, Reginald Gay 137, 138
Bennett, F. 143
Berry, Edwin Gibbs 143
Besley, Burdon 133
Bethell, Ray 145
Biffin, Harry 132

Bingham, Duncan Henry 143
Bingham, Henry G. 143
Bingham, S. 143
Binning, Jack 145
Birch, George 141
Bird, Joseph Sidney 144
Bishop, Norman 135
Blaber, G. 131
Blower, Neil 133
Board, Francis William 138
Boobyer, Frank 130
Bosley, Sidney Joseph 139
Bowles, Bill 145
Boyd, Roland John Lere 138
Bradfield, Jack 135
Bradford, Bill 133
Brailey, A. 137
Branch, Edmund Dury 'Jack' 140
Brawn 129
Braybrook 129
Brean, Allan 137, 138
Brean Frederick Thomas 143
Brean, Jack 137
Brean, Norman Edward 143
Brean, Thomas Henry 143
Brean, William 143
Brewer 129
Brice, Ray 134
Brice, Robert Henry 144
Brice, Thomas Edward 144
Bridges, V. 139
Bridson, Thomas Ridgway 144
Briffett, Edwin John 142
Brimicombe, Bob 130
Brooks, Arthur George 139
Brooks, Colston 145
Brooks, George Leonard 132
Brooks, Percy 140
Brown, Gilbert 134
Browning 129
Brunt, Charles Thomas 138
Bryne, Stanley 145
Buckton, J. 130
Buncombe, Don 131
Buncombe, George Clifford 142
Buncombe, Harold 133
Buncombe, J. 129
Buncombe, N. 129
Buncombe, S. 131
Burbridge, Don 136
Burdge, Cliford James 138
Burland 129
Burns, William 136, 138, 139
Bush, James Edward 137, 138
Bush, William 'Bill' John 137, 138
Butcher, Bernard 134
Buxton, Gilbert 137, 138
Buxton, Robert James 143

Callow, Jim 133, 145
Campbell-Kaye, Roderick 138
Cann 129
Cannon, Jim 135
Carpenter, H. 139
Cattell, Bill 145
Cave, Tommy 132
Challoner 130
Chamberlain, Arthur 138
Chamberlain, Charlie 137

Champion, Philip 130
Champion, Richard 142
Champney, Austin 133, 145
Channon, Pat 135
Chaplin, A. 139
Chapman, Douglas Harry W. 144
Chedgey, Bill 132
Chick, Herbert 130
Chick, Stan 134
Chick, Wally 130
Clapp, James 'Jim' 145
Clapp, Roy 136
Claridge, George Ormston 141
Clark, Dennis 137
Clark, Donald 138
Clark, Jack F. 137, 138
Clarke, Albert 135
Clarke, John 135
Clay, H. 130
Cleeves, Albert James 142
Cleeves, George Henry 142
Cleeves, Raymond John 142
Cleeves, Robert Charles 142
Cleeves, Thomas 144
Cleverdon, Wilfred Laurier 141
Cockayne, Allan 145
Cockram, Gordon Percival 144
Cockram, William Henry A. 141
Coggins, Gilbert 130
Cole, Ern 137
Cole, Philip Sidney 138
Coleman, W. 131
Coles 129
Coles, Albion Charles 138
Coles, Arthur Francis 139
Coles, Ernest George 138
Coles, Leonard Alfred 137, 138
Coles, William 138
Collier, Morris W. 138
Collins, Bill 130
Collins, Henry George 144
Comer, Joe 136
Conibere, Edmund Victor 140
Cook, Arthur 137
Cook, Ern 132
Cook, Fred 144
Cook, Jeff 145
Cook, Les 131
Cook, Maurice 132
Cook, Sid 145
Coombes, Stan 131
Corfield, Francis George 144
Cornelius, Frederick 142
Cornish, E.J. 129
Corp, Frederick Joseph 138
Corrick, Albert E. I. G. 144
Cosh 134
Cox 129
Cox, Austin 131
Cox, James Sandys 142
Cox, Sidney Hugh 144
Cox, Ted 131
Cox, William 142
Crabbe, Keith Wilfred 139
Croaker, Ted 135
Crocker, Arthur Henry 143
Crocker, Charles Douglas 138
Crocker, Clifford 144
Crocker, E. 137

Crocker, Edward 'Ted' J. 137, 138
Crocker, Gilbert 143
Crocker, Gordon 143
Crocker, Henry 143
Croker, H. 144
Croker, J. 144
Crook, Frederick Arthur 144
Cross, Francis Edmund 138
Cross, Kenneth Edmund James 138
Crowther 129
Curry, Reginald Walton 142
Cutler, Tom 133

Daffern 133
Davies, David 'Dewey' 135
Davis, Frank 138
Davis, Victor 145
Daw, Raymond 135
Day, Donald Sidney 138
Day, Ernest Henry 140
Day, Francis William A. 137, 138
Day, George 'Lou' 133
Day, Joe 132
Day, Norman Alfred 144
Day, P. 130
Day, Rowland Edward 140
Day, Thomas 142
Day, Tom 132
Deakin, Thomas Meyrick 144
Dean, George 145
Dean, Ted 144, 145
Denbee, Tom 145
Denvers, Rewfroth Silvey 137, 138
Dicker, Arthur T. 136, 138, 139
Dicks 132
Difford 134
Dill, N. 130
Dobson, John Frederick 144
Downey, Bernard 137
Dredge 129
Drew, Ernest 136
Duckett, George Wookey 145
Duckett, John 145
Duckett, Randolph 145
Dunn 129
Durbin, Charles George 137, 138
Durbin, Edward 138
Durston, Edmund 133
Dyer, A. 131
Dyer, Samuel John 141
Dyer, Sidney Francis 142
Dyke, Ron 134

Edson 134
Edwards, Reginald Ernest 141
Edwards, Stanley George 141
Edwards, William Charles 141
Ellis 143
Ellis, Melvin Howard 141
Emerson, Bertram Neil 142
Emery 133
Evans 134
Evans, Eddie 135
Evans, Met 134
Evans, Reg 134
Eveleigh 138

Fairhurst, Stephen Samuel 141
Farr, William 133

Farthing 134
Fear 129
Fear, Austin 145
Fear, Cliff 145
Fear, Frederick 138
Fear, H. 143
Febrey, Alec George 142
Ferris, Thomas Henry 144
Ferris, William 'Bill' 133
Filer, John William 138
Filer, Reginald Arthur 138
Filer, William Leslie 138
Fisher, Reginald 141
Fisher, Ted 131
Fitzgeorge 134
Flint, William Herbert 142
Flower, Frederick 138
Foord, Frank 140
Foord, Gilbert 140
Foord, Percy William 140
Ford, Charles Adrian 141
Ford, Colin 140
Foot, Jimmy 134
Foster, Joe P. 130
Fountain, Edward George 140
Fountain, Mervyn 140
Fountain, Sidney 'Cecil' 140
Fox 129, 130
Francis, Miss 133
Freke 130
Frith, James Stratton 136, 141, 142
Frost, Albert 139
Frost, Herbert 142
Frost, Kenneth Stanley C. 139
Frost, Philip 130
Furness, G.H. 130

Gardiner 141
Gardiner, Raymond 142
Gardner, Walter Leonard 142
Garrett, Derrick Mark 140
Garrett, Peter Laurie 140
Gatehouse, John 133
Gibbs, Archibald James 137, 138
Gibbs, Guy 136
Gibbs, Joseph Councell 136
Gibbs, R.G. 137
Giblett 129
Gill, Dennis Sidney 141
Gill, Percy Nunny 141
Gilling, Frederick James 139
Gilling, George 134
Gilling, James 138
Golby, John Ernest 141
Goodenough, E. 144
Gough, Aubrey 134
Gough, Douglas 134
Gower, Charlie 133
Grant, Wally 133
Green, Wilfred Victor James 138
Greenslade, Alfred J. 136, 137, 138
Greenslade, Kenneth J. 137, 138
Gregory, Cyril 134
Gregory, Frederick 138
Griffin, Lionel Murlif 141
Griffiths, Graham Charles 142
Grimes 129
Grimstead, Albert 145
Grundy, Samuel 139

Gulliver, Robert James 138
Gunning, Lionel George 144

Haddrell, Edmund Charles 138, 139
Hain, Charles George 140
Haines, H. 131
Hale, Fred 138, 139
Hale, Mervyn Leonard 142
Hall, Douglas Charles Oliver 141
Ham, Donald 136, 145
Hamblin, Jack 141
Hamlin, Trevor 142
Hamlin, William John E. 142
Hancock, George Edward 142
Hancock, William E. H. 138, 139
Harding, C. 143
Harding, F. 143
Harding, Stanley Edward 140
Hares, Henry Roland 140
Hares, Ted 133
Harper, Christopher Withington 139
Harris, Alvan Henry 138
Harris, Archibald Beaumont 138
Harris, Arthur 130
Harris, Ben 130
Harris, George 145
Harris, Gilbert 145
Harris, Michael 130
Harris, Rupert William 130
Harris, Stanley 135
Harse, Percy 142
Harvey, Harold Edward 141
Harvey, Wilfred Evan George 139
Hawkins, Mark 132
Hector, Gilbert 131
Hedges, D. 139
Hembury, Maurice 135
Hemmens, Alfred 137
Hemmens, Henry 137
Hemmens, J. 137
Hemmings 143
Hendon, Richard 141
Henniker, A.M. 129
Hess, S.H. 129
Hewlett, Henry George 142
Hewlett, Wyndham C. 138, 139
Hibbard, Charles P. L. 138, 139
Hicks, Percy 132
Higgins 129
Hiles, Aldwyn William 142
Hill, Cecil 132
Hill, Ronald Sidney 139
Hill, Tim 134
Hobbs, E.F. 129, 130, 132
Hole, Ray 144, 145
Holland 130
Holland, S. 130
Hollier, Bert 137
Hollier, Frank Henry 138
Holloway, Walter Fred 142
Holmes 129, 130
Holmes, H.W.H. 129
Holt, George 132
Hope-Simpson, J.B. 137
Horler, Leslie Alexander 142
Horsham, Norman 133
Houlden, W.E.L. 129
House 131

Howard 134
Howell, Russell Percival 138
Hucker, Arthur John 143
Hudson, Alfred 143
Hunt 141, 142
Hunt, Frederick 142
Hunt, James George Hunt 142
Hunt, Ken 135
Hurn 133
Hurt 140

Jackson, Robert Dunnett 138, 139
Jakeway, Lyn 133
Jarman, Anthony Edgar 141
Jenner 129
Jones, Alan 132
Jones, E. 130
Jones, Frank 132
Jones, James William Stewart 138
Jones, Leonard 135
Jones, Reginald Beaman 137, 138
Jones, Robert Jesse 142
Jones, S.R. 136, 139
Jones, William Edward 141

Keate, Frank 135
Keel, Ivor 139
Keel, Reginald Frank 139
Keel, William Walter 142
Kennedy, Toby 144, 145
Kerridge, Bill 145
Kerton, Jim 130
King 129
King, Clifford 133
King, Leslie John 142
Kingman, Archibald J. 137, 138
Kingston, Eric 144, 145
Kington, Albert Edward 138, 139
Kirby, Norman Kitchener 139
Kitchen, Charles Edgar 143
Kitley, William 133, 145
Knapp 132

Lack, Tom 135
Ladbrook, John Howard 138
Lane, Montague 142
Lane, William 136
Langford, Sam 133
Larder, Frank 133
Larder, William 'Bill' 145
Law 129
Lee, A. 130
Lee, R. 139
Legge, B. 139
Leigh, Albert 145
Leigh, Eli 145
Leigh, Harold Frank 144, 145
Leigh, S. 131
Lenthall, Ernest Ronald 140
Lenthall, Gilbert Ronald 140
Lewis, Arthur Reginald (or R.A.) 144
Lewis, Dick 134
Lewis, Garn 134
Lewis, George Arthur J. 137, 138
Lewthwaite, James 138
Light, Francis Henry 137, 138
Light, Wilfred James 138
Lindsay, Jack 133
Linham 130

Lintern, Jack 133
Lintern, Joseph George 139
Litton 129
Lock, Arthur Edward George 142
Lock, Charles Henry 142
Lock, Frederick Silvester 142
Lock, Gilbert 140
Lock, Philip Charles 142
Lock, Stanley Christopher W. 142
Lock, Walter 142
London, John Henry 138
Lovell 133
Lovell, Daniel Reece 138
Lowis, Robert James 143
Luke, B. 131
Lutley, Edward James Reece 142
Lyne, Robert Francis 136, 137
Lyons, Arthur Raymond 138
Lyons, Benjamin Watts 138

Macdonald, Miss 133
Maclaren, R. 137
Major, Harry 131
Mansfield, George 134
Mansfield, Tom 133
Marchent 129
Mark, Roland 144
Markland, D.R. 143
Marks, Charlie 137
Marsh 129
Marsh, Clifford 131
Marshall, Arthur 142
Marshall, Frank 142
Marshall, Gilbert 143
Martin, Norman John 141
Martin, Reuben 139
Matthews, John 131
Matthews, Sidney Theodore 138
May, Bill 132
Meaker, Fred 132
Meller, Grahame Temple 137, 138
Milkins, Billy 133
Millard 135
Millard, Arthur Raymond 136, 139
Millard, Gus 145
Millard, Leonard 144
Millard, Oliver John 144
Millard, Roy W. 138, 139
Miller, Frank 132
Mills, S.J. 133
Milton, Walter 142
Mitchell 129
Mitchell, Joseph George Henry 138
Monk, William George 138
Morgan, 'Muddy' 133
Morris 132
Morris, Daven 145
Morris, Gilbert 137
Moss, John 'Jack' Lapthorne 140
Murdoch, James Borthwick 138
Murphy, James 137, 138

Neads, George 135
Neath, Frank John 141
Needs, Buster 132
Newman, Victor 132
Newphry, Lou 133
Newton, Frank 135
Newton, Victor Clarence 138, 139

Nichols, Elton 133
Nichols, Robert 'Bob' 145
Nigh, Reg 133
Nipper, Arthur Herbert 144
Norton, Edward George 139
Norton, Herbert Charles 141

Ogbourne, H. 143
Ogbourne, Reginald James 143
Oliver, Charles Richardson 142
Organ, Richard Kenneth 144
Organ, William Henry 136, 144
Ormerod, H.J. 129, 130
Owens, Edward Maurice 144

Packer, Albert 145
Packer, Ernest 134
Packer, Walter 145
Padfield, Ernest 145
Palmer, Walter Henry 141
Parker, Arthur William 142
Parker, Percival Sidney 142
Parker, Sidney 142
Parkin-Bell, John Frank 138
Parsons, George (Berrow & Brean) 130
Parsons, George (Congresbury) 141
Parsons, Gilbert Charles 138
Parsons, Robert Cecil 138
Parsons, Ron 130
Patch, B. 137
Payne, Frank 133, 145
Payne, Maurice 137
Pearce 129, 130
Pearce (or Pearse), Francis J. F. 137, 138
Pearce, William Herbert 137, 138
Pell, Leslie John 142
Perkins, Oliver 140
Perrett, John 130
Perry, Arthur William John 143
Phelps 129
Phippen, William Thomas 141
Pickering 129
Pickford, Arthur James 144
Pike, Frank 145
Pike, Kenneth John 141
Pincott, Eric Mervyn 141
Pitman 134
Pitman, James Reginald G. 138
Pitty, Horace 130
Plumley, King Edward K. 139
Plumley, Richard Thomas 144
Pollitt, William John 141
Popham, Ernest 136
Pope, Ernest Charles 133
Pope, Hubert 132
Porter, Wilfred H. 131, 132
Pulsford, Charles William 140
Poulsom, George 142
Price, William Alfred Charles 141
Pring, Frederick Ernest 139
Puddy, Don 131
Puddy, George Sidney 144
Puddy, Henry 129 130
Puddy, Herbert 145
Puddy, Jack 145
Puddy, Reg 131
Purnell, Herbert John 139

Raines, Leslie George 142
Rains, Donald 135
Reason, Charles Herbert 139, 140
Redfern, Foster 140
Redgers, Charles Henry 138
Redgers, Sidney Thomas 137, 138
Rendell, Celia 133
Rice, Cyril 145
Rice, G. 131
Rice, Ivan 145
Rice, Reg 135
Richards, Alfred Thomas 141
Richards, Arthur A. 141
Robbins, L.H. 141
Roe 139
Roe, James Percival 144
Roe, Walter 133
Rogers, Bob 132
Rollison, D. 130
Roper, Albert 145
Roper, Joseph Francis 140
Rouse, Reginald John 139
Rowden, Wilf 132
Roynon, Thomas Shorland 138, 139
Rudeman, H. 143
Rugman 143
Russell, C. 131
Russell, Edward James 138

Sainsbury, Victor 138
Saint, Ross 135
Salter 133
Salter, William 133
Salvidge, S. 131
Saunders 130
Sawtell, Bevis 140
Seabright, Bill 133
Seaton, R. 139
Seymour, Jack 133
Sharp, Edmund Michael 138
Shepherd, John Henry 143
Sheppard, George 133
Shepstone, Archie
Sherstone, Olive 133
Shipsey, Dick 137
Short, James 144
Simmons 133
Simms, Percy 133
Skinner, Rowland Frank 138
Small, Douglas Stedman 138
Small, R. 139
Smith 129
Smith, George Worsley 140
Smith, Joseph Hilton 139
Smith, Les 132
Smith, Robert Hilton 139
Smith, Toby 130
Smith, William John 144
Somers, Bertram Frederick 137, 138
Sparex, Wiliam James 141
Spence, Harold 140
Stabbins, Bob 135
Stacey, Arhibald 141
Star, George 142
Starr, C. 131
Starr, Harold 134
Steer, Harry 144
Steer, Sidney 135
Stephen, Phil 133

Stevens (or Stephens) 132
Stevens, Cyril Randolph Mark 138
Stevens, George Rowland 143
Stevens, L.M. 129, 130
Stevens, Victor 145
Stiles, Arthur Eric 143
Stitch, Reg 145
Stokes, Frederick James 142
Stokes, William Hopkin 142
Stone, Glyn 137
Stowell, Wilfred 145
Sugg, Arnold 145
Sydenham, Albert James 141

Tabbrett, Bill 135
Talbot 130
Tanner, Dick 133, 145
Taylor 143
Taylor, Alfred James 138, 139
Thatcher, Albert 141
Thatcher, Reg 134
Thiery, George William 140
Thomas, Arthur Rowland 140
Thomas, John Henry 141
Thomas, M. 131
Thomas, Raymond Albert 140
Thompson 130
Throssell 143
Tidball, Ern 131
Tidball, Ray 131
Tidman 136, 143
Tidman, Harold 143
Tincknell, Ernest 144
Tincknell, Ronald William 144
Tincknell, Stan 145
Tincknell, William 144
Toothill, Alfred Roy S. 136, 138, 139
Trapnell, Robert George 142
Tratt, Leonard Fred 142
Tregidgo, Kenneth John 138
Tricks, Dennis Norman F. 137, 138
Tripp, Roy B. 144
Trott 129
Tucker Cyril 138
Tucker, Doug 133
Tucker, E. 131
Tucker, W.W. 129, 130
Turk 129
Tyley, James Arthur 138

Urch, Bett 133
Urch, Peter 133, 145

Varney, Alf 134
Vauden, Harold Arthur 143
Veal 133
Venn (née Cooper), Doreen 133
Vigar, Robert 131
Villis, Maurice Albion 138
Vowles, Frank E. 144
Vowles, Thomas Edgar 144

Wade, Anthony Philip Samuel 140
Wade, Roger Frederick 140
Waddon, H. 130
Wall, Albert 131
Wall, Edwin 144, 145
Ward 129

Warford, Ronald Leslie 138
Watts, Don 145
Watts, Wallace George 140
Watts, Walter 145
Watts, William Henry 142
Wear, Frederick James 142
Weaver, Jonathon George 138
Webber, Bob 131
Weeks, R.V. 133
Welland, F.B. 130
Wensley, J. 131
West, Jack 131
Westbrook, Ernest Charles J. 138
Westcott, T. 130
Westlake, S. 139
Wheadon, George 132
Wheatley, Henry 145
Wheeler, Albert Edgar 141
Wheeler, Tom 141
Whitcher, George 133
White, Albert 'Bert' 133
White, Frank 143
White, Graham John 140
White, H. 134
Whitting, G. 131
Wilkins, C. 143
Wilkins, Edwin Sylvester 143
Wilkins, George Sylvester 143
Williams 129
Williams, Clifford Charles 138
Williams, G.V. 129
Williams, Reverend 130
Williams, Richard 139
Williams, S. 130
Williamson, John 138
Williamson, Laurie Hunter 137, 138
Wills, John Desmond 144
Wilson, Chris 133
Wilson, Ernest P. 139
Wilson, Frank 133
Winter, Len 134
Wood, Dubric 144
Wookey, Edwin James 138
Wookey, Frederick George 139
Wookey, Harry Clement 136, 139
Wright, James William 138
Wyatt, Edward John 143, 144

Yarde, Kenneth 140
Yates, Norman 130
Yatman, A.H. 129
Yeeles, Thomas William 138
Young, Edward Thomas 140
Young, James 142
Young, Reginald William C. 139

South Somerset Sector

Aitkin, J.J. 146
Allfrey, H.I.R. 146
Barrington 146
Broadmead 146
Bushell, T.A. 146
Chedzoy, Stanley 146
Downes, Mrs. A. 146
Drew, B.C.H. 146
Foster, Joan 146
Fouracre 146
Geary 146
Harries, A.N. 146
Hembrow, D. 146
Hold 146
Hughes, C.F.W. 146
Lyon, C.D.G. 146
Mogford 146
Norman, C.L. 146
Parker, T.E. 146
Paul 146
Porter 146
Taylor, J.B. 146
Tolman, L.J. 146
Trim 146
Unmack, R.C. 146
Wheeldown, Mrs. 146
Williams, V.D.S. 146

1st (Minehead) Battalion

Abbott, C. Hardy 171
Ackland, E.L.Dyke 147, 148, 161
Ackland, Walter Frederick G. 163
Ackland-Troyt, John 170
Adams, Cyril 173
Adams, G. 153
Agers 177
Alan, Percy 167
Alderman, John 163
Alexander, R.D. 147, 148, 149, 159, 161
Alford, Tom 158
Allen, Harold Richard George 163
Allen, Harold Stanley 163
Ames, Leslie 168
Amies, Stanley 162, 163
Amor, 'Lofty' 153
Andrews, Edward Percy 163
Andrews, Herbert 175
Aplin, Jack 173
Arscott, Mervyn 150
Arthur, J.S.W. 147
Arthurs, W.P. 148, 176
Ashwin, W.H. 147
Atkins, Noah 153, 156
Atkinson 166
Attiwell, Frederick Redvers 163
Ayre, Thomas Douglas 175
Ayres, Reg 154, 159

Bach, P. 153
Bacon, Ernest John 163
Bacon, Walter Sidney 163
Badcock, T. 153
Baggett 177
Bailey, Fred 167
Baker 153, 166
Baker, Bill 155
Baker, Hubert 169
Baker, Kempton 173
Baker, S.R. 168
Baker, Stanley S.W. 148, 161, 162, 168
Baker, W. 153
Baldwin, Bruce 149
Baldwin, Charlie 154, 155, 158
Bale, Albert 163
Bale, Jack 159
Balman, Harold 167
Balmond, Fred 176
Banbury, Arthur 167
Barr, Robert Young 154, 158
Barter, Eddie 170
Bartlett, Charles 148, 153
Bartlett, John 'Jack' Arthur 162, 163
Barwick, Clifford 148
Barwick, Joe 159
Bass, Sid 148
Bates 148, 157
Bates, Elton 154, 155, 158
Bawden, Bert 172, 173
Bawden, John 159
Bawden, K. 172
Bawden, Ken 176
Bawden, Percy 176, 177
Bawden, Tom 159
Bawler, Bill 154
Bear, F.G. 170
Beckett, Stan 151, 153
Bedford, Henry Edward 163
Bellamy, Ern 150
Bennett, Leonard 150
Bennett, Sid 166, 167
Berry, Cyril 169
Besley, Fred 169
Besley, Jack 170
Besley, Lionel 154, 157, 158
Billinger 170
Binding, Albert John 163
Binding, Arthur 163
Binding, Robert John 163
Binding, Sidney Arthur 163
Binding, William Henry 163
Bindon, Basil Charles 162, 163
Bindon, Ernest 163
Bindon, Reginald 158
Bird, R.J. 161, 166
Bishop, Clifford 163
Bishop, Frank 167
Bishop, Jack 167
Bishop, Leslie 158
Bissell, Jack H. 160, 161, 162
Blackmore, Alfred John 163
Blackwell, H.J. 151, 153
Bladderwick, Mrs. 166
Blanchflower, Margaret 162
Blue, Harold 170
Bolsom, Bernard 172
Bond, Harry 177
Bond, Transvaal William 163
Bosley, Geoffrey 163
Bosley, Lawrence Stuart 163
Bowden, William Thomas 163
Bowles, Alf 158
Boys, Ernest Edward 163
Boys, Ernest Lewis 163
Bradner, George 169, 170
Bray, Clifford 160
Bray, J. 178, 179
Bray, Johnny 178, 179
Brewer 173
Brewer, Jim 166, 167
Brooks, Charlie 148
Broom, E. 170
Broom, J. 170
Brown, Bill 169
Brown, C. 153
Browning, Reginald John 163
Browning, Robert 163
Brownsey, Charles Levi 163
Bryant 160
Bryant, Alfred Lionel 163
Bryant, Fred 'Daisy' 167
Bryant, James 162
Bryant, Morris 167
Bryant, Percy 167
Bryant, Ray 166
Bryant, Tom 154
Bryne, Morris 160
Buckingham, Reg 173
Bucknell 179
Bullard, Eddie 179
Bullen, E.T. 148
Bulpin 160
Bulpin, Thomas William 162, 163
Bulpin, Walter Henry 162, 163
Bulpin, William Henry 163
Bulpin, William John 163
Burge, Bill 167
Burge, Richard Henry 163
Burnell, Jimmy 160
Burnell, W.G. 158
Burnett, Arthur 167
Burnett, Wilfred George 163
Burns, Michael 173
Burston, Ted 169
Bushen, George 148
Butter, Mrs. M. 147
Butterfield 154, 155
Butterfield, F.C. 154, 158
Byrde, Maybely 169, 170

Cabe, C. 151, 153
Calloway, A.J. 'Bert' 169
Catford, George 153
Capper, A.S. 169
Carey, Bill 176
Carey, Sid 176
Carter, J. 178, 179
Carter, John 179
Carter, L. 178, 179
Cavil, A. 168
Chamberlain 153
Chambre, Eric Chris A. 163
Champion, Chris 155
Chaplin, Frank 154, 159
Chapman 154
Chapman, D. 170
Chichester, B.F. 178, 179
Chidgey, Alf 167
Chidgey, Frederick Shewan 163
Chidgey, Leonard 166
Chidley, W.C. 168
Chilcot 172
Chilcott, Francis 163
Chiplin 179
Chiswell, Bill 148
Choke, Clifford 150
Chubb, Philip 163
Chubb, Walter 175
Clapp, S. 170
Clarke, Chris 167
Clarke, Nobby 166
Clatworthy, J.F. 148, 176
Clavey, Douglas H.J. 'Jack' 162, 163
Clayton, E.R. 147, 162
Cole, Monty 153
Coleman 153, 179
Coleman, E.H. 168
Coles 153, 170
Coles, Bill 160
Coles, G. 153
Coles, Herbert 163
Coles, Norman 160, 161
Collier, E.S. 154
Colman, Edward 174
Colman, W. 151, 153
Conibeare, William H.E. 168
Connett, Sidney 148, 160, 161, 162
Cook, Alfred 149
Coombs, A.C. 161
Coomer, Bill 166
Cooper, R.A. 168
Copp, Cyril 154
Copp, Jimmy 155
Cording, Bill 175
Corney, Bill 153
Couch, Rev. A. 166
Court, Bill 160
Court, J. 160
Coward, F. 177
Cox, Frederick Percival 163
Cox, H.J. 161
Cox, Russell G. 160
Cozens, A. 172
Crane, P.C. 168
Crawford 'Jock' 164
Creech, Dick 150
Cressey, John 176
Criddle, Ernie 176
Cridland 166
Crockford, Jack 150
Cromer, Earl of 151, 153
Crook, Bert 173
Crook, Ken 176
Cross, Alf 169, 170
Crossman, Ern 173
Crossman, Tom 179
Crudge, Cecil 179
Cubbon, Archie 166
Curtis 175
Curtis, George 176

Danby, Victor E. 148, 161, 162, 163
Dane, William Herbert 163
Darch 172
Dascombe, Herby 179
Dascombe, Hubert 169
Davey, Hubert 174, 175
Davey, Ted 174
Davey, Wilfred 174
Davidge, Albert Leslie 163
Davies 167
Davies, George 150
Davies, Jack 167
Davis 153
Davis, Edwin Herbert 148, 162
Davis, H.E. 159
Davis, Harry 160
Davy, Bert 155
Day, Francis James 163
Dear, K. 170
Delve, Bill 175
Dennett, Stanley 166, 167
Doble, Lionel George 160
Double 177
Down, Harold 154, 155
Down, Reg 179
Downer, George 157
Downer, George (Jnr.) 157, 158
Downer, Jim 154, 155, 157, 158
Driver, E.M. 147, 148, 169
Duddridge, Ernest J.H. 163
Duddridge, Jesse Manning 163
Duddridge, Stanley 162
Dulborough 169
Durrant, B. 168
Dyer, Archie 158
Dyte, Wallace 163

Edmunds, Cyril 169, 170
Edwards, Arthur James 163
Edwards, D.C.H. 148, 176, 177
Edwards, Samuel Victor 163
Elford 154
Ell, Clifford 156
Elliott, F. 156
Erskine-Collins, J. 148, 161, 162
Escott, Raymond 154, 155, 157
Evans, Gilbert 175
Evans, Gwyn Elwyn 163
Evans, Reg 175
Eveleigh, Leonard 162, 163
Everard, Christopher 173
Evett, Harry 174, 175

Farmer, Charlie 173
Farmer, Gordon 157
Farmer, Jack 148, 149, 150
Farmer, Phil 172
Farmer, Tom 150
Farquhar 179
Farrant, Bert 159
Farrant, Jeff 148
Fenwick 157
Ferris, Sid 148
Ferris, Stanley 173
Fevre 166
Follett, Herbie 179
Follett, Maurice 179
Ford 177
Ford, Frank 176
Fowler, Ned 159
Fox, Charlie 148
Foy, C. 153
Frankham, George N. 169
Frayne, Fred 179

Gadd, M.W. 170
Gadd, Sam 167
Gale, Richard 174, 175
Gardener, Bill 170

Gardner, F. 178
Gardner, Herbert William 163
Gardner, Redvers Donald 163
Gardner, Walter John 163
Gardiner 160, 161
Garnish, George 149
Gayton, Eric John 163
Geary, M. 161
German, Ron 172
Gibbons, Bert 'Tacker' 148
Gibbons, Sid 148
Gibbs 175
Gibbs, George 175
Gibbs, K. 175
Gibbs, Len 178
Gibbs, Sid 174, 175
Gibbs, Wilfred 175
Giles, Thomas 163
Gill, Geoff 170
Gill, Harold 154, 155
Gilman, John 166
Glascow 148
Gliddon, Laity 160
Goacher, George 159
Godfrey 173
Goldsmith, F. 153
Golf, Fred 179
Goostrey, John Dickinson 163
Goss, Jack 170
Gough 179
Gould, Jack 150
Gould, Ossie 154, 155
Grabham, Ken 158
Grabham, R. 170
Grabham, Sid 170
Greenslade, Robert 156
Greenslade, Walter Lancelot 163
Gregory, Herbert 158
Gregory, Thomas Foster 163
Gregory, Walter 154
Greswell, W.T. 148, 160, 161, 162, 167
Griffiths, Frank 158
Griffiths, Geoff 178
Griffiths, Ted 154, 158
Griffiths, Walter 157
Griffiths, William Albert 163
Groves, Arthur John Morgan 163
Gubb 153
Gudge, Kenneth 179
Gulliver, Arthur 166, 167
Gunter, Bert 154, 157
Gunter, Bill 150
Gunter, Charlie 173
Gunter, Clifford 173

Hale, Tony 150
Hall, A.G. 168
Hall, Bert 169
Hall, E.B.D. 169
Hall, George 148
Harding, Wally 150
Harris, Herbert 179
Harris, Tom 148
Harrison 178
Harrison, K.D. 168
Hart, Henry 170
Harvey 169, 170
Harvey, Bill 173

Harvey, William 172
Hawkins, Bill 'Ganger' 169, 170
Hawkins, Jimmy 160
Hayes, Bill 173
Hayes, Ernie 167
Hayes, Frank (or B.) 167
Hayes, Gordon 174
Hayes, Harold 174
Hayes, Jack 166, 167
Hayes, Jeff 167
Hayes, John 174, 175
Hayes, Lionel 170
Hayward, Eric Reginald 163
Hayward, Ron 173
Headford, Ernest William 163
Headon, E. 170
Heard, Harold 159
Heard, Kenneth 154, 159
Heard, Vic 153
Hembrow, Percy 160
Henson, James 168
Herniman, Herbert 168
Hewett, D.P. 147
Hewett, H.P. 148
Hewlett, A. 168
Heywood, Frank 175
Heywood, George 174
Heywood, Jack 158
Hill, Edmund Murray 151, 152, 153
Hill, Jack 166, 167
Hill, Richard 153
Hill, Roland 173
Hill, Tom 150
Hill, W. 170
Hill, Wilf 179
Hill, William (Wheddon Cross) 159
Hill, William (Stogumber) 166, 167
Hills 153
Hobbs 153
Hodge, Barry 173
Holden, R.C. 147
Hole, Arthur 174, 175
Hole, Cyril 173
Hole, Ivor Charles 163
Hole, Leslie 175
Hole, Rob 174
Hole, Walt 160
Holland, E.F. 170
Holland, S. 170
Holmes, Reg 153
Holt, Geoffrey 150, 151, 153
Hooper, Leonard 163
Hooper, Stan 148
Hope, Jack 170
Hopkins, Rees 163
Horsey, Jim 167
Horsey, Ron 153
House 160, 177
House, Oliver Walter 163
House, William Wallace 163
Howe 148
Howe, Ern 174
Howe, J. 172
Howe, Rex 167
Hunt 160
Hunt, Fred 155
Hunt, Joseph Walter 162, 163
Hunt, Reginald John 163
Hunt, S.J. 170

Hunt, Stan 'Sniffer' 160
Huntley, Reg 148
Hurcock, J. 174
Hurford 148
Hurley, William C. 160, 162
Hutchins 169
Hutchins, A. 178, 179
Hutchins, John 166
Hutchins, Roger 167
Hutchins, W. 178, 179
Hutchinson, J.R. 160, 161, 166, 167
Hutter, Charles 173
Huxtable, Dudley 154
Hyatt, Leslie 166, 167

Jacobs, Jack or Walt 169, 170
James, Frank 176
James, Tom 176
Jarman, S. 178, 179
Jefferies, James 154, 155
Jenkins, Charlie 160
Jennings, Maurice 153
Johnston, Reg R.L. 154, 157
Jones, Alfred James 163
Jones, Dai 173
Jones, Jack 154, 155, 156
Jones, Joe 177
Joslin, Henry Codd 163
Joyce, Patrick 148

Keal, Alfie 148
Keal, Bill 148
Keal, Eddie 150
Keal, Raymond 148
Kemp, William Leslie 163
Kempster, Charles Henry 163
Kent, Fred 148
Keynton, H.S. 147, 148
Kievill, Mrs. M. 147
Killie, Hubert 153
Kingdom, Jack 170
Kingdon, Arthur 150
Kingdon, Herbert 148
Kingdon, Jack 150
Kirby, Elias 164

Ladd, Arthur 154, 156
Ladd, Stan 154, 155
Laidlaw 148, 153
Land, G. 172
Lang, Walter 170
Langdon, G. 168
Langdon, Leslie George 164
Langdon, W.T. 164
Langrish, Vivian 148
Laramy, Arthur 157
Lazrath 172
Leach, Peter 148
Lee, Arthur 149
Lee, Ern 169, 170
Lee, Jack 175
Lee, Jimmy 162
Lee, William John E. 162, 163, 164
Leonard, Arthur Thomas 164
Lewis, Bert 169
Lewis, Bill 167
Lewis, Harry 157, 158
Ley, Ernest Robert 164

Little, A. 178, 179
Little, S. 178, 179
Lloyd, Norton D. 164
Lloyd, W. 156
Lloyde, David 177, 178
Lock, A. 170
Lock, Bill 174, 175
Lock, Eddie 174
Lock, Fred 176
Lock, Sid 175
Locke, Bill 170
Lofthouse 153
Loosemore, F.R. 172
Loosemore, Jack 169, 170
Love, A.T. 161
Luxton, Fred 154, 159
Lyddon, Padre 153
Lyne, Bob 166

McNalley 153
Maddock, Lionel 173
Maddocks, Dick 160
Maddocks, Miss 166
Maggs, F.J. 176
Maidment, G. 156
Malet, C.H.W. 168
Manley, Victor 149
Marden, Mrs. 166
Marle (or Morle), Frank 169
Marley, Dick 176
Marshall 179
Martin 153, 178
Martin, Hubert John 172, 175
Martin, Billy 153
Mason, Wilf 177
Maunder, Ron 175
May 177
May, George 160
May, Ron 154
Mead, Bill 170
Meade, Jack 148
Meade-King, W.T.P. 147
Meadows, Alec 176
Meddick, Carl 154, 155
Meredith 153
Merson, H. Jim 168
Middleton, Bill 157
Middleton, Fred 148
Miles, William 164
Millard, J. 161
Mills, Stafford 150
Milton, Herbert 164
Moore 177
Moore, Arthur 150
Moore, Philip 150
Moore, Rob 148, 176
Moore, Ron 150
Morgan, Lewis Lawrence 163, 164
Morris, W. 156
Moule, Bob 176
Muirhead, C.A. 151
Mullins, W. 176
Mullis, Fred 153
Murphy, Kevin Maurice 164
Muxworthy, Bill 175
Muxworthy, Fred 175
Muxworthy, R. 170
Muxworthy, Russell 175
Mylne, E.C. 172, 173

Nation 177
Nation, George 175
Nation, Jim 167
Naylor, Bart 177
Neal, Joe 166
Neale, John 164
Neale, Richard 164
Needs 153
Needs, George 155
Nelder, Edith May 174
Nelder, Reginald Charles 171, 172
Nelder, Robin 171, 173
Newcombe, Cyril 153
Newton, Arthur 153
Nicholas, Cyril Keen 164
Nicholas, Edwin John 164
Nicholl, George 179
Nicholls, H. 170
Nichols 159
Nichols, Roland 164
Noble, Don 170
Norman, Edgar Maurice 164
Norman, Fred 154, 159
Norman, Geoffrey William F. 164
Norman, Harold 164
Norman, Hedley 174
Norman, J. 170
Norman, Jim 175
Norman, K. 170
Norman, Leslie 174
Norman, Russell Clifford 164
Norman, Thomas 164
Norman, Victor or William 175
Norman, William 173
Norton, F.H. 148, 176
Nuthall, G.F. 148, 169
Nutt, Cliff 170

Odam, William George 164

Parfitt, Jack 173
Parker, D. 153
Parker, Doug 153
Parkman, Ernest 170
Parkman, Phil 175
Parsons 148
Parsons, Bill 148, 149
Parsons, Dudley 154, 158
Parsons, John 172, 174
Parsons, Jimmy 154, 155, 156
Parsons, William H.P. 168
Paski, George 157
Passmore, A. 153
Passmore, Frank 157
Payne, Henry Arthur 164
Payne, William C. 168
Pearce, Eric 157, 158
Pearce, Robert James 164
Peppin, Cecil James 164
Perriott, Bill 175
Perry, Cuthbert 158
Perry, Jack 170
Pertwee, Roland 170
Philips, Eddie 176
Philpott 172
Pike, Arthur 173
Pincott, Bill 178
Pinkham, Ern 175
Pollard, Ernest 149

Pollard, Harry 149
Poole 179
Poole, F. 153
Poole, Walter 158
Pope, George Henry 163, 164
Pope, John Alfred 164
Pope, Walter 158
Potter, Colin 154, 157
Potter, E.H. 147
Potter, Ernest 153
Priscott 153
Priscott, Bill 158
Priscott, Harold 150
Prole, Arthur Henry 164
Prole, Ernest William 164
Prole, G. 170
Prole, Ivor John 162, 164
Prole, Ronald Henry 162, 163, 164
Prole, William 163, 164
Prout, Harry 177
Pugsley, Dennis George 164
Pugsley, Henry 157
Pulsford, Frank 169
Pulsford, Sid 169
Pulson, Donald 169, 170
Putt, Frederick Raymond 164
Puttock 177

Quartley, Jack 172, 173
Quick, Frank 173

Radford, E. 156
Radford, Ken 154, 155, 156
Raffel, Albert 170
Rashly, W. 178, 179
Rawle, Harry 148
Rawle, J.W. 147
Rawle, Sid 148
Rawle, Tom 150
Rawlings, Ted 150
Ray, Ernie 154
Red, Nichol 166
Redwood, Jack 167
Reed 154, 155, 157
Reed, Edgar 153
Reed, Sutherland 166
Rice 173
Rich, Raymond 177
Richards, Dudley 148
Ridd, Sid 176
Ridley 154, 157
Rigg 166
Roberts, Jack 149
Roberts, Rev. 173
Rolle 179
Rollings, John Alfred 164
Routley, Arthur 167
Routley, Bernard 167
Rowe, Bill 170
Rowe, Clifford 154, 155, 156
Rowen, Harold 170
Rowen, Jack 170
Rowle, Dick 177

Salmon, Arthur William 162, 164
Salter, Frank 157, 158
Salter, Tom 174
Sandford 148
Sankins, J. 178, 179

Saunders, Alfred 175
Saunders, Ray 173
Scott, Bill 160
Scudamore 154, 155
Scudamore, Dick 154
Sealey, Harry 169, 170
Sedman, Percy 150
Sellick, Jeff 167
Shapland, Chris 169, 170
Sharland, Jack 169, 170
Sharp, Albert Thomas 164
Sharp, Tom 'Squeaker' 173
Shephard, Tommy 170
Shepherd, Arthur 169
Shire, George 173
Shopland, Stanley 169, 170
Short, Frances Edwin 164
Short, Harold 159
Simons, Harry 154, 157, 158
Skinner 173
Slader, Ron 154, 159
Smallridge, Arthur 173
Smart, Rev. J.A. 148
Smith, Arthur 158
Smith, Bert 170
Smith, S.H. 168
Smith, W.G. 168
Snell, Charlie 174
Snell, George 174
Soaper 173
Sobey, Stanley Hume 164
Southwood, Bill 179
Sowden, Percy 179
Sparkes, Bert 166
Spencer, Albert 179
Spencer, Frank 179
Squibbs, Bill 160
Stacey, Alexander 164
Stanley, P.E. 147, 148, 159
Starks, Alfie 150
Steer, Dick 177
Steer, Herb 176, 177
Steer, Jim 176
Steer, Peter 176
Stephens, Percy 173
Stephenson, Joe 157, 158
Stevens, Bert 154, 155, 158
Stevens, E. 161
Stevens, Ernest 162, 166, 167
Stevens, Fred 153
Stevens, Ray 174, 175
Stevens, Ted 166, 167
Stewart 153
Stoate 148, 177
Stoate, Richard 164
Stockwell, Alf 160
Stone 153, 160
Stone, Bill 172
Stone, Jack 170
Stone, Raymond George 164
Storey 154
Storey, W. G. 'Pop' 154, 155, 156
Suchley, Louis William 164
Sulley, Frank 170
Sully, A. 156
Sully, Arthur 160
Sully, Bert 160
Sully, Bill 160
Sully, Ernest 148

Sully, Gerald 155
Sully, J. 160
Sully, Roy 155, 156
Sully, Rufus Sidney 164
Sully, Tom 148
Sully, William James 164
Summerfield, Bill 167
Summerfield, Bob 167
Summerfield, Tom 167
Summers, John 173
Sweetland, Leslie 160

Tackle 179
Tackle, Albert 179
Tame, Bill 148, 150
Tame, Reg 150
Tancock, Bert 148
Tapp, Herbert 179
Tarr, Eddie 172
Tarr, Harold 170
Tarr, John 170
Tarr, R.J. 168
Tayler, R. Kingsley 147, 148, 153, 155, 169, 172, 175, 176
Taylor, Arthur 157
Taylor, B. 148, 161
Taylor, H.J. 147
Taylor, Jack 159
Taylor, John 159
Thackeray 154
Thale 153
Thomas, A.A. 172, 175
Thomas, Bill 148
Thomas, Bill (Snr.) 148
Thomas, C.F. 148, 161
Thomas, Cyril 162, 166, 167
Thomas, Jack 173
Thomas, John 169, 170
Thomas, M. 153
Thomas, Preston 154, 159
Thomas, Ron 174
Thomson, W.D. 147, 148, 162, 164
Thorne 153
Thorne, E.G. 178, 179
Thorne, Tom 169
Thrush, William 157, 158
Thrush, Tom 154, 157
Tidly 157
Tipler, Ronald Herbert 164
Toogood, Reg 176
Tooze, Ern 170
Tooze, Herbert 174
Touchins, G.H. 168
Tout 170
Tout, Fred 172
Tozer, John 157
Trebble, Bob 160
Trebble, Maude 162
Tremlett, Clifford 167
Tucker, Bill 150
Tuckfield, William 168
Tucker, Geoff 176
Tudball, Arthur William 164

Upham, Bill 160
Upham, Johnny 159

Vaulter, Charlie 173
Vaulter, Donald 154, 155

Vaulter, Jim 174
Vaulter, Reg 155
Vellacott, Reg 179
Venn, Beryl 162
Venn, Bill 173
Venn, William J.D. 161, 162
Venn, Clarence, 153
Venner, Fred 179
Venton, Arthur 170
Veysey, Sid 175
Viara 166
Vinnell, Jack 176
Vowles, A.C. 147, 148
Vowles, Alfred 153

Ward, Arthur 148
Warman, Cyril 169
Warren, Frederick W.J. 162, 164
Watts, Colin 154, 157
Watts, Jimmy 169, 170
Watts, Percy 167
Watts, Stanley 164
Watts, William John 162, 164
Webb, Henry 148
Webber 153
Webber, Albert James 164
Webber, Arthur T. 154, 159, 164
Webber, Charles 164
Webber, D.R. 168
Webber, Fred (Wheddon Cross) 154, 159
Webber, Fred (Wiveliscombe) 169
Webber, Harold Edward 162, 164
Webber, Henry George 164
Webber, Hugh 148, 149
Webber, J. 156
Webber, L. 160
Webber, Sidney 150, 159
Webber, Stanley 158
Webber, Tommy 160
Webber, William John 164
Wedlake, A. 161
Wedlake, Alfred Leslie 162, 164
Wells, Harry 153
Wells, Percival Thomas 164
Welsh, Charlie 155
Wescott, Hubert John 162, 164
Westcott, Cecil 148
Westcott, Ike 170
Westcott, W. 178, 179
Western, Cyril Herbert 162, 164
Western, Sidney 159
Western, Wilfred 154, 159
White 155, 173
White, Francis 148
White, Wallace J.H. 164
Whitmore 175
Wilkins, Jim 156
Wilkins, Leonard James 164
Williams 160
Williams, Arthur James 164
Williams, Bill 174
Williams, Bob 150
Williams, Clem 177
Williams, D. 153
Williams, Gordon 176
Williams, Joe 154, 155, 157
Williams, Percy 164
Williams, Sid 157

Willicombe, F.H. 148, 163, 164
Willicombe, George 162, 163, 164
Willicombe, James Frederick 164
Willis 153
Willis, W. 170
Willmot, S. 170
Wilson, Jim 148
Winter, Bert 170
Winter, Harold 170
Winter, Harry 170
Winter, Stanley 157, 158
Winter, Tommy 154, 155, 156
Winzer, Bill 176
Winzer, George 176
Woodberry, Jesse 154
Wyatt, Bob 169, 170
Wyatt, Bunny 170
Wyatt, Dick 170
Wyatt, Harold 170
Yandle, Bert 169, 170

Yeandle, Bill 148
Yeandle, Clifford 157
Yeatons 170
Yendell, William 'Shaver' 166, 167
Yerbury, William 174

2nd (Taunton) Battalion

Abbott, W. 205
Ackland, Leonard 199
Adams, H. Goldsworthy, H. 200
Adams, Jack 189
Alford, W. 200
Alibone, Fred 197
Allen, A. 208
Allsop, John 212
Alway, B.T.S. 200
Andrews, Albert 199
Anon, J. 210
Antrobus, T. 200
Arbuthnot, A.G. 189
Are, W. 200
Arnold, Ken 212
Atkins, Arthur 191
Attrill, Dennis 183
Authers, Reg J. 199, 200
Auton, Jack 205, 207

Babb, Victor Henry 195
Baker, Bob 191
Baker, Fred 190, 191
Baker, G. 208
Baker, Harry 190
Bale, S. 184
Bale, Stan 184
Bale, W. 184
Ball, T.J. 200
Balls, R. 212
Barber, B. 205
Barham, Don 212
Batchelor, V. 189, 190
Batten, J. 206
Batten, Sid 191
Bauler, Reub 192
Bawden, Jeff 189
Bealey 183
Beer, Bert 208

Bendal 208
Bennett, W. 184
Benson, R. 180
Berry, Bill 199
Berry, H. 210
Berry, Jim 182
Berry, L. 186
Berry, Reg 199
Berry, Tom 206
Besley, Don 189
Betty, Ken 188
Bevan, J.D. 180, 195
Bew, Harry 189
Bickham, F. 204
Biffin, Frank 185
Bishop, 'Cubby' 192
Bishop, Roy 191
Blackmore, Fred 191
Blackmore, H. 210
Blackmore, R. 200
Blake, A.H. 180
Blaney 208
Boak, D. 184
Board, Bill 208
Bodger, John 'Jack' 195
Bodger, Thomas William 195
Boles, Gerald 190
Bond, A. 197
Bond, Bill 210
Bond, Eddie 197
Bond, H. 208
Bonner, 'Teddy' 185
Boon, Frank 189
Bosley, Sid 208
Bowditch, Alec 209
Bowditch, Ted 208
Bowerman 211
Bowerman, E.W. 200
Bowey, Ernest 208
Bowie, S. 206
Boyer, Horace 212
Bradbeer 185
Braddick, Leonard 199
Bradford, Bill 199
Braddick, C. 206
Braddick, E. 206
Bragg, F. 184
Bragg, T. 184
Brassington, W. 212
Bray, R. 205
Brayley, C.E. 182
Brice, F.A. 208
Bridgwater, T. 210
Briers, George 208
Bristow, Stan 205
Brookes, Perce 192
Brooks 212
Brooks, Ivor 192
Brooks, L.C. 180
Broom 204
Budden, A. 208
Burford, W. 211
Burgess, S. 190
Burnett 200
Burnett, Bill 191
Burnett, Bob 191
Burnett, Charlie 190
Burnett, Percy 190
Burston, H. 200

Burt, G. 208
Bushell, T.A. 180, 187

Callow, W. 208
Carrow, Bill 185
Carey, Harry 212
Cavill, Bert 211
Cavill, Frank 189
Cavill, Joe 191
Challice, Mike 198
Chalker 185
Chandler, A.H. 180
Chapman, Peter 183
Chard, Alfred 199
Chave, Edward 205
Chedzoy, L. 186
Chick, F.L. 200
Chiplin, Sid 190
Churchill, V. 210
Clark, R.E. 212
Clarke 208
Clarke, G.P. 180
Clay, A. 212
Clist, Den 206
Cload, Ern 205
Cload, Stan 205
Clute, Jeff 191
Coggins, Walt 189
Cole, M. 208
Coles, Charlie 188
Coles, Cyril 189
Coles, Dennis 208
Coles, Ernie 190
Coles, S. 208, 210
Collard, Harold 189
Collard, Walter 197
Colman, F. 207
Comer, A. 206
Connett, C.G. 209, 210
Cook, Bill 190
Cook, Bob 189
Cook, Jim 199
Cook, Phil 212
Cook, W.W. 182
Cooke, C. 186
Coombes, Lance 192
Cooper, Ted 212
Cornish, C. 184
Cornish, Cyril 204
Cornish, G. 200
Cornish, Jack 189
Cornish, Leslie 195
Cornish, Lionel 189
Cornwell 192
Cort, S. 184
Cottey, Edwin 199
Cottrell 212
Counsell, A. 208
Cousins, F.G. 180, 183, 184, 187
Cousins, Harold W. 199, 200
Cousins, Jack 198
Cox, Stan 188
Cozens, Jack 197
Cozens, Jim 208
Crabb, G. 199
Crang, John 190
Cross, G. 210
Cross, Howard 199
Cross, Walter 199

Cruwys, William 192
Cundy, D. 210
Curry, Bill 188
Curry, Harry 188
Curtis, Frank 191

Darlow, Fred 190
Davey, Fred 197
Davey, Jim 197
Davies, Rev. 181
Davies, Rev. Rees 204
Davis, Charles 190
Davis, Ray 197
Dawe, Bill 183
Dawe, Leo G. 'Pukka' 199
Day, Cyril 197
Day, Leslie 197
Day, Mark 190
Day, Ron 197
Day, Roy 197, 198
Deacon, C. 200
Denham, John 188
Derman, Herb 198
Derrick, Bill 208
Dick, M.I. 199, 200
Dilliston 183, 185
Dimon, Fred 188
Dodd, Bill 212
Dollin, P. 200
Dollings, Dick 191
Dommett, Harold 199
Dommett, J. 211
Done, H.R. 180
Donovan, R.J. 200
Douglas 188
Drew, Norman 192
Drew, P. 208
Drew, R.F. 180, 188
Drew, Roy 208
Dryden, Harry 210
Duddridge, Arthur 205
Duddridge, Jim 205
Dunlop 188
Dunn, Edward Frank 184
Dunn, Henry 204
Dunn, Ken 191
Dunn, Reg C. 200
Duthie, G.F. 180
Dyer, C. 200

Eason, Walt 189
Eastment, Ern 199, 200
Edmonds 180, 186
Edney 186
Edwards, B. 206
Elkington, Arthur 197
Elkins 199
Ellett, H. 208
Ellison, C.E.M. 180
Elston, Bill 212
Elston, H. 204

Faulkner, G. 212
Fisher 192
Fletcher, P. 212
Flood, Arthur 190
Flood, Walt 190
Floyd, Jim 204
Fooks, Geoff 183

Ford, Charlie 197
Forrester, G.H. 189
Forsdyle, John 212
Foster, F. 208
Fouracre, Bob 197, 198
Fox, J. 188
Fox, T. 199
Fox W. 200
Foxwell, Tristram 192
Fudge, Fred 184
Fyfield, Charlie 208

Gaine 186
Gange, Ted 191
Gardner, J.R. 209, 210
Garland 212
Garland, George 208
Garland, Stan 186
Garnsworthy 205
Gay, Jim 189
Gazlett 212
Gibb 197, 198
Gidney, George 205
Gilbert 189
Giles, J. 200
Giles, W. 200
Gillard, Sid 189
Gilles, Eric 212
Ginnings, Arthur 212
Glade-Wright, C.W. 195
Glanville, P. 188
Glanville, Vic 188
Glencross, J.B. 208
Gold 185
Goldsworthy, H. 200
Goldworthy, Jack 197
Goodhall, Jack 212
Goodhind, Lewis 205
Gordge, Roland 208
Gould 183
Grabham, W. 199
Gready, Ben 185
Greed, P. 208
Greed, R. 188
Greedy, Bert 189
Green 212
Green, J. 200
Green, W. 207
Greenwood 212
Griffin, D.E. 200
Grinter, Dennis 183
Groves, Dick 197
Groves, Harold 212
Guppy, Bill 185
Gwyther, W. 207

Haddon, Baldwin L. 199, 200
Hake, Claude 201
Hake, Samuel James 201
Hake, Terry 201
Halse, Frank 212
Ham, Bill 183
Hamblin, Bill 197
Hankey, R.B. 204
Hannaford, John 199
Hargreaves 180, 185
Hartley, H. 188
Hartley, W. 188
Hartnell, L. 205

Hartnell, Roy 204
Hatcher 212
Hawkins 183
Hawkins, Jack 204
Hayes, C. 199
Hayes, Percy 199
Hedderwick, Cedric E. 189, 191
Heenan, J. 210
Hellard, George 189
Hellings, Ken 205
Hellings, Len 205
Heman, L. 186, 188
Hemmingshaw 212
Hender, Derrick 183
Henderson, G. 212
Herman, L. 180
Hewings, Douglas 208
Heywood, Harold 208
Hick 200
Hill, C. 188
Hill, Jack 190
Hill, Len 205
Hill, William 206
Hilliard 208
Hilton-Green, H.F.L. 180, 206
Hime, L.J. 182
Hind 193
Hinds, W.F. 'Porky' 199, 200
Hitchcott, Bill 208
Hoare, F. 208
Hoare, J. 210
Hobbs 190
Hockey, F. 200
Hockey, P. 207
Hodge 211
Hodge, B. 206
Holden, Jimmy 188
Holden, Johnny 186
Honeybun, George 190
Hookway, Ernest 'Basil' 199, 200
Hooper, Dick 191
Hooper, Fred 191
Hooper, George 191
Hooper, Les 191
Hooper, 'Toosey' 192
Hopkins, J. 186
Hordle, Walter 188
Horrell, Jack 205
Hort, L. 188
Hosegood 184
Hoskins, Reginald 185
Huddle, George 212
Hughes, O.S. 'Oscar' 199
Hull, Tom 183
Humphries, Arthur 199
Hunt, Bill 192
Hunt, Eddie 208
Hunt, Frank 208
Hunt, Fred 192
Hunt, Ted 197, 198
Hunt, Thomas John 'Basher' 193
Huntington, Ulick 189
Huntley 185
Hussey, Fred 208
Hussey, Walter 208
Hutchins, Ben 205
Hutchins, Bill 205
Hutchins, J. 205
Hutchins, Tom 204

Hutchinson 212
Hutchinson, John 212
Hutton, W.S. 200
Huxtable, Jack 182

Indemaur 188
Innocent, Jack 191

Jackson, Tom 197, 198
James, F. 190
Jefferies, T. 207
Jenkins, Charlie 199
Jenkins, S. 206
Jennings, Reg 189
Jewell, Freddie 192
Johns 205
Johnson, E. 207
Johnson, Lewis 206
Jolly, Keith 212
Jones 188, 211
Jones, A. 210, 211
Jones, Jesse 188
Jones, L. 188
Jones, Sid 204
Jordan 186
Jordan, J. 200
Jordan, S. 200
Jury, Bob 183

Keitch, Alec 210
Keitch, Jim 191
Kelland 212
Kenner, Maurice 183, 185
Kerslake 207
Kerswell, Bill 191
King, Bill 190
King, J. 184
Kingdom, W.A. 180, 181
Kinnersley, S.K. 200
Kitson, R. 190
Knight 191
Knight, Frank 211
Knight, George 189

Lambert, F.L. 209
Land, H. 205
Lane, J. 200, 207
Langdon, George 197, 198
Langdon, Ray 197, 198
Langham, Frank 200
Laverock, Jack 183
Lawrence, G. 205
Leamon, Fred 212
Leavey, Stan 212
Leavey, V. 212
Lee 191
Lee-Michel, Frank 200
Lever 191
Ling, H. 200
Ling, Theo 208
Lipscombe, J.H. 180
Lock, Ernest William 195
Lock, F. 208
Lock, Ray 190
Lock, T. 211
Lock, T.F. 200
Lock, Tom 204
Long, Gerald 197, 198
Long, Norman 183

Lord, J. Alec 180, 182, 186, 188
Lubbick 199
Lucas, Arthur 206
Luscombe, W. 182
Luxton, A. 207
Lye, Bob 199
Lynas, Arnold 185
Lyons, Jack 199

McHardy, Jim 186
Major, Jack 183
Male, H. 200
Male, Reg 197
Manners, Stan 183
Manning 185
Manning, R. 186
Marchant, Mac 192
Marks, Reg 204
Martin, A. 212
Martin, Perce 191
Matravers, Leslie 208
Matravers, Ted 208
Matterson, C.A. 180
Matthews, Clement Charles 195
Mead, Bob 193
Mead, Maurice 189
Meade, Cecil 189
Medhurst 186
Meikle, John 183
Mellor, G.F. 180
Merriman, A.D.N. 180
Millard, Tom 183
Millen, Bob 198
Miller, A. 210
Milton 190
Milton, Fred 189
Milton, G. 200
Milton, Jim 189
Mitchell, A. 192
Mitchell, J. 186
Mitchell, Len 192
Mitford, E.B. 180, 195, 211
Moore, Barrington 180
Morris, Alan 189
Morse, B. 208
Mortimer, L.A. Jones 180
Mortimer-White 193
Mott, R.J.K. 197, 198
Murray, B. 208
Mutter, Charles 197, 198

Nickerson, P. 206
Norman, Ken 192, 193
Norman, C.L. 180
Norrish, V. 199
Northam, D. 205
Northam, N. 200
Northam, S. 205

Orrell, T. 210
Osmond 197
Overton, W. 211

Palmer 184
Palterman, C. 186
Panton, James 199
Parker 206
Parker, 'Ginger' 212
Parker, Les 191

Parker, Percy 189
Parminter, H. 200
Parr, C. 200
Pascoe, Donald S. 181, 185
Paterson, W. 182
Pavey, Bill 204
Pavey, Frank 212
Pavey, Fred 197
Payne 208
Payne, J. 199
Payne, S. 212
Percy 192
Perrot, William 206
Perry, Ern 199, 200
Perry, H. 200
Peters, Robin H. 205
Peters, T. 199
Phillips 185
Phillips, S.F. 200
Phippen, Bill 182, 183
Pilgrim 188
Pike, E. 205, 207
Pike, E.J. 'Ted' 190
Pike, Eli 190
Pinney, Tom 208
Pitcher, C.T. 180
Pitman, J. Verdun 199
Pole, Lionel 188
Pollard 185
Pollard, H. 192
Pook 186, 188
Pook, Edgar 188
Poole, Frank 189
Porter, Bill 191
Porter, W. 200
Potter, Gilbert 208
Potter, H.J. 180
Potter, Harold 210
Power, Bob 189
Power, Don 183
Pratt, Trevor 183
Prettejohns, Francis 205
Price, Bill 191
Prideaux, Ernest 199, 200
Prideaux, L. 199
Pring, W.G. 182
Prosser, T. 211
Puffet, W. 184, 187
Pulman, Fred 204
Purchase, Sam 200
Purchase, Walter 189

Quick, Bill 183
Quick, R. 200

Radford, H.K. 207
Radford, W. 'Bill' G. 204, 207
Rattray, A. 180
Rawle, G. 208
Rayson, H. 184
Reading, Toby 191
Redstone, H.G. 189
Reed, Herb 197, 198
Reed, John 189
Reed, R. 200
Reynolds, Bert 191
Rich, G. 199
Rich, John 205
Rich, Trugg 190

Richards, Archie 191
Richards, Bert 191
Ridler 211
Rivington 188
Rivett, Tom 212
Roberts, Henry 206
Roberts, J. 206
Roberts, J.R. 180
Roberts, Les 212
Rogers, Bill 190
Rogers, Harry 191
Rosewarne 210
Rosewell, G. 199
Rosewell, H. 199
Rowlands, A. 211
Rowlands, S. 200
Rowsell, Bill 188
Rowsell, Clifford 208
Rowsell, J. 183
Rugg, R.T. 200
Russell 200
Russell, D. 188

Sadgrove, K.H.O'R. 208
Sadler 184
Sanders, Reg J. 200
Sandford, George 192
Saunders, Bill 189
Saunders, H. 188
Saunders, R.J. 199
Saunders, W. 184
Sealy, Tom 189
Searle, Rex 212
Sears, R. 212
Sedgebeer, George 189
Sedgebeer, Jack 189
Sellick, T. 184
Shapland, Jack 205
Shapland, Peter 183
Sharland, Harold 204
Shattock, H. 208
Shattock, Ralph 189
Shattock, Ted 189
Sheldon, D. 184
Sheppard, A. 190
Shire, Abraham 206
Shire, H. 199
Shire, R. 199
Shire, Walter 199
Shorney, Stan 189
Short, P. 210
Shute, W. 186
Silvester, E. 188
Simmons, A. 190
Simons, Albert 189
Simons, Arthur 189
Singleton, E. 188
Skeens, H.C. 180
Slade, H. 200
Sleep, Bert 197
Smith, A.E. 188
Smith, Bert 183
Smith, Richard John 195
Smith, Ron 192
Smith, Sam 197
Snell, Claud 189
Snow, E.M. 207
Sobers 188
Southcott, S. 200

Sparkes, Albert 199
Sparkes, E. 200
Sparks, L. 204
Sparks, Maurice 199
Sparrow, Alfred 188
Sparrow, W. 180, 186
Spence, P.H. 189, 190, 209, 210
Spiller 200, 208
Spiller, Bill 183
Stapleford 208
Staples, D. 210
Starkes, T. 184
Stenhouse, T. 'Jock' 199
Stenson, Bill 208
Stevens, Edward 204
Stevens, Harry 209
Stevens, Jim 208
Stevens, Ron 208
Stokes 189
Stokes, George 208
Stone 211
Stone, J. 184
Stone, Leslie 204
Stone, Phil 190
Stone, Reg 189
Stone, Rupert 189
Stott 186, 188
Stowell, William 199
Stratton, Van 212
Strickland, Ron 191
Strickland, T. 210
Stutt, Don 197, 198
Sully 211
Sully, Bill 190
Summers, Gordon 195
Supman, Sidney 212
Swain, George William 195
Sweet, C.J. 182
Sweet, Fred 190
Sweeting, Jack 192
Sweeting, S. 192
Sweetland 211
Sydenham, Tom 206
Symonds, Ted 190
Symons, Bob H. 206
Symons, Jack 206
Symons, William 206

Tancock, W. 184
Tarr, Bill 205
Tarr, Cecil 190
Tarr, Charles 204
Taylor 208
Taylor, F. 199, 200
Taylor, Jack 192
Taylor, Wally 190
Thomas, Bill 199
Thomas, Harold 192
Thompson 184
Thomson, Charles John 195
Thomson, Colin George 195
Thorne, Albert 189
Thresher, Tom 190
Tidball, N.F. 200
Titcombe, Les 188
Tolley 183, 185
Tong, Kenneth 183
Tooze, Bill 189
Tooze, Fred 189

Townsend, J. 212
Towsey, C. 212
Tregaskis, Tosh 199, 200
Trembath, N. 200
Trenchard, Sid 205
Trevelyan, David 205
Triggol, Ernie 190
Trim 211
Trim, Bill 199
Trim, James 199
Troake 184
Trotman 180
Trott, Bert 210
Tucker 211
Tucker, Cyril 205
Tuffin, H.R. 'Dick' 189, 190
Turier, A.S. 180

Underhill, A. 206
Underhill, Bill 184
Underhill, J. 207
Underhill, P. 206
Unwin 185

Vallacott, J. 210
Venn 208
Venn, A. 199
Venn, H. 199
Venton 211
Venton, Lou 189
Vickery 210
Vickery, Clifford 208
Vile, W. 208
Villar, A. 208
Virgin 197, 198

Wadham, C. 210
Wadham, Jim 192
Wakely, Cliff 188
Wakely, John or Brian 192
Wall 205
Walmesley, C.T.G. 197, 198
Walsh, Reg 183
Walton, F. 188
Ware, W. 200
Warner, Bill 212
Warner, Clem 197
Warren, Bill 197, 198
Warren, F. 206
Warren, Joe 198
Warren, Reg 199, 200
Waterworth, G.F. 208
Watkin, Peter 182
Watts 185
Waygood, F. 210
Waygood, Gordon 190
Waygood, H. 200
Waygood, R.T. Merlin 190
Waygood, W. 200
Weaver, Arthur 185
Weaver, Bill 185
Webb, Ern 210
Webb, Nelson 199
Webber, Cyril 206, 208
Webber, Courtney 208
Webber, E. 211
Webber, Ernie 208
Welch, Ron 192
Welland, Len 212

Wellstead, Richard 212
West, T. 184
Wheadon, Robert 192
Wheeler 188
White, Ron 189
White, S. 188
Whiting 185
Whitmore, W. 190
Wickenden, H.J. 182
Wide, George 185
Wilcox, T. 210
Wilkinson, G. 210
Willey, Jeff 212
Williams, Bill 188
Williams, Fred 212
Williams, George 186
Williams-Freeman, F.C.P. 208
Willis, Dennis 190
Willis, H. 180
Windsbrow, Bert 212
Winter, Bill 204
Winter, Bob 204
Winterton, A. 199, 200
Wiscombe, R. 190
Withinshaw, L.W. 197, 199
Wood, Walter 208
Woodley, S. 210
Woods, Bill 190
Woollen, Harry 189
Wyatt, F. 211
Wyatt, Harold 192

Yard, G. 184
Yates, Rupert 185

Zeisburger 191
Zelley 208

3rd (Yeovil) Battalion

Abbott 233
Abbott, Fred 217
Abbott, Stan 215
Ackermann, Fred 217
Acourt, W. 227
Aldridge 228
Anderson, A.L.B. 'Ginger' 222-3
Andrews 220
Apsey, Stanley 221
Ashford, F. 227
Atkins, J. 233
Atkinson, L.E. 235
Axe, A. 215
Axe, Charles 226

Baker 233
Baker, Charles 221
Baker, Ern 220
Baker, Roger 231
Ball, E. 220
Ball, Vic 213
Banfield 214
Banfield, L.R. 223
Banfield, Reg 224
Barlow, F. 213
Barnes, E. 224
Bartlett, Ken 232
Batten, H.C.C. 213, 216
Baywell, P. 236

Beames, Edgar 232
Beaton, Bob 224
Beaton, C. 227
Beaumont, R. 232
Beazley, L. 213
Best, Billy 217
Best, G. 227
Bethel, Joe 224
Bex 233
Biggin, Jeff 221
Bilby 213
Blackmore, W. 236
Blake, J.H. 228
Boles, D.C. 213
Bond, Arthur 224
Bowditch 227
Bowditch, Arthur 236
Boxall 224
Bradford 227
Brake, Bill 224
Branston 227
Bridle, E. 236
Brock, Charlie 224
Bromfield, Jim 232
Bromfield, Raymond 232
Bromfield, Vernon 232
Brooks, R.B. 223
Broome, Ted 225
Brown, F. 227
Brown, J. 233
Brown, Len 232
Brown, Peter 234
Brownsey, M. 221
Brunt, Tony 232
Burge, Bill 216
Burge, Bill (Jnr.) 216
Burt, Redvers 234
Burt, Sammy 224
Burton, Lindley 232
Bush, H. 227
Bush, John 233
Buttle 215

Cable, G. 230
Cake, Ernie 224
Cannon, Norman 230
Carey, A.H. 225
Case, George 230
Champion, Tony 232
Chant, Godfrey 225, 226
Chant, J. 236
Chappel 233
Chilcott 214
Clark, G. 224
Clark, Henry 224
Clarke, Walter 226
Clayton 233
Clayton, Fred 220
Cleal, Fred 236
Coke 226
Collard 233
Collie, Bob 233
Collings 223
Collins, Harry 232
Collins, J. 220
Cook, Jack 214
Cook, N.G. 223
Coombes, Eric 217
Coombs, Austin 236

Cornelius, Alan 216
Cornelius, Jack 216-8
Cornish, N.P.R. 223
Cousins, W. 233
Cox, G. 236
Cox, Leslie 232
Cox, Wilf 224
Craven, A.E.L. 228, 229, 230
Craven, Jonathan 229
Cressey, Harold 221
Crouch 213, 218
Culpitt, Archie 232
Curtis 233
Cutler, Roy 217

Dabinett, S. 227
Darch, G. 221
Daskford, Bob 215
Davies, L. 227
Davies, P. 227
Davis, S. 227
Day 236
Day, Eric 218
Day, George 215, 216
Day, Kenneth 225, 226
de la Perrelle 233
Denman, Bert 216
Denmead 220
Denning, John 224, 235
Dewberry, Charlie 236
Dickinson 229
Doble, Jim 226
Didge 233
Dodge, Percy or Andrew 230
Dodge, Ray 218
Doe 214
Dowding 236
Down, F. 218
Dowsett 233
Drake, Cecil 217
Draper, Bob 232
Drayton 214, 215
Drew, Sidney Leonard 214
Duncan, A.W. 213
Dunford, R. 227
Dunning, E. 220
Dunning, John 220
Dunster 236
Dyer, A. 227
Dyer, S. 227

Eades, Jim 224
Eason, R.J. 223
Eason, Steve 220
Ebsworth, Eric 233
Edgeley, John 233
Edwards, Malgwyn 233
Ellen, C. 233
Elliott 214
Elliott, D. 227
Elswood, Harry 230
Etchells, R.H. 213
Evans, Bert 224
Evans, Harold 224
Evans, William 224
Ewens 225

Farnham, L. 227
Farr, Oliver 230

Ferguson 232
Fishlock, A. 227
Fishlock, E. 227
Folkard, F. 233
Ford, Arthur 226
Ford, Charles Benjamin A. 225-6
Ford, Dennis George 235
Ford, H. 227
Fowler, Charlie 236
Frampton, A.T. 228
Frampton, Doug 236
Freestone, Cyril 224
Frost, Ted 233, 234
Fry 214
Fry, Harold 226

Gale, Bill 236
Gale, Fred 236
Gard, George 224
Gardner 233
Gardner, Vic 233
Garrett, Bert 236
Garvey, Basil M.C. 233
Gay, Francis 'Frank' 216
Gaylard, B. 227
Gaylard, G. 227
Gaylard, H. 227
Gaylard, P. 227
Gaylard, R. 227
Gear, Stan 232
Gibbons, Ted 233
Giles 234
Gillard, Maurice 224
Gilley, Fred 217, 225
Gillham, Harry 236
Gillman 225
Gosney 214
Gosney, L.T. 236
Gosney, Tom 236
Gould, Alfred 226
Gould, Charles 226
Grundy, Bill 232
Grunhill 219
Gummer, H. 22
Guppy, F. 223

Haines, G.W. 223
Hall 214
Hancock, T. 221
Harrison 233
Hawker, Fred 230
Hawkins, Jack 226
Hayward 232
Hayward, C.R. 213
Henry, H.R. 222
Higgins, A.G. 223
Hill, A.J. 223
Hillier, John Robert 235
Hockey 233
Hodder 214, 215
Hodge, W.G. 223
Hodgson, C.G.S. 213
Holland, Arthur 224
Hooper, Bill 230
Hooper, Bob 236
Hoskins, Ernie 233
Hubbard, Fred 224
Hughes, Frederick George 235
Hurford, W. 236

Hutchins, George 235
Hutchins, Percy 230

Ing, G.H.A. 213
Ingram, F.R. 223

Jeanes, C. 227
Jenkins, Reg 236
Jones 233
Jones, Harry 214, 215
Jones, J.A. 213
Jones, John 235

Keetch, A. 227
Knapper, 'Sapper' 234
Knight, R. 223

Lacey, Percy 230
Lacy, Cecil 226
Lacy, George 226
Land, A. 227
Lane 233
Langdon, Bert 217, 218
Langdon, Cecil 230
Langdon, Fred 225, 226
Langdon, Wilfred 225, 226
Larcombe, Ernest 226
Last, Ron 224
Laver, V.J. 223
Lawrence, Harry 230
Lawrence, Wilf 230
Le Lohe 233
Lea, Dennis 233
Leamon, Gordon 232
Leamon, John 232
Legg 233
Leighton, Keith 232
Lewis, C.F. 223
Little, Jack 224
Little, Jock 236
Little, Lionel 225
Loader, Eric George 235
Lobb, Ernie 214, 215
Lock 214, 215
Lock, F. 227
Lock, Graham 220
Lock, L. 227
Loman 233
Lord 224
Lucas, Bill 236
Lumb, F.G.E. 222

McConnell 220
McKenn, Donald 215
McLean, Donald 236
Malliphant, Rev. 227
Manning, Frank 232
Marks, John 226
Marples, F.C. 221, 222
Marsh, W.F. 223
Martin, William Bramwell 235
Mason, B. 232
Masters, Fred 224
Masters, Gerald 224
Matthews, Gordon 218
Mattock, A. 227
Maunder, J. 227
Maunder, R.J. 223
May, Jack 224

Mayled, Thomas James 227
Meadon 233
Meech, S. or Charlie 232
Mellish, T. 236
Mickleburgh, T. 232
Miller, John 224
Mines, George 226
Mitchell, Bert 230
Mitchell, Ron 215
Mitchem, R.J. 223
Moon, P. 220
Moore 215
Moore, R.B. 221
Moores, J.C. 223
Morey, C. 227
Morgan, B.M. 223
Morgan, Rowland 221

Napper, William 230
Nash, F. 233
Neville, Archie 218
Noble 219
Noble, W.C. 213, 214
Norris, Rosina 234
Nutland 220

Oaksford, Bob 218
Oliver, H.C.E. 213
Osborne 236
Osborne, A. 230
Osborne, Ernie 230
Oxenbury, Thomas David 235

Paley 233
Palmer, Nigel Leonard 235
Palmer, W. 227
Pape, Frank 233
Parker, F.G. 213
Parker, Reg 236
Parker, Sid 236
Parkman, Leslie 232
Parsons, E. 227
Parsons, Tony 224
Paterson, D.G. 235
Pattemore, Harry 230
Patten, A.E. 223
Pauley, Bill 236
Paull, Leonard 230
Pavey, A.L. 213
Peach, Aldred 'Sam' 214
Peach, Arthur 232
Penfold 214
Penny, G. 233
Percy, Charlie 236
Perrett, H. 227
Perrott, J. 233
Petley 233
Pickford, E.J. 223
Pickford, Fred 224
Pickford, W.C.S. 223
Pike, Charlie 232
Pike, Frank 215
Pike, Kenneth 'Ben' 215, 216
Pilkington 233
Pilton, J. 220
Pittard, Douglas 213, 214, 216
Pittard, John 213
Pittard, Norman 230
Plenty, R.O. 223

Pond, H.G. 223
Powell 233
Pulman, Cecil 217
Purchase, Cecil 232
Purchase, 'Tiffer' 218

Quarterman, Bill 215
Quinton, Reg 215
Radford, Albert 226

Rand 236
Raper, Godfrey 232
Rasmussen, Hermann 224
Rawlins 213, 214
Raymont, Cecil 224
Raymont, Cliff 224
Reeves, Clifford 215
Reid, A. 227
Rendell, Kingsley 217
Rice, Charlie 220
Rice, Dick 220
Rice, Eddie 220
Ring, Cyril 236
Robbins, A.E. 223
Rodford, Reg 232
Rodford, Sam 232
Rogers 214, 225
Rogers, K. 225
Rossiter, Ted 236

Sacker, Johnny 233
Sadler, F.H. 230
Samways, Bill 230
Satherley, W. 227
Savidge, A. 223
Scammell, Glyde 235
Seymore 233
Shiner, Jack 230
Shiner, Thomas 230
Shire, Carol 226
Shouldham, W.F.Q. 225
Sibley, Harold 221
Simkins, F.W. 213
Sinnick, R. 220
Smart, Harry 224
Smith, Cecil 236
Smith, Charlie 236
Smith, Ern 236
Smith, Frank 236
Smith, Reg 230
Snell, C. 213
Snell, John 213, 220
Southcombe 226, 230
Sperway 227
Spilsbury 233
Starke, Bernard 224
Stephens, Frank 224
Steed, R. 227
Stevens 214, 215
Stevens, Ron 224
Stirling, Maurice D. 213
Stone, W. 227
Stradling 214
Straw, Jack 233
Strickland, T. 227
Stubbs, Rev. Gerald 225
Swain, Edwin 230
Sweet, J. 223
Taylor, Fred 216

Tetlow, B. 233
Tewkesbury 224
Thompson 215
Thompson, Alan 217
Thorne, B. 220
Thorne, Ted 215
Tilley, J. 223
Trask, Ralph 232
Trion, Les 214, 215
Tuck, W. 223
Turnbull 236
Turner 215
Turner, G.R. 233

Underwood, C. 227
Upshall, F. 236
Urwick, Gerald 221

Vaughan, E.J.F. 222
Vaughan, W. 227
Vickers 233
Vincent, Walter 224

Wadman, Selwyn 221
Walker, Bob 233
Wallbridge 218
Wallis, E. 232
Warner, G. 227
Warren 214
Warry, G.F.C. 223
Watts 233
Watts, Ernie 230
Way, George 213, 215
Weller, T. 236
West 224
Wetherall, Jack 224
Wetherall, Roy 224
Whetham, Alan 217
Whetham, Arthur Frank 235
Whetham, William Henry A. 235
Wheway, George 231
White 233
White, Bob 224
White, D. 227
White, Eric F.C. 225
White, F. 225
White, F.L. 223
White, Kenneth 226
White, R. 227
White, Wyatt 236
Whiting 236
Whittaker, H.T. 213
Wigmore 224
Wigmore, Albert 224
Wigmore, Alfie 224
Willcox, R.J. 213
Williams, Bill 233
Williams, J. 227
Williams, Tony 233
Willis, Doug 233
Willmott, Don 232
Wills 224
Wills, Billy 232
Wills, Wally 224
Wilmont 233
Wilmot, A.S. 235
Wilson, J. 220
Wilson, Tony 232
Wiscomb, L. 233

Woodman, Bert 236
Woodruff, F. 223
Woolacott, Harry 214, 215
Wray 219

Yates, Tony R. 233
Young, Alfred 226

10th (Bridgwater) Btn.

Ackland 239
Ackland, Ted 238
Adams, Jack 252
Addicott 242
Addicott, Len B. 252, 253, 254
Aitkenhead, A. 237
Aldridge, Cyril 262
Aldridge, Harry 245
Alford, Ray 245
Allen, Ernest 262
Allen, Lambert 244
Andrews, Jack 259
Arnold, Alfie 260
Ash, Fred 244
Ashford, Herbert 261, 262
Ashman, F.J. 252, 253, 254
Ashman, H.F. 253, 254
Attwater, R. 241
Atyeo, Harold 261
Atyeo, Stanley 261
Austin 237
Avery, D.G. 237, 238, 257
Avery, V. 244

Bacon, G. 241
Bagg, Leonard 260
Bailey, Bert 254
Bailey, L.J. 253, 254
Bailey, S.B. 253
Baird 242
Baker, A. 261
Baker, D.W.J. 253, 254
Baker, E. 238
Baker, H. 261
Baker, R.E. 253,
Baker, R.F. 253,
Baker, R.J.G. 253
Baker, Ralph 262
Baker, Reginald 254
Ballance, G.F. 237
Banfield, J.R. 237
Barnett, M. 237, 249
Bartholomew, Albert 239
Bawdon, Dennis 241
Bawden 262
Bawden, Ernest 261
Bawden, Sidney 260
Bax, William 240
Beard, Raymond George 254
Beavan, A.W. 257
Beechey, E.T. 253
Bell, H.G. 253, 254
Bell, Ivor 247, 248
Bell, K. 253
Bell, K.J. 253
Bellringer, John 238
Berry 253
Berry, Jack 245

Betty, F. 257
Biddiscombe, A. 237, 249
Bird, John 241
Birt, A.C. 237
Bishop, Ern 241
Bishop, George 239
Blake, Fred 264, 265
Board, Donald 249
Board, Ralph 249
Bodley, Jack 259
Bold, H. 257
Bollon, O.J. 237
Bond 253, 260
Boobyer, Frank 262
Boobyer, Sidney 260
Bottle, H.A. 253
Bown, Cecil 260
Bown, Maurice 261
Bowyer 254
Bradbury, P.H. 237, 249, 254
Braddick, Jack 245
Braddick, Stan 245
Bradford 258
Bradford, Pete 245
Bradford, W. 251
Branfield, Howard 262
Braston, F.A. 237
Bridgman, Edward 239
Brimson, G. 237, 249
Brooks, E. 261
Broom, D. 253, 254
Broom, E.G. 253
Broughton, A.G. 237
Broughton, Geoffrey 242, 243
Broughton, Benjamin R. 237, 243
Brown 239, 244
Brown, H. 239
Brown, Jack 262
Browning, E.F. 244
Bryant, Arthur 238
Bryant, Bob 250, 251, 258
Bryant, Frank 241
Bryant, Roy 259
Budd, Bill 259
Buller, Eric 240
Buller, Sid 240
Buncombe, Miss 244
Burge, Bob 240
Burge, Charlie 240
Burge, George 265
Burge, Jack 240
Burge, S. 259
Burland, Bill 239
Burland, Geoff 241
Burnett, G.H. 253
Burrows 262
Burrows, Harry 260
Burrows, Norman John 260
Burrows, Reg 242
Burston, Bill
Burston, John 245
Bury, Eric W. 262
Bury, Roland 262
Butcher, L. 261
Butt, G. 261
Buttle, Ernest 265

Came-Williams, W.A. 237, 242, 243
Carver, Jesse Edwin 264, 265

Cary, C. 261
Cattle 262
Cave, Ted 259
Cavill, Bill 238
Cavill, Jack 241
Chalk, E.H. 257
Chamberlin, R. 237, 250, 253, 256, 260, 262
Chappel 261
Chappell, Jack 258, 264
Chard, A.H. 265
Chedzoy 265
Chidgey, Bob 241
Chidgey, E. 244
Chidgey, Jack 238
Chidgey, Percy 237, 240
Chilcott 259
Chilcott, Bill 238
Chilcott, Norman 238
Chilcott, Sam 244
Chilcott, T. 240
Chilcott, Tommy 240
Chilcott, Victor 240
Chilvers, W. 253, 254
Chivers, J.H. 253
Christopher, G. 237, 262
Churchill, Jack 260, 262
Clapp, E. 261
Clark, Walter 247
Clarke, W. 247
Claverly 244
Coleman, C. 253, 254
Coles 264, 265
Coles, Frank 240
Collard, Dennis 242
Collard, H. 261
Collard, W.H. 261
Collier, J. 253
Collins, Arthur 259
Collis, C.G. 237
Collum, H.W.A. 237, 258, 260
Conibeare, Alf 239
Conibeare, Bill 239
Conibeare, Gordon 239
Cook, V. 247
Cook, Walter 247
Coombes, Freddie 247
Cooze, Harry 252
Cornish 239
Cornish, W. 253, 254
Cottrell 259
Court, Ray 247
Cousins, Frank 238
Coward, S.W. 253, 254
Cox 244
Cox, Edward 247
Cox, F. 249
Cox, Fred 262
Cox, R.R. 247
Cox, W. 248
Crawford, A.J. Dirom 237, 238, 239
Creedy, D. 253
Cridge, Stanley 240
Crocker, H.W. 257
Croker, W.H. 253, 254
Crompton, R. 253, 254
Crosby, Jim 240
Cross, Fred 245
Crouch, E.J. 253

Cruise, Jack 238
Culverwell, R. 253, 254, 258
Curtis, L.F. 237

Dando, J.T. 253, 254
Dare, Fred 238
Dart 254
Davey, C.R. 253
Davey, Roy 260, 262
Davey, T. 253
Davies, A. 261
Davies, F.R. 253, 256
Davies, W. 261
Davis 262
Davis, Howard 261
Davis, Jack 261
Davy 258
Day, Cecil 238
Day, E. 253, 254
Day, Harry J. 257
Day, R. 253, 254
Day, R.D. 253
Day, W.D. 238
Denman, J. 259
Devas, C.E. 242
Dickenson, H. 253, 254
Difford, D. 244
Dorse, Alvin 261
Dorse, Graham 261
Dorse, Wesley 261
Dosson, Jack H. 237
Down, Jack 238
Duckham, Geoffrey 239
Duddridge, Jack 260, 261
Duddridge, Len 259
Durston, Clifford L. 237, 245
Dyer 262
Dyer, W. 253
Dyer, Walt 245

Edwards, Jim 244
Elworthy, Jack 262
England, W.J. 237, 262
Escott, A.T. 254
Escott, C.R. 253, 254, 258
Evans, Raymond 262
Evans, S.F. 257
Evans, William 239

Facey, R. 253
Fackrell, T. 241
Fackrell, Tom 241
Farrance, H.W. 253, 254
Farrer 259
Farthing, Alfred 242, 243
Farthing, Mervyn 258, 264
Fernie, J. 253
Fewings, J. 247, 248
Field, Jack 245
Finch, N.R. 253, 254
Finnemore 243
Fisher, Cyril 245
Fisher, Francis 247, 248
Fisher, T. 247, 248
Ford, J.C. 237, 262
Fowler 261
Fox, B.M. 237, 244
Fox, Bernard Arthur Wilfred 262
Francis, W.A. 250

Fry, Cecil 244
Fry, Henry 260
Fry (née Gillard), Mrs. 248
Fudge 239
Furze, G.C. 237, 239

Gardener, J. 253, 254
Gardiner 258
Gardiner, Henry 239
Gardiner, Jack 245
Gardiner, Sam 245
Gardiner, Tom 265
Gaylor 252
Gaylor, A.E. 253, 254
Gaylor, H.G. 253, 254
Gibbs, Ben 242
Gibbs, Elijah Albert 262
Gibbs, G. 256
Gigg, L. 261
Gigg, S. 261
Gilbert, Bert 262
Gilbert, Harry 245
Gill 242
Gill, P. 237
Gillard, Bert 260
Gillard, Ern 247
Gillard, Don 262
Gillard, Horace 260
Gillard, Jack 260, 262
Gillard, R. 247
Godwin, Noah 264, 265
Goodman 239
Gough, Gerald 239
Govett, Clement 240
Gower, Jim 259
Graham, R.S. 237
Graham, Robert 262
Grant, E. 247
Gray, L. 253
Greed, Jim 241
Green, K. 253, 254
Greener, W.J. 237, 244, 249
Greenhalgh, F. 237, 249
Greenhill, C.H. 244
Gregory, E.R. 237, 253
Groves, Bill 260
Groves, Charles 238, 239
Groves, Leslie 260
Groves, Ted 260
Guias, C.F. 253, 254
Gulliver, Leslie 244
Gulliver, Mr. and Mrs. 244
Gumbrell, V.E. 237, 251, 260, 262
Gunningham, Billy 240
Gunningham, Stanley 240
Guntripp 261

Haggett, C. 244
Haggett, H.G. 237
Haggett, Raymond 245
Haggett, W.A. 253, 254
Hall, C. 260
Hall, L. 249
Ham, P.R. 253, 254
Ham, Tom 238
Hamblyn 264, 265
Hamlin, F. 244
Hancock 258
Hancock, Bill 265

Hanham 261
Hardiman, S.V. 249, 250, 257
Hare, David 247
Harries, R.F. 253
Harris, Bert 241
Harris, C.C. 237, 264
Harris, Fred 264, 265
Harris, G. 256
Harris, Stephen 241
Harvey, H.T. 250, 251
Harwood, E. 244
Hawkes, Harold 250
Hawkins, Ern 241
Hawkins, H. 253
Hay, W.D. 237, 238
Haydon, Harold 265
Hayes, Len 247, 248
Haywood, Harold 239
Hazel, J. 260
Head, William 261
Heard, Leslie 262
Heavery, B.J. 253
Hector, G. 249
Hembury, Albert 244
Hembury, Stan 245
Hern, Rupert 240
Hesmer, D. 253, 254
Hesmer, E. 254
Hesmer, R. 253
Hibberd 249
Higgins 242, 243
Hill, Bertie Cecil 254
Hill, H. 261
Hillman, Dick 262
Hinds, F.J. 250
Hobbs, D.H.W. 253
Hobbs, G.H. 237
Hobbs, W.J. 252, 253, 254, 256
Hodge, Rodney 264, 265
Hodges, R.V. 253, 254
Holderness, G. 253
Hole, Tom 240
Holley, Bert 244
Holman, C.E. 251
Holman, K. 253, 254
Hook, Victor 241
Hooper 261
Hooper, K.M. 253, 254
Hooper, M. 259
Horn, Leslie 241
Horseman 253
Houghton 262
House, G. 261
House, Jim 240
Howell, C.N. 253, 254
Hucker, E. 261
Huggins, Phil S. 249, 250, 253, 254
Hughes, Owen 265
Humphreys, Wally 258, 264
Hurford, F.J. 253, 254
Hurford, W.J. 251
Hurley, Arthur 239
Husband, C.T. 257
Hutchings, L.F. 253
Hutchins, Leonard F. 250
Hynam, Alfred 247

James, Clifford 253
James, G.S. 237, 244

Jamieson, J. 249
Jarvis, M. 259
Jeanes, Albert 241
Jeanes, Frank 241
Jeanes, Metford 241
Jefferies 261
Jenkins, J. 241
Jenkins, Tom 241, 242
Jones, A.H. 237, 249, 250, 253, 264
Jones, Basil 240
Jones, Gordon 240
Jones, Joe 240
Jones, Norman 240

Kearle, E.J. 253
Keirl, William 'Bill' 261
Keirle 242, 260
Kelly, Andrew M. 252, 253, 254
Kelly, Len 259
Kendle, N.C. 253
Kidner, Eddie 260
King 264
King, C.E. 257, 258
King, R. 257
Kingston, Ivor 259
Kingston, W. 259
Kinnersley, Ken 241
Knight, Bill 259
Knight, Sid 238
Knox, Frank 240, 241

Lampert 261
Lane, Ted 238
Lane, W.I.E. 237, 249, 251, 252
Lang, William 260
Langford, George 260
Lawrence 249
Lee, Frank 247
Lee, Robert 252
Lee, W.F. 247, 248
Lee, W. 'Bill' R. 253, 254
Leggatt, N.J.S. 237
Leicester, B. 237
Letham, D. 253, 254
Lewis, E. 256
Lewis, H. 256
Lewis, Jim 241
Lewis, L.A. 253
Lewis, Phil 238
Lindsay, G.M. 250, 256
Ling, O. 262
Lock, A. 262
Lock, Dicky 242, 243
Lock, Fred 260, 262
Lock, John 'Jack' 250, 253, 254, 256
Lock, Stan 252, 253, 254
Lockyer, A. 261
London, V. 262
Long (née Kick), Joan 244
Lovibond, Charles 260, 261
Lowe 260
Lowndes, Mrs. 244
Lukins, Jim 240
Lush, George 256
Lush, Gilbert C. J. 'George' 264, 265
Lyon, Ben 264, 265

Male 259
Marker, Reg C.D. 252, 253, 254, 256

Marsh, Arthur 245
Martin, Wallace 261
Mather, G.R. 237
Maunder, Charles 259
May 260, 262
May, Cecil 260, 262
Mayled, Sid 244
Mead, Harry 245
Meade, R. 237, 261
Mildon, Fred 241
Mildon, Jack 241
Millener, Bill 245
Millett, E. 247
Mitchell, N. 253, 254
Mogg, Reg 245
Moon, J.W. 237, 249, 251
Moore, Tom 238
Moote, Ken 242
Morgan, F. 253
Morgan, W. 261
Morse, D. 261
Mortimer, Ernest 262
Mortimer, Sidney 262
Moverley, F. 237
Moxey, Alan (Jnr.) 247
Moxey, Alan (Snr.) 247
Moxey, Harry 247
Moxey, Nelson Rufus 247, 248
Moxey, Norman A. 247
Moyse, Ernie 259
Musgrave, L.W. 260, 262

Newberry, Gerald 240
Newbury, R.J. 253
Newton 261
Newton, John 240
Norman, John 242, 243
Norman, S. 253, 254
Norman, Wilf 244
Norris, A.C. 247, 248
Norris, A.J. 247, 248
Norris, Roland 247
Nosworthy, P. 251
Nurden, Ted 245
Nutt, E. 244

Oldridge, Cyril John Edwards 262
Osmond 242
Owen, Sidney 250
Owens, T.J. 253, 254
Overd, H. 261

Paisey, J.J. 253
Paling, Harold 250
Palmer, Harold 238
Palmer, Jim 238
Palmer, Lionel George 265
Palmer, R.C.B. 253, 254
Palmer, Raymond 238
Palmer, Ted 262
Pardoe. J.C. 237
Pardoe, W.A.L. 237
Parker 243
Parker, Cecil 254
Parker, W. 244
Parkhouse, W. 244
Parsons, W.M.T. 237
Parsons, Percy 241
Parsons, Wilfred 247

Patten, Thurston Walter 254
Payne, F.J. 253
Payne, Ken 238
Payne, Mervyn 240
Pearce 239
Pearce, E.H. 237, 249, 257
Pearce, Frank 261
Pearce, Harold 240
Peppard, Bert 260
Percy, C. 254
Percy, F. 253, 254
Perkins, E. 249
Perks, A.C. 253, 254
Perrot 240
Perrot, Phil 240
Perry, C. 252, 253, 254
Peters, Beryl 244
Pettitt, W.R. 237, 256, 264
Phelips, R.M. 237, 260
Phillips, H. 262
Phillips, Wilfred 262
Picton, Tom 259
Pike, E.J. 249
Pinchen, L. 261
Pitman, Cecil 262
Pitman, Ernie W. 252, 253, 254
Pitman, H. 249, 251
Pittey 260
Pocock, Jim 260, 262
Pole, H.S. 249
Pollard, A.F. 247
Pollard, H. 251
Pollard, Ralph 247, 248
Pollard, Victor 247, 248
Pollard, W.H. 237, 249
Pomeroy 261
Pook, J. de C. 237, 247, 248, 249
Poole, H. 237, 249
Poole, J. 244
Pope 258
Pople, Dennis 262
Pople, Herbert 239
Pople, Les 239
Pople, Metford 239
Porter 242
Porter, A.E. 237
Porter, G. 244
Porter, Horace 241
Porter, Jack 241
Porter, Tom 245
Powell, A.J.C. 237
Powell, William 244
Priddle, Frank 260
Pring, R. 253, 254
Prosser, C.H. 253
Prosser, H.J. 253
Prosser, L.W. 253
Prowle, F. 261
Prowse, Harry 238
Prowse, John 238
Purves, F. 237

Quartley 239

Rabjohns, F.G. 253, 254
Rainey, M. 257
Rawle, D.V. 253
Rawlinson, E. 253
Read, Leonard 260

Reasons, Eddie 244
Reasons, George 244
Redman, C.E. 253, 254
Redman, Harold 265
Reed, Clem 262
Reed, Ivor 262
Rees, G. 237
Rendle, G. 253
Rendle, Graham 265
Rendle, N.C. 264, 265
Rice, Hubert 'Taffy' 247
Rich, Ed 238
Rich, Horace 240
Rich, Sam 240
Richards, Ted 262
Riddell 244
Ridgemount 258
Ridgment, Cyril Thomas 264, 265
Ridler-Rowe, Bob 240
Roe, Bill 241
Rogers, W.R. 253, 254
Rood, Jim 241
Rooke, S.J. 253
Rose, R.A. 253, 254
Rosewell, Percy 262
Rowles, H.J. 254
Rowles, H.V.A. 252, 253, 254
Rowles, R. 253, 254
Rowles, W.T. 253
Rowley, R.M. 237, 257
Rugg, Walter J. 252, 253
Rycroft, G. 253, 254

St. Audries, Lord 237, 238
Salisbury, W.T. 253
Salvage, Ed 238
Salvidge, W. 249
Sandford, Charlie 247, 248
Sandy, Reg 244
Saunders, G. 253
Saunders, Ted 241
Scone, R.A.G. 253
Scorey, Ralph 255
Scott, Cyril 240
Scott, F.R. 253, 254
Sealey, D.D.G. 253
Searle, H. 253
Searle, Tom 265
Sellick 242, 243
Sellick, Fred 260
Selway, Robert 262
Setter, H.J. 253
Seymour, Jack 265
Seymour, R.C. 237, 238
Shapter, S.E. 253
Sharkey, H.V. 251
Sharkey, M.G. 251
Sharkey, W.J. 253, 254
Shaw, R.N. 237
Shephard 239
Shepherd, Edward 240
Shepherd, H.L. 237, 244
Sherwood, E.F. 237, 260
Shorney, Maurice 245
Short, William 261
Showbrook 239
Skuse, L. 249
Sloman, E.J. 251
Smaldon, Fred 241

Small, Maurice 244
Small, Wilfred 241
Smith, A.W. 247
Smith, G.L. Lyon 237, 238, 260, 264
Smith, N.A. 237
Smith, Percy 244
Snook, Harold 241
Solomon, Eric 249
Somers 239
Sparkes, Clifford 245
Sparkes, Gordon 240
Sparkes, H. 257
Sparkes, Terry 259
Sparks, Ern 241
Spearing, Ron 259
Speed, Reg 241
Spender, M.D.T. 253
Spiffle, W.R. 250
Spoors, J. 253, 254
Spraggs, Percy 262
Sprankling 254
Squires, Bert 259
Stabbins, Henry 262
Stabbins, John 262
Stacey, Bert 238
Stacey, Horace 264
Stafford, Howard 260, 261
Standerwick, Jim 264, 265
Staples, Doris 244
Steer, P.W. 253, 254
Stepney 240
Stevens, Leslie 241
Stevens, W. 259
Stockham, Fred 238
Stockham, P. 244
Stockham, Phillip George 238
Stokes 261
Stokes, B. 261
Stone 249, 261
Stone, F. (Bridgwater) 253, 254
Stone, F. (Stogursey) 240
Stone, F.C. 261
Stone, F.G. 261
Stone, G.C. 261
Stone, H. 253
Stoodley, C.H. 253
Stoodley, Charles 253, 254
Stratton, G. 237
Stuart, N. 253
Sulley, Bill 240
Sullivan, M. 261
Summers, R. 260
Sweet, Fred 258
Sweetland, Harry 247
Symonds, W.J. 253

Taghill, Eric 245
Talbot, Jim 259
Tamlyn, W.H. 237, 249, 250, 253
Tarr, Jack 240
Tarr, Lester 240
Taylor, Ernest 238
Thomas, Sam 259
Thoms, N.W.B.B. 237, 264
Thomson, Geoffrey 242, 243
Thorne, Gilbert 241
Thorne, Peter 241
Thorne, William J. 253, 254, 256

Thyer, Reg 247
Tidball, B. 247, 248
Tidball, Vic 247
Tilley, E. 257
Timbrell 249, 261
Todham 241
Tratham, A.H. 256
Tratt, Charles 247, 248
Trenchard, C.C. 237
Trickey, William 238
Triggol, Alvin 240
Triggol, E. 261
Trout, Jack 238
Trynan, A.E. 247
Tucker, Arnold 247
Tucker, Bill (Cossington & Bawdrip) 245
Tucker, Bill (Sedgemoor) 260
Tucker, F. 261
Tucker, William 238
Turner, B. 257
Tyler, J. 247

Vale, J.H. 237
Van Trump, H.W. 251
Varney, R. 237, 253, 254
Venn, Albert 238
Venner, Edward 239
Venner, Herbert 239
Venner, Wilf 239
Vernon, Fred 262
Villis, Joe 238, 239
Villis, Sid 238
Villis, William 238
Vinnicombe, Maurice 237, 249, 258
Vowles, Bill 247
Vowles, F. 247, 248
Vowles, G. 249
Vowles, G.F. 237
Vowles, Peter 238

Walker, Wyndham 245
Walter, C.J. 253
Wardell, C.G.V.M. 237, 249
Ware, Tom 238
Ware, Walter 238
Warner, G.H.C. 253
Warren, Edgar L. 253, 254, 256
Warren, G. 253
Waterman, Fred 241, 242
Waterman, Jack 241
Watts, Bill 262
Watts, M. 247
Webb, Mr. and Mrs. 244
Webber, Bill 241
Webber, W.L. 253, 254
Webber, Walter 262
Wegg, Ernie 254
Welsh, F.W. 257
Westcombe, Tom 240
Westman, Eric 245
Whitcombe, H. 237, 244
White 262
White, Charlie 260
White, E.N. 253, 254
White, Frank 238
White, Peter 238, 239
White, Reg 245

Wilkins, Cliff 244
Wilkins, Harry 238
Williams, C.A.E. 253
Williams, Ivor 245
Williams, K.B. 257
Williams, Stan 259
Willicombe, Donald 240
Willis, Tom 247
Wills, Edward 237, 249, 253, 254, 255
Wilson, Arthur 254
Winn, H. 262
Winn, M. 262
Winslade, Percy 262
Winter, Bert 253, 254
Woodhouse, Geoffrey C. 237, 241
Woodrow, Harry 245
Woolaway, R.T. 252, 253, 254
Wooley, Sidney 238
Wyatt, George 238
Wyatt, Gerald 238
Wynn, F.J. 244
Wynn, Len 264, 265

Young, Rev. A. 249
Young, R. 257

11th (Ilminster) Btn.

Adams, George 275
Adams, H. 268
Allen, S. 267

Bailey, B. 268
Baker, Cyril 272
Baker, Don 269
Baker, Eddie 273
Baller 268
Barnaby, Arthur 275
Barnes 272, 273
Barrington 272
Barrington, Roy 267
Bartram, E. 267
Beacham, Robert William 269
Beak, D. 268
Beasley, Leslie 275
Beer, Wilfred 'Buffy' Beer 277
Beeston, Mary G. 266, 270, 271
Beeston, William H. 266, 270, 271
Bellringer, A. 267
Benjafield, Douglas 275
Bennett, Douglas 275
Berry, Fred 275
Bettridge, Ivor 275
Bewell, Arthur 275
Bidgood, Ken 275
Bond, Arthur 269
Boobyer, R. 268
Boobyer, S. 268
Boobyer, V. 268
Bowditch, Charlie 275
Bowey, B. 268
Bowey, H. 267
Boyland, Len 275
Bragge, Nelson 272, 273
Brice, Fred 269
Bright, Gordon 275
Broad, Leslie 275

Brodrick 275
Brown 275
Brown, B. 268
Brown, Ernie 275
Brown, Les 275
Browne, E.D. 274
Bulgin, Frank 272
Buller, Frank 276
Butler, Fred 277

Champion, F. 268
Channing 267
Chedzoy, A. 268
Chedzoy, E. 268
Chedzoy, F. 268
Chedzoy, L. 268
Chick, Jack 275
Choak 273
Chubb 276
Chubb, Ernie 272
Chubb, Harry 277
Close, Bill 272
Coate, Dan 267
Coate, F. 268
Coate, P. 268
Cole, R.A.L. 273
Coleman, Tom 273
Coles, R. 268
Collins 276
Connett, Bert 275
Cork, Harold 275
Corley, Charlie 275
Cottell, P. 268
Cousin, F. 268
Cox, A. 273
Cox, Cyril 273
Cox, Dick 269
Cox, H. 268
Crabb, Jack 269
Crabb, Sam 269
Creech, Sidney 277
Curwood, Doug 275

Daniel, F.R. 266
Dare, C.W. 267
Dare, J. 268
Dare, S. 268
David, B. 268
David, Edwin 'Ted' 267
Davidson 277
Davie, J.C. 270, 272, 273
Davie, S. 268
Denman, F. 267
Derby, Fred 275
Derham, A. or H. 267
Derham, Martin 267
Dibble 268
Dickson, Charles 275
Doble, F. 268
Doble, Sid 273
Dobson, F. 275
Doore, Ralph 277
Doster, C. 268
Doster, J. 268
Dowell, Les 275
Down, Edgar 276
Down, Percy 276
Duddridge, F. 268
Duke, Cuthbert 267

Duke, Edmund 267
Duke, J. (Ilminster) 266, 270
Duke, J. (North Curry) 267
Dunell, W. 268

Eastwood, Donald 275
England 273
England, Fred 273
Evans, Jim 277
Evans, Reg 275

Falkner, Sid 269
Faulkner, Charlie 273
Farr 269
Forsey, Ern 277
Foster, E. 267
Fowler 268
Fowler, Jack 275
Frampton, F. 268
Franklin, Vernon 275
Freeman, L.G.H. 266
Froud 277

Gale, Clifford 275
Galpin, Jim 275
Garland, M. 268
Garwell, Jack 267
Garwood, Alfie 275
Geanes, R. 267
Gibson, W.T. 266
Gillingham, G. 273, 275
Gillingham, Jeff 275
Gollop, Albert 275
Gollop, Harold 275
Grant-Davie, C. 276, 277
Gridley, B. 267
Gridley, H. 267
Griffen, Leslie 277
Groves 272
Groves, L. 268
Gudge, Charlie 273
Gudge, Ned 272, 273
Gummer, E. Robert 272, 273
Gundry, W. 266, 270
Gurdon, J. 274

Hake 275
Hall, 'Johnny' 277
Hallett, Albie 276
Hallett, Jim 276
Halliday 272
Hansford 273
Harris, 'Bunny' 276
Harris, H. 273
Harris, L.J. 266
Harris, T. 267
Harvey, Dick 275
Harvey, Rex 272, 273
Hawkins, Lindole 266, 270, 272
Hearn, G. 268
Hebditch, R. or D. 267
Hembrow, F. 268
Hembrow, L.J. 267
Hickman, Prebendary Gerald 270
Hill, Arthur 275
Hill, H.T. Copinger 267
Hill, Reg 273
Hill, Tom 273
Hill, William 275

Hoare 276
Hobbs, Wilfred 275
Holland 275
Holley, Phil 272
Hooper 272
Hopgood, Ernest 275
Hopkins, Scott 276
Horsey, Jack 277
Horsey, Tom 269
Hounsell, Douglas 275
Hounsell, Percy 275
House, D. 268
Howells, Mervyn 275
Hubbard, B. 268
Huish, Edward 275
Huish, George 275
Huish, Jesse 275
Hutchins, Stewart 275

Irish, P. 272

Jeanes, A. 267

Keirle, C. 268
Keirle, I. 268
Knott, Ernest 277

Land, Harold 276
Lane, Cyril 273
Lane, R. 267
Lane, Reg 267
Larcome, Percy 273
Lawrence, Sidney 277
Lawson, F.T. 266
Lewis, F. 267
Long, Alec 275
Long, Andy 277
Long, Bill 275
Long, Henry 275
Long, Les 275
Long, Reuben 275
Love, Bob 276
Loveless, Ernie 272
Loveridge, R. 267
Lowe, E.H. 276
Luther, A.C.G. 270, 276, 277

Maclean, Donald C. 266, 270
Madge, Hubert E. 272, 273
Manderson, R.W. 270
Manning, H. 268
Marriot, E. 275
Marshalsea, Sam 266
Martin, George 277
Martindale, Tom 275
Masters, Dick 276
Matravers, F. 268
Matravers, P. 268
Matthews, Jim 275
May, A.W. 267
May, Alan 269
Mear, Clifford 275
Meare, A. 268
Meare, D. 268
Meech, Fred 277
Moore, C.H. 266
Morecombe, Wilf 275
Morgan, Leslie 277
Morris, M. 268

333

Morton 275
Musgrove, C. 268
Musgrove, V. 268
Musgrave, W. 268

Newis, A. 268
Newman 269
Newton, Courtney 277
Nicholas, A. 268
Nichols, George 277

Offer, Vic 269
Oram, B. 268

Painter, W.H. 266
Parsley, Michael 275
Parsons, Anthony Clifford 272
Parsons, Will 273
Partridge, Eddie 277
Passmore 276
Patten, G. 268
Patten, M. 268
Pattimore, Walter 275
Paull, F. 267
Pavey, Ben 275
Peach, P. 268
Pearce, John 272
Peard, J.C. 267
Penfold, Arthur 275
Pennecard, George 277
Perrin, Vince 269
Perry, Charles 267
Perry, J. 267
Perry, L. 268
Perry, N. 268
Phelps, Alfred 277
Phelps, Charles 'Mumbler' 277
Phelps, Charles (Snr.) 277
Phelps, Frank 273
Phippen, Charles 275
Pierce, Gordon 275
Pike 273
Pine, John 267
Pipe, V. 267
Plyer, Frank 272, 273
Plyer, William 275
Portal, Andrew Wallace 269
Potts 272
Powell, Dick 277
Powell, Ivor 275
Pownall, John 275
Priddle, E. 268
Priddle, S. 268
Priddle, T. 267
Pringle, J.C. 276

Rainbow, William 275
Restorick 276
Richards, Jack 267
Rocket, Harold 273
Rocket, Tom 272, 273
Rogers, Percy 272
Rogers, Rex 275
Rogers, Roy 275
Rose 270, 272, 273
Rowe, Les 277
Rowley, P. 273
Rowley, Percy 273
Roy, Lionel 272

Sawyer, Cyril 277
Scott 276
Scott, Eddie 273
Scott, Mickey 276
Shannon 277
Sheppard 270, 272, 273
Sibley, Arthur 277
Singleton, Reg 277
Skeens, Hugh 266
Skinner, Raymond 275
Slade, A. 268
Smith, Bill 273
Smith, George 273
Smith, H.H. 266, 271
Smith, S. 274
Smith, Sid 273
Snook, J. 267
Snook, W. 267
Spearing, Tom 267
Stacey, Jack 275
Staple, E. 268
Staple, R. 268
Stenson, H. 267
Stevens, H. 267
Stevens, John 275
Stokes, F. 268
Stone, G. 267
Stonham, Charlie 276
Stonham, Jack 276
Strawbridge 273, 275
Strawbridge, Graham 277
Summerhay, F. 273
Sumption, George 273
Sutton, J. or P. 267
Symes 273

Tancock, John 269
Tarr 272
Taylor, Harold Owen 275
Thompson, Guy 273
Totterdell, C. 267
Townsend, Ernest George 'Johnny' 275
Townsend, L.P. 274
Trenchard, Jim 275
Tratt, Jack 275
Trott, Harold 269
Trott, Herbie 272, 273
Trott, Reg 269
Tubbs 277
Tucker, Tim 275
Turner, Ern 272
Turner, Wilfred 275
Tutcher, Les 272

Venn, L. 268
Vile, Wilfred 273

Wakeham, Bill 272
Wakley, P. 267
Wallford, Albert 275
Warfield, Fred 269
Warfield, 'Old' Vic 269
Warfield, 'Young' Vic 269
Warren, Derrick 276
Washington-Metcalfe, Thomas 266, 270, 277
Wellington, Leslie 275
Wembridge, Tom 267

Wheaton, Ray 277
White, Edward 275
White, Jack 275
White, Ronald 275
White, W. 276
Whitehead, Arthur 275
Woodland, Arthur 275
Woodland, B. 275
Woodland, Harry 272, 273
Woodland, P. 268
Wood, Cyril 275
Woods, A. 268
Woods, Arthur 268
Wyatt 275
Wyatt, W. 267

Yard, Arthur 268
Yarde, C. 268
Yeo, W.M. 267

12th (Somerton) Btn.

Adams, Bert 283
Adams, Henry 284, 285
Adams, Leonard 295
Agar, L.E. 299, 301
Aldworth, George 287
Alexander, C. 294
Alford, Perce 289, 291
Allen, T. 283
Alway, J.H. 293
Alway, M.G. 293
Amor, Frank 283
Andrews, F. 299
Andrews, W. 298
Appleby, Alex 301
Apsey, A.G. 293
Archer, E.W. 278
Arnold, Cecil 300
Arnold, J. 299
Arnold, L. 296
Arnold, R. 299
Arthur, George 289, 290
Ashman, K. 298
Atyeo, Don 289
Atyeo, Edric 289, 290
Atyeo, Ralph 289, 290
Avery, H. 300
Axe, H. 298

Bacon, Cecil 291
Badelow, T.G. 287
Badman 284
Bailey, A. 278, 279
Bailey, Raymond 289, 292
Baker 289, 290, 300
Baker, Len 278, 279, 280
Banting, W. 300
Bargery, E. 299
Barker, Roger 288
Barnard, Bill 'Brassy' 279, 280
Barnard, Eric 278
Barnard, Jim 278
Barnes, C.G.S. 278, 279, 280, 281, 283, 299
Bartlett, G.J. 293
Bartlett, J. 298
Bartlett, R.D. 293

Bartlett, T. 293
Bastable, M. 299
Bastable, Mervyn 300
Batten, George 297
Beach, W.J. 293
Beacon, Arthur 288
Bendle, William 297
Bennet, Dick 300
Bennett, Charles 287
Bennett, Dick 301
Bennett, Fred 301
Bennett, George 287
Bennett, Ron 288
Biddiscombe, Bill 297
Biggs, Arthur 297
Biles, G. 299
Bisgrove, Reg 291
Bishop, B. 294
Blow, W. 299
Board, Maurice 289, 290
Bond, E. 298
Bond, Jack 288
Bonning, Ernie 280
Boobyer, Harold 278
Bown, Frank 279
Bowyer, Percy 294
Boyce, Joe 289
Boyes, Jim 291
Bradford, Bert 281
Bradford, Will 281
Brain, E.S. 293
Brake, Albert 281
Brake, Arthur 281
Bray, E.A. 278
Bristol, H. 299
Brixey, Percy 299
Broadway, Weston 297
Brooks, Ed 286
Brooks, R. 294
Brown, Alan 297
Brown, Bill 291
Brown, J. 299
Brown, Sid 301
Bryant, Mrs. 289, 291
Bryant, Ronald 287
Buck, John 297
Buckingham, T. 299
Buckland, Tim 288
Buckley, L. 293
Budgell, A. 294
Bullock, Reg 297
Bundy, W. 298
Burfitt, Bill 288
Burge, Hubert 278
Burge, Jim 283
Burt, Allan 287
Burt, Charles 284, 287
Burt, Edward 287
Burt, Jack 288
Burt, Redvers Charles 284, 287
Burt, William 287
Burton, Arthur 289, 291
Burton, Henry 289, 291
Burton, John 289, 291
Burton, Percy 289, 291
Burton, William 289, 291
Butcher, B. 300
Button 297

Cabble, Harry 289, 290, 292
Cabble, Philip 289, 292
Cabell, Hugh 'Litty' 297
Cable, C. 283
Candy, E.J. 293
Candy, Norman 300
Candy, S. 299
Candy, Stanley 300
Carpenter 294
Carpenter, Donald 294
Carr 294
Catley 296
Catley, Derek 300
Chalker, H.W. 293
Chamberlain 296
Chamberlain, J.S. 293
Chandler, Sidney 300
Chant, Aubrey 297
Chant, W. 298
Chaplin, Jack 300
Chard 283
Chard, Jack 283
Chedzoy, Jack 283
Cheeseman, Charles 287
Childs, Arthur 288
Chivers 294
Chubb 279
Chudleigh, R.N. 287, 288
Churchill, Lou 284, 285
Clark, A.C. 299, 301
Clark, Fred 284, 286
Clark, H.B. 293
Clarke, D. 299
Clarke, Percy 281
Clases 297
Cleal, F. 298
Clothier, Bruce 295
Clothier, C. 298
Clothier, Dan 295
Clothier, G. 293
Clothier, P.C. 293
Clowes, H.M. 287, 288
Cluet, D. 294
Coate, Arthur 289
Coates, Cecil 289, 292
Cocks, C.J. 293
Coe, Charlie 284
Coffin, Frank 300
Coffin, Jack 300
Coggan, D. 299
Cole, A. 300
Coleman, J. 294
Coles, V. 298
Collins 300
Collins, Bill 301
Collins, Bob 301
Collis, J. 298
Comer, Stan 289
Cook 278
Cook, Bert 297
Cook, Ern 290
Cook, F.W. 293
Coombes, David 286
Cooper, Bill 297
Cornelius, Fred 284
Cornell, Ray 283
Corp, Richard 289
Cousins, Reg 278
Coward, Charlie 294

Coward, E 298
Cox, A.H. 293
Cox, Bruce 284
Cox, Dick 296
Cox, Eddie 289, 292
Cox, Fred 284, 287
Cox, George 284, 285
Cox, Hubert 284, 287
Cox, Joseph 287
Cox, Mrs. 289
Cox, Walter 297
Crab, Jim 289, 291
Crab, Wilf 289
Crang, Arthur 289, 291
Crang, Cecil 289, 291
Creed, B. 296
Creed, D. 298
Crocker, H. 299
Crocker, Henry 284, 286
Crofts, D. 298
Croom, Harold 289, 290
Croom, Walter 289, 290
Cross (née Cox), Cathleen 289, 291
Crossley 297
Crossman, Norman 286
Crumb 284, 285
Cullen, Albert 284, 286
Cullen, Fred 283
Cullen, Jack 284, 286
Curtis, William 287

Dabinett 278
Dabinett, Charlie 278
Dabinett, Jeff 289
Dabinett, Theo 283
Dare, Albert 278
Dauncey, Eddie 294
Davey, George 289, 290
Davey, Maurice 289, 290
Davey, Reg 289, 290
Davey, William 289, 290
Davies 284
Davis, Alec 297
Davis, Bert 284
Davis, E.H. 293
Davis, J.R. 278
Davis, K. 293
Davis, L. 293
Davis, W. 298
Day, A.H. 293
Dayment, Ted 289, 291
Deacon, Bert 288
Denning, Doug 289, 290
Derby, Jeff 281
Dewberry, W. 298
Dewfall, W. 298
Dibben 298
Dike, D. 299
Dimond 284
Doddington, Jack 298
Doe, F. 299
Dowding, Stan 297
Duck, Bob 281
Duck, Doug 283
Duck, Ern 281
Duck, Ken 281
Duck, Len 281
Duddridge, Ken 286
Dukes, J. 301

Dunford, C. 300
Dunford, D. 299
Dungey 297
Dunkling 283
Dunn, Len 291
Dunston, F. 299
Durrant, Percy 297
Dyer, Sidney 289, 291
Dyer, W.J. 293
Dyke, B.B. 297, 298
Dyke, J. 294
Dyke, Bob 283
Dykes 289

Eades, Cyril 290
Eades, Percy 289, 290
Edwards, D.R. 300
Edwards, J. 294
Edwards, W. 287
Elford, G.H. 293
Elliott, Charlie 281
Elliott, Reg 297
Elliott, Ted 281
Elmer 287
Escott, Fred 288
Escott, John 289, 290
Evans, L.G. Lavington 278
Eves, L. 299

Feltham, George 289, 291
Feltham, Mrs. 289, 291
Fevin, Arthur 288
Findley 278
Follett, Mick 281
Foot, G. 298
Foot, J. 298
Fowler, G. 294
Fowler, H. 296
Fox, B. 293
Franklin, D. 283
Frazer, J. 299
Freke, Alan L. 278, 289, 291
Freke, Mrs. 289, 291
Freke, William G.A. 289, 291
Frost, Eric 297

Garland, W. 295
Garrett, W. 298
George, John 289
Gibbs, George 289, 291
Gibbs, Henry 289, 291
Gillard, Harry 283
Gillett, Bert 281
Glover 283
Glover, J.L. 278
Glover, Norman 288
Goddard, Charlie 288
Golledge, K. 295
Gooding, Fred 288
Gooding, Jack 288
Goodland, Ern 294
Goodland, Tom 294
Gould, Maurice 286
Gould, Ted 286
Green, D. 294
Grey, Harold 283
Griffin, G. 293
Griffin (née Webb), Violet 289
Grimes, Lionel 297

Grinter, Will 281
Groves, J. 298
Gullidge 278
Gullidge, Joe 279
Guppy, Bert 297

Haines, Roy 288
Hale 284, 285
Hall, John 295
Hallett 297
Hallett, Fred 281
Hallett, Harry 291
Hallett, Mrs. 297
Hallett, Percy 297
Hallett, William 289, 290
Ham, Bernie 297
Hamblin, Douglas 300
Hamblin, M. 299
Hammond, A.G. 278
Hanham, George 289
Hannam, Stan 297
Hansford, Eric 297
Hardinge, F.B. 289, 292
Harris, R. 298
Hart, Charles 289, 290
Hartland, George 278, 279, 280
Harvey, Bill 283
Harvey, Dennis 286
Harwood, Cecil 278
Harwood, Maurice 279
Harwood, Stan 278, 279
Hasell, Wilf 289, 291
Haskett, Bill 288
Haskett, J. 299
Hatcher, K. 295
Hatcher, Roy 295, 296
Hatchley, Jim 301
Hawker, Jim 288
Hawker, W. 'Bill' J. 287, 288
Hawkins, C. 301
Hawkins, Jim 301
Hawkins, Norman 291
Hayter, F. 299
Hazard 301
Hebditch, John 281
Hebditch, Joseph 281
Hector, Les 284
Hedditch, F. 294
Hellings, Arthur 289, 291
Helps, Reg 291
Henderson, L. 293
Heritage, George 297
Herman, A.M. 293
Hewson, John 288
Hibberd, E.P. 299
Hibberd, Reginald 299
Hibberd, T. 299
Hide, Bill 297
Higgins, Arthur 297
Higgins, D. 299
Higgins, G.A. 293
Higgins, Nat 294
Hoare, Charlie 301
Hobbs 283
Hobbs, R. 294
Hockey, R.W. 293
Hodder, Bert 281
Hodges, Bill 289, 291

Hodges, Bob 289, 290
Hodges, Edward 289, 290
Hodges, Fred 289, 290
Hodges, Stanley 289, 290
Hodges, T. 298
Hookings, W. 299
Hooper, Bill 291
Hooper, Fred 291
Hoskings, H. 278, 279, 280
Hoskins, H. 294
Hoskins, Jim 296
House 294, 300
House, C. 293
House, T. 293
Hughes, M. 300
Hunt, Jim 289, 290
Hunt, R.J. 293
Hurd, Maurice 286
Hurst, W. 299
Hussey 284

Ingram, Alfred 289, 290
Ingram, Fred 289, 290
Ingram, Mrs. 289, 290
Isgrove, Norman 295

Jackson, Stuart 'John' 286
Jacobs, Leonard 281
James, B. 296
James, E. 295
James, F. 299
James, Ivor 291
James, Jack 289, 291
Jefferies, Charles 289, 291
Jefferies, H.G. 280, 284
Jeffrey, Stan 291
Jennings, Frank 281
Johnson, Harry 286
Jones, Albert 284, 285
Jones, C.W. 298
Jones, Jack E.S. 294, 295, 296
Jones, Roy 280
Jones, W. 298
Jones, W.E. 278
Jotcham, John 284, 285
Jotcham, R. 284, 285

Keech, Peter 283
Keen, B. 299
Keen, D. 299
Kempster, W.C. 293
Kidd, Charles Meade 291
King, Donald L. 297
King, Dick 301
King, Ivor 301
Knap, Bert 278
Knight, Ashton 280, 284, 285
Kynaston, C. 298
Kynaston, R. 298

Lamb, C. 298
Lamb, Charlie 297
Lamb, H. 298
Lamb, R. 298
Lamb, R.C. 283
Lambert, Arthur 289, 292
Lambert, Fred 283
Lampert 284
Lane 297

Lane, H. 294
Langford 284
Langford, Bill 278, 279
Langford, Cecil 278, 279, 280
Langford, Charles 278, 279, 280
Langford, Jack 278
Langford, Raymond 279
Langford, Sam 289, 292
Langford, Sid 286
Langford, William 278
Lavis, Austin 286
Lawrence, Ambrose 294
Lawrence, Charlie 288
Lawrence, Claude 294
Lawson, Sir Digby 300
Leach, K. 299
Legg, Cecil 281
Lewis 297
Lewis, Albert J. 287
Lewis, 'General' 284
Lewis, Len 301
Lintern, H. 294
Lloyd, Reginald 300
Lock, Archie 278
Lock, Bill 287
Lock, C. 298
Lock, D. 298
Lock, Dennis 284
Lock, Fred 281
Lock, Harry 281
Lock, Harry 'Henny' 281
Lock, Herbie 281
Lock, Percy 278, 279, 280
Lock, Walter 281
Locke, A. 289
Lockyer, John 286
Lockyer, Ted 284, 286
Loman, W. 'Bill' 280, 284, 285
Lombard, Frank 278
Lucas, F. 298
Lucas, W. 298
Lucas, William 295, 297
Luffman, R.J. 287
Lukins 289

McCreadie, Lloyd 300
McCreadie, R. 300
McEvoy, R.J. 280, 284, 285
Maddox, J. 299
Maggs, Mrs. Doris 289, 291
Maggs, Ralph 289, 291
Maidment, J. 298
Maidment, W. 298
Male 280
Male, Alfie 283
Male, Lewis 281
Marchetti 279
Marsh 297
Marsh, Les 294
Marsh, R. 283
Marsh, Vivian 294, 296
Marshall, G. 293
Marshall, Tom 283
Martin, Bob 281
Martin, Bruce 278
Martin, Eddie 284
Martin, George 297
Martin, Harold 284, 285
Martin, W. 300

Masters, Eddie 297
Masters, Ossie 297
Mathews, Gilbert 300
Matthews, Eric 288
Maybee, Doug 301
Mead, F. 298
Miles, Jim 294
Miles, Les 288
Millard, George 278, 279
Miller, H.R. 293
Miller, Sid 283
Miller, T. 298
Mills, William 297
Milton, Edgar 283
Mitchel 294
Mitchell 297
Mitchell, Albert 297
Mitchell, R.F. 293
Mitchell, Ray 286
Mitchell, Samuel 287
Mitchell, Wally 284
Mitchell, Warburton 286
Moger, K. 296
Mogg 289, 290
Mogg, Harry 289, 290
Moldram, Leslie 300
Moorse, W. 298
Morrison, J. 294
Mounter, Bob 281
Mounter, Jack 281
Mounter, Will 281
Moxham, Bill 295
Mullin, S. 299

New 298
Newbury, Gerald 288
Newman, Albie 301
Newman, Reg 301
Newman, W. 300
Newport, C. 298
Newport, F. 298
Newport, S.A. 293
Newport, W. 298
Norman, Geoff 295
Norris, C. 298
Norris, Tom 280, 281

Oaten, Ben 281
Oram, Bill 296
Oram, Jeff 286
Osborne 294
Osborne, S. 293
Osborn, W.A. 293

Packe, Maurice 281
Paddock, Brian 289, 290
Paddock, William 289, 290
Pangbourne, G.W. 287
Paramore, Don 288
Parham, Ken 291
Parker, E.W. 293
Parker, Fred 284, 285
Parker, Harry 289, 292
Parker, J. 298
Parris, Frank 280, 281
Parsons, J. 298
Parsons, Percy 287
Parsons, W. 299
Partridge, C. 298

Paul, F. 298
Paul, Harry 289, 290, 292
Paull, Fred 281
Paull, Norman 281
Paull, W. 300
Pavey, Ted 284, 285
Payne, Frank 283
Payne, R. 294
Payne, Ted 296
Paynter, S. 293
Peake, Jack 300
Pearce, T. 296
Pembourne, Gerald 288
Penny, C. 294
Penny, F. 298
Peppard, Bill 286
Peppard, George 286
Perry 278, 280
Perry, F. 298
Perry, R. 294
Perry, T. 294
Perry, Walter 289, 290
Pester, Charlie 283
Phillips, Frank 289, 291
Phillips, Gerald 291
Phillips, Stanley 291
Pickford, Chris 289, 291
Pickford, Jack 289, 291
Pitman, I.T. 293
Pitman, W.E. 293
Pittard, Albert 288
Polden, A. 300
Polly, George 301
Pomeroy, F. 294
Pope, Bert 287
Powell, Alec 294
Priddle, Eddie 283
Priddle, Hubert 286
Priddle, Ken 278, 279, 280
Priddle, Tommy 278
Prince, P.E. 278
Pritchard, G. 298
Pullen, Stan 289, 291

Quantock 281
Quinnell, G.A.F. 278

Raison, Lionel 297
Raymond, G. 293
Reading, Ray 284, 286
Reed, Fred 281
Reeves, F. 294
Reeves, George 289, 291
Rendall, J. 287
Rendell, A.B.C. 293
Rendell, J. 298
Rendell, L. 298
Rendle, Fred 301
Richards, Bill 278, 286
Richards, C. 295
Richards, Don 291
Richards, Henry 'Rocky' 279, 280
Richards, J. 298
Roun, Fred 297
Rouse, W. 284
Rowden, J. 300
Russ, Charles 281
Russ, Fred 281
Russ, T. 296

Ryall, E.C. 293

Salway, Bert 278
Salway, Morris 283
Salt, Tom 280, 281
Sargeson 297
Satterly, Percy 281
Savage, Headley 281
Saywell 301
Scammell, Archie 297
Scott, Tom 279, 280
Scriven, Charlie 284, 286
Seager, William S.V. 278, 289, 290
Sealey, Bert 289, 290
Searle 288
Sevior, Perce 289, 290
Shepherd, Cliff 291
Shepherd, Sid 286
Shepherd, Ted 295
Shepherd, W. 295
Sheppard, Charles 287
Shergold, S. 298
Sherston, Peter 301
Shipper, George 294
Shire, Bill 294
Shire, Percy 287
Shoemark 298
Showers, Charlie 283
Silk, H. 298
Simmonds, Jim or Reg 278, 279
Sly, Frank 296
Small, Fred 287
Small, George 289
Small, Harry 299
Smith, A. 284
Smith, F. 284
Smith, Harry 297
Smith, Jack 281
Snadden, B. 295
Snell, Bob 295, 296
Snook, Bert 297
Snook, C. 300
Snook, H.W. 293
Snook, L.W. 293
Southcombe, Hector G. 297, 298
Southway, Ken 289
Sparey, F. 293
Sparey, H. 293
Spearing, Ken 289, 291
Spencer, G. 298
Spiller, Reg 288
Squire, Jack 284, 287
Squires, Bill 288
Stanier, Frank 297
Starks 298
Stephens 298
Stevens, D. 294
Stickland, R.E. 293
Stone, Albert 297
Stone, Bill 281
Stoodley 291
Stoodley, George H. 289, 290
Stott, S. 299
Street, W. 299
Stroud, Frank 279
Stuckey, Len 281
Sturgeon, Claude or Richard 278, 280
Sugg, J. 294

Suter, Reg 284, 287
Swain, J. 298
Sweet, Arthur 288

Talbot, Bert 281
Talbot, Ron 281
Talbot, S. 299
Tapp, John 295
Tapscott, Ron 286
Taylor 284
Taylor, B. 299
Taylor, R. 283
Teagle 288
Thomas, Don 281
Thomas, Fred 287
Thompson 297
Thompson, G. 298
Thompson, J. 299
Thresh, George 289
Thrush, Joe 291
Tilley 278
Tilly 298
Tindall, W. 278
Toop, M. 294
Tovey 284
Townsend, Walter 281
Travis or Travers, Cecil 296
Treasure, Bert 278
Trim, N. 299
Trim, Robert 278, 280
Trim, Stanley 300
Troakes, A.M. 293
Trott, Gerry 278
Tuck, Ted 297
Tucker, J. 299
Tyndall, Walt 296

Vaux, Charlie 287
Vearncombe, Dick 285
Venner, Bill 291
Vigar, Albert 287
Vigar, Gordon 286
Vigar, Henry 286
Vigar, Sid 286
Vile 284
Vincent, Stan 296
Vining, Bill 290
Vining, Jack 290

Wainwright, Bill 284, 285
Wainwright, Roly 288
Wake, Jack 294
Walker, Sir C.E. 278
Waltham, John 297
Waltham, Richard 297
Walter, G.J. 293
Walters, Ernie 284
Warner, William 287
Warr, L. 298
Warren, George 289, 291
Warry, George 289, 291
Watts, Charlie 281
Watts, George 287
Watts, T. 298
Watts, Vic 300
Weaver, Bill 278
Webb, Bill 278, 279
Webb, T. 299
Webb, V. 299

Webb, Vigar 286
Webber 284
Webber, D.J. 280
Webber, Don 285
Weeks, Edgar 289
Weller, Bill 297
Wembridge, Fred 283
West, Len 297
Westlake 288
Westlake, Herb 281
Whaites, Bill 283
Whaites, Ern 283
White, J. 299
White, R. 298
White, Sid 297
Whitehead, Alec 289, 291
Whitehead, E.J. 293
Whitfield, F.F. 295, 296
Whitlock, Vic 301
Willcocks, Bernard 291
Willcox, Robert 289
Willey, George 283
Williams, S. 298
Willmott, Fred 289, 292
Willmott, Harry 284
Wills, C.G. 293
Wilton, L. 298
Wiltshire, Jack 290
Windsor, F. 293
Windsor, Percy 286
Wines, Jack 289
Wingham, E. 298
Wood 278
Woodland, Stan 283
Wright, Rev. John 294
Wyatt, F. 299

Yarde, Bert 283
Yarde, Bill 283
Yarde, Reg 283

Somerset MT Column

Beacham, Reg 302
Beacham, Ron 302
Bodman, Sid 302
Burns, C.H. 302
Chantler, Les 302
Craddock, Frank 302
Doel, C. 302
Duck, Jack 302
Durnford, N.S.M. 302
Evemy, A.W. 302
Frampton, H. 302
Gale, Tom 302
Glade-Wright, M.C. 302
Hillier, Jim 302
Hutt, Horace 302, 303
Jenkins, C.D. 303
Lambert, Jack 302
Lancaster, R.T. 302
Leat, Albert Samuel 302
Perkins, Frank 302
Rabbetts, Jack 302
Ridler, C.N. 302
Smith, C. 302
Starling, Ted 302
Symons, G. 302
Turner, Ivan 302